Institutions and Governance in Comparative Policy Analysis Studies

Volume Two

Volume Two of the *Classics of Comparative Policy Analysis* contains chapters concerned with "Institutions and Governance in Comparative Policy Analysis Studies". They highlight that at the core of any policy making, the different institutions and modes of governance have a significant effect.

Questions about the impact of governance have become more central to comparative policy analysis as scholars have given more attention to globalization, organizational cultural differences, policy learning, transfer, and diffusion. The chapters included in this volume tackle the nature of policies and policy analytic practices within and across organizations, actors and institutions as well as among governance modes.

The chapters demonstrate the ways in which institutions and governance in the public and private sectors, shape policies, and conversely, how policy choices can shape the institutions associated with them. Other chapters focus on how the diffusion of knowledge and lesson drawing address challenges of policy making, cooperation and harmonization.

"Institutions and Governance in Comparative Policy Analysis Studies" will be of great interest to scholars and learners of public policy and social sciences, as well as to practitioners considering what can be reliably contextualized, learned, facilitated or avoided given their own institutional or governance systems.

The chapters were originally published as articles in the *Journal of Comparative Policy Analysis* which in the last two decades has pioneered the development of comparative public policy. The volume is part of a four-volume series, *the Classics of Comparative Policy Analysis* including Theories and Methods, Institutions and Governance, Regional Comparisons, and Policy Sectors. But, each volume also showcases a new chapter comparing interrelated domains of study with comparative public policy: political science, public administration, governance and policy design, authored by JCPA co-editors Giliberto Capano, Iris Geva-May, Michael Howlett, Leslie Pal and B. Guy Peters.

Iris Geva-May has been recognized by Thomson Reuters for having pioneered the field of comparative policy analysis since 1998, when she founded the now high indexed *Journal of Comparative Policy Analysis*. She serves as its Founding Editor and the Founding President of the Scholarly Society for International Comparative Policy Analysis (ICPA-Forum). She has published among others *The Logic and Methodology of Policy Analysis, An Operational Approach to Policy Analysis (with Wildavsky), International Library of Policy Analysis Series, Routledge Handbook of Comparative Policy Analysis,* and *Policy Analysis as a Clinical Profession.* She is Professor Emerita at Simon Fraser University, Vancouver, Canada and currently an Honorary Visiting Professor at SPPA, Carleton University, Ottawa, Canada, and the Wagner School NYU, USA.

B. Guy Peters is Maurice Falk Professor of Government at the University of Pittsburgh, USA, and an Honorary Editor of the *Journal of Comparative Policy Analysis*. He is also the Founding President of the *International Public Policy Association* and Editor of the *International Review of Public Policy*. Among his seminal publications are as follows: *Comparative Politics Theory and Methods, Institutional Theory in Political Science, The Politics of Bureaucracy: A Comparative Perspective, An Advanced Introduction to Public Policy,* and *The Next Public Administration*.

Joselyn Muhleisen serves as the Awards Coordinator for the International Comparative Policy Analysis Forum and the *Journal of Comparative Policy Analysis*. She is a Doctoral Lecturer at the Marxe School of Public and International Affairs, Baruch College, City University of New York (CUNY), USA. She earned her doctorate in political science from The Graduate Center, CUNY, USA. She is the former Assistant Director of the European Union Studies Center, CUNY, USA. She has published work about the development of comparative policy analysis and its relationship to international studies.

Institutions and Governance in Comparative Policy Analysis Studies
Volume Two

Edited by
Iris Geva-May, B. Guy Peters and
Joselyn Muhleisen

With
Foreword by Laurence E. Lynn, JCPA Founding Co-Editor
Introduction to the Series, Iris Geva-May, JCPA Founding Editor,
B. Guy Peters Co-Editor, Joselyn Muhleisen Co-Editor

And
Part 2, New Contribution: The Rise of the Governance Mantra and
Comparative Policy Analysis, Giliberto Capano, JCPA Co-editor

Sponsored by

LONDON AND NEW YORK

First published 2020
by Routledge
2 Park Square, Milton Park, Abingdon, Oxon, OX14 4RN

and by Routledge
52 Vanderbilt Avenue, New York, NY 10017

Routledge is an imprint of the Taylor & Francis Group, an informa business

© 2020 The Editor, Journal of Comparative Policy Analysis: Research and Practice

All rights reserved. No part of this book may be reprinted or reproduced or utilised in any form or by any electronic, mechanical, or other means, now known or hereafter invented, including photocopying and recording, or in any information storage or retrieval system, without permission in writing from the publishers.

Trademark notice: Product or corporate names may be trademarks or registered trademarks, and are used only for identification and explanation without intent to infringe.

British Library Cataloguing-in-Publication Data
A catalogue record for this book is available from the British Library

ISBN13: 978-1-138-33274-4

Typeset in Times
by codeMantra

Publisher's Note
The publisher accepts responsibility for any inconsistencies that may have arisen during the conversion of this book from journal articles to book chapters, namely the inclusion of journal terminology.

Disclaimer
Every effort has been made to contact copyright holders for their permission to reprint material in this book. The publishers would be grateful to hear from any copyright holder who is not here acknowledged and will undertake to rectify any errors or omissions in future editions of this book.

 Printed in the United Kingdom by Henry Ling Limited

Contents

Citation Information	viii
Notes on Contributors	xii
Foreword to the Book Series: *The Classics of Comparative Policy Analysis*	xvi
Laurence E. Lynn, Jr.	

PART 1
An Introduction to the Classics of Comparative Policy Analysis Book Series — 1

   Why the Classics of Comparative Policy Analysis Studies?   3
   Iris Geva-May, B. Guy Peters and Joselyn Muhleisen

PART 2
Lesson Drawing Relationships: Comparing Associated Disciplines and Comparative Policy Analysis — 11

   The Rise of the Governance Mantra and Comparative Policy Analysis   13
   Giliberto Capano

PART 3
The Classics: Institutions and Governance in Comparative Policy Analysis Studies — 25

1. Bringing Governments Back in: Governance and Governing in Comparative Policy Analysis   27
   Giliberto Capano, Michael Howlett, & M Ramesh

2. Comparative Analyses of Infrastructure Public-Private Partnerships   38
   Anthony E. Boardman, Carsten Greve, & Graeme A. Hodge

3. Public–Private Partnerships in the Us and Canada: "There Are No Free Lunches"   45
   Aidan R. Vining, Anthony E. Boardman and Finn Poschmann

CONTENTS

4 Comparing Public–Private Partnerships and Traditional Public Procurement: Efficiency vs. Flexibility — 67
Thomas W. Ross & Jing Yan

5 The Determinants of Privatization: a Comparative Analysis of Developing Countries — 86
Michael Breen & David Doyle

6 Comparative Implementation Research: Directions and Dualities — 106
Peter Hupe & Harald Sætren

7 Organizing for Policy Implementation: The Emergence and Role of Implementation Units in Policy Design and Oversight — 116
Evert Lindquist

8 Policy Harmonization: Limits and Alternatives — 130
Giandomenico Majone

9 Exploring the Concept of Governability — 148
Jan Kooiman

10 Can Corruption Be Measured? Comparing Global Versus Local Perceptions of Corruption in East and Southeast Asia — 168
Min-Wei Lin & Chilik Yu

11 Introduction – Public Personnel Policies: Impact on Government Performance — 186
Greta Nasi

12 Government Effectiveness in Comparative Perspective — 192
Soo-Young Lee and Andrew B. Whitford

13 Federalism, Political Structure, and Public Policy in the United States and Canada — 225
Beryl A. Radin and Joan Price Boase

14 Towards Harmonization or Standardization in Governmental Accounting? The International Public Sector Accounting Standards Board Experience — 246
Iluminada Fuertes

15 Trust and Distrust as Distinct Concepts: Why Studying Distrust in Institutions is Important — 265
Steven Van De Walle & Frédérique Six

16 Sustainable Development and Transnational Communication: Assessing the International Influence on Subnational Policies — 282
Sander Happaerts and Karoline Van Den Brande

CONTENTS

17 Accountable Climate Governance: Dilemmas of Performance Management across Complex Governance Networks — 300
Asim Zia and Christopher Koliba

18 Beyond Welfare Effort in the Measuring of Welfare States — 319
Jon Olaskoaga, Ricardo Alaez-Aller & Pablo Diaz-De-Basurto-Uraga

19 Beyond Compliance: The Europeanization of Member States through Negative Integration and Legal Uncertainty — 333
Susanne K. Schmidt

20 Governance in the European Union: A Policy Analysis of the Attempts to Raise Legitimacy through Civil Society Participation — 343
Eva G. Heidbreder

21 Policy Transfer and Accession: A Comparison of Three International Governmental Organisations — 362
Peter Carroll

22 Agency Fever? Analysis of an International Policy Fashion — 379
Christopher Pollit, Karen Bathgate, Janice Caulfield, Amanda Smullen, and Colin Talbot

23 Networks for Regulation: Privacy Commissioners in a Changing World — 396
Charles D. Raab

24 Four Styles of Regulation and their Implications for Comparative Policy Analysis — 415
Christian Adam, Steffen Hurka, & Christoph Knill

25 Global Governance Indices as Policy Instruments: Actionability, Transparency and Comparative Policy Analysis — 433
Tero Erkkilä

26 Informing Institutional Design: Strategies for Comparative Cumulation — 454
Aidan R. Vining and David L. Weimer

Index — 473

Citation Information

The chapters in this book were originally published in the *Journal of Comparative Policy Analysis*. When citing this material, please use the original page numbering for each article, as follows:

Chapter 1
Bringing Governments Back in: Governance and Governing in Comparative Policy Analysis
Giliberto Capano, Michael Howlett, M Ramesh
Journal of Comparative Policy Analysis, volume 17, issue 4 (2015) pp. 311–321

Chapter 2
Comparative Analyses of Infrastructure Public-Private Partnerships
Anthony E. Boardman, Carsten Greve, Graeme A. Hodge
Journal of Comparative Policy Analysis, volume 17, issue 5 (2015) pp. 441–447

Chapter 3
Public–private partnerships in the US and Canada: "There are no free lunches"
Aidan R. Vining, Anthony E. Boardman, Finn Poschmann
Journal of Comparative Policy Analysis, volume 7, issue 3 (2005) pp. 199–220

Chapter 4
Comparing Public–Private Partnerships and Traditional Public Procurement: Efficiency vs. Flexibility
Thomas W. Ross, Jing Yan
Journal of Comparative Policy Analysis, volume 17, issue 5 (2015) pp. 448–466

Chapter 5
The Determinants of Privatization: a Comparative Analysis of Developing Countries
Michael Breen, David Doyle
Journal of Comparative Policy Analysis, volume 15, issue 1 (2013) pp. 1–20

Chapter 6
Comparative Implementation Research: Directions and Dualities
Peter Hupe and Harald Sætren
Journal of Comparative Policy Analysis, volume 17, issue 2 (2015) pp. 93–102

Chapter 7
Organizing for policy implementation: The emergence and role of implementation units in policy design and oversight
Evert Lindquist
Journal of Comparative Policy Analysis, volume 8, issue 4 (December 2006) pp. 311–324

Chapter 8
Policy Harmonization: Limits and Alternatives
Giandomenico Majone
Journal of Comparative Policy Analysis, volume 16, issue 1 (2014) pp. 4–21

Chapter 9
Exploring the Concept of Governability
Jan Kooiman
Journal of Comparative Policy Analysis, volume 10, issue 2 (June 2008) pp. 171–190

Chapter 10
Can Corruption Be Measured? Comparing Global Versus Local Perceptions of Corruption in East and Southeast Asia
Min-Wei Lin, Chilik Yu
Journal of Comparative Policy Analysis, volume 16, issue 2 (2014) pp. 140–157

Chapter 11
Introduction – Public Personnel Policies: Impact on Government Performance
Greta Nasi
Journal of Comparative Policy Analysis, volume 13, issue 1 (February 2011) pp. 5–10

Chapter 12
Government Effectiveness in Comparative Perspective
Soo-Young Lee, Andrew B. Whitford
Journal of Comparative Policy Analysis, volume 11, issue 2 (June 2009) pp. 249–281

Chapter 13
Federalism, political structure, and public policy in the United States and Canada
Beryl A. Radin, Joan Price Boase
Journal of Comparative Policy Analysis, volume 2, issue 1 (2000) pp. 65–89

Chapter 14
Towards Harmonization or Standardization in Governmental Accounting? The International Public Sector Accounting Standards Board Experience
Iluminada Fuertes
Journal of Comparative Policy Analysis, volume 10, issue 4 (December 2008) pp. 327–345

Chapter 15
Trust and Distrust as Distinct Concepts: Why Studying Distrust in Institutions is Important
Steven Van De Walle, Frédérique Six
Journal of Comparative Policy Analysis, volume 16, issue 2 (2014) pp. 158–174

Chapter 16
Sustainable Development and Transnational Communication: Assessing the International Influence on Subnational Policies
Sander Happaerts, Karoline Van Den Brande
Journal of Comparative Policy Analysis, volume 13, issue 5 (November 2011) pp. 527–544

Chapter 17
Accountable Climate Governance: Dilemmas of Performance Management across Complex Governance Networks
Asim Zia, Christopher Koliba
Journal of Comparative Policy Analysis, volume 13, issue 5 (November 2011) pp. 479–497

Chapter 18
Beyond Welfare Effort in the Measuring of Welfare States
Jon Olaskoaga, Ricardo Alaez-Aller, Pablo Diaz-De-Basurto-Uraga
Journal of Comparative Policy Analysis, volume 15, issue 3 (2013) pp. 274–287

Chapter 19
Beyond Compliance: The Europeanization of Member States through Negative Integration and Legal Uncertainty
Susanne K. Schmidt
Journal of Comparative Policy Analysis, volume 10, issue 3 (September 2008) pp. 299–308

Chapter 20
Governance in the European Union: A Policy Analysis of the Attempts to Raise Legitimacy through Civil Society Participation
Eva G. Heidbreder
Journal of Comparative Policy Analysis, volume 17, issue 4 (2015) pp. 359–377

Chapter 21
Policy Transfer and Accession: A Comparison of Three International Governmental Organisations
Peter Carroll
Journal of Comparative Policy Analysis, volume 16, issue 3 (2014) pp. 280–296

Chapter 22
Agency fever? Analysis of an international policy fashion
Christopher Pollit, Karen Bathgate, Janice Caulfield, Amanda Smullen, Colin Talbot
Journal of Comparative Policy Analysis, volume 3, issue 3 (2001) pp. 271–290

Chapter 23
Networks for Regulation: Privacy Commissioners in a Changing World
Charles D. Raab
Journal of Comparative Policy Analysis, volume 13, issue 2 (April 2011) pp. 195–213

Chapter 24
Four Styles of Regulation and their Implications for Comparative Policy Analysis
Christian Adam, Steffen Hurka, Christoph Knill
Journal of Comparative Policy Analysis, volume 19, issue 4 (2017) pp. 327–344

Chapter 25
Global Governance Indices as Policy Instruments: Actionability, Transparency and Comparative Policy Analysis
Tero Erkkilä
Journal of Comparative Policy Analysis, volume 18, issue 4 (2016) pp. 382–402

Chapter 26
Informing institutional design: Strategies for comparative cumulation
Aidan R. Vining, David L. Weimer
Journal of Comparative Policy Analysis, volume 1, issue 1 (1998) pp. 39–60

For any permission-related enquiries please visit:
http://www.tandfonline.com/page/help/permissions

Contributors

Christian Adam is an Assistant Professor at the Geschwister Scholl Institute of Political Science at the Ludwig-Maximilians-Universität München, Germany.

Ricardo Alaez-Aller is a Professor of Economics at the Universidad Pública de Navarra, Pamplona, Spain.

Karen Bathgate is a Social Researcher in the Welsh Government.

Anthony Boardman is the Van Dusen Professor of Business Administration in the Strategy and Business Economics Division at the University of British Columbia, Vancouver, Canada.

Michael Breen is a Lecturer in the School of Law and Government at Dublin City University, Ireland.

Giliberto Capano serves as co-Editor of the *Journal of Comparative Policy Analysis*. He is a Professor of Political Science and Public Policy at the University of Bologna, Italy. His most recent books are *Making Policies Work* (Edward Elgar 2019), *Designing for policy effectiveness* (Cambridge 2018), and *Changing Governance in Universities* (Palgrave 2016).

Peter Carroll is a Research Professor in the Faculty of Business at the University of Tasmania, Hobart, Australia.

Janice Caulfield is a Writer on creative practice; Editor on reports and grant applications; and Public Sector Consultant on public policy and administration, local government, and regional development.

Pablo Diaz-de-Basurto-Uraga is a Lecturer at the Universidad del País Vasco, Bilbao, Spain.

David Doyle is a Lecturer in the School of Law and Government at Dublin City University, Ireland.

Tero Erkkilä is an Assistant Professor of Political Science at the University of Helsinki, Finland.

Iluminada Fuertes is a Senior Lecturer in Accounting and Finance at the Jaume I University, Castellón de la Plana, Spain.

Iris Geva-May has been recognized by Thomson Reuters for having pioneered the field of comparative policy analysis since 1998, when she founded the now high indexed *Journal* *of Comparative Policy Analysis.* She serves as its Founding Editor and the Founding President of the Scholarly Society for International Comparative Policy Analysis (ICPA-Forum). She has published among others *The Logic and Methodology of Policy Analysis, An Operational Approach to Policy Analysis (with Wildavsky), International Library of Policy Analysis Series, Routledge Handbook of Comparative Policy Analysis,* and *Policy Analysis as a Clinical Profession.* She is Professor Emerita at Simon Fraser University, Vancouver, Canada and currently an Honorary Visiting Professor at SPPA, Carleton University, Ottawa, Canada, and the Wagner School NYU, USA.

Carsten Greve is a Professor of Public Management and Governance in the Department of Organization at Copenhagen Business School, Denmark.

Sander Happaerts is a Policy Analyst on sustainable growth at the European Commission's Directorate-General Regional and Urban Policy, Belgium.

Eva G. Heidbreder is a Professor for 'multilevel governance in Europe' at the Otto von Guericke University of Magdeburg, Germany.

Graeme A. Hodge is a Professor of Law at Monash University, Melbourne, Australia.

Michael Howlett serves as co-Editor of the *Journal of Comparative Policy Analysis.* He is Burnaby Mountain Professor and Canada Research Chair (Tier 1) in the Department of Political Science at Simon Fraser University, Vancouver, Canada. His most recent books are *Designing Public Policies* (Routledge 2019) and *Making Policies Work* (Edward Elgar 2019).

Peter Hupe teaches Public Administration at Erasmus University, Rotterdam, the Netherlands.

Steffen Hurka is an Assistant Professor at the Geschwister-Scholl-Institute of Political Science at the Ludwig-Maximilians-University Munich, Germany.

Christoph Knill is a Professor of Empirical Theory of Politics at the University of Munich, Germany.

Christopher Koliba is a Professor in the Community Development and Applied Economics Department at the University of Vermont (UVM), Burlington, USA.

Jan Kooiman was a Professor of Public Organizations and Management at the Faculty of Business Administration of the Erasmus University, Rotterdam, the Netherlands.

Soo-Young Lee is a Professor of Public Management Theory, Organization Behavior, Personnel Administration in the Graduate School of Public Administration at Seoul National University, South Korea.

Min-Wei Lin is a PhD Student in the Department of Public Administration at National Chengchi University, Taipei, Taiwan.

Evert Lindquist is a Professor and Director of the School of Public Administration at the University of Victoria, British Columbia, Canada.

Laurence E. Lynn, Jr. is the Founding Co-editor of the *Journal of Comparative Policy Analysis.* He is the Sydney Stein, Jr. Professor of Public Management Emeritus at the University of Chicago, USA. He chaired the Masters in Public Policy Program at Harvard's Kennedy School of Government. He has been a Fellow of the National Academy of Public Administration and of the Council on Foreign Relations, as well as APPAM President.

He has been honored by Lifetime Academic Achievement Awards by the American Political Science Association, American Society for Public Administration, and the Public Management Research Association. He published, among others, *Public Management as Art, Science, and Profession* from the Academy of Management, *Oxford Handbook of Public Management*, and (with Hill) *Public Management: Thinking and Acting in Three Dimensions*.

Giandomenico Majone is a Professor of Public Policy, Emeritus, at the European University Institute, Florence, Italy.

Joselyn Muhleisen serves as the Awards Coordinator for the International Comparative Policy Analysis Forum and the *Journal of Comparative Policy Analysis*. She is a Doctoral Lecturer at the Marxe School of Public and International Affairs, Baruch College, City University of New York (CUNY), USA. She earned her doctorate in political science from The Graduate Center, CUNY, USA. She is the former Assistant Director of the European Union Studies Center, CUNY, USA. She has published work about the development of comparative policy analysis and its relationship to international studies.

Greta Nasi is an Associate Professor in the Department of Policy Analysis and Public Management at Bocconi University, Milan, Italy.

Jon Olaskoaga is a Lecturer in Economics and Business administration at the Universidad del País Vasco, Bilbao, Spain.

B. Guy Peters is Maurice Falk Professor of Government at the University of Pittsburgh, USA, and an Honorary Editor of the *Journal of Comparative Policy Analysis*. He is also the Founding President of the *International Public Policy Association* and Editor of the *International Review of Public Policy*. Among his seminal publications are as follows: *Comparative Politics Theory and Methods, Institutional Theory in Political Science, The Politics of Bureaucracy: A Comparative Perspective, An Advanced Introduction to Public Policy,* and *The Next Public Administration*.

Christopher Pollitt held a number of academic positions in prestigious institutions before retiring as a Professor at the Public Management Institute, KU Leuven, Belgium, and the Scientific Director at the Netherlands Institute of Government, Enschede, the Netherlands.

Finn Poschmann is an Associate Director of Research at C.D. Howe Institute, Toronto, Canada.

Joan Price Boase has retired from the Political Science Department at the University of Windsor, Canada, where she is now Professor Emerita.

Charles D. Raab is a Professorial Fellow in the Department of Politics and International Relations at the University of Edinburgh, UK.

Beryl A. Radin is a member of the faculty at McCourt School of Public Policy of Georgetown University in Washington, DC. An elected member of the National Academy of Public Administration, she is the former President of the Association of Public Policy and Management. She also served as a Special Advisor to the Assistant Secretary for Management and Budget of the US Department of Health and Human Services and other agencies. She is the Editor of the Georgetown University Press book series, Public Management and Change, and the author of several books, including *Policy Analysis in the Twenty-First Century: Complexity, Conflict, and Cases; Beyond Machiavelli: Policy Analysis Reaches Midlife,* and *Federal Management Reform in a World of Contradictions*.

CONTRIBUTORS

M Ramesh is UNESCO Chair of Social Policy Design in Asia in the Lee Kuan Yew School of Public Policy at the National University of Singapore.

Thomas W. Ross is UPS Foundation Professor of Regulation and Competition Policy in the Sauder School of Business at the University of British Columbia, Vancouver, Canada.

Harald Sætren is a Professor in the Department of Administration and Organization Theory at the University of Bergen, Norway.

Susanne K. Schmidt is a Professor of Political Science at the University of Bremen, Germany.

Frédérique Six is an Associate Professor in the Faculty of Social Sciences, Political Science and Public Administration, and an Associate Professor of New Public Governance at Vrije Universiteit Amsterdam, the Netherlands.

Amanda Smullen is a Senior Lecturer in Policy and Governance in the Crawford School of Public Policy at Australian National University, Canberra, Australia.

Colin Talbot is a Professor of Government at the University of Manchester, UK.

Steven Van de Walle is Research Professor of Public Administration and Public Management at the Public Governance Institute at KU Leuven, Belgium.

Karoline Van den Brande is a Counsellor in the Department of Strategy and Coordination, within the Department of Economics and Innovation for the Flemish Government, Belgium.

Aidan R. Vining is the Centre for North American Business Studies (CNABS) Professor of Business and Government Relations in the Beedie School of Business at Simon Fraser University, Vancouver, Canada.

David L. Weimer is the Edwin E. Witte Professor of Political Economy at the University of Wisconsin-Madison, USA.

Andrew B. Whitford is the Alexander M. Crenshaw Professor of Public Policy and a Professor of Public Administration and Policy at the University of Georgia, USA.

Jing Yan is an Associate Professor at the Central University of Finance and Economics, Beijing, China.

Chilik Yu is a Professor of Public Policy and Management, and a Vice President (Academic Affairs) of Shih Hsin University, Taipei, Taiwan.

Asim Zia is serving as a Professor of Public Policy and Computer Science in the Department of Community Development and Applied Economics, with a secondary appointment in the Department of Computer Science at the University of Vermont (UVM), Burlington, USA.

Foreword to the Book Series: The Classics of Comparative Policy Analysis

LAURENCE E. LYNN, JR.
Founding co-Editor, *Journal of Comparative Policy Analysis*
Sydney Stein, Jr. Professor of Pubic Management Emeritus
The University of Chicago, USA

The Classics of Comparative Policy Analysis Series is both a record of and a milestone in the development of the theories and methods not only of comparative public policy analysis but, as well, of comparative studies in public affairs-related disciplines and professions, which the *Journal of Comparative Policy Analysis (JCPA)* has advanced. Having been present at the founding of the field of public policy analysis in the 1960s and of comparative policy analysis studies through the *JCPA* in 1998, and having been contributed to a field of research, public governance, which is heavily influenced by comparative perspectives, I am pleased that this series calls attention to the extent to which public affairs research has been influenced by the intellectual ambitions of the kinds of scholarship represented in the four volumes of this series.

Publication of this series of research papers that appeared in volume 20:1 of the *JCPA*, 2018, marks and celebrates the twentieth anniversary of the journal. Selections of classic papers provide not only models for scholars, they are of immense value to teachers in creating reading lists and study assignments. As well, they reinforce awareness of the dimensions and content of a vital field of public affairs research.

Especially welcome are new chapters in each volume authored by the *JCPA* co-editors, highlighting the emerging symbiotic relationships between established disciplines and professions and comparative policy studies. These developments advance the fulfillment of an early intention of the policy analysis movement: promoting the integration of the social sciences in public affairs research. Also important in this regard is the attention in the *Classics of Comparative Policy Analysis* to recent development in research fields, such as policy design and governance, harkening back to the emergence in the original policy analysis movement of implementation studies and program evaluation, with their comparative bent. These newer research studies now appear not only in *JCPA* but in a patulous number of public affairs-oriented academic journals and conference agendas.

It is noteworthy that the *Classics of Comparative Policy Analysis Series* appears in unsettled and unsettling times in national and international affairs. The intellectual developments celebrated in this series have been taking place in a relatively stable and liberal global order. Beginning in the aftermath of World War II, various forms of international cooperation gradually took shape, including regional and the United Nations-sponsored governance and shared sovereignty institutions. This order is now challenged by the seemingly ascendant emergence of nationalism and authoritarianism in many of the world's largest and oldest nations and democracies. These developments threaten the rule of law and the rule of reason, both of which have largely come to be taken for granted in the teaching and research of public affairs-oriented disciplines and professions. Activism and tribalism are competing with analysis and democratic deliberation in the shaping of public policy, and it appears at the expense of fairness and social justice and institutional stability.

But the current political context could also provide opportunities for comparative policy studies. Its scholars have perspectives, models, and methods, as well as the disposition, to study the dynamics of instability, changing institutional and organizational environments and their consequences for policymaking and public administration. For example, researchers on federalism, already informed by comparative studies at subnational levels of governance and international institutions, have the tools to address new questions posed by evolving patterns of governance.

As depicted by Geva-May, Peters, and Muhleisen in their introduction to the series and evident throughout the four volumes, the comparative perspective is producing the kinds of intellectual capital that may be of unique value in policy formulation and design. Lesson drawing is increasingly appropriate in an era of worldwide reinventing of governance. Through the publication of this series, and through papers accepted for publication in future volumes of the *JCPA*, the journal will continue to be a pilot light for imaginative and pathbreaking research that sustains the momentum of the development of comparative policy studies.

Part 1

An Introduction to the Classics of Comparative Policy Analysis Book Series

Why the Classics of Comparative Policy Analysis Studies?

IRIS GEVA-MAY, B. GUY PETERS AND JOSELYN MUHLEISEN

The Classics of Comparative Policy Analysis is a collection of the most representative articles in the *Journal of Comparative Policy Analysis (JCPA)* on its twentieth anniversary. The *JCPA* has "pioneered the domain of comparative policy analysis" studies since 1998[1] and is still the only journal explicitly devoted to promoting comparative policy studies. The articles published in the *JCPA* have become classics in the field of comparative policy analytic studies, and have established it as a distinctive field of study since (Thomson Reuters 2008; Radin 2013; Geva-May, Hoffman and Muhleisen 2018). The papers published over the last two decades in *JCPA* are explicitly comparative and could be viewed as cornerstones of comparative public policy analysis theory, methodology, policy inter-disciplinarity, and inter-regional scholarship. Contributors include founders of the field of policy analysis, comparative politics, and comparative public administration and management from which comparative policy analysis (CPA) has derived: Peter deLeon, Duncan McRae, Laurence E. Lynn, B. Guy Peters, Beryl Radin, David Weimer, Frans Van Nispen, Yukio Adachi, as well as second- and third-generation policy analysis scholars who have set high scholarship bars in advancing the field.

The term "comparative" has normatively been associated with descriptive accounts of national similarities or dissimilarities with respect to content or to features of the public policy process requiring information sharing. At the research level, it has traditionally been concerned with cross-national generalizations or explanations of differences among policies. As the founding editors of the *JCPA* declare in the first volume, "JCPA seeks to go beyond these confines and offer an intellectual arena for analyzing comparative explanatory frameworks and research methods, testing models across spatial structures … and comparing different instruments for achieving similar ends".[2]

The collections of articles included in the volumes of this series support the aim and scope of the *JCPA* to establish points of reference for aspects of comparative policy analytic studies. The four volumes compile, respectively, those foundation articles which contribute to the four main aspects of CPA scholarship advanced by the *JCPA*: (a) Apply or develop comparative methodologies and theories; (b) Investigate valid and reliable means of performing inter-regional or inter-social units comparisons; (c) Investigate the connection among public policy, institutions, and governance factors that can explicate similarities or differences in policymaking; (d) Finally, they focus on the application or utilization of comparative public policy analysis in a variety of policy sectors such as immigration, technology, healthcare, welfare, education, economics, and many others.

Although the chapters included in each volume are classified according to a specific overarching topic, we do find overlaps between, for instance, regional comparisons and methodology or theories, or linkages to institutions as independent variables and policy sectors as dependent variables – thus transcending the single focus of the research presented in each of the volumes.

There is one more aspect that has been explicitly covered neither in the *JCPA* (except for its anniversary Vol 20:1) nor as a separate volume in the present series: the linkages among comparative public policy and the more established fields of comparative politics (political science) and public administration, as well as the newly emerging (or diverging) domains such as governance – from public administration and policy design – from public policy. To open a window to further comparisons among inter-related public domains we introduce a new chapter in Part II of each volume. Authored by the *JCPA* co-editors, the four chapters embrace the notion that the established political science and comparative politics, as well as public administration and comparative public administration, have much to offer to policy studies and to the developing field of CPA studies. It is also noteworthy that the comparative policy analytic studies domain is seen as a source of lesson drawing for the increasing interest in policy design and in governance. The cross-fertilization between these domains can range anywhere between theoretical, conceptual, methodological, and empirical. Identifying points of similarity or difference in enhancing lesson drawing, adaptation, transfer and borrowing, or missed opportunity thereof.

These fundamentals common to all domains of study are addressed by Guy Peters and Geva-May who note down the prospective gift of (comparative) political science to CPA and reciprocal missed opportunities in Volume One; Capano contributes a new chapter on governance, regimes, and comparative public policy in Volume Two; Leslie Pal writes about comparative public administration and comparative public policy in Volume Three; while Howlett addresses the newly emerging branch of policy design and what can be derived from comparative public policy in Volume Four.

In today's politics and policymaking, the reality of global policy convergence, economic competition, and political fads, the cross-national sources of information have proliferated to the extent that any policy analyst, public policy scholar, or policy decision-maker in any given country is bound to be aware of developments that happen in a different "social unit" as Ragin and Zaret (1983) label units of social analysis. Comparisons between social units may be nations or institutions, or points of reference such as policy goals, actor interference, market failures, or intervention in public policy issues of concern. The main reason is lesson drawing in order to maximize utility of policy solutions, avoid failure, or utilize information to seek advantage. Comparative cross-national policy analysis can extend insights, perspectives, or explanations that otherwise would be difficult or impossible to obtain. Lesson drawing (Rose 1991; Geva-May 2004), transfer, borrowing, adoption or adaptations, or sheer inspiration (DeLeon 1998; Geva-May 2002a) increases effectiveness and efficiency, and avoids fallacies. Notwithstanding this stipulation, there is a word of warning: CPA done badly has an immediate effect on the public, and can be financially wasteful or dangerous to the social units and populum immediately involved. Furthermore, it can be detrimental to the credibility of policymaking, as well as to policy analysis as a practical and scholarly domain.

One more contention is that in the *Classics of Comparative Policy Analysis Studies* the terms policy analysis, policy studies, and policy analytic studies are often used by authors interchangeably for a number of reasons: Foremost, because these domains are often similar in their possible points of linkage to the comparative aspects that they cover. Additionally, in today's third generation of policy analysis studies, the borderlines between policy studies, policy design, and policy analysis have frequently blurred and the terminology used has often been transposable. The terms used contain a wider perception of public policy within which domains and sub-domains complement one another despite their very distinct roles. Except for those actually studying or working in these sub-fields, the scholarly work refers to them frequently interchangeably.

We selected the articles in the series not only by thematic relevance and excellence, but also based on how they serve the aim and scope of the *JCPA* (Geva-May and Lynn 1998) which set clear intellectual avenues towards the development of the field beyond the mere prevalent perception of "comparative" as the comparison of two objects – whether institutions or regions. Proven valid enough to have served as scholarly cornerstones in the development of comparative policy studies for two decades, each respective *JCPA* aim drives the focus of each respective volume in the series. **Volume One** presents selections focused on **comparative theory and methodology** development, and comparative **theory testing**: two central aims of the *JCPA*. **Volume Two** addresses **institutions and questions about modes and types of governance** which speaks about the aim of examining the inter-relations between institutions and policy analysis either as dependent or independent variables. **Volume Three** builds on comparative empirical research, as well as lesson drawing and extrapolation, and evaluates comparative research methods through articles on regional policy differences or similarities. **Volume Four** touches on almost all the aims of *JCPA* through studies of specific policy sectors – healthcare, immigration, education, economics, welfare, technology, etc., – particularly allowing for lesson drawing, extrapolation, and possible avoidance of failures within sectors.

Volume One: Theory and Methodology

CPA depends upon the various theoretical and methodological approaches to public policy. The same theoretical perspectives such as the advocacy-coalition framework, multiple-streams models, and agenda-setting are important for understanding national and international policymaking and public policy comparatively. These are applied through lesson drawing and policy transfer, for instance, among others, by Pal (2014), and Wolf and Baehler (2018).

Of particular interest are the linkages of policy theories with various academic disciplines, including economics, political science, sociology, and law, all of which bring their own theoretical perspectives to bear on public policy. Each of the articles included in the first volume demonstrates the need to make difficult theoretical and methodological choices in the study of CPA.

Perhaps the most important aspect of these articles is that the researcher had to make a conscious choice about theory and method, and had to justify those choices. The articles also indicate how they frame policy problems and how they overcome methodological challenges in CPA (Ira Sherkansky 1998; Hoppe 2002; Green-Pedersen 2004; Peters 2005; Saurugger 2005; Stiller and van Kersbergen 2008; Capano 2009; Howlett and

Cashore 2009; Greer et al. 2015; among others). In doing so, many address another aim of the *JCPA*: the evaluation of comparative research methods. One way to both evaluate the aptness of research methods and to test theory is to conduct empirical studies. For example, Green-Pedersen contends with the dependent variable problem in the context of social welfare research (Green-Pedersen 2004).

Volume Two: Comparative Policy Analysis and Institutions

"Evidence-based policymaking" is more difficult than sometimes assumed, depending, as it does, on understanding both the dynamics of public policy and the institutional contexts. Despite this difficulty, there has been a surge of interest in policy designed on the basis of "scientifically" demonstrated effectiveness and the ability to identify those successful policies within various structures.

Drawing on the larger institutionalism and governance literatures, many selections in the second volume are concerned with distinct forms of governance and types of political institutions. Governance and institutions are treated both as independent and dependent variables (Weimer and Vining 1998; Ng 2007; Radaelli 2008). The latter make an important distinction between first-order and second-order instruments. The first are those known to policy analysts, the second less transparent depend on features of institutions that "facilitate or constrain" the adoption of first-order policies. The authors contend that in order to make meaningful comparisons, it is important to analyze the usefulness of policy analysis against the analysis of the institutional features that condition policy choice. While public policy scholars and politicians have given increasing attention to new, innovative governance apparatuses, empirical work basically intends to document whether these instruments are effective in specific jurisdictions and institutional contexts and what can be extrapolated from one milieu to another.

One of the chief institutional explanations of policy variation is the nature of political and bureaucratic institutions within which the policies are developed or implemented. CPA has also considered the influence of particular governance arrangements, for example, public-private partnerships on policy outcomes (Vining and Boardamn 2018). But governance structures and institutions are also reflective of the societies, cultures, and polities that constitute them (Hoppe 2002; Geva-May 2002b). Other studies focus on the determinants of certain governance mechanisms, such as privatization (Breen and Doyle 2013), and the impact of the participation of certain societal groups in the policymaking process (Heidbreder 2015). Thus, public policy, institutions, and society are in complex and reciprocal relationships that require a great deal of care to properly disentangle and analyze.

Major themes that underscore several contributions in the volume on institutions and governance will be unsurprising to policy scholars; many selections are especially concerned with effectiveness, efficiency, and mechanisms of compliance (Lee and Whitford 2009; Ross and Yan 2015).

Volume Three: Comparative Inter-regional Policy Analysis Studies

The selections included in this volume make policy comparisons within and across regions. In fact, CPA studies are mostly regarded as comparisons across political systems, whether they are countries, provinces, cities, or another jurisdiction. Likewise, much of the policy analytic research focuses on how policies have fared in specific jurisdictions (Laguna 2011; Saetren 2015) and which factors that contribute to a policy's success can potentially be applied in other contexts.

This mode of analysis brings CPA closer to comparative politics and sociology, and focuses on many of the variables used in the other social sciences to explain observed similarities or differences in the policy choices made by different political systems. The policy choices of federalist systems, for example, are compared by Radin and Boase (2000); Boushey and Luedtke (2006); Sheingate (2009); and Capano (2015). The latter, for instance, compare the Canadian and US federal systems in order to identify similarities and differences between them that explicate the divergence in their social and economic policies. The argument is based on two typologies – Lowi's typology refers to different types of policies, and Deil Wright's typology refers to different models of intergovernmental systems. Here, we also glance at how other theories and related typologies can be applied to CPA across units of comparative analysis.

Focusing on regional comparisons can offer a solid methodological basis for comparative studies by eliminating sources of variation and allowing scholars to isolate more clearly the influence of independent variable(s). To the extent that countries in a region share culture, language, history, or institutional design, inter-regional studies can also target alternate explanations for policy differences. Alternatively, where there is a high degree of policy similarity in very different countries, the existence of a regional power or institution may explain policy convergence. Several studies included in this volume take this approach when considering the phenomenon of Europeanization, for instance, which considers both regional and institutional policy determinants (Mendez et al. 2008; Raedelli 2008; Sarugger 2005). Many contributions compare the policies or policymaking process in a domain across jurisdictions (Ng 2007; Smith and Williams 2007). Other scholars rather focus on tendencies towards regional agglomeration (May et al. 2005) or policy convergence (Clavier 2010).

The *JCPA* has contributed substantially to the body of inter-regional comparative public policy literature and has devoted a number of Special Issues to the topic. This is reflected in the diversity of regions addressed by this volume's selections: Latin America, North America, East Asia, Southeast Asia, Southern Africa, the Baltic states, the Nordic states, Western Europe, Central Europe, Eastern Europe, and Europe as a whole. Dedicated to CPA, the wide range of cases published in the *JCPA*, and the attempt to understand policy and policymaking in many contexts, has served as a major object of interest among authors, readers, and researchers of comparative inter-regional studies.

Volume Four: Comparing Policy Sectors

Our volume on comparative policy sectors focuses on the major areas of strength in the *JCPA*: markets, money and economy, healthcare, welfare, education, migration, and biotechnology policy. These articles explicitly compare policies within policy sectors. The reader can readily identify the marked differences between more technical domains such as technology (Allison and Varone 2009), and more politicized domains such as immigration (Scholten and Timmermans 2010; Geddes and Scholten 2015), healthcare (Marmor et al. 2010), and higher education (Levy and Zumeta 2011).

Many of the articles in this volume deal with comparisons of differences and similarities in various policy disciplines and sectors within and among political systems. For example, Gornick and Heron (2006) compare working time policies across eight European countries, the US, and Japan. Sheingate (2009), on the other hand, compares biotechnology policy decision-making in the European Union and the US, which are treated in his analysis as different styles of federalist regimes.

The absence of papers that explicitly compare *across* policy sectors is noteworthy in the *JCPA*. This is why the *JCPA* anniversary Special Issue Vol. 20:1 and Part One of each volume in this series have been devoted to the comparison of policy, politics, and administration studies. Yet, we still do not find comparative papers between healthcare and immigration, or policy analysis and psychology, or medicine, or law (Geva-May 2005).

To some extent, this phenomenon represents the difficulties of scholars to master the details of any other policy domain, much less several that might be appropriate for comparison. This does not come as a surprise. To cite Gary Freeman (1985), indeed, the differences across domains within a single country would, on average, be greater than differences between the same domain across countries. That was a rather bold claim, but there are some reasons to expect policy domains to be significantly different, and therefore more difficult to compare. For example, some policy domains – such as defense or taxation – tend to be dominated by the government itself, while others – education, social policy – tend to have significant direct influence by citizens. Still other policy domains such as health and technology will be dominated by expert professionals who can reduce some of the role of government in policy. We could add to this list of variables, but the fundamental point remains that the nature of the policy does influence the ways in which policy is made and implemented. That said, differences across political systems do continue to show up in these domains, and it remains crucial for the student and the researcher of CPA to be sensitive to several sources of variation in process and outcomes.

In sum, the four volumes in the *Classics of Policy Analysis Studies* seek to present scholars the most salient work that the *JCPA* has covered in the last two decades and illustrate the multiple levels of study on which we can pursue the intellectual dialogue on comparative public policy. First, the series offers a centralized resource of work that furthers the aims of the new discipline of CPA and the inter-related fields of political science, sociology, and economics. Second, it contributes to the database of knowledge by investigating, applying, or developing theories and methodologies that ensure the validity and reliability of the comparative policy studies. Third, it extends case studies that enrich the ongoing discussions about what can be learned through comparative policy analytic studies to increase efficiency, effectiveness, transparency, and equity in public policy.

We wish the readers of the *Classics of Comparative Policy Analysis Studies* an interesting journey, from which they can adopt, adapt, borrow, transfer, extrapolate, or be inspired for their comparative studies.

Notes

1. Thomson Reuters. (2008). *Whos Who*.
2. Geva-May, I., & Lynn, E. L, Jr. (1998). Comparative policy analysis: Introduction to a new journal. *JCPA*, *1*(1), 1.

References

Allison, C. R., & Varone, F. (2009). Direct legislation in North America and Europe: Promoting or restricting biotechnology? *Journal of Comparative Policy Analysis, 11*(4), 425–449.

Boushey, G., & Luedtke, A. (2006). Fiscal federalism and the politics of immigration: Centralized and decentralized immigration policies in Canada and the United States. *Journal of Comparative Policy Analysis, 8*(3), 207–224.

Breen, M., & Doyle, D. (2013). The determinants of privatization: A comparative analysis of developing countries. *Journal of Comparative Policy Analysis: Research and Practice, 15*(1), 1–20.

Boardman, A. E., Greenberg, D.H., Vining, A.R. & Weimer, D.L. *Cost-Benefit Analysis: Concepts & Practices*, 2018, Cambridge University Press: Cambridge, UK.

Capano, G. (2009). Understanding policy change as an epistemological and theoretical problem. *Journal of Comparative Policy Analysis, 11*(1), 7–31.

Capano, G., Howlett, M., & Ramesh, M. (2015). Bringing governments back in: Governance and governing in comparative policy analysis. *Journal of Comparative Policy Analysis: Research and Practice, 17*(4), 311–321.

Clavier, C. (2010). Bottom–up policy convergence: A sociology of the reception of policy transfer in public health policies in Europe. *Journal of Comparative Policy Analysis, 12*(5), 451–466.

DeLeon, P., & Resnick-Terry, P. (1998). Comparative policy analysis: Déjà vu all over again?, *Journal of Comparative Policy Analysis: Research and Practice*, 1:1, 9–22.

Dunn, W. N. (2008, 2015). *Public Policy Analysis: An Introduction* (4 ed.). Upper Saddle River, NJ: Pearson Prentice Hall.

Freeman, G. P. (1985). National styles and policy sectors: Explaining structured variation. *Journal of Public Policy, 5*(4), 467–496.

Geddes, A., & Scholten, P. (2015). Policy analysis and Europeanization: An analysis of EU migrant integration policymaking. *Journal of Comparative Policy Analysis: Research and Practice, 17*(1), 41–59.

Geva-May, I. (Ed.) (2005). *Thinking Like a Policy Analyst: Policy Analysis as a Clinical Profession*. New York: Palgrave Macmillan.

Geva-May, I. (2002a). Comparative studies in public administration and public policy. *Public Management Review, 4*(3), 275–290.

Geva-May, I. (2002b). From theory to practice: Policy analysis, cultural bias and organizational arrangements. *Public Management Review, 4*(4), 581–591.

Geva-May, I. with Wildavsky, A. (1997, 2001, 2011). *An Operational Approach to Policy Analysis: The Craft: Prescriptions for Better Analysis*. Kluwer Academic Publishers.

Geva-May, I., & Lynn, L. E. Jr. (1998). Comparative Policy Analysis: Introduction to a New Journal. *Journal of Comparative Policy Analysis, 1*(1).

Geva-May, I., Hoffman, D. C., & Muhleisen, J. (2018). Twenty years of comparative policy analysis: A survey of the field and a discussion of topics and methods. *Journal of Comparative Policy Analysis: Research and Practice, 20*(1), 18–35.

Green-Pedersen, C. (2004). The dependent variable problem within the study of welfare state retrenchment: Defining the problem and looking for solutions. *Journal of Comparative Policy Analysis: Research and Practice, 6*(1), 3–14.

Greer, S., Elliott, H., & Oliver, R. (2015). Differences that matter: Overcoming methodological nationalism in comparative social policy research. *Journal of Comparative Policy Analysis: Research and Practice, 17*(4), 408–429.

Heidbreder, E. G. (2015). Governance in the European Union: A policy analysis of the attempts to raise legitimacy through civil society participation. *Journal of Comparative Policy Analysis: Research and Practice, 17*(4), 359–377.

Hoppe, R. (2002). Cultures of public policy problems. *Journal of Comparative Policy Analysis: Research and Practice, 4*(3), 305–326.

Howlett, M., & Cashore, B. (2009). The dependent variable problem in the study of policy change: Understanding policy change as a methodological problem. *Journal of Comparative Policy Analysis, 11*(1), 33–46.

Laguna, M. I. (2011). The challenges of implementing merit-based personnel policies in Latin America: Mexico's civil service reform experience. *Journal of Comparative Policy Analysis, 13*(1), 51–73.

Lee, S. Y., & Whitford, A. B. (2009). Government effectiveness in comparative perspective. *Journal of Comparative Policy Analysis, 11*(2), 249–281.

Leslie A. Pal (2014). Introduction: The OECD and policy transfer: Comparative case studies. *Journal of Comparative Policy Analysis: Research and Practice, 16*(3), 195–200.

Levy, D. C., & Zumeta, W. (2011). Private higher education and public policy: A global view. *Journal of Comparative Policy Analysis: Research and Practice, 13*(4), 345–349.

Marmor, T. R. (2010). Introduction: Varieties of comparative analysis in the world of medical care policy. *Journal of Comparative Policy Analysis, 12*(1–2), 5–10.

May, Peter, Jones B. D., Beem, B. E., Neff-Sharum, E. A. & Poague, M. K. (2005). Regional Policy Agglomeration: Arctic Policy in Canada and the United States, *Journal of Comparative Policy Analysis: Research and Practice,* 7(2), 121–136.

Mendez, C., Wishlade, F., & Yuill, D. (2008). Made to measure? Europeanization, goodness of fit and adaptation pressures in EU competition policy and regional aid. *Journal of Comparative Policy Analysis, 10*(3), 279–298.

Ng, M. K. (2007). Sustainable development and governance in East Asian world cities. *Journal of Comparative Policy Analysis, 9*(4), 321–335.

Peters, G. B. (2005). The problem of policy problems. *Journal of Comparative Policy Analysis, 7*(4), 349–370.

Radaelli, C. M. (2008). Europeanization, policy learning, and new modes of governance. *Journal of Comparative Policy Analysis, 10*(3), 239–254.

Radin, B. A. (2013). *Beyond Machiavelli: Policy Analysis Reaches Midlife.* Georgetown University Press.

Radin, B., & Boase, A. (2000). Federalism, political structure, and public policy in the United States and Canada, *Journal of Comparative Policy Analysis: Research and Practice, 2*(1), 65–89.

Ragin, C. C. (1994). Introduction to qualitative comparative analysis. *The Comparative Political Economy of the Welfare State, 299,* 300–309.

Ragin, C. and Zaret, D. (1983) Theory and Method in Comparative Research: Two Strategies. *Social Forces, 61* (3), 731–754.

Rose, R. (1991). What is lesson-drawing? *Journal of Public Policy, 11*(1), 3–30.

Ross, T. W., & Yan, J. (2015). Comparing public–private partnerships and traditional public procurement: Efficiency vs. flexibility. *Journal of Comparative Policy Analysis: Research and Practice, 17*(5), 448–466.

Rothmayr Allison, C., & Varone, F. (2009). Direct legislation in North America and Europe: Promoting or restricting biotechnology?. *Journal of Comparative Policy Analysis, 11*(4), 425–449.

Saurugger, S. (2005). Europeanization as a methodological challenge: The case of interest groups. *Journal of Comparative Policy Analysis, 7*(4), 291–312.

Scholten, P., & Timmermans, A. (2010). Setting the immigrant policy agenda: Expertise and politics in the Netherlands, France and the United Kingdom. *Journal of Comparative Policy Analysis, 12*(5), 527–544.

Sheingate, A. D. (2009). Federalism and the regulation of agricultural biotechnology in the United States and European Union. *Journal of Comparative Policy Analysis, 11*(4), 477–497.

Smith, A. J., & Williams, D. R. (2007). Father-friendly legislation and paternal time across Western Europe. *Journal of Comparative Policy Analysis, 9*(2), 175–192.

Stiller, S., & van Kersbergen, K. (2008). The matching problem within comparative welfare state research: How to bridge abstract theory and specific hypotheses. *Journal of Comparative Policy Analysis: Research and Practice, 10*(2), 133–149.

Thomson Reuters (2008). Iris Geva-May, *Who's Who.*

Vining, A. R., & Weimer, D. L. (1998). Informing institutional design: Strategies for comparative cumulation. *Journal of Comparative Policy Analysis, 1*(1), 39–60.

Wolf, A., & Baehler, K. J. (2018). Learning transferable lessons from single cases in comparative policy analysis. *Journal of Comparative Policy Analysis: Research and Practice, 20*(4), 420–434.

Part 2
Lesson Drawing Relationships: Comparing Associated Disciplines and Comparative Policy Analysis

The Rise of the Governance Mantra and Comparative Policy Analysis

GILIBERTO CAPANO

Introduction

Comparative policy analysis (CPA) is the systematic study of the processes by which policies are made and of their outputs and outcomes. Thus, CPA is one of the ways to study how policies are steered and how societies are governed. The intellectual mission of the CPA, as outlined by Geva-May and Lynn 1998, has given rise, among others, to the analytical interest on the concept of governance and comparative governance. One could say that CPA and governance have been traveling companions: with the growing interest in governance scholarship, the two new domains of CPA and governance have triggered and structured a reciprocal and fruitful interaction.

Governance has been, and partially still is, one of the "new" concepts that has been acquiring prominence in the social sciences. The governance shift has represented a relevant watershed in the development of various disciplines, such as political science and public administration and, obviously, even for public policy analysis. Governance has become a pivotal topic for researchers who have begun to focus on the governance "of everything" and governance "everywhere". Transnational governance, good governance, governance without government, collaborative governance, horizontal governance, multi-level governance (MLG), co-governance, hybrid governance, and meta-governance are some of the concepts and labels that have been forged in the age of governance. It has become a kind of "magic" word (Pollit and Hupe 2011) that has triggered a mantra capable of enchanting all of us, redirecting many research strategies and designs, and pushing to reconceptualize the existing bulk of theories concerning politics and policy.

Deciding whether and how the governance mantra has been a substantial shift in political and policy studies, or if it has been one of the recurrent fashionable events that characterize the diachronic developments in social sciences, is a topic of endless discussion.

However, when a new (or renewed) concept is widely adopted, there is some real motivation in exploring it further. In the case of governance, its popularity is clearly due to the need for conceptually bordering and grasping the effects of those socio-economic and political processes that have generated the growing problems of governability, of government overload, and of social complexity since the 1970s and 1980s (Peters and Pierre 2018). All in all, this conceptual challenge has characterized even the perspective of CPA: the crisis in governability, government overload, and increasing social complexity have radically impacted policymaking (that is, how to define collective problems, to decide how to deal with them, and to implement decisions taken), social expectations, and policy outcomes.

Thus, the governance mantra has been, and still is, something relevant also for public policy and, consequently, for CPA. In this essay, I discuss and take stock of the reciprocal interaction that has occurred between the literature on governance and CPA. In the following section, I summarize the rise of the governance literature and its implications for public policy analysis. In the third section, I outline the reciprocal influences between governance and CPA, while in the fourth concluding section I argue what CPA should still do when studying governance.

The Rise of the Governance Mantra and Its Implication for Public Policy

The Mantra and the Battle for Meaning

Governance, as a word and thus as a concept, has recently entered the language of social sciences and is in fact an elitist term (Hirst 2000). It is not the case that governance is, in common language, considered as a synonym for government; in fact, according to Webster's Dictionary, governance means "the act or process of governing, specifically authoritative direction and control", or the "lawful control over the affairs of a political unit (as a nation)", or "the act or activity of looking after and making decisions about something". Substantially, then, governance is synonymous with government and has started to be used, in the social sciences, to define something new or at least perceived as new. Thus, this word has been rediscovered to try to interpret, grasp, design, and order the drastic changes in the political world since the 1970s. The first evidence of the fiscal crisis of the Welfare State, together with the long-term effects of the democratization in western countries and the massive internationalization and globalization of many public policies, along with the explosion in social demands, has effected significant changes in political and policy processes. Thus, it appears that the normal categories for analysing politics have almost become obsolete.

What was perceived as hierarchically ordered and linearly governed has suddenly appeared to be fragmented and intricate; governments' capacity to steer their societies and their international role appears to be weaker and in some ways elusive. To deal with these upheavals, social scientists have started to recur to new concepts, and governance (together with networks) is at the top of their list. Thus, governance has become the word used to define how societies are governed currently in this age of "crisis".

Thus, the governance mantra has exploded and numerous definitions have been proposed. There are at least five common uses for the word, according to Hirst (2000); some scholars, on the other hand, present six definitions of the term (Rhodes 1996), while van Kersbergen and van Waarden (2004) counted nine possible definitions of the concept of "governance": economic governance, "good" governance, corporate governance, governance as minimal State, governance as socio-cybernetic system, governance as a self-organizing system, network governance, and so on. Indeed, there is considerable danger of constructing a true Tower of Babel as far as the definition of governance is concerned.

It is well known that the battle for the definition of governance has been fought over the difference between government and governance. This government/governance dichotomy seems to be a cornerstone of most of the definitions proposed in political and social science studies. The basic definition was proposed by Pierre (2000), who distinguished between state-centric "old governance" and society-centric "new governance". The former is characterized by a state-centric perspective (where the focus is on how the political-institutional system steers society and public policies). The "society-centric" perspective, meanwhile, places the focus on the ability of society to govern itself. At some point the battle assumed a radical shape, when some scholars stated that governance means "a change in the nature of the meaning of government" (Bevir and Rhodes 2003:45), whereas government and governance are conceptualized as the two poles in a continuum of different possible ways of governing and coordinating the policymaking process: the extreme case from this perspective – but one that is considered to be realistic, nevertheless – is that of "governance without government", meaning the actual coordination of a complex policymaking process without the presence of any form of hierarchy.

This battle is well summarized by some of the various definitions of governance in politics and policy: "the traditions and institutions by which authority in a country is exercised for the common good" (Kaufmann 2005:82); "the processes and institutions, both formal and informal, that guide and restrain the collective activities of a group" (Keohane and Nye 2000:12); "the tools, strategies and relationships used by governments to help govern" (Bell and Hindmoor 2009:2);

> the reflexive self-organization of independent actors involved in complex relations of reciprocal interdependence, with such self-organization being based on continuing dialogue and resource-sharing to develop mutually beneficial joint projects and to manage the contradictions and dilemmas inevitably involved in such situations;
>
> (Jessop 2002: see also Rhodes 1996:652–653)

"the pursuit of the collective interest" (Peters and Pierre 2018:11). All these definitions, in some way or another, show how the substance of the debate on governance lies in Pierre's definition, which clearly grasps the empirical aspect of the ongoing debate on governance: how is a new way of governing societies – "new governance" – eclipsing the old governance model? Is "government" – meaning the hierarchical governance framework – truly losing its central role in the policymaking process, to be replaced by a more decentralized, self-governing form of governance (Hill and Lynn 2005)? All in all, the battle for definitions cannot hide the underlying normative afflatus: what has been at stake for years is a "normative" goal of scholars regarding how the means of steering democracy should develop.

Currently, after the battle for a definition has decreased its intensity and even in its normative, almost ideological, basis, there is a sufficiently shared view that governance is not a new way to govern, nor a new theory of governing but

> is about establishing, promoting and supporting a specific type of relationship between governmental and non-governmental actors in the governing process. Thus, governance is about actors and their interactions, and the ideas and instruments through which policy processes are coordinated. In other words, governance is another way of ordering reality, of explaining how public policies are decided and implemented, and of indicating those actors with a role in such policy-making, and the interaction between these policy-makers.
>
> (Capano, Howlett and Ramesh 2015a:313)

Thus, there is common agreement in considering that governance is not a new theory on how societies are governed but simply a new way to organize political and policy analysis, as the governance lenses allow for a better understanding of "what is worthy to study" (Stoker 1998:18).

The Five Faces of Governance: Structure, Dynamics, Policy Instruments, Capacity, and Strategy

Thus, the governance mantra has produced a significant revision of what should be studied to better understand the reality of political phenomena by focusing on the different dimensions of the way societies are steered. The rise of the analytical attention on governance indicates that scholars should focus on governance intended as structure, dynamics, policy instruments, strategy, and capacity.

The focus on governance as structure has meant rethinking and reconceptualizing the institutional arrangements through which societies, and thus policies, are coordinated. From this point of view what is relevant, then, is that the governance perspective has pushed to redesign how the fundamental principles of social coordination are institutionalized in a specific socio-political system and, consequently, in its own policy system. Here, what matters are the structure or the institutionalized characteristics through which societal and policy steering is channeled. They have been defined as governance modes/arrangements (Howlett 2009; Capano 2011), regimes of laws and administrative practices (Lynn, Heirich and Hill 2001), and the set of stable institutional and ideational parameters and related actor constellations (Zurn, Walti and Enderlein 2010). Governance as structure helps to reconsider the various components the institutional arrangements by taking into consideration not only the formal institutions but also institutionalized practices, interactions, and actors' roles.

The structure of governance can also be distinguished according to the prevailing principle of coordination and thus according to the prevalence of hierarchy, market, or self-steering (network) (Peters 1996; Considine and Lewis 1999; Newmann 2001; Kooiman 2003; Capano 2011). This way of considering the structural characteristics of governance is, however, immediately challenged by empirical analysis, whereas what emerges is that the description of a specific governance structure in terms of the prevailing principle of coordination could be very misleading because, in reality, hybridity is what prevails. There is no pure, "real" hierarchical or market-driven or network-driven governance structure/regime/arrangement/mode, but there are governance mixes (Capano, Rayner, and Zito 2012) that impose a more fine-grained analysis on governance structures.

The focus on the intrinsic dynamic characteristics of governance allows to see the structure of governance in action and thus to escape the static views of the institutional evolution of the governance arrangements that are too often analysed from a punctuated perspective. This tendency is evident in the recurrent debate on the demise/return of the State (Evans, Rueschemeyer and Skocpol 1985; Evans 1997) or in the radical change in the actual way of steering policies, as attested by the New Public Management (NPM) literature that initially underlined NPM as a definitive epochal watershed in how to steer policies and public administration (Aucoin 1990; Lane 2000; Barzelay 2001) but subsequently significantly changed this interpretation by admitting that NPM has been only a partial shift in pre-existing governance characteristics (Ongaro 2009; Pollitt and Bouckaert 2011). Thus, governance should be conceived not only as a structure, and, thus, as an institutionalized set of actors and distribution of powers, ideas, and practices but also as an ongoing process through which changes occur (Levi-Faur 2012; Capano, Howlett and Ramesh 2015b).

A focus on the instrumental side of governance has been advanced when scholars began researching how governance truly operates. In fact, when underlining the developments of new, more horizontal and less hierarchical governance arrangements, scholars have observed that this processes has been undertaken through the shift from hard to soft policy instruments (Rhodes 1997, Stoker 1998; Salamon 2002). When this divide has been overcome, and it becomes clear not only that in new governance arrangements hierarchy is still present but also that the distinction between hard and soft instruments is not helpful in grasping the reality of governing, the instrumental dimension of governance can be analysed in a less normative way and thus can express its full potential. What has emerged here is that governance impacts the reality of policy through policy instruments that are the concrete means through which governance arrangements and dynamics drive the characteristics of policies and steer them towards the expected effects. Thus, the debate over the tools of government (Hood 1983) has shifted to the tools of governance (Salamon 2000, 2002). Obviously, this dimension of governance has acquired great interest in public policy, where the connection among governance arrangements, policy design, and policy instruments is pivotal to understanding how policies work and could work (Howlett 2009, 2014, 2019).

By considering governance as strategy, we find two different analytical perspectives. On the one hand, governance as strategy means "governancing" the activity of continuously redesigning the governance arrangements of a specific policy/political context (Levi-Faur 2012). On the other hand, governance can be seen as a strategic dimension of policymaking, whereas "strategic" captures the power dimension of the governance arrangements. This means that actors are aware that the features of governance arrangements and the types of policy instruments adopted have an impact on the interests they are pursuing, and that the positions/roles they have in the existing governance arrangements represent a fundamental source of power and/or influence. This awareness justifies the emphasis that all governments and policy actors have placed on continually redesigning governance arrangements within policy fields in order to better accomplish their goals. At the same time, this awareness underlies the ongoing battle over policy instruments and the features of governance arrangements (Capano, Howlett and Ramesh 2015b).

The capacity dimension of governance focuses on its effectiveness in delivering what is expected. This dimension has been analysed as good governance (World Bank 1994; Fukuyama 2013; Pierre and Peters 2005), as State or government capacity (Besley and Person 2011), as quality of government (Rothstein 2011), as systemic sustainability in governing pooled resources (Ostrom 1990), and as the capacity to produce optimal or effective regulation (Jordana and Levi Faur 2004). All these definitions help us grasp specific characteristics of governance capacity that can more generally be used to assess whether and how a governance arrangement is capable of achieving its declared goals and to obtain and maintain the necessary political consensus among the actors involved in the specific policy field in question. Thus, governance capacity represents a fundamental concept to grasp whether and how a specific governance arrangement is capable of reaching/maintaining its policy goals as well as its political legitimacy (Capano, Howlett and Ramesh 2015b).

The different faces of governance show how, thanks to this concept, it is possible to reconceptualize the different dimensions of political and policy processes in a very dense and interactive way. The governance mantra, then, can be considered not only for its "magical" side but even for its effective capacity in having encouraged an analytical reordering of the complexity of the political phenomenon by assembling its substantial basic dimensions.

CPA and the Five Faces of Governance: Reciprocal Lessons

The five faces of governance have risen and developed together with CPA. All in all, what do policy scholars do if not analysing, understanding, explaining, and sometimes prescribing how governance works? Whatever governance is defined, public policy can be considered to study it in all its aspects and dimensions. Moreover, precisely because public policy is intrinsically comparative, the study of comparative governance can be considered as a part of CPA. In addition, this is surely true, although with a different degree of intensity, for all five faces of governance listed above. All in all, governance and CPA have been growing up together, almost intertwined: they need each other.

The governance mantra, in fact, has redesigned the way we see policymaking as well as its interactions with political processes. It has obliged us to re-think the role of the State as well of the "market". It has obliged us to include in any analytical perspective the increased complexity of policy-making, and thus the awareness that other, different principles of coordination could coexist with hierarchy and market (like networks). It has obliged us to rethink the role and the process of selection of policy instruments and thus of designing policies. This reorientation has interacted with CPA in two different ways. On the one hand, governance studies needed to be an object of comparative research to gain empirical relevance and reliability; on the other hand, it has offered a new analytical framework (even in terms of "what" to be studied) for those interested to do CPA.

The two sides of the relationship between the governance mantra and CPA have been reinforcing each other. In fact, thanks to governance literature suggestions, CPA has developed interesting and enlightening comparative research on how governance truly works and develops, while thanks to the research agendas developed by scholars of CPA, the concept of governance has acquired a greater analytical and empirical basis and thus has decreased the risk of appearing more of a fashion than of a real shift in analytical perspective.

Furthermore, CPA, by directly including the governance shifts in its theoretical lenses, has greatly deepened our knowledge of the five faces of governance. Moreover, in CPA, very often the different faces of governance are taken into consideration together as analytical elements. That said, below I try to summarize how the inclusion of the governance perspective has increased the potentiality and the analytical quality of CPA, by focusing on the five faces of governance discussed above.

CPA has developed and deepened the structural dimension of governance in various ways, two of them in particular: MLG and modes of governance. The comparative policy literature on MLG is substantial, not only in the case of the abundant research on MLG carried out in the EU but in the case of the comparison of specific policy fields as well as the decentralization of policymaking. MLG and European Public Policy are substantially the same thing, and all the relevant literature cannot be summarized here (see Bache 2012; Stephenson 2013). What is relevant here is that the dense empirical analysis compares how MLG works in different EU countries even with respect to the supranational level has helped us understand how the structure of governance arrangements has changed over time and how this has implications for the characteristics of policymaking, especially for its outputs and outcomes. This focus on MLG has been applied even in comparing the process of reforms in different policy fields, for example, tobacco control policy (Studlar and Carney 2019) or environmental policy (Duit 2014). As for modes of governance, this topic has been at the centre of many comparative studies in different policy fields, especially in terms of focus on governance shifts (Capano 2011; Giest and Howlett 2013; Ozerol et al. 2018). Furthermore, it must be underlined how the interest of CPA in changes in governance modes has encountered and intertwined with two other streams of the literature focusing on the rise of neoliberal policies (Evans, Richmond, and Shields 2005) and on administrative reforms (Pollitt and Bouckaert 2011).

Governance dynamics has increasingly been the object of CPA. Previous decades have seen major reforms and changes in the way policies are steered and thus a focus on dynamics, that is, the process through which governance develops has been a must for policy scholars. The literature here is truly immense, as "governance" can be operationalized in many ways when the focus is on such dynamics as administrative reforms, regulatory reforms, and welfare reforms. What is relevant here is that CPA has been capable of unpacking the meaning of governance dynamics by focusing not only on the content of reforms produced through the dynamics but also on the characteristics of the process, the role of interest groups and other stakeholders, the networking of the set of policy actors, and the different political and policy trade-offs at stake. Thanks to CPA, then, we know a great deal about not only the determinants of policy dynamics but also their outputs.

In terms of policy instruments, CPA has worked particularly effectively on the changes to the policy instruments adopted from a comparative perspective in different policy fields. CPA has shown how the policy mixes, through which polices are steered, have been redesigned. Here, the role of CPA has been particularly fruitful in grasping and describing the incredible variety of policy instruments that are adopted in various policy fields. Thus, thanks to CPA, we know how rich the instrumental and operative side of governance is.

Governance capacity from a comparative perspective has been a field in which not only scholars but also international organizations, such as the Organization for Economic Cooperation and Development and the World Trade Organization, have constantly shown a comparative commitment. It must be underlined, however, that CPA on governance capacity has been a latecomer with respect to the long-lasting stream of research on mainstream political science, where the problem of governance capacity has been operationalized in terms of "quality" of governance – very often operationalized by emphasizing the quality of government (Rothstein and Teorell 2008; Rothstein 2011; Holmberg and Rothstein 2012; Fukuyama 2013) – or, in a more broad sense, has been conceptualized in terms of quality of democracy (Diamond and Morlino 2005). CPA on governance capacity has been developing recently based on the theoretical focus on policy capacity, which is defined as

> the set of skills and resources – or competences and capabilities – necessary to perform policy functions. Skills or competences can be categorized into three types: analytical, operational and political. Each of these three competences involve resources or capabilities at three different levels: individual, organizational, and systemic capacity.
> (Wu, Howlett and Ramesh 2018:3)

Thanks to this analytical framework, governance capacity can be unpacked and analysed in its various dimensions, which are multi-level and multi-actor. This overlapping of governance capacity with policy capacity is not only very relevant from a theoretical point of view (also because it clearly unifies policy and governance) but also because it is quite useful in understanding and explaining how capacity truly works when policies need to be steered (Capano and Pritoni 2016; Dunlop 2018; Yap 2018). Furthermore, the focus on governance capacity can also be approached in terms of characteristics of policy design, where the analytical capacity of governments or its will can be considered as a relevant driver of governance capacity (Howlett, Mukherjee, and Woo 2015; Capano 2018). On the analytical side of governance capacity, CPA has deepened the analysis of the advisory system (Craft and Howlett 2012; Craft and Wilder 2017) and of the use of evidence-based policymaking (Tagney and Howes 2016; Wiseman and Davidson 2018).

As for the strategic dimension of governance, CPA has been working less well than expected, at least if compared with the substantial work carried out on the other four faces of governance. Obviously one could say that when focusing on dynamics, scholars necessarily take into consideration the strategic will or behaviour of governments and other policy actors involved. However, this could be said for any analysis of governance, where in one way or another the different faces can be touched on at least marginally. The lack of autonomous focus on the strategic dimension of governance (among the few existing works, see Capano 2015; Lewis 2015; Natali 2015) could be because this face requires a significant focus on the role of governments as well as a research design capable of gathering high-quality information and data on the strategic motivations of all the actors involved. Thus, this is a very demanding research strategy. Or it could be due to a certain theoretical dis-attention by comparative policy scholars to the strategic motivations of actors and especially of governments.

What CPA Should Still Do When Studying Governance

As I have tried to show, albeit in a very synthetic way, the governance mantra has had some useful and fruitful effects from a CPA perspective: in reality, for CPA to take into consideration its analytical tools, the governance matter has represented a trigger for better research design and for enlarging the analytical lenses in formulating comparative public policy.

However, there are some gaps that CPA has still not filled when governance is the object of research.

First, there is the issue of fully implementing the suggestion that Freeman (1985) proposed when analysing the relevance of policy style from a comparative perspective: working not only to compare the governance of national systems but to compare sectorial governance, as the governance structure is not necessarily the same for all policy fields in the same countries. Here, CPA has still not developed its full potential. This is a real pity because the governance perspective could be very useful to enlarge one's perspective when explaining whether and how a national governance style prevails with respect to a sectorial one, or, better, why and how some policy fields are more impermeable than others with respect to their governance structure, dynamics, and instruments. Here, the governance perspective allows for a broader and more receptive lens of analysis with respect to the Freeman focus (which was on the politics/policy prominence), and a deep and substantial research effort on the theme could say something more about how governance arrangements develop and change over time. All in all, what is missing here is a systematic comparative analysis of governance systems.

Second, there is the too often forgotten or marginalized question of the performance of governance. Whatever the "face" of governance is taken into consideration, too often policy scholars forget to relate governance structure, dynamics, instruments, strategy, and even capacity to the real effects that an analysed, compared, governance "thing" is capable of producing. This is quite surprising, if we consider that in the last decades there has been a "feast" of reforming governance. Governance has been repeatedly changed under the assumption, at least in the rhetoric of the reformers, that it was the best way to change the performance on the policies delivered. This dis-attention to governance performance can only be partially justified because policy scholars prefer to pay attention to the characteristics of the process and related outputs rather than on outcomes (on the basis of the assumption that the causal relation between outputs and outcomes is very loose). To fill the gap in the performance of governance from a comparative perspective would be important, I would say pivotal, to understande whether and how governance reforms have had similar/dissimilar performances in similar/dissimilar countries/policy fields.

Lastly, there is at the moment a certain tendency to proceed that is separated among those scholars working on specific types of governance or on different levels of governance. For example, there is an unexpectedly deep divide among relevant streams of research on governance, such as comparative regulation, global/transnational governance, collaborative governance, national/sectorial governance, comparative design, and policy instruments. This divide is surely justified by the natural and necessary path to specialization, but at the same time can represent a great loss in terms of a general understanding of governance as well as a limitation in developing a more integrated conceptualization (in terms of interconnecting the five faces of governance). Here, probably, a collective effort towards more communication and interactions among the different streams could be useful, and, from the CPA point of view, it could be very exciting to work on a more integrated analytical framework when empirically studying governance.

I know perfectly well that this expectation may appear as naïve. At the same time, I must underline that precisely because governance is a descriptive concept, to agree on a shared descriptive/analytical framework (whereas the causal linkages are left to one's individual epistemological choice) would be a fundamental step in making the contribution of CPA to governance more effective.

References

Aucoin, P. (1990) Administrative Reform in Public Management: Paradigms, Principles, Paradoxes and Pendulums. *Governance*, 3(2), 115–137.

Bache, I. (2012) Multi-level Governance, in D. Levi-Faur (ed.) *Oxford Handbook of Governance*, Oxford: Oxford University Press, pp. 628–641.

Barzelay, M. (2001) *The New Public Management: Improving Research and Policy Dialogue*. Berkeley: University of California Press.

Bell, S., and Hindmoor, P. (2009) *Rethinking Governance: The Centrality of the State in Modern Society*. Cambridge: Cambridge University Press.

Besley, T., and Persson T. (2011) *Pillars of Prosperity: State Capacity and Economic Development*. Princeton, NJ: Princeton University Press.

Bevir, M. R., and Rhodes, R. A. W. (2003) *Interpreting British Government*. London: Routledge.

Capano, G. (2011) Government Continues to Do Its Job. A Comparative Study of Governance Shifts in the Higher Education Sector. *Public Administration*, 89(4), 1622–1642.

Capano, G. (2015) Federal Strategies for Changing Governance in Higher Education: Australia, Canada, and Germany Compared, in G. Capano, M. Howlett, M. Ramesh (eds.) *Varieties of Governance*, London: Palgrave, pp. 103–130.

Capano, G. (2018) Policy Design Spaces in Reforming Governance in Higher Education: The Dynamics in Italy and the Netherlands. *Higher Education* 75(5), 675–694.

Capano, G., Howlett, M., and Ramesh, M. (2015a) Bringing Governments Back In: Governance and Governing in Comparative Policy Analysis. *Journal of Comparative Policy Analysis* 17(4), 311–321.

Capano, G., Howlett, M., and Ramesh, M. (2015b). Rethinking Governance in Public Policy, in G. Capano, M. Howlett, M. Ramesh (eds.) *Varieties of Governance*, London: Palgrave, pp. 3–26.

Capano, G., and Pritoni, A. (2016) Mirror, Mirror on the Wall, Who is the 'Most' Reformist One of All? Policy Innovation and Design Coherence of the Renzi Government. *Italian Contemporary Politics* 8(3), 289–302.

Capano, G., Rayner, J., and Zito, A. (2012) Governance from the Bottom Up: Complexity and Divergence in Comparative Perspective. *Public Administration* 90(1), 56–73.

Considine, M., and Lewis, J. (1999) Governance at Ground Level: The Frontline Bureaucrat in the Age of Markets and Networks. *Public Administration Review* 59(6), 467–460.

Craft, J., and Howlett, M. (2012) Policy Formulation, Governance Shifts and Policy Influence: Location and Content in Policy Advisory Systems. *Journal of Public Policy* 32(2), 79–98.

Craft, J., and Wilder, M. (2017) Catching a Second Wave: Context and Compatibility in Advisory System Dynamics. *Policy Studies Journal* 45(1), 215–239.

Diamond, L. J., and Morlino, L. (2005) *Assessing the Quality of Democracy*. Baltimore: Johns Hopkins University Press.

Duit, mA. (2016) The Four Faces of the Environmental State: Environmental Governance Regimes in 28 Countries. *Environmental Politics* 25(1), 69–91.

Dunlop, C. (2018) Building Organizational Political Capacity Through Policy Learning: Communicating with Citizens on Health and Safety in the UK, in X. Wun, M. Howlett, M. Ramesh (eds.) *Policy Capacity and Governance*, London: Palgrave, pp. 265–284.

Evans, P. (1997) The Eclipse of the State? Reflections on Stateness in an Era of Globalization. *World Politics* 50(1), 62–87.

Evans, P., Rueschemeyer, D., and Skocpol, T. (1985) *Bringing the State back in*. New York: Cambridge University Press.

Freeman, G. (1985) National Styles and Policy Sectors: Explaining Structured Variation. *Journal of Public Policy* 5(4), 467–496.

Fukuyama, F. (2013) What is Governance. *Governance* 26(2), 347–368.

Giest, S., and Howlett, M. (2013) Comparative Climate Change Governance: Lessons from European Transnational Municipal Network Management Efforts. *Environmental Policy and Governance* 23(6), 341–353.

Hill, J. C., and Lynn, L. E. Jr. (2005) Is Hierarchical Governance in Decline? Evidence from Empirical Research. *Journal of Public Administration Research and Theory* 15(2), 173–195.

Hirst, P. (2000) Democracy and Governance, in Jon Pierre (ed.) *Debating Governance: Authority, Steering and Democracy*, Oxford: Oxford University Press, pp. 13–35.

Holmberg, S., and Rothstein, B. (2012) *Good Government: The Relevance of Political Science*. Cheltenham and Northampton: Edward Elgar.

Hood, C. (1983) *The Tools of Government*. Chatham, NJ: Chatham House.

Hooghe, L., and Marks, G. (2001) *Multi-level Governance and European Integration*. New York: Rowman & Littlefield Publishers.

Howlett, M. (2009) Governance Modes, Policy Regimes and Operational Plans: A Multi-Level Nested Model of Policy Instrument Choice and Policy Design. *Policy Sciences*, 42(1), 73–89.

Howlett, M. (2014) From Old to New Policy Design: Design Thinking Beyond Markets and Collaborative Governance. *Policy Sciences*, 47(3), 197–207.

Howlett, M. (2019) *Designing Public Policies; Principles and Instruments*. London: Routledge. 2nd ed.

Howlett, M., Mukherjee, I., and Woo, J. J. (2015) From Tools to Toolkits in Policy Design Studies: The New Design Orientation towards Policy Formulation Research. *Policy & Politics* 43(2), 291–311.

Jessop, B. (2000) Governance Failure, in G. Stoker (ed.) *The New Politics of British Local Governance*, Basingstoke: Palgrave, pp. 11–32.

Jordana, J., and Levi-Faur, D. (2004) *The Politics of Regulation: Institutions and Regulatory Reforms for the Age of Governance*. Northampton, MA: Edward Elgar.

Kaufmann, d. (2005) *Myths and Realities of Governance and Corruption*. Washington: World Bank.

Keohane, R. O., and Nye, J. S. (2000) Introduction, in J. S. Nye, J. D. Donahue (eds.) *Governance in a Globalizing World*, Washington, DC: Brookings Institution, pp. 1–44.

Kooiman, J. (2003) *Governing as Governance*. London: Sage.

Lane, J. E. (2000) *New Public Management*. London: Routledge.

Levi-Faur, D. (2012) From "Big Government" to "Big Governance"?, in D. Levi-Faur (ed.) *The Oxford Handbook of Governance*, Oxford: Oxford University Press, pp. 3–19.

Lewis, J. (2015) Research Policy as "Carrots and Sticks": Governance Strategies in Australia, the United Kingdom and New Zealand, in G. Capano, M. Howlett, M. Ramesh (eds.) *Varieties of Governance*, London: Palgrave, pp. 131–150.

Lynn, L. E., Jr., and Geva-May, I. (1998) Introduction to the Journal of Comparative Policy Analysis, *Journal of Comparative Policy Analysis: Research and Practice*, 1(1), pp. 5–8.

Lynn, L. E., Jr., Heinrich, C. J., and Hill, C. J. (2001) *Improving Governance: A New Logic for Empirical Research*. Washington, DC: Georgetown University Press.

Natali, D. (2015) Changing Multi-level Governance: The Regained Centrality of National Policy-makers in Recasting Pensions in Central Eastern Europe. in G. Capano, M. Howlett, M. Ramesh (eds.) *Varieties of Governance*, London: Palgrave, pp. 151–169.

Newmann, J. (2001) *Modernising Governance: New Labour Policy and Society*. London and Newbury Park, CA: Sage.

Ongaro, E. (2009) *Public Management Reform and Modernization: Trajectories of Administrative Change in Italy, France, Greece, Portugal and Spain*. Cheltenham and Northampton, MA: Edward Elgar.

Ostrom, E. (1990) *Governing the Commons: The Evolution of Institutions for Collective Action*. New York: Cambridge University Press.

Özerol, G., Vinke-de Kruijf, J., Brisbois, M. C., Casiano Flores, C., Deekshit, P., Girard, C., Knieper, C., Mirnezami, S. J., Ortega-Reig, M., Ranjan, P., Schröder, N. J. S., and Schröter, B. (2018) Comparative Studies of Water Governance: A Systematic Review. *Ecology and Society* 23(4): 43.

Peters, B. G. (1996) *Governing: Four Emerging Models*. Lawrence: University Press of Kansas.

Peters, G., and Pierre, J. (2018) *Comparative Governance*. Cambridge: Canbridge University Press.

Pierre, J. (2000) Introduction, in Jon Pierre (ed.) *Debating Governance: Authority, Steering and Democracy*, Oxford: Oxford University Press, pp. 1–10.

Pierre, J., and Peters, B. G. (2005) *Governing Complex Societies: Trajectories and Scenarios*. Basingstoke: Palgrave-Macmillan.

Pollitt, C., and Bouckaert, G. (2011) *Public Management Reform: A Comparative Analysis*. Oxford: Oxford University Press.

Pollitt, P., and Hupe, P. (2011) Talking About Government. *Public Management Review*, 13(5), 641–658.

Rhodes, R. A. W. (1996) The New Governance: Governing Without Governance. *Political Studies* 44(4), 652–667.

Rhodes, R. A. W. (1997) *Understanding Governance*. Milton Keynes: Open University Press.

Rothstein, B. (2011) *The Quality of Government: Corruption, Social Trust and Inequality in a Comparative Perspective*. Chicago: University of Chicago.

Rothstein, B., and Teorell, J. (2008) What is Quality of Government: A Theory of Impartial Political Institutions. *Governance* 21(2), 165–190.

Salamon, L. (2000) The New Governance and the Tools of Public Action: An Introduction. *Fordham Urban Law Journal* 28(5), 1611–1674.

Salamon, L. (ed.) (2002) *The Tools of Government. A Guide to the New Governance*. Oxford: Oxford University Press.

Stephenson, P. (2013) Twenty Years of Multi-level Governance: 'Where Does It Come From? What Is It? Where Is It Going?' *Journal of European Public Policy* 20(6), 817–837.

Stoker, g. (1998) Governance as Theory: Five Propositions. *International Social Science Journal* 50(1): 17–28.

Studlar, D., and Cairney, P. (2019) Multilevel Governance, Public Health and the Regulation of Food: Is Tobacco Control Policy a Model? *Journal of Public Health Policy* 40(2), 147–165.

Tagney, P., and Howes, M. (2012) The Politics of Evidence-based Policy: A Comparative Analysis of Climate Adaptation in Australia and the UK. *Environment and Planning C: Government and Policy* 34(6), 1115–1134.

Van Kersbergen, K., and Van Waarden, F. (2004) Governance' as a Bridge between Disciplines: Cross-disciplinary Inspiration Regarding Shifts in Governance and Problems of Governability, Accountability and Legitimacy. *European Journal of Political Research* 43(2), 143–171.

Yap, F. (2018) Government's Credible Accountability and Strategic Policy Capacity: Evidence from the Asian NICs of Taiwan, South Korea, Malaysia, and Singapore, in X. Wun, M. Howlett, M. Ramesh (eds.) *Policy Capacity and Governance*, London: Palgrave, pp. 203–228.

Wiseman, A., and Davidson, P. (eds.) (2018) *Cross-nationally Comparative, Evidence-based Educational Policymaking and Reform*. Emerald Publishing Limited.

World Bank (1994) *Governance: The World Bank's Experience*. Washington: World Bank.

Wu, X., Howlett, M., and Ramesh, M. (eds.) (2018) *Policy Capacity and Governance: Assessing Governmental Competences and Capabilities in Theory and Practice*. London: Palgrave.

Zürn, M., Wälti, S., and Enderlein, H. (2010) Introduction, in H. Enderlein, S. Wälti, M. Zürn (eds.) *Handbook of Multilevel Governance*, Cheltenham: Edward Elgar, pp. 1–13.

Part 3
The Classics: Institutions and Governance in Comparative Policy Analysis Studies

Bringing Governments Back in: Governance and Governing in Comparative Policy Analysis

GILIBERTO CAPANO, MICHAEL HOWLETT, & M RAMESH

ABSTRACT *In many visions of governance, governments are portrayed as playing a "steering", rather than "rowing", role. The widespread use of privatization, deregulation, decentralization and third-party governments are often mentioned as concrete manifestations of the broad transformation which has led to new forms of governance. Examined more closely, however, the large and growing body of literature on governance has done little to clarify what is "new" about "new governance". Does it indicate a clean break from institutions and processes of the past, or is it merely chronicling an assortment of instrument changes necessary for governments to adapt to changing socio-economic conditions? Do the changes really indicate the emergence of a new system in which the government is merely another player on a par with societal and international counterparts? More fundamentally, is governance a normative framework reflecting the hopes and desires of those who prefer smaller governments, or an empirical description of an existing reality? This article briefly surveys existing studies in the field as an introduction to the articles in this special issue. These articles provide strong arguments in support of the view that governments continue to play a pivotal role in policy-making, and that if this fact is not taken into consideration then the perception is of governance risk being anchored to a merely normative or prescriptive view rather than an empirically robust one.*

Introduction

Traditional public policy and administrative processes are now often said to have given way to something "new", encapsulated in the catchy but elusive term "governance". Under the new rubric, policies are often described as being made and implemented in markets or in state–society networks in a form of "collaborative governance" rather than by government agencies as envisioned by traditional studies of public policy and administration. In this new vision, governments are often portrayed as playing a "steering", rather than "rowing", role. The widespread use of privatization, deregulation, decentralization and third-party governments are often mentioned as concrete manifestations of broad transformations which have led to and informed new forms of governance. While the details vary depending on the case and jurisdiction examined, this broad narrative is remarkably similar in most writings in this vein.

Examined more closely, however, this large and growing literature has done little to clarify what is new about "new governance". Does it indicate a clean break from institutions and processes of the past or is it merely chronicling an assortment of instrument changes necessary for governments to adapt to changing socio-economic conditions rather than a more fundamental transformation? Do the changes really indicate the emergence of a new governance system in which the government is merely another player on a par with its societal and international counterparts? More fundamentally, is governance a normative framework reflecting the hopes and desires of those who prefer smaller governments or an empirical description of an existing reality?

The large and growing literature on the subject has not convincingly addressed these questions, much less answered them conclusively. Indeed, recent empirical studies of privatization and deregulation cast serious doubts on the purported decline of the state and the emergence of "governance without government" first postulated by Rhodes (1996). There is plenty of evidence suggesting that while the role of the state may indeed have changed to adapt to and accommodate more complex and rapidly changing environments, the dominant role of government in these new governance arrangements remains intact. In fact recurrent security and economic crises since the 1990s have underscored the need for the continued active role of the state, and have arguably taken it to an unprecedented level (Kennett 2008).

The unanswered questions can only be resolved through a more clearly focused conceptualization of, and more rigorous empirical research into, current governance arrangements than presently exists. The purpose of the research should be to shed light on how to understand the changes that have come about in policy processes without, a priori, denigrating the possibility of a continuing central, indeed leading, role of the state in many such arrangements. The fundamental hypotheses of this collective effort to study this question is that there are many ways to coordinate public policies, that some of these may have changed in recent years, but that the role of government is still pivotal in any specific new articulation of governance arrangements.

This special issue brings together a broad group of scholars working on comparative public policy in order to examine and report on the changing face of governance in a variety of regions and sectors. The issue is intended not only to enlighten theoretical issues but also to empirically show how different modes of governance have been constructed and operate in different sectors and regions. This broad and detailed comparative perspective is the best way to understand how governance really works and to advance theorization on the subject.

From Government to Governance?

Governing is what governments do: controlling the allocation of resources between social actors; providing a set of rules and operating a set of institutions setting out "who gets what, where, when and how" in society; and managing the symbolic resources that are the basis of legitimacy. Governing thus involves the establishment of a basic set of relationships between governments and their citizens which can vary from highly structured and controlled by governments ("hierarchical modes") to arrangements that are monitored only loosely and informally, if at all ("network" or "market" modes). Thus, in its broadest sense, "governance" is a term used to describe the *mode* of government coordination exercised by state actors in their effort to solve familiar problems of collective action inherent to government and governing (Kooiman 1993, 2000; de Bruijn and ten Heuvelhof 1995; Rhodes 1996; Majone 1997; Klijn and Koppenjan 2000; Colebatch 2014). That is, "governance" is about establishing, promoting and supporting a specific type of relationship between governmental and non-governmental actors in the governing process. Thus governance is about actors and their interactions, and the ideas and instruments through which policy processes are coordinated. In other words, governance is another way of ordering reality, of explaining how public policies are decided and implemented, and of indicating those actors with a role in such policy-making, and the interaction between these policy-makers.

However, the ongoing debate, especially in the field of political science, has for a long time focused on the government/governance dichotomy. The basic definition of this dichotomy was given by Pierre (2000), who distinguished between state-centric "old governance" and society-centric "new governance". The former is characterized by a state-centric perspective (where the focus is on how the political-institutional system steers society and public policies). The latter, "society-centric", perspective places the focus on the ability of society to govern itself. Other significant definitions have been proposed by Peters (1996), Considine and Lewis (1999), Newmann (2001) and Kooiman (2003); however, the substance of the governance debate lies in Pierre's definition, which clearly grasps the empirical aspect thereof. The question is: in what way is the new way of governing societies – "new governance", meaning the development of market and network forms of interactions – eclipsing the old governance model? Is "government" – meaning the hierarchical governance framework – really losing its central role in the policy-making process, to be replaced by a more decentralized, self-governance model (Hill and Lynn 2005; Joardan et al. 2005)?

This important debate has developed over the last couple of decades, in the search for different formulations of the concept of governance. The most enthusiastic interpretations have focused on the non-hierarchical potentiality of "governance", and have underlined the belief that governance means "a change in the nature of the meaning of government" (Bevir and Rhodes 2003, p. 45), whereby government and governance are perceived as the two extremities of a continuum of different possible ways of governing and coordinating the policy-making process. The very extreme case, from this perspective – but one that is considered to be realistic nevertheless – is that of "governance without government", meaning the actual coordination of a complex policy-making process without the presence of any form of hierarchy. Furthermore, there is the belief that "the growth of governance reduced the ability of the core executive to act effectively" (Rhodes 2007, p. 1248).

This interpretation, however, is potentially very misleading from the point of view of the analysis of politics and policies. Any crisis of "central government", for example, undoubtedly implies the weakening, but not necessarily the disappearance, of government's "command and control" approach to policy-making. Governments (conceived as central political institutions) may find themselves overburdened with social demands so that "hierarchical governance" – that is, a policy framework whereby the most important actors are governments and the state implements policies by ordering and sanctioning – may no longer prove efficient or effective. However, this does not necessarily imply a shift of the locus of power and authority from governments to non-governmental actors or structures.

That is, at some point or other all democratic countries have witnessed a gradual shift away from the traditional state-centric way of governing society towards other forms of governing. This process of transition has been characterized by attributes such as the decentralization of powers, the greater distribution of authority, the blurring of the borders between public institutions and private organizations, and the inclusion of new stakeholders, self-governing mechanisms and so on. And political science scholars have had to try and grasp this changing reality, and these processes of change in the way policies are created and implemented, and in the way complex political and policy systems are governed. However, the existence of different modes of governing does not mean that the role of the "government" function has radically changed, as supporters of the governance hypothesis have suggested: rather, what has changed is above all the "way" of governing – that is, the strategies and instruments adopted in order to pursue public goals (and to put order in the political and policy dynamics). Any government/governance dichotomy therefore could be empirically misleading and thus theoretically inappropriate and involve the improper "stretching" of the concept itself.

In other words, the "government" perspective simply focuses on the way of governing and coordinating policy-making that may have taken place in the past, where the main political and administrative actors take centre stage, adopting specific approaches to creating and implementing public policy (the command/control steering approach). Changing times have brought about substantial changes in the way that policy-making is coordinated, and new ways of governing may have emerged but these exist alongside the more traditional ones and reversion to these earlier models always remains a distinct possibility.

It is more useful from both the theoretical and empirical points of view to assume that governance is simply a broader concept than government (Borzel 1998; Benz 2004; Klijn 2008), in that the latter defines the actions taken by those institutional actors officially in charge of the decision-making process, whereas the former concept focuses on the "process" in which decisions are formulated and especially implemented through the interaction of all the actors involved. The contraposition of "old government" and "new governance" could radically divide past from present, and distort any description or explanation of either period of decision-making and policy-making processes.

To sum up, we believe that many scholars place excessive emphasis on the idea of governance as a new theoretical tool. According to this interpretation, scholars have to single out the individual features of each specific governance arrangement, by focusing on the number of key actors, the nature of their interaction, the policy strategies adopted, and so on. This means that so-called "old government" is simply a specific governance arrangement characterized by the strategic role of central political-administrative institutions acting directly, and in particular implementing hierarchical, top-down policy strategies; on the other hand, so-called "new governance" is characterized by the heterarchic or polycentric participation of several actors/stakeholders at different institutional and systemic levels. And this structural configuration of policy-making is expected to produce very different policy dynamics (based on a mix of soft regulation, contracts and negotiation, persuasion, etc.). So, from this perspective, "government" is only one component of any governance arrangement, without recognizing that it is usually the most important and has the latent power to "verticalize" any process, thus bringing hierarchy back into the equation.

Certain aspects of governance thinking, however, should not be taken for granted. For example, the role of the "political-institutional centres" of the systems (governments) has to be empirically investigated, since they do not necessarily lose their weight and power during the shift to a more decentralized system of policy coordination: it may be that government's role continues to be one of strategic relevance, albeit within a different environment and through the use of different policy strategies. Public policy goals may remain the same, while only the way they are pursued is changed by modifying the governance arrangements and methods within a specific policy field (Richards and Smith 2002). Governments (or, more generally, public institutions) thus continue to have prime responsibility for governing society, but they may choose to modify the way they perform this duty.

Meta-Governance and the Role of the State in Contemporary Policy-Making

There is no one way of governing, and the direct involvement of public institutions is not strictly necessary. Governments may choose to steer from a distance (Kickert et al. 1997). From this point of view, the "hollowing out" of the state (Rhodes 1994, 1997) can be read as a diversification of the way in which public institutions act. The hollowed-out process suggests a dynamics of extraction which leaves government with a limited core business, while producing a fragmented environment within which a great many policy issues remain bereft of their traditional "providers". In this fragmented landscape, there is structural pressure to foster collaboration and create partnerships between public and private policy actors (Skelcher 2000). However, such collaboration is pursued and enforced under the umbrella either of the governments or of other political-institutional centres.

The basic assumption concerning the persistence of the major role of governments and political-institutional centres in governance dynamics behind this collection of article is confirmed by the growing body of studies focusing on the concept of "meta-governance". The fact that something over and above the normal dynamics of governance is being searched for also means that those supporting the view of more horizontal, less hierarchical governance modes have problems in explaining how such governance modes and inter-actor cooperation work. As has been pointed out, there are at least three streams of literature calling for better understanding of meta-governance arrangements (Sørensen and Torfing 2007). Firstly, there is the interdependency approach whereby the need for meta-governance emerges from at least two different directions. Those involved in network governance – that is, the supporters of the more radical version of the new governance perspective – have to admit that the high cost of actors' transactions and relations involves a significant combination of process design and management, or the need to manage networks (Kickert et al. 1997; Sorensen and Torfing 2009; Sørensen et al. 2012). On the other hand, there is the more "governmental" perspective, which assumes that the state (governments and political-institutional centres of power) not only has the power to decide which mix of governance modes is to be adopted, but also the latent power to reintroduce hierarchy into the equation in order to avoid the failure of governance (Jessop 2002; Meuleman 2008, 2009).

The second stream of literature is more focused on the problem of governability (Scharpf 1993, 1997; Kooiman 2003; Mayntz 2004). These authors observe how the tendency to more horizontal governance modes needs to be structured as a "game" or set of incentives and disincentives designed to elicit specific types of behaviour from policy actors and targets (through specific institutional design or positive incentives). Here it is quite clear that the games involved in non-hierarchical modes of governance are played under the "shadow of hierarchy" or the potential reintroduction at any moment of state primacy and authority.

The third stream of thought is of a more normative nature – from March and Olsen (1995) to Foucault (1991). Here the emphasis is on understanding the "hegemonic norms and ideas about how to govern and be governed" (Sørensen et al. 2012, p. 131), which include considerations of "governmentality" (Foucault 1991) or the ability of governments to drive and lead policy discourses and practices. Here, the role of governments and political-institutional centres is less apparent, but no less real, since the production of narratives needs to be institutionalized (and hence the role of institutional design by government is important).

This special issue, supported among other things by the theoretical assumptions of the meta-governance perspective, follows the premise that government and governance are not the two poles of a continuum of the various possible ways of governing and coordinating the policy process, but are rather two different concepts centred upon substantially different phenomena. Governance refers to the possible ways in which policy actors, including governments, combine to solve collective problems and thus affect the ways in which policy processes are steered. Governance modes can be based on different mixes of coordination principles (hierarchy, market and network), but even in the more extreme horizontal arrangement they need to be steered – that is, they need to be led towards constructive, positive coordination. Government, on the other hand, is not just one of the possible actors in systemic governance but *the* central player, whether it chooses to play that role or not. Its role in any governance arrangement may vary considerably, and change, depending on the context. It is a core determinant and element of governance, rather than something existing in opposition to, or outside of, governance. Government has the inescapable task of defining what governance is, or can be (Capano 2011), and may choose to allow a higher degree of freedom to other policy actors with regard to the goals to be pursued and the means to be employed.

In other words, government is an independent variable rather than a constant or a dependent one (Pierre and Peters 2000) and the role of government is a determinant one affecting the structure of governance. And, as the articles in this issue show in a variety of context and governance modes, governments – or, more generally, public or state institutions – have prime responsibility for governing society, although they may choose to modify the way they perform this role (Kickert et al. 1997). In this sense, governments can be thought of as "designing" the systemic mode of governance of a policy sector, through a combination of their pursuit of strategic goals and their choice of the means to implement such goals.

The Content of the Special Issue

The authors of the contributions to this special issue provide us with empirical evidence of the role of governments and political-institutional centres, in different policy fields and countries. We have not asked them to adopt any specific theoretical approach to governance modes, even if some of them have elaborated their own framework and typologies in the past (see, for example, Howlett et al. 2009; Capano 2011). Rather, we have simply asked them to identify the role of government; and these studies show that different policy fields offer highly specific combinations of governance modes and policy instruments, especially when different fields are compared and different levels of (micro and macro) analysis are taken into consideration. This common enterprise is designed to show how governments continue to play significant roles in all governance modes, and in various different fields.

Two studies are comparative analyses dealing with education and health governance reforms. Giliberto Capano analyses three decades of governance reforms in education in three federal countries (Australia, Canada and Germany). The focus on federal political systems makes this paper particularly interesting, due to the multilevel institutional arrangements of these countries, and the different distribution of powers and responsibilities between federal government and sub-federal units. What emerges from this analysis is revealing from the point of view of governance studies. First of all, the paper clearly shows that in all three countries, governance reforms have involved the increasing role of both federal and state/provincial governments, albeit as a result of different federal dynamics which have structurally influenced the process and the content of the reforms themselves. In some cases, this increased power is the result of the direct centralization of the governance mode (greater hierarchy), while in other cases it has been achieved through the adoption of a softer approach (either steering at a distance or voluntary cooperation). However, what clearly emerges in all three cases is that governments hold a strategic, pivotal role in all resulting governance arrangements, and that they are very careful with regard to the risk of failure of the existing governance modes. Furthermore, this article shows how governance arrangements in policy-making can be redesigned, in federal countries, without changing the written constitution but driven by changes in intergovernmental relations, and how they depend on the capacity of both the levels of government to design effective strategies through complex and ongoing intergovernmental interactions.

The same conclusion, albeit in a different policy field and geopolitical context, is reached by Ramesh, Wu and Howlett in their essay regarding developments in the governance of health policy in China, India and Thailand. The authors' empirical analysis starts from an interesting description of the failures afflicting all governance modes. They then show how, in specific geopolitical contexts, the role of governments in steering healthcare policy is essential to avoiding the intrinsic weakness of market and network modes of governance. The different directions taken by Thailand on the one hand, and by China and India on the other hand, show how hierarchy (be it directly or indirectly exercised) is necessary to guarantee results in this complex, socially important policy field.

Eva Heidbreder further clarifies the intrinsically hierarchical aspect of policy-making by analysing cooperative governance dynamics within the EU policy-making sphere; specifically focusing on two empirical cases of the Open Method of Coordination, which is a governance strategy based on voluntary cooperation, benchmarking, activation and the large-scale consultation of stakeholders; and the activation of the participation of civil society in EU policy-making. The article shows how EU strategy has been based on the attempt to design a series of normative provisions which legitimize a more cooperative governance mode, which in turn represents a means by which to increase the democratic legitimization of EU policy-making. The empirical evidence suggests that, lacking a central government actor, this approach has been ineffective, failing to produce results in terms of either legitimization or policy performance. Our perception of democratic legitimization cannot be reinforced through the top-down involvement of civil society (weak narrative compared to the historically rooted narrative of electoral legitimization); and there is no room for any real improvement in policy performance at EU level without the clear role of government in a supporting position at the very least.

The similar persistence of government's steering role within the context of the planned reduction of hierarchical governance, but this time through market-based reforms, also emerges from the comparative analysis conducted by Zhang of vegetable retailing in two Chinese cities. In this particular study, the previous, strongly hierarchical system has undergone substantial changes based on liberalization and privatization. He finds the new market system, characterized by plurilateral dynamics, to be significantly influenced, from many points of view, by local government steering through that level of government's continued involvement in shaping the structural features of the new system, and in maintaining its strict regulation of those urban areas in which the vegetable retail trade is conducted. What is interesting here is that the failure of the former hierarchical mode of governance has been used to justify the adoption of the new privatization policy, whilst at the same time preserving the hierarchical steering of certain aspects of policy-making so as to avoid the failure of the new approach to governance.

A different government strategy towards transforming existing hierarchical modes is offered by Sarah Giest in her analysis of the way in which the Swedish government has deliberately established networks of governance in regard to national energy policy, through the "National Network for Wind Power" project. In this case, government has decided to favour the establishment of a network, and to manage that network. That is, rather than emerge autonomously or spontaneously, current network governance has emerged as government has used its powers (hierarchy) to establish a non-hierarchical governance mode (network governance), whilst continuing to support and steer it from a distance.

Conclusion

Rather than focus on one or two modes of governance, the essays in this issue all attempt to answer one rather important, yet unresolved question: what roles do governments actually play in the multiple modes found in contemporary governance? The essays address questions such as: which governance modes exist, and how do their various different aspects (principles, strategies, instruments, actors and their interactions) evolve? When, how and why does government decide to change its mode of governance? How effective are the new governance modes in coordinating policies? And how do the changes in governance mode affect the economic and political contexts of governance, and vice versa?

Many authors have suggested that governance emerged from a distinct historical trajectory that began with the "crisis of command and control" in its mid-twentieth century form characterized by public provision of goods and services and detailed, prescriptive regulation of markets and ended with network steering (Kooiman 1993, 2000; Klijn and Koppenjan 2000). Many assume that a new way of governing society – "new governance" – has supplanted the old governance model and represents "a change in the nature of the meaning of government" (Bevir and Rhodes 2003, p. 4). On the other hand, there are those who genuinely doubt that "government" – meaning a hierarchical framework of government – is losing its central role in the policy-making process, to be replaced by a more decentralized, "self-governing" variety of governance (Hill and Lynn 2005; Goetz 2008; Héritier and Lehmkuhl 2008). However, we need to avoid using governance as a catch-all description, or assuming its superiority over earlier forms a priori, if the concept is to be useful. New forms of governance are not necessarily better, more effective or efficient, or even more democratic, than their predecessors.

Moreover, as the discussion above and the contents of the works contained in this special issue suggest, there are other possible historical trajectories besides the hierarchy to pluriformity one, including arriving at network governance via experiments with market or regulatory arrangements or failing to shift out of another quadrant at all. A shift to a network mode of governance thus represents only one alternative to other possible forms of state–societal coordination. Many of these alternate trajectories are clearly visible in many policy sectors over the past two decades where the initial promotion of market governance accompanied by privatization, deregulation, contracting out and other activities associated with the "new public management" (NPM) ethos of the late twentieth century (Jordana and Levi-Faur 2004), for example, quickly reverted to other modes of governing (Hira et al. 2005; Ramesh and Howlett 2006; Capano 2014).

The essays in this issue address the "governance problem" by focusing on the different governance modes – i.e. the ways of coordinating policy-making – and the different ways government goals are pursued and the means adopted in a variety of hierarchical, market and network contexts. The essays underline how the governance concept, freed of its ideological connotations and preferences for non-governmental modes of governing is a powerful conceptual tool which can help to order and analyse the multifaceted ways through which policies are coordinated (decisions are made and implemented, and services are delivered) in comparative policy research and analysis.

By submitting important data and evidence concerning the situations found in many countries and sectors, the essays in this issue, as a whole, find that governments still matter, that governance arrangements have not been "degovernmentalized" but continue to work under the shadow of hierarchy, that many governance modes are multilevel arrangements which limit some possible alternative arrangements, and that all arrangements are not static, but are dynamic, continuously evolving entities. This empirical variety emphasizes that we need to be more careful when theorizing new governance modes, and that theoretical analysis should avoid considering governments' role in coordinating the policy-making process as being irrelevant or less powerful than in past eras. Governments are still very much in charge, in every governance mode. They may act directly or indirectly (as suggested by meta-governance studies), but they nevertheless continue to act significantly in every mode of governing, from hierarchical to market and network forms.

References

Benz, A., 2004, Path-dependent institutions and strategic veto players: National parliaments in the European Union. *West European Politics*, **27**, pp. 875–900. doi:10.1080/0140238042000283283

Bevir, M. R. and Rhodes, R. A. W., 2003, *Interpreting British Government*. (London: Routledge).

Borzel, T. A., 1998, Organizing Babylon – On the different conceptions of policy networks. *Public Administration*, **76**, pp. 253–273. doi:10.1111/1467-9299.00100

Capano, G., 2011, Government continues to do its job. A comparative study of governance shifts in the higher education sector. *Public Administration*, **89**, pp. 1622–1642. doi:10.1111/j.1467-9299.2011.01936.x

Capano, G., 2014, The re-regulation of the Italian university system through quality assurance. A mechanistic perspective. *Policy & Society*, **33**(3), pp. 199–213.

Colebatch, H., 2014, Making sense of Governance. *Policy & Society*, **33**(4), pp. 307–316.

Considine, M. and Lewis, J., 1999, Governance at ground level: The frontline bureaucrat in the age of markets and networks. *Public Administration Review*, **59**, pp. 467–460. doi:10.2307/3110295

de Bruijn, J. A. and ten Heuvelhof, E. F., 1995, Policy networks and governance, in: D. L. Weimer (Ed) *Institutional Design* (Boston, MA: Kluwer Academic Publishers), pp. 161–179.

Foucault, M., 1991, Governmentality, in: G. Burchell, C. Gordon, P. Miller (Eds) *The Foucault Effect: Studies in Governmentality* (Hemel Hempstead: Harvester Wheatsheaf), pp. 87–104.

Goetz, K. H., 2008, Governance as a path to government. *West European Politics*, **31**, pp. 258–279. doi:10.1080/01402380701835066

Héritier, A. and Lehmkuhl, D., 2008, Introduction: The shadow of hierarchy and new modes of governance. *Journal of Public Policy*, **38**, pp. 1–17.

Hill, C. J. and Lynn, L. E., 2005, Is hierarchical governance in decline? Evidence from empirical research. *Journal of Public Administration Research and Theory*, **15**(2), pp. 173–195. doi:10.1093/jopart/mui011

Hira, A., Huxtable, D., and Leger, A., 2005, Deregulation and participation: An international survey of participation in electricity regulation. *Governance*, **18**, pp. 53–88. doi:10.1111/j.1468-0491.2004.00266.x

Howlett, M., Rayner, J., and Tollefson, C., 2009, From government to governance in forest planning? Lessons from the case of the British Columbia great bear rainforest initiative. *Forest Policy and Economics*, **11**, pp. 383–391. doi:10.1016/j.forpol.2009.01.003

Jessop, B., 2002, *The Future of the Capitalist State*. (Cambridge: Polity Press).

Jordan, A., Wurzel, R. K. W., and Zito, A., 2005, The rise of "New" Policy instruments in comparative perspective: Has governance eclipsed government?. *Political Studies*, **53**, pp. 477–496. doi:10.1111/j.1467-9248.2005.00540.x

Jordana, J. and Levi-Faur, D. (Eds), 2004, *The Politics of Regulation* (Cheltenham: Edward Elgar).

Kennett, P., 2008, *Governance, Globalization and Public Policy*. (Cheltenham: Edward Elgar).

Kickert, W. J., Klijn, E., and Koppenjan, G. F. (Eds), 1997, *Managing Complex Networks: Strategies for the Public Sector* (London: Sage).

Klijn, E.-H., 2008, Governance and governance networks in Europe: An assessment of ten years of research on the theme. *Public Management Review*, **10**, pp. 505–525. doi:10.1080/14719030802263954

Klijn, E. H. and Koppenjan, J. F. M., 2000, Public management and policy networks: Foundations of a network approach to governance. *Public Management*, **2**, pp. 135–158. doi:10.1080/146166700411201

Kooiman, J., 1993, Governance and governability: Using complexity, dynamics and diversity, in: J. Kooiman (Ed) *Modern Governance* (London: Sage), pp. 35–50.

Kooiman, J., 2000, Societal governance: Levels, models, and orders of social-political interaction, in: J. Pierre (Ed) *Debating Governance* (Oxford: Oxford University Press), pp. 138–166.

Kooiman, J., 2003, *Governing as Governance* (London: Sage).

Majone, G., 1997, From the positive to the regulatory state: Causes and consequences of changes in the mode of governance. *Journal of Public Policy*, **17**, pp. 139–167. doi10.1017/S0143814X00003524

March, J. G. and Olsen, J. P., 1995, *Democratic Governance*. (New York: The Free Press).

Mayntz, R., 2004, Governance im modernen Staat, in: A. Benz (Ed.) *Governance – Regieren in Komplexen Regelsystemen: Eine Einführung* (Wiesbaden: Verlag für Sozialwissenschaften), pp. 65–76.

Meuleman, L., 2008, *Public Management and the Metagovernance of Hierarchies, Networks and Markets: The Feasibility of Designing and Managing Governance Style Combinations* (Dordrecht: Springer).

Meuleman, L., 2009, 'Metagoverning Governance Styles: Increasing the Metagovernors' Toolbox. Paper presented at the panel 'Metagoverning Interactive Governance and Policymaking', ECPR general conference 10–12 September 2009, Potsdam.

Newmann, J., 2001, *Modernising Governance: New Labour Policy and Society*. (London: Sage).

Peters, B. G., 1996, *Governing: Four Emerging Models*. (Lawrence, KS: University Press of Kansas).

Pierre, J., 2000, Introduction, in: J. Pierre (Ed) *Debating Governance: Authority, Steering and Democracy* (Oxford: Oxford University Press), pp. 1–10.

Pierre, J. and Peters, B. G., 2000, *Governance, Politics and the State*. (New York: St. Martin's Press).

Ramesh, M. and Howlett, M., 2006, *Deregulation and Its Discontents: Rewriting the Rules in Asia*. (Aldershot: Edward Elgar).

Rhodes, R. A. W., 1994, The hollowing out of the state. *Political Quarterly*, **65**, pp. 138–151. doi:10.1111/j.1467-923X.1994.tb00441.x

Rhodes, R. A. W., 1996, The new governance: Governing without government. *Political Studies*, **44**, pp. 652–667. doi:10.1111/j.1467-9248.1996.tb01747.x

Rhodes, R. A. W., 2007, Understanding governance: Ten years on. *Organization Studies*, **28**, pp. 1243–1264. doi:10.1177/0170840607076586

Richards, D. and Smith, M., 2002, *Governance and Public Policy*. (Oxford: Oxford University Press).

Scharpf, F. W., 1993, *Games in Hierarchies and Networks: Analytical and Empirical Approaches to the Study of Governance Institutions* (Frankfurt-am-Main: Campus-Verlag).

Scharpf, F. W., 1997, *Games Real Actors Play: Actor-centered Institutionalism in Policy Research*. (Boulder, CO: Westview Press).

Skelcher, C., 2000, Changing images of the state: Overloaded, hollowed-out, congested. *Public Policy and Administration*, **15**, pp. 3–19. doi:10.1177/095207670001500302

Sorensen, E. and Torfing, J., 2009, Making governance networks effective and democratic through metagovernance. *Public Administration*, **87**, pp. 234–258. doi:10.1111/j.1467-9299.2009.01753.x

Sørensen, E. and Torfing, J., 2007, *Theories of Democratic Network Governance*. (Basingstoke: Palgrave Macmillan).

Sørensen, E., Torfing, J., Peters, B. G., and Pierre, J., 2012, *Interactive Governance: Advancing the Paradigm*. (Oxford: Oxford University Press).

Weaver, R. K. and Rockman, B. A., 1993, When and how do institutions matter?, in: *Do Institutions Matter? Government Capabilities in the United States and Abroad* (Washington, DC: Brookings Institutions), pp. 445–463.

Williamson, O. E., 1975, *Markets and Hierarchies*. (New York: Free Press).

Williamson, O. E., 1985, *The Economic Institutions of Capitalism: Firms, Markets, Relational Contracting*. (New York: Free Press).

Williamson, O. E., 1996, *The Mechanisms of Governance*. (Oxford: Oxford University Press).

Introduction

Comparative Analyses of Infrastructure Public-Private Partnerships

ANTHONY E. BOARDMAN, CARSTEN GREVE, & GRAEME A. HODGE

Infrastructure public–private partnerships, also known as PPPs or P3s, continue to be a fascinating aspect of public policy around the globe. It has been more than two decades since John Major's government in the UK adopted the idea of privately funding and delivering infrastructure services using long-term contracts. In fact, PPPs shifted from being simply an option for governments towards being a policy preference at the heart of the government's consciousness (Smith 1999).

Internationally, there is increased interest in PPPs. The UK presented a renewed "PF2" policy in late 2012 (HM Treasury 2012). The OECD (2012) issued guidelines for how governments should proceed with PPPs. ASEAN (2014) countries, which received assistance from the OECD, developed a new framework for PPPs. Many Asian countries are looking to the PPP policy option in their infrastructure policy. The new president of the European Commission, Mr. Jean-Claude Juncker, has launched an ambitious "Investment Plan for Europe" that will be presented in full in the next few years (European Commission 2014). This plan will entail encouraging private financing of public infrastructure programmes on a grand scale. In the USA, the Obama administration is considering different policy options, including a new tax proposal and administrative action that will attract private finance to help address the huge infrastructure investment challenges that the federal government faces (New York Times 2015). All of these initiatives will inject private finance into programmes and projects that governments want to be delivered.

And yet, like their policy cousins, privatization and outsourcing, PPPs remain controversial today. They are both widely praised and loudly criticized. Debates continue over fundamental matters such as what defines a PPP, the resulting value-for-money (VfM) of PPPs, as well as the legitimacy and policy lessons learned to date. And it is difficult to sort the cheap advertising bluster and ideological criticism from the rational policy commentary and solid technical advances.

Some of this confusion is due to the fact that PPPs constitute not a single technique for infrastructure delivery, but a phenomenon which covers many meanings. Hodge and Greve (2013) argue that the language of PPPs is adopted at four levels: when we discuss a specific project; when we refer to a specific infrastructure delivery technique; when we speak of a policy preference; or when we debate it as a governing mechanism. In practice, whilst we may all use the same words, these can carry very different meanings. It also means that the PPP phenomenon is a big target in debates. If a commentator does not support a particular project, the arrangement used to deliver the project, the policy of using the particular delivery arrangements or the long-term governing effects of contracts, then PPP is criticized. Alternatively, if any of these are supported, then PPP is praised. Little wonder that there is so much contestation noise.

Another reason for the contest, though, is the breadth of the PPP delivery options available. Whilst some governments refer to PPPs as a very particular type of long-term (design, build, finance, operate and maintain - DBFOM) infrastructure contract type, the reality is that there are many possible different contractual arrangements. Contracts may differ in terms of whether the public or private sectors complete a particular task or activity from initial planning through to the final maintenance operations, the extent of finance from each sector, the specific project to be delivered, which party bears which risks, the strength of incentives for performance, as well as issues of transparency. The fabric to be applied to accountability and governance matters as well and adds to this long list of fundamental dimensions. Even so-called "leading PPP jurisdictions", such as Canada and Australia, employ a variety of different arrangements, rather than having one national PPP model (Hodge 2013; Siemiatycki 2013). So, in a scientific sense, we ought to acknowledge up front that there is no such thing as "the" PPP model. Of course researchers will no doubt continue to use the PPP label as shorthand when discussing long-term bundled infrastructure contract arrangements. But the ambiguity is palpable.

What this means for public policy scholars is that careful learning is required in the international PPP arena. Detailed specification of the PPP arrangement under discussion is required, and its context and jurisdictional characteristics acknowledged. Importantly, too, analysts need to be willing to deal not solely with the formal numerical engineering, economic or financial details, but also with ideas from other disciplines such as political science, sociology and public policy which study more ambiguous, fluid and rhetorical tools of persuasion and power in society (Hodge et al. 2010).

The five articles in this special issue of the *Journal of Comparative Policy Analysis* were initially presented at an international conference conducted in Vancouver, Canada. Organized by the Sauder School of Business (University of British Columbia), the Copenhagen Business School and Monash University, the conference was part of the ongoing International PPP Scholars Network.

Each article contributes to comparative policy analysis in a different way using a different methodology. Briefly, Ross and Yan compare PPPs to traditional public procurement using economic theory; Reeves compares the goals of PPPs in Ireland before and after the global financial crisis (GFC), and draws comparisons to the UK; Albalate, Bel, Bel-Piñana and Geddes compare the transfer of different types of risk in transportation PPPs in many South American and European countries; Acerete, Gasca, Stafford and Stapleton compare the organizational and financial arrangements of healthcare PPPs in two regions of Spain; and Hellowell and Vecchi compare the agency problems that lead to budgetary problems with PPP hospitals in the UK and Spain. Each article has important policy implications. For example, Ross and Yan provide conditions under which government should choose PPPs over traditional procurement, which is of fundamental importance given the billions of dollars that will be spent on new infrastructure; Reeves finds that there has been a fundamental shift in the Irish government's motives for PPPs following the GFC towards levering private funds for investment and job creation; Albalate, Bel, Bel-Piñana and Geddes highlight the importance of risk-mitigation strategies and of institutional quality and stability; although focussed on healthcare rather than transportation, Acerete, Gasca, Stafford and Stapleton find significant differences in institutional quality across regions within the same country and conclude that great care is needed when making inferences about the transferability of policies to different regions; Hellowell and Vecchi's research suggests that government should consider carefully the political and organizational pressures on state employees during the financial appraisal process. Ross and Yan contribute to comparative theory development and derive practical implications from theory-based research. Acerete, Gasca, Stafford and Stapleton present theory-based empirical research, taking a critical analysis approach. The other articles draw on theory and empirical observation of comparative situations to derive important policy lessons. We now discuss each article in more detail.

A major debate around PPPs is the issue of the initial choice of infrastructure delivery method – when should a government choose a PPP arrangement in preference to a "traditional arrangement"? Ross and Yan acknowledge that one of the longstanding potential problems with PPPs is "the loss of flexibility that comes with the long lived contractual obligations governments must respect when changing circumstances may require significant change in the way the public service is provided". They develop the first formal model that considers analytically the trade-off between loss of flexibility to adapt to changing needs and the potential productive efficiencies available through a PPP. Importantly, Ross and Yan show that PPPs will be superior to government provision (in terms of VfM or social surplus) when the potential efficiencies of a PPP are large, the probability that there will need to be changes to the project is small, the gains to project redesign are small and when the government's bargaining power in renegotiation is greater. They suggest that PPPs ought to be more attractive for roads or bridge projects, where there is little chance that a redesign will be needed, and less attractive for more dynamic projects such as healthcare or information technology projects. These results, whilst theoretical, have a certain pragmatic sense to them. Furthermore, Ross and Yan show that the choice between a PPP or traditional delivery can depend on whether government's main aim is to maximize total social surplus or VfM.

Reeves reminds us that there is much to be learned from countries that have gone down the PPP road (pardon the pun). Examining the motivations for PPPs and their performance in Ireland, he describes the origins of the policy prior to the GFC and points to the government's desire to alleviate infrastructure delivery capacity constraints, to effect "speedy delivery" of infrastructure, and to achieve VfM. He concludes that, in contrast to the UK and prior to the GFC, PPPs did make a contribution to infrastructure investments over and above that which would have occurred anyway. However, the stock of Ireland's infrastructure initially lagged that of many other EU countries. Furthermore, the procurement process was slow and relatively few PPPs have been completed. Reeves' VfM analysis was hampered by the lack of a formal requirement for public agencies to put details in the public domain and other factors. Nonetheless, his analysis provides reasonable grounds for scepticism of official VfM estimates. He nominates the principal lesson from the Irish experience as being that "PPP does not represent a quick fix for the problems of infrastructure deficits or difficulties with traditional procurement methods".

In a fascinating account of the post-GFC experience, Reeves outlines how the Irish economy took a dramatic downturn and government debt more than doubled to 91 per cent of GDP. The government launched an economic stimulus plan in 2012, which included a renewed wave of PPPs. Unlike the policy prior to the GFC, the new objectives were to add economic stimulus and create employment in a stagnant economy. In addition, PPPs continued to provide off-balance sheet financing of public capital investment and neatly circumvented formal European fiscal constraints. Finally, with ongoing concerns around the scarcity of critical performance information (even to government ministers and parliamentary committees!), Reeves concludes that "greater transparency is possibly the most important challenge to be addressed if PPP is to succeed in meeting the objectives set by its advocates".

One of the most powerful rationales for PPPs is the potential to transfer risk to the party most able to bear it – that is, the party that can best manage it or mitigate it. Albalate, Bel, Bel-Piñana and Geddes directly examine the distribution of various risks in motorway concession PPP contracts in many countries and draw lessons on the use of different contractual options and mitigation strategies. Spain suffered from strong instability of PPP regulation; many early PPPs bore significant risks and became bankrupt while, later, the government bore most of the financial risks. Early French concessions in the 1970s were subsequently renationalized in the 1980s, largely due to poor demand forecasting and the oil crises. More recently, in a stable regulatory environment, the French government was able to successfully transfer risks to the private partners. Chile is posited as a successful example of a well-functioning institutional and regulatory design with the reward of successfully attracting international private capital for PPP projects. Widespread renegotiations at the end of the 1990s, however, saw the pioneering use of variable term demand mitigation strategies. The stability of Brazil's experience is contrasted with Argentina's "widespread renegotiations and civil protests" with PPPs. Interestingly, in Argentina, cost overrun risks and demand risk were shared, while maintenance and operational risks were borne by the state. The Polish experience provides a further contrast, given the heavy influence of its communist past. Here, financing challenges along with weak legal protections have inhibited private participation in PPPs. The article infers, perhaps predictably, that "countries with higher institutional quality and stability are able to engage in PPPs with fewer guarantees or less need for sharing the risks associated with the demand, cost overrun and maintenance and operation".

Albalate, Bel, Bel-Piñana and Geddes provide some important policy conclusions. First, they point out that diversifiable risks are likely to be "more tolerable" to private investors than other risks, such as regulatory and environmental permitting risks. They suggest that construction risks should be transferred to the private partner, while other risks are "idiosyncratic" – that is, their allocation may depend on the governing legal framework. While they suggest risk sharing of variation in traffic level, they also propose variable-term contracts as a way to share demand risk and reduce the likelihood of renegotiations. Finally, they stress the importance of institutional quality (i.e. an independent special purpose regulatory agency) and careful assessment of VfM, not simply at the time of the initial project construction stage, but also during the ongoing operation of the project as well as for extensions or later proposed projects.

Acerete, Gasca, Stafford and Stapleton undertake a critical analysis approach to examine healthcare PPPs in Spain, an acknowledged international leader in using PPPs for healthcare. Spain pioneered the "Alzira model" in which the PPP provides clinical services, with potentially attractive revenue streams, as well as physical infrastructure. The regional government has been extremely pleased with the performance of the Alzira Hospital and it has attracted considerable international interest. However, Acerete et al. tell a rather different story. They analyse and compare the organizational and financial arrangements of healthcare PPPs in two regions of Spain, Valencia and Madrid. The authors highlight the complex nature of PPP organizational structures and the inability of the public to access relevant information. Further, in Spain, there is lack of public accountability. Despite extensive searches, the authors were unable to find any information about any Valencian PPP contracts (except the Alzira hospital, 1999–2004). Key financial information was difficult to procure for various reasons: often, it is consolidated or is simply not available to the public. Thus, private sector partners can obscure the effect of any opportunism. One of the particularly interesting and unique characteristics of Spanish PPPs is that regional savings banks are shareholders in many contracts, with the consequence that some PPPs are closer to public–*public* partnerships than public–private partnerships. In terms of financial performance, they find some evidence that PPPs provide cheaper healthcare in Valencia, but they argue that it is due to special circumstances. Importantly, it is not transferred to other regions in Spain. For example, in Vademoro, which is part of Madrid, the PPP continues to make losses. They note that integrated contracts, where primary and specialist healthcare are included in the capitation model, have performed best. However, they caution that the longer term financial success of some of the Spanish healthcare arrangements may not be transferable internationally given the unique and highly specific characteristics of these arrangements and of the institutional environments. They conclude that "care is needed to avoid unwarranted inferences about claimed benefits of lower costs while maintaining sustainable quality ... these projects continue to carry ongoing risks for all governments". Such cautionary experiences ought to be taken seriously and regarded as relevant to all western jurisdictions rather than as quaint and esoteric news from afar.

In the final article, Hellowell and Vecchi investigate the reasons PPPs tend to create budgetary problems for the state (i.e. government) partner. They note that PPPs have long been advocated on the grounds that they reduce the extent to which "strategic misrepresentation" occurs with public projects, with costs being deliberately underestimated and benefits deliberately overestimated in order to ensure favoured projects gain approval for funding. Since governments impose hard(er) budget constraint on PPPs, the actual outcomes should be closer to estimated outcomes, and evidence supports this theory. However, there is also considerable evidence that governments often find that PPP projects are unaffordable and impact on their capacity to provide socially-defined objectives. Importantly, then, Hellowell and Vecchi ask a simple question: why would a public authority agree to sign a contract at a price which is unaffordable? Based on English and Italian evidence, they find that there is strategic behaviour by government employees during the appraisal process which focuses on whether the government agency has the capacity to pay the forecast price. In particular, they highlight the over-indexation of payments (where the proportion of the payment indexed to inflation is larger than the inflation-sensitive element of the operator's costs – enabling private sector bidders to offer a lower initial price, and recoup payments later in the contract period). Such behaviour may promote managerial utility (e.g. the career objectives of local politicians and bureaucrats), but is unlikely to serve the public interest.

Several themes arise through this collection of articles. Differing definitions of PPPs clearly exist with distinct legal environments and policy contexts in different jurisdictions. Vastly different arrangements for financing and risk sharing exist. Perhaps most importantly, there are significant cross-national differences in institutional arrangements and the extent of public accountability. This collection emphasizes that PPP scholars need to consider carefully the institutional arrangements in each region or state and should drill down to understand the incentives faced by individual players (see also van den Hurk et al. 2015). Policy makers should understand the incentives of individuals during the negotiation phase as well as during the post-contractual stage.

Another theme from this collection is that accurate, relevant data on PPPs are often hard for researchers to obtain. Particular problems arise with obtaining performance and cost data as well as institutional arrangements. The lack of such data limits our ability to draw cross-national policy lessons. It also opens up the opportunity for lazy advocates or critics to cherry-pick PPP successes or failures and hold them up in support of their opinions.

Another theme is the existence of multiple stakeholders with multiple objectives that shift over time. Whilst this phenomenon has been noted previously (Hodge 2010), it is nonetheless salient to see new empirical evidence coming to the fore illustrating the inherently political nature of PPP projects around the globe and the importance of a political economy perspective (Boardman and Vining 2012). A continuing theme from past research is the contrast between the sophisticated theorizing and formal number crunching calculus on the potential advantages expected from PPPs and the actual reality of poorly calibrated economic and financial models and the visible lack of reliable VfM findings as well as other crucial performance information. These observations occur in the midst of the continuing political attractiveness of PPPs as a policy option and evidence-based suggestions that strategic misrepresentation continues with privately funded PPP projects, contrary to current mythology. All of this suggests that PPPs will remain a major challenge for scholars and public servants alike. And whilst these five articles extend previous work and provide exciting new results and insights, there is equally no doubt that wide debate around the worth and value of PPPs will continue. In this light, there is much research still to be done.

Acknowledgement

We would like to thank the reviewers of the submitted articles.

Funding

We would like to thank the Social Sciences and Humanities Research Council of Canada [grant number 646-2012-0305], which provided funds for a Conference on Public–Private Partnerships held at the

University of British Columbia, June 2013. The articles in this special issue were initially presented at this conference. We would also like to thank the Sauder–CBS Partnership fund for its support of some participants at this conference and of the International PPP Scholars Network.

References

ASEAN, 2014, *ASEAN Principles for PPP Frameworks* (Jarkata: The Asean Secretariat).

Boardman, A. E. and Vining, A. R., 2012, The political economy of public-private partnerships and analysis of their social value. *Annals of Public and Cooperative Economics*, **83**(2), pp. 117–141. doi:10.1111/apce.2012.83.issue-2

European Commission, 2014, *An Investment Plan for Europe* (Brussels: European Commission).

HM Treasury (UK), 2012, *A New Approach to Public-Private Partnerships* (London: HM Treasury).

Hodge, G. A., 2010, Reviewing public-private partnerships: Some thoughts on evaluation, in: G. A. Hodge, C. Greve, A. E. Boardman (Eds) *International Handbook on Public-Private Partnerships* (Cheltenham, UK: Edward Elgar), pp. 81–112.

Hodge, G. A., 2013, Keynote presentation to Global Challenges in PPP: Cross-Sectoral and Cross-Disciplinary Solutions?, 6–7 November 2013, Universiteit Antwerpen, City Campus, Hof Van Liere.

Hodge, G. A. and Greve, C., 2013, Introduction: Public-private partnership in turbulent times, in: C. Greve, G. Hodge (Eds) *Rethinking Public-Private Partnerships: strategies for Turbulent Times* (London: Routledge), pp. 1–32.

Hodge, G. A., Greve, C., and Boardman, A. E. (Eds), 2010, *International Handbook on Public-Private Partnerships* (Cheltenham, UK: Edward Elgar).

New York Times, 2015, Obama proposes tapping private investors to fund infrastructure projects. Available at: http://www.nytimes.com/2015/01/17/us/politics/obama-proposes-tapping-private-investors-to-fund-infrastructure-projects.html?_r=3 (accessed 16 January).

OECD, 2012, *Recommendations of the Council on Principles for Public Governance of Public-Private Partnerships* (Paris: OECD).

Siemiatycki, M., 2013, Is there a distinctive Canadian PPP Model? Reflections on Twenty Years of Practice. Paper presented at the Second CBS-Sauder-Monash PPP Conference, Vancouver, BC, 13–14 June.

Smith, A. J., 1999, *Privatized Infrastructure: The Role of Government* (London: Thomas Telford).

van den Hurk, M., Brogaard, L., Lember, V., Petersen, O. H., and Witz, P., 2015, National varieties of Public–Private Partnerships (PPPs): A comparative analysis of PPP-supporting units in 19 European countries. *Journal of Comparative Policy Analysis: Research and Practice*, published online 23 March. doi:10.1080/13876988.2015.1006814

Public–Private Partnerships in the US and Canada: "There Are No Free Lunches"[1]

AIDAN R. VINING, ANTHONY E. BOARDMAN and FINN POSCHMANN

ABSTRACT *Governments in many industrialized nations have made concerted efforts to reduce their immediate expenditures and to reduce the cost of major infrastructure projects. Public–private partnerships (P3s) are one emerging method that might do so. Despite the increased use of P3s, there is little independent research on the effectiveness of P3s as a public policy instrument. This article considers the major rationales for P3s, including cost savings and keeping project financing off government budgets. It then presents a transaction cost model that suggests that P3s can often be prone to conflict, high contracting costs, opportunism and failure. Evidence from six major infrastructure projects and a summary analysis of US prisons is then presented. These cases confirm that contracting costs have been high, as predicted by the model. Specifically, high contracting costs reflect the presence of complexity/uncertainty, asset specificity, the potential for ex post bilateral opportunism and a lack of contract management skills by governments. Given these circumstances, the private sector can behave opportunistically at the expense of the public sector as there has sometimes been a political imperative to prevent projects from terminating. Public partners have also behaved opportunistically after projects are in place. Unless public sector managers recognize that they must design contracts that both compensate private sector partners for risk and then ensure that they actually bear it, P3s have little chance of being efficient or effective service delivery mechanisms.*

Introduction

Governments in many industrialized nations, and at all levels, have made a concerted effort to reduce their budgets and their budget deficits (Grout and Stevens 2003: 220). Because public-private partnerships (P3s) reduce direct government expenditures (at least in the short run) without necessarily reducing services, they have attracted growing interest from governments. Budgetary savings, however, are not the only reason for this increasing interest. P3s are "part of a wider trend to decentralization and autonomization" (Pollitt *et al.* 2001: 275) that aims to improve public procurement as well as other aspects of government performance (Gruening 2001). This article reviews the emerging experience regarding the implementation and operation of P3s in the US and Canada, focusing primarily on cases of major infrastructure projects. While projects with partnership characteristics began to emerge in the 1980s, it was not until the mid-1990s that P3s really began to take hold. Since then, P3 projects have taken root in many jurisdictions. How effective have these initial P3s been? What lessons can be learned?

A wide range of relationships between the public sector and for-profit private firms could potentially be labeled as P3s.[2] The critical feature of P3s is that they involve an *ongoing* relationship between a public sector entity and a private sector entity *with some degree of joint decision making and financial risk sharing*. In contrast, contracting out involves a "purchase" from the private sector by the public sector (Globerman and Vining 1996). However, there is no "bright line" that distinguishes these or other forms of government procurement (Warner and Hebdon 2001). In practice, one organizational form merges into the other. We argue that P3s and contracting out can share many of the same features that can raise costs, result in conflict between the participants and lead to poor performance outcomes.

Infrastructure P3s are typically structured by an explicit contract – between a government entity and one or more private sector firms – where the private sector entity agrees to finance, build and operate some facility for a specific period of time, after which ownership is transferred to the public sector.[3] These projects are frequently referred to as Build–Operate–Transfer projects or BOTs. The governmental entity is sometimes the (intermediate) customer for the project's output and is sometimes responsible for the payment of the user fees. In other cases, toll roads, for example, the public sector party negotiates the contract and sometimes specifies unit prices, but road users pay the private entity directly.

The paper proceeds as follows. It first considers government rationales for P3s. Second, it considers a "positive" model of P3s based on the fact that P3s have similar characteristics to two other contracting relationships between government and private sector entities – contracting out by governments and "mixed" enterprises (enterprise owned by government and private shareholders). These relationships "partner" participants with conflicting goals; as a result contracting costs (a form of transaction cost) are likely to be high. Third, a number of P3 examples are then considered in light of this positive model. They suggest that the prognosis for future P3s is somewhat pessimistic under current practice in North America. As discussed in the conclusion, these findings are similar to those emerging from the scholarly literature in Europe. In sum, governments have generally found it difficult to *effectively* reduce their financial and budgetary exposure through the use of P3s. Furthermore, in some cases, governments have faced significant increased political risk, rather than reduced risk as they had hoped. At the same time, the for-profit private sector partners have had difficulty making adequate rates of return, although this is a tentative conclusion as they have usually had incentives to publicly emphasize losses and to be secretive about profits. One common outcome is the dissolution of the P3 more quickly than envisioned in the original contract, whether through a government buy-out, private entity bankruptcy or otherwise. Another common outcome is protracted conflict, with high contracting costs borne by one party or both.

Can these problems be solved, or at least mitigated? The fundamental goal conflict is not going to disappear. Clearly, if decision-making authority and financial risk bearing are not carefully matched, incentives will be misaligned and effective outcomes are unlikely. Unless there is government learning (both across and within levels), governments will be doomed to constantly repeat both the high contracting costs and the poor outcomes. In the conclusion, we discuss some ways that governments might start to control these high contracting costs.

Government Rationales for P3s

There is a history of private franchising in the United States (see Boardman et al. 2005). In Canada, there has been a long history of public subsidies for large-scale private infrastructure, such as railroads (Hardin 1974, Mylvaganam and Borins 2004). Close linkages between the public and private sectors re-emerged in the US and Canada in the mid-1990s in the form of P3s. North American governments, like those in Europe and Australia, have been most attracted to P3s in capital-intensive areas, such as transportation, water and wastewater, to minimize the expenditure of large amounts of public capital (Norment 2002).

Why do governments argue that it makes sense to utilize P3s rather than more direct means of public provision? While there may well be an element of faddism in the move to P3s (Pollitt et al. 2001), governments have presented five specific reasons. As mentioned in the introduction, a major reason for P3s is to keep public sector budgets, and especially budget deficits, down. Indeed, most US states have constitutional or legislative requirements to balance budgets. Even in the absence of constitutional constraints, most governments perceive that there are political benefits from keeping large capital projects "off-budget" (Li et al. 2005). Second, governments usually argue that P3s can provide both infrastructure and on-going services at a lower cost, resulting primarily from superior private sector scale efficiencies and technical efficiency, also called X-efficiency (Frantz 1992). A third reason is financial risk reduction. This pertains to both the cost of the project and the future revenue stream. Various agencies of the UK government have generally argued that this risk transfer should be the primary benefit flowing from the use of infrastructure P3s (usually called Private Finance Initiatives, or PFIs in the UK) (UKNAO 1999, NHS 1999, HM Treasury 2000). Relevant to both rationale two and three, large government infrastructure projects in a wide variety of jurisdictions have often cost far more than anticipated or budgeted (Boardman et al. 1994, Flyvbjerg et al. 2002, USGAO 2003, UKNAO 2003). Furthermore, revenue streams from these projects have often turned out to be much lower, higher or more volatile than expected. If revenues do not meet expectations, a public project would have to be cross-subsidized out of general revenue. A fourth reason is governments' desire to avoid up-front capital costs – it is easier to raise private capital than additional tax revenues or government loans. Bond issues in the US are often subject to voter referendum. But, voters may simultaneously demand more services and vote against bond proposals (Pozen 2003: 264). While this rationale is obviously closely related to the desire to avoid on-budget commitments, it is distinct. Fifth, governments may believe (or at least want to believe) that private sector provision of financing means that it is easier for a private entity to impose user fees, resulting in less political cost to government. The reasoning is that voters will accept that the private sector needs to raise revenue to make a profit and repay its debt, but they are less willing to accept the argument that the public sector needs to do so. This rationale is best assessed after the implementation of P3s; we briefly consider the evidence on this later.

Are the first four rationales well-founded? Concerning the first rationale for P3s – keeping the project off the public balance sheet – the government will normally account for the project in accordance with public sector accounting principles. However, it is important to recognize that, regardless of the accounting conventions used, the underlying economic reality is not altered. For example, a government or health care provider that constructs a new hospital using a P3 will have to pay for it at some point in time either via a rent charge or a user charge. This charge will normally have to recompense the private entity for all the construction risk it bore. This reflects the fact that no matter who finances the project, whether in the public or private sector, "the overall cost of capital ... is determined wholly by the underlying risks associated with the activity" (Jenkinson 2003: 325). Thus, the present value of this payment is likely to be *at least* equivalent to the real risk-adjusted cost of constructing the hospital. This risk charge might actually be lower for many governments because of their ability to spread construction risk over a large number of similar projects, that is, from their superior risk-pooling capacity (see Perold 2004: 6–12). However, it is possible to postulate that global firms would have superior risk-pooling capacity for highly specialized projects. In these situations, provided that the project is not globally unique, the firm would be able to avail itself of economies of scale and learning that are not available to governments. Thus, while there may be a political benefit in keeping the debt off-budget, this is normally not a fundamental economic rationale for P3s.

The next three rationales for P3s relate to the relative (non-financing) costs of the public sector versus the private sector. There are certainly a number of theoretical reasons to expect that P3 delivery could lower costs that are not related to financing. There are a number of related strands to this cost superiority argument. The major argument for cost superiority is that private sector firms may be able to utilize superior scale, scope or learning economies. Private sector firms often enjoy project-specific economies of scale and scope advantages compared to most governments. Their advantage is particularly strong in comparison to sub-national governments, which by definition are limited in the geographic scope of their operations – unless they can engage in (costly) contracting with adjacent governments (Globerman and Vining 1996). Large multinational firms may engage in many similar projects and be global in scope. In contrast, many governments at the sub-state level cannot realistically achieve minimum efficient scale. Large firms not only benefit from these scale effects directly, but they also allow them to utilize learning economies – specialized knowledge accumulated through learning and experience (Lapre and Van Wassenhove 2003). These cost advantages are likely to be most important during the construction phase of projects, but they can also be important in reducing the cost of raising equity and debt capital (in other words, before construction).

Another cost superiority argument is that the private sector normally has superior incentives to minimize costs, holding constant any scale, scope or learning effects.

Put another way, the private sector has lower agency costs (Jensen and Meckling 1976), as is clearly illustrated in the recent privatization literature (Megginson and Netter 2001). Nonetheless, as we discuss below, specific incentive structures can negate or reverse these normal incentives. Because of the cost-reduction profit incentives, they may have more cost-efficient operations, including procurement policies, and better project management skills. These technical efficiency cost advantages are likely to be relatively most important during the operational and management phases of projects. They may also have lower wage costs, possibly due to hiring non-union labor (Hundley 1991, Gregory and Borland 1999). It is often argued that these superior incentives show up most clearly over time in cost-reducing innovation, or *dynamic* technical efficiency (Dosi 1988).

Second, critics argue that the cost of financing may be lower for the public sector. US tax policy generally favors the public sector because state and local governments may issue bonds that are exempt from state and federal taxes. Canadian tax policy does not provide such tax benefits, but provincial bonds generally carry a lower interest rate than corporate bonds. After a comprehensive review of the issues, de Bettignies and Ross (2004: 146–147) conclude that it is not at all clear that governments are generally able to borrow at a lower cost than the private sector.[4] Additionally, there is a trend for some governments to provide equivalent tax-exempt status to P3 projects, further leveling the playing field.

Although the cost rationales for using P3s have some prima facie merit, some critics would not accept them and have directly rejected P3s on more fundamental normative grounds (Rosenau 1999, Teisman and Klijn 2002). While these debates are important, they are not the major focus of this article. Rather, in the next section, we explicitly focus on a positive theory analysis (Vining and Weimer 2001).

A Positive Theory Perspective: Incorporating Contracting Costs

The public and private participants in a P3 inevitably have conflicting interests (Teisman and Klijn 2002, Reeves 2003, Trailer *et al.* 2004). Studies have shown that in other interorganizational contexts with similar conflicting interests, the result can be high bargaining costs, opportunism, failure to achieve goals and partnership dissolution. For example, mixed enterprises that are jointly owned by private shareholders and government can result in "the worst of both worlds", achieving neither high profitability nor worthwhile social goals (Eckel and Vining 1985, Boardman and Vining 1989, Sueyoshi 1998). Contracting out by government in relatively unfavorable circumstances has also been shown to be prone to high bargaining costs (Globerman and Vining 1996, Brown and Potoski 2003, Boardman and Hewitt 2004). Even private sector joint ventures where the participants both have profit goals experience conflict, opportunism and have high failure rates (Geringer and Herbert 1991, Inkpen and Beamish 1997, Shenkar and Yan 2002).

The likelihood that a P3 will provide a project at lower cost to government or the rest of society depends not only the private sector partner having the appropriate incentives to minimize costs, but also the incentives to pass some of these cost savings on to the public sector partner. But, firms are interested in profit maximization, rather than cost minimization. If they are remunerated on a "cost-plus" basis, whether deliberately or because of a lack of foresight, then they will have an incentive to raise, rather than lower, costs (McAfee and McMillan 1988). If they can achieve lower costs, they have no intrinsic desire to pass on these lower costs as lower prices. Sophisticated private sector equity investors are especially wary of engaging in contracts with prices that do not fully compensate them for all the risks they assume. Additionally they can strategically minimize their risk in (at least) two ways: (1) by forming a stand-alone corporation that is isolated from their other corporate activities, thereby reducing the costs of bankruptcy if it becomes necessary; (2) by limiting their equity participation through the utilization of extensive third-party debt financing (Roll and Verbeke 1998). As we discuss below, both strategies are consistent with either a transaction cost theory or agency theory perspective with respect to the P3 relationship (Jensen and Meckling 1976, Trailer et al. 2004).

The critical issue in evaluating the success of a P3 is whether the total cost of the P3 is lower than the total cost of the counterfactual of government provision. Transaction cost economics provides a useful framework because it emphasizes that in interorganizational contexts total contract cost equals production cost plus transaction costs (Williamson 1975).[5] Transaction costs include the cost of negotiating, monitoring and, if necessary, re-negotiating contracts with profit-maximizing firms.[6] Many of these transaction costs, however, are not included as a cost of the project in the project budget. Some of these contracting costs may be captured in other government budgets, for example, in government legal and procurement departments. But, they are frequently not allocated to the P3. From a social perspective, all costs, including the private sector's transactions costs, should be included when evaluating the "success" of P3s (Globerman and Vining 1996).

As discussed earlier, proponents of P3s have tended to focus on the potential ability of P3s to deliver projects more promptly and at lower construction costs than can governments. There is some evidence to support this argument (UKNAO 2003). While these two measures do represent some degree of success, and are dimensions where traditional public sector projects are weakest, they are too narrow as they do not include transaction costs. In sum, they are not equivalent to a social benefit-cost analysis. Independent studies of P3 performance that use comprehensive measures of performance are rare and admittedly difficult.

Transaction costs are substantively important because many P3 infrastructure projects present complex contracting situations. Indeed, one way of thinking of P3s is simply government contracting out under relatively unfavorable conditions. Transaction cost theory suggests that contracting costs are likely to be high when the infrastructure has the following characteristics: high asset specificity, high degrees of complexity/uncertainty and low *ex ante* competitiveness (Williamson 1975, Globerman and Vining 1996, Broadbent et al. 2003). The difficulty in managing these issues is greater if the government initiating the P3 has poor contract management skills (Boardman and Hewitt 2004, Leiblein and Miller 2003). After the P3 contract has been signed, contestability is low and the risk of holdup is high. Thus, aggregate contracting costs are likely to be high. Governments with weak contracting ability and experience will not have the skill to anticipate these contracting problems and contract for them *before* the contract is finalized. Many P3s, especially infrastructure projects, are likely to have some or most of these characteristics.

Six P3 Project Reviews

We provide reviews of six specific projects. They were selected because of the availability of information, the size and profile of the projects and the lessons they offer for P3 contract theory, design and implementation. Three are in the US: the Dulles Greenway in Virginia, Route 91 in Orange County and the Tampa Bay Seawater Desalination Plant in Florida, and three in Canada: the Alberta Special Waste Management System, Highway 407 in metropolitan Toronto and the Confederation Bridge linking Price Edward Island with the Canadian mainland.

Dulles Greenway

US federal law essentially banned private toll roads until 1991 (USCBO 1997). In that year the passage of the Intermodal Surface Transportation Efficiency Act explicitly authorized their use. In spite of this, the United States General Accounting Office (USGAO) recently concluded that "[a]ctive private sector sponsorship and investment has been used to a limited extent in the United States to fund, construct, and operate major highway and transit projects; as a consequence, the nation's experience with active private sector sponsorship and investment has been limited" (USGAO 2004: 3). The USGAO identified only two major recent highway projects that included for-profit private partners (USGAO 2004: 11). These are the Dulles Greenway toll road in Virginia and Orange County State Route 91 Express Lanes in southern California.

The Dulles Greenway (formerly the Dulles Toll Road extension) is a fourteen and a half mile toll road that runs from Dulles International Airport to Leesburg in Virginia. Apart from $3.5 million in state funds, its owner, the Toll Road Investors Partnership II (a partnership of local interests, the Italian toll road operator Autostrade SPA and Kellogg, Brown and Root), raised $360 million in private capital to finance the startup. However, the project only involved approximately $40 million in equity financing (USGAO 2004: 14). At the time it was raised, none of the financing qualified as a tax-exempt bond (Taliaferro 1997).

Construction was originally scheduled to start in 1989 and to be completed by 1992, but financing and environmental concerns postponed the start of construction until September 1993. The highway opened in September 1995, six months ahead of schedule. However, early ridership was lower than projected, and the project went into default in July 1996 – within a year of its opening.

Demand forecasts were based on an independent consultant's report conducted in the late 1980s, prior to the economic downturn in the early 1990s. This report assumed demand would be approximately 20,000 vehicles per day at a toll of $1.50 for the first year, rising to 34,000 per day at the same toll rate by 1995 (Wooldridge et al. 2002). The delay in opening the road was ignored and ridership was forecast at 34,000 per day (Pae 1995).

To increase ridership, tolls were lowered from an initial $1.75 to $1.00. While trips increased, this had a marginal impact on revenues due to the lower tolls. In 1998/99, debt was restructured and did qualify for tax-favorable treatment, thus lowering carrying costs.[7] Usage has increased over the six-year period since the highway's completion from about 10,000 per weekday to about 60,000 (Brumback 2003).

Nevertheless, the partnership's losses have been about $30 million per year, and future profitability will depend on the ability of future revenue growth to cover capital and operating costs.

The Dulles Greenway P3 illustrates a "vicious cycle" that seems to afflict quite a few highway projects: tolls are set high in an attempt to cover financing and operating costs, demand is overestimated at that toll, the toll discourages usage and thus total revenues are not high enough to cover financing and operating costs. Tolls are lowered, as a result demand increases, but total revenues do not increase substantially and still do not cover financing and operating costs; the builder/operator requests some form of bailout by government and if it does not get it the firm slides into technical default.

The potential for this cycle is not as common in more incremental reforms to highway procurement contracting that introduce some greater degree of incentive compatibility between government and highway construction firms. Various forms of performance-based contracting do seem to improve highway procurement (Batelle 2003).

SR 91, Orange County

State Route (SR) 91 was authorized by the California legislature in 1991.[8] A ten-mile stretch of the California freeway opened in 1995 with the median lanes of the highway dedicated as the SR 91 Express Lanes. These lanes were operated as a P3. Access to these lanes was restricted and operated as an electronic toll road. Toll rates were not regulated, but the operator could not earn a return in excess of 17 per cent. The agreement included a non-compete clause which restricted improvements to the freeway or nearby roads except for safety reasons (Poole 2000).

The developer and operator of the project was the California Private Transportation Company (CPTC). CPTC was a limited partnership that included Peter Kiewit Sons (a large construction firm), Cofiroute (a French toll road company) and Granite Construction (a local Californian firm). The public sector partners were the California Department of Transportation (Caltrans) and the Orange County Transportation Authority. Upon completion in 1995, the state owned the lanes, but CPTC was to operate, maintain and police the road for 35 years. After the 35-year period, roadway management would revert to the government. Initial private financing raised approximately $125 million, although only $20 million was CPTC's equity (USGAO 2004: 14).

Volume on SR 91 increased steadily from 7.3 million trips in 1999 to 9.5 million trips in 2002, while over the same period annual revenue grew from $19.5 million to $29 million (USGAO 2004: 43). In 1999, there was an attempt to sell CPTC to a newly created non-profit entity for $260 million. There was a public outcry over the perception that this was a non-arms-length "sweetheart" deal and the sale was cancelled. Over this period, the Orange County government came under increasing political pressure because of the contract conditions. The manifest focus of conflict was the non-compete clause, but CPTC's profitability also seems to have been a latent issue. Caltrans essentially decided to ignore the non-compete clause and tried to expand capacity in 1999, claiming that safety was an issue. However, CPTC sued and Caltrans was forced to settle after the discovery process revealed Caltrans internal documents admitting there was no significant safety issue (Poole 2000). There were other lawsuits filed by Riverside County as well as two unsuccessful legislative attempts to void the non-compete clause and acquire the tolls lanes via condemnation. In 2002, the Orange County Transportation Authority finally reached an agreement with CPTC to purchase SR 91 for $207.5 million. The road continued to be managed by a successor corporation to CPTC named Cofiroute Mobility.

It could be argued that SR 91 was successful – the lanes were built quickly and at projected cost. Riders use the lanes every day. The ultimate sale back to government was certainly portrayed as a "win–win" situation by both sides. Looked at from a broader public policy perspective, however, it is hardly a model example of partnership between the public and private sectors. Both parties exhibited opportunistic behavior and the transaction costs, including legal costs and negotiation costs, were enormous.

Tampa Bay Seawater Desalination Plant

The Tampa Bay region decided in the mid-1990s to solve a looming water shortage by constructing a major water desalination plant. The plant was projected to process 25 million gallons a day, or approximately 10 per cent of the volume that West Coast Regional Water Supply (now Tampa Bay Water), the region's water supplier, provided to the cities of Tampa Bay, St. Petersburg and New Port Richey, as well as surrounding counties. At the time, the desalination process was still an emerging technology and was expected to be considerably more expensive than incremental conventional groundwater sources (Johnson 2003). However, the Southwest Florida Water Management District was putting pressure on jurisdictions to reduce groundwater pumping and was prepared to provide subsidies for desalination. No other utility in the United States provided water by desalination on a regular basis.

The water utility wished to proceed with a P3 that protected it from financial risk. The project was divided into two separate components: an engineering–procurement–construction project and a 30-year operations and maintenance contract. Initial bids offered to provide water at $2 to $3 per 1,000 gallons. These price quotes were considerably below the price that the water utility expected to pay because contractors appear to have hoped to gain an early lead in the desalination market. Covanta Tampa Construction was selected for both the construction contract and a 30-year operations-maintenance contract.

The relationship between the utility and the contractor appears to have been fraught with mistrust, partly brought about by constant delays in completing the plant. Eventually, Covanta filed for bankruptcy in October 2003 with the operations and management contract (worth approximately $350 million) as its only asset. One reason for the bankruptcy filing was to prevent Tampa Bay Water from terminating Covanta's contract and replacing it with another firm.

Construction of the plant was completed in 2003. Although the plant has begun producing water, Tampa Bay Water refused to approve the plant during a 14-day acceptance test, claiming major deficiencies (Wright 2003). The main problem appeared to be that the purification membranes clogged easily and needed replacement much more frequently than forecast. Without this approval, Covanta was blocked from beginning the operations and management contract. In 2003, a US Court ordered the parties into mediation, but by 2004 the partnership had terminated with Tampa Water paying Covanta $4.4 million of the $7.9 million it had retained from the construction contract.

At the time of writing, the plant was producing 22.4 million gallons a day, not far off its projected volume of 25 million gallons, albeit at higher than projected costs. Tampa Bay Water is negotiating with a number of firms concerning repairs to the filters and other problems. These repairs are forecast to cost somewhere between $8 million and $20 million (Pittman 2004). The *St. Petersburg Times* concludes: "The dumbfounding part of the troubled odyssey in opening this important desalination plant is that the contract arrangement was designed to limit the public's financial liability" (*St. Petersburg Times* 2003: 14A).

The Alberta Special Waste Management System

The Alberta Special Waste Management System (ASWMS) was created in 1987. It was jointly owned by a provincial corporation (40 per cent) and BOVAR Inc., a private firm (60 per cent). ASWMS built an integrated hazardous waste-treatment facility at Swan Hills, Alberta. BOVAR was to collect 60 per cent of the profits and all of the net earnings of the operator (Chem-Security). Under the agreement, BOVAR also received a guaranteed minimum return on capital linked to the current prime rate regardless of the profitability of the venture (Mintz 1995). Furthermore, the provincial government provided debt guarantees for BOVAR, as well as indemnity against any future remediation or insurance liabilities in excess of $1 million. This arrangement followed from the Alberta government's belief that a private sector entity could build and operate the plant more efficiently than the public sector, although it recognized that the plant would not be commercially viable without subsidies.

The parties later modified the agreement to permit a large capacity expansion. Partly as a result of this expansion, the subsidy turned out to be considerably larger than expected – approximately $445 million in total between 1986 and 1995 (Mintz 1995: 17). Importantly, the additional capacity turned out to be excessive.[9] The plant has operated at about 50 per cent of its capacity through most of its life. In 1995, the Alberta government bought out BOVAR's ownership interest for $150 million. The contract's return-on-capital provisions provided a clear incentive for overcapitalization. BOVAR's profits did not depend on revenue exceeding costs: earnings were a function of capital investment, rather than efficiency or profitability.[10] BOVAR also had no incentive to encourage cost reductions by the plant operator. As a result, BOVAR received a high guaranteed rate of return although it was exposed to little risk.[11]

Because there was no useful sharing of risk and reward, it is hard to classify Swan Hills as a successful P3. The result was a waste treatment facility with capacity that exceeded Alberta's needs, having been built and operated under terms very costly to provincial taxpayers.

The Highway 407 Express Toll Route[12]

Highway 407 is a controlled-access 108-kilometer highway that crosses the north side of metropolitan Toronto. The request for proposals (RFP) was announced in the fall of 1993, when the Province of Ontario was emerging from a recession which had left it in an extremely weak financial position (Mylvaganam and Borins 2004). The recession and the province's high debt load made a toll road politically viable. The 407 project was managed through the Ontario Transport Capital Corporation, a special-purpose entity created by the Ontario government. The original RFP proposed that the province would be responsible for land assembly and related costs. The private partner would provide financing, guarantee a maximum construction price and operate the highway. It would be remunerated from toll revenues, but neither traffic levels nor toll revenues were guaranteed. Under this original RFP, the private partner would have been financially exposed to the operating risk. The RFP specified few characteristics of the highway, in an attempt to encourage private sector innovation.

In the responses to the RFP, it became clear that credible private partners were unwilling to assume the financing risks in addition to construction and operating risks. Indeed, both of the two qualified consortia sought extensive provincial backing for the project debt. Without a toll-revenue guarantee, a private firm would have had to pay at least 75 basis points more for debt financing than would the province (Hambros 1999). These realities were used to rationalize the province's assumption of the financing of the project.[13] Subsequently, one consortium was allocated the contract for construction and highway maintenance, while the other was contracted to manage the toll system. This removal of financial risk fundamentally transformed the nature of the project. Once the bulk of the capital cost and financial risk shifted to the province, the project necessarily lost much of its P3 quality. The private partner was now tendering a fixed-price construction project.

The province also retained the operational risk during the first 18 months of operation. The risk to the province was reduced only when it sold the highway's operating concession to a Canadian–Spanish–Australian consortium for $3.1 billion (Mendoza et al. 1999). The concession term was for 99 years, after which ownership of the asset reverts to the government. The operating consortium appeared to negotiate a unilateral right to set tolls. In 2004, the consortium announced that it intended to raise tolls, claiming it was losing money (Mackie 2004). In the meantime, the province had gone through a change of government and the new government decided to fight the toll increase. The dispute is now before the courts (Mylvaganam and Borins 2004).

The 407 project has been successful to the extent that the highway was built quickly and without major cost overruns. The highway generates 300,000 daily vehicle trips, and it shifts nearly 200 million kilometers in travel per month from un-tolled public highways.[14] Given that each vehicle kilometer is billed to users and that no part of the highway exercises an effective monopoly, these figures suggest there is significant demand for the road. The 407 design process appears to have saved substantial provincial money in the initial construction phase, perhaps in the order of $300 million (Hambros 1999). Some of these savings were not realized, however, because design changes were needed before the highway opened. These changes were charged to the province because the parties agreed they were not part of the initial price-guaranteed contract. The full extent of savings is therefore unclear. Innovative design features such as short entrances and narrow radius ramps certainly reduced land assembly and construction costs. While there were some claims that these changes might jeopardize safety, these fears appear not to have materialized (Mylvaganam and Borins 2004).

Overall, the 407 does not stand out as an exemplary P3 owing to the failure of the government to effectively transfer financing risks; the construction phase turned into a conventional develop, design and build contract. However, the Canadian Council for Public–Private Partnerships certainly regarded it as a success and awarded it a gold medal. Those who focus on the lack of risk transfer, such as Boase (1999), regard it as a P3 failure. Mylvaganam and Borins (2004) present a mixed assessment.

The Confederation Bridge

Prince Edward Island (Canada's smallest province) joined the Canadian federation under a constitutional agreement that guaranteed ship service to the island in perpetuity.[15] Beginning in the 1980s, there was ongoing debate over whether to substitute a fixed link for a weather-dependent ferry. In early 1988, a plebiscite approved such a link. Later in that year, the federal government selected three bids out of seven proposals for further development. Strait Crossing Development Inc. (SCDI), a consortium of Canadian, Dutch, French and American interests, submitted the winning bid.

The selected bid was essentially a BOT agreement. The contract specified a $41.9 million (1992 Canadian dollars) annual payment from the federal government to the operator, notionally representing the avoided cost of ferry operation. SCDI was entitled to all toll revenues for 35 years, after which bridge operation and ownership of its revenue (and cost) stream would revert to the federal government. The government provided an annual $13.9 million revenue guarantee. SCDI initially took on most of the construction and operational risk, as well as toll revenue risk beyond the $13.9 million level. The federal government agreed to bear a number of the residual risks from enemy attack, nuclear catastrophe, earthquake and environmental injunctions, and regulatory risk. The federal payment to SCDI was to begin whether or not the bridge was in service in 1997, but if the bridge was not substantially completed, SCDI was required to pay the ferry subsidy. SCDI was required to post performance bonds and guarantees for specific contingencies.

Principal financing was secured in 1993 through the sale of $640 million of real return bonds by Strait Crossing Finance Inc (SCFI). SCFI was established as a special purpose Crown Corporation of the province of New Brunswick. Its bonds were guaranteed by the federal government and received high credit ratings, providing a financial structure sufficiently durable to survive the 1996 pullout of the American private partner, Morrison Knudsen. Fabrication began in late 1993 and the bridge opened in 1997. Initial tolls were set at the ferry price for comparable vehicles and passengers. Annual increases were, and are, permitted at 75 per cent of the rate of consumer price inflation. The Canadian government estimated its incremental costs for project management to be $46 million.

This P3 is clearly a success to the extent that it delivered a functioning bridge on schedule. While there have been weather closures and some unexpected repairs, the bridge itself is functioning as expected, entirely supplanting the prior ferry service. The Canadian government claims that the Confederation Bridge entailed no incremental cost to government and required no direct funding from government.

The basis for the claim is the argument that the guaranteed payments to the SDCI are the same as the avoided cost of ferry provision, which the government was constitutionally required to pay anyway. The accuracy of this particular argument depends on the cost of (hypothetical) future ferry service provision.

Because SCFI's bonds are guaranteed by the Canadian government, financial risk has remained largely with government. The bonds were sold at a 4.5 per cent interest rate, at a time when similar federal issues were priced at 4.1 per cent. Moreover, SCFI paid a sales commission of 1.75 per cent, compared to a typical rate of 0.6 per cent for federal real return bonds. SCFI's higher rate and fees would not be an issue if the Canadian government had eliminated equivalent risk (in other words, if the federal government had acquired a put option against the risk of project default) or if the consortium's capital requirement had imposed on the private partners an incentive to minimize project capital. However, because the money was raised by a special purpose government agency and was guaranteed by government, there was no net reduction in risk exposure. It is difficult to escape the conclusion that the structure was primarily chosen in an effort to achieve off-balance-sheet financing.[16]

The project was completed and put in service very quickly. Again, however, it is not clear that the Canadian government laid-off risks that matched its financial exposure.

US Prison P3s

This section briefly reviews the evidence concerning P3s in the US prison system based on a number of sources. Admittedly, this evidence is at a highly aggregated level, rather than individual case studies of prison P3s. Some of the earliest private prison arrangements concerned only the delivery of imprisonment services in facilities that were built and owned by government, in other words, standard contracting out. In the 1980s, however, US federal and state governments undertook a large prison building program with private sector participation. This expansion was largely a result of a need to reduce overcrowding: in mid-1991, 40 states were operating prisons in violation of the Constitution's prohibition on "cruel and unusual punishment" (McDonald 1994, Pozen 2003). A number of private corporations financed, constructed and operated the new prisons. In some cases, there were also lease-buyback arrangements. As a result of this building expansion, the number of prisoners in private facilities grew from 0.5 per cent of all prisoners 8.5 per cent of all prisoners between 1985 and 1997 (Schneider 1999: 196). By the end of 2002, 6.5 per cent of all prisoners (approximately 94,000 in total) were being held in private facilities – 12.4 per cent of federal prisoners and 5.8 per cent of state prisoners (Harrison and Beck 2003: 8).

Pozen (2003: 72) concludes that "private prisons have a decent if patchy record in the United States." Rates of escape are similar at public and private prisons. Although attempts at cost comparison have been fraught with methodological problems, most empirical studies conclude that the cost of private prisons has been lower than, or similar to, the cost of public prisons: "these studies show a slight advantage to the private prisons and illustrate (in Texas, at least) that a state may realize a reduction in per inmate cost, over time" (Schneider 1999: 201). Many states, including Florida, require private firms to provide services at a cost savings of some specific amount (usually 5–10 per cent).[17] The data on quality as measured on a number of dimensions (administrative compliance, escapes, assaults on staff, vocational programs, etc.) suggest that private prisons are better than, or equal to, publicly operated prisons. Interestingly, Lanza-Kaduce, Parker and Thomas (1999) find lower recidivism rates in private prisons, which they attribute to higher completion of rehabilitation programs. McDonald et al.'s (1998: 56) survey suggests that prison contract administrators thought that they were generally "getting what they ask for in privately operated prisons." Finally, the presence of private prisons has been credited with helping to improve the cost and quality of public prisons.

Lessons from the US and Canadian Cases

Individual P3 Lessons

There is one note of caution concerning P3 lessons from these six examples. Our analysis is based on the availability of public information, whether in journals, newspapers or on the web. Conflict and problems are inherently more newsworthy than co-operation and everyday delivery of services. Therefore, we would not claim that this is an unbiased sample of P3s. However, these six examples clearly illustrate many of the difficulties of implementing effective or "successful" P3s that deliver services at lower risk-adjusted total costs than direct government provision or traditional contracting out. As described in the introduction, a major expected benefit of P3s is the private sector's ability to have lower production costs due to economies of scale, more experience, better incentives and better ability to innovate. However, as we also pointed out, the critical test from a social perspective is whether P3s have lower total costs, including production costs *and* all of the transaction costs associated with managing external suppliers of services.

These P3s illustrate that contracting difficulties make it difficult for the public sector to actually realize lower *total* costs, that is, including all transaction costs. It is useful to consider the factors that are likely to have raised contracting costs in these case studies. First, we consider the issue of complexity/uncertainty. (Complexity and uncertainty are conceptually different, although in practice they are often treated as a single variable.) Many highway projects are relatively predictable from a construction cost perspective, but are highly uncertain from a usage perspective. For example, there was relatively little problem in constructing the Dulles highway on schedule. However, use levels on the toll road were significantly lower than anticipated (10,000 per day during the initial month versus 34,000 per day projected). This P3 essentially involved bundling a relatively standard highway construction project with a much more uncertain (and complex) operating project that involved demand estimation and pricing expertise. Bundling of these two very different kinds of "projects" resulted in a relatively complex project. SR 91 also illustrates this kind of bundling problem. Neither party had experience with variable price electronic tolling in the United States. Revenues and demand were highly uncertain. The feasibility and cost of electronic tolling was also uncertain, although this uncertainty has gone down quickly as a dominant design has emerged. The Tampa Bay water project again illustrates the bundling problem, although in this case it was the construction of the Tampa Bay water project that was complex (because large-scale desalination is an emerging technology), while usage demand and price were guaranteed. The intrinsic complexity of the construction phase resulted in costs that were far higher than expected.

It is generally argued that it is preferable to specify contracts in terms of outcomes or outputs rather than inputs, as it minimizes the potential for opportunism and other problems (Milgrom and Roberts 1992: 125–247). However, in the presence of high complexity and uncertainty, this is essentially impossible. P3s potentially have special merit in infrastructure provision because imperfect information makes it difficult to specify *ex ante* the best design, construction techniques, or even the optimal investment in physical plant as opposed to later operational and servicing costs. In these circumstances, leaving design and investment decisions to private agents with expertise can be optimal (in providing incentives for innovation and efficient allocation of capital) – provided the public partner can adequately specify the desired service level. However, the Highway 407 example illustrates how complexity can actually be increased by specifying performance in terms of outcomes, rather than inputs. The lack of specification on the "how" in the RFP was presumably intended to draw out private sector innovation, but it increased complexity substantially. In turn, it had the effect of reducing *ex ante* competitiveness, as indicated by the fact that there were only two qualified bidders (even though each of the two consortia included quite a few firms).

Second, we consider asset specificity. Many infrastructure P3s are likely to have high asset specificity as such facilities have a high degree of "sunkness" – their value in any other use is low or zero. A related critical issue is whether the specific government that has initiated the contract is effectively the sole potential purchaser. The Tampa Bay desalination plant was characterized by locational asset specificity and the government was the only possible buyer. Government could also use its wider powers to strengthen its bargaining position. The city would not approve the plant and the private sector contractor could not sell the water to any other customer due to its location. Thus, the contractor was subject to government opportunism or holdup.

Highways, similarly, involve a high degree of locational asset specificity as they cannot be used for anything else of value other than a highway in that location. Transaction cost theory would predict that this would lead to a potential problem and, indeed, it has often turned out to be a problem during the construction phase. Here, either side can face the risk of holdup. The government partner can be held up because it is generally a lot cheaper for the initial contractor to finish the job than to bring in a new contractor. The existing contractor has a great deal of specific knowledge about the particular project, i.e., there is considerable human capital asset specificity. However, once the infrastructure has been constructed (and approved), this aspect of the asset specificity problem is reduced because there are many users. However, as in the desalination example, the government has a high degree of potentially opportunistic bargaining power once construction is complete because the private partner cannot remove a highway. Even the threat of opportunistic behavior can be opportunistic! These kinds of problems appear to be a major reason why US turnpike companies in the nineteenth century were generally quite unprofitable (Klein 1990, Klein and Yin 1996).

Third, we consider contract management skills. A lack of contract management effectiveness may relate either to the lack of general contracting expertise or to more specific subject-matter expertise. A lack of contracting expertise is a common problem for governments with limited P3 experience. Many public agencies cannot achieve relevant economies of scale and are, therefore, "learning-by-doing" on a steeper part of the learning curve; the result is higher unit cost. This lack of experience tends to encourage opportunism by private sector firms. In the Alberta Special Waste Management System project, BOVAR received a very high guaranteed return on capital. Taxpayers essentially paid twice for the project. Furthermore, the project capacity was too large, having operated at about 50 per cent of capacity most of the time. Here, lack of government contract skills led to a contract where the private partner had inappropriate cost incentives.

Opportunism can impact contract management effectiveness in many other ways. If governments are under a political and media microscope, they will be unlikely to "pull the plug" on projects, even if they are failing. Indeed, there may be an escalation of commitment (that is, a tendency to throw good money after bad). It is very hard politically for governments to stop P3 infrastructure projects in the middle – the bigger the project, the harder it is to stop (Ross and Staw 1993). Of course, this is also true for pure public sector projects (Boardman *et al.* 1993). If the private sector firm knows the public sector is committed to continuing the project regardless of escalating cost, it has an opportunity to behave opportunistically. But the SR 91 case suggests that governments can also be tempted to behave opportunistically when the private partner is too successful. Government is vulnerable to political charges of having made a "sweetheart deal" with, or being duped by, the private partners. These political costs tempt politicians to renege on contracts, no matter what the financial cost.

In summary, the risk of holdup is high when uncertainty/complexity and asset specificity are high and contract management effectiveness is low. This appears to be more likely to happen during the construction phase of P3s, than during the operating phase. While there may be uncertainty during the operating phase, this factor alone may not be too bad. Contestability is often reasonably high and the risk of holdup quite low. If one private sector operator fails, government can bring in another.

Prison P3 Lessons

The evidence suggests that P3 prisons are as cost-effective, or more so, than public prisons. The main reasons appear to be that economies of scale and better cost-containment incentives allow the private sector to operate with lower costs. These advantages do not appear to be offset by the transaction costs that have bedeviled other forms of P3. Contracting costs are reasonably low. There are a number of reasons: the core tasks are not very complex (both in terms of construction and operations), uncertainty is low, asset specificity is low and competition, or at least contestability, is quite high. Complexity is low because the tasks can be specified clearly. Uncertainty is reasonably low because demand is reasonably easy to forecast. This also reduces asset specificity and increases competition. In fact, competition is quite high, as evidenced by the number of private prison firms that are traded on the stock exchange (Schneider 1999: 196). As a result, P3s in prisons generally appear to have worked reasonably well. Of course, there have been some problems in private prisons, including several riots, but these problems also occur in some public prisons.

Conclusion: No Free Lunches

Since the mid-1990s most infrastructure P3s in the US and Canada have occurred most frequently in the areas of transportation (roads, airports and bridges), water and wastewater, power and energy, and for hospital and other facilities. Some of the reasons why governments are drawn to P3s – especially lower cost provision – clearly have some validity. But, even if valid, it is important to emphasize that from a social perspective the key issue is whether the total cost of the P3 is lower than the total cost of government provision, including production costs and all contracting costs. To investigate this issue we examined six North American infrastructure P3s (all those we could gather reasonable information on from secondary sources). The evidence suggests that these potential benefits are often overwhelmed by contracting costs and opportunism. The reality that "there are no free lunches" applies to P3s as much as it does to anything else.

This case evidence should not be surprising. Profit-making private sector entities, whether they are construction firms, operating entities or whatever, are adept at ensuring that they are fully compensated for risk taking. Thus, in practice, there has been considerable variation in the degree to which financial risk has been shifted to the private sector. In some cases, in spite of the initial intentions of the public partner, projects have ended up largely or completely financed with the public sector bearing the risk. Private sector participants frequently go to considerable lengths to *avoid* risk, especially those associated with usage, even when that was the primary motivation for the public sector to utilize the P3 form. At the extreme, this means that private sector actors tend to establish "stand-alone" operating firms when carrying out P3 contracts that entail large risks from technological or demand uncertainty. These stand-alone private sector entities can avoid large losses when things go badly wrong by declaring bankruptcy or by *threatening* to go bankrupt. The evidence suggests that the public sector has difficulty in anticipating this form of opportunism (perhaps because it is something the public sector – with its taxing power – rarely has to deal with). However, the case studies illustrate that governments can also succumb to opportunism, especially when a P3 becomes a high-profile political issue.

Although our findings are based on a limited number of case studies in the US and Canada, the fragmentary evidence from other P3s in North America appears to be similar (e.g. Bartelme 2004). The findings are also quite similar to the emerging case study evidence in the United Kingdom (Broadbent and Laughlin 2004, Grout and Stevens 2003: 230), Ireland (Reeves 2003), the Netherlands (Klijn and Teisman 2003) and Denmark (Greve and Ejersbo 2003). One particularly significant international finding from both the UK (Asenova and Beck 2003, Edwards and Shaoul 2003) and Australia (English and Guthrie 2003) is that governments have not been particularly successful at shifting risk to private sector partners. Additionally, Li (2003) found that in the UK that contract negotiations associated with attempts to shift risk were extremely costly. Thus, the evidence, in total, suggests that our findings in North America are similar to those from Europe. This raises the question of whether governments can learn, individually or collectively, to adequately specify contract conditions and institutional conflict resolution mechanisms *ex ante* so that the past is not prologue.

How Can Government Do Better?

Unless public sector managers can design contracts that both compensate private sector partners for risk and *then ensure that they actually bear it*, P3s will not improve allocative efficiency and make society better off (Globerman and Vining 1996). To do so, governments need to be much more honest. If they are going to encourage agencies to use P3s, they must be honest on the transaction costs. The most senior level of government with authority is best able to do this.

Acknowledgement

We would like to thank Michael Volker for research assistance.

Notes

1. This article builds on five cases that are forthcoming in Boardman, Poschmann and Vining (2005). A sixth case has been added as well as the US prison study. The theoretical framework is largely new.
2. For example, the US General Accounting Office includes conventional contracting out of government services and even privatization – the complete withdrawal of government provision and financing – as P3s (USGAO 1999). Additionally, the USGAO has treated non-profit entities as being "private" sector entities in P3s (USGAO 2004).
3. Specifically, we do not include the following relationships as P3s: (1) service contracts or other forms of contracting out by the public sector; (2) privatization in the form of the sale of public assets; (3) regulation (including franchise contracting) by public sector entities of privately owned natural monopoly facilities; or (4) the construction of facilities by the private sector and the leasing or sale of those facilities to the public sector based upon fixed, certain terms (including lease/purchase or turnkey agreements).
4. Governments cannot borrow infinite amounts of capital without affecting their credit rating. Raising funds for a P3 project may raise the cost borrowing for subsequent projects. Such costs should be included in the "full" cost of the P3.
5. The transaction cost language is more appropriate than agency language because P3s have the character of a relationship between independent organizational entities. Agency, or principal–agent theory, language is appropriate for intraorganizational hierarchical contexts.
6. Vining and Weimer (2005) distinguish between *ex ante* transaction costs, which can be called governance costs, and *ex post* transaction costs, which can be called opportunism costs or holdup costs.
7. Hall (1998) quotes the Chief Financial Officer of the private firm that operated the road as saying: "We haven't made any debt payments in so long I've forgotten how much we owe now."
8. Assembly Bill 680. This section primarily draws on USCBO (1997) and USGAO (2004).
9. Chem-Security said the reasons for this included generators' pursuit of lower-cost options for waste disposal (NRCB 1994: 6–8).
10. If Chem-Security and BOVAR could have earned profits higher than the guaranteed rate of return, they would have had an incentive to control costs. However, Mintz (1995: 33 and Appendix) shows that even with some positive probability of profit, they have an incentive to over-invest.
11. Mintz (1995) estimates a weighted return on equity of 15.9 per cent for the period 1989 to 1994, far above the risk-free return.

12. This section draws on Poschmann (2003).
13. Note that the logic is flawed. The province's taking on of the financing necessarily brought risks and costs not featured in the government's analysis (de Bettignies and Ross 2004).
14. Per http://www.407etr.com (accessed August 28, 2004).
15. This discussion follows Loxley (1999).
16. This was the Auditor General of Canada's conclusion, and the government did not ultimately succeed in keeping the financing off-book (Receiver General for Canada 1995).
17. Nonetheless, the USGAO (1996) concluded that the evidence on cost savings was "inconclusive."

References

Asenova, D. and Beck, M., 2003, The U.K. financial sector and risk management in PFI projects: a survey. *Public Money & Management*, **23**(3), 195–203.

Batelle, 2003, Performance-based contracting for the highway construction industry: an evaluation of the use of innovative contracting and performance specification in highway construction. February.

Bartelme, T., 2004, A marriage that didn't work. *Journal of Commerce*, January 5, 1–2.

Boardman, A. and Hewitt, R., 2004, Problems with contracting out government services: lessons from orderly services at SCGH. *Industrial and Corporate Change*, **13**(6), 917–929.

Boardman, A. and Vining, A., 1989, Ownership and performance in competitive environments: a comparison of the performance of private, mixed and state owned enterprises. *Journal of Law and Economics*, **32**(1), 1–34.

Boardman, A., Vining, A. and Waters, W. II, 1993, Costs and benefits through bureaucratic lenses: example of a highway project. *Journal of Policy Analysis and Management*, **12**(3), 532–555.

Boardman, A., Mallery, W. and Vining, A., 1994, Learning from *ex ante/ex post* cost–benefit comparisons: the Coquihalla highway example. *Socio-Economic Planning Sciences*, **28**(2), 69–84.

Boardman, A., Poschmann, F. and Vining, A., 2005, North American infrastructure P3s: examples and lessons learned, in: G. Hodge and C. Greve (Eds) *The Challenge of Public–Private Partnerships: Learning from International Experience* (Cheltenham, UK: Edward Elgar).

Boase, J., 1999, Beyond government? The appeal of public–private partnerships. *Canadian Public Administration*, **43**(1), 75–92.

Broadbent, J., Gill, J. and Laughlin, R., 2003, The development of contracting in the context of infrastructure investment in the UK: the case of the private finance initiative in the national health service. *International Public Management Journal*, **6**(2), 173–197.

Broadbent, J. and Laughlin, R., 2004, Perils of partnership. *Australian CPA*, **74**(4), 56–58.

Brown, T. and Potoski, M., 2003, Managing contract performance: a transaction cost approach. *Journal of Policy Analysis and Management*, **22**(2), 275–297.

Brumback, T., 2003, SCC weighs toll road rate ceiling. *Leesburg Today*, December 4.

de Bettignies, J.-E. and Ross, T., 2004, The economics of public–private partnerships. *Canadian Public Policy*, **30**(2), 135–154.

Dosi, G., 1988, Sources, procedures, and microeconomic effects of innovation. *Journal of Economic Literature*, **26**(3), 1120–1171.

Eckel, C. and Vining, A., 1985, Elements of a theory of mixed enterprise, *Scottish Journal of Political Economy*, **32**(1), 2–94.

Edwards, P. and Shaoul, J., 2003, Partnerships: for better or worse. *Accounting, Auditing & Accountability Journal*, **16**(3), 397–421.

English, L. M. and Guthrie, J., 2003, Driving privately financed projects in Australia: what makes them tick? *Accounting, Auditing & Accountability Journal*, **16**(3), 493–511.

Flyvbjerg, B., Holm, M. and Buhl, S., 2002, Underestimating costs in public works projects: error or lie? *Journal of the American Planning Association*, **68**(3), 279–293.

Frantz, R., 1992, X-efficiency and allocative efficiency: what have we learned? *American Economic Review*, **82**(2), 434–438.

Geringer, J. M. and Hebert, L., 1991, Measuring performance of international joint ventures. *Journal of International Business Studies*, **22**(2), 249–263.

Globerman, S. and Vining, A., 1996, A framework for evaluating the government contracting-out decision with an application to information technology. *Public Administration Review*, **56**(6), 40–46.

Gregory, R. and Borland, J., 1999, Recent developments in public sector labor markets, in: O. Ashenfelter and D. Card (Eds) *Handbook of Labor Economics* (Vol. 3C) (Amsterdam: North-Holland).

Greve, C. and Ejersbo, N., 2003, when public–private partnerships fail – the extreme case of the NPM-inspired local government of Farum in Denmark. Paper for Nordisk Kommunalforskningskonference, Odense, Denmark, November 29–December 1.

Grout, P. and Stevens, M., 2003, The assessment: financing and managing public services. *Oxford Review of Economic Policy*, **19**(2), 215–234.

Gruening, G., 2001, Origin and theoretical basis of new public management. *International Public Management Journal*, **4**(2), 1–25.

Hall, T., 1998, Red ink floods greenway. *Washington Business Journal*, **17**(18), 1–2.

Hambros, 1999, Public–private partnerships for highways: experience, structure, financing, applicability and comparative assessment. Objective one: final report. Report to the Council of Deputy Ministers Responsible for Transportation and Highway Safety.Ottawa: Transport Canada.

Hardin, H., 1974, *A Nation Unaware: The Canadian Economic Culture* (Vancouver, BC: J. J. Douglas).

Harrison, P. and Beck, A., 2003, Prisoners in 2002. *Bureau of Justice Statistics Bulletin*. US Department of Justice, Office of Justice Programs, available at: http://www.ojp.usdoj.gov/bjs/pub/pdf/p02.pdf (accessed August 26, 2004).

HM (Her Majesty's) Treasury, 2000, *Public Private Partnerships – the Government's Approach* (London: HM Stationary Office).

Hundley, G., 1991, Public- and private-sector occupational pay structures. *Industrial Relations*, **30**(3), 417–434.

Inkpen, A. C. and Beamish, P. W., 1997, Knowledge, bargaining power and international joint venture instability. *Academy of Management Review*, **22**(1), 177–202.

Jensen, M. and Meckling, W., 1976, Theory of the firm: managerial behavior, agency costs and ownership structure. *Journal of Financial Economics*, **3**(4), 305–360.

Jenkinson, T., 2003, Private finance. *Oxford Review of Economic Policy*, **19**(2), 323–334.

Johnson, N., 2003, As seawater desalination plant readies for day 1, eyes turn to Tampa. *Knight Kidder Tribune Business News*, January 6.

Klijn, E.-H. and Teisman, G., 2003, Institutional and strategic barriers to public-private partnerships: an analysis of Dutch cases. *Public Money and Management*, **23**(3), 137–146.

Klein, D., 1990, The voluntary provision of public goods? The turnpike companies of early America. *Economic Inquiry*, **28**(4), 788–812.

Klein, D. and Yin, C., 1996, Use, esteem, and profit in voluntary provision: toll roads in California. *Economic Inquiry*, **34**(4), 678–692.

Lanza-Kaduce, L., Parker, K. and Thomas, C., 1999, A comparative recidivism analysis of releases from private and public prisons. *Crime and Delinquency*, **45**(1), 28–47.

Lapre, M. and Van Wassenhove, L., 2003, Managing learning curves in factories by creating and transferring knowledge. *California Management Review*, **46**(1), 53–72.

Leiblein, M. J. and Miller, D. J., 2003, An empirical examination of transaction and firm-level influences on the vertical boundaries of the firm. *Strategic Management Journal*, **24**(9), 839–859.

Li, B., 2003, Risk management of public/private partnership projects. Unpublished PhD, School of the Built and Natural Environment, Glasgow Caledonian University.

Li, B., Akintoye, A., Edwards, P.J. and Hardcastle, C., 2005, The allocation of risk in PPP/PFI construction projects in the UK. *International Journal of Project Management*, **23**(1), 25–35.

Loxley, S., 1999, An analysis of a public private sector partnership: the confederation bridge. A report prepared for the Canadian Union of Public Employees.

McAfee, R. and McMillan, J., 1988, *Incentives in Government Contracting* (Toronto: University of Toronto Press).

McDonald, D., 1994, Public imprisonment by private means: the re-emergence of private prisons and jails in the United States, the United Kingdom, and Australia. *British Journal of Criminology*, **34**(1), 29–48.

McDonald, D., Fournier, E., Russell-Einhourn, M. and Crawford, S., with the assistance of Nelson, J., Gaes, G., Camp, S. and Saylor, W., 1998, *Private prisons in the United States: an assessment of current practice* (Cambridge, Mass: Abt Associates Inc).

Mackie, R., 2004, McGinty shrugs off highway toll spat. *Toronto Globe and Mail*, August 12, A4.

Megginson, W. and Netter, J., 2001, From state to market: a survey of empirical studies of privatization. *Journal of Economic Literature*, **39**(2), 321–389.

Mendoza, E., Gold, M., Cater, P. and Parmar, J., 1999, The sale of Highway 407 express toll route: a case study. *Journal of Project Finance*, **5**(3), 5–14.

Milgrom, P. and Roberts, J., 1992, *Economics, Organization and Management* (Englewood Cliffs, NJ: Prentice-Hall).

Mintz, J., 1995, An evaluation of the joint venture agreement establishing the Alberta special waste management system. University of Toronto Faculty of Management, mimeo, October.

Mylvaganam, C. and Borins, S., 2004, *If You Build It: Business, Government and Ontario's Electronic Highway* (Toronto: University Centre for Public Management).

Natural Resources Conservation Board, 1994, Receipt of hazardous waste from other Canadian jurisdictions by the Alberta special waste management system. Decision Report: Application #9301 – Chem-Security (Alberta) Ltd. Calgary: Natural Resources Conservation Board, November.

NHS (National Health Service), 1999, *Public Private Partnerships in National Health Service: The Private Financial Service: Good Practice* (London: Her Majesty's Stationary Office).

Norment, R., 2002, PPPs-American style. *The PFI Journal*, **39**, 26–27.

Pae, P., 1995, Drivers put the brake on toll road's promise. *Washington Post*, December 26, A1, A18, A19.

Perold, A., 2004, The capital asset pricing model. *Journal of Economic Perspectives*, **18**(3), 3–24.

Pittman, C., 2004, Contractors differ over cost to fix desal plant. *St. Petersburg Times*, March 16, 1B.

Pollitt, C., Bathgate, K., Caufield, J., Smullen, A. and Talbot, C., 2001, Agency fever? Analysis of an international policy fashion. *Journal of Comparative Policy Analysis: Research and Theory*, **3**(3), 271–290.

Poole, R. Jr., 2000, Caltrans had no choice but make deal with 91 express lane firm. *Los Angeles Times (Orange County Edition)*, April 23, 13.

Poschmann, F., 2003, Private means to public ends: the future of public-private partnerships. *C. D. Howe Institute Commentary 183* (Toronto: C. D. Howe Institute).

Pozen, D., 2003, Managing a correctional marketplace in the United States and the United Kingdom. *Journal of Law and Politics*, **19**, 253–284.

Receiver General for Canada, 1995, *Public Accounts of Canada, 1995. Volume 1* (Ottawa: Canadian Government Publishing).

Reeves, E., 2003, public–private partnerships in Ireland: policy and practice. *Public Money & Management*, **23**(3), 163–170.

Roll, M. and Verbeke, A., 1998, Financing of the trans-European high-speed rail networks: new forms of public-private partnerships. *European Management Journal*, **16**(6), 706–713.

Rosenau, P., 1999, Introduction: the strengths and weaknesses of public-private policy partnerships. *American Behavioral Scientist*, **43**(1), 10–34.

Ross, J. and Staw, B., 1993, Organizational escalation and exit: lessons from the Shoreham nuclear power plant. *Academy of Management Journal*, **36**(4), 701–732.

St. Petersburg Times, 2003, A troubled water odyssey. October 31, 14A.

Schneider, A., 1999, Public–private partnerships in the U.S. prison system. *American Behavioral Scientist*, **43**(1), 192–208.

Shenkar, O. and Yan, A., 2002, Failure as a consequence of partner politics: learning from the life and death of an international cooperative venture. *Human Relations*, **55**(5), 565–601.

Sueyoshi, T., 1998, Privatization of Nippon Telegraph and Telephone: was it a good policy decision? *European Journal of Operational Research*, **107**(1), 45–61.

Taliaferro, R. Jr., 1997, Greenway runs into financial troubles. *Richmond Times Dispatch*, September 28, A-17.

Teisman, G. and Klijn, E.-H., 2002, Partnership arrangements: governmental rhetoric or governance scheme. *Public Administration Review*, **62**(2), 197–205.

Trailer, J., Rechner, P. and Hill, R., 2004, A compound agency problem: an empirical examination of public-private partnerships. *Journal of American Academy of Business, Cambridge*, **5**(1/2), 308–315.

UK National Audit Office (UKNAO), 1999, *Examining the Value for Money of Deals Under the Private Finance Initiative* (London: National Audit Office).

UK National Audit Office (UKNAO), 2003, PFI: construction performance. Report by the Comptroller and Auditor General, HC 700, Session 2002–2003 (London: HMSO).

US Congressional Budget Office, 1997, *Toll Roads: A Review of Recent Experience* CBO Memorandum (Washington, DC: Congressional Budget Office).

US Government Accounting Office (USGAO), 1996, Private and public prisons: studies comparing operational costs and/or quality of service. Washington DC.

US Government Accounting Office (USGAO), 1999, Privatization: lessons learned by state and local governments. GAO/GGD-97-48, Washington DC. Report to the Chairman, House Republican Task Force on Privatization.

US Government Accounting Office (USGAO), 2003, Federal-aid highways: cost and oversight of major highway and bridge projects – issues and options. GAO-03-764T. Washington, DC. Testimony before the Subcommittee on Transportation, Treasury and Independent Agencies, Committee on Appropriations, House of Representatives; Statement for the Record by JayEtta Z. Hecker, Director, Physical Infrastructure Issues.

US Government Accounting Office (USGAO), 2004, Highways and transit: private sector sponsorship of and investment in major projects has been limited. Report to Congressional Requesters, GAO-04-419, Washington, DC.

Vining, A. and Weimer, D., 2001, Criteria for infrastructure investment: normative, positive and prudential perspectives, in: A. Vining and J. Richards (Eds) *Building the Future: Issues in Public Infrastructure in Canada* (Toronto: C. D. Howe Institute), 131–165.

Vining, A. and Weimer, D., 2005, Economic perspectives on public organizations, in: D. Ferrin, L. Lynn and M. Pollitt (Eds) *Oxford Handbook of Public Management* (Oxford and New York: Oxford University Press), pp. 209–233.

Warner, M. and Hebdon, R., 2001, Local government restructuring: privatization and its alternatives. *Journal of Policy Analysis and Management*, **20**(2), 315–336.

Williamson, O., 1975, *Markets and Hierarchies: Analysis and Antitrust Implications* (New York: The Free Press).

Wooldridge, S., Garvin, M., Cheah, Y. and Miller, J., 2002, Valuing flexibility in private toll road development: analysis of the Dulles Greenway. *Journal of Structured and Project Finance*, **7**(4), 25–36.

Wright, A., 2003, Desalination dispute leaves a bitter taste; judge orders Tampa Bay Water and Covanta to name a mediator to work out plant dispute. *Engineering News-Record*, **251**(23), 12.

Comparing Public–Private Partnerships and Traditional Public Procurement: Efficiency vs. Flexibility

THOMAS W. ROSS & JING YAN

ABSTRACT *Public–private partnerships (PPPs) have become an increasingly popular way for governments to procure for their citizens certain public services. Supporters argue that the private sector can provide services more efficiently while critics complain that the long-term contracts involved reduce governments' ability to adapt to changing needs. This paper shows that the optimal choice between a PPP and traditional public procurement depends on a number of factors, including the likelihood that changes will be necessary, the productivity of non-contractible effort exerted by private sector partners, and the bargaining power of government vis-à-vis private parties. It also shows that this choice may depend on whether the government's objective is to maximize "value for money" or to maximize total social surplus.*

Introduction

Continuing a movement that had earlier involved the privatization of many state-owned firms, the deregulation of major industries and the more widespread use of contracting out, in the early 1990s a number of governments began to experiment with another innovation involving expanded use of the private sector in the delivery of public services: public–private partnerships (PPPs).[1] A large and diverse set of definitions of PPPs exist today, but one that conveys the main idea simply defines a PPP (optimistically) as an agreement between the government and one or more private partners (which may include the operators and the financiers) according to which the private partners deliver the service in such a manner that the service delivery objectives of the government are aligned with the profit objectives of the private partners and where the effectiveness of the alignment depends on a sufficient transfer of risk to the private partners.[2] For infrastructure projects (our focus here) this involves allocating the various tasks associated with the provision of the public services – for example, financing, design, construction, operation, maintenance – between public and private sector partners in ways that will provide the desired services at lower cost.[3] Very long-term, and frequently complex, agreements typically govern the relationship between the private and public partners in infrastructure PPPs.

The increased private involvement in the provision of public sector infrastructure and related services has become a global phenomenon. Data from the *Infrastructure Journal* suggests that major PPP projects with a combined value of US$394 billion have been undertaken worldwide since 2005.[4] In both higher and lower income countries, common industries for this kind of private participation included those related to power, transportation, water and telecommunications. Various kinds of social infrastructure such as hospitals, prisons and schools are common as well.

Advocates of the PPP model argue that such arrangements, by giving a larger set of tasks to the private sector under competitive bidding, will unleash the superior power of competitive, for-profit enterprises to minimize costs and to find innovative approaches to addressing social needs. Critics of the PPP model have pointed to a number of potential problems with this model of public sector procurement. One of these – our focus here – is the loss of flexibility that comes with the long-lived contractual obligations governments must respect when changing circumstances may require significant changes in the way the public service is provided.

This suggests a trade-off faced by governments choosing whether to proceed with a project as a PPP or by traditional public procurement: while PPPs might have the potential to generate substantial productive efficiencies, they may limit a government's ability to react to changing demands for the public service. This trade-off is the subject of this paper. Our model allows us to illustrate the trade-off very simply and to explore various factors which will influence that trade-off. We can show that the optimal choice of procurement mode will depend on the exact nature of the government's objective function. In this regard, we study two commonly proffered objectives: (i) minimizing the cost to taxpayers (or users) of the service and (ii) maximizing total social surplus. We also demonstrate that the relative advantages of the PPP mode will depend on the nature of the PPP contract considered – that is, whether the private partner is compensated based on simply having completed the project or based on the actual usage of the facilities.

Some Background on PPPs

Essentially, a PPP involves contracting out at a scale and complexity well beyond what is normal for governments.[5] As suggested, the alleged benefits of PPPs derive from their potential to apply the forces of competition and higher-powered incentives to generate higher levels of efficiency and innovation. While the experiences of governments with PPP are varied, there is evidence to suggest that the PPP model can be successful in the right circumstances.[6]

To date, a great deal of the work by economists on PPPs has been concerned with the optimality of "bundling" of the various tasks so that one private partner tackles multiple tasks (e.g. building and operating) rather than having each task performed by a single independent private partner.[7] While, to some researchers, it may be the bundling of tasks that defines a PPP, our focus is on the "privatization" aspect of PPPs – that they involve the outsourcing of tasks that might otherwise have been performed by public sector agencies and their employees.[8]

Critics of PPPs point out that any efficiencies coming from the increased role of the private sector come at some cost. For example, many have argued that upon entering into long-term partnership arrangements governed necessarily by complicated, detailed and still incomplete contracts, governments lose control of key aspects of service delivery that they may wish to adjust in the future. To make changes requires negotiation, and not only will the renegotiation process involve a new set of transaction/bargaining costs, it will also involve bargaining without competition on the selling side. In this sense, we say PPP agreements lack flexibility. The flexibility question strikes us as particularly important in dynamic industries such as healthcare, where the kind of hospital services appropriate today may not closely resemble the services we will be demanding in 20 or 50 years, given advances in medical knowledge and technologies.[9] On the other hand, flexibility may be less important for other kinds of projects, such as roads and bridges.[10] This paper is about how the government might trade off flexibility for efficiency – a question we believe has not been formally analyzed to this point.

A great deal of experience suggests that flexibility challenges are very real in PPP delivery. Specifically, it would appear that renegotiation is frequent and often costly. A review by Guasch (2004), for the World Bank Institute, of more than 1,000 PPP concessions granted between 1985 and 2000 in Latin America and the Caribbean reported that renegotiation "was extremely common among the concessions in the sample, occurring in 30 percent of them".[11] Another review of changes made in PPP-type projects in the United Kingdom by the National Audit Office (UK) (2008, p. 4) concluded that changes undertaken in UK projects in 2006 involved extra payments to contractors of approximately £180 million. While much of this spending provided additional value to taxpayers and users, the National Audit Office (UK) (2008, p. 5) noted that "several components of the cost of changes were problematic".[12]

While many writers have mentioned the potential costs to the public sector of lost flexibility in lengthy PPP contracts, there has been very little formal modeling to our knowledge.[13] The paper most closely related to the questions addressed here is, in fact, not about public sector procurement. Bajari and Tadelis (2001), hereafter BT, study private sector procurement, emphasizing an example from the construction industry. As here, they emphasize the trade-off between contracts that provide maximum flexibility to incorporate changes and those that provide the strongest incentives for cost minimization. They find advantages to fixed-price contracts in terms of efficiency, but also recognize the greater flexibility in contracts of the cost-plus variety. While there are many parallels between the analysis of BT and that provided here, there are several important points of differentiation. First, our focus on the special problems associated with public sector procurement creates differences. For example, we consider different possible governmental objective functions and how they might lead to different choices of procurement mode. Second, our modeling approach is different in a number of ways. For example, we use a less "reduced form" model that, while less general in some respects, provides for a larger set of specific and intuitive comparative statics results on the importance of key parameters. Third, the source of the inefficiencies that can arise in PPP or fixed-price contracts differs in our two models. Fourth, we model the renegotiation process differently.[14]

Finally, we note that there is clearly a relationship between our model of costly renegotiation and models of transaction costs. Indeed, the costs of renegotiation can be viewed as an important element of the transaction costs associated with using the PPP model, and high levels of transaction costs have previously been flagged as a problem associated with the PPP model by, for example, Vining and Boardman (2008).[15] As flexibility issues can, in principle, be dealt with by developing more costly (because of transaction costs) contracts, this paper can be thought of a special case of the choice between low production costs (from private producers) and low transaction costs (by using the public sector and avoiding costly contracts).

In what follows, the next section lays out the general model, while the following section studies the two special cases, PPP and public provision, that form the core of our analysis. The article then extends the basic model in two directions. The last section concludes.

General Model

We take a fairly general approach to the problem of a government, "G" (as principal), procuring certain public services (e.g. an infrastructure "project") from a firm, "F" (the agent). Special cases of this model will correspond to provision via public–private partnerships (denoted PPPs) and more traditionally by public agencies (PUB).[16] To be clear, our model of traditional public procurement (PUB) is essentially one in which the provision of services is kept in-house by the public sector – that is, we are focusing on the degree to which the PPP model "privatizes" aspects of service delivery rather than on bundling or other potential differences between PPPs and other procurement models.

Basic Setup

The (net present value of the) gross social benefit of the project, which is neither verifiable nor contractible, is given by b_i with $b_i \epsilon \{b_L, b_H\}$ and $b_H > b_L > 0$. The government can contract with F to deliver these services. There are in general many identical firms willing to compete to provide these services.

The firm's cost to deliver the project depends, in part, on the non-contractible level of effort or innovation, e, chosen by the firm, and the productivity of that effort.[17]

$$C = K - \delta e$$

where K is the observable innate cost of the project (including cost of materials, labor, etc.) and $\delta > 0$ captures the marginal productivity of the firm's effort. We assume that δ is the firm's private information, and hence that it is not known by the government, *ex ante*. The monetary value of the disutility costs of this effort for the firm is $\emptyset(e)$. For simplicity, we assume that these costs can be represented by a quadratic disutility function:

$$\emptyset(e) = \frac{e^2}{2}$$

The non-verifiability of effort will generate familiar moral hazard problems.

Firms wishing to secure the contract to deliver this project will bid competitively. The firm winning the project will be paid a lump sum α by the government and then be responsible for project costs. The firm's profits are taxed by the government at the rate $t \in [0, 1]$. We will explore the consequences of different rates of taxation but assume the level is set by forces outside the model. A firm winning the contract to deliver the project will have after-tax profits given by:

$$\pi = (1-t)(\alpha - K + \delta e) - \emptyset(e)$$

The original specification of the project comes from government and the government can be right or wrong about this specification. If the government specifies the project correctly, the social benefits will be b_H. However, there is a chance – with probability μ – that the government will have incorrectly specified the project, or that circumstances will change such that a different design is appropriate. We will refer to this as an unexpected change in the nature or level of demand for the services.[18]

While the change in demand is public information, we assume that because demand could have changed in so many different ways, contracts cannot practically be made contingent on changes in demand. Adapting to the new design will restore the b_H benefits. However, if the project is not changed, the lower social benefit b_L will be realized.

There are many reasons why projects may need to be redesigned or adjusted. In some cases, demand may have been badly estimated or technological changes may alter the way services should be delivered (common in healthcare, for example). While we will model this adjustment, if it is needed, as occurring before any services have been delivered, this is a modeling device meant only to capture the need for change sometime during the long life of the project.

If demand changes, efficiency dictates that the project adapt. Since this change represents a change in the contract between G and F, it must be negotiated. We model the negotiations using the familiar Nash bargaining model: the parties will bargain over the surplus created by efficiently adapting to the demand changes.[19] We assume that there are real economic costs associated with switching to a new project design (this could include the renegotiation costs) and each of the two parties will bear this cost by paying an amount of $s \geq 0$.[20] After the contracts are settled and, if necessary, any design changes negotiated, the firm picks its level of effort, costs are incurred, contracts honored and payoffs received.

Timing

Reviewing the timing of the game, then, we have:

1. Government announces it has a project for which it wishes to receive bids.
2. Firms bid for the project, and it is awarded to the firm offering to provide it at the lowest fixed fee, α_0.
3. Nature may move to change demand – if no change, proceed to 5.
4. If demand changes, α_0 is renegotiated (to α_1) via Nash bargaining and the design is changed, both parties incur switching costs, s.
5. F chooses level of effort, e.[21]
6. Benefits are realized and the government honors its contract.

The objective of the firm in this model is straightforward. It will make decisions to maximize its profits subject to honoring its contracts. The government's objectives are more interesting. In much of the literature on public–private partnerships, it is argued – often just assumed – that a PPP will dominate the public procurement method in a particular case if the PPP form provides "value for money" (VFM) relative to traditional methods of procurement. Value for money in this context is typically taken to mean that services of the quality desired are provided at a lower cost to the ultimate payers – taxpayers or (in the case of tolled services) end users. This will be our starting point here: we will look for conditions under which a PPP can provide services at a lower cost to the government.

Value for money as an objective can be contrasted with the objective of maximizing total social surplus (TSS) that is often applied in cost–benefit analysis. The key differences arise due to transfers that will not matter under a TSS standard but will affect VFM. For example, firm profits will hurt VFM by pushing up the price the government pays for the project, but as simple transfers from taxpayers to firms will not affect TSS. A later section of this paper will consider how the choice between PPP and traditional methods (PUB) can depend on the government's objective function.

Solving the Model

After solving this model for the more general case, we will focus on two specific special cases that will allow us to highlight the differences between public–private partnership and traditional public procurement. Traditional public procurement, PUB, will correspond to the case in which $t = 1$ (so that all profits revert to the government) and all bargaining power remains with the government (as it can order its employees to take actions without the need for renegotiation required with an outside contractor). We will contrast this with something more "private", here by considering as our PPP example the case in which $t = 0$ and the bargaining weights are more equal.

We solve the model backwards, beginning with the firm's choice of effort.

Firm's optimal effort (e^*): Given α, F chooses a level of e to maximize its profit. This gives us the incentive compatibility constraint:
$$\max_e \pi = \max_e (1-t)(\alpha - K + \delta e) - \varnothing(e)$$

subject to $e \geq 0$

The optimal level of effort is then given by:
$$(1-t)\delta = \varnothing'(e^*) = e^* \qquad (1)$$

Clearly, higher rates of taxation discourage effort. At the extreme, when $t = 1$, $e^* = 0$. To be clear, under our assumptions $e^* = (1-t)\delta$ is the profit-maximizing choice of effort for either the original or a revised design, as the costs of delivering to either design are described by the same cost function and the effort decision is made after any required renegotiations.

Renegotiation (if needed): As indicated, with probability μ there is a shift in demand which requires that changes be made to project design to preserve the maximum social benefits (b_H). In such a case, if switching costs are not too large – which is assumed [22] – G and F will renegotiate and sign a new contract with payment α_1 going from G to F. Under Nash bargaining, G's threat point is: $b_L + t(\alpha_0 - K + \delta e^*) - \alpha_0$. If renegotiation fails, G gets only b_L of social benefit from the project but still pays α_0 to F as provided in the initial contract. It also collects taxes on F's profits to reduce its net cost of the project. Correspondingly, F still receives α_0 and its optimal cost-reducing effort remains the same. Thus F's threat point will be given by:

$$(1-t)(\alpha_0 - K + \delta e^*) - \frac{(e^*)^2}{2} = 0$$

We allow for the possibility that the government and the firm have unequal bargaining power, represented by differing bargaining weights in the Nash Product (NP). It may be, for example, that governments will have larger weights given their powers to enact and revise laws and regulations and even to rewrite contacts while shielding themselves from actions for damages. In other cases, however, sophisticated and highly motivated private partners may be able to retain higher quality advisory services to assist in their renegotiations, in the process capturing a larger share of the surplus generated.[23] To explore the implications of unequal bargaining power, suppose G has a bargaining weight λ, and F has the weight $1 - \lambda$, where $0 \leq \lambda \leq 1$.

The Nash Product will then be:

$$\text{NP} = [(b_H + t(\alpha_1 - K + \delta e^* - s) - \alpha_1 - s) - (b_L + t(\alpha_0 - K + \delta e^*) - \alpha_0)]^\lambda$$

$$* \left[\left((1-t)(\alpha_1 - K + \delta e^* - s) - \frac{(e^*)^2}{2}\right) - \left((1-t)(\alpha_0 - K + \delta e^*) - \frac{(e^*)^2}{2}\right) \right]^{1-\lambda}$$

Maximizing this with respect to α_1 yields:

$$\alpha_1 = \frac{1-\lambda}{1-t}(b_H - b_L) + \frac{2\lambda - 1 - t}{1-t}s + \alpha_0 \qquad (2)$$

Initial payment (α_0): Assuming perfectly competitive bidding and no uncertainty about which design is optimal, we would expect potential private partners to bid down to the level of costs (which would be perfectly known to the firm and revealed through bidding), leaving the firm with zero profits. When we introduce uncertainty in the efficient design and the opportunity for renegotiation in the absence of competition, however, the picture is more complicated. Renegotiation under Nash bargaining, if needed, will necessarily involve moving to the new, superior design and to a readjustment upward of the fixed fee (to α_1) to share the gains of the renegotiation with the private partner. If the original contract was going to provide zero profits to the private partner (because it had been competitively bid), the renegotiated contract will necessarily generate positive profits.

Clearly, the potential for this renegotiation – and the new profits it will provide the private partners – could affect the original bidding. In a world in which private, risk-neutral, bidders could commit to honoring their promises to complete projects regardless of the subsequent profitability of those projects – perhaps by posting bonds – these prospective profits in renegotiation would translate into lower prices being bid in the initial round. The result would be that *ex ante* expected profits of bidders would still be zero – and if the design did not need to be changed, the private partner would in fact suffer losses *ex post*. However, it is not clear that such commitment – particularly on large projects – is possible. Private partners will often be able to walk away from projects once the anticipated profits turn negative, or to at least make credible threats to walk away if subsidies are not forthcoming. This behavior is facilitated by the "special purpose vehicle" (SPV) structure that is adopted for many large PPP projects in which the SPV can simply declare bankruptcy and close down without there being any remaining claims on the SPV's joint-venture parents.

Therefore, we invoke a limited liability constraint, familiar in the contracting literature, and assume here that the government will not accept as a winning bid any offer that would not allow the private partner to at least break even without any renegotiations.[24] Governments, in their scrutiny of bids, will need to be persuaded that the contract can be honored without the necessity for any renegotiations. Therefore, if we assume that a private firm has limited liability and no wealth it can commit – that is, it cannot be pushed to negative profits (or it would exit) – F will again bid up to the point where it will break even without renegotiation. The limited liability/wealth approach to the agency problem has been applied by many others as an alternative to introducing risk aversion on the part of one or both players.[25]

We can then write the limited liability constraint as:[26]

$$(1-t)(\alpha_0 - K + \delta e^*) - \frac{(e^*)^2}{2} = 0$$

And the winning bid is given by:[27] $\alpha_0 = K - \delta e^* + \frac{(e^*)^2}{2(1-t)}$

Given that $e^* = (1-t)\delta$, we can see that:

$$\alpha_0^* = K - \frac{\delta^2}{2}(1-t) \tag{3}$$

This result suggests that the winning bid will be lower when tax rates are lower, because of the higher levels of effort that follow lower taxes.

Value for money (VFM): Given the costs of the contract to the government with and without renegotiation, we can easily determine the expected value for money. If there were no change in demand, the value for money would be simply given by the difference between the benefits of the project and the government's costs to procure it (α_0 minus any tax collected on profits):

$$\text{VFM} = b_H + t(\alpha_0^* - K + \delta e^*) - \alpha_0^* = b_H - K + \frac{\delta^2}{2}(1-t^2)$$

If the project does change, the new contract price, α_1^*, will be given by, substituting (3) into (2):

$$\alpha_1^* = \frac{1-\lambda}{1-t}(b_H - b_L) + \frac{2\lambda - 1 - t}{1-t}s + K - \frac{\delta^2}{2}(1-t) \tag{4}$$

And the VFM after renegotiation will then be given by:

$$\text{VFM} = b_H + t(\alpha_1^* - K + \delta e^* - s) - \alpha_1^* - s = \lambda b_H + (1-\lambda)b_L - K + \frac{\delta^2}{2}(1-t^2) - 2\lambda s$$

Combining the VFM results with and without a change in project design, we see that the *ex ante* expected VFM is then:

$$E(VFM) = \mu\left(\lambda b_H + (1-\lambda)b_L - K + \frac{\delta^2}{2}(1-t^2) - 2\lambda s\right) + (1-\mu)\left(b_H - K + \frac{\delta^2}{2}(1-t^2)\right)$$

$$= (1-\mu(1-\lambda))b_H + \mu(1-\lambda)b_L - K + \frac{\delta^2}{2}(1-t^2) - 2\mu\lambda s \quad (5)$$

A set of intuitive results regarding the determinants of VFM of a project follow directly.

Result 1:[28] The value for money of a project will be greater: the lower is the cost of the project (K), the greater is the gross benefit of first- and second-best projects (b_H and b_L), the greater is the cost-reducing effect of effort (δ), the smaller is the probability (μ) the project design will need to change, the smaller is the switching cost (s), and the lower is the tax rate (t). Assuming that the net benefit of renegotiation ($b_H - b_L - 2s$) is always positive – that is, renegotiation is efficient and therefore always occurs when there are changes in demand – VFM is higher when the government is in a stronger bargaining position (i.e. when λ is greater).

Most of these results are easily understood and relate to the simple point that the greater the benefits and/or the lower are the costs of the project, the greater will be its VFM. The least obvious results here are those related to the tax rate, the bargaining weights and the likelihood of the need for renegotiation. By discouraging effort, higher tax rates actually hurt the achievement of VFM, even though the taxes received reduce government net expenditures. By limiting the ability of the private partner to drive up prices in renegotiation, a greater government bargaining weight increases expected VFM. Finally, the more likely it is that the project will need to be modified, the less attractive it becomes *ex ante* from a VFM perspective, even though the final gross benefits and costs of production will be in the same in any case.

Comparing PPPs and Traditional Public Procurement

We turn now to the key results of the paper: considering two special cases of the model above will allow us to compare the relative costs and efficiency of a PPP and more traditional methods of public procurement (PUB).

By taxing back all the profits (t approaching 1) and granting the government full power in renegotiation ($\lambda = 1$) we essentially transform the firm into an arm of the government and create the traditional public procurement scenario, PUB.[29] By contrast, when taxes are lower and bargaining weights more balanced, we have more private interests and control in the project.[30] To fix ideas here, we take the case in which $t = 0$ and $0 \leq \lambda \leq 1$ to represent the PPP model. Recall that for a given level of λ, lower taxes raise VFM, so indeed in a PPP scenario in which the government is ceding some control rights (i.e. $\lambda<1$), the government will maximize VFM by setting the tax rate to zero.[31]

Setting $t = 0$ we can solve for the chosen level of effort, from (1), the original contract price, from (3), and the renegotiated price, from (4):

$$e^{PPP} = \delta; \; \alpha_0^{PPP} = K - \frac{\delta^2}{2},$$

$$\alpha_1^{PPP} = (1-\lambda)(b_H - b_L) + K - \frac{\delta^2}{2} + (2\lambda - 1)s$$

This will provide an expected VFM in the PPP case given by:

$$E(\text{VFM}^{PPP}) = (1 - \mu(1-\lambda))b_H + \mu(1-\lambda)b_L - K + \frac{\delta^2}{2} - 2\mu\lambda s \tag{6}$$

Then, by setting $t = 1$ and $\lambda = 1$, we can construct the PUB alternative. This will yield:

$$e^{PUB} = 0; \; \alpha_0^{PUB} = K; \; \alpha_1^{PUB} = K + s$$

As a result of the lack of profit incentives for F, no effort or innovation will be forthcoming. The fact that it holds all the bargaining power, however, does mean that G will have to pay no more than the costs actually incurred by F. The expected VFM under PUB will be given by:

$$E(\text{VFM}^{PUB}) = \mu(b_H - K - 2s) + (1-\mu)(b_H - K) = b_H - K - 2\mu s \tag{7}$$

Our second, and key, set of results highlights the intuitive trade-off between efficiency and flexibility in the choice of procurement mode.

Result 2: Under the objective of maximizing VFM, a PPP procurement will dominate public procurement (PUB) when:

$$E(\text{VFM}^{PPP}) - E(\text{VFM}^{PUB}) = \frac{\delta^2}{2} - \mu(1-\lambda)(b_H - b_L) + 2(1-\lambda)\mu s > 0 \tag{8}$$

Therefore, procurement using a PPP is more likely to dominate procurement under PUB: the greater is the cost-reducing effect of effort (δ), the smaller is the probability the project design will need to change (μ); the greater is the switching cost (s), and the smaller is the difference between the social values of the best project and the other project ($b_H - b_L$). Assuming that the net benefit of renegotiation ($b_H - b_L - 2s$) is always positive, then the VFM of a PPP is relatively higher when government is in a stronger bargaining position (λ).

The basic trade-off between the efficiency of private providers and the flexibility of public providers comes through very clearly here. When flexibility does not matter because demand is extremely unlikely to change ($\mu = 0$), $E(\text{VFM}^{PPP}) > E(\text{VFM}^{PUB})$, implying that PPP procurement must dominate PUB because of its efficiency benefits. On the other hand, when the need to provide extra incentive for efficiency is less important, perhaps because there is little potential for innovation in the project ($\delta = 0$), procurement via PUB will dominate – that is, $E(\text{VFM}^{PPP}) < E(\text{VFM}^{PUB})$.

Other intuitive results follow from (8) quite simply. When the difference between the "right" project and the "wrong" one ($b_H - b_L$) is large, it is more important for G to renegotiate – improving the terms that F can extract and reducing the VFM benefits of the PPP. Greater bargaining power on the part of the government expands the range of parameter values under which PPP procurement is preferred by the VFM standard as greater bargaining power on the part of the government limits the ability of the private partner to raise the government's costs in renegotiation. Finally, higher levels of switching costs (s), other things being equal, tend to favor the PPP mode. Under PUB, the public provider bears the full switching costs of both partners. However, under the PPP structure – and given Nash bargaining in renegotiation – the private partners will end up sharing the loss of surplus associated with higher switching costs. Less than 100 per cent of this cost is then passed on to the public sector.

We can illustrate the efficiency–flexibility trade-off with a simple graph based on values of δ (capturing the importance of effort for efficiency) and μ (capturing the need for flexibility) that lead the PPP and PUB procurement modes to deliver identical levels of VFM – i.e. that set condition (8) equal to zero. These levels will be given by $\delta = (2\mu(1-\lambda)(b_H - b_L - 2s))^{\frac{1}{2}}$, which is illustrated in Figure 1, where the area under the curve (shaded) is the range within which PUB dominates PPP while the area above represents values such that the PPP mode dominates. Other aspects of *Result 2* can be illustrated with this graph. For instance, increases in $b_H - b_L$ or decreases in s rotate the curve upward (around the origin), which expands the area in which PUB dominates.

The interpretation of *Result 2* is therefore quite straightforward. Under a PPP contract, F has incentives to exert cost-reducing effort because it captures the gains of its efforts. Those incentives are absent under PUB. The disadvantages of the PPP, however, derive from the incompleteness of the contract. For the government, this involves new costs – the extra surplus that must be transferred to the private partner under Nash bargaining, which lowers the government's VFM.

Therefore, PPPs will be more attractive when there is little chance for a need to redesign the project – road or bridge projects may come to mind as examples. On the other hand, when it is more likely that the kind of services needed in the future could be very different from those anticipated *ex ante* – as might be the case for sophisticated healthcare projects, for example – the flexibility of public procurement contracts may make them superior.

Figure 1. The efficiency–flexibility trade-off

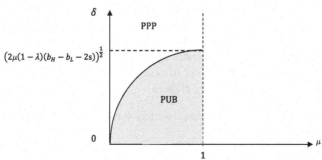

Extensions

A Total Social Surplus (TSS) Objective[32]

In the baseline case, the government pursues a value-for-money objective, a measure widely used in the PPP literature and by PPP practitioners. However, this is not the most commonly assumed objective for governments in normative policy work by economists. More typically, government objectives would be modeled as the maximization of some measure of social welfare or total social surplus. This is a different measure than value for money to be sure – principally differing as a result of transfers from one party to another. It has been argued – for example, by public sector labor unions – that PPPs facilitate the substitution of poorly paid private sector labor for more highly paid (and unionized) public sector labor. To the extent that this happens, these transfers do improve value for money, but do not represent increases in total social surplus. Profits earned by private providers, on the other hand, would harm value for money but not necessarily affect total social surplus.

To study this alternative objective, however, we need to add a deadweight cost of government financing (from tax revenues), $\gamma > 0$, which represents the additional cost to the economy when a government extracts \$1 to pay for the project. This is because without some shadow price of public funds that incorporates the cost of raising revenue, there will not be a unique solution to the question of what price the government will pay for the services provided.

To facilitate comparison with VFM analysis, we continue to focus on the two special cases: (i) PUB with $\lambda = 1$, $t = 1$, and (ii) PPP with $0 \leq \lambda \leq 1$, $t = 0$. By applying similar analysis as in the VFM case above but adding in this cost of government financing, we get:

$$E(\text{TSS}^{\text{PUB}}) = b_H - (1+\gamma)K - 2(1+\gamma)\mu s$$

$$E(\text{TSS}^{\text{PPP}}) = b_H + (1-\lambda)b_L - (1+\gamma)(K - \frac{\delta^2}{2}) - 2(1+\gamma)\lambda\mu s$$

Comparison of $E(\text{TSS}^{\text{PUB}})$ and $E(\text{TSS}^{\text{PPP}})$ leads to a set of results similar to those in Result 2. A new result relates to the added parameter, the marginal deadweight loss of government funding (γ). It is straightforward to show that increases in γ favour the PPP alternative. This is because increases in the deadweight loss of government funding will favour the procurement mode that involves the lowest cost to government. The PPP mode lowers the cost of production because of the higher levels of effort, and it also shares the switching costs with the private partner whose financing does not create deadweight loss.

Would a government pursuing a VFM objective adopt the PPP mode when the PUB approach would yield greater total surplus under the TSS objective? Comparing the TSS and VFM results provides our third set of results, which demonstrate that the different objectives can indeed lead to different choices.

Result 3: When the public and private partners have different bargaining weights the following cases become possible:

(i) When the government has the greater bargaining weight (i.e. $\lambda > \frac{1}{2}$) it is possible for a PPP to maximize VFM while PUB maximizes TSS;

(ii) When the government has the lesser bargaining weight (i.e. $\lambda < \tfrac{1}{2}$) it is possible for a PPP to maximize TSS while PUB maximizes VFM.
(iii) When the government and firm have equal bargaining weight (i.e. $\lambda = \tfrac{1}{2}$), comparisons under VFM are the same as those under TSS. They are also the same if the deadweight cost of government financing (γ), the probability of change (μ) and/or the switching costs (s) are zero.

Some intuition for this result comes from considering the case in which the government has a limited amount of bargaining power (λ is close to 0). In such cases, the government will pay a high price for any changes it makes, pushing down the VFM, but not necessarily damaging TSS much since most of the high renegotiated prices are simply transfers.

Toll Revenue PPPs

In the PPP model we have used to this point, the private partner is paid a fixed sum to deliver the project. This could have been in the form of a lump sum or a stream of "availability payments" (i.e. payments dependent only on the facility operating but not on the actual demand for that facility or the extent of its usage). In many PPP arrangements, however, private parties are paid according to the use of the services. Road projects funded by tolls are a common example in which users rather than the government pay the private partners. In other cases private partners are paid according to demand or use of the facilities, but are paid by the government.[33]

In cases in which the private partner is paid based on the project's success in terms of meeting demand, we can imagine that this player will be much more willing – even eager – to amend the project if demand changes make design changes optimal. Similarly, users (or the government if it pays) are not as disadvantaged by a failure to adapt to change since they will not have to pay as much. Put another way, the players' threat points are different in such a situation.

In exploring a toll-based PPP alternative, we will continue to assume that $t = 0$ in the PPP mode with tolls. Suppose that, under the PPP contract, the fraction of the benefit that F gets (via usage fees) is τ_0. The government's VFM objective here then will be to secure the best project by surrendering the smallest fraction of the benefits to the private partner.

Given τ_0, F chooses an optimal level of effort to maximize its profit. Once again F's incentive compatibility constraint is:

$$\text{Max } \pi = \text{Max } \tau_0 b_H - (K - \delta e) - \frac{e^2}{2}$$

and the optimal effort level is again $e^{PPP} = \delta$.[34]

Potential private partners will bid according to what level of τ_0 they are willing to accept, with the contract going to the lowest bidder. We maintain the assumption that the winning firm, F, will have bid to the point where it will break even (its limited liability constraint) without renegotiation. This implies:

$$\pi = \tau_0 b_H - (K - \delta e^{PPP}) - \frac{(e^{PPP})^2}{2} = \tau_0 b_H - K + \frac{\delta^2}{2} = 0$$

$$\text{so } \tau_0^* = \frac{1}{b_H}\left(K - \frac{\delta^2}{2}\right)$$

If changes in demand materialize, G and F renegotiate and sign a new contract. G's threat point is $(1 - \tau_0^*)b_L$. If we think of $\tau_0^* b_L$ as G's payment to F, then G actually "pays" less now as $\tau_0^* b_L < \tau_0^* b_H$. In this sense, we say that G has a stronger bargaining position than it would in an availability case. If the firm does not agree to change the contract, its payoff is $\tau_0^* b_L - K + \frac{\delta^2}{2}$, which is negative, as $b_L < b_H$. Consistent with our earlier assumption, we assume that F can walk away. So in this case F's threat point still generates zero profits (in this case through exit). Assume that the target of G is to maximize VFM. The Nash Product is then:

$$NP = [(1 - \tau_1)b_H - s - (1 - \tau_0^*)b_L]^\lambda [\tau_1 b_H - K + \frac{\delta^2}{2} - s - 0]^{1-\lambda}$$

The new toll rate, τ_1^*, will then be given by:

$$\tau_1^* = \frac{1}{b_H}\left((1-\lambda)(b_H - b_L) + (\lambda b_H + (1-\lambda)b_L)\frac{1}{b_H}\left(K - \frac{\delta^2}{2}\right) - (1 - 2\lambda)s\right)$$

Therefore, the expected VFM of the toll contract is:

$$\begin{aligned} E(\text{VFM}_{\text{toll}}^{\text{PPP}}) &= \mu((1 - \tau_1^*)b_H - s) + (1 - \mu)(1 - \tau_0^*)b_H \\ &= ((1 - \mu(1 - \lambda))b_H + \mu(1 - \lambda)b_L)(1 - \tau_0^*) - 2\lambda\mu s \\ &= ((1 - \mu(1 - \lambda))b_H + \mu(1 - \lambda)b_L)\left(1 - \frac{1}{b_0}\left(K - \frac{\delta^2}{2}\right)\right) - 2\lambda\mu s \end{aligned}$$

We can now ask whether a toll contract or an availability contract generates greater VFM for the government. Recall that expected VFM of the availability contract, for clarity here now labelled $E(\text{VFM}_{\text{avail}}^{\text{PPP}})$, is given by (6).

This leads to our fourth set of results.

Result 4: When the objective of the government is to maximize VFM, the toll contract dominates the availability contract. (Proof provided in the online Appendix.)

Thus, the toll contract dominates the availability contract in terms of VFM. Additionally, we see that the advantage of the toll contract over the availability contract is greater: the more likely it is that the project will need to change (higher μ), the greater the cost of the project (bigger K), the smaller the cost-reducing effect of effort (δ) and the greater the percentage difference between the "right" and "wrong" project (larger $(b_H - b_L)/b_H$). This is because under the toll contract, the government essentially pays less if renegotiation fails and hence the government is in a stronger bargaining position. Finally, as λ gets larger, renegotiation is less costly to G, with the result that the VFM advantages of the toll contract are greater when G has less bargaining power (i.e. when λ is small).

It follows trivially, then, that when tolling is to be used to pay for the project, the PPP model will dominate traditional public provision under an even broader set of conditions than would an availability payments-based PPP.[35]

Conclusions and Directions for Future Research

Public–private partnerships are being used to deliver public services in many sectors, such as transportation, water, healthcare, education and prisons. In this paper, we have examined an important trade-off associated with the choice between PPP and more traditional public procurement methods (PUB). While the PPP model provides the private contractor with greater incentives for cost-reducing effort and innovation, it locks the government into a long-term contract that may be costly to renegotiate if changing circumstances make a project redesign optimal. We show that the PPP model will be superior when possible efficiencies are large, the probability there will be a need to change the project is small, the gains through project redesign are small and when the government's bargaining power in renegotiation is greater. This result holds whether government's objective is to maximize value for money (VFM) or total social surplus (TSS), though the different objectives can imply different choices between the PPP and PUB approaches. Our analysis has also demonstrated that PPP contracts based on usage-sensitive payments (e.g. tolls) can generate higher VFM for the government.

To our knowledge, this paper is the first to offer a formal model that focuses on this trade-off, though the idea that efficiency comes at the price of flexibility is very intuitive and appears in other contexts (e.g. in the choice of flexible vs inflexible production technologies). Our results may shed some light on why PPPs have become popular in some sectors such as roads and water – where it could be argued that the need for large changes to designs is likely to be relatively smaller – while they remain less common (and more controversial) in areas that might seem more dynamic, such as healthcare and information technology.

A key issue for further work relates to some of the strategies that public and private sector partners employ to deal with the deficiencies of the PPP and PUB models presented above. For example, in PPP projects the parties may anticipate the need to renegotiate in the future and may then put into place mechanisms (e.g. third-party arbitration) to limit the ability of the private partner to take advantage of its strong position to extract much higher payments. A particularly promising innovation directed at reducing the costs of adapting to changing economic (particularly, but not exclusively, demand-related) conditions is the "Least-Present-Value-of-Revenue (LPVR) auctions" of Engel et al. (2001). Under this mechanism, which has been applied in South American projects, private parties bid on the lowest net present value of revenues they will accept to undertake the project. The winning bidder then holds the contract, collecting tolls or other payments, until this net present value threshold is reached. It is easy to see how this mechanism can help avoid costly renegotiation due to demand shocks, for example. If demand is greater than expected, which might otherwise have created great public pressure to prevent a private windfall, the concession period is automatically shortened without any further negotiations necessary. Similarly, if demand is lower than anticipated, rather than threatening to shut down to avoid losses on an existing contract, the private partner will simply see its concession extended to allow it to recover its sunk investments over a longer period.

PUB modes can also be improved by creating incentives for innovation and effort on the part of public sector providers. Indeed, a great deal of effort has been put into making governments more efficient providers of services generally – for example, by giving managers more authority for the way their units operate but also making them more accountable for the quantity and quality of the services provided.

Finally, though it would require a model different from ours here, it would be worthwhile to explore some of the potential benefits of the relative inflexibility of PPP contracts. The fact that these arrangements are more difficult to change may actually yield benefits of at least two types: (i) they compel governments to make decisions based on efficient life-cycle cost analyses rather than building assets today and worrying about operations and maintenance costs later; and (ii) they may provide a commitment vehicle which assures that critical maintenance is not deferred – a very common problem with public infrastructure assets.[36]

Acknowledgments

The authors gratefully acknowledge helpful discussions on this topic with Jean-Etienne de Bettignies, Larry Blain, Anthony Boardman, Nicholas Hann, Elisabetta Iossa, Michael Riordan, Alan Russell and Ralph Winter; comments received at conference and seminar presentations at Zhejiang University, the University of British Columbia, the Copenhagen Business School and from anonymous reviewers; the capable research assistance of Jennifer Ng; and the financial support of the Phelps Centre for the Study of Government and Business, in the Sauder School of Business at the University of British Columbia.

Supplemental Data

The Appendix for this article can be accessed at http://dx.doi.org/10.1080/13876988.2015.1029333

Notes

1. An early version of PPPs was the Private Finance Initiative (PFI) pioneered in the UK from the early 1990s.
2. Organization for Economic Cooperation and Development (OECD) (2008). For an interesting discussion of the wide range of PPP models and some of the history behind public–private cooperation in delivering public services, see Hodge and Greve (2013) and the references cited therein.
3. The private sector partner is typically a consortium of firms acting through a special purpose vehicle to deliver the assets and associated services. One major way PPPs differ from one another is according to which of the tasks are assumed by the private partner. For example, in the common "DBFOM" form the private partner "designs, builds, finances, operates and maintains" the assets but in other cases the private partner will assume a smaller set of tasks.
4. Infrastructure Journal Project Database, http://www1.ijonline.com (accessed July 25, 2011).
5. See, e.g., De Bettignies and Ross (2004) for a discussion of what distinguishes modern PPPs from classical contracting out.
6. There has not been enough work done to properly evaluate the success of PPP projects *ex post*, in part because these are generally very long-lived – and on-going – agreements, and a full accounting cannot really be done until the agreements have expired. The UK was an early adopter of the model and work by the National Audit Office there suggests some success with the private finance initiative (PFI) version of the PPP model – there are many NAO reports at http://www.nao.org.uk/. Australia has also been a leader in the

use of the PPP model, and there is evidence of success there as well, see e.g. Infrastructure Partnerships Australia (2007).
7. For example, see Benz et al. (2002), Hart (2003), Hart et al. (1997), Bennett and Iossa (2006) and Iossa and Martimort (2015). For a discussion of other aspects of PPPs studied by economists, see De Bettignies and Ross (2011).
8. Not surprisingly, it is this aspect of PPPs that led to them being strongly opposed by public sector unions. For example, see "The case against PFI" from the website of the largest public service union in the UK (UNISON): http://www.unison.org.uk/pfi/caseagainst.asp.
9. In the UK, PPP (or PFI) is not recommended for the provision of information technology services, in part because of the high probabilities and costs of changes (see Yescombe 2007, p. 27). From HM Treasury (2006, p. 32): "the PFI procurement structure is unlikely to deliver value for money ... where authorities require a significant degree of short-term flexibility due to fast-changing service requirements".
10. Making the point that the surrendering of decision-making authority to the private sector in PPPs makes it more difficult for the public sector to adapt to changing demands for public services, see e.g. Organization for Economic Cooperation and Development (OECD) (2008, pp. 65–69), Yescombe (2007, section 2.12) and PricewaterhouseCoopers (2005, Chapter 2).
11. Excluding concessions in the telecommunications sector "because practically all telecommunication projects were privatized rather than concessioned, raises the incidence of renegotiation to 41.5%" (Guasch 2004, p. 12). Guasch studied various aspects of these renegotiations, including which party initiated the renegotiation, the form of bidding that resulted in the concession award, the incidence of renegotiation in different sectors, and the average time before contracts are renegotiated. In their study of 61 PPP road concession contracts in Chile, Colombia and Peru between 1993 and 2010, Biltran et al. (2013) find that 50 of the contracts had been renegotiated at least once – and in total there were 540 renegotiations on these contracts. In 80 per cent of the cases the renegotiations were triggered by the government with higher costs then imposed on the public sector.
12. From page 8 of the NAO report: "Under PFI, almost any requested change, even as small as a new electrical socket, has to be processed through the SPV as it manages the asset during the contractual period and bears the risk of failing to meet service obligations. Often lacking the option of going to a different supplier, even for major changes, there is a risk that the public sector will have reduced leverage in negotiation and that the SPV or FM provider may not be incentivised to keep down the cost of changes or to process them quickly." This report goes on to list the kinds of changes that come up frequently in long-term PPP contracts.
13. Two papers consider flexibility issues quite different from those studied here. Iossa and Martimort (2015) consider the advantages of negotiating sequentially (i.e. with more flexibility) with a builder and operator versus bundling the two tasks. Athias and Saussier (2010) look at the optimal degree of pricing flexibility within PPP contracts.
14. We will highlight the differences between this paper and the analysis of BT at various points below.
15. See also Vining et al. (2005). Going back further, there are clear parallels as well with the "administered contracts" work of Goldberg (1976), who recognized that large value, long-term contracts will almost certainly be incomplete, opening them up to renegotiation for any of a variety of reasons. In some cases this may need to be addressed through some form of regulatory mechanism.
16. In BT's private sector procurement model, they consider fixed price contracts which have properties similar to our PPP contract, and cost-plus contracts which have incentive properties similar to our PUB arrangements.
17. It is possible that effort is observable. Here we only assume that effort is not contractible, i.e. that its value cannot be demonstrated for a court or any contract enforcement mechanism.
18. In fact, the most interesting cases involve changes in the nature of demand – i.e. the kinds of services to be provided. A bridge redesigned to accommodate more bicycles and fewer cars might be an example. Uncertainty about simply the level of demand for a project can often be dealt with in carefully drafted contracts.
19. In contrast, BT use a "take-it-or-leave-it" renegotiation model.
20. If this is solely a renegotiation cost, it may seem likely that s would be smaller (or even zero) when the changes can simply be ordered by the government under a traditional public procurement process. In such a case it is not difficult to show that higher renegotiation costs (that do not apply under PUB) will make PUB a relatively more attractive option.

21. It is not difficult to show that, because effort affects only costs and not benefits in our model, an alternative timing in which effort decisions are made before changes and renegotiations would produce identical results to those derived here.
22. This requires that the total benefits of making the change ($b_H - b_L$) exceed the costs of making the change ($2s$).
23. A common concern raised about PPPs, particularly when the public partner is an under-resourced government department of a developing country, is that the private partners will have more legal and technical "firepower" at the table than will the government.
24. This is not to deny that there can be a problem of firms adopting strategies in which they win the contract with an apparently attractive bid, only to threaten later that the deal must be renegotiated or they will not continue. However, sophisticated governments will be alert to this possibility, and will want to scrutinize bids carefully to assure themselves that they are feasible. Also, in a world in which most of these private sector PPP players wish to continue to win future bids with the same or other governments, such gaming could be damaging to their reputations as trustworthy partners.
25. The classic reference is Sappington (1983). See also the text by Laffont and Martimort (2002). It can be shown, as well, that the key trade-off between efficiency and flexibility remains even if firms are permitted to bid down to zero *ex ante* expected profits (and can commit to their bids) as long as there are costs associated with renegotiation.
26. If the limited liability constraint is satisfied it is very easy to see that a participation or individual rationality constraint (requiring firms to earn non-negative profits in expectation *ex ante*) will never be binding. For this reason we do not include participation constraints here.
27. As suggested, this does require that the winning bidder can credibly convince the government that its bid will allow it to break even in the absence of any renegotiations.
28. All proofs are contained in the online-only Appendix.
29. If we allow t to exactly equal 1 we lose uniqueness to our solutions – since the government taxes back every dollar of profit, it does not care what price it pays. Therefore, when we speak of $t = 1$ here, we more precisely mean $t = 1 - \varepsilon$, where ε can be an arbitrarily small but positive quantity.
30. An alternative modeling technique could simply involve assuming that under PUB, the government does not need to renegotiate changes and can just order them. This approach, taken in an earlier version of this paper, produces essentially identical results.
31. To be clear, we do not see λ as a choice variable except to the extent that a government can choose to procure using traditional public methods, thereby effectively setting λ to one. Any form of private provision will involve, for the purposes of our model, a bargaining weight that is exogenous to the government.
32. Details on some of the steps not fully reported in this subsection are contained in the online Appendix.
33. Shadow tolls (where use is measured but the tolls are paid by the government) on road and bridge projects would be an example.
34. The optimal effort is the same here in part because effort does not affect demand in this model. It would be interesting to explore the implications of having effort influence demand as well as costs.
35. This is also shown in the online Appendix.
36. We are grateful to an anonymous referee and editor for stressing these important points to us. This referee also suggested a number of interesting supply-side issues worth exploring in future work, including the role of infrastructure pricing (e.g. tolling) on the supply response in PPP arrangements and how PPP arrangements affect the speed of that supply response.

References

Athias, L. and Saussier, S., Contractual Flexibility or Rigidity for Public Private Partnerships? Theory and Evidence from Infrastructure Concession Contracts, Discussion Paper, EPPP DP No. 2010-3, IAE Pantheon, Sorbonne, 2010.

Bajari, P. and Tadelis, S., 2001, Incentives versus transaction costs: A theory of procurement contracts. *The RAND Journal of Economics*, **32**, pp. 387–407. doi:10.2307/2696361

Bennett, J. and Iossa, E., 2006, Building and managing facilities for public services. *Journal of Public Economics*, **90**(10–11), pp. 2143–2160. doi:10.1016/j.jpubeco.2006.04.001

Biltran, E., Nieto-Parra, S., and Robledo, J. S., 2013, Opening the black box of contract renegotiations: An analysis of road concesssions in Chile, Colombia and Peru, OECD Development Centre, Working Paper No. 317, April 26. doi:10.1787/5k46n3wwxxq3-en

De Bettignies, J.-E. and Ross, T. W., 2004, The economics of public-private partnerships. *Canadian Public Policy / Analyse de Politiques*, **30**, pp. 135–154. doi:10.2307/3552389

De Bettignies, J.-E. and Ross, T. W., 2011, The economics of public-private partnerships: Some theoretical contributions, in: G. Hodge, C. Greve, A. Boardman (Eds) *International Handbook of Public-Private Partnerships* (Northampton, MA: Edward Elgar Publishing), pp. 132–158.

Engel, M. R. A., Fischer, R. D., and Galetovic, A., 2001, Least-present-value-of-revenue auctions and highway franchising. *Journal of Political Economy*, **109**, pp. 993–1020. doi:10.1086/322832

Goldberg, V., 1976, Regulation and administered contracts. *The Bell Journal of Economics*, **7**, pp. 426–448. doi:10.2307/3003265

Guasch, J. L., 2004, *Granting and Renegotiating Infrastructure Concessions: Doing it Right* (Washington, DC: World Bank Institute).

Hart, O., 2003, Incomplete contracts and public ownership: Remarks, and an application to public-private partnerships. *The Economic Journal*, **113**, pp. C69-C76. doi:10.1111/1468-0297.00119

Hart, O., Schleifer, A., and Vishny, R., 1997, The proper scope of government: Theory and applications to prisons. *Quarterly Journal of Economics*, **112**(4), pp. 1127–1161. doi:10.1162/003355300555448

Hodge, G. and Greve, C., 2013. Public-private partnership in developing and governing mega-projects, chapter 9. in: H. Priemus, B. Van Wee (Eds) *International Handbook on Mega-Projects* (Northampton, MA: Edward Elgar Publishing).

Hodge, G., Greve, C., and Boardman, A. (Eds), 2011, *International Handbook of Public-Private Partnerships* (Northampton, MA: Edward Elgar Publishing).

Infrastructure Partnerships Australia, 2007, *Performance of PPPs and Traditional Procurement in Australia*. Available at www.infrastructure.org.au/content/PPP.aspx (accessed 23 March 2015).

Iossa, E. and Martimort, D., 2015, The simple microeconomics of public–private partnerships. *Journal of Public Economic Theory*, **17**, pp. 4–48. doi:10.1111/jpet.12114

Laffont, J.-J. and Martimort, D., 2002, *The Theory of Incentives: The Principal-Agent Model* (Princeton, NJ: Princeton University Press).

National Audit Office (UK), 2008, *Making Changes in Operational PFI Projects*, Report by the Comptroller and Auditor General, 17 January.

Organization for Economic Cooperation and Development (OECD), 2008, *Public-Private Partnerships: In Pursuit of Risk Sharing and Value for Money* (Paris: OECD).

PricewaterhouseCoopers, 2005, *Delivering the PPP Promise: A Review of PPP Issues and Activity* PricewaterhouseCoopers, November.

Sappington, D., 1983, Limited liability contracts between principal and agent. *Journal of Economic Theory*, **29**, pp. 1–21. doi:10.1016/0022-0531(83)90120-5

Treasury, H. M., 2006, *PFI: Strengthening Long-Term Partnerships* (London: HM Treasury).

Vining, A. and Boardman, A., 2008, Public-private partnerships in Canada: Theory and evidence. *Canadian Public Administration*, **51**, pp. 9–44. doi:10.1111/j.1754-7121.2008.00003.x

Vining, A., Boardman, A., and Poschmann, F., 2005, Public-private partnerships in the US and Canada: 'There are no free lunches'. *Journal of Comparative Policy Analysis*, **7**, pp. 199–220. doi:10.1080/13876980500209363

Yescombe, E. R., 2007, *Public-Private Partnerships: Principles of Policy and Finance* (Boston, MA: Butterworth-Heinemann, Elsevier).

The Determinants of Privatization: a Comparative Analysis of Developing Countries

MICHAEL BREEN & DAVID DOYLE

ABSTRACT *Privatization has altered the traditional relationship between the state and the productive sector. However, only a handful of empirical studies concerned with the determinants of privatization exist, and explanations have tended to diverge. Drawing on the new World Bank database on privatization transactions, we estimate the main determinants of privatization across 77 developing world economies, between the years 1988 and 2008. Our findings indicate that the initial decision to privatize is driven primarily by exogenous factors while the extent and scale of privatization is shaped by a range of domestic political and economic conditions.*

The last four decades have witnessed the revision of the traditional relationship between the state and the productive sector. Triggered by the problems associated with state-led industrialization, many developing economies, from the 1970s onwards, began to adopt structural reforms that significantly reduced the presence of the state in the national economy. Privatization, the sale of state-owned assets, was centripetal to this process, and it has repeatedly proven to be a catalyst for fractious distributional and political battles (Przeworski 1991). The scale of state divestiture has been notable. Between 1988 and 1999, the average revenue generated by privatization was US$349 million per annum, per country, across 77 developing world economies. Between the years 2000 and 2008, privatization proceeds averaged US$399 million per annum, across 41 developing world countries. The decision of embattled administrations to sell, or re-nationalize, state-owned assets continues to generate heated debates. Given the political and economic importance of this issue, particularly in light of the current global economic downturn, it is essential that we understand what shapes the adoption and extent of privatization.

There is a large literature on privatization. In particular, the potential efficiency gain from privatization has received considerable attention from economists (see for example, Dewenter and Malatesta 2001). There are now a growing number of empirical studies that explore the determinants of privatization across countries and across time (see Boix 1997; Brune and Garrett 2000; Biglaiser and Danis 2002; Bortolotti, Fantini and Siniscalco 2003; Brune, Garrett and Kogut 2004; Meseguer 2004; Henisz, Zellner and Guillén 2005; Schneider, Fink and Tenbücken 2005; Murillo and Martínez-Gallardo 2007; Zohlnhöfer, Obinger and Wolf 2008; Doyle 2010; Bjørnskov and Potrafke 2011). The majority of these studies, however, focus exclusively on the advanced industrialized nations and many of them have been hampered by methodological limitations coupled with the lack of reliable, comparable and temporal data on privatization. Consequently, quantitative studies have produced divergent explanations for cross-national variation in levels of state divestiture.

We build on this empirical literature, and contend that this divergence is partly rooted in the manner in which these studies operationalize privatization. Privatization is generally modeled as a single homogenous transaction and in addition, the measurement of state divestiture has tended to vary widely across this literature. In contrast, we argue that privatization is best modeled as a two-stage process.[1] There is the first stage, involving the initial decision to either adopt to reject privatization as a reform measure, followed by a second stage, concerning what to sell and how much. What is more, the incentives that shape the initial decision to privatize will not necessarily have a similar effect on the scale of state divestiture.

We utilize the comprehensive global dataset on privatization from the World Bank as a reliable cross-national and temporal measure of state divestiture. We model privatization as a two-stage process, involving an initial decision over whether or not to privatize, and a subsequent decision over the size of asset sales. Utilizing a probit model, together with a time-series cross-sectional model, we estimate the effect of endogenous and exogenous political and economic pressures on privatization across 77 developing world economies between the years 1988 and 1999, and 41 developing economies between the years 2000 and 2008. We find that the initial decision to privatize is largely shaped by exogenous variables, perhaps no surprise given the international context, while the scale of state divestiture is primarily a product of political battles and domestic economic realities.

The paper is structured as follows. The first section discusses trends in privatization around the world; the second section considers the empirical work on state divestiture, while the third section presents both the data and the method. The fourth section discusses the results of these estimations, while the final section presents the conclusion and discusses the wider implications of this research.

The Revenue from Privatization

The World Bank has recorded the proceeds from individual privatization transactions, including full and partial divestitures, concessions, management contracts and leases since 1988.[2] From these individual transactions, we have constructed a time-series cross-sectional dataset covering 77 emerging economies between 1988 and 1999, and 41 developing economies from 2000 to 2008, with one observation on the proceeds of privatization, as a percentage of GDP, for each country, for each year in question.[3] It is important to note that privatization is a multifaceted concept. In this paper, we are interested in material transactions that generate revenue for the government from privatization, or private sector participation in an existing state-owned asset. Privatization can also encompass formal transactions, involving an amendment to the legal status of a company, but not share sales, and functional transactions, involving contracts such as public–private partnerships (see Zohlnhöfer, Obinger and Wolf 2008: 97).[4]

It was necessary to split the analysis into two periods, 1988–1999 and 2000–2008, as the data are qualitatively different in each period. In the earlier period, the World Bank has included voucher transactions and smaller transactions under $1 million. We split the sample because we were unable to identify all of the voucher transactions. Even if it were possible to do so, excluding them would sacrifice important variation in the data, as they were a central component of several waves of privatization in the 1990s. The comprehensive coverage of this data allows us to illustrate, in Figure 1, trends in privatization over the last two decades.

As can be seen from this graph, the revenue generated by national asset sales has increased, with some troughs, over time. In 1988, the first year of our sample, revenue from privatization amounted to a little over US$1.2 billion and involved only 14 countries, but by 1997, over 60 countries were engaged in privatization, generating some US$33 billion in total revenue for that year. In the early years of our second sample, while the total number of countries selling state assets fell, the revenues from privatization remained rather large. For example, for every year bar 2002, revenues from privatization exceeded US$10 billion. In fact, the largest single volume of revenue recorded in a given year, US$38 billion, was as recently as 2008.

Figure 1. Privatization across the globe.

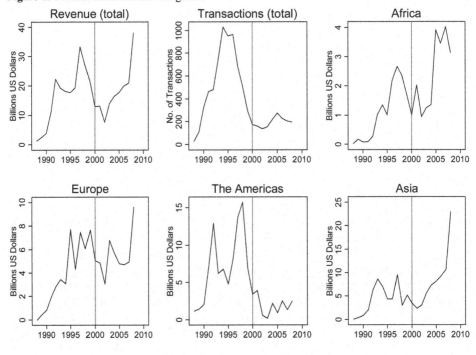

There is also significant regional variation in privatization. The first region to generate significant revenue from privatization was Latin America, with a sharp initial peak in the early 1990s, driven by the rapid and aggressive privatization programs of Argentina and Mexico. Following a brief hiatus, revenues peaked again in the late 1990s, this time driven by the privatization program of Brazil and to a lesser extent Colombia. Interestingly, revenues fell sharply after 1999, and remained quite low throughout our second sample period.[5]

In Africa, the initial adoption of privatization was far slower, and revenues far smaller. However, with the onset of privatization programs in Nigeria, Ghana, Egypt and Morocco from 1993, the proceeds from state divestiture across the region increased steadily, a trend maintained through the 1990s, as these countries were joined by South Africa, Tanzania and Senegal. From the early 2000s, we can observe a rather rapid increase in revenues, driven by large waves of privatization in Nigeria, the North African states of Egypt, Tunisia and Algeria, and in Ghana and Kenya to a lesser extent.

In the transition economies of Central and Eastern Europe, revenue increased until the mid-1990s, primarily driven by the small, but consistent privatization programs of Hungary and the Czech Republic, before revenues rose sharply, as Russia, Poland and Slovakia joined their neighbors in the sale of state assets. The temporary hiatus of privatization in Russia in the early 2000s caused a drop in revenue, but revenue soon climbed sharply again, as Bulgaria, Serbia and Romania began privatizing and Russia once again raised very large sums through asset sales.[6]

During the 1990s, privatization proceeds in Asia, like that of Latin America, displayed two distinct peaks. The first peak in the early 1990s can be explained by the onset of privatization programs in China, Indonesia, India and Malaysia, while the second peak, in the late 1990s, shortly after the East Asian financial crisis, can be partly explained by increased sales in China and Thailand. More significantly however, after 2000, we can observe a precipitous rise in the income raised by asset sales. The revenue during this period accounts for nearly half of all global proceeds from privatization. The burgeoning privatization programs of developing world giants, such as India and Pakistan and, most notably, China, drive this trend, and this near vertical increase in revenue across Asia shows no signs of abating.

Clearly then, privatization continues to remain an important source of revenue for national governments, but what explains these trends?

Why do States Privatize?

There is an extensive literature on privatization, the majority of which is primarily concerned with the economic utility of state divestiture (see Dewenter and Malatesta 2001).[7] There is a small but growing body of quantitative work that focuses on the causal factors driving privatization across countries and across time. This literature offers a number of explanations for state divestiture, the most prominent of which include partisanship (Boix 1997; Doyle 2010), the pressures of liberalization (Schneider, Fink and Tenbücken 2005), diffusion (Meseguer 2004), domestic economic conditions (Brune and Garrett 2000; Zohlnhöfer, Obinger and Wolf 2008) and the design of legal institutions (Bortolotti, Fantini and Siniscalco 2003).

We contribute to this empirical literature, and suggest that the different results produced by these quantitative studies can be partly explained by the operationalization of state divestiture as a single transaction in econometric estimations, involving a unitary decision process. We contend that privatization is best modeled as a two-stage process, involving an initial decision over whether to adopt privatization or not, and if adopted as a reform measure, a subsequent decision over the scale and extent of what to divest (see also Meseguer 2004; Doyle 2010). What is more, at each stage of this process endogenous and exogenous variables will generate different incentives. Therefore, the factors that influence the initial decision to adopt privatization may not necessarily have a similar effect regarding the scale and extent of asset sales.

Let us consider the initial decision to select privatization as a reform measure. A national government, when contemplating such a move, will be confronted with a combination of incentives and constraints. Firstly, trade liberalization may place downward pressure on governments to adopt privatization. The logic is straightforward. Large state sectors cushion market mechanisms, distorting prices and wages. To sustain state sectors, governments must raise taxes or increase borrowing, thereby forcing interest rates to rise and depressing economic activity, deleteriously affecting output and employment (Garrett 1998: 792). Therefore, the efficiency concerns of increasing trade competition generate incentives to privatize. This pressure is exacerbated by the liberalization of capital controls. The imperative to attract mobile capital in today's globalized markets may convince national governments to implement privatization as a means to woo capital with investment opportunities, often at significantly reduced prices and in near-monopolistic market conditions. In fact, the empirical evidence of Schneider, Fink and Tenbücken (2005: 718–719) indicates that the main driver of infrastructure privatization in OECD states was the liberalization of capital markets.

Secondly, the initial decision to select privatization may be shaped by processes of international diffusion and emulation (Brune and Garrett 2004; Meseguer 2004). Governments may choose privatization as a consequence of bounded learning, or cognitive heuristics, whereby governments place exaggerated stock in a measure's superiority and simply adopt it wholesale, regardless of its relevance for their own context (Weyland 2005). Emulation can also be social, whereby states herd simply on the behavior of their peers (Meseguer 2004: 312). For developing countries, given the international context at the beginning of the 1990s, this incentive may have been exacerbated, due to the debt crisis in Latin America, and the process of market liberalization in Eastern Europe after the collapse of the Soviet Union. Emulative processes played a large role in the initiation of privatizations across Latin America (see Meseguer 2004; Doyle 2010), while peer dynamics had a significant effect on the adoption of pension privatization across Eastern Europe and Central Asia (see Brooks 2005).

The international financial institutions can also directly influence a government's decision to adopt privatization (Henisz, Zellner and Guillén 2005). The debt crises of the 1980s witnessed the IMF launch the first structural adjustment programs (SAPs), which included measures to liberalize, privatize and deregulate economic activity in borrowing countries (Henisz, Zellner and Guillén 2005: 872). Structural conditionality, of which privatization became an important component, went on to become a common feature of both IMF and World Bank programs. For both institutions, the principal rationale for privatization is the assumption that the private sector will be able to increase the efficiency of production (Biersteker 1990: 485). Conditionality, then, is a tool to pressure borrowing countries to privatize inefficient state enterprises and empirical evidence has demonstrated the positive correlation between the likelihood of adopting majority privatization and exposure to multilateral lenders in 71 countries between 1977 and 1999 (Henisz, Zellner and Guillén 2005).

The initial decision to privatize will also be shaped by domestic politics. As privatization is often associated with fractious political processes, the potential political leverage privatization may afford, will affect the strategic behavior of governments and, consequently, the adoption of reform (Murillo and Martínez-Gallardo 2007). Domestic opposition, in the form of public sector unions and domestic export industries, will have to be overcome. For example, in India the militancy of public sector unions undermined repeated attempts to initiate privatization (Gupta 2008). In Argentina, during the administration of Raúl Alfonsín, some of the fiercest opposition to privatization came from the rent-seeking *patria contratistas* or *capitanes de la industria* (Captains of Industry) who benefited enormously from lucrative contracts with the public sector (Corrales 1998). In Kenya, Uganda and Tanzania, domestic industry was initially very hesitant to support privatization for fear their businesses would be unable to compete with privatized firms (Bennell 1997: 1797).

Initiating an unpopular measure such as privatization will also be partly a product of the institutional limitations that national governments face. For example, in Uruguay in 1992, the attempted privatization of the state telecom company, ANTEL, was prevented by public plebiscite, while in 2003, legislation to end the monopoly of the state oil company, ANCAP, was again overturned by referendum (see Bensión 2006). The probability of policy adoption is dependent upon the number of veto players in a political system, and the similarity of their preferences (Tsebelis 2002).

Finally, fiscal distress may prompt a government to adopt privatization. When heavily indebted, privatization can provide states with the means to pay creditors, to finance current expenditure and to reduce deficits (Bortolotti, Fantini and Siniscalco 2003: 309). The resultant reduced levels of external debt will send signals of credibility to the market, improving a country's credit rating and generating lower interest payments (Biglaiser and Brown 2003: 80). Likewise, stagnant or negative growth rates, or repeated bouts of price instability may induce states to consider divestiture (Biglaiser and Danis 2002: 91), as not only will such transactions generate much-needed revenue for the state, but also because privatization is often seen as a growth-stimulating measure (Zohlnhöfer, Obinger and Wolf 2008: 103).

Once the decision has been made to begin privatizing, governments are then faced with a second decision regarding how much to actually divest. What is more, what drives the initial decision to adopt privatization may not necessarily drive the scale of privatization revenue in a similar manner. Let us begin with the perspective of the seller. Once a national government has decided to privatize, electoral incentives will prompt governments to act strategically, and therefore the core clientele of the governing party will shape the decision of how much to sell. Left-leaning governments will be associated with lower volumes of privatization, given the negative dislocating effect that privatization will have on their core support (Boix 1997; Zohlnhöfer, Obinger and Wolf 2008; Doyle 2010, 2012; Bjørnskov and Potrafke 2011), while right-leaning parties will be associated with higher volumes of privatization (Boix 1997; Bortolotti, Fantini and Siniscalco 2003).

Secondly, the international financial institutions may also serve the very useful role of political alibi for much-needed reform (Vreeland 2003). In this scenario, governments, irrespective of their partisan hue, will attempt to ameliorate domestic political tensions by scapegoating the IMF for privatization. Governments enter into IMF agreements even when they do not need foreign exchange, in order to utilize IMF conditions to push through large privatizations (Vreeland 2003; Doyle 2012). Therefore, privatization revenues may prove to be larger when a government is part of an IMF agreement or indebted to a multilateral institution.

Thirdly, once the decision to privatize has been made, and privatizations have begun, the attitude of domestic interest groups may change considerably. For example, in Argentina, Menem, in order to overcome the opposition of rent-seeking indigenous industry, began to involve them in privatizations on highly preferential terms, and within a short time period domestic industry became vocal advocates of privatization (Treisman 2003: 97). In Mexico in the early 1990s, to pave the way for the sale of the state telecom company, TELMEX, the Carlos Salinas administration co-opted the union leaders with resources generated by this privatization (see Clifton 2000). In Ghana, the acquiescence of workers in state-owned firms was secured with guarantees of very large benefits (Bennell 1997: 1797), while in India, the ability to purchase shares in newly privatized firms increased support amongst the middle classes for the sale of state assets (Gupta 2008: 185–186).[8]

Finally, just as institutional limitations can hamper attempts to introduce privatization, the interests of veto players may impede the size and extent of national governments' privatization plans. Take the government of Victor Ciorbea in Romania in 1996 as an example. A range of veto players hostile to state divestiture, combined with weak institutional and bureaucratic structures, repeatedly hampered his administration's attempts to expand the scale of privatization (Pop-Eleches 2009: 230–233).

The revenue generated by privatization will also be shaped by the incentives that potential investors face. The scale of revenue may not just be driven by the coercive effects of conditionality per se, but also by the important signaling and credibility effects of conditionality. Participation in an IFI-sponsored program should send a positive signal to market actors who may be interested in undertaking the sort of long-term investment that privatization implies (Brune, Garrett and Kogut 2004). Evidence indicates that investors are willing to pay a premium for divested assets in countries that are subject to IMF conditionality, as they view conditionality as a signal of credible policy reform (Brune, Garrett and Kogut 2004).

The scale of privatization also rests on the ability of national governments to demonstrate a credible commitment to reform, thus ameliorating the fear of expropriation for potential investors. Without sufficient credibility, a government will simply find it too difficult to attract interest from buyers. Biglaiser and Danis (2002) for example, demonstrate that democratic regimes, due to the transparency of their legal institutions, durable constraints on political actors and respect for property rights, are associated with a greater propensity to privatize than their authoritarian counterparts. A well-functioning stock market, and a legal system that facilitates privatization transactions and protects the purchasers of divested state assets from future opportunistic behavior, are also necessary for the success of any privatization program (Bortolotti, Fantini and Siniscalco 2003). In addition, healthy economic fundamentals can signal stability and sound economic governance, creating a far more hospitable investment climate (Brune and Garrett 2000; Biglaiser and Danis 2002).

The next section will discuss our empirical strategy for modeling privatization as the two-stage process described above.

Data and Method

We utilize the World Bank (2011) database on privatization as a cross-national measure of state divestiture. From this we have generated two unbalanced panel datasets, covering 77 developing economies during the period 1988–1999, and 41 developing economies during 2000–2008. In all of our statistical tests, the number of countries and observations is based on data availability. We model privatization as a two-stage process, and estimate a probit model together with a time-series, cross-sectional model, on both the decision to implement privatization, and the subsequent extent of asset sales.

The Variables

Our dependent variable, *privatization revenue as a percentage of GDP*, is taken from the World Bank's Privatization Database (World Bank 2011).[9] It has been used in previous studies (see Brune, Garrett and Kogut 2004) and allows us to differentiate among countries that have privatized in small quantities versus those that have undertaken large-scale privatization programs. As this variable is highly dispersed, we use its natural log transformation.

We build upon previous studies by considering two further measures: *privatization revenue as a percentage of employment* and *privatization as a percentage of value added*. This is to ensure that our analysis is sensitive to the different ways in which the implementation of privatization can affect the amount of revenue generated. Governments must select from a range of options including: initial public offerings on stock exchanges, cash auctions, auctions where the winner extends a loan to the government, investment tenders, the distribution of vouchers to the population, or the retention of 'golden shares'. Given this range of options, it is very likely that politics is decisive. For example, a left-leaning government might select a method of privatizing that protects workers but generates less revenue for the same asset as a right-leaning government that selected a strategy that generated more revenue at the expense of labor. It makes sense, therefore, to also examine *privatization as a percentage of employment*, and as *a percentage of value added* to account for variations in the way revenue is generated by the state.[10]

Although our dependent variable is a useful proxy for the scope of privatization, we argue privatization is best modeled as a two-stage process, whereby a government must first decide on whether or not to privatize in a given year, before deciding on the scope of asset sales. Therefore, to capture the first stage of the privatization process – that is, whether or not to select privatization as a reform measure – we utilize a simple binary variable, where a year in which a privatization transaction occurred is coded as '1' and all other years are coded as '0'.

In order to explain the cross-national variation in both the adoption and extent of state divestiture, we include a range of explanatory variables. Firstly, we consider one of the main challenges for quantitative studies on privatization: the initial size of the state-owned sector. Both the decision to privatize and the extent of any subsequent privatization should be influenced by the existing stock of state-owned enterprises. However, little cross-national data exists on this issue and previous studies have employed indices of economic freedom as proxies for the size of the state sector. One problem with such indices, however, is that countries with large state-owned sectors may score highly, as the indices also capture the quality of regulation and the business environment. We use *domestic credit to the private sector as a percentage of GDP*, from the World Bank's Development Indicators (2011). Although by no means a perfect proxy, it does allow us to control for the importance of the domestic private sector in an economy. However, this variable also has its issues. It may reflect the health of the banking system, rather than the size of the public sector.

Secondly, we capture exogenous pressures by controlling for *trade* and the level of *capital mobility*. Taken together, these variables capture the extent of a country's economic interdependence with the rest of the world. Trade is simply *imports plus exports as a percentage of GDP*, and is taken from the World Bank's Development Indicators (2011), while we use the Chinn and Ito (2008) index of capital account openness, based on information from the IMF's Annual Report on Exchange Arrangements and Exchange Restrictions, in order to capture the degree of capital mobility.

Previous empirical studies have suggested that a relationship exists between the IMF and increased levels of privatization (Brune, Garrett and Kogut 2004). Therefore, we include *IMF credit as a percentage of GDP* in our specifications (World Bank 2011). This variable represents the reliance of some developing markets on IMF support. In line with previous research, we expect to find a positive and significant association between IMF lending and privatization revenue.

Thirdly, we consider the preferences of political actors, the structural characteristics of political systems, and the institutional make-up of the state. The decision to privatize has long been associated with political parties on the right. As a consequence, although this is a crude proxy, we control for the ideological orientation of the executive (right, center, left) (see Marshall and Jaggers 2002).[11] Second, we include a variable that accounts for the number of veto players that can potentially hamper government action on privatization. This is the *checks* variable from the database of political institutions (Beck et al. 2001). Third, we control for the effect of an election to the legislative or executive branch. Governments should wait until after an election to push through privatization measures in order to reduce the political backlash that might ensue. This is a dummy variable, coded as 1 for any year in which a presidential or legislative election was held (Beck et al. 2001).

We also consider the origin of a country's legal system and employ a dummy variable to control for British legal heritage. La Porta, López-de-Silanes and Shleifer (2008) find that legal heritage is correlated with a broad range of economic outcomes, including the protection of investors, shareholders and creditors from expropriation. For the most part, common law systems tend to provide greater protection for investors, so we expect that countries with a British legal heritage will generate larger volumes of revenue from national asset sales.

Finally, we include several economic variables that capture long- and short-term domestic economic conditions, including *CPI inflation (logged)*, *GDP growth (per cent)*, *GDP per capita (constant USD, 2000, logged)* and *external debt as a percentage of GDP*. We expect for example, that a high level of inflation will prompt the state to divest public assets to combat economic malaise. By contrast, a high level of external debt might result in privatization in order to raise revenue for debt service and reduce the primary deficit. All of these variables are taken from the World Bank's Development Indicators (2011).

The Model

We model privatization in two stages: an initial stage involving decisions over whether or not to adopt privatization, followed by a second stage, involving decisions over how much to sell. One advantage of this approach is that many developing world states have never bothered with privatization. Without taking into consideration the profile of countries that never privatized, a statistical analysis would only capture some of the substantial variation in this outcome. It might even add bias, inflating the importance of the attributes of countries that privatized while ignoring specific attributes of those that did not. In other words, the decision to undertake privatization and the decision over the subsequent scope of privatization are not independent. In order to correctly analyze both decisions and the systematic relationship between each decision, we begin by estimating a probit model on the decision to privatize. We follow Carter and Signorino's advice (2010: 1559) and use cubic polynomial approximation to address the problem of time dependence in the binary data. From the probit model, we generate the inverse mills ratio – Heckman's (1979) correction. We include this as a control variable in the second stage of the statistical analysis, where our dependent variable is *privatization revenue* (as a percentage of GDP, employment and value-added). Doing this allows us to examine systematic differences between the countries that received something from privatization, and those that received nothing at all.

Although the Heckman selection model is appropriate for this task, it performs poorly without an exclusion restriction – a variable that enters the selection equation but does not enter the outcome equation (Sartori 2003: 112). We use *regional emulation* as our exclusion restriction. This variable measures the number of countries in the region that privatized in the previous year. It is a good exclusion restriction because it is unlikely to affect the actual scale of privatization. It would make little sense for a state to emulate the precise scale of its neighbors' efforts, when each faces a very different set of political, economic and social obstacles. Rather, it is more likely that diffusion operates at a more general level, pushing neighboring countries to adopt broadly similar strategies but adapt these strategies to their own unique circumstances. Therefore, the inclusion of this variable in the selection equation is justified on theoretical grounds and is not merely a practical measure to improve model fit.

In the second stage of our analysis, we utilize ordinary least squares (OLS) with panel-corrected standard errors to correct for panel heteroscedasticity and spatial correlation (see Beck and Katz 1995). We do not include a lagged dependent variable in our models, as to do so would bias our estimator. Rather, we follow Achen (2000), who recommends leaving out the lagged dependent variable and correcting for first-order autocorrelation. We also repeat our specifications with fixed effects to account for possible time-invariant, country-specific unobserved factors that affect privatization. Finally, we lag all independent variables by one year to avoid simultaneity. The basic form of this equation is as follows:

$$Revenue_{it} = \alpha_i + b_{1it-1} + b_{2it-1} + \ldots + b_{nit-1} + \mu_{1it}$$

In the equation above, α represents country dummies, b is the parameter estimate for the independent variables, while μ represents the error term. The dependent variable will be observed if the γ of $PRIV_{it}$, that is the decision to privatize or not in a given year, plus the second error term, $u_{2it} > 0$, where:

$$u_1 \sim N(0, \sigma)$$

$$u_2 \sim \begin{matrix} N(0,1) \\ corr(u_1, u_2) = p \end{matrix}$$

Results

Tables 1 and 2 present our findings for 1988–1999 and 2000–2008, respectively. The first column of each table presents estimates from the probit model on the initial decision to privatize. The other columns present estimates using our three dependent variables. For each dependent variable, we specify three models: one with country-specific fixed-effects, another with the Gaussian first-order autoregressive process/ AR(1) correction and another with both. The results are remarkably consistent across our three measures of privatization. For the most part, the coefficients maintain the same direction, level of statistical significance, and magnitude. One minor difference is that an increase in GDP per capita is associated with a slightly higher increase in revenue from privatization as a percentage of employment. This suggests that richer states might place fewer restrictions on sales in order to increase asset values because they are less interested in protecting workers.

Firstly, let us consider the relationship between the first stage, the initial decision to privatize, and the second stage, concerning the scope of state divestiture. Across every single specification of the Time-series cross-sectional (TSCS) models for the 1988–1999 sample, the selection effect from the probit model is statistically significant. Clearly, the decision to select privatization as a reform measure is related to the subsequent scale of asset sales, justifying our contention to model privatization as a two-stage process. However, in the second sample, 2000–2008, the selection effect does not reach levels of statistical significance, suggesting that the

Table 1. Privatization 1988–1999

	Probit estimates	Privatization/GDP				Privatization/Employment			Privatization/Value Added		
	(1)	(2)	(3)	(4)	(5)	(6)	(7)	(8)	(9)	(10)
Private sector/GDP$_{t-1}$	0.02***	−0.03***	−0.01**	−0.03***	−0.03***	−0.01**	−0.03***	−0.01	−0.01	−0.01
	(0.00)	(0.01)	(0.01)	(0.01)	(0.01)	(0.01)	(0.01)	(0.01)	(0.01)	(0.01)
Inflation (log)$_{t-1}$	0.05	−0.11	−0.11	−0.11	−0.11	−0.12*	−0.11	−0.15*	−0.08	−0.15**
	(0.04)	(0.07)	(0.07)	(0.07)	(0.07)	(0.07)	(0.07)	(0.08)	(0.08)	(0.08)
Capital mobility$_{t-1}$	0.10**	−0.11	−0.01	−0.11	−0.11	−0.02	−0.11	−0.09	−0.06	−0.09
	(0.05)	(0.11)	(0.10)	(0.11)	(0.11)	(0.10)	(0.11)	(0.12)	(0.10)	(0.12)
Trade/GDP$_{t-1}$	−0.01***	0.01	0.01***	0.01	0.01	0.01***	0.01	0.01	0.01**	0.01
	(0.00)	(0.01)	(0.00)	(0.01)	(0.01)	(0.00)	(0.01)	(0.01)	(0.00)	(0.01)
External debt/GDP$_{t-1}$	−0.00*	0.02**	0.01***	0.02**	0.02**	0.01***	0.02**	0.01	0.01***	0.01
	(0.00)	(0.01)	(0.00)	(0.01)	(0.01)	(0.00)	(0.01)	(0.01)	(0.00)	(0.01)
GDP per capita (log)$_{t-1}$	0.17**	−0.13	0.20	−0.14	0.65	1.23***	0.65	−1.84	0.17	−1.78
	(0.08)	(0.98)	(0.13)	(0.99)	(0.98)	(0.14)	(0.98)	(1.55)	(0.11)	(1.52)
GDP growth (%)$_{t-1}$	0.02*	0.01	0.02	0.01	0.01	0.02	0.01	0.03	0.03	0.03
	(0.01)	(0.02)	(0.02)	(0.02)	(0.02)	(0.02)	(0.02)	(0.02)	(0.02)	(0.02)
Checks$_{t-1}$	−0.01	−0.04	0.01	−0.04	−0.04	0.00	−0.04	−0.00	0.00	−0.00
	(0.03)	(0.05)	(0.05)	(0.05)	(0.05)	(0.05)	(0.05)	(0.06)	(0.04)	(0.06)
Election$_{t-1}$	−0.02	−0.40**	−0.47**	−0.40**	−0.41**	−0.47**	−0.41**	−0.36**	−0.36**	−0.37**
	(0.12)	(0.17)	(0.19)	(0.17)	(0.17)	(0.19)	(0.17)	(0.18)	(0.18)	(0.18)
Government ideology$_{t-1}$	0.08**	−0.50***	−0.10	−0.50***	−0.49***	−0.12	−0.49***	−0.48**	−0.01	−0.47**
	(0.04)	(0.18)	(0.08)	(0.18)	(0.18)	(0.08)	(0.18)	(0.19)	(0.12)	(0.19)
UK legal system	0.29**	3.18***	−0.29	3.18***	2.66*	−0.30	2.66*	−3.61	−0.52*	1.79
	(0.13)	(1.19)	(0.30)	(1.20)	(1.44)	(0.30)	(1.45)	(2.75)	(0.30)	(1.60)
IMF/GDP$_{t-1}$	0.05***	−0.04	0.04*	−0.04	−0.04	0.04	−0.04	0.01	0.06**	0.02
	(0.01)	(0.05)	(0.03)	(0.05)	(0.05)	(0.03)	(0.05)	(0.07)	(0.03)	(0.07)
Selection effects		−2.06***	−1.30**	−2.06***	−2.07***	−1.29**	−2.07***	−1.58**	−1.19*	−1.60**
		(0.63)	(0.62)	(0.63)	(0.63)	(0.60)	(0.63)	(0.69)	(0.64)	(0.68)
Exclusion restriction	0.07***									
	(0.01)									
Observations	720	378	378	378	377	377	377	309	309	309
R-squared		0.516	0.281	0.516	0.666	0.357	0.665	0.552	0.278	0.555
chi2	150	17293	219	5729	3201	114714	9489	382	217	1792
AR1	N/A	N	N	N	N	Y	Y	N	N	Y
Fixed effects	N/A	Y	N	Y	Y	N	Y	Y	N	Y
No. countries		77	77	77	76	76	76	62	62	62

Standard errors in parentheses. Time controls for probit model not displayed. ***$p < 0.01$, **$p < 0.05$, *$p < 0.1$.

Table 2. Privatization 2000–2008

	Probit estimates	Privatization/GDP				Privatization/Employment				Privatization/Value Added		
	(1)	(2)	(3)	(4)	(5)	(6)	(7)	(8)	(9)	(10)		
Private sector/GDP$_{t-1}$	0.00 (0.00)	0.01 (0.03)	-0.01*** (0.00)	0.02 (0.03)	0.01 (0.03)	-0.01*** (0.00)	0.02 (0.03)	0.01 (0.03)	-0.01*** (0.00)	0.02 (0.03)		
Inflation (log)$_{t-1}$	0.02 (0.06)	-0.48** (0.21)	-0.22* (0.13)	-0.53** (0.21)	-0.49** (0.22)	-0.24** (0.13)	-0.54*** (0.21)	-0.48** (0.21)	-0.23* (0.13)	-0.53** (0.21)		
Capital mobility$_{t-1}$	0.03 (0.05)	-0.38 (0.23)	0.04 (0.05)	-0.38* (0.22)	-0.39* (0.23)	0.03 (0.05)	-0.39* (0.22)	-0.38 (0.23)	0.04 (0.05)	-0.38* (0.22)		
Trade/GDP$_{t-1}$	-0.01*** (0.00)	0.03 (0.02)	0.01*** (0.00)	0.03 (0.02)	0.03 (0.02)	0.02*** (0.00)	0.03 (0.02)	0.03 (0.02)	0.02*** (0.00)	0.03 (0.02)		
External debt/GDP$_{t-1}$	-0.00 (0.00)	-0.00 (0.01)	0.01 (0.01)	-0.01 (0.01)	-0.00 (0.01)	0.01 (0.01)	-0.01 (0.01)	-0.00 (0.01)	0.01 (0.01)	-0.01 (0.01)		
GDP per capita (log)$_{t-1}$	0.31*** (0.08)	5.16*** (1.73)	0.04 (0.19)	5.42*** (1.64)	6.19*** (1.73)	1.05*** (0.19)	6.45*** (1.64)	5.16*** (1.73)	0.05 (0.19)	5.42*** (1.63)		
GDP growth (%)$_{t-1}$	0.04*** (0.02)	-0.14* (0.08)	0.05 (0.03)	-0.16** (0.08)	-0.14* (0.08)	0.03 (0.03)	-0.16** (0.08)	-0.14* (0.08)	0.04 (0.03)	-0.16** (0.08)		
Checks$_{t-1}$	0.06 (0.04)	-0.27*** (0.07)	-0.11* (0.06)	-0.29*** (0.06)	-0.28*** (0.07)	-0.11** (0.07)	-0.30*** (0.06)	-0.27*** (0.07)	-0.11** (0.06)	-0.29*** (0.06)		
Election$_{t-1}$	-0.29** (0.13)	-0.81*** (0.26)	-0.60** (0.29)	-0.87*** (0.27)	-0.82*** (0.26)	-0.60** (0.29)	-0.87*** (0.27)	-0.81*** (0.26)	-0.59** (0.29)	-0.86*** (0.27)		
Government ideology$_{t-1}$	0.08* (0.05)	0.26 (0.21)	-0.25*** (0.09)	0.31* (0.18)	0.26 (0.21)	-0.29*** (0.09)	0.30* (0.18)	0.26 (0.21)	-0.25*** (0.09)	0.30* (0.18)		
UK legal system	0.09 (0.15)	-3.77*** (1.28)	0.13 (0.34)	-8.02** (3.77)	-3.68*** (1.28)	0.25 (0.35)	10.69*** (2.71)	-3.75*** (1.28)	0.12 (0.34)	10.20*** (2.69)		
IMF/GDP$_{t-1}$	0.07*** (0.02)	0.01 (0.08)	-0.05 (0.05)	0.03 (0.08)	0.02 (0.08)	-0.05 (0.05)	0.04 (0.08)	0.01 (0.08)	-0.05 (0.05)	0.03 (0.08)		
Selection effects		-0.66 (0.88)	0.30 (0.82)	-0.74 (0.96)	-0.67 (0.88)	0.25 (0.83)	-0.75 (0.95)	-0.66 (0.88)	0.28 (0.82)	-0.73 (0.96)		
Exclusion restriction	0.08*** (0.02)											
Observations	553	139	139	139	139	139	139	139	139	139		
R-squared		0.639	0.422	0.700	0.713	0.375	0.772	0.641	0.423	0.700		
chi2	70.1	603	284	569	1551	1575	621	922	319	575		
AR1	N/A	N	Y	Y	N	Y	Y	N	Y	Y		
Fixed effects	N/A	Y	N	Y	Y	N	Y	Y	N	Y		
No. countries		41	41	41	41	41	41	41	41	41		

Standard errors in parentheses. Time controls for probit model not displayed. ***$p < 0.01$, **$p < 0.05$, *$p < 0.1$.

importance of deciding whether to adopt privatization or not has waned as this structural reform has become more widespread.

What is more, there are clearly different mechanics at play during the initial decision to adopt privatization, and the subsequent scale of state divestiture. The initial decision to choose privatization as a reform measure is largely a product of exogenous variables, while the scale of subsequent privatizations is primarily driven by economic conditions and domestic political interaction.

As we can see from column one in both tables, *IMF* is positively signed and statistically significant. The larger the volume of IMF loans to country i, the greater the likelihood of country i adopting privatization at time t_{+1}. However, we find little evidence that IMF support is associated with the scale of privatization. There are several potential explanations for this. The IMF might successfully push governments to adopt a privatization strategy, but governments may not properly implement this strategy. Alternatively, IMF programs are possibly failing borrowing countries by not catalyzing the investment necessary for governments to sell state assets.

Several further exogenous factors are also significant determinants of the likelihood of privatization. The exclusion restriction – that is, emulative diffusion – is positively signed and statistically significant in the probit model across both samples. States herd on the behavior of their peers, and choose to adopt privatization because their neighbors have done so.[12] In the first sample, capital mobility is positively signed and statistically significant, indicating that during this period privatization was a means for developing economies to attract investors. The level of trade competition is also statistically significant, but it is negatively signed in both probit models.[13] States that are more integrated in global trade are less likely to embark on privatization, as they must first overcome domestic opposition from those who benefit from a large state presence in the economy.

In contrast, variation in the scale of asset sales, across both samples, is primarily shaped by domestic political and economic concerns. Firstly, *trade* is statistically significant across both samples, although it is not robust to fixed effects. However, the direction of this effect differs from the probit models. After overcoming the initial hurdle, states that are more integrated with global trade derive more revenue than others in similar circumstances. States that are more integrated with global trade may firstly have to confront powerful sectional interests that favor a greater role for the state in the economy. Once this hurdle has been cleared, however, export-oriented interests have probably tipped the domestic political balance away from policy that favors a large role for the state in the economy. This finding confirms the importance of employing a two-stage process to model privatization. Clearly, there are systematic differences among states that privatize public enterprises and those that do not. The substantive effect of trade competition on privatization revenue is notable. A shift from the 10th to the 90th percentile in levels of trade leads to a one standard deviation increase in the logged value of privatization revenue as a percentage of GDP.

The importance of domestic politics can also be observed in the results for *election*, which are negatively signed and statistically significant in every single TSCS model, across both samples. Governments are evidently cognizant of the damaging political after-effects of state divestiture and so, in an election year, will reduce the scale of asset sales. An election year will result in a decrease in privatization revenue of half a standard deviation.

The ideology of the government in power also affects the volume of revenue from privatization. Government ideology is negatively signed in every TSCS model across the first sample, and reaches levels of statistical significance in six of the nine specifications. During this period, left-leaning governments are associated with lower levels of state divestiture. The difference between a government of the left in power and a government of the right in power is over half a standard deviation in the logged value of revenue as a percentage of GDP. In the second sample, although government ideology is negatively signed and statistically significant in three models, it also changes signs across the remaining specifications. These results echo those of Schneider, Fink and Tenbücken (2005), who found that partisan effects on infrastructure privatization disappeared, as privatization became a widely accepted phenomenon.

The inability of the executive to negate potential veto players also has a statistically significant effect on privatization. *Checks* is negatively signed and statistically significant in all nine of the panel estimations across the second sample. When the level of checks on the executive moves from the 10th to the 90th percentile, the volume of revenue generated by privatization will fall by over half a standard deviation. Politics is often a struggle over how to divide the spoils or manage the distributional consequences of government policy. The evidence on privatization clearly points towards domestic distributional conflict over the scale of economic reform, rather than the existence of reform measures per se, although the importance of veto players is only statistically significant from 2000 to 2008. When taken together, however, domestic political variables are key drivers of the scale of privatization across both time periods.

Domestic economic conditions also clearly shape the extent of state divestiture. In the first sample period, *debt* is positively signed in all estimations, and statistically significant in seven of the nine models. When levels of external debt shift from the 10th to the 90th percentile, then the proceeds from privatization will increase by nearly two standard deviations.

In contrast, in the second period *GDP per capita* is positively signed and achieves levels of statistical significance in seven of the nine specifications, while inflation is negatively signed and statistically significant across all nine specifications. The difference between levels of inflation at the 10th and 90th percentile equates to a reduction in privatization revenue of nearly one standard deviation. Much of the privatization literature argues that poor states privatize to address an ailing economy, but our results suggest that, initially, states employed privatization as a means to raise revenue to service the external debt and reduce the primary deficit, but over time, once pressing economic demands have been met, privatization revenues were greater in wealthier, more macro-economically stable states.

Finally, our proxy for the initial size of the state sector, *domestic credit to the private sector*, is negatively signed in every specification for the earlier sample, and statistically significant in six of them. In the later sample, this variable changes signs across the models, and only achieves a level of statistical significance in three of them. Clearly, the initial size of the state sector was an important determining factor in the early phase of state divestiture, but this waned in importance, as privatization became a standard policy instrument.[14]

Robustness

For the sake of robustness, we also estimated a number of alternative specifications. Firstly, we repeated the Panel-corrected standard errors (PCSE) models with the alternative Generalized Least Squares (GLS) estimator.[15] The results remained very similar. We also ran collinearity diagnostics, which indicated that this was not an issue in any of the models. Secondly, we added a number of additional control variables to the base specification, including: a dummy variable to capture the presence of an autonomous region and a dummy variable to capture the presence of multiple levels of subnational government. Our rationale was to account for the effect of federalism on the level of privatization. We also included the XCONST variable from Polity IV (Marshall and Jaggers 2008); a dummy variable to capture the presence of a functioning stock market; and the Rule of Law index from the Worldwide Governance Indicators, for the later sample (2000–2008) (Kaufman, Kraay and Mastruzzi 2009). We also substituted UK legal origin with a dummy variable that records French legal origin. Even with these additional controls, the core results remained unchanged.[16]

Thirdly, we controlled for the effect of regime type. According to Biglaiser and Danis (2002), regime type is an important determinant of privatization. We added the level of democracy (POLITY) to the base specification (Marshall and Jaggers 2008). POLITY was positively signed but statistically insignificant. Otherwise, the results remained the same.

We also included an alternative measure for the initial size of the state-owned sector, taken from the index of economic freedom (Gwartney, Lawson and Norton 2008). In addition, we substituted the variables that measure IMF lending with *World Bank lending and grants as a percentage of GDP*, and *multilateral lending as a percentage of GDP*; replaced capital mobility with *FDI as a percentage of GDP*; and included regional dummies to capture any regional effects. Finally, we repeated our main specifications with *publicly guaranteed debt as a percentage of exports* and *public and publicly guaranteed debt service as a percentage of GNI*. Once again, the results remained unchanged.

Discussion/Conclusion

Few other reform measures have altered the relationship between the state and the productive economy as successive waves of privatization have, and continue to do, across the developing world. State divestiture is now a defining tenet of the modern liberal economy. However, quantitative studies on the determinants of privatization have been limited by data and methodological restrictions. We built on this literature and utilized the comprehensive dataset on privatization from the World Bank as a reliable, cross-national measure of state divestiture over time. We modeled the decision to privatize as a two-stage process, involving an initial decision over whether or not to privatize, and a subsequent decision over how much to sell, and estimated the main determinants of privatization across 77 developing world economies between the years 1988 to 1999, and 41 countries between 2000 to 2008.

Our results generate a number of important insights. Firstly, exogenous and endogenous pressures have different roles to play at different stages of the decision-making process. The initial decision to privatize in developing countries is largely shaped by exogenous incentives. The degree of capital mobility, the desire to emulate privatizing neighbors, and the influence of the IMF, all induced developing economies to adopt privatization as a reform measure. The extent of privatization, however, or what to sell and how much, was shaped by different incentives again. The politics of trade remain important for the volume of revenue generated by state divestiture, but our results also indicate that this stage of the decision-making process is conditioned by domestic variables. It is no surprise that the impetus to adopt a fractious structural reform such as privatization would emanate from outside the political system, while the factors determining the scale of privatization, once the decision to adopt such a reform has been made, would primarily be a function of domestic political and economic concerns.

This has important implications for the existing empirical literature on privatization. If we return to the explanations for privatization, it is clear that they all have some relevance for the story we present here. This suggests that there is no single uniform explanation for privatization, but rather that different incentives for state divestiture exist at different stages of the decision-making process and across different time periods (see also Meseguer 2004; Doyle 2010). Therefore, in order to adequately understand privatization, we must disaggregate this process into its component parts, rather than treating it as a single transaction. This also has potential implications for other reform measures, such as labor and tax reform.

So what does this mean for a broader understanding regarding the determinants of privatization? Our results for trade competition are interesting. States that are more integrated in global trade are less likely to embark on privatization, but when they commit to privatization their efforts are more extensive. After overcoming the initial hurdle, states that are more integrated with global trade derive more revenue than others in similar circumstances. Clearly, states seek to reap the benefits from international economic integration, but this is also conditional.

The IMF has a role in encouraging states to adopt privatization, but there is little evidence that it takes an active part in overruling government decisions regarding what to divest and on what scale. Rather, this is primarily a product of domestic politics: electoral concerns, the strategic interest of political parties and the ability of the governing administration to negate potential veto players. What is more, during the first phase of privatization, these political battles occurred against a backdrop of pressing external debt obligations, whereby developing world economies divested state enterprises in order to raise revenue to pay creditors and reduce their primary deficit. However, during the second phase of privatization, although the political struggles remained prevalent, the economic realities underpinning privatization altered. During this period, increased revenue from state divesture was associated with wealthier, more macro-economically stable states. When pressing macroeconomic concerns have been addressed, and privatization is more widespread, the purchasers of divested state assets began to seek stable political environments and the protection of property rights (see Jensen 2008; Biglaiser and Staats 2009).

Notes

1. Scholars have long analyzed policy as a multi-stage process. In this paper, by a two-stage process, we are explicitly referring to the manner in which privatization is modeled in quantitative analyses.

2. Many previous empirical studies on privatization have been limited by a lack of reliable and comparable data. The new World Bank Privatization Database has taken existing data on privatization between 1988 and 1999, from the old World Bank Privatization Transactions Database, and combined it with newly released data on privatization in the developing world between 2000 and 2008.
3. A full list of all countries included in this analysis can be found in the online appendix at the author's website http://www.dcu.ie/~doyled.
4. The vast majority of the data represents proceeds raised by central governments only, bar a handful of exceptions for state level utilities in a small number of major countries.
5. In this section, we discuss those countries with the largest share of revenue from privatization by region.
6. See Clifton, Comín and Díaz Fuentes (2006) who note that EU liberalization directives largely determined the timing and scale of privatization in the EU states.
7. The World Bank alone accounts for a vast amount of research on this topic.
8. Graduate economic training of civil servants in the US and Europe may also have contributed to the re-evaluation of privatization.
9. Descriptive statistics, plus full descriptions for all variables, can be found in the appendix.
10. Every so often, states have nationalized, expropriated, or confiscated private property. Unfortunately, no adequate data exists on the extent to which states have nationalized or rolled back on privatization so it is not possible to calculate *net privatization*.
11. Taken from the Polity IV dataset; right was coded as 1, center as 2 and left as 3.
12. Although we cannot identify the exact causal mechanism underlying this process.
13. *GDP per capita* is also positively signed and statistically significant across both probit models.
14. *Capital mobility* changed signs across the specifications and only reached levels of statistical significance in a handful of them. Likewise *GDP growth* and the *UK legal system*.
15. The results of these robustness tests can be found in the appendix.
16. The presence of a functioning stock market had a strong and significant effect on the decision to privatize but not on the scale of privatization.

References

Achen, C. H., 2000, Why lagged dependent variables can suppress the explanatory power of other independent variables. Paper presented at the annual meeting of the Political Methodology Section of the American Political Science Association, Los Angeles, July 20–22, 2000.

Beck, N. and Katz, J. N., 1995, What to do (and not to do) with time-series-cross-section data in comparative politics. *American Political Science Review*, **89**(3), pp. 634–647.

Beck, T., Clarke, G., Groff, A., Keefer, P. and Walsh, P., 2001, New tools in comparative political economy: The database of political institutions. *World Bank Economic Review*, **15**(1), pp. 165–176.

Bennell, P., 1997, Privatization in sub-Saharan Africa: Progress and prospects during the 1990s. *World Development*, **25**(11), pp. 1785–1803.

Bensión, A., 2006, Las reformas económicas de Uruguay (1974–2004), *CEPAL: Serie Macroeconomía del Desarrollo*, **50**, pp. 1–81.

Biersteker, T. J., 1990, Reducing the role of the state in the economy: A conceptual exploration of IMF and World Bank prescriptions. *International Studies Quarterly*, **34**, pp. 477–492.

Biglaiser, G. and Brown, D., 2003, The determinants of privatization in Latin America. *Political Research Quarterly*, **56**(1), pp. 77–89.

Biglaiser, G. and Danis, M. A., 2002, Privatization and democracy: The effects of regime type in the developing world. *Comparative Political Studies*, **35**(1), pp. 83–102.

Biglaiser, G. and Staats, J., 2010, Do political institutions affect foreign direct investment? A survey of U.S. corporations in Latin America. *Political Research Quarterly*, **63**(3), pp. 508–522.

Boix, C., 1997, Privatizing the public business sector in the eighties: Economic performance, partisan responses and divided governments. *British Journal of Political Science*, **27**(4), pp. 473–496.

Bjørnskov, C. and Potrafke, N., 2011, Politics and privatization in Central and Eastern Europe: A panel data analysis. *Economics of Transition*, **19**(2), pp. 201–230.

Bortolotti, B., Fantini, M. and Siniscalco, D., 2003, Privatization around the world: Evidence from panel data. *Journal of Public Economics*, **88**(1–2), pp. 305–322.

Brooks, S. M., 2005, Interdependent and domestic foundations of policy change: The diffusion of pension privatization around the world. *International Studies Quarterly*, **49**, 273–294.

Brune, N. and Garrett, G., 2000, The diffusion of privatization in the developing world. Paper presented at the Annual Meeting of the American Political Science Association. Washington DC, 30 August–3 September.

Brune, N., Garrett, G. and Kogut, B., 2004, The International Monetary Fund and the global spread of privatization. *IMF Staff Papers*, **51**(2), pp. 195–219.

Carter, D. B. and Signorino, C. S., 2010, Back to the future: Modeling time dependence in binary data. *Political Analysis*, **18**, pp. 271–292.

Chinn, M. D. and Ito, H., 2008, A new measure of financial openness. *Journal of Comparative Policy Analysis*, **10**(3), 309–322.

Clifton, J., 2000, On the political consequences of privatization: The case of Teléfonos de Mexico. *Bulletin of Latin American Research*, **19**(1), pp. 63–79.

Clifton, J., Comín, F. and Díaz Fuentes, D., 2006, Privatizing public enterprises in the European Union 1960–2002: Ideological, pragmatic, inevitable? *Journal of European Public Policy*, **13**(5), pp. 736–756.

Corrales, J., 1998, Coalitions and Corporate Choices in Argentina, 1976–1994: The Recent Private Sector Support of Privatization. *Studies in Comparative International Development*, **32**(4) (Winter), pp. 24–51.

Dewenter, K. and Malatesta, P. H., 2001, State-owned and privately owned firms: An empirical analysis of profitability, leverage and labor intensity. *American Economic Review*, **91**(1), pp. 320–334.

Doyle, D., 2010, Politics and privatization: Exogenous pressures, domestic incentives and state divestiture in Latin America. *Journal of Public Policy*, **30**(3), pp. 291–320.

Doyle, D., 2012, Pressures to privatize? The IMF, globalization, and partisanship in Latin America. *Political Research Quarterly*, **65**(3), pp. 572–585.

Garrett, G., 1998, Global markets and national politics: Collision course or virtuous circle? *International Organization*, **52**, pp. 787–824.

Gupta, N., 2008, Privatization in South Asia, in: G. Roland (Ed.) *Privatization, successes and failures* (New York: Colombia University Press), pp. 170–199.

Gwartney, J., Lawson, R. and Norton, S., 2008, Economic freedom of the world: 2008 annual report. *The Fraser Institute*. Available at http://www.freetheworld.com (accessed 30 November 2010).

Heckman, J. J., 1979, Sample selection bias as a specification error. *Econometrica*, **47**(1), pp. 153–161.

Henisz, W. J., Zelner, B. A. and Guillén, M. F., 2005, The worldwide diffusion of market-orientated infrastructure reform 1977–1999. *American Sociological Review*, **70**(6), pp. 871–897.

Jensen, N. M., 2008, Political regimes and political risk: Democratic institutions and expropriation risk for multinational investors. *Journal of Politics*, **70**(4), pp. 1040–1052.

Kaufmann, D., Kraay, A. and Mastruzzi, M., 2009, Governance matters viii: Aggregate and individual governance indicators 1996–2008. *Policy Research Working Paper Series*, The World Bank (4978).

Marshall, M. G. and Jaggers, K., 2002, *Polity IV project: Political regime characteristics and transitions, 1800–2002*. University of Maryland, Center for International Development and Conflict Management: College Park, MD.

Meseguer, C., 2004, What role for learning? The diffusion of privatization in OECD countries and Latin American countries. *Journal of Public Policy*, **24**(3), pp. 299–325.

Murillo, M. V. and Martínez-Gallardo, C., 2007, Political competition and policy adoption: Market reforms in Latin American public utilities. *American Journal of Political Science*, **51**(1), pp. 120–139.

La Porta, R., López-de-Silanes, F. and Shleifer, A., 2008, The economic consequences of legal origins. *Journal of Economic Literature*, **46**(2), pp. 285–332.

Pop-Eleches, G., 2009, *From economic crisis to reform: IMF programs in Latin America and Eastern Europe* (Princeton, NJ: Princeton University Press).

Przeworski, A., 1991, *Democracy and the market: Political and economic reforms in Eastern Europe and Latin America* (Cambridge: Cambridge University Press).

Sartori, A. E., 2003, An estimator for some binary-outcome selection models without exclusion restrictions. *Political Analysis*, **11**(2), pp. 111–138.

Schneider, V., Fink, S. and Tenbücken, M., 2005, Buying out the state: A comparative perspective on the privatization of infrastructures. *Comparative Political Studies*, **38**(6), pp. 704–727.

Treisman, D., 2003. Cardoso, Menem, and Machiavelli: Political tactics and privatization in Latin America. *Studies in Comparative International Development*, **38**(3), pp. 93–109.

Tsebelis, G., 2002, *Veto players: How political institutions work* (Princeton, NJ: Princeton University Press).
Vreeland, J., 2003, *The IMF and economic development* (Cambridge: Cambridge University Press).
Weyland, K., 2005, Theories of policy diffusion: Lessons from Latin American pension reform. *World Politics*, **57**(1), pp. 262–295.
World Bank, 2011, *World Bank privatization database*. Available at http://rru.worldbank.org/Privatization/ (accessed 30 November 2010).
Zohlnhöfer, R., Obinger, H. and Wolf, F., 2008, Partisan politics, globalization, and the determinants of privatization proceeds in advanced democracies (1990–2000). *Governance*, **21**(1), pp. 95–121.

Introduction to the Special Issue

Comparative Implementation Research: Directions and Dualities

PETER HUPE & HARALD SÆTREN

ABSTRACT *The study of policy implementation developed steadily and considerably in the 1970s and 1980s through two generations of research. Since then progress towards a more rigorous scientific "third generation research paradigm", assumed to be crucial for further theoretical development, has been much slower and more uneven. Comparative studies figure prominently in this respect. On one hand they are strongly encouraged but on the other they are difficult to conduct according to best practice advice in the textbooks. Comparative implementation research is the theme of this special issue. In this Introduction the articles included are presented, focusing on how they deal with some of the issues posed by the norms of a rigorous "third generation" approach. Reasons for the state of affairs in implementation research are discussed. Some inherent dualities and tensions in contemporary comparative implementation research are identified as particular challenges.*

Policy Implementation: Towards Comparative Research

Political science has been surprisingly slow in discovering the translation of public policies into practice as a relevant and interesting research topic. According to the conventional story it happened with the book by Jeffrey Pressman and Aaron Wildavsky terming this policy stage *Implementation*. The book was published in 1973 in the wake of emerging and rapidly expanding American welfare state programs, such as President Johnson's *Great Society* and *War on Poverty*. The "great expectations" behind these programmatic visions and declarations roused the curiosity of policy researchers with respect to their subsequent fate (Hill and Hupe 2014).

Pressman and Wildavsky's case study would come to have an enormous influence on the policy scholarship that would follow. The result was a new and fast expanding field of study – *implementation research*. It would develop into a new "growth industry" (Hill and Hupe 2014). This sudden and rapidly surging interest among political scientists in the new research topic did not last long. It peaked and even declined somewhat already in the early to mid-1980s, before it subsequently stabilized at this level in quantitative terms (Sætren 2005). As a conference and workshop theme the decline of interest in implementation research during the same period was much more dramatic. Why? There are probably several reasons. An important one may have been that ambitions and expectations of many policy scholars drawn to this new research field were simply too high and unrealistic. The idea that implementation studies would enable sound prescriptive policy recommendations to political authorities and practitioners in public administration would lead to disillusionment, disappointment and eventually exit from the scholarly field (O'Toole 2004).

Development of implementation research in more *qualitative* terms has been summed up by some scholars in terms of a *research generations* metaphor (Goggin 1986; Lester et al. 1987; Goggin et al. 1990; Hill and Hupe 2014). *First generation* denotes studies during the 1970s and earlier, with a qualitative, explorative, a-theoretical character and a focus on a single case. *Second generation* investigations emerged during the early 1980s in the wake of the first analytical-theoretical frameworks (e.g. Van Meter and Van Horn 1975; Sabatier and Mazmanian 1979; Mazmanian and Sabatier 1981, 1983). These involved an even stronger empirical focus on implementation phenomena now commonly anchored in theoretical constructs and a substantial increase in the propensity to formulate and test hypotheses with some statistical techniques on quantitative data. The empirical and normative *failure* bias stemming from Pressman and Wildavsky's seminal single case study would later be characterized as "misery research" (Rothstein 1998, p. 62). It was corrected to some extent by a doubling of comparative studies that asked why a policy would "succeed" in one context and "fail" in another (Sætren 2014).

Notwithstanding these substantial changes in implementation research epitomized in second generation studies, important challenges remained. Conceptual disagreement on what implementation as a study object was all about, that had plagued this new research field from the beginning, remained unsolved (O'Toole 1986). The mushrooming of a different analytical-theoretical framework during the late 1970s and early 1980s led to a proliferation of potentially relevant explanatory factors most vividly illustrated by one scholar who conceived of no fewer than 44 potentially important factors related to his own single policy case (Chase 1979). Another consequence was that implementation researchers tended to coalesce into two different schools of thoughts with opposing ideas on both empirical-methodological and normative issues related to the study of policy implementation – the *top-down* and *bottom-up* perspectives, respectively. Although perhaps necessary and useful at an early stage, this analytical-theoretical divide soon became counterproductive in terms of promoting theory building.

This triggered a plea for a *third generation* of implementation research premised on the notion that more *rigorous* scientific research designs were the crucial step towards further theoretical progress (Goggin 1986; Lester et al. 1987; Goggin et al. 1990).

Key elements in the third generation research paradigm are the following:

- Variables (dependent and independent) must be *clearly defined.*
- *Hypotheses* derived from theoretical constructs should guide empirical analysis.
- More use of *multivariate statistical analysis* on quantitative data to supplement qualitative data.

- More *careful* consideration and *selection* of cases for *comparison* both across different units of analysis (countries as well as their political-administrative subunits) and different policy sectors.
- More *longitudinal* research designs (i.e. studies with a time frame of at least five years and preferably longer).

Assessments of the policy implementation literature by O'Toole (2000, 2004), Winter (2012a) and Sætren (2014) reveal that progress towards the third generation research paradigm has been mixed and much less impressive than the transition from first to second generation studies. They also agree that observed progress relates more to research methods than conceptual issues and theory development. With regard to conceptual matters so crucial to theory development Winter (2012a, 2012b) notes some recent slowly emerging consensus towards how to define and delimit the concept of implementation. The same can perhaps be said with respect to how to define the slippery normative concepts like implementation "success" and "failure" (Matland 1995; Winter 2012a, 2012b).

As to theory development, the unproductive schism between top-down and bottom-up perspectives in implementation research seems to have dissipated, as recognition that both are valid and needed gained more ground since the 1990s. Instead, a synthesized integrative analytical framework (Winter 1990, 2012b) has emerged as a standard reference in handbooks, textbooks and journal articles. Although not a theory, Winter's framework is a heuristic device and roadmap that guides investigators in the direction of a handful of *clusters of variables* that has repeatedly shown up in the research literature to be important in explaining policy implementation.

Sætren (2014) has noted changes in type of theories referenced and subjected to some sort of empirical testing before and after the launching of the third generation research design by Goggin et al. (1990). Much less reference to and empirical testing of early top-down theoretical frameworks, and substantially more of the same with respect to institutional and network/governance constructs, were most prominent in this respect. These are hardly surprising changes, as they are very much aligned with similar developments in political and social sciences more generally. Another equally clear but more surprising trend after 1990 is that implementation scholars are much less prone to make connections to the research literature on the earlier policy stages, like agenda setting and policy formation.

Leading implementation scholars disagree on how to interpret the increasing plethora of theoretical frameworks, perspectives, models etc. after 1990. O'Toole (2000, p. 268) clearly deplores this situation by saying "what has not happened is a careful winnowing of the mass of potential explanatory variables towards parsimonious explanation". Winter (2012a, p. 265) on the other hand argues that what O'Toole hopes for is premature; theoretical diversity is a strength, rather than a weakness. Thus he suggests that implementation research can be improved by "(1) accepting theoretical diversity rather than looking for one common theoretical framework, and (2) developing and testing partial theories and hypotheses rather than trying to reach for utopia in constructing a general implementation theory".

Taking Winter's point of view with respect to theory development, there has been a steadily positive trend consistent with his advice in terms of theoretically informed hypotheses formulation and statistical testing during the last three decades of implementation research (Sætren 2014, Table 2). As to the other equally important research designs embedded in the third generation paradigm – *comparative* studies regardless of type and *longitudinal* studies – the same author reported very little change since 1980. One could of course always say that the fact that 50 per cent of all studies of policy implementation have a comparative dimension to them is positive in itself. This argument, however, misses the important point that the scientific value of comparison hinges much more on quality and rigor of methodology than on quantity. Selection of units of analysis for comparison is just one crucial issue in this respect that impacts on the internal and external validity of such research. The same is the case with the longitudinal studies so essential to causal analysis; they constituted around 17 per cent of all studies both in the 1980s and the 2000s. In this context it is relevant to note that the longitudinal research design was somewhat more common during the first generation studies before 1980 (22 per cent) than later (Sætren 2014, pp. 9–10; see Table 4).

Cross-national comparison is especially important with regard to furthering theory development for implementation research. It is the closest to the most rigorous research methodology of all – laboratory experiments in the "hard" sciences – that comparative social sciences at their best can only aspire to approximate. Equally important, it provides a wider range of cultural and political contexts and variables crucial to general theory building. One illustrative example is the consideration of institutional and constitutional factors at the macro level that are common and constant features within a given country but that can vary substantially across national boundaries. In this respect it is worthwhile noting that even Winter's otherwise laudable integrative analytical framework has no reference to such macro systemic features that might explain how and why policies are implemented differently in various national settings. It probably reflects the fact that 90 per cent of implementation research even as late as in the 2000s studied and compared policies *within* a given country (Sætren 2014).

The great inherent potential of cross-national research remains largely untapped because it is especially rife with many suboptimal selection criteria. This has been the case with this type of research in general (Dierkes et al. 1987) and there is no reason to believe that implementation scholars are faring better in this respect. Nevertheless, there are several exemplary studies comparing policy implementation across national boundaries (Siedentorpf and Ziller 1988; May 1995; Knill and Lenschow 1998; Falkner et al. 2008; Sætren 2009). The one by Siedentorpf and Ziller (1988) stands out here as particularly ambitious, well-crafted and comprehensive, studying the implementation of 17 randomly selected EU directives in all member states in the mid-1980s. At the same time there is an issue here: whether many other EU studies than those mentioned here are actually studying "implementation", or rather what happens in an earlier stage of the policy process, the one of "policy co-formation" by nation-states as legitimate political actors in their own right (Hill and Hupe 2014).

Since the early 1970s knowledge about the logic and procedures related to comparative research in general, is easily available and elaborated on in textbooks and journals (Przeworski and Teune 1970; Lijphart 1971; George 1979; Ragin 1987; Collier 1991; King et al. 1994; George and Bennett 2005). Maybe due to this fact Winter (2012a) does not say much about how to improve implementation research through comparative studies except to briefly mention their importance in general. Hence, we will limit our discussion to a few but nevertheless important issues facing contemporary and future comparative implementation research. We will do so after having presented the articles to follow in this special issue.

Variants of Comparative Implementation Research: Contents of the Special Issue

The first article is by Harald Sætren and titled "Crucial Factors in Implementing Radical Policy Change: A Comparative Longitudinal Study of Nordic Central Agency Relocation Programs". In his study he applies some of the guidelines inherent in the third generation research paradigm in an attempt to explain the marked differential fates of governmental efforts to relocate central agencies in a Scandinavian context. The study is comparative and synchronically based on the most-similar-systems research design (Finland, Norway and Sweden), as well as diachronically and longitudinally, as relocation programs in each country are investigated over more than one policy cycle encompassing several decades. This cross-national comparative and longitudinal research design is combined with another – crucial – case logic to identify the key factors that account for both what is perceived as policy "successes" and "failures". These are found to be a combination of factors related to macro-institutional arrangements, policy entrepreneurship and timing relative to contextual circumstances. Type of government and its relation to vested interest groups is a factor that is found to be of particular importance in this respect.

Ingrid Helgøy and Anne Homme, in the second article, titled "Path-dependent Implementation of the European Qualifications Framework in Education. A Comparison of Norway, Germany and England", have chosen to study the implementation of the same education policy program in three countries with quite different welfare regimes and political economies. National implementation processes are analyzed in terms of three diffusion concepts: (1) norm emergence, (2) norm cascade and (3) internalization. The authors conclude that all three countries seem to have adopted and implemented parts of the European Qualification Framework, that there is variation in the speed with which this has happened and that there also seems to be a common national institutional resistance towards full implementation. Cross-national variation appears here to be as much a function of policy legacy and path dependency as differences in welfare regime and political economy.

The third article, by Keith Baker and Gerry Stoker, titled "A Comparison of State Traditions and the Revival of a Nuclear Power in Four Countries", also explores the role macro-institutional factors play – in this case national governing traditions. The latter influence – through the selection of policy instruments – the networks of international companies constituting the nuclear power industry on which national nuclear power programs depend. Four quite different Western liberal democratic countries involved in this type of energy policy – Finland, France, the UK and the US – with markedly different governing traditions are compared. Although governing traditions did influence selection and deployment of policy instruments, some other factors also played an important role.

The fourth article, by Vancoppenolle et al., is titled "The Politics of Policy Design and Implementation: A Comparative Study of Two Belgian Service Voucher Programs". Two similar programs (subsidized childcare and home cleaning) adopted at approximately the same time within the same country (Belgium) and type of policy (voucher systems), but with strikingly different results, are compared in order to explain why one program was considered an indisputable success and the other an equally clear failure. The study points to the different target groups of the two programs and the deeply flawed nature of the Flemish childcare voucher system relative to its special target groups that made it almost impossible to implement. Thus the critical connection between policy design, program implementation and target groups is vividly illustrated.

The last article, by Jan Froestad and associates, follows up the important policy formation/implementation link of the previous article, as their title, "Policy Design and Nodal Governance: A Comparative Analysis of Determinants of Environmental Policy Change in a South African City", suggests. Their point of departure is a failed attempt to implement a solar water heater bylaw in a major South African city despite broad-based initial support. This apparent policy paradox is explained through an investigation of the two agencies involved in the sub-process of policy formation and their sharply different way of thinking regarding the desirability and feasibility of the policy measure in question. The authors conclude that at an early stage of policy formation insufficient attention was given to the fact that both agencies would have to cooperate closely and that inputs from both were critical to the policy's success. Although not comparative in the same manner (i.e. cross-national) as the other articles in this special issue we have nevertheless included it due to its intriguing case history in a policy context outside the Western hemisphere that is still rare in the implementation literature (Sætren 2005).

Comparative Implementation Research: Dualities Identified

Large-n *or Small*-n *Comparison*

A perennial issue in the research methodology literature is at stake here, often with a preference bias towards large-*n* comparative studies. This is unfortunate, as the right choice here is not self-evident. The respective relevance and merits of large- and small-*n* comparison, we would argue, depends on the research questions pursued. Hence, since they are complementary both are needed. Given the bias towards large-*n* a few arguments in favor of small-*n* comparisons contained in this special issue might be worth mentioning.

First, the classical argument against small-*n* comparison, their assumed over-determined research design (i.e. too few cases and too many variables), misses the point that one or a few cases (e.g. a country) can be disaggregated to many subcases (provinces, states or even lower level political-administrative subunits), thus substantially increasing units of observation (*n*) and thereby also mitigating the relevance of this argument. Similarly, one policy can be disaggregated into a number of similar constituent policy programs, as illustrated in the articles by Sætren and Vancoppenolle et al. in this special issue.

Second, the organizational and contextual richness of details so crucial to understanding policy processes that small-*n* case analysis can provide is almost impossible in large-*n* comparison. In the latter instance this easily translates into measurement and validity issues with respect to salient theoretical variables, not just related to qualitative data but quantitative data as well.

Third, the complex, dynamic relationship between various factors impacting on the policy process is easier to observe in in-depth analysis of a few cases compared to a much larger number of cases. Nevertheless, as two experienced large-*n* policy researchers concluded some years ago, it is not the size of *n* per se that matters but rather their inherent opportunities and limitations relative to research questions and skills of the researcher in this respect (Nicholson-Crotty and Meier 2002).

Most-Similar-Systems Design (MSSD) or Most-Different-Systems Design (MDSD)

This is another classical issue in comparative research. Should the selection of units of analysis to be compared be based on their differences or similarities? Ideal-typically each focuses on an intriguing and apparently paradoxical comparative observation. The first (MSSD) asks how we can explain that when quite similar units of analysis (e.g. countries) try to do the same thing (e.g. adopt a common policy), researchers end up with strikingly different results (policy outputs and outcomes). The other (MDSD) asks how we can explain that quite different units of analysis in most respects nevertheless end up with the same policy results. Although there seems to be a preference for the MSSD comparative design because it offers many control variables through its similarity principle, the choice here should really be guided by topical interest, the research question at hand and even theoretical ambitions. MDSD scholars tend to be more interested in common phenomena on almost any level of analysis that are invariant across many if not all available units of analysis. This again may reflect an interest in and ambition to develop more universally general theories in the social sciences. Those employing MSSD on the other hand are probably more skeptical towards the feasibility of developing grand theories and tend to think that middle-range context contingent theories are the best we can hope for. Hence their interest in explaining empirical variation among otherwise similar units of analysis implies important nuances within the many similarities, like for example institutional, organizational arrangements and policy legacies.

In practice it may not be so easy to follow the guidelines of these two different comparative research designs consistently. Often convenience and pragmatic considerations seem to play a more important role in the selection of units of analysis to be compared rather than what constitutes an optimal research design in terms of explanatory ambitions. That applies also to some extent to articles in this special issue. It should be mentioned too that the two comparative research designs can be fruitfully combined, although as far as we know that is not often done.

Comparative versus Longitudinal Research Design

The third generation research design exhorts the application of both more comparative (across jurisdictions, etc.) and longitudinal (over time) research designs. Sætren (2014), however, found that comparative studies in general are less prone to have a longitudinal research design than others. This is no doubt due to the fact that comparative studies to a larger extent are based on quantitative data that tend to be cross-sectional survey data. Causal analysis of policy processes becomes problematic when there is no time dimension in the data collected. Panel survey data stretching over several years or institutionally based time series data on agency activities and performance results – although perhaps more resource demanding to obtain – are sometimes used to counteract this adverse impact of comparison on the longitudinal dimension. Sætren's article illustrates how the comparative and longitudinal research design dimensions can be combined in a theoretically fruitful manner.

Macro- versus Lower Level Institutional Factors

The paucity of higher level institutional and constitutional factors in efforts to explain cross-national differences in policy implementation is striking. We do not a priori know the impact of the way the political system is organized or the type of government it has at any particular time, compared to the role of institutional and organizational arrangements at lower layers in the political-administrative system. At the same time their impact on policy performance cannot simply be ignored. In this special issue Sætren in his cross-national comparative study tries to sort out the relative impact of both higher and lower level institutional factors in this respect.

Policy Formation and Implementation

With the seminal work by Pressman and Wildavsky (1973) the focus in policy research shifted away from policy formation towards policy implementation. This happened, even although the authors themselves in a postscript of their book warned against this by emphasizing how important the earlier stage in the policy process could be to understand what was going on in the latter. Several implementation scholars have made efforts to correct this pendulum, swinging back towards a more balanced focus that include both policy stages and their interaction. These efforts have not been all that successful, especially after 1990, as Sætren (2014) found in his investigation of the implementation literature. This trend does not bode well for the prospect of developing a more all-embracing theory of policy processes research of which both policy design-*cum*-decision-making, as policy formation, and implementation must be part. At the same time, several articles in this special issue do incorporate the policy formation/implementation relationship in their research designs.

Conclusion

This special issue shows the variety of forms comparative implementation research takes – as indicated in the previous section. The collection of articles represents a small and modest range of efforts to move implementation research further in the direction of the norms implied by the "third generation research paradigm", especially where a comparative approach is concerned. They reflect an implicit consensus that the only way to winnow down the plethora of explanatory factors contained in the implementation literature towards more parsimonious theoretical constructs lies in the application of more rigorous comparative research designs.

The progress booked since Goggin and his colleagues (1990) formulated their "third generation" research agenda is obviously mixed. Much has been achieved but there is still a lot to do. Dualities and tensions have been pointed out that are trade-offs, implying they cannot easily be solved. In any case, the only way to deal with those dualities and tensions in actual research is to address them as such.

Acknowledgments

The guest editors of this special issue have since 2010 had the privilege to organize a Permanent Study Group on Public Policy within the frame of the European Group for Public Administration (EGPA). In successive years they have chaired workshops at the EGPA conferences in Toulouse (2010), Bucharest (2011), Bergen (2012), Edinburgh (2013) and Speyer (2014). Particularly the 2011 workshop in Bucharest, with the theme "Policy implementation in varying institutional settings", formed the basis for the articles in the present special issue. The editors of the *Journal of Comparative Policy Analysis* are gratefully acknowledged for enabling this publication. The guest editors also thank the anonymous reviewers for their comments on earlier versions of the included articles.

References

Chase, G., 1979, Implementing a human services program: How hard will it be? *Public Policy*, **27**(4), pp. 385–435.
Collier, D., 1991, The comparative method: Two decades of change, in: D. A. Rustow and K. P. Erickson (Eds) *Comparative Political Dynamics: Global Research* (New York: Harper Collins).
Dierkes, M., Weiler, H. N., and Antal, A. B., 1987, *Comparative Policy Research: Learning from Experience* (New York: St. Martins Press).
Falkner, G., Treib, O., and Holzleithner, E., 2008, *Compliance in the Enlarged European Union. Living Rights or Dead Letters?* (Aldershot: Ashgate).
George, A. L., 1979, Case studies and theory development. The method of structured focused comparison, in: P. G. Lauren (Ed), *Diplomatic History: New Approaches* (New York: The Free Press).
George, A. L. and Bennett, A., 2005, *Case Studies and Theory Development in the Social Sciences* (Cambridge, MA: MIT Press).
Goggin, M. L., 1986, The "too few cases/too many variables" problem in implementation research. *The Western Political Quarterly*, **39**(2), pp. 328–347. doi:10.2307/448302
Goggin, M. L., Bowman, A. O. M., Lester, J. P., and O'Toole, J. L. J., 1990, *Implementation Theory and Practice: Toward a Third Generation* (Glenview, IL: Scott Foresman/Little, Brown and Company).
Hill, M. J. and Hupe, P. L., 2014, *Implementing Public Policy: An Introduction to the Study of Operational Governance*, 3rd ed. (London: SAGE). 2nd ed., 2009.
King, G., Keohane, R. O., and Verba, S., 1994, *Designing Social Inquiry. Scientific Inference in Qualitative Research* (Princeton, NJ: Princeton University Press).
Knill, C. and Lenschow, A., 1998, Coping with Europe: The impact of British and German administrations on the implementation of EU environmental policy. *Journal of European Public Policy*, **5**(4), pp. 595–614. doi:10.1080/13501769880000041
Lester, J. P., Bowman, A. O. M., Goggin, M. L., and O'Toole, L. J., 1987, Public Policy implementation: Evolution of the field and agenda for future research. *Review of Policy Research*, **7**(1), pp. 200–216. doi:10.1111/j.1541-1338.1987.tb00038.x
Lijphart, A., 1971, Comparative politics and the comparative method. *The American Political Science Review*, **65**(3), pp. 682–693. doi:10.2307/1955513
Matland, R. E., 1995, Synthesizing the implementation literature: The ambiguity-conflict model. *Journal of Public Administration Research and Theory*, **5**(2), pp. 145–174
May, P. J., 1995, Can cooperation be mandated? Implementing intergovernmental environmental management in New South-Wales and New Zealand. *Publius*, **25**(1), pp. 89–113
Mazmanian, D. A. and Sabatier, P., 1981, *Effective Policy Implementation* (Lexington, MA: Lexington Books).
Mazmanian, D. A. and Sabatier, P., 1983, *Implementation and Public Policy* (Glenview, IL: Scott, Foresman).
Nicholson-Crotty, S. and Meier, K. J., 2002, Size doesn't matter: In defense of single-state studies. *State Politics and Policy Quarterly*, **2**(4), pp. 411–422. doi:10.1177/153244000200200405
O'Toole Jr., L. J., 1986, Policy recommendations for multi-actor implementation: An assessment of the field. *Journal of Public Policy*, **6**(2), pp. 181–210. doi:10.1017/S0143814X00006486
O'Toole Jr., L. J., 2000, Research on policy implementation: Assessment and prospects. *Journal of Public Administration Research and Theory*, **10**(2), pp. 263–288. doi:10.1093/oxfordjournals.jpart.a024270
O'Toole Jr., L. J., 2004, The theory-practice issue in policy implementation research. *Public Administration*, **82**(2), pp. 309–329. doi:10.1111/j.0033-3298.2004.00396.x
Pressman, J. L. and Wildavsky, A., 1973, *Implementation: How Great Expectations in Washington Are Dashed in Oakland (...)*, 3rd ed., 1984. (Berkeley, CA: University of California Press).
Przeworski, A. and Teune, H., 1970, *The Logic of Comparative Social Inquiry* (New York: John Wiley & Sons).
Ragin, C. C., 1987, *The Comparative Method* (Berkeley: University of California Press).
Rothstein, B., 1998, *Just Institutions Matter: The Moral and Political Logic of the Universal Welfare State* (Cambridge: Cambridge University Press).
Sabatier, P. A. and Mazmanian, D. A., 1979, The conditions of effective implementation. A guide to accomplishing policy objectives. *Policy Analysis*, **5**(4), pp. 481–504.
Sætren, H., 2005, Facts and myths about research on public policy implementation: Out-of-fashion, allegedly dead, but still very much alive and relevant. *The Policy Studies Journal*, **33**(4), pp. 559–582. doi:10.1111/j.1541-0072.2005.00133.x

Sætren, H., 2009, Explaining radical policy change against all odds: The role of leadership, institutions, program design and policy windows, in: J. A. Raffel, P. Leisink, and A. E. Middlebrooks (Eds) *Public Sector Leadership: International Challenges and Perspectives* (Cheltenham, UK: Edward Elgar).

Sætren, H., 2014, Implementing the third generation research paradigm in policy implementation research: An empirical assessment. *Public Policy and Administration*, **29**(2), pp. 84–105. doi:10.1177/0952076713513487

Siedentorpf, H. and Ziller, J., 1988, *Making European Policies Work: the Implementation of Community Legislation in the Member States* (London: SAGE).

Van Meter, D. S. and Van Horn, C. E., 1975, The policy implementation process: A conceptual framework. *Administration & Society*, **6**(4), pp. 445–488. doi:10.1177/009539977500600404

Winter, S., 1990, Integrating implementation research, in: D. J. Palumbo and D. J. Calista (Eds) *Implementation and the Policy Process: Opening Up the Black Box* (New York: Greenwood Press).

Winter, S., 2012a, Implementation, introduction to part 5, in: B. G. Peters and J. Pierre (Eds) *Handbook of Public Administration* (London: SAGE), pp. 255–263.

Winter, S., 2012b, Implementation perspectives: Status and reconsideration, Chapt. 16, in: B. G. Peters and J. Pierre (Eds) *Handbook of Public Administration* (London: SAGE), pp. 265–278.

Organizing for Policy Implementation: The Emergence and Role of Implementation Units in Policy Design and Oversight

EVERT LINDQUIST

ABSTRACT The leaders of governments in the United Kingdom, Australia, and Queensland recently created "implementation" or "delivery" units at the centre, ostensibly to advise, monitor, and ensure better implementation of policy initiatives. This collection of papers seeks to explore the emergence, roles, functions, and accomplishments of policy implementation and delivery units, as well as their prospects. This overview paper provides a framework for analyzing and assessing the work of these units to date, beginning with a synopsis of the evolution of thinking on implementation, and turning to the new environment for governance, policy development, and implementation. It casts policy implementation and delivery units as one of several "adhocracies" that populate the centre of government, which may take on quite different roles. The paper provides an overview of the case studies and key findings.

Introduction

Over 40 years ago the spotlight was put on gathering scholarly interest on policy implementation with the publication of Pressman and Wildavsky's (1973) seminal book on *Implementation: How Great Expectations in Washington Are Dashed in Oakland*.[1] In its slipstream came Bardach's (1977) *Implementation Game* outlining the myriad ways in which policy initiatives could be diverted, deflected, dissipated, and delayed. Despite his pessimism about the promise of big policy solutions more generally, and the prospects for improving implementation in particular, Bardach nevertheless suggested creating capabilities related to implementation in two institutional locations for the purpose of "game-fixing": in staff policy analysis and evaluation units in pertinent department budget offices and, in an environment of policy-capable US legislatures, in policy or appropriation committees with low turnover in staff and representatives. There, he speculated, officials might have the incentive, perspective, expertise, and resources to mitigate dysfunctional implementation dynamics.

Forty years later, in very different institutional contexts, the leaders of governments in several jurisdictions – the United Kingdom, Australia, and Queensland – have created "implementation" or "delivery" units at the centre, ostensibly to advise, monitor, and ensure better implementation of policy initiatives. In the UK, the Prime Minister's Delivery Unit was established by Prime Minister Tony Blair in the Cabinet Office in 2001. In Australia, a Cabinet Implementation Unit was installed by Prime Minister John Howard in the Commonwealth's Department of Prime Minister and Cabinet in 2003, and an Implementation Unit was established in March 2004 in the Queensland Department of Premier and Cabinet under Premier Peter Beattie.

The emergence of policy implementation units is intriguing, if only because they seem to have been at the instigation of prime ministers and premiers, and not the result of a recent call by policy scholars to build new capacities. Indeed, although implementation analysis has long been a staple in the tool-kit taught in graduate policy programmes and textbooks, and should be an essential feature of decision briefs prepared for ministers, arguably the implementation literature has lost considerable profile and steam, with a small band of insightful contributors refining and elaborating theoretical propositions (Hill and Hupe 2002). Relatively little attention has been paid to questions of capacity and doing better at making initiatives work in ever more complex policy environments. This, of course, has been a top concern of political leaders, who have adopted new performance regimes, the language of the New Public Management, and project management techniques to ensure priority initiatives are realized. Against this backdrop, the emergence and nomenclature of policy implementation units, however intriguing, seems like a throwback – one would have thought that the wave of such units would have hit in the 1980s in response to the original insights of Bardach, Pressman, Wildavsky, and many others writing at that time.

The purpose of this collection of papers is to explore the emergence, roles, functions, and accomplishments of policy implementation and delivery units, as well as their prospects. It does not argue that such units should be established as a feature of modern central government, but rather that their emergence is worthy of note and understanding. Proceeding under the auspices of first ministers, these capabilities can be seen as a critique of existing management, implementation, and monitoring capabilities of the larger governance and public service systems where policy priorities are concerned, and the latest instrument unsheathed by some first ministers to design, assist, and embed critical policy initiatives. But policy implementation units join the panoply of different capabilities leaders have experimented with to drive policy agendas and co-ordinate government activities, and, in the modern era, where policy is often recognized as inherently complex, share some similarities with capabilities intended to manage horizontal and whole-of-government initiatives. Indeed, a key goal of this collection is to ascertain what policy implementation units actually do, and whether they will endure, recognizing that capabilities with the same names may play completely different roles in different systems, presumably reflecting the ecology of their respective institutional environments and the strategic needs of their progenitors.

The cases in this collection reflect the universe of known "named" policy implementation units. Despite the preponderance of Westminster systems serving as the backdrop for these cases (with the exception of the European Union case), they have considerable diversity with respect to the motivations of political leaders who established them, the bureaucratic capabilities and roles that were installed, and the governance environments in which they have operated (unitary, federal, and multi-level governance). This paper seeks to provide a framework for analyzing and assessing the work of these units to date. It begins by with a brief synopsis of the evolution of thinking on implementation, and then considers the new environment for governance, policy development, and implementation. With this backdrop, the paper casts policy implementation and delivery units as one of several "adhocracies" that populate the centre of government (Desveaux et al. 1994, Lindquist 2004), and distinguishes among different functions because, despite their labels, implementation units may take on quite different roles. The paper then provides an overview of the genesis case studies and key findings.

Evolving Perspectives on Implementation

There has been no shortage of reviews of the implementation literature. Generally, it is suggested that the modern literature has moved through three phases (e.g., Goggin et al. 1990, Hill and Hupe 2002, Howlett and Ramesh 2003, Schofield and Sausman 2004). The first phase was triggered by the contributions of Pressman and Wildavsky (1973), Bardach (1977), and others. A flurry of writing emerged on the gap between policy intentions and the reality of programme delivery in the US and other jurisdictions, considerable introspection about the limitations of social science research and ambitious ideas and solutions informing policy-making and the design of programmes, and strong interest in discerning what interventions worked. Recognition of and debate over the implementation challenge was a defining moment for the modern policy literature, producing important strands of inquiry on implementation, evaluation, and knowledge utilization that not only since defined the field and been insinuated into the "policy cycle" heuristic (see Howlett and Ramesh 2003, Pal 2001, Bridgman and Davis 2000, Hogwood and Gunn 1984) but also distinguished it from the early policy sciences approach (Lerner and Lasswell 1951).

A second stream of writing focused on searching for useful theoretical perspectives and frameworks on implementation. This included work seeking to determine the most productive vantage points for thinking about how to anticipate and work through implementation challenges, which included the interesting debate over "top-down" (forward-mapping) and "bottom-up" (backward-mapping) approaches (Elmore 1979, Berman 1978), increasingly sophisticated efforts to develop frameworks and more sophisticated analytic tools that addressed the complexity of implementation (Mazmanian and Sabatier 1983), and the sustained efforts to find better means to monitor and measure the impact of policy interventions (e.g., Williams et al. 1982). Arguably, this latter stream of research has built the most momentum over the years, particularly in the US, leading to a huge consulting industry dedicated to evaluation and quasi-experiments of programme implementation, and effectively has defined the work supported by the Association for Public Policy Analysis and Management for the last two decades.

Like all fields, many of its early strands of writing endure as important lines of thinking in their own right. Howlett and Ramesh (2003) have suggested that more recent inquiry on implementation has tapped into game theory, public choice and principal/agent models to frame implementation challenges and guide empirical research. Considerable attention has focused on how instruments can be wielded and used in combination to achieve policy goals as well as different sectoral and national styles for approaching design and implementation (Linder and Peters 1990, Howlett 1991, Howlett 2005). Recently, there has been renewed interest in implementation in the context of whole-of-government and multi-level governance perspectives (Schofield and Sausman 2004) and the challenge of managing complexity and networks more generally (Kickert *et al.* 1997, O'Toole 2004).

However, like the knowledge utilization literature (though not as thoroughly), one senses that the literature on implementation has dissipated as a coherent field into specific lines of inquiry, effectively a victim of its success. Despite its status as a foundation stone in the policy tool-kit, many of the themes associated with implementation are taken up under different rubrics, such as horizontal management, whole-of-government, evaluation research, governing instruments, network analysis, etc. (Hill and Hupe 2002). Relatively few scholars march forward waving the implementation flag. And, despite the interesting theorizing still occurring, and recent resurgence in interest in implementation (Schofield and Sausman, 2004), there is little evidence of applying implementation theory in practice and engaging practitioners in the emerging challenges of implementation, a style that was the hallmark when the literature first emerged (O'Toole 2004).

For the purposes of this collection of papers, this sketch of the implementation literature should suggest that contributors have done a good job of recognizing complexity over the years, and thinking carefully about the analytic challenges of anticipating implementation issues; the mix, qualities, and merits of different policy instruments for an implementation perspective; and the evolutionary and emergent quality of handling implementing policies and programmes, a process of negotiation, adjustment, and learning as managerial strategies. All of these themes and lessons should resonate even more in today's arguably more complex policy-making landscape. However, Bardach's early musings about building the right organizational and institutional capacities to mitigate implementation challenges has not received much attention over the years, and at best is only implicitly addressed in the field. This, combined with the lack of dialogue with practitioners on implementation challenges in recent years and the fact that several governments have recently considered or created units in their core executive to inform the upstream of policy development and to provide central oversight of implementation, suggests that the study of implementation units at the apex of governments is a timely and potentially fruitful line of inquiry.

Evolving Contexts, New Rationales for Implementation Units

Innovations like policy implementation and delivery units do not spring out of thin air; they are responses of first ministers to perceived challenges, signals about how they expect policies should be designed and implemented. Whether such innovations are well conceived and live up to their promise is one matter, one that will be addressed by the case studies. Here we consider how the policy environment might have changed to stimulate such action in several different jurisdictions.

In the late 1980s and 1990s, a common challenge for many OECD countries concerned stemming the growth in the size of government budgets and either cutting or rationalizing programmes. Public bureaucracies were depicted as having their own incentives, resistant to efforts by governments to control growth in programmes, and political leaders unwilling or unable to take decisive steps. This led to the argument that governments should assert political priorities and control over public service institutions, buttressed by theoretical perspectives such as public choice and agency theory. As tough fiscal decisions were made by many governments, their focus was less about implementing new policies and more about scrutinizing and changing existing policy regimes, and meeting aggressive expenditure targets and reorganization timelines. In this context policy implementation naturally received less attention, executive careers were increasingly based on managerial performance as opposed to policy shrewdness, and policy capabilities (not to mention labour negotiation capabilities) in public service institutions waned in many jurisdictions. For similar reasons focused less on the challenges of policy design and implementation (Barrett 2004) and more on scrutinizing alternative ways to deliver government services, ensuring that big service transformation projects were on time and budget, and adopting performance regimes.

As some governments turned the corner in their efforts to stabilize deficits and climb back to surplus positions, this raised the possibility of investing in new policy initiatives. With the pain of cuts fresh in the minds of decision makers, there were likely to be higher tests for what constituted prudent and worthwhile spending, and for ensuring that the funds led to intended results. Arguably, too, by the end of the twentieth century policy makers had a much better sense of the interconnectedness of issues, the need for alignment in the use of different governing instruments, and the reality that many policy solutions required working across the boundaries of departments and agencies within and across levels of government (United Kingdom 2001, Australia 2004, Canada 2004). Whether such appreciation for complexity and the need for horizontal and whole-of-government thinking emerged from lessons from downsizing and restructuring, the frames emanating from hypertext and we-based models, or systems thinking from the likes of Peter Senge and others does not matter. The important observation is that more citizens and policy makers sought to be more careful about how new policy initiatives were designed, how well aligned new instruments were with existing ones, and how quickly such initiatives could be put in place.

With this sketch of the recent evolution and swings in the governance environment for many OECD jurisdictions, we can venture several different hypotheses for establishing policy implementation and delivery units. They include:

- *Meeting government commitments.* Since the 1990s many political leaders have campaigned for office committed to policy platforms with specific commitments (i.e., the Liberal "Red Book" in Canada; Gingrich's "Contract with America", British Columbia's "New Era Commitments", etc.). Delivery and implementation units can be seen as another tool for first ministers and their governments to ensure that key commitments get met and they keep focused on its agenda and message.

- *Asserting political control.* This hypothesis would be rooted in the presumption that departments and agencies would resist adopting new policies because they might compete with existing programmes or not reflect the preferences of public service leaders. The goal of an implementation unit would be to bring pressure to bear and a spotlight on the public service.
- *Anticipating design challenges.* This hypothesis would argue that there is a need to vet policy proposals from departments and agencies for whether they fully account for the complexity of problems and the interaction of pertinent policy instruments, perhaps wielded by other governments or with other sectors.
- *Navigating implementation challenges.* The more complex a policy initiative, the more likely that it will require capacity to manage and co-ordinate implementation in a multi-level governance context.
- *Promoting cultural change.* Another hypothesis would suggest that the ultimate goal of implementation units is to change how front-line service delivery units do their work, to increase focus on better serving clients, improving the measuring and monitoring of results, and, as a result, to change their values and culture.
- *Addressing political optics.* Given the loss of credibility of government with citizens, and the perceived need for governments to become more "business-like", implementation units might be established to project a new image and focus on getting programmes in place on time and within budget.

Interestingly, each hypothesis implies that a government might staff an implementation or delivery unit with different kinds of talent and expertise, where they are located at the centre, and what processes they engage with. That said, the case studies may reveal that governments had overlapping and reinforcing reasons for creating the units, and that, no matter the initial goals driving inception, they evolved over time.

Implementation Units and the Ecology of Central Capabilities

The "centre" in most governance systems is comprised of a constellation of central agencies and secretariats dedicated to serving first ministers, and supporting and co-ordinating the government and the public service as corporate entities. Implementation units cannot be understood and evaluated on their terms because they are insinuated into an ecology of capabilities at the centre of government.

This observation is important for three reasons. First, implementation units may have emerged as a critique of other central units in the systems. Second, in a complex and "congested" central state apparatus, such units have to compete for resources and the attention of ministers and departments alike. Third, any unit may be called on to take up different tasks and roles in the upstream or downstream of the policy-making process. In what follows we consider the ecology of capabilities that such units have to navigate and consider the different roles that implementations units might play.

Traditional Cabinet Secretariats. Perhaps the most important, if the least exciting, central capabilities are the secretariats that handle the upstream and downstream logistics for the meetings of cabinet and its committees. Typically, these units are dedicated to ensuring that proper notice, sign-off, consultation, and proper documentation and analysis occur before initiatives are tabled for ministers to consider. Depending on the size of the cabinet and its jurisdiction, there can be many secretariats, some serving cabinet as a whole and others serving particular standing and ad hoc committees. Usually, these units function as gate-keepers and process managers, and do not have the capacity to undertake policy and implementation analysis, nor can they to monitor or hold to account the performance of ministers and departments assigned responsibility for implementation.

Other Standing Cabinet Secretariats. Cabinet offices typically have responsibility for advising the first minister and cabinet secretary on the overall direction of public service institutions. In this connection there usually are secretariats that provide advice and support on the appointment of top executives across the public service, the overall structure of ministerial portfolios and the machinery of government, and broader reform initiatives such as renewal and public service reform. Finally, there will be secretariats dedicated to co-ordinating the assessment and evaluation of ministers and top officials.

Co-ordinating Secretariats. First ministers often establish several policy units at the centre of government, such as national advisors or secretariats on security, science, Aboriginal affairs, and the environment. These are different from the traditional standing secretariats responsible for supporting cabinet and its committees (although co-ordinating secretariats may support ad hoc committees of cabinet). These secretariats can function as focal points to move issues higher on the government agenda and clear the path for policy development; what Bakvis and Juillet (2004) have depicted as a "catalytic" or champion role. However, Lindquist (2004) suggests that without strong political will such capabilities will quickly become seen as "symbolic" (Myer and Rowan 1977).

Policy Adhocracies in Departments. The lead responsibility for developing, framing, and advocating a major policy initiative – even one that is clearly horizontal – will typically be assigned to a lead department or ministry, unless it is determined by the first minister that it is prudent or necessary for a central co-ordinating units to be established. Such units are responsible for assembling expertise and undertaking analysis, developing a coherent and politically sensitive policy plan, and dealing with and managing the central agencies and cabinet. It is in this latter role that such policy units will encounter and perhaps clash with policy implementation units.

Scrutiny and Challenge. Central agencies may tend to defer to departments for their policy and operational expertise, but one time-honoured role of the centre is scrutinize and challenge new proposals and often their implementation plans, even if approved by the cabinet. Such scrutiny emerges from the responsibilities of departments of finance and treasuries – particularly in the expenditure management and budget office functions – to ensure that funds are well spent and provide good value for money. This challenge role can be exercised as part of informing cabinet deliberations when considering proposals, but it can also take place once policy decisions have been made, and finer-grained budget and human resource allocation decisions have to be made in the downstream to decisions. The extent to which this takes place will also depend on how potent the budget office and finance ministries are in the implementation process; in some jurisdictions, managerial flexibilities and traditions of autonomy may circumscribe this role.

Facilitation Advice. In some systems, central capabilities are established to support horizontal initiatives, either by providing advice, training or lesson-drawing. They could facilitate learning, the dissemination of best practices, and function as a "centre of excellence". This could be relevant to implementation initiatives since there could be learning and support informed by previous experience. Such capacity could assist officials leading a horizontal initiative at the formative stage, but such a role should be seen as distinct from the catalytic, champion, and implementation roles identified above.

Downstream Co-ordination. The implementation of policy initiatives are usually assigned to lead departments, but sometimes their complexity and horizontality may require that the centre establish a co-ordination secretariat, either located with a lead department and sometimes in the cabinet office. In a parallel way, central agencies may often agree to co-ordinate across "service" lines, particularly if key oversight functions and policies are distributed across different central agencies, to streamline the approvals and reporting associated with a particular initiative.

Monitoring and Evaluating Performance. The line between monitoring progress on specific implementation initiatives and evaluating the performance of ministers and their executive teams can be blurry, but the latter activity focuses on more global assessment and reporting, whereas the former may involve remedial steps by the centre to ensure that implementation occurs. This might involve working with ministers and their departments to identify milestones and performance indicators for specific initiatives, and, more generally, developing accountability frameworks for departments and executive teams, and reviewing indicators to inform the annual assessments of executive performance. It may also involve identifying broad outcome indicators for gauging the impact of government policies and programmes in different domains over a longer period of time.

The foregoing leads us to see that there is a significant difference between creating capacity to promote priorities, assign responsibilities for horizontal initiatives, design significant policy interventions, co-ordinate approvals, facilitate progress, provide information, monitor implementation, and assess outcomes. These are distinct roles for co-ordinating units to play in government, and itemizing them in sequence lays bare the inherent complexity for properly managing policy initiatives from the centre. It is in this context that we need to consider the role of policy implementation units at the centre for government. But even here we can have functional differentiation, and in this connection it is useful to identify two different potential roles that such units could play:

- *Upstream implementation.* First ministers in Australia and Queensland have created implementation units in cabinet offices seemingly intended to ensure that *when* new initiatives are proposed, the administering organizations are properly identified, constructed and located, and that the right questions have been asked

about a variety of implementation issues (Shergold 2003). These implementation units provide *ex ante* quality control, to ensure the priority issues of government are properly addressed.
- *Downstream implementation.* A related, but distinct, function is to monitor progress on implementation and, when necessary, invoke central authority to clear the path for horizontal initiatives as they evolve. The best example of dedicated capabilities for this purpose is the Delivery Unit in the British government, initially attached to the British Cabinet Office along with other policy and reform capabilities, and later moved over to the Treasury (Burch and Holliday 2004).

It should be understood that implementation units could play one or both of these roles, or their focus could evolve over time depending on the interests of first ministers, and, of course, the competition and comparative advantage of other central capabilities.

More generally, we can see that there is great potential for implementation units, however defined and mandated, to overlap with and perhaps assume the responsibilities of other central actors in governance systems. Indeed, implementation units may have been established precisely to compensate for, and constitute a critique of existing central capabilities. This implies potential for overlap and rivalry for implementation units, and suggests that other central capabilities may exert pressure or attempt re-build capabilities to compete with or absorb implementation units. Moreover, there is no end to ongoing demand to create adhocracies and secretariats at the centre, and considerable pressure and incentive – particularly symbolic in nature – to retain them (Lindquist 2004). However, prime ministers and top advisers also have to ask, "How do you cull and re-align the centre?", so that governments can maintain their focus, and the time of central actors, departments, and agencies can be utilized more effectively. In short, this canvassing of central capabilities suggests a degree of precariousness for these new units. These are important empirical questions to explore in the case study contributions of this collection.

The Cases: Overview and Approach

The empirical part of this project focused on three case studies. Authors familiar with central structures and initiatives were invited to prepare papers. The annex to this paper contains the questions sent to contributors to guide the drafting of their cases. Their findings were presented at the Second Annual International Comparative Policy Analysis (ICPA) Workshop on October 3, 2005 in Vancouver. The papers included:

- *David Richards* and *Martin Smith* (Sheffield University), "Central Control and Policy Implementation in the UK: A Case Study of the Prime Minister's Delivery Unit". This paper chronicles the emergence of the Delivery Unit (PMDU), but first considers larger trends in the governance of UK's core executive. The authors show how the design of the PMDU and its direct reporting to the prime minister (even though it has been located in the Cabinet Office and the Treasury) was a response not only to the arrival and challenge of New Public Management themes to the Westminster style of governance and to significant fragmentation in the delivery of services. They see the PMDU as a concerted effort of the prime minister to work *directly* and negotiate with delivery agencies on implementation of priority initiatives because the departments of the core executive had failed to bring about a necessary culture shift to improve delivery performance. Richards and Smith see the PMDU and its monitoring activities as reflecting Tony Blair's "personalism" in carrying out his duties as prime minister.

- *John Wanna* (Australian National University), "From Afterthought to Afterburner: Australia's Cabinet Implementation Unit". This paper examines the decision of Prime Minister John Howard and his top political and public service advisors to create a capability to encourage ministers and public servants to focus attention on the delivery or implementation aspects of policy decisions. This interest arose close to Howard's second term, and was addressed in the transition planning for his third government. The author describes how Prime Minister Howard and top officials learned from the UK experience with the PMDU and located a small Cabinet Implementation Unit (CUI) in the Department of Prime Minister and Cabinet. The CUI can be seen as one of many strategies that Howard employs for running a "disciplined" cabinet system. While the officials do not seem to be the high-flyers found in the PMDU with direct access to the prime minister, the unit does review all proposals going to cabinet for implementation analysis and risk assessment, and the unit maintains a "traffic light" system to the prime minister and cabinet for about 30 per cent of all proposals that the cabinet has approved.
- *Anne Tiernan* (Griffith University), "Working With the Stock We Have: The Evolving Role of Queensland's Implementation Unit". This paper provides some background on Queensland's history and governance challenges, including recent efforts to modernize public sector governance and administration. Premier Peter Beattie's interest in implementation arose from several embarrassments during the second term of his government, revealing a disconnection between cabinet decisions and on-the-ground service delivery. This interest emerged as Beattie shifted from a collaborative style of governing to a far more directive and populist approach, running against the performance of the public service and working hard to keep his ministers in line. Beattie and his top officials were very well aware of Blair's PMDU and Howard's Cabinet Implementation Unit. However, they chose to reorganize standing policy and reporting capabilities to establish an Implementation Unit in the Department of Premier and Cabinet's Policy Division. An interesting feature of the Queensland experience concerns how the premier sought to have this capability work through the "desk officers" in DPC responsible for liaising with departments and agencies.

Not long after the workshop was held, I presented the framework and broad findings from this project at the Annual Research Meetings of the Association for Public Policy Analysis and Management in November 2005 in Washington, DC. There I learned of research by *Steven Kelman* (Harvard University) on PMDU and its monitoring of front-line service delivery agencies in a paper on "Central Government and Frontline Performance Improvement: The Case of Performance Targets in the United Kingdom". In a highly serendipitous way, Kelman's paper effectively takes up the final observation in the Richards and Smith paper in the collection: "Real improvements in delivery will only come about with greater attention paid to the resources and culture of those who operate at street level." Kelman does so in two ways. First, he reviews the organization theory literature to develop a framework that captures how central units might control, regulate, or facilitate entities delivering services. His four-part framework includes: decision making/design; monitoring/ approval; knowledge creation and transfer; and value infusion. Second, using that framework, he reports on interview findings from a host of officials at the centre, in departments, and in front-line roles with respect to several specific case studies in the UK involving the negotiation and monitoring of performance targets. Though less focused on the emergence of PMDU as a new central phenomenon, Kelman's framework nicely complements the one advanced in this paper.

While small in number, this set of papers is interesting for exploring the emergence, role, and evolution of this wave of implementation units. There is variation in jurisdictional complexity, ranging from sub-national jurisdictions (Queensland), to a unitary national system (the United Kingdom), and to a federal system (Commonwealth of Australia). At the level of nation-states, it appears that implementation units have emerged mainly in parliamentary systems, although obviously this is a small sample from which to draw any conclusion. It is well understood that first ministers in many parliamentary countries have sought to exert further increase in control over government priorities and managing the public service as a whole even as the challenge of doing so seems to steadily grow more daunting (Savoie 1999, Weller 2003, Burch and Holliday 2004). This suggests that jurisdictions with "strong" centre traditions are more disposed to such experimentation (Peters 2003, Lindquist 2000), in contrast to the more autonomous agency traditions and weaker central institutions often associated with Western European governments. It is also the case that first ministers and their cabinets in other jurisdictions have similar concerns but rely on functional equivalents to cabinet implementation and delivery units.

This last possibility is taken up in the concluding paper to this collection, which not only compares the information from the four papers with respect to their character and roles of central implementation units in three jurisdictions, particularly with respect to how the actual roles and activities support the hypotheses outlined earlier in this paper. It also considers the lessons and prospects for cabinet implementation units, and explores some implications for the literature.

Acknowledgements

On behalf of the contributors to this special issue, I want to thank: Iris Geva-May and Nancy Olewiler of Simon Fraser University's Public Policy Program for hosting the ICPA Forum in Vancouver in October 2005 where the case studies in the collection were first presented and valuable comments were received from session chairs and discussants; staff at SFU's Public Policy Program and University of Victoria's School of Public Administration for handling all of the logistics; Peter May of the University of Washington for his comments on *all* of the papers; the Knowledge Links program of the University Presidents Council of British Columbia for providing travel support for the ICPA Forum and Joy Illington for making the connection; and to JCPA's anonymous reviewers and editorial team of Iris Geva-May, Michael Howlett, and Diana Walker for their suggestions, guidance and support.

Note

1. See Hill and Hupe (2002) for an excellent description of the genesis of this literature, including precursors to the work of Pressman and Wildavsky.

References

Australia, Management Advisory Committee, 2004, *Connecting Government: Whole of Government Responses to Australia's Priority Challenges* (Canberra: Commonwealth of Australia).

Bakvis, H., and Julliet, L., 2004, *The Horizontal Challenge: Line Departments, Central Agencies and Leadership* (Ottawa: Canada School of Public Service).

Bardach, E., 1977, *The Implementation Game: What Happens After a Bill Becomes Law* (Cambridge, MA: MIT Press).

Barrett, S. M., 2004, Implementation studies: time for a revival? Personal reflections on 20 years of implementation studies. *Public Administration*, **82**(2), 249–262.

Berman, P., 1978, Macro- and micro-implementation. *Public Policy*, **26** (Spring), 165–179.

Bridgman, P. and Davis, G., 2000, *The Australian Policy Handbook* (Sydney: Allen Unwin).

Burch, M. and Holliday, I., 2004, The Blair government and the core executive. *Government and Opposition*, **39**(1), 1–21.

Canada, 2004, *Policy Development and Implementation in Complex Files* (Ottawa: National Homelessness Initiative and Canada School of Public Service).

Desveaux, J., Lindquist, E. and Toner, G., 1994, Organizing for policy innovation in public bureaucracy: AIDS, energy, and environmental policy in Canada. *Canadian Journal of Political Science*, **27**(3) (September), 493–538.

Elmore, R. F., 1982, Backing mapping: implementation research and policy decisions, in: W. Williams, R. F. Elmore, R. P. Nathan, S. A. MacManus and M. Kirst (Eds) *Studying Implementation: Methodological and Administrative Issues* (Chatham, New Jersey: Chatham House).

Goggin, M., Lester, J., O'Toole, L. and Bowman, A. (Eds), 1990, *Implementation Theory and Practice: Toward a Third Generation* (Glenview, IL: Scott, Foresman, Little, Brown).

Hill, M. and Hupe, P., 2002, *Implementing Public Policy* (London: Sage).

Hogwood, B. W. and Gunn, L., 1984, *Policy Analysis for the Real World* (Oxford: Oxford University Press).

Howlett, M., 1991, Policy instruments, policy styles, and policy implementation: national approaches to theories of instrument choice. *Policy Studies Journal*, **19**(2), 1–21.

Howlett, M., 2005, What is a policy instrument? Tools, mixes and implementation styles, in: P. Eliadis, M. Hill and M. Howlett (Eds) *Designing Government: From Instruments to Governance* (Kingston and Montreal: McGill-Queen's University Press).

Howlett, M. and Ramesh, M., 2003, *Studying Public Policy: Policy Cycle and Policy Subsystems*, 2nd edition (Toronto: Oxford University Press).

Kelman, S., 2005, Central government and frontline performance improvement: the case of "Targets in the United Kingdom", Paper presented to the Annual Research Meetings of Association for Public Policy Analysis and Management, November 5 Washington, DC.

Kickert, W. J. M., Klijn, E.-H. and Koppenjan, J. F. M. (Eds), 1997, *Managing Complex Networks: Strategies for the Public Sector* (London: Sage).

Lerner, D. and Lasswell, H. D. (Eds) 1951, *The Policy Sciences: Recent Developments in Scope and Method* (Stanford, CA: Stanford University Press).

Linder, S. H. and Peters, B., G., 1990, Research perspectives on the design of public policy: implementation, formulation, and design, in: D. J. Palumbo and D. J. Calista (Eds) *Implementation and the Policy Process: Opening Up the Black Box* (New York: Greenwood Press).

Lindquist, E. A., 2000, Reconceiving the center: leadership, strategic review and coherence in public sector reform, in OECD. *Government of the Future* (Paris: OECD), pp. 149–183.

Lindquist, E. A., 2004, Strategy, capacity and horizontal governance: lessons from Australia and Canada. *Optimum Online: The Journal of Public Sector Management*, **34**(3) (December) at http://www.optimumonline.ca/

Mazmanian, D. A. and Sabatier, P. A., 1983, *Implementation and Public Policy* (Glenview: IL: Scott, Foresman).

Meyer, J. W. and Rowan, B., 1977, Institutionalized organizations: formal structure as myth and ceremony. *American Journal of Sociology*, **83**, 340–363.

O'Toole, L. J. Jr., 2004, The theory-practice issue in policy implementation research. *Public Administration*, **82**(2), 309–329.

Pal, L. A., 2001, *Beyond Policy Analysis: Public Issue Management in Turbulent Times*, 2nd edition (Toronto: Nelson).

Peters, B. G., 2003, Administrative traditions and the Anglo-American democracies, in: J. Halligan (Ed) *Civil Service Systems in Anglo-American Countries* (Cheltenham: Edward Elgar).

Pressman, J. L. and Wildavsky, A. B., 1984, *Implementation: How Great Expectations in Washington are Dashed in Oakland*, 3rd edition (Berkeley: University of California Press).

Rose, R., *Lesson-Drawing in Public Policy: A Guide to Learning Across Time and Space* (Chatham, New Jersey: Chatham House, 1993).

Savoie, D. J., 1999, *Governing From the Centre: The Concentration of Power in Canadian Politics* (Toronto: University of Toronto Press).

Schofield, J. and Suasman, C., 2004, Symposium on implementing public policy: learning from theory and practice: introduction. *Public Administration*, **82**(2), 235–248.

Shergold, P., 2003, A foundation of ruined hopes? Delivering government policy, Address to Public Service Commission SES Breakfast Briefing, October 15.

United Kingdom, Cabinet Office, 2001, *Wiring it Up: Whitehall's Management of Cross Cutting Policies and Services* (London: Performance and Innovation Unit).

Weller, P., 2003, Cabinet government: an elusive ideal? *Public Administration*, **81**(4), 701–722.

Williams, W., Elmore, R. F., Nathan, R. P., MacManus, S. A. and Kirst, M. (Eds), 1982, *Studying Implementation: Methodological and Administrative Issues* (Chatham, NJ: Chatham House).

Annex: A Guide for Drafting Case Study Papers

The goal of this collection of papers is to describe and analyze the emergence and roles of implementation and delivery units in the UK, Australia and Europe, to understand how they differ from each other, and how they evolved and fared. Their arrival undoubtedly reflected broader developments in the management and evolution of central institutions in each jurisdiction, so some background on this would be useful. The authors of the case studies were asked to address several points identified as best they could, but were encouraged to develop their analysis and narrative in the way that made the most sense to them. Here are the guiding questions:

- What was the rationale for establishing these units? Did they reflect the specific interests of first ministers or other leaders? Did particular failures or scandals lead to their creation, or was there a more general critique in the air? Was their emergence partially as a critique of the inability of other central agencies to make these kinds of assessments?
- What is the location of implementation and delivery units in the immediate organizational ecology of the core executive? Did this evolve over time? Why?
- What kind of leaders and staff were chosen to fill these units? What was the size of these units? Did the type of leader change over time?

- What is the specific role of the units in policy development, agenda management, and oversight processes by first ministers and their governments? Does the label "implementation unit" really reflect their role? Are they working the upstream of developing policy initiatives, or do they operate more fully in the downstream with the actual implementation of initiatives, or both? Or are they monitoring the progress of other entities – such as departments, ministries, or agencies – as they seek to implement a policy initiative? Are they reserved for dealing only with certain kinds of policy initiatives?
- How do these units carry out their mandates in complicated, shifting institutional environments with a multitude of delivery agents but also a good number of other core executive agencies and units? Can you point to instances where these units successfully carried out their roles? Are there instances where they were marginal or ineffective? Has their effectiveness evolved over time?
- Are there functional equivalents or competitors to implementation units, such as central processes or other units and central agencies that provide implementation thinking in the upstream of policy development and then monitor progress?
- Has "lesson-drawing" taken place across jurisdictions (Rose 1993), when the units were created, or as they took up their mandates?
- What does the future appear to hold for these units? Is the existence of these units precarious, at the whim of first ministers and certain governments? Or do they appear have the promise of becoming institutionalized? If so, where?

Discourse and Dialogue

Policy Harmonization: Limits and Alternatives

GIANDOMENICO MAJONE

ABSTRACT *Globalization is an important reason for the current interest in the harmonization of national policies. In the European Community/Union harmonization of the national laws and policies of the member states was one of three legal techniques the Rome Treaty made available for establishing and maintaining a common market. The long history of policy harmonization in the EC/EU provides a good empirical basis for a more general analysis of the benefits and costs of a centralized approach to transnational policymaking. The main alternative to centralized harmonization is competition among different approaches to comparable policy problems.*

Harmonization and Its Modes

Harmonization may be defined as making the regulatory requirements or governmental policies of different jurisdictions identical or at least more similar. It is one response to the problems arising from policy/regulatory differences among political units; it is also one form of inter-governmental cooperation. A "harmonization claim", according to David Leebron (1996), is a normative assertion that the differences in the laws and policies of two, or more, jurisdictions should be reduced: either by assigning decisions to a common political authority; or by different countries adopting similar laws and policies, even in the absence of such a common authority. Leebron distinguishes four main types of harmonization. First, harmonization of specific rules and regulations prescribing how certain activities should be performed – e.g. pollution regulations for chemical factories can be made more similar in different countries, or different jurisdictions of the same country. Second, more general governmental policy objectives – e.g. concerning the ambient air quality standards, or minimum occupational health and safety standards to be maintained – can be harmonized. A third type of harmonization concerns certain general principles that are to be followed in policymaking. Thus, the "polluter pays principle", aiming at the internalization of pollution costs, was adopted by both the European Community and Organisation for Economic Co-operation and Development (OECD) in the 1970s. More recently, and more controversially, the European Union adopted the Precautionary Principle as the basic approach in risk regulation – a principle which was however rejected by the World Trade Organization, and by most developing and developed countries, including the US (Majone 2005: 124–142). The fourth category concerns the harmonization of structures and procedures, often as a means of reinforcing other types of harmonization. Thus the monopoly of legislative initiative enjoyed by the EU executive, the European Commission, since the 1957 Treaty of Rome, was clearly meant to facilitate (or even to make possible) the first kind of harmonization: harmonization of the national policies of the member states.

Here I am mainly interested in policy harmonization, but the distinctions made above can be quite helpful in the analysis of specific harmonization problems. On the other hand, the taxonomy presented so far assumes only one type of harmonization: ex ante harmonization, achieved by a centralized authority, or by different governments or sub-national jurisdictions. But even more important for the present argument is ex post harmonization achieved through a variety of competitive processes. In this second, ex post, sense harmonization may be viewed as an aspect of the problem of optimal policy areas.

Ex Post Harmonization through Policy Competition

In an important book on politics and public finance the Canadian economist Albert Breton (1996) argues that democratic governments compete with one another because they have to respond to their citizens' interests and preferences. In fact, inter-jurisdictional competition has been a key feature of the history of the Old Continent, with the European states system of the early modern age preserving important aspects of the cooperative competition which characterized the Middle Ages. Individuals and whole populations sometimes "voted with their feet" by shifting their allegiance to that country which was governed best. Hence the fairly rapid diffusion of policy and institutional innovations throughout the continent in the period preceding the full development of the national state (Jones 1987). Unfortunately, the prophets of European integration were too concerned with the tragic consequences of twentieth century nationalism to pay attention to the earlier history of Europe. As a consequence, their opposition to nationalism did not lead them to explore alternative ways of organizing inter-state relations, but rather to transfer as much as possible of the received national model of statehood to the supranational level. Hence their preference for positive integration, legal centralism, and ex ante harmonization of national policies at the supranational level. Quite revealing in this respect is the preference for total harmonization – i.e. for measures designed to regulate exhaustively a given problem to the exclusion of previously existing national measures – in the early stages of the integration process. The EU's harmonization bias is still evident enough to have caught the attention of Breton, who in his *Competitive Governments* criticizes the EU for what he calls its excessive policy harmonization:

> I believe that the European Union is quite stable but that the stability has been acquired by the virtual suppression of intercountry competition through excessive policy harmonization ... To prevent the occurrence of instability, competition is

minimized through the excessive harmonization of a substantial fraction of social, economic, and other policies ... If one compares the degree of harmonization in Europe with that in Canada, the United States, and other federations, one is impressed by the extent to which it is greater in Europe than in the federations. (Breton 1996: 275–276)

Today we know that even excessive harmonization has not been sufficient to ensure the stability of the EU. Indeed, one could argue that excessive harmonization has been the immediate cause of the present instability: monetary union is, after all, an extreme form of total harmonization, see below. At least since the *Cassis de Dijon* judgment[1] in 1979, attempts have been made to reduce the dependency on harmonization as the main tool of policy integration in Europe. Indeed, the principle of mutual recognition was supposed to reduce the need for ex ante, top-down harmonization, and to facilitate regulatory competition among the member states. Supposedly a cornerstone of the Single Market programme, mutual recognition requires member states to recognize regulations made by other EU members as being essentially equivalent to their own, thus allowing activities that are lawful in one member state to be freely pursued throughout the Union. In this way, a virtuous circle of regulatory competition would be stimulated, which should raise the quality of all regulation and drive out rules offering protection that consumers do not, in fact, require. The end result would be ex post harmonization, achieved through competitive processes rather than by administrative measures. However, the high hopes raised by the *Cassis de Dijon* judgment and by what appeared to be the Commission's strong endorsement of this doctrine of the EU Court of Justice were largely disappointed. For political, ideological, and bureaucratic reasons, ex post, market-driven harmonization was never allowed to seriously challenge the dominant position of centralized, top-down harmonization. While the *Cassis* doctrine was greeted enthusiastically at a time when the priority was to meet the deadline of the Single Market ("Europe '92") project, institutional and political interests militate against wholehearted support of mutual recognition and regulatory competition. Instead of viewing competition as a discovery procedure (Hayek 1984), the tendency has always been to assert that integration can be only one way to prevent a "Europe of Bits and Pieces" (Curtin 1993). In a sense, the reluctance of politicians and bureaucrats to rely on competition is understandable, since "competition is valuable only because, and so far as, its results are unpredictable and on the whole different from those which anyone has, or could have, deliberately aimed at ... the generally beneficial effects of competition must include disappointing or defeating some particular expectations or intentions" (Hayek 1984: 255).

The Open Method of Coordination (OMC), codified and endorsed by the Lisbon European Council in March 2000, was another attempt to add a competitive dimension to the traditional methods of integration. The philosophy underlying the OMC and related "soft law" methods is that each state should be encouraged to experiment on its own, and to craft solutions to fit its national context. Advocates of the new approach argue that the OMC can be effective despite – or even because of – its open-ended, non-binding, non-justiciable qualities (Trubek and Trubek 2005). In fact, the new method seems to have fallen far short of expectations even in areas where one might have presumed it to have yielded the most significant results. Many observers judge the whole OMC procedure to be too bureaucratic to stimulate genuine interstate competition.

The evidence from these two attempts to move beyond harmonization in a systematic way suggests that the notion of competitive governments is foreign to the ideology of European integration espoused by the founding fathers. It is of course true that rules on market competition have always been a key element of EU law, but a moment's reflection shows that the reason for the importance attached to such rules is strictly utilitarian: not a commitment to a genuine free-market philosophy, but the realistic assessment that it would be impossible to integrate a group of heavily regulated economies without limitations on the interventionism of the national governments (Majone 2009: 96–97). What is at any rate clear is that competition between different national approaches to economic and social regulation has played hardly any role in the European integration process. Indeed, a distinguished specialist of EU law has argued that competition among regulators is incompatible with the notion of undistorted competition in the internal European market. Hence the UK – the member state which has most consistently defended the benefits of inter-state competition – has been accused of subordinating individual rights and social protection to a free-market philosophy incompatible with the basic aspirations of the European Community/Union: "Competition between regulators on this perspective is simply incompatible with the EC's historical mission" (Weatherill 1995: 180).

In this context it is important to keep in mind that governments operating in a common market cannot compete vigorously unless the authority to make economic policy remains largely in their hands, while the supranational institutions must have the instruments to prevent the national governments using their regulatory authority to erect trade barriers against the goods and services from other member states. According to Weingast (1995), a common market, national responsibility for the economy, monitoring by the supranational level, and tight budget constraints are crucial conditions of economic development. In addition to a game-theoretic argument, this American political economist provides interesting historical evidence in support of his thesis. Thus, the enormous expansion of the American economy during the nineteenth century was based on the division of labour between the federal state and the states of the federation. The federal government was responsible for establishing and maintaining the common market, but before the 1880s it interfered little in economic affairs, while the states were the promoters and entrepreneurs of economic development. Also Louis Hartz writes in his classic study of the economic policy of the state of Pennsylvania between 1776 and 1860: "Despite the significant restrictions which the federal constitution imposed upon the states, it reserved to them, both by implication in the enumerated powers of the [federal] government and by the express provisions of the Tenth Amendment, a large authority to deal with economic issues" (Hartz 1948: 3–4). Even the stunning economic growth of modern China, according to Weingast (1995: 21–24), seems to be due to the central government's acceptance of the loss of political control over regional economic policymaking. The degree of support of decentralization among the Peking authorities led to a variety of experiments in economic development. As these proved successful, and the central government did not revoke them, they were expanded and imitated.

By way of contrast, we saw that Albert Breton came to the conclusion that in the EU inter-country competition has been virtually suppressed through excessive policy (ex ante) harmonization. More generally, the Canadian economist suggests that part of the widespread opposition to the idea that domestic governments, national and international agencies, associations of various kinds, vertical and horizontal networks, and so on, should compete among themselves derives from the notion that competition is incompatible with, even antithetical to, cooperation. Breton cogently argues that this perception is mistaken. Excluding the case of collusion, cooperation and competition can and generally do coexist, so that the presence of one is no indication of the absence of the other. In particular, the observation of cooperation and coordination does not per se disprove that the underlying determining force may be competition. If one thinks of competition not as the *state* of affairs neoclassical theory calls "perfect competition", but as an *activity* – à la Schumpeter, Hayek, and other Austrian economists who developed the model of entrepreneurial competition – then it becomes plain that "the entrepreneurial innovation that sets the competitive process in motion, the imitation that follows, and the Creative Destruction that they generate are not inconsistent with cooperative behaviour and the coordination of activities" (Breton 1996: 33). Given the appropriate competitive stimuli, political entrepreneurs, like their business counterparts, will consult with colleagues at home and abroad, collaborate with them on certain projects, harmonize various activities, and in the extreme case integrate some operations – all actions corresponding to what is generally meant by cooperation and coordination.

Exit and Voice as Alternative Mechanisms of Competition

As was mentioned in the preceding section, inter-jurisdictional competition in medieval and early modern Europe was activated by exit: individuals and whole populations sometimes "voted with their feet" by shifting their allegiance to that city or country which was governed best; hence the fairly rapid diffusion of policy and institutional innovations throughout the continent in the period preceding the full development of the national state. However, the rise of the modern welfare state has significantly increased the economic and social costs of the exit option. In advanced modern economies competition stimulated by exit will take place mostly at the sub-national level, between different communities. According to the so-called Tiebout hypothesis, inter-jurisdictional competition results in communities supplying the goods and services individuals demand, and producing them in an efficient manner. In Tiebout's model communities below the optimum size seek to attract new residents while those above optimum size do the opposite. As a result, the population distributes itself in such a way that in each community all residents tend to have identical, or at least similar, preferences. The idea of horizontal intergovernmental competition seems to have entered the literature of public finance and public choice with Tiebout's (1956) seminal paper on local public goods. But, Breton (1996) points out, the effectiveness of the entry and exit mechanism for intergovernmental competition may be quite weak beyond the local level because of the limited mobility of persons across national borders, as well as for other more technical reasons. Therefore, the notion of inter-jurisdictional competition has to be extended to apply to situations where Tiebout's potential entry and exit mechanisms do not work effectively, for instance because mobility is limited by language and/or cultural and social cleavages, as in the EU. One such extension is Salmon's external benchmark mechanism. This extension consists in assuming that the citizens of a jurisdiction can use information about the goods and services supplied in other jurisdictions, or in other comparable countries, as a benchmark to evaluate the performance of their own government; and that the same citizens decide to support or to oppose their government on the basis of that assessment. The first assumption corresponds, more or less, to the idea of information exchange also underlying the EU's Open Method of Coordination, but since national parliaments are largely excluded from the OMC process, European citizens are unable in practice to use information about the performance of other member states to induce their government to improve its own performance.

It should also be noted that in any jurisdiction there always are many subgroups whose preferences with respect to certain goods and services, and corresponding policies, are the same as those of subgroups in other jurisdictions, even in other countries. This observation has two significant implications. First, as Breton points out, one can assume that the stimulus to compete based on external benchmarks exists. The strength of the mechanism will naturally depend on the ability of citizens to make inter-governmental performance comparisons. To quote Breton (1996: 234–235): "The existence of 'iron' or 'bamboo' curtains – measures designed to ensure that policy implemented elsewhere is not used as external norms to evaluate internal performance – is evidence that the Salmon mechanism is not only operative but powerful". The second implication is that any discussion about the benefits and costs of policy harmonization – the main costs resulting from the fact that the harmonized policy is a sort of average and as such it may match the preferences of some subgroup only in a very rough sense – must start from the realization that policy harmonization can take place in the context of two very different modes of integration: by territory or by function.

Functional vs. Territorial Integration

A functional approach to international integration was advocated by David Mitrany in the 1940s. A territorial union, Mitrany argued, "would bind together some interests which are not of common concern to the group, while it inevitably cuts asunder some interests of common concern to the group and those outside it". To avoid such "twice-arbitrary surgery" it is necessary to proceed by "binding together those interests which are common, where they are common, and to the extent to which they are common". Thus the essential principle of a functional organization of international activities "is that activities would be selected specifically and organized separately, each according to its nature, to the conditions under which it has to operate, and to the needs of the moment" (citations in Eilstrup-Sangiovanni 2006: 57–58). On the other hand, Mitrany was sceptical about the advantages of political union. His main objection to schemes for continental unions was that "the closer the union the more inevitable would it be dominated by the more powerful member" (in Eilstrup-Sangiovanni 2006: 47). This point, which has been largely overlooked by later writers on European integration, is directly linked to the discussion of Germany as a potential (if reluctant) hegemon (Majone 2014: chapter 8).

Mitrany's ideas were resurrected and applied to the case of European integration by Ralph Dahrendorf in the 1970s. While still a member of the European Commission, Dahrendorf wrote a series of newspaper articles (published in 1973 under the *nom de plume* Weiland Europa) in which he severely criticized the European institutions and their strategy of "integration by stealth" – political integration under the guise of economic integration. The first of the four principles he advocated as a means of accelerating the process of political integration was that it is more important to solve problems than to create institutions. This was a clear, if implicit, criticism of federalists like Paul-Henri Spaak and Jean Monnet, for whom what mattered most was the creation of European institutions – regardless of what these institutions might do. It was his third principle that expressed the idea of integration *à la carte*, meaning that "everyone does what he wants and ... no one must participate in everything", a situation that "though far from ideal is surely much better than avoiding anything that cannot be cooked in a single pot" (cited in Gillingham 2003: 91–92). Concretely this meant that there would be common European policies in areas where the member states have a common interest, but not otherwise. This, said Dahrendorf, must become the general rule rather than the exception if we wish to prevent continuous demands for special treatment, destroying in the long run the coherence of the entire system – a prescient anticipation of the present practice of moving ahead by granting opt-outs from treaty obligations. Dahrendorf's suggestion that under the mode of integration he envisaged "everyone does what he wants" should not be taken literally, of course: even a mere free-trade area presupposes some generally accepted rules. The key point is that "no one must participate in everything"; hence integration *à la carte*, although it presupposes some general rules accepted by everybody, does not assume a common final destination – not even in the sense of an open-ended process of "ever closer union". Beyond the common agreement to form, say, a customs union with elements of a common market, member states would be free to cooperate in specific functional areas on the basis of shared interests.

Neither Mitrany nor Dahrendorf based their ideas of functional integration on formal theory. Such a theory is available today; it is the economic theory of clubs, originally developed by James Buchanan (1965), and later applied by Alessandra Casella (1996) to study the interaction between expanding markets and the provision of product standards. Casella argues, inter alia, that if we think of standards as being developed by communities of users, then "opening trade will modify not only the standards but also the coalitions that express them. As markets ... expand and become more heterogeneous, different coalitions will form across national borders, and their number will rise" (Casella 1996: 149). The relevance of these arguments extends well beyond the narrow area of standard-setting. In fact, Casella's emphasis on heterogeneity as the main force against harmonization and for the multiplication of "clubs" suggests an attractive theoretical basis for the mode of integration advocated by Dahrendorf and Mitrany. To see this more clearly we need to recall a few definitions and key concepts from Buchanan's theory of clubs.

Public (or collective) goods, such as national defence or environmental quality, are characterized by two properties: first, it does not cost anything for an additional individual to enjoy the benefits of the public goods once they are produced (joint-supply property); and, second, it is difficult or impossible to exclude individuals from the enjoyment of such goods (non-excludability). A "*club good*" is a public good from whose benefits individuals may be excluded; an association established to provide an excludable public good is a *club*. Two elements determine the optimal size of a club. One is the cost of producing the club good – in a large club this cost is shared over more members. The second element is the cost to each club member of the good not meeting precisely his or her individual needs or preferences. The latter cost is likely to increase with the size of the club. The optimal size is determined by the point where the marginal benefit from the addition of one new member – i.e. the reduction in the per capita cost of producing the good – equals the marginal cost caused by a mismatch between the characteristics of the good and the preferences of the individual club members. If the preferences and the technologies for the provision of club goods are such that the number of clubs that can be formed in a society of given size is large, then an efficient allocation of such excludable public goods through the voluntary association of individuals into clubs is possible. With many alternative clubs available each individual can guarantee herself a satisfactory balance of benefits and costs, since any attempt to discriminate against her would induce her exit into a competing club. The important question is: what happens as the complexity of the society increases, perhaps as the result of the integration of previously separate markets? It has been shown that under plausible hypotheses the number of clubs tends to increase as well, since the greater diversity of needs and preferences makes it efficient to produce a broader range of club goods, such as standards. The two main forces driving the results of Casella's model are heterogeneity among the economic agents, and transaction costs – the costs of trading under different standards. Harmonization is the optimal strategy when transaction costs are high enough, relative to gross returns, to prevent a partition of the community of users into two clubs that reflect their needs more precisely. Hence harmonization occurs in response to market integration, but possibly only for an intermediate range of productivity in the production of standards, and when heterogeneity is not too great.

Think now of a society composed not of individuals, but of independent states. Associations of independent states (alliances, leagues, confederations) are typically voluntary, and their members are exclusively entitled to enjoy certain benefits produced by the association, so that the economic theory of clubs is applicable to this situation. In fact, since excludability is more easily enforced in the context envisaged here, many goods that are purely public at the national level (e.g. national defence) become club goods at the international level (Majone 2005: 20–21). The club goods in question could be collective security, policy coordination, common technical standards – or a common currency: several proposals on how to resolve the euro crisis boil down to changing the nature of monetary union, from a public good to a club good. In these and many other cases, countries unwilling to share the costs are usually excluded from the benefits of inter-state cooperation in a particular project. Now, as an association of states expands, becoming more diverse in its preferences, the cost of uniformity in the provision of such goods – e.g. the total harmonization of monetary policies – can escalate dramatically. The theory predicts an increase in the number of voluntary associations to meet the increased demand of club goods more precisely tailored to the different requirements of various subsets of more homogeneous states. In sum, the key idea of the theory of clubs is that aggregate welfare is maximized when the variety in preferences is matched by a corresponding variety of institutional arrangements.

But of course clubs, in the sense of the theory sketched here, need not be formed by governments. In fact, the theory explains why a number of important tasks which used to be assigned to central governments are today performed by private, increasingly transnational, organizations. Although there is a strong historical link between standardization and the emergence of the sovereign territorial state (Spruyt 1994), current views of standardization have changed radically as a result of the advance of globalization, the development of technology, and the growing variety and sophistication of technical standards. Standards are indeed public goods – in the sense that they fulfil specific functions deemed desirable by the community that shares them – but this does not mean that they must be established by government fiat. A good standard must reflect the needs, preferences, and resources of the community of users, rather than some centrally defined vision of the "common interest".

Let me now come back to the issue of policy harmonization in the EU. In preparation for the "big bang" enlargement at the beginning of the new century there was a determined attempt to minimize the risks entailed by a high level of heterogeneity among the member states. The more optimistic Euro-leaders – among whom figured prominently members of the German government and of the European Commission – claimed that geographical widening and policy deepening were not just compatible, but mutually reinforcing aspects of the integration process. Other European leaders who neither shared this view, nor wished to follow the euro-sceptics in supporting enlargement as a way of preventing further "deepening", tended to view enlargement primarily as an organizational or managerial problem, to be solved by better institutional design and more effective decision-making procedures. What all leaders were reluctant to admit, at least in public, was that each enlargement of the EU necessarily changes the calculus of the benefits and the costs of integration – the reduction of transaction costs made possible by harmonized rules, on the one hand, and the welfare losses entailed by rules that are less precisely tailored to the resources and preferences of each member state, on the other. To repeat an important point: as long as resources and preferences are fairly similar across countries, the advantages of common rules are likely to exceed the welfare losses caused by harmonization, but when heterogeneity exceeds a certain threshold the reverse will be true. There are indications that in the present EU this threshold has been exceeded. This may explain the growing opposition to harmonization, even of the minimum type; and also the current popularity of voluntary methods of coordination and cooperation, and other "soft" modes of governance.

Normative Arguments in Favour of Policy Harmonization

So far I have considered policy harmonization primarily from an efficiency perspective: the maximization of the welfare of individuals. One of the standard arguments in favour of centralized harmonization of national social policies and regulations, however, is the need to prevent the possibility that the member states take advantage of the Single European Market (or, more generally, of globalization) to engage in "social dumping", or in a competitive lowering of social standards, in order to attract foreign investments. Indeed, many, perhaps most, measures of positive integration in the areas of health, safety, and environmental regulation have been justified by the argument that without EU-level harmonization member states would engage in a socially undesirable "race to the bottom". The notion of social dumping is notoriously vague. In a report entitled *The Social Dimension of the Internal Market*, published in 1988, the European Commission defined social dumping in the following terms: "the fear that national social progress will be blocked or, worse, that there will be downward pressure on social conditions (wages, levels of social protection, fringe benefits, etc.) in the most advanced countries, simply because of the competition ... from certain countries, where average labour costs are significantly lower" (cited in Sapir 1996: 559). A vivid demonstration that this fear was well-founded seemed to be provided in 1993, when the US-owned domestic appliances group Hoover Europe, faced with the need to close either its factory in Scotland or one in the Dijon region of France, decided to transfer the production of the French plant to Scotland. One of the reasons for the company's decision was a new collective agreement at the Scottish plant, where unions agreed to a wage freeze, greater flexibility, and a ban on strikes. The French workers and their government reacted angrily, protesting that what was involved was a British attempt to compete on low labour costs and lax social standards – "social dumping", as the French Prime Minister denounced the day after Hoover's choice became known. Intervention by the European Commission, headed at the time by the formidable Jacques Delors, himself a Frenchman, was demanded. But Delors could do little more than express sympathy when, at the peak of the crisis, he received a delegation of workers from Hoover France. The truth, he pointed out, was that differentials in labour costs between member states could not be eliminated, or even mitigated, by existing EU social legislation. Neither the Social Charter nor the Protocol and Agreement on Social Policy annexed to the Treaty of Maastricht, even if they had been ratified by the United Kingdom at the time, could have prevented Hoover from relocating from France to the United Kingdom in order to lower its labour costs. Only EU-wide minimum wages could have helped to reduce differentials across member states, but the Union has no competence to legislate on such matters. Besides, the process of relocation is a normal, and desirable, phenomenon in an integrated market. The objective of the Single European Market project – Jacques Delors' main, if partial, achievement – was precisely to facilitate the mobility of the factors of production. Ironically, at the same time as the Hoover decision to transfer production to Scotland, the Swiss multinational Nestlé announced that it planned to transfer part of its operations from Scotland to France!

An argument which is often used to justify centralized harmonization of social standards, not only in the EU but in most federal states, is that harmonization is needed to prevent member states from competing for industry by offering social standards that are too lax relative to the preferences of their citizens. Such competition is said to lower the level of social protection that states would pursue if they did not face international or inter-jurisdictional competition. It is not difficult to show, however, that the race-to-the-bottom argument is theoretically unsound. Following Revesz (1992) we may take the simplest case of two states that are identical in all relevant aspects, including (say) the level of environmental quality desired by their citizens. State 1 initially sets its standard of pollution control at the level that would be optimal if it were a completely independent country rather than member of a federation. State 2 decides to set a less stringent standard, and we assume that industrial migration from State 1 to State 2 will ensue. To recover some of the lost jobs and tax revenues, the first state in turn considers competing on its own standard, and lowers it accordingly. The process of adjustment continues until an equilibrium is reached. The equilibrium outcome will be that the two states will not have experienced any net inflow or outflow of industry, but will have adopted suboptimal standards that do not correspond to the preferences of their citizens. In this sense a "race to the bottom" may be considered a case of the "prisoners' dilemma", where both players will find it convenient to defect in every round of the (finitely repeated) game, even though both would gain by honouring their commitment. If the two states in our example could enter into a cooperative agreement to adopt the optimally stringent standard, they could maximize social welfare without engaging in "unfair" competition for industry – assuming that the agreement is enforceable, and that preferences for environmental quality are exactly the same in the two jurisdictions. If the agreement is enforceable, for example because the two jurisdictions are part of the same federation, the suboptimal outcome could be avoided if the environmental standards were harmonized at the higher level, *provided* the harmonized standard were equal to the level the two jurisdictions would find independently optimal. Article 95(3) of the EC Treaty attempted to offer such a solution, at least for the richer members of the Union, stating that in proposing harmonization measures concerning health, safety, environmental protection, and consumer protection, the Commission "will take as a base a high level of protection ...Within their respective powers, the European Parliament and the Council will also seek to achieve this objective".

The proviso about the harmonized standards corresponding to the actual preferences of the member states is crucial. If states have different preferences for environmental or other social standards, as is to be expected in a highly heterogeneous Union, then standards that maximize aggregate welfare will have to be different. A uniform European rule, even one that sets a minimum standard and allows the member states to adopt more stringent national standards, will not be optimal – unless the minimum standard is low enough to be exceeded by all the national standards, in which case it is practically irrelevant. So it is quite possible that even if there is a race to the bottom, a European standard might still reduce aggregate social welfare. As a matter of fact, there is no convincing empirical evidence of a race to the bottom in social standards, even at the international level. For example, econometric analyses of trade patterns failed to find evidence of industrial migration to countries with lower environmental standards. Several possible reasons for this have been offered: corporations doing business in a variety of jurisdictions find it more cost-effective to operate according to the most stringent regulations rather than designing different production processes for each location; environmental compliance costs are too small, relative to other costs, and too similar across countries to weigh heavily in location decisions; multinational corporations believe that most countries are just a few years (less than the lifetime of a factory) behind the most advanced countries in environmental-standards stringency, so that it is better to invest now than be forced to retrofit later (Majone 2005: 153–154).

Especially the last reason – the fact that environmental quality is a "superior" good, the demand for which grows as incomes increase – makes the race-to-the-bottom argument highly implausible in the case of economically advanced countries. Thus, a detailed study on the future of the European "Social Model" in the global economy found that "[s]o far, there are few signs that [a] race to the bottom is occurring; rather the race has been in the other direction, with the southern countries (in particular, Portugal) upgrading to northern European levels of [social] expenditure" (Ferrera et al. 2001: 174). Moreover, the race-to-the-bottom argument, is not only theoretically weak and empirically unsupported, but also, as Revesz points out, incomplete. That is because the argument fails to consider the existence of alternative means of attracting foreign direct investments, other than by lowering social standards. The "race model" implicitly assumes that states compete over one variable only, e.g. environmental quality or labour costs. But it seems more reasonable to assume that if harmonization prevents competition on the social dimension, then states would try to compete over other variables, e.g. lower taxation of corporate profits. To avoid the possibility of any form of inter-state competition, the central regulators would have to harmonize all forms of national rules. This would amount to eliminating any trace of national autonomy: the race-to-the-bottom becomes, in the end, an argument for centralization and against national sovereignty.

Naturally, the fear of social dumping or, generally, of a race to the bottom is not the sole rationale for harmonization. A more plausible argument for EU-wide harmonization of social standards is the need to dismantle non-tariff barriers to trade within the Single Market. Even in this respect, however, ex ante, top-down harmonization probably has been pushed too far. A number of case studies have shown that the costs imposed by social standards are only a minor consideration in the location decisions of large multinational firms: quality of infrastructure, education of the labour force, or political stability are much more important influencing factors. Today it is also recognized that an initial difference in health, safety, or environmental standards need not distort international trade;

rather, trade should lead to their eventual convergence. The reason is that social standards are positively correlated with the standard of living. Hence, as wealth grows as a result of trade, the endogenous demand for higher social standards grows as well.

The Competitive Advantage of Nations

In the EU centralized policy harmonization was always seen as an important step towards political union. In turn, political union was and is seen as a protecting wall built around a group of countries that are said to be too small to count on a world scale, and economically and demographically too weak to take care of themselves. Thinking of the EU as an international actor, Commission President Barroso, in an article in *The Observer* of 13 November 2011, wrote that the crisis of monetary union confronts Europeans with the choice: "either unite or face irrelevance". The status quo will not do and the EU must "move on to something new and better". Three noted scholars are also worried about the international role of Europe and, even more, about the future of the European welfare state:

> The peoples of Europe must learn that they can only preserve their welfare-state model of society and the diversity of their nation-state cultures by joining forces and working together. They must pool their resources if they want to exert any kind of influence on the international political agenda and the solution of global problems. To abandon European unification now would be to quit the world stage for good. (Bofinger et al. 2012)

The standard formula to overcome the present difficulties is "more Europe" – pretty much along the lines that have been followed for more than half a century. Such an approach diverts attention from the structural flaws of the European construction and the many errors of the past. It also attaches too much importance to formal powers, and not enough to flexibility, to the benefits of institutions and policies tailored to specific national needs, to shared values and common traditions. Joining forces and working together can produce results only if there is general agreement about the goals and the best means for achieving them, which is certainly not the case in the EU of today. Above all, the advocates of "more Europe" ignore Tocqueville's warning that the real weakness of confederal governments increases in direct proportion to the growth of their nominal powers (Majone 2014: chapter 9). This being the situation, as long as the peoples of Europe are not willing to support something like a full-fledged federal solution, we must still rely on the problem-solving capacity of the national states and hence must avoid too rigid limits on their freedom of action.

Indeed, Michael Porter, of the Harvard Business School, has convincingly argued that neither globalization nor European integration have reduced the central role of the national state in economic development and innovation. To support his thesis, Porter starts from the empirical observation that the leaders in particular industries and segments of industries tend to be concentrated in a few nations and sustain their competitive advantage for many decades. This competitive advantage is created and sustained in a highly localized (national or even sub-national) process:

> Differences in national economic structures, values, cultures, institutions, and histories contribute profoundly to competitive success …While globalization of

competition might appear to make the nation less important, instead it seems to make it more so. With fewer impediments to trade to shelter uncompetitive domestic firms and industries, the home nation takes on growing significance because it is the source of the skills and technology that underpin competitive advantage ... The home base [for successful global competitors] is the nation in which the essential competitive advantages of the enterprise are created and sustained. It is where a firm's strategy is set and the core product and process technology (broadly defined) are created and maintained. (Porter 1990: 19)

These propositions are supported by an impressive amount of statistical and descriptive material showing how a nation provides the environment in which its firms in a particular industry are able to improve and innovate faster than foreign rivals. The sample includes ten important trading nations – from Asia (Japan, Singapore, Korea), Europe (the United Kingdom, Germany, Italy, Denmark, Sweden, Switzerland), and the United States – and over 100 industries. The theoretical core of Porter's approach is a critique of the static (neoclassical) view of competition in which a nation's factors of production are fixed and firms deploy such factors in industries where they will produce the greatest return. In actual competition, Porter points out, the essential character is innovation and change: "Instead of simply maximizing within fixed constraints, the question is how firms can gain competitive advantage from changing the constraints" (Porter 1990: 21). To expand the range of feasible choice, however, both firms and national governments must enjoy considerable freedom of action. Given sufficient freedom of action, even small countries can achieve extraordinary economic results.

Thus, by the early decades of the twentieth century Switzerland, with a population of about 7 million, had emerged as an industrial country of importance far beyond its small size, and in the post-World War II period it became one of the richest industrialized countries. By some measures it actually had the highest per capita income in the world by the 1960s. Swiss companies, among them Nestlé, Sandoz, Ciba-Geigy, and Lindt, are among the most global of any country, and generally employ far more people outside the country than in Switzerland. The Swiss case, writes Porter (1990: 307–308), "vividly illustrates how a small nation, without a large home market as in Japan or America, can nevertheless be a successful global competitor in many important industries. Switzerland is also an economy that has continuously upgraded itself to support a rising standard of living". Also Sweden, not significantly larger than Switzerland in terms of population, is the home base of a striking number of large, global companies. Its economy supports a very high standard of living, as well as one of the most highly developed welfare states in the world.

The American business economist concludes that nations enjoy a competitive advantage in industries that draw most heavily on unique elements of their histories and characters. Moreover, the influence of the national environment becomes even more vital as competition becomes more knowledge-based. This environment shapes the way opportunities are perceived, how specialized skills and resources are developed, and the pressures on firms to mobilize resources in rapid and efficient ways: "It is the creation of knowledge and the capacity to act, which are the result of a process that is highly localized, that determines competitive success". In sum, "globalization makes nations more, not less, important" (Porter 1990: 736). Such a view of the competitive advantage of nations contradicts the one-size-fits-all philosophy and the emphasis on the harmonization of national policies which have characterized the process of European integration since the 1950s. More recent research provides additional support for the thesis that economic development is possible only by preserving and even strengthening the policymaking autonomy of the national governments.

As Dani Rodrik, an economist teaching at Harvard's Kennedy School of Government, writes: "Markets are most developed and most effective in generating wealth when they are backed by solid governmental institutions. *Markets and states are complements,* not substitutes, as simplistic economic accounts would have it" (Rodrik 2011: 16; italics in the original). Analysing a huge set of economic data from both advanced and developing countries, Rodrik found a strong positive correlation between a country's exposure to international trade and the size of its government. In other words, "governments had grown the largest in those economies that were most exposed to international markets" (Rodrik 2011: 17). Thus countries heavily engaged in international trade, like Sweden or the Netherlands, devote the highest proportion of their resources to the public sector – between 55 and 60 per cent of GDP. How can we explain this rather counterintuitive finding? Rodrik considers many possible explanations and in the end concludes that the evidence points strongly towards the social insurance motive: "People demand compensation against risk when their economies are more exposed to international economic forces; and governments respond by erecting broader safety nets ... If you want markets to expand, you need governments to do the same" (Rodrik 2011: 18). In the decades following the Great Depression of the 1930s, industrial states erected a wide array of social protections – unemployment compensation and other labour markets interventions, health insurance, family support, etc. – that mitigate demand for cruder forms of protection such as sheltering the economy behind high tariff walls, as was done during the Great Depression. This is the reason why today protectionism can be kept under control, in America as in Europe.

The European paradox is that while the EU does not have either the financial resources or the legal powers to provide similar compensations against the risks of globalization, at the same time it pretends to limit the autonomy of the member states by imposing increasingly stringent constraints on national policymaking. Since the very beginning of European integration the emphasis has been on the top-down harmonization of the laws and policies of the member states rather than on a healthy competition between different national approaches to problem solving. As a consequence, inter-jurisdictional competition has hardly played a role in the integration process. Indeed, according to some legal experts, such as Stephen Weatherill (1995), competition among national regulators is incompatible with the notion of undistorted competition in the internal European market (see above).

Harmonization and Regional Integration

The importance of understanding the advantages and limits of policy harmonization has been significantly enhanced by the recent worldwide diffusion of regional integration. The two-volume collection of economic and legal analyses of various aspects of harmonization, titled *Fair Trade and Harmonization* and edited by Bhagwati and Hudec in 1996, is a good example of the international relevance of this topic. The revival of regional integration in the 1980s – which Jagdish Bhagwati (1993) labelled the "Second Regionalism", in contrast to the "First Regionalism" of the 1960s – raises a number of issues, starting with the question why the first regionalism failed (with the notable exception of the European Economic Community), while this time regionalism is likely to endure. The conversion of the United States to regionalism is of major significance in this respect. As the key advocate of multilateralism through the post-war years, its decision to travel the regional integration route seems to have tilted the balance at the margin from multilateralism to regionalism. A second important factor has been the widening and deepening of the European Community/Union. Thus, the fear that European investments would be diverted to Eastern Europe was cited by President Salinas of Mexico as a factor decisively pushing him toward the North American Free Trade Agreement (NAFTA). He felt that a free trade area embracing all of North America would enable Mexico to get the investments needed from the United States and Canada, as well as from Japan (Bhagwati 1993; Vega Cànovas 2010). In his comment on Bhagwati's (1993) article, Robert Baldwin (1993: 54) considered the likelihood of a gradual drift of the North American regional bloc to include a number of other Latin American countries. This enlargement would be driven by pressures from these countries to tap into the US market but another important factor that might drive the expansion of an American-centred bloc, according to Baldwin (1993), "would be the growing influence of the European Community in trade, macroeconomic and foreign policy matters. U.S. political and economic leaders may adopt the view that it is necessary to expand such a bloc in order to match the increasing political and economic power of the Community" (p. 55).

A distinguishing characteristic of the new regionalism is the movement from shallow integration – integration based on the removal of barriers to trade at the border, and limited coordination of national policies – to deeper integration, concerned with behind-the-border issues such as regulation of services and environmental and labour standards. This feature of the new regionalism has tempted a number of analysts, such as Robert Baldwin, to envisage a "European" model of the future of regional integration. According to this model "intensified economic integration implies stronger, more formal institutions that become wider and wider in scope. Institutions become more effective as they become more 'state-like'" (Kahler 1995: 19). In reality, far from adopting the EC/EU model, the new or revived regional groups are seldom supported by significant supranational institutions or elaborate mechanisms for common decision-making. This is true also of regional organizations designed to be more than free trade areas or customs unions. Thus, MERCOSUR (Mercado Comùn del Sur) was established by Brazil, Argentina, Paraguay, and Uruguay in 1995 with the objective of establishing a full common market in goods, capital, and people. However, executive power within MERCOSUR is with the national governments rather than with a European-style Commission. The highest decision-making body is the MERCOSUR Council, made up of the foreign and finance ministers of the four countries.

Even more striking (because more successful) is the Australia–New Zealand Closer Economic Relations Trade Agreement (ANZCERTA), which despite its ambitious aims of deeper integration, including full liberalization of trade in services and harmonization of regulatory practices, "is almost defiantly lacking in formal institutional development" (Kahler 1995: 108). ANZCERTA provides strong support for the thesis, espoused by a number of distinguished economists, that ambitious programmes of trade liberalization, including behind-the-border policies, do not require the support of significant supranational institutions, elaborate mechanisms for common decision-making, or even extensive ex ante policy harmonization. Thus the economic agreement between Australia and New Zealand is the clearest example of a model of regional integration that is explicitly alternative to the EU model. After the late 1980s, ANZCERTA entered a very ambitious phase in dealing with behind-the-border barriers to trade and issues of deep integration. By 1990 nearly all barriers to a single market were removed. Harmonization took place in regulatory practices, customs procedures, government purchasing, and technical barriers to trade.

In terms of economic integration, the Common Market of South America (MERCOSUR) has been much less successful than either NAFTA or ANZCERTA. According to some analysts this is due, at least in part, to the reluctance of Brazil to use its economic and political position as the regional leader to assume active regional leadership (Mattli 1999). As an increasingly influential member of the BRIC (Brazil, Russia, India, China) group of countries, however, Brazil may be willing to play a more active role in the near future. On the other hand, it seems unlikely that it will abandon its staunch opposition to any plan to accept for MERCOSUR anything like a EU-style Commission or supranational courts, not to mention a common currency and other forms of total policy harmonization.

In sum, despite repeated suggestions to the effect that "the study of economic integration has been inspired if not dominated by the European example" (Pelkmans 1997: 2), the empirical evidence points to the fact that the European example has elicited defensive reactions rather than emulative responses. In terms of comparative regionalism, the EU appears be the outlier rather than the model. The emphasis on process rather than concrete results, as well as the deep ambiguity about ends, go a long way towards explaining the lack of attraction of European-style regional integration.

Traditionally, the alleged comparative advantage of the EU model with respect to other regional organizations has been attributed to the extent of the powers delegated to the supranational institutions. But a high level of supranational institutionalization entails high transaction costs, so that in terms of the *net* benefits of integration the superiority of the European model is far from obvious. The results achieved by regional organizations such as NAFTA and ANZCERTA show that extensive economic integration is possible without elaborate institutional and legal superstructures, and with limited policy harmonization. Distinguished economists, such as Harry Johnson (Johnson 1958), had argued the same point in the early days of the European Economic Community, without however influencing the public discourse. Unless we are willing to assume that the founding fathers of communitarian Europe were either naïve or uninformed we must conclude that the rationale behind the unique institutional development of the European supranational institutions was political rather than economic.

The problem is that a politically integrated Europe, in the sense in which "political integration" is commonly understood today, was and continues to be an elitist project. In the course of more than half a century of integration efforts a certain Europeanization of intellectual, economic, and political elites has taken place, yet this process has hardly touched the vast majority of European citizens. All attempts to induce a transfer of loyalties from the national to the supranational level – not only by propaganda and cultural actions but, more concretely, by such measures as the direct election of the European Parliament, various social policy measures, including the "welfare state for farmers" represented by the Common Agriculture Policy, or policies of regional aid – failed completely in this respect, when they did not increase the degree of conflict among the member states of the EU. In the early stages of integration the reaction of the Euro-elites to this unsatisfactory situation was to claim that popular support was not, after all, necessary. Thus Ernst Haas and his neo-functionalist school argued that the bureaucratized nature of European states implies that all crucial decisions are made by elites: public policymakers, as well as economic elites, trade unions, professional associations, business lobbies, etc. Public opinion at large, on the other hand, was deemed to be unimportant. The basic problem for the neo-functionalists, but also for some political leaders, was not how to "Europeanize the masses", but how "to make Europe without Europeans" (Schmitter 2005, p. 255) Thus Paul-Henri Spaak, Belgian political leader and ardent federalist, maintained that supranational institutions had become indispensable for peace and prosperity in West Europe, regardless of what those institutions might be or do. "For me", he once told a group of journalists, "everything which tends towards European organizations is good" (cited in Milward 1992: 324).

Unfortunately neo-functionalist scholars and integrationist leaders alike overestimated the effectiveness of supranational institutions. The superior problem-solving capacity of these institutions – a superiority assumed a priori rather than supported by concrete evidence – was supposed to produce a sufficient normative basis for the integration project by inducing the progressive transfer of the loyalties and political demands of social groups from the national to the European level. Since the 1970s, however, the effectiveness of the supranational institutions has been increasingly questioned. Today most opinion surveys show that the supranational institutions in Brussels and Frankfurt are increasingly perceived less as potential sources of solutions than as causes of some of the problems that most concern the citizens of the EU. In addition, the available evidence supports the growing conviction that an ever-widening and deepening integration process has proved impotent to arrest the decline of Europe's economy relative to its major competitors. What is increasingly questioned is less the general idea of integration than the particular integration method followed so far. As discussed above, a promising alternative approach to regional integration is based on a functional, rather than territorial, approach. And on inter-jurisdictional competition rather than ex ante harmonization.

Note

1. The Cassis de Dijon judgment upholds the principle of mutual recognition of national rules in the sense that goods which are legally produced and marketed in one EU country must also be permitted in the other EU countries.

References

Baldwin, R., 1993, Comments on Bhagwati "Regionalism and multilateralism: an overview", in: J. De Melo and A. Panagariya (Eds) *New Dimensions in Regional Integration* (Cambridge: Cambridge University Press), pp. 54–56.
Bhagwati, J., 1993, Regionalism and multilateralism: an overview, in: J. De Melo, and A. Panagariya, (Eds) *New Dimensions in Regional Integration* (Cambridge: Cambridge University Press),pp.22–50.
Bhagwati, J. N. and Hudec, R. E. (Eds), 1996, *Fair Trade and Harmonization*, (Cambridge, MA: The MIT Press).
Bofinger, P., Habermas, J. and Nida-Ruemelin, J. (2012) Einspruch gegen die Fassandendemokratie (Protest against a would-be democracy), *Frankfurter Allgemeine Zeitung* 4 August.
Breton, A., 1996, *Competitive Governments*, (Cambridge: Cambridge University Press).
Buchanan, J. M., 1965, An economic theory of clubs. *Economica*, **32**(1), pp.1–14.
Casella, A., 1996, Free trade and evolving standards, in: J. N. Bhagwati and R. E. Hudec (Eds) *Fair Trade and Harmonization*, Vol. 1. (Cambridge, MA: The MIT Press), pp.119–156.
Curtin, D., 1993, The constitutional structure of the union: A Europe of bits and pieces'. *Common Market Law Review*, **30**(1), pp.17–69.

Eilstrup-Sangiovanni, M., 2006, *Debates on European Integration*, (New York: Palgrave).
Ferrera, M., Hemerijck, A. and Rhodes, M., 2001, The future of the European 'social model' in the global economy. *Journal of Comparative Policy Analysis*, **3**(2), pp.163–190.
Gillingham, J., 2003, *European Integration, 1950–2003*, (Cambridge: Cambridge University Press).
Hartz, L., 1948, *Economic Policy and Democratic Thought*, (Cambridge, MA: Harvard University Press).
Hayek, F., 1984, Competition as discovery procedure, in: C. Nishiyama and K. R. Leube (Eds) *The Essence of Hayek* (Stanford, CA: Hoover Institution Press), pp.254–265.
Johnson, H. G., 1958, The gains from freer trade with Europe: an estimate. *The Manchester School*, **26**(3), pp.247–255.
Jones, E. L., 1987, *The European Miracle: Environments, Economies and Geopolitics in the History of Europe and Asia*, 2nd ed. (New York: Cambridge University Press).
Kahler, M., 1995, *International Institutions and the Political Economy of Integration*, (Washington, DC: The Brookings Institution).
Leebron, D. W., 1996, Lying down with Procrustes: An analysis of harmonization claims. in: J. N. Bhagwati and R. E. Hudec (Eds) *Fair Trade and Harmonization* (Cambridge, MA: The MIT Press), pp.41–118.
Majone, G., 2005, *Dilemmas of European Integration*, (Oxford: Oxford University Press).
Majone, G., 2009, *Europe as the Would-Be World Power: The EU at Fifty*, (Cambridge: Cambridge University Press).
Majone, G., 2014, *Rethinking the Union of Europe Post-Crisis: Has Integration Gone Too Far?*, (Cambridge: Cambridge University Press).
Mattli, W., 1999, *The Logic of Regional Integration*, (Cambridge: Cambridge University Press).
Milward, A. S., 1992, *The European Rescue of the Nation State*, (London: Routledge).
Pelkmans, J., 2006, *European integration: methods and economic analysis*. (Pearson Education).
Porter, M. E., 1990, *The Competitive Advantage of Nations*, (New York: The Free Press).
Revesz, R. L., 1992, Rehabilitating interstate competition: Rethinking the 'race-to-the-bottom' rationale for federal environmental regulation. *New York University Law Review*, **67**, pp.1210–1254.
Rodrik, D., 2011, *The Globalization Paradox*, (Oxford: Oxford University Press).
Sapir, A., 1996, Trade liberalization and the harmonization of social policies: Lessons from European integration. in: J. N. Bhagwati and R. E. Hudec (Eds) *Fair Trade and Harmonization*, Vol. 1. (Cambridge, MA: The MIT Press), pp.543–570.
Schmitter, P. C., 2005, Ernst B. Haas and the legacy of neofunctionalism. *Journal of European Public Policy*, **12**(2), pp.255–272.
Spruyt, H., 1994, *The Sovereign State and Its Competitors*, (Princeton, NJ: Princeton University Press).
Tiebout, C. M., 1956, A pure theory of local expenditures. *The Journal of Political Economy*, **64**(5), pp.416–424.
Trubek, D. M. and Trubek, L. G., 2005, Hard and soft law in the construction of social Europe: The role of the open method of co-ordination. *European Law Journal*, **11**(3), pp.343–364.
Vega Cànovas, G., 2010, *El Tratado De Libre Comercio En America Del Norte*, (Mexico D.F: El Colegio de Mexico).
Weatherill, S., 1995, *Law and Integration in the European Union*, (Oxford: Clarendon Press).
Weingast, B. R., 1995, The economic role of political institutions: Market-preserving federalism and economic development. *The Journal of Law, Economics,& Organization*, **11**(1), pp.1–31.

Exploring the Concept of Governability

JAN KOOIMAN

ABSTRACT *In this paper a start is made in developing a conceptual model for the governability of a particular societal system based upon the (inter)active perspective on governance. Governability is seen as consisting of three main components, a system-to-be-governed (SG), a governance system (GS), and the interactions between these two (GI). The basis for conceptualizing the GS is the primary processes in which societal sectors specialize. These processes show characteristics by which they can be analyzed, such as their diversity, dynamics and complexity. The GS can be operationalized according to aspects of governance activities: elements, modes and orders of governance, and in the three major societal governance institutions: state, market, civil society and increasingly hybrid forms among them. The article also discusses the GI where one input is from the SG to the GS, defined as participatory interactions, and another from the GS to the SG which is seen as policy and management driven forms of interactions. Together these major governability components form a conceptual basis to analyze and eventually assess the governability of a particular societal sector, such as a fishery, a coastal zone or in fact any societal sector.*

Introduction

This paper grew out of a program directed at inter-disciplinary research on the governance of fisheries, and a subsequent project on the governability of fisheries, aqua-culture and coastal zones.[1] Central to these projects was addressing the question of what kind of factors have contributed to failure to slow depletion of the resource despite the great policy and management efforts by public authorities all over the world. Answers suggest that not only are policies usually inadequate, but that the institutions formulating and implementing these policies are weak or lacking and the value foundations of all these efforts are contradictory, to say the least.

These findings led to the realization that not only policy and management are at stake, but so also is governance of the fisheries system as a whole. In our terminology, the fishery system includes the system to be governed (SG – the fish chain from catching to consuming fish); the governing system (GS – state, market and civil society institutions governing this chain); and the interrelations between the two (GI – all interactions between those involved in the chain). All of these play a role in what we call governability, which, in the case of fisheries, has a weak capacity for governance (Jentoft 2007b).

The framework outlined in this paper is designed to facilitate the comparative assessment of the governance capacity of a societal sector such as fisheries; however, it can also be seen as a contribution to developing a conceptual context for policy analytical purposes. The paper aims at continuing a discussion as formulated in the "Introduction to a Symposium on Comparative Social-political Governance and Policy" in this Journal in 2003, in which my work was partly used, saying:

> There can certainly be little doubt that the socioeconomic, political, cultural, and natural environments that now prevail in most advanced liberal democracies are much changed from any that have existed before. All these societies have become more diverse, dynamic, and complex, so the role of governments have changed... The response has been a gradual transition away from traditional modes of governing towards new patterns of state-society interactions... When one considers the increased plurality of agents of government and civil society participating in the policy process, and the growing complexity of issues to be decided upon, it is perhaps not surprising that some contributors to this debate question whether modern societies are in fact governable. (Dixon et al. 2003: 101–102)

As stated this way, features of governance and governability become major contextual factors for policies and for policy connected concepts such as policy problems, policy processes, policy arenas, and may become even a part of a general conceptual framework for the policy sciences (Pielke 2004: 218).

The paper starts by establishing the relation between governability and its 'mother' concept governance. This is followed by a systematic discussion of its major components SG, GS and GI. In the conclusion the potential role of the framework for policy analysis is taken up again.

Governability

Background

Governability as a concept has several pedigrees. The first one has a somewhat dubious scholarly standing, notwithstanding the high status of its contributors, Crozier, Huntington and Watanuki (1975). The concept served as a carrier for a semi-political movement promoting the idea that modern democracies had become ungovernable because of an overload of public tasks. This did not contribute to its scholarly reception (Dahrendorf 1980). Its second lineage is in the German discussion on governance and governability under the title *Steuerung* and *Steuerungsdefizit* (governability failure). Luhmann and his followers attributed this failure to the basic *autopoietic* nature of societal (sub)systems, while Mayntz and her collaborators put the blame on the difficulty of governing the special dynamics of complex modern societies and the capacity of highly organized policy fields to resist political guidance

(Mayntz 1993, Luhmann 1995, Dunsire 1996). Most recently a third source for conceptualizing governability can be found in relation to democracy, in particular for Latin American countries (Figuerdo 2006). In all instances governability has been coupled in one way or another to the state as governance agency.

The ideas underlying the concept of governability pursued in this article by distinguishing a SG and a GS builds on the important discussion on *Steuerbarkeit*, governability, in the German context, as summarized by Mayntz (2005: 16–17) in a recent state of the art survey of governance research. She argues that the change in perspective from *Steuerung* to governance, in which the separation between *Steuerungsobjekt* and *Steuerungssubjekt* has disappeared, has made it much more difficult to address the *Steuerbarkeitsproblematik* in a systematic manner. This sophisticated discussion of governability, unfortunately hardly recognized elsewhere, is important and a far cry from the short-lived and ideological one of the 1970s.

The governability concept as sketched in this paper builds on this German contribution and my own earlier suggestions (Mayntz 1993, Kooiman 1993). My exploration of governance (2003) ended with a short conceptual note on governability. This paper takes that as a starting point and continues this exploration by extending it based upon the experiences with the governance of fisheries worked out in a number of papers, and applying it to fisheries, coastal zones and aqua-culture in a few settings in the South (see the examples below). These efforts show its potential capacity as a conceptual base for comparative research in different fields and as an element in a framework for comparative policy analytical purposes as suggested above.

The Concept

The idea of relating governability to qualities of the object of governance, to its subject and to the relation between these two led us to conceive governability of any societal system or entity as the propensity for its successful governance. Governors, the governed and the interactions among governors and the governed all contribute to governability, as do all kinds of external influences. Governability can therefore be defined as: "*the overall capacity for governance of any societal entity or system*".

Its conceptual starting point is to look at three major sets of variables contributing to governability of societal entities, including the natural resources valued by those entities: those entities themselves considered as system-to-be-governed (SG), those governing these entities labeled the governance system (GS), and the inter-relation between these two, worked out in terms of governing interactions (GI). All three add in varying degrees to governability.

Governability is always changing, depending on external and internal factors. What may be high governability at a given time may be low governability at another. Similarly, what may be effective governance in one place may be ineffective in another. Governability as a whole, or any of its components, can be influenced by acts of governance. However, many external factors influence governability as well, some of which can only be poorly handled in governance, or not at all. This often enhances uncertainty with respect to the governability of a societal system or entity.

As sources for variables for SG I use earlier work on complexity, diversity and dynamics and general literature on environment and natural resources to give a first global idea of the possibility to conceptualize the SG component of governability. The variables for GS are taken from my earlier work on governance as the emphasis there was on aspects of those responsible for governance. The variables for GI are a broadening of the interaction concept as developed earlier. Policy and participation literature are the main sources for this, as well as some classical ideas on pressure and some recent ones on impact assessment. For all three components the chosen variables can be considered as a conceptual middle way for on the one hand the richness of potential variables, and on the other to limit the number of them as the model serves as a basis for going into the field and assess governability in concrete situations.[2]

Interactive governance, in keeping with its basic assumptions, considers governability as a property of systems as wholes: that is, systems that are defined as the totality of inter-relations among given entities. Societal systems imply interactions, and interactions are conditions for the existence of those systems. In interactive governance, interactions and systems belong together (Kooiman 2003).

What a system looks like, how it can be broken down, and what its boundaries and other qualities might be, depends on the perspectives of its observers. The systems concept in this paper is to be considered as a heuristic tool, without any teleological, functional or reification connotations (Jervis 1997, Jentoft 2007b). Any system – societal, natural or combinations of the two – is part of a hierarchy of nested systems. Where in the hierarchy one wants to locate a particular system also exists in the eyes of its beholders. The more beholders with comparable ideas about a system, the stronger the concept becomes, for study and for practical purposes (see Figure 1).

This article describes the concept of governability as an integrated whole, while explaining that each of its components (SG, GS and GI) has a conceptual basis on its own. It might be held that only people (and not nature) "govern". However it can also be argued that, because of the nested hierarchy of systems, nature in the end

Figure 1. Integrated framework for governability

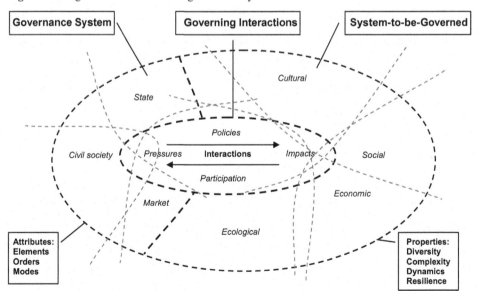

governs all societal governance. These are fundamental issues only a full-fledged study of governability can deal with in a serious manner. Here it is mentioned, because in operational terms what belongs to the GS or what to the SG might come up in an actual analysis of the governability of a particular societal-natural system, such as a fishery, or in fact any other societal entity.

Governability and the System-to-be-Governed (SG)

The key consideration with the SG is to determine which dimensions decide if a system is governable or not. On the one hand one would think that this is relatively simple because any societal activity in theory and in practice can be considered as an SG. On the other hand defining the SG is complicated because what we could consider as potentially relevant for governability is almost unlimited. By focusing on societal interactions as our prime conceptual tool we hope to make the analysis of SG workable. Interactions can be instrumental in ordering societal activities, and they can serve to – at least conceptually – limit the scope of what we need to look at.

Governability of SG and Societal Primary Processes

Societal subsystems as systems of interactions exist around specific societal activities. Such a basic undertaking can be labeled a "primary process": educating children, taking care of sick people, catching fish, producing bicycles, handling a bank account. All such processes have increasingly become more diverse, dynamic and complex and take place at different scales – not only quantitatively but also qualitatively. How this works out in fisheries is shown in Box 1.

Box 1. Scales in fisheries and governability

> The scales of capture fisheries can be described in many ways, for example, by the size of the resource (small local stock vs. large wide-ranging stock), the types of vessels used (small, inshore vs. large, ocean-going), the nature and state of technological development of fishing gear (manual, home-made vs. advanced electronic and hydraulic), and their administrative arrangements (small vs. large fisheries departments and national vs. regional and international administrations). These highly variable scales form the complex, multi-dimensional space in which fishers fish.
>
> Problems arise when aspects of capture fisheries are scaled up or down without careful consideration of the consequences for functionality. For example, some small developing countries have attempted to replicate large-country fisheries department capacity in small departments, with the result that few function effectively. A lack of fit between some fisheries' management practices and the scales at which they are applied can contribute to real or perceived failures. By taking different spatial, temporal, and organizational scales in capture fisheries into account, their governability might be greatly enhanced.

Source: Johnson *et al.* 2005.

Operationalizing factors to take into consideration in interaction systems around primary processes at different levels of abstraction is not a simple matter. Fortunately the impact assessment literature (Becker and Vanclay 2003) might help with this, as this is the field of research where occurrences having an impact are studied systematically. Social impact assessment, for example, maps people's way of life, their culture, their community, their political systems, their environment, their health and well-being, their personal and property rights, and their fears in a researchable manner. Recently this literature (Van Schooten et al. 2003) has also distinguished a wide variety of societal processes (i.e., interactions) that are useful for assessing a SG and its governability.

In our own research, the concept of the (fish) chain from ecosystem to the consumer, enabled analysis of ecological, social, economic, cultural, ethical and political aspects of fisheries systems by scholars from different disciplines and persons having different points of view (Kooiman et al. 1999, Kooiman et al. 2005).

Governability of SG and Common Properties

It is the inter-relationships and interactions among the economic, social, ecological and other components of a SG – often studied as individual components – that constitute the SG as a whole. Each of these components has specific major variables and terminology. For studying the systemic qualities of a SG by focusing on overlaps, linkages, interactions and interdependencies among its components, it is essential to find common concepts, descriptors and measures for the properties of the SG and these components. The interactive governance perspective considers diversity, complexity, dynamics and scale to be such commonalities.

To understand interactive governance and governability, in particular on the boundaries between its social, political and natural facets, one must recognize and confront their diversity, complexity, dynamics and scale (Kooiman 1993, 2003, Bavinck and Kooiman 2005). *Diversity* calls attention to the specific and varying qualities of actors and other entities in an SG, its GS and GI between them. It is a source of creation and innovation, but also carries the danger of disintegration. *Complexity* invites examination of societal structures, interdependencies and inter-relations and is a condition for combining interdependencies. The difficulty is how to reduce it in an effective and responsible manner. By introducing the *dynamics* of systems we call attention to the regularity or irregularity with which developments within and around systems take place. Dynamics create the potential for change, but can have disruptive consequences. *Scale* concerns their dimensions in space or time for a specific analytical or applied purpose. It represents the level at which the combined effects of diversity, complexity and dynamics can be best observed and analyzed. Governability as a component of societal systems is itself also diverse, complex and dynamic. They are features that emerge at different scales of those systems. The role of diversity, complexity and dynamics for governability in aquaculture is shown in Box 2.

Other common characteristics are also in use. Robinson and Tinker (1997) argue, for example, that a number of attributes apply to a greater or lesser extent to all three primary systems they look at (the biosphere, the economy and human society). They discuss attributes such as the capacity to change (with respect to) diversity, stability,

Box 2. The diversity, complexity and dynamics of aqua-culture

> Aqua-culture operations vary from homestead and farm ponds of less than 100 m^2 to cage, pen and pond farms covering hundreds of hectares. Small-scale aqua-culture, sometimes as a part-time occupation, makes large contributions to poverty alleviation in Asia. Cold-water aqua-culture (for example, trout and salmon farming) and warm-water aqua-culture (for example, tilapia farming) mirror the broad differences between temperate and tropical agriculture. Organic aqua-culture is also developing rapidly.
>
> Aqua-culture also has considerable complexity, largely because of the complex life histories of aquatic organisms and the complex technical requirements of providing for these in captivity. Farmed fish are bred in breeding programs, striving for genetic improvement of commercial traits. Fish hatcheries produce seed and fish nurseries grow those to juveniles of more viable size. Fish farmers then proceed to raising those juveniles to marketable size. Arrangements among hatchery, nursery, farming and post-harvest operations are complex because of seasonal and other shifts in supply and demand and the advent of new technologies and products.
>
> Inter-relationships among aqua-culture and other sectors are highly dynamic, especially those concerning land and water use, environmental impacts, farm workers health and safety, and farmed fish health, quality and safety for consumers. Aqua-culture is often risky. Unpredictable climatic conditions, operator error, equipment failure, and largely uncontrollable events such as toxic algal blooms, the spread of aquatic diseases and pollution all cause mass mortalities of farmed fish.

Source: Pullin 2005.

resilience and self-organization in response to stress. They also assert the existence of more or less inflexible outer limits for such properties beyond which a system will collapse. Using essentially the same kind of ideas on generic properties, Holling *et al.* (1998: 352) state that for natural resources management "Characteristically, problems tend to be systems problems, where aspects of behavior are complex and unpredictable and where causes, while at times simple (when finally understood), are always multiple".

Examples of common properties used across a wide range of disciplines are: capital, capacity, capability, function, chain, impact, resilience, sustainability, uncertainty, vulnerability, memory, and risk. Two examples show their usefulness for our purpose. Vulnerability might reveal the problematic side of governability, while resilience is symbolic of its opportunity side.

Resilience. Holling (1973) introduced the concept of resilience into ecology to facilitate assessments of ecosystem behavior in the face of disturbances and change. Resilience was initially conceived with the assumption of stable states – that is, an ecosystem returning to its original situation after a disturbance. Now it has become a more dynamic concept, allowing for changes taking place after a disturbance, and it has been broadened to include social and economic aspects as well as ecological ones. Key properties in recent studies of resilience are adaptive renewal cycles, emphasizing feedback loops, uncertainty and surprise, self-organization, learning and innovation (Berkes *et al.* 2003). Social resilience is also conceived of as a central category of analysis and is related to resource dependency and risk (Adger 2000).

A SG with higher resilience might be thought to have higher governability than one with lower resilience, because the former copes better with disturbances, is better at organizing (that is, governing) itself, and has a higher learning capacity, and so on. But are there direct and positive correlations between governability, self-governance and resilience? In the interactive governance perspective, it is assumed that most modern SGs are, in the face of a complex, dynamic and diverse world, characterized by mixes of three modes of governance, among which self-governance is only one (see the section on modes of governance). For a SG to be more governable, self-organizing is important but not entirely sufficient.

Vulnerability. Vulnerability is a concept used in ecology, economics and social science. It is a measure of weakness, often compared with and related to resilience as a measure of strength. From their conservation perspective, Wilson *et al.* (2005) define vulnerability as a threatening process, implying risk as a loss: the likelihood or imminence of bio-diversity loss to current or impeding threatening processes. They distinguish three dimensions of vulnerability: exposure, intensity and impact. Adger (1999: 249) approaches vulnerability from social and economic points of view, saying "[s]ocial vulnerability is the exposure of groups or individuals to stress as a result of social and environmental changes and disruption to livelihoods". In this approach, social as well as physical impacts are included. The distinction between individual and collective dimensions of vulnerability is also important, with separate determinants, consequences, and thus indicators, as hinted at in the example on coastal zones given in Box 3.

Governability and the Governance System (GS)

Governability from the point of view of the GS is the capacity to bring about, organize and carry out governing interactions in the face of societal and natural diversity, complexity and dynamics in terms of elements, modes and orders of governance as attributes (Kooiman 2003). This applies to all three of the major components, state, market and civil society, and to the hybrid forms among them. How do governing images, instruments and action elements used by governors contribute to governability? In which way do fact and value systems, resources and social capital contribute to the way governing images are formed, instruments developed and action potential employed? At the structural level are the three modes of governance, self-, co- and hierarchical governance, fully exploited? And are the three governing orders, problem solving/opportunity creation, care for institutions and meta-considerations complementary, or are they at odds, and thus is their contribution to governability low, medium, or high? Questions like this point to the combination of norms and practice in the governability aspect of the GS.

Box 3. Vulnerability of coastal zones

> The ecological, social and economic conditions of coastal zones are such that the chain of (natural and human) producers of various coastal products and services to consumer may be better described as "coastal webs". The intricacy of these webs is enhanced by a multitude of interactions: among living organisms in coastal ecosystems, among coastal stakeholders, and between humans and ecosystems. As systems become more vulnerable with alteration and extraction by natural and anthropogenic causes, an understanding of these interactions is required to increase governability of coastal zones. Such interactions also imply that coastal management goals may be short term and long term. Given their features and these multiple interactions, there are high risks associated with decision making for coastal zones. Managing coastal activities to minimize risk and damage to ecosystems, and controlling undesirable ecological, social and economic impacts, might be more attainable than trying to achieve ideal and holistic goals. Both reactive and proactive approaches can be applied in risk-management situations, however, particularly where coastal resources are highly vulnerable and the cost of damages may be too high.

Source: Chuenpagdee *et al.* 2005.

Governability and Attributes of GS

Elements. Governors govern in and through interactions, and in those interactions three elements can be distinguished: images, instruments and action. In every governance interaction all three play a role: images as sets of ideas where a governor wants to go, instruments giving these ideas substance, and action needed to let these instruments do their work.

Images constitute the guiding lights for the how and why of governance. Images come in many types: visions, knowledge, facts, judgments, presuppositions, hypotheses, convictions, ends and goals. They not only relate to specific issues but also contain assumptions about fundamental matters such as the relationships between society and nature, the essence of humankind, and the role of government (see Box 4). *Instruments* link images to action. Instruments are not neutral. Their design, choice and application frequently elicit strife. Instruments may be "soft" or they may be "hard" and their choice is not free: positions in society determine their available range. *Action* is the putting of instruments into effect. This includes the implementation of policies according to a set of guidelines. However, action may also consist of mobilizing actors in new and uncharted directions.

We should not forget that for governability structural conditions might be even more important than the actual governing interactions themselves. From which sources do images come? From what kinds of resources do instruments come, and which of those resources are limited and/or renewable? What kinds of action patterns belong to a particular political culture and which ones do not? Together these resources form the base on which governing entities can draw for actual use.

Box 4. The Tragedy of the Commons

> The Tragedy of the Commons is undoubtedly the most influential image governing fisheries (and maybe natural resources in general) as coined by Hardin (1968) explaining the inevitably of depletion of a natural resource if the exploitation is left to those using it. It is (economically) rational for all fishermen to individually catch more fish even when the harvest is already on the decline, thus causing a tragedy for all. One response is for the state to impose restraining measures; others, however, propose privatizing the commons, arguing that private ownership will provide sufficient incentive for restrained behavior. Both lines of argument have come under critique. The tragedy itself has been attacked because of its behavioral and other untested assumptions – thus it is not a tragedy but a tragicomedy. Governance regimes in between the two just mentioned options are promoted, for example co-management, as a more effective strategy against over-fishing in the long term.

Source: McGoodwin 1990: 89–96.

Modes of governance. Interactive governance recognizes three main modes: hierarchical governance, self-governance, and co-governance. Of the three, the hierarchical mode is the most familiar and classic mode of governance. Co-modes are emerging more and more and being experimented with, while societal self-governance is the subject of much misunderstanding, theoretical as well as political-ideological (see Box 5).

All societies not only demonstrate these three modes; they also require them. A considerable step forward in our knowledge about societal governability could be taken when governance qualities of societies would be considered as mixes of the three, and not as any one of these modes in particular. The limits of hierarchical governance we see every day around us, where more and more rules and regulations become less and less effective. Experiences with co-governance, such as co-management in fisheries governance, and public-private partnerships have become widely used to fill the gaps in hierarchical governance (see the section on Forms of Interactions). Self-governance is probably the most ubiquitous mode, but also the least well known and understood in its contribution to governability. Theoretical work and empirical research is needed to specify under which conditions what kinds of mixes of the three governance modes might contribute to societal governability or hamper it.

Orders of governance. Governing activities can focus on different sorts of things, and these can be categorized in three 'orders': first-order, second-order, and meta-governance.

First-order governance deals with day-to-day affairs. It takes place wherever people and their organizations interact in order to solve existing societal problems and to create new opportunities. Of course there are many other primary governing tasks, but these serve as examples of how other tasks can be conceptualized as well.

Second-order governance focuses on the institutional arrangements within which first-order governance takes place. Here, the term 'institution' denotes the

Box 5. Modes of governance in capture fisheries

> In capture fisheries, the three major modes of governance (self-, co- and hierarchical) all influence governability. *Self-governance* in fisheries has been common worldwide, with its basis usually in local communities. The main reason is the use of fisheries resources as a commons, and the need to regulate their use, for technical reasons and/or to avoid conflicts. In the North, this mode of governance in its purest form has become rare, though remnants are still in operation in some parts of southern Europe. *Hierarchical* governance in fisheries is also widespread, particularly in the North where interventionist interactions by the state are the order of the day. However, this involvement by the state is not unchallenged. Erosion of traditional self-governing modes and their replacement with state-run management systems often does not work well. Although hierarchical governance is mainly connected with the state, it is also common in the market sector, particularly by multi-national companies. In such cases, hierarchical governance by the state is replaced by hierarchical governance by the market. Co-management, as a form of *co-governance*, means that government agencies and fisher people share responsibility for resource management functions. It tries to steer a middle course between government regulation and community-initiated regulation. Co-management is not as informal as community-based management, it requires fishermen to establish organizations with formal leadership and an executive staff. But this leadership is participatory rather than hierarchical, and (where feasible) decentralized rather than centralized.

Source: author.

arrangements of agreements, rules, rights, and procedures applied by first-order governors to make decisions. One might say that state, market and civil society are high-level expressions of such institutional arrangements in a society.

Third-order or meta-governance feeds, binds, and evaluates the entire governance exercise. Many principles or criteria guide governance. Some are of a more 'applied' nature: such as rationality, efficiency, effectiveness or performance. Others may have a more fundamental or even ethical stance, such as equity, responsibility or justice. In meta-governance, governors and the governed alike take each other's measure in formulating the norms by which they want to judge each other and the measuring process itself.

With respect to governability, the three orders of governance (first-, second- and meta-) cannot survive without each other. If no problems are solved or no opportunities created, governing institutions become hollow shells. If institutions do not renew and adapt, they will hamper rather than help in meeting new governance challenges. If these two different sets of governing activities are not put against the light of normative standards in the long run they will become pillars without foundations, blown away or falling apart in stormy weather or chaotic times (see Box 6).

Box 6. Code of conduct for responsible fisheries

> In response to recent developments and concerns in world fisheries, the Food and Agriculture Organization (FAO) of the United Nations developed a Code of Conduct for Responsible Fisheries (CCRF). The goal was to establish principles and international standards for responsible fisheries, defined in relation to the effective conservation, management and development of living aquatic resources, with due respect for the ecosystem and bio-diversity. The CCRF states that fisheries management should promote the maintenance of the quality, diversity and availability of fishery resources. The CCRF was shaped in conformity with the United Nations Convention on the Law of the Sea (UNCLOS). It applies to all fisheries, whether on the high seas, within the Exclusive Economic Zone (EEZ), in territorial waters or in inland waters. Its main target is the regulation of professional fisheries, though it also voices the intention to cover recreational fisheries.

Source: Bavinck and Chuenpagdee 2005.

Governability and Sub-systems of GS

States are still the most central and omni-present societal governance sub-systems.

They steer and control from the local to international levels in complex ways, and for all practical purposes the concept of a homogeneous societal institution, denoted as "the state" and governed by uniform rules, has to be replaced by other models, allowing variety and differentiation as well as certain degrees of independence and interdependence. Changes show the dynamics of the modern state, and "[w]hilst the state...may be in retreat in some respects, its activity may be increasing in others. And nowhere...has its key decision-making role been seriously undermined" (Müller and Wright 1994: 1).

Markets, as governance institutions, also consist of many mixes of interactions, each with their own diverse, complex and dynamic features. Williamson's (1975) view of governance, in which institutional economics provide the institutional framework, consists broadly of markets, hierarchies and mixed forms of these, through which transactions are channeled. This amounts to getting away from general economic laws explaining market interactions, but showing some of their governance aspects.

The governance roles of *civil society* can be conceived as a societal domain which is predominantly characterized by governing interactions that are rather spontaneous, semi-formalized, mainly horizontal, and non-interventionist. In principle, it is not the formal status of individuals or organizations, but rather the ways in which they interact with each other, that are decisive in deciding if they belong to civil society or not. Cohen and Arato (1992) have shown state and market as successful in institutionalizing their autonomy and task differentiation, civil society less so. The dynamics and balance between state and civil society are in constant flux such that "neither of the two can monopolize public life without provoking a reaction from the opposite realm to retain political space" (Biekart 1999: 36–37).

Hybrids between the three societal institutions such as public and private have always been present. Other hybrids where the state withdraws and leaves some of its servicing tasks to companies with private or mixed ownership are also common, often in the same countries. For governability this hybridization of institutions and the way they are institutionalized on the borderline between state, market and civil society are important and are challenging to assess (Van Tulder and Van der Zwart 2006).

Governability and Governance Interactions (GI)

Governing Interactions

Interactions between the SG and the GS are a basic element of governance, and important for assessing governability. Those governed, through their participation, try to exert influence on those governing. Governing entities try to influence those governed through their policies and management efforts. Recently, interactions of a more collaborative governance nature have become the order of the day (Box 7).

Power relationships and social-political cultural traditions find their expression in governance interactions. For example, it is often said that "Anglo-Saxon"

Box 7. Interactions in aqua-culture

> Aqua-culture operations and institutions depend upon multiple interactions with each other. These interactions are largely shaped by market forces. For example, fish breeding in government research stations and seed production in private hatcheries can function well as public-private partnerships. Expansion of aqua-culture has inevitable consequences for equitable sharing of natural resources. Small-scale fish seed producers and farmers cannot easily compete with larger operators. Aqua-culture has been the world's fastest growing form of food production for over 20 years (about 9% per year). It could not have achieved this without multiple interactions. However, the persistent image of aqua-culture as a special "thing in itself", still often administered as a sub-sector of fisheries, is limiting interactions that could further revolutionize food production.
>
> Moreover, many of the world's institutions are established in ways that limit interaction between conservation of bio-diversity and food production, in terms of policy making, administrative arrangements and budgets. The Convention on Biological Diversity (CBD) regards all wild and farmed organisms and their supporting ecosystems as bio-diversity. The fish that humans consume, as well as the agro-ecosystems from which more and more are derived through aqua-culture, are indeed bio-diversity. However, the interactions of aqua-culture do not yet reflect this well, because institutions are still fostering its separation from agriculture and its false alliance with capture fisheries. The score for the presence of governing interactions in aqua-culture is high.

Source: Pullin 2005.

social-political culture does not stimulate formal interactions between governors and governed, in contrast to the "continental" tradition, where those are enabled and often institutionalized. Such differences may also explain why co-governing interactions, such as co-management schemes as in fisheries, are more common in some political cultures than in others (Wilson *et al.* 2003). Scale may also be an important feature in governance interactions. Market parties, such as multinational companies may interact with NGOs at the global level, while at the local or national level they do not interact at all.

This points to an important analytical distinction in governance interactions: an action or intentional level and a structural or contextual level. This distinction, although the subject of heated social science debates, such as in terms of agency structure, is a useful one. Any conceptualization of the constituent actors in a governance interaction necessarily involves an idea of its structural and agency component. In the literature on interest groups there are at least five structural explanations for their role in modern policy making: pluralist, neo-pluralist, Marxist, neo-Marxist, elitist and corporatist or neo-corporatist (Granados and Knoke 2005). And a heated debate on the role of agency, structure or contextual levels of explanation for the effects of policy networks also shows that the distinction between more than one dimension of governance interactions might be a sensible one (Marsh and Smith 2000, 2001).

Modalities of GI

In the reality of modern governance an enormous variety in interactions can be observed. From the GI perspective they can be ordered in a few major types: participatory, collaborative and policy or management interactions (see Kooiman 2003 for the conceptual basis of this distinction).

For governability, it is important to know how social-political entities – such as individuals, organizations, groups, movements or other forms of collective action – *participate* in governing interactions. Where does such participatory action come from? Who acts and who reacts? The character of the interaction is determined by the responsiveness of those governing and what has been called the "repertory" of resources and activities which the governed command (Barnes and Kaase 1979). This repertory is wide, and varied: voting, letter writing and protesting in sit-ins and boycotts and participating in a movement or being a member of a focus or action group. I see participatory interactions as directed from the SG to the GS. Social movements are the classical example of this kind of spontaneous, loosely organized form of governance interaction.

The importance of *collaborative* forms of governance interactions is growing. Why, for governance purposes, are groups, organizations and authorities willing to share their activities and aim to do things together instead of doing them alone? Often mutual interdependencies are mentioned as the main reason for such collaborative or co-operative interactions. Partnerships between public and private entities are a popular form of such collaboration. But collaborative interactions between companies and NGOs can also be found, although their motives may differ. Companies seem to be compliance-, risk-, value- or opportunity-driven, while motives for NGOs are more in terms of funding, capabilities or mission (Austin 2006).

Policy and *management* interactions are the collective variables for all hierarchical interactions by GS aimed at having an impact on SG. Public authorities at all levels have numerous interactions, dressed in policy terms, at their disposal to bring about politically preferred societal changes (Mayer *et al.* 2005). Management is seen as a way to organize these interactions according to criteria of efficiency and effectiveness. Stakeholder identification, for example, has become a popular (interventionist) tool in this respect (Bryson 2004: 32–33).

Systems of GI

Interactive governance considers governance and governability as a property of societal systems. To understand what is going on in the governance of modern societal systems, and thus systems of GI, one must confront head-on issues connected with their diversity, complexity and dynamics. Too often, in more traditional approaches to governing, these features have been ignored or have lip-service paid to them. We can not solve all issues related to them, but we can at least put them at the center of our approach to governance and governability.

There is an important argument for taking the *diversity* of values, goals and interests of those involved in interactions into account. This points to processes of ordering and re-ordering of aspects of diversity. For example, such a process led Buanes *et al.* (2004) to test this diversity searching approach for stakeholders in coastal zones of Norway into several distinct categories.

More often than not, *complexity* is considered not to mean anything more than that something is difficult to understand, or complicated to handle. However, complexity is more than that: it is a basic aspect of the phenomena we deal with, and, as such, it has baffled practitioners and scholars alike. We assume that there are limits to the human capacity to know and to act. This means that, in coping with complexity, we have to follow the path of combined strategies (LaPorte 1975).

Dynamics can be seen as a composition of forces which sometimes turn into gradual developments, but more often result in non-linear patterns of change. Insights in societal dynamics have direct or indirect relevance for governance and an assessment of the role of the GI in governability. For example in his study of interactions between state and society De Vries (2005) distinguished four (macro) types of policy interactions between government and society in the Netherlands by crosstabulating (dis)parity of power and authority (vertical, horizontal) and perceived interests (antagonistic, congruent). These four types were characteristic only for a certain period during the last 50 years, and after some time changed into another system of policy interaction, a transition which expresses the dynamic nature of governance interactions.

Influence of GS on SG

Among the many controversies in political science, and to some extent in sociology, few can compete with the so-called "power or influence" debate that raged in the 1960s and 1970s. Although it has never ended in anything really satisfying, it resurfaces regularly, and understandably, because applying influence and bringing power into play are facts of life in general, not only in politics. However, the story of research on influence and its "ugly sister power", the term coined by Wootton (1970: 73), shows, as Baumgartner and Leech (1998: 3) state, that substantial progress has been made but serious gaps in our knowledge remain in the study of interest groups and their influence in politics. Influence, pressure and power remain, nevertheless, fascinating subjects for social science scholars; some of whom mourn their neglected status in areas such as fisheries governance (Jentoft 2007a).

Impact or Effect of GS on SG

A summary of the multiple interactions between the GS and the SG can be obtained by looking at the effects or impacts of these interactions on the SG. The concept of impacts enables us to bring order to the changes governors try to bring about in SG

Box 8. Sea tenure, social organization and power in South Indian fisheries

> Sea tenure systems present different ways of regarding and organizing the use of marine resources. They tend also to correspond to different modes of social and economic organization.
>
> Small-scale fisheries along the Coromandel Coast – as in most developing countries – are predominantly a rural affair, rooted in pre-colonial formations and in a village style of life. Here a fisher, if he has done well on a particular day, tends to stay home the next, as his family's needs have basically been met. Kinship and ties of residence structure social interactions and influence individual decision making. The division of labor is elementary and communities are egalitarian in nature. Religious attitudes permeate everyday life in many ways.
>
> The trawler fisheries of the region are quite dissimilar. Here the laws of capitalism color the dynamic. This is brought out by the pattern of fishing. As soon as craft have returned from a fishing trip, they are prepared for the next one – after all, time wasted is money lost. Every participant's ambition is to maximize returns. There is a high degree of labor differentiation, with boat owners, and the back-lying providers of capital, calling the tune. Here life has a raw flavor, and people largely have to fend for themselves.
>
> Power is an essential ingredient in both forms of social organization and sea tenure, and also plays an important role in the relationship between the fisheries sub-sectors. The Fisheries Department, as one arm of government, has deeply influenced the balance of power at sea, which already tends toward the party with the bigger craft and engine power. The Department lent essential support to trawler fishers particularly in the sub-sector's formative phase, rebutting the waves of anger and successfully deafening small-scale fishers' protest. But the Fisheries Department has not always sided with the trawler fishers, often striving to play a mediating role. This is motivated also by the fact that small-scale fishers constitute a substantial vote bank, and cannot be ignored politically.

Source: Bavinck 2005.

by means of their policy or management interactions. Impact analysis might help in operationalizing the effect of governing efforts by a GS on the SG (Boothroyd 1995, Becker and Vanclay 2003). Impact analysis or assessment looks at the effects or potential effects of such efforts. It has been applied in many areas, such as social, environmental, ecological, technology, and risk impact assessments, all with their own specialized methodologies and technical requirements.

Recently interest in building a common theoretical and conceptual basis for impact assessment has been growing, and it is this effort which fits best with our aim of using impacts as a variable in the governability model (Slootweg et al. 2003). The synthesis known as policy assessment (Boothroyd 1995) is particularly relevant to applying impact assessment analysis to the operationalization of governance efforts. Policy assessment is a combination of policy evaluation and impact assessment aimed at intended as well as unintended outcomes of policies. As such it deepens the systemic awareness of impact chains. These developments are significant because for designing analytical tools for assessing the impacts or effects of governing efforts by the GS on the SG we first need sound conceptual and, for preference, broad and interdisciplinary-oriented frameworks for them.

Conclusion

In this paper the conceptual contours of governability as part of an interactive governance perspective have been sketched. In principle, all societal systems or activities can be looked upon from the point of view of their governability. They can be characterized by variables such as the diversity, complexity and dynamics of their primary processes and by properties like resilience, vulnerability, risk and others. The same applies to variables describing the main qualities of the way they are governed by institutions such as state, market and civil society and other features describing their GS. GI is of special importance, because it is the part of governability of any system where the policy aspects of governance interactions find their place.

We may assume that not all societal systems are equally diverse, complex and dynamic, or show the same patterns of governing interactions or institutional involvement. The next step in working with the framework is to make it applicable for assessment and comparison purposes. For several variables like resilience and risk, policies and participation, and the governance role of institutions, sufficient literature is available for this task. Others like complexity, diversity and dynamics or modes of governance have to be adapted or even invented. Assessing and comparing will be a longer-term research task.

This brings me to a final point. In the Introduction a potential role of this governability framework for policy, policy analysis and comparative policy analytical work in this field was suggested. Since the basic features of the framework have been sketched now, it might be clearer what this role might be: a contextual one. As part of a "renaissance" in comparative policy analysis DeLeon and Resnick-Terry mention all kinds of possibilities for a new generation of comparative policy analysis, using new conceptual approaches and theoretical perspectives. "The concept that *context* counts has become a guiding principle in the second 'generation' of comparative policy analysis" (1999: 18; emphasis added). Governance theorizing, with its broad orientation to factors involved in policy and policy making is certainly a candidate for defining such a context. The link between governance and governability on the one hand and policy and comparative policy analysis on the other, may become a strong one if we keep in mind the call made by Geva-May (2002: 257):

> for a comparative research agenda that will look into (1) what variables are inherent in 'political cultures/cultural bias' or 'ways of life' that affect public policy analysis in various contexts; (2) what their common manipulable denominator is; (3) the ways in which these variables can be manipulated when normative policy analysis methodology is employed; and (4) how we can develop an awareness for culturally sensitive variables in policy arena interactions.

This comes close to aims of the governability framework as sketched above, and opportunities in establishing links between its further development and continuous work on comparative policy analysis certainly come to mind. Such a framework might create a conceptual and, eventually even a theoretical link between policy and governance or policy analysis and governability assessment, preferably in a comparative manner, links which so far have not received much attention. This paper is a modest step in filling this gap.

Acknowledgements

I would like to express my gratitude to members of the Fisheries Governance Network, to James Meadowcroft, and to the reviewers of JCPA for their comments on earlier versions of this paper, and to Roger Pullin and Derek Johnson for their editorial help.

Notes

1. The concept of governance presented in this paper is based upon, and a follow-up to the interactive governance perspective developed by Kooiman (2003), and applied to fisheries in Kooiman *et al.* (2005) as part of the work of Fisheries Governance Network (www.fishgovnet.org). Governability has been discussed in Kooiman (2003); applied to fisheries, aqua-culture and coastal zones in Chuenpagdee and Kooiman (2005) and used for assessing governability in three papers presented at the MARE Conference "People and the Sea", July 2005 in Amsterdam: Chuenpagdee, Kooiman and Pullin (2005), Mahon (2005), Bavinck and Salagrama 2005 (see: www.marecentre.nl). The cases in this article are derived from the work of this Fisheries Governance Network.
2. A proposal for a project with the purpose of continuing this work and assessing the governability of fisheries in four areas in the South has been filed with a potential donor.

References

Adger, W. N., 2000, Social and ecological resilience: are they related? *Progress in Human Geography*, **24**, 347–364.

Adger, W. N., 1999, Social vulnerability to climate change and extremes in coastal Vietnam. *World Development*, **27**, 249–269.

Austin J. E., 2006, Sustainability through partnering: strategic alliances between businesses and NGOs. Paper presented at the Royal Netherlands Academy of Arts and Sciences Colloquium: Partnerships for Sustainable Development. Amsterdam, June 6.

Barnes, S. H. and Kaase, M., 1979, *Political Action* (Beverly Hills, CA: Sage).
Baumgartner, F. R. and Leech, B. L., 1998, *Basic Interests* (Princeton, NJ: Princeton University Press).
Bavinck, M., 2005, Understanding fisheries conflicts in the south – a legal pluralist perspective. *Society and Natural Resources*, **18**, 805–820.
Bavinck, M. and Chuenpagdee, R., 2005, Current principles, in: J. Kooiman, M. Bavinck, S. Jentoft and R. Pullin (Eds) *Fish for Life: Interactive Governance for Fisheries* (Amsterdam: Amsterdam University Press), pp. 245–264.
Bavinck, M. and Kooiman J., 2005, The governance perspective, in: J. Kooiman, M. Bavinck, S. Jentoft and R. Pullin (Eds) *Fish for Life: Interactive Governance for Fisheries* (Amsterdam: Amsterdam University Press), pp. 11–24.
Bavinck, M. and Salagrama, V., 2005, Assessing the governability of capture fisheries in the Bay of Bengal. Paper presented at MARE Conference "People and the Sea", University of Amsterdam, Amsterdam July.
Becker, H. A. and Vanclay, F. (Eds), 2003, *The International Handbook of Social Impact Assessment* (Cheltenham: Edward Elgar).
Berkes, F. Colding, J. and Folke, C. (Eds), 2003, *Navigating Social-Ecological Systems* (Cambridge: Cambridge University Press).
Biekart, C. H., 1999, *The Politics of Civil Society Building* (Utrecht: International Books).
Boothroyd, P., 1995, Policy assessment, in: F. Vanclay and D. A. Bronstein (Eds) *Environmental and Social Impact Assessment* (Chichester: Wiley), pp. 83–125.
Bryson, J. M., 2004, What to do when stakeholders matter: stakeholder identification and analysis technique. *Public Management Review*, **6**, 21–54.
Buanes, A., Jentoft, S., Karlsen, G. R. and Søreng, A., 2004, In whose interest? An exploratory analysis of stakeholders in Norwegian coastal zone planning. *Ocean and Coastal Management*, **47**, 207–223.
Chuenpagdee, R. and Kooiman, J., 2005, Governance and governability, in: J. Kooiman, M. Bavinck, S. Jentoft and R. Pullin (Eds) *Fish for Life* (Amsterdam: Amsterdam University Press), pp. 325–350.
Chuenpagdee R., Kooiman J. and Pullin R., 2005, Exploring governability of capture fisheries, aquaculture and coastal zones. Paper presented at MARE Conference "People and the Sea", University of Amsterdam, Amsterdam, July.
Cohen, J. L. and Arato, A., 1992, *Civil Society and Political Theory* (Cambridge, MA: MIT Press).
Crozier, M., Huntington, S. P. and Watanuki, J., 1975, *The Crisis of Democracy: Report on the Governability of Democracies to the Trilateral Commission* (New York: New York University Press).
Dahrendorf, R., 1980, Effectiveness and legitimacy: on the governability of democracies. *The Political Quarterly*, **51**, 393–402.
DeLeon, P. and Resnick-Terry, P., 1999, Comparative policy analysis. *Journal of Comparative Policy Analysis*, **1**, 9–22.
De Vries, M. S., 2005, Generations of interactive policy-making in the Netherlands. *International Review of Administrative Sciences*, **71**, 577–591.
Dixon, J., Kouzmin, A. and Goodwin, D., 2003, Introduction to the Symposium: Comparative Sociopolitical Governance. *Journal of Comparative Policy Analysis*, **5**, 101–105.
Dunsire, A., 1996, Tipping the balance: autopoiesis and governance. *Administration and Society*, **28**, 299–334.
Figuerdo, D. S., 2006, Democratic governability in Latin America: limits and possibilities in the context of neoliberal domination. *Critical Sociology*, **32**, 105–124.
Geva-May, I., 2002, Cultural theory: the neglected variable in the craft of policy analysis. *Journal of Comparative policy Analysis*, **4**, 243–265.
Granados, F. J. and Knoke, D., 2005, Organized interest groups and policy networks, in: T. Janoski, R. Alford, A. Hicks and M. A. Schwarz (Eds) *The Handbook of Political Sociology* (New York: Cambridge University Press), pp. 287–309.
Hardin, G., 1968, The tragedy of the commons. *Science*, **162**, 1243–1248.
Holling, C.S., 1973, Resilience and stability of ecological systems. *Annual Review of Ecology and Systematics*, **4**, 1–23.
Holling, C. S., Berkes, F. and Folke, C., 1998, Science, sustainability and resource management, in: F. Berkes and C. Folke (Eds) *Linking Social Systems and Ecological Systems* (Cambridge: Cambridge University Press), pp. 352–378.
Jentoft, S., 2007a, In the power of power: the understated aspect of fisheries and coastal management. *Human Organization*, **66**, 426–437.

Jentoft, S., 2007b, Limits to governability? Institutional implications for ocean and coastal governance. *Marine Policy*, **4**, 360–370.

Jervis, R., 1997, *System Effects: Complexity in Political and Social Life* (Princeton, NJ: Princeton University Press).

Johnson, D., Bavinck, M. and Veitayaki, J. 2005, Fish capture, in: J. Kooiman, M. Bavinck, S. Jentoft and R. Pullin (Eds) *Fish for Life: Interactive Governance for Fisheries* (Amsterdam: Amsterdam University Press), pp. 71–92.

Kooiman, J. (Ed.), 1993, *Modern Governance* (London: Sage).

Kooiman, J., 2003, *Governing as Governance* (London: Sage).

Kooiman, J., Van Vliet, M. and Jentoft, S. (Eds), 1999, *Creative Governance: Opportunities for Fisheries in Europe* (Aldershot: Ashgate).

Kooiman, J., Bavinck, M., Jentoft, S. and Pullin, R. (Eds), 2005, *Fish for Life* (Amsterdam: Amsterdam University Press).

Laporte, T. R. (Ed.), 1975, *Organized Social Complexity* (Princeton, NJ: Princeton University Press).

Luhmann, N., 1995, *Social Systems* (Stanford, CA: Stanford University Press).

McGoodwin J. R., 1990, *Crisis in the World's Fisheries* (Stanford, CA: Stanford University Press).

Mahon, R., 2005, Governability of fisheries in the Caribbean Paper presented at MARE Conference "People and the Sea", University of Amsterdam, Amsterdam, July.

Marsh, D. and Smith, M., 2000, Understanding policy networks: towards a dialectical approach. *Political Studies*, **48**, 4–21.

Marsh, D., and Smith, M., 2001, There is more than one way to do political science: on different ways to study policy networks. *Political Studies*, **49**, 528–541.

Mayer, I., Edelenbos, J. and Monnikhof, R., 2005, Interactive policy development: undermining or sustaining democracy. *Public Administration*, **83**, 179–199.

Mayntz, R., 1993, Governing failures and the problem of governability: some comments on a theoretical paradigm, in: J. Kooiman (Ed.) *Modern Governance* (London: Sage), pp. 9–20.

Mayntz, R., 2005, Governance Theory als fortentwickelte Steuerungstheorie? in: G. F. Schuppert (Ed.) *Governance Forschung* (Baden-Baden: Nomos), pp. 11–18.

Müller, W. C. and Wright, V., 1994, Reshaping the state in Western Europe. *West European Politics*, **17**, 1–11.

Pielke, R. A. Jr., 2004, What future for the policy sciences. *Policy Sciences*, **37**, 209–225.

Pullin, R., 2005, Aquaculture, in: J. Kooiman, M. Bavinck, S. Jentoft and R. Pullin (Eds) *Fish for Life: Interactive Governance for Fisheries* (Amsterdam: Amsterdam University Press), pp. 93–108.

Robinson, J. and Tinker, J., 1997, Reconciling ecological, economic and social imperatives: a new conceptual framework, in: T. Schrecker (Ed.) *Surviving Globalism* (Houndmills: MacMillan), pp. 71–94.

Slootweg, R. F., Vanclay, M. and Van Schooten, M., 2003, Integrating environmental and social impact assessment, in: H. A. Becker and F. Vanclay (Eds) *The International Handbook of Social Impact Assessment* (Cheltenham: Edward Elgar), pp. 56–73.

Van Schooten, M., Vanclay, F. and Slootweg, R., 2003, Conceptualizing social change processes and social impacts, in: H. A. Becker and F. Vanclay (Eds) *The International Handbook of Social Impact Assessment* (Cheltenham: Edward Elgar), pp. 74–91.

Van Tulder, R. and Van der Zwart, A., 2006, *International Business-Society Management* (London: Routledge).

Williamson, O. E., 1975, *Markets and Hierarchies* (New York: Free Press).

Wilson, C. D., Nielsen, J. R. and Degnbol, P. (Eds), 2003, *The Fisheries Co-Management Experience* (Dordrecht: Kluwer Academic Publishers).

Wilson, K., Pressey, R.L., Newton, A., Burgman, M., Possingham, H. and Weston, C., 2005, Measuring and incorporating vulnerability into conservation planning. *Environmental Management*, **35**, 527–543.

Wootton, G., 1970, *Interest-Groups* (Englewood Cliffs, NJ: Prentice Hall).

Can Corruption Be Measured? Comparing Global Versus Local Perceptions of Corruption in East and Southeast Asia

MIN-WEI LIN & CHILIK YU

ABSTRACT *Since Transparency International first released its annual Corruption Perceptions Index (CPI) in 1995, the CPI has quickly become the best known corruption indicator worldwide. The CPI has been widely credited with making comparative and large-N studies of corruption possible, as well as putting the issue of corruption squarely in the international policy agenda. Despite its enormous influence on both academic and policy fronts, the CPI is not without critics. One often noted critique is that the CPI relies solely on surveys of foreign business people and the expert assessments of cross-national analysts; as such, the CPI mainly reflects international experts' perceptions, not the perceptions of each country's citizens. This study examines the above critique in closer detail. Data from the Asian Barometer Survey is employed to analyze whether international experts' corruption perceptions were similar to those of domestic citizens. The Asian Barometer Survey is a public opinion survey on issues related to political values, democracy, and public reform in 13 different areas around East and Southeast Asia (Cambodia, China, Hong Kong, Indonesia, Japan, South Korea, Malaysia, Mongolia, the Philippines, Singapore, Taiwan, Thailand, and Vietnam). Data analysis indicates that global and local perspectives are only moderately aligned in the 13 areas studied. International experts and domestic citizens differ, to varying degrees, in their evaluation of the extent of public sector corruption in several areas, suggesting the presence of a corruption perception gap. Four implications about the existence of this gap can be drawn for future corruption measurement.*

Introduction

Corruption is increasingly regarded as a major challenge for many countries in Asia (and indeed much of the developing world) and is one of the foremost obstacles to Asia's political, economic, and social development (Diamond 1999; Bhargava and Bolongaita 2004). Despite Asian economies having rebounded from the late 1990s financial crisis,

Quah (2006) argues that the problem of corruption remains symptomatic throughout the region, "significantly cramping the extent and potential of Asia's 'rise'".

One widely used measure of the severity of corruption is provided by Transparency International's (TI) Corruption Perception Index (CPI). The CPI ranks countries and territories around the world based on international experts' and business people's perceptions of the level of public sector corruption. Table 1 depicts the 2005–2011 CPI scores for 17 countries/territories located in East and Southeast Asia. CPI scores range from 0 (highly corrupt) to 10 (very clean). As seen in Table 1, Asia is home to countries perceived to be highly corrupt (e.g. North Korea and Myanmar), and countries that are seen as very clean (e.g. Singapore). The CPI scores from 2005–2011 reveal that a given country/territory's scores typically do not vary much year to year. Generally, TI considers a CPI score of 5 to be the transition point differentiating countries that do and do not have a serious corruption problem. In the 2011 CPI, 11 of the 17 countries/territories listed fail to score above 5.

The CPI data reported in Table 1 indicates that the perceived level of public sector corruption is relatively high for a majority of East and Southeast Asian countries/territories. A fundamental, but seldom addressed, question is whether the domestic population of these countries/territories hold views corresponding with the CPI scores. As often noted by critics, because the CPI is an aggregate index constructed predominantly from international expert assessments and opinion surveys of business executives, it represents only a very narrow range of perceptions.

Table 1. Performance of East and Southeast Asian areas on the CPI, 2005–2011

Country/territory	2005 score (rank)	2006 score (rank)	2007 score (rank)	2008 score (rank)	2009 score (rank)	2010 score (rank)	2011 score (rank)
Cambodia	2.3 (130)	2.1 (151)	2.0 (162)	1.8 (166)	2.0 (158)	2.1 (154)	2.1 (164)
China	3.2 (78)	3.3 (70)	3.5 (72)	3.6 (72)	3.6 (79)	3.5 (78)	3.6 (75)
Hong Kong	8.3 (15)	8.3 (15)	8.3 (14)	8.1 (12)	8.2 (12)	8.4 (13)	8.4 (12)
Indonesia	2.2 (137)	2.4 (130)	2.3 (143)	2.6 (126)	2.8 (111)	2.8 (110)	3.0 (100)
Japan	7.3 (21)	7.6 (17)	7.5 (17)	7.3 (18)	7.7 (17)	7.8 (17)	8.0 (14)
Korea (North)	NA	NA	NA	NA	NA	NA	1.0 (182)
Korea (South)	5.0 (40)	5.1 (42)	5.1 (43)	5.6 (40)	5.5 (39)	5.4 (39)	5.4 (43)
Laos	3.3 (77)	2.6 (111)	1.9 (168)	2.0 (151)	2.0 (158)	2.1 (154)	2.2 (154)
Macau	NA	6.6 (26)	5.7 (34)	5.4 (43)	5.3 (43)	5.0 (46)	5.1 (46)
Malaysia	5.1 (39)	5.0 (44)	5.1 (43)	5.1 (47)	4.5 (56)	4.4 (56)	4.3 (60)
Mongolia	3.0 (85)	2.8 (99)	3.0 (99)	3.0 (102)	2.7 (120)	2.7 (116)	2.7 (120)
Myanmar	1.8 (155)	1.9 (160)	1.4 (179)	1.3 (178)	1.4 (178)	1.4 (176)	1.5 (180)
Philippines	2.5 (117)	2.5 (121)	2.5 (131)	2.3 (141)	2.4 (139)	2.4 (134)	2.6 (129)
Singapore	9.4 (5)	9.4 (5)	9.3 (4)	9.2 (4)	9.2 (3)	9.3 (1)	9.2 (5)
Taiwan	5.9 (32)	5.9 (34)	5.7 (34)	5.7 (39)	5.6 (37)	5.8 (33)	6.1 (32)
Thailand	3.8 (59)	3.6 (63)	3.3 (84)	3.5 (80)	3.4 (84)	3.5 (78)	3.4 (80)
Vietnam	2.6 (107)	2.6 (111)	2.6 (123)	2.7 (121)	2.7 (120)	2.7 (116)	2.9 (112)
Regional average	4.38	4.48	4.33	4.33	4.31	4.33	4.21
Number of countries and territories surveyed	159	163	180	180	180	178	183

Source: Transparency International's Corruption Perception Index, 2005–2011. CPI scores are scaled from 0 (highly corrupt) to 10 (very clean). A country or territory's rank indicates its position relative to the other countries and territories included in the index. A useful heuristic is that an index score below five indicates the presence of a serious corruption problem.

To shed light on the above question, this study examines domestic citizens' and international experts' perceptions of corruption in East and Southeast Asia. For local perspectives on corruption, data from the 2005–2008 Asian Barometer Survey (ABS) was utilized. The ABS was a regional, applied research program based at National Taiwan University that investigated the politically relevant attitudes and behaviors of Asian citizens. For the current study, public opinion data was extracted from ABS results for 13 different areas in East and Southeast Asia: Cambodia, China, Hong Kong, Indonesia, Japan, South Korea, Malaysia, Mongolia, the Philippines, Singapore, Taiwan, Thailand, and Vietnam. Data on global perspectives of corruption in these 13 areas, on the other hand, was taken from TI's Corruption Perception Index. Before presenting data analysis results, an overview of the relevant literature on corruption measurement is provided in the next section.

Measuring Corruption

Developing Indicators/Indices of Corruption

While there is general consensus about the threat corruption poses to the effectiveness of national governance, understanding corruption's true patterns, causes, and consequences has been hampered by the twin fundamental problems of definition (Johnston 1996, 2001, 2005; Brown 2006; Philp 2006) and measurement (Jain 2001; Kurer 2005; Miller 2006; Sampford et al. 2006; UNDP 2008). The process of either defining or measuring corruption is notoriously difficult, largely because (a) corruption is usually illicit and concealed, and (b) what constitutes corrupt or unethical behavior varies according to cultural, legal, and other factors (Svensson 2005). Caiden (2001), for instance, has attempted to identify the 19 "most commonly recognized forms of corruption", but these efforts have not closed the definitions debate since there is simply no universal consensus on the meaning of corruption (UNDP 2008). In fact, the United Nations Convention against Corruption (UNCAC) has deliberately steered clear of defining corruption explicitly or comprehensively, relying instead on enumerated acts to characterize the different types of corruption.

Even if substantial issues over the definition of corruption remain unsettled, scholars and practitioners interested in the multi-faceted and complex phenomenon of corruption have not been deterred from attempting to measure it. Early efforts were based on obtaining objective (or hard) measurements such as number of arrests and convictions for corruption, counts of newspaper stories on corruption, and other official records and statistics. The main difficulty with this approach is that such hard empirical evidence is often a sign of an effective criminal justice system (i.e. anti-corruption agencies, prosecutors, and judges) or the presence of a free and independent press to investigate and expose corruption, rather than a reflection of the actual corruption levels. In highly corrupt countries, there may be virtually no arrests for or media reports on serious corruption, whereas in very clean countries, there may be frequent arrests and convictions for relatively minor offenses.

As a result of these inherent deficiencies in using objective indicators, much research over the past 20 years has focused on utilizing subjective measures of corruption as a substitute. Two main types of subjective measures have been developed – perception-based and experience-based measures. Broadly speaking, perception-based measures are indicators based on the subjective opinions of experts and/or citizens about the extent of corruption in a country, whereas experience-based indicators attempt to measure the citizens' and firms' actual experiences with corruption (such as whether they have paid or been solicited for a bribe in exchange for a public service).[1]

The most widely used perception-based measure of corruption is the Corruption Perception Index, produced annually by Transparency International, a non-governmental organization based in Berlin dedicated to raising public awareness about the severity of the worldwide corruption problem. First released in 1995, the CPI has quickly become the best known of TI's corruption measurement tools. The CPI is a composite index (a survey of surveys) that draws on existing global expert evaluations and business opinion surveys from a variety of third party sources, including commercial risk rating agencies, think tanks, NGOs, and international organizations. Under the working definition of corruption being "the abuse of entrusted power for private gain", the CPI ranks countries and territories around the world yearly according to the perceived level of public sector corruption as determined by experts, business people, and analysts (Heinrich and Hodess 2011). The main rationale for combining and aggregating measures from several data sources is to attenuate concerns about potential measurement errors and biases arising from a single source (Lambsdorff 2007).

After TI's introduction of the CPI, researchers at the World Bank also began publishing an international index of corruption as part of its Worldwide Governance Indicators (WGI) project, which was an elaborate effort to measure, compare, and rank the governance of countries/territories around the world. This indicator, known as Control of Corruption (CC), is one of the six dimensions of governance, defined broadly as "the traditions and institutions by which authority in a country is exercised" (Kaufmann et al. 1999). The CC governance indicator shares some of the same primary sources as the CPI, although it uses slightly different estimation and aggregation procedures (Kaufmann et al. 2010). However, unlike the CPI, the World Bank's CC governance indicator employs a more heterogeneous set of questions about the different types of corruption and incorporates a few data sources that survey ordinary citizens' perceptions of corruption.[2]

The wide accessibility of these two perception-based corruption indices have thus stimulated a substantial amount of academic research on corruption and advanced its study over the past two decades (for excellent reviews, see Svensson 2005; Lambsdorff 2006, 2007; Treisman 2007). Since both the CPI and World Bank's CC governance indicator cover a large number of countries and territories, they have not only made large-N studies of the causes and consequences of corruption possible, but have also placed the issues of combating corruption and improving governance squarely on the international policy agenda of governments and private enterprises. Nevertheless, while these composite indices represent a major step forward in understanding and measuring corruption, strong concerns about the adequacy, validity, reliability, and ultimate usefulness of these perceptual measures persist (for a partial list of critiques, see Lancaster and Montinola 2001; Sik 2002; Arndt and Oman 2006; Galtung 2006; Soreide 2006; Knack 2007; Andersson and Heywood 2009; Langbein and Knack 2010; Pollitt 2010; Razafindrakoto and Roubaud 2010; Hawken and Munck 2011). It is not the intention of the present paper to defend the use of global perception-based corruption indices, or to provide yet another critique on their numerous inherent conceptual and methodological shortcomings. Rather, the purpose of the paper is to address a more mundane, but critical question: Do citizens' perceptions of corruption differ from the experts' perceptions, and, if so, to what extent are they different?

Whose Perceptions Count: Experts or Citizens?

As noted earlier, one often-cited weakness of aggregate indicators of corruption such as the CPI or the Control of Corruption governance indicator is that they give greater weight to the opinions of international business executives and the expert assessment of cross-national analysts. As such, both indices primarily reflect the opinions of mostly foreign experts and business elites, which may be disconnected from the views of the general public in each country under evaluation.

To address such shortcomings, beginning in 2003 TI supplemented the CPI with the Global Corruption Barometer (GCB), a large worldwide survey across dozens of countries that investigates and tracks ordinary people's views toward, and experience of, corruption. TI's own analysis of the GCB and CPI data indicates that, contrary to the above criticism, there is indeed a statistically significant correlation between citizens' and international experts' assessments of the extent of public sector corruption across all countries (Transparency International 2010).[3] Moreover, international experts' general opinions on corruption were also found to align strongly with the local public's specific experiences with bribery – in countries or territories where the experts perceive corruption to be rampant, a higher proportion of citizens reported paying bribes in the past year (Transparency International 2010).[4] The message from TI thus seems clear; since the CPI and the GCB correlate, expert perceptions of corruption were arguably not too dissimilar from average citizens' perceptions, thereby establishing the validity for each of these indicators.

In the literature, a number of studies using other international public opinion surveys have corroborated TI's findings, although none focused on East or Southeast Asia specifically. In a review of major international corruption indices, Ko and Samajdar (2010) compared the CPI with public opinion data taken from two multi-region surveys: the World Values Survey (WVS) and the International Crime Victimization Survey (ICVS). Their analyses show that CPI scores are highly correlated with local people's responses to the bribery questions respectively found in the WVS ($r = -0.86$) and in the ICVS ($r = -0.75$). The authors thereby concluded that, as far as petty bribery is concerned, international corruption indices "can reflect [a] significant variation of domestic perceptions". Also, in a study of the level of government corruption in seven Latin American countries, Canache and Allison (2005) found that there was a similar high degree of correspondence between expert and local judgments.

A recent innovative study conducted by Razafindrakoto and Roubaud (2010) in eight African countries, however, has produced findings that directly challenge the above studies. Surveying both the general public and the so-called experts of those countries, they found that the expert perceptions did not correlate with the ordinary citizens' views at all, but instead were more closely associated with international corruption indicators such as the CPI and the CC governance indicator.[5] More importantly, the authors found that experts – whether domestic or foreign – systematically overestimated the actual extent of, and the local population's tolerance for, corrupt practices. Based on these results, Razafindrakoto and Roubaud posit that most experts were basing their assessments on an erroneous cultural model of "how Africa operates" and/or acting on their personal ideological inclinations.

Moreover, in an analysis of evaluator characteristics within the various data sources of the Worldwide Governance Indicators, Hawken and Munck (2011) discovered that different classes of evaluators systematically generate higher or lower estimates of the level of corruption in countries around the world. For example, they found that experts from commercial risk assessment agencies generally provide stricter assessments of the extent of corruption in a country than those from non-governmental organizations and that only expert ratings from the multilateral development banks can be considered indistinguishable from general public opinion. Hawken and Munck also detected important evaluator differences in regional comparisons as well. For instance, Southeast Asia as a whole received relatively unfavorable assessments from experts in commercial risk rating agencies and in surveys of business executives, but more favorable assessments from surveys of the public. East Asian countries, on the other hand, were favored by experts from multilateral development banks, but disfavored by other business executives and by the citizens at large. The main reason for differences in expert ratings within or between regions is unclear, but the implication is that in most geographical areas, expert and common citizen's perceptions differ, and noticeable variations exist among different classes of experts.

That a discrepancy may exist between expert and the general public's judgments is neither new nor exclusive to studies of corruption. For some time now, it has been well known in environmental policy and the sociology of risk literature that, for whatever reason, experts and lay people frequently disagree on risk perceptions and risk assessments (Bostrom 1997; Sjoberg 1999). The most illustrative example is the case of nuclear power in the 1960s. Scientific opinion at the time declared the risks of nuclear energy to be low, but the general public was alarmed about the safety of this new technology, perceiving the risks of a nuclear disaster to be high. Risk managers and theorists have since been preoccupied with explaining this gap between expert and lay perceptions, and also finding avenues to bridge it. In the policy arena, citizens also frequently disagree with policy experts on important public issues quite frequently, even though the latter is presumed to have the best-informed opinion (Darmofal 2005).

There are common-sense reasons to trust expert assessments. By definition, experts are individuals who, through education, training, and experience, possess extensive specialized knowledge or skills in a particular subject, and thus can act as a reliable information source or adviser. Kaufmann and Kraay (2008) provide three advantages that expert assessments offer over public opinion when measuring multifaceted concepts such as governance or corruption: (1) lower costs (i.e. no need to carry out surveys of individuals or firms across 100 or more countries and territories); (2) the ability to tailor assessments for cross-national comparability; and (3), given the complexity of the concept in question, experts can be more readily called upon to provide technical or specialized information.

Still, expert assessments do have their fair share of important limitations. One is that expert assessments (and the experts themselves) are subject to ideological, cultural, institutional, and other biases. The CPI, for instance, has been severely criticized for relying on data sources whose samples were disproportionally pro-business and male, thereby overlooking the perspectives of most women, the poor, and the disenfranchised (Galtung 2006). Donchev and Ujhelyi (2013) found evidence that, for a given level of corruption, corruption indices based on expert perceptions were not only systematically biased in favor of more economically developed and traditional Protestant countries, but they also tended to penalize larger countries. The second concern is that experts, being a small and relatively homogeneous group, may lack familiarity with the local customs and language, or worse, may only have a superficial knowledge of them (Sik 2002), particularly for smaller countries (Knack 2007). The third issue with expert assessments (and to a lesser extent with citizens' subjective evaluations) is a danger of the echo chamber problem. Individuals assessing corruption levels end up simply repeating conventional wisdom, thus reinforcing a vicious cycle of prior (mis)conceptions (Johnston 2002). Knack (2007) also claimed that, rather than being independent evaluations, expert judgments are often based on experts from different institutions consulting with one another, reading each other's reports, and possibly being influenced by each other's ratings.

By contrast, there are three main reasons local citizen surveys may provide superior indications of corruption levels. One is that citizen opinions are extremely valuable because they represent internal stakeholders who may choose to act upon those views (Kaufmann and Kraay 2008), and governments are less likely to dismiss the views of their citizens (as opposed to external expert assessments, which are often ignored). Second, the views of randomly chosen members of the general public – unlike expert opinions – are more likely to be independent from, and uncontaminated by, other types of judgments (Knack 2007). Third, household surveys of citizens are extremely helpful for assessing the prevalence of petty or low-level corruption (UNDP 2008).

Yet cross-national surveys of citizens face several potential problems that threaten their validity and reliability. First, since most forms of corruption are illegal, some respondents may not answer questions truthfully, especially those in authoritarian countries or in societies where the public acceptance of corruption is low (Mishler and Rose 2008). Second, the general public is also more prone than experts to be influenced by the media and the country's overall political and economic climate (Galtung 2006). The possibility of a home country bias is one of the justifications for using international experts, on the premise that outside reviewers can be expected to act in a more neutral and competent way when evaluating many different countries according to a set of universal standards (Lambsdorff 2007). Third, like all empirical social science research based on subjective data, surveys of citizens are subject to three forms of systematic measurement error: respondents' cognitive problems in understanding/answering questions, respondents' inclination to give socially desirable responses to sensitive questions, and respondents' lack of an informed opinion on a particular issue (Bertrand and Mullainathan 2001).

Nevertheless, scholars and practitioners alike will continue debating over whose perceptions, the global experts or the local citizens, better capture the actual level of corruption in a country. Each has its own strengths and weaknesses for certain purposes. Moving forward, more restraint will be needed when using these two forms of perceptions in academic or policy contexts. In the next section, the central question of the present study is considered: do East and Southeast Asian citizens' perceived levels of corruption mirror those of the global experts?

Perceptions of Corruption in East and Southeast Asia

To gauge individual citizens' perceptions of corruption in society, the Asian Barometer Survey[6] asked respondents the following two questions:

1. How widespread do you think corruption and bribe-taking are in the national government [in the capital city]?
2. How widespread do you think corruption and bribe-taking are in your local/municipal government?

For both questions, respondents were presented with four choices: "hardly anyone is involved", "not a lot of officials are corrupt", "most officials are corrupt", and "almost everyone is corrupt". The original coding scheme was retained, so that higher values would indicate higher levels of perceived corruption. Table 2 presents the data on the

Table 2. Citizens' perceptions of corruption and bribe-taking in the national government

Country/territory	How widespread is corruption and bribe-taking in the national government? (1 to 4 scale)				Valid respondents Total
	Hardly anyone is involved	Not a lot of officials are corrupt	Most officials are corrupt	Almost everyone is corrupt	
Cambodia (Year: 2008; n = 1000; percentage missing = 22.4%)	11 (1.4%)	251 (32.3%)	**348 (44.9%)**	166 (21.4%)	776
China (Year: 2007–2008; n = 5098; percentage missing = 60.8%)	816 (40.9%)	**893 (44.7%)**	229 (11.5%)	58 (2.9%)	1996
Indonesia (Year: 2006; n = 1598; percentage missing = 12.5%)	94 (6.7%)	**616 (44.0%)**	489 (35.0%)	200 (14.3%)	1399
Japan (Year: 2007; n = 1067; percentage missing = 10.3%)	11 (1.1%)	**529 (55.3%)**	367 (38.3%)	50 (5.2%)	957
South Korea (Year: 2006; n = 1212; percentage missing = 5.3%)	15 (1.3%)	**585 (51.0%)**	410 (35.7%)	138 (12.0%)	1148
Malaysia (Year: 2007; n = 1218; percentage missing = 10.0%)	47 (4.3%)	**561 (51.2%)**	356 (32.5%)	132 (12.0%)	1096
Mongolia (Year: 2006; n = 1211; percentage missing = 7.3%)	31 (2.8%)	251 (22.4%)	**482 (42.9%)**	359 (32.0%)	1123
Philippines (Year: 2005; n = 1200; percentage missing = 6.2%)	103 (9.1%)	276 (24.5%)	**457 (40.6%)**	290 (25.8%)	1126
Singapore (Year: 2006; n = 1012; percentage missing = 13.6%)	**443 (50.7%)**	416 (47.6%)	11 (1.3%)	4 (0.5%)	874
Taiwan (Year: 2006; n = 1587; percentage missing = 13.3%)	43 (3.1%)	411 (29.9%)	**763 (55.5%)**	159 (11.6%)	1376
Thailand (Year: 2006; n = 1546; percentage missing = 15.8%)	193 (14.8%)	**725 (55.7%)**	280 (21.5%)	103 (7.9%)	1301
Vietnam (Year: 2005; n = 1200; percentage missing = 19.3%)	115 (11.9%)	**688 (71.0%)**	143 (14.8%)	23 (2.4%)	969

Source: Asian Barometer Survey, 2005–2008.
Note: Cell entries are frequencies, and numbers in parenthesis are percentages. The largest group of responses for each country is highlighted in **bold**. Because of rounding, percentages may not add up to 100. Data was not available for Hong Kong. n = country/territory sample size.

distribution of individual responses to the question about corruption in the national government, disaggregated by country, with the largest share of responses highlighted in bold.

Most local citizens surveyed in the ABS did not think that corruption was widespread in their respective national governments. As depicted in Table 2, a majority of respondents in China, Indonesia, Japan, South Korea, Malaysia, Singapore, Thailand, and Vietnam believed that few national government officials were involved in corruption. Expectedly, Singapore was the only country where more than half of respondents felt that hardly any government official was engaged in corrupt behavior. Conversely, over 66 per cent of the respondents in Cambodia, Mongolia, the Philippines, and Taiwan believe that most or almost all government officials are corrupt. Although no country had the "almost everyone is corrupt" as the most popular response, Mongolia came closest with 32 per cent, followed by the Philippines at 26 per cent). Indonesia was interesting because its citizens were the most evenly split between those who perceived corruption in the national government to be high and those who deemed it to be low (49 per cent versus 51 per cent).

The distribution of individual responses for each country on this corruption perception question nevertheless produced some interesting and unexpected results, especially when compared to the CPI scores (from Table 1) or conventional wisdom. For instance, the percentage of Chinese, Thai, and Vietnamese respondents who believed that corruption is *not* pervasive in their national governments were all above 70 per cent. Additionally, a large majority of Taiwanese citizens (approximately 67 per cent) perceived that most or almost all national government officials *are* corrupt. These two sets of findings certainly defy these countries' performance and placements in the CPI. In the ensuing discussion, these four countries will be used as illustrative cases in the current study's attempt to explore why experts' and citizens' perceptions differ.

What factors explain the perplexing percentages above? While ensuring that underlying data met the necessary research requirements, the problem of missing data as triggered by nonresponses to questionnaire items was noticed. An inspection showed that only 39 per cent ($n = 1996$) of China's respondents provided useful answers to the question regarding corruption in the national government. Assuming that data collection was conducted properly and data entry errors were kept at a minimum, this means that as much as 61 per cent of Chinese respondents – the highest percentage of abstainers in the ABS – did not answer the question. Those that responded provided mostly favorable assessments of their national government officials. Missing information makes Chinese responses on corruption problematic, and any analysis using this questionnaire item must be treated with caution.[7] Item nonresponse because of respondent error or reticence to answer was less of an issue for Taiwan, Thailand, and Vietnam. Missing values accounted for less than 20 per cent in these countries' surveys.[8]

One explanation that may have impacted the overall pattern of responses was the time period during which the ABS was implemented in each country. This factor partly explains why in the 2006 ABS Survey, two out of three Taiwanese respondents felt their national government was overrun by corrupt officials. There was severe political turmoil in Taiwan during 2006, with a series of corruption scandals involving then President Chen Shui-bian and his close associates being uncovered. As a result, people's indignation toward the Chen administration lingered for months (for more information, see Chu 2007; Yu et al. 2008).

In Thailand, the ABS was conducted a few months before the Thai military staged a successful coup to overthrow Prime Minister Thaksin Sinawatra, a lightning-rod politician who, despite enormous popularity in rural areas, was intensely distrusted by opposition leaders, academics, journalists, and middle-class Bangkok residents. They saw Thaksin as gradually undermining Thailand's democratic institutions, weakening media independence, and establishing a regime extensively fueled by corruption (Ockey 2007). However, without additional context, the events of 2006 do not fully explain why Thai respondents believed that corruption was not a serious public concern and yet ousted Thaksin's administration in 2006, at least partly over corruption. According to a Thai author, this was precisely the source of the problem: it was not the acts of corruption themselves, but the fact that tolerance of corruption was "too deeply ingrained" in Thailand, permeating all sectors of Thai society, as citizens were "easily bored and indifferent toward corruption by politicians and bureaucrats" (Hengkietisak 2010). People's greater acceptance of corruption may constitute another explanation for the difference in perceptions between experts and average citizens.

As for Vietnamese perceptions that corruption was not widespread in the national government, the timing of the survey appears to have been a critical factor. For most of 2005, Vietnam continued its push toward greater economic growth, improved its governance, and intensified the dialogue between the state and society concerning global integration (Luong 2006). In that particular year, there was extensive coverage of major corruption cases by the media, and the Vietnamese authoritarian state toughened its anti-corruption and anti-waste stance by passing the country's first comprehensive anti-corruption legislation (Fritzen 2006). These developments, arguably, provided the Vietnamese ABS respondents with reason to perceive their government leaders as committed to cracking down on graft. Under this scenario, Vietnamese citizens are perhaps more trusting of their government's anti-corruption efforts than the external experts.

Table 2 contains a mixture of both anticipated and unanticipated results. Being cautious, it remains unclear whether the unexpected results should be labeled as citizens' perceptual errors, or as indications of something else, such as wider tolerance of corruption or greater faith in government. In Table 3, the distribution of citizen responses about the existence of widespread corruption in local or municipal governments is reported. Here the data from Hong Kong is included but not Singapore's (the question was omitted from the Singaporean survey due to the country's small size). The percentages in Table 3 closely resemble those in Table 2. First, contrary to perceptions of government corruption at the national level, most Cambodian and Mongolian citizens believed corruption was less rampant at the local level. Second, there were considerably more Chinese respondents believing corruption and bribery to be prevalent in local governments (although item nonresponse was still a problem). On the other hand, citizens of Taiwan and the Philippines carried over their perceptions that corruption and bribe-taking behavior by public officials was just as prevalent in local as in national government.

Citizens' perceptions of corruption in both national and local governments can be aggregated and then averaged to form a measure that captures the citizen's overall evaluation of the severity of public sector corruption in a particular country/territory. This mean perceived corruption from the ABS data can then be compared with expert-based indices of corruption such as the CPI (Table 4). Because countries were surveyed at different times, this study calculates their CPI value as the average of their CPI scores for the two years immediately following their ABS implementation year.[9] The correlation

Table 3. Citizens' perceptions of corruption and bribe-taking in the local/municipal government

Country/territory	How widespread is corruption and bribe-taking in your local/municipal government? (1 to 4 scale)				Valid respondents Total
	Hardly anyone is involved	Not a lot of officials are corrupt	Most officials are corrupt	Almost everyone is corrupt	
Cambodia (Year: 2008; n = 1000; percentage missing = 6.0%)	65 (6.9%)	**420 (44.7%)**	320 (34.0%)	135 (14.4%)	940
China (Year: 2007–2008; n = 5098; percentage missing = 39.5%)	372 (12.1%)	**1226 (39.7%)**	1143 (37.1%)	344 (11.2%)	3085
Hong Kong (Year: 2007; n = 849; percentage missing = 16.0%)	139 (19.5%)	**486 (68.2%)**	83 (11.6%)	5 (0.7%)	713
Indonesia (Year: 2006; n = 1598; percentage missing = 12.4%)	228 (16.3%)	**620 (44.3%)**	388 (27.7%)	164 (11.7%)	1400
Japan (Year: 2007; n = 1067; percentage missing = 8.2%)	20 (2.0%)	**554 (56.5%)**	366 (37.3%)	40 (4.1%)	980
South Korea (Year: 2006; n = 1212; percentage missing = 5.1%)	35 (3.0%)	**626 (54.4%)**	377 (32.8%)	112 (9.7%)	1150
Malaysia (Year: 2007; n = 1218; percentage missing = 10.0%)	63 (5.7%)	**567 (51.1%)**	342 (30.8%)	137 (12.4%)	1096
Mongolia (Year: 2006; n = 1211; percentage missing = 8.4%)	161 (14.3%)	**438 (39.0%)**	351 (31.3%)	173 (15.4%)	1109
Philippines (Year: 2005; n = 1200; percentage missing = 6.4%)	161 (14.2%)	294 (26.0%)	**451 (39.9%)**	224 (19.8%)	1123
Taiwan (Year: 2006; n = 1587; percentage missing = 10.6%)	56 (3.9%)	423 (29.8%)	**822 (57.9%)**	118 (8.3%)	1419
Thailand (Year: 2006; n = 1546; percentage missing = 15.7%)	358 (27.5%)	**684 (52.5%)**	199 (15.3%)	63 (4.8%)	1304
Vietnam (Year: 2005; n = 1200; percentage missing = 17.8%)	385 (39.0%)	**539 (54.6%)**	54 (5.5%)	9 (0.9%)	987

Notes: Cell entries are frequencies, and numbers in parenthesis are percentages. The largest group of responses for each country or territory highlighted in **bold**. Because of rounding, percentages may not add up to 100. Data was not available for Singapore. n = country/territory sample size.
Source: Asian Barometer Survey, 2005–2008.

Table 4. Analysis of perception differences in the ABS and CPI data using z-scores

Country/territory	Mean perceived corruption (ABS)	ABSZ	CPI score (2-year average)	CPIZ	CPIZ' = −1 × CPIZ	ABSZ − CPIZ'	Absolute value of (ABSZ − CPIZ')
Philippines	2.74	1.05	2.50	−0.93	0.93	0.12	0.12
Singapore	1.51	−2.25	9.25	2.00	−2.00	−0.25	0.25
Cambodia	2.66	0.85	2.05	−1.12	1.12	−0.28	0.28
Mongolia	2.76	1.10	3.00	−0.71	0.71	0.38	0.38
Hong Kong	1.94	−1.11	8.15	1.52	−1.52	0.41	0.41
Malaysia	2.51	0.42	4.80	0.07	−0.07	0.49	0.49
China	2.28	−0.19	3.55	−0.47	0.47	−0.66	0.66
Indonesia	2.45	0.28	2.45	−0.95	0.95	−0.67	0.67
South Korea	2.54	0.52	5.35	0.31	−0.31	0.82	0.82
Thailand	2.10	−0.66	3.40	−0.54	0.54	−1.19	1.19
Taiwan	2.72	1.00	5.70	0.46	−0.46	1.46	1.46
Japan	2.45	0.28	7.50	1.24	−1.24	1.52	1.52
Vietnam	1.87	−1.28	2.60	−0.88	0.88	−2.17	2.17
Regional mean (μ)	2.35		4.64				
Standard deviation (σ)	0.37		2.30				

Notes: ABSZ and CPIZ are the respective z-scores calculated from the ABS and CPI values. The CPIZ was then reversed to produce CPIZ' so that higher values indicate more corruption. In the table, countries are ordered from low to high according to the absolute value of the difference between their ABS and CPI z-scores. The closer the absolute value of the difference in z-scores is to zero (= more congruence), the smaller the perception gap between citizens and experts.

Source: Transparency International; Asian Barometer Survey, 2005–2008.

coefficient between ABS's mean perceived corruption and the CPI values equaled -0.507, suggesting a medium level of perceptual correspondence between the two. However, ABS/CPI correlation was not statistically significant at the usual 0.05 level ($p < 0.077$).

To understand how each country compares to others in the region, standard z-scores were computed for all countries (labeled ABSZ and CPIZ in Table 4).[10] After a few elementary math operations to get the correct signs, the two z-scores were subtracted from one another to obtain an estimate of the corruption perception gap between citizens and experts. For easier interpretation, the absolute value of the differences in z-scores was taken. These results are listed in the rightmost column of Table 4.

As can be seen from the table, the Philippines, Singapore, and Cambodia have the smallest values when the two z-scores were subtracted from one another, indicating a greater congruence in corruption perception between the citizens and experts. The countries where experts and citizens most diverged were Thailand, Taiwan, Japan, and Vietnam – they all had z-score differences greater than one standard deviation.

Results show that only *some* commonality between local people's aggregate perceptions of corruption and global experts' views as provided by the CPI. The lack of a direct, strong correspondence between the two is displayed in Figure 1, where countries' ABS z-scores are plotted against their CPI z-scores. The 45 degree diagonal in the figure is used to indicate perfect congruence between ABS and CPI.

As can be seen from the figure, four types of combinations between (global) expert and (local) citizen perceptions can be identified: (1) both groups perceived corruption in the country to be high (quadrant I); (2) both groups perceived corruption to be low (quadrant II); (3) experts, but not the citizens, perceived corruption to be high (quadrant III), and (4) citizens, but not the experts, perceived corruption in the country to be high (quadrant IV). The distribution of Asian countries across the four quadrants is telling.

Figure 1. A typology of perception differences.

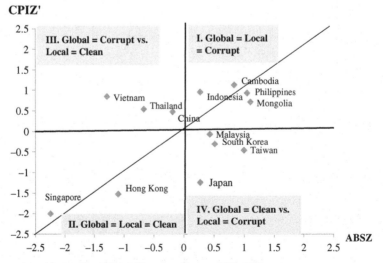

Source: Transparency International; Asian Barometer Survey, 2005–2008.
Note: ABSZ and CPIZ are the respective z-scores calculated from the ABS and CPI values. The CPIZ was then reversed to produce the CPIZ' so that higher values indicate greater corruption.

Asian citizens' aggregate perceived corruption aligned with the expert (CPI) view in only half of the countries (quadrants I and II). Among the countries that performed more poorly in the CPI rankings, only citizens from four countries (the Philippines, Cambodia, Mongolia, and Indonesia) agreed with the experts that corruption was rampant in their governments. Among places that score high on the CPI (lower perceived corruption), citizens from Singapore and Hong Kong also collectively perceived the level of public corruption to be low. For quadrants III and IV, on the other hand, global and local perspectives disagreed, sometimes sharply. In quadrant III are the countries that performed poorly in the CPI rankings (Vietnam, Thailand, and China), while citizens perceived their government to be relatively clean. In quadrant IV, citizens in Japan, Taiwan, South Korea, and Malaysia viewed their government to be relatively corrupt, but the experts believe otherwise. This typology of perception differences between global experts and local citizens should be useful for future research, and the reasons for the existence of or lack of perception gaps for these countries deserves further investigation.

Conclusions

Increasing worldwide concerns about reducing corruption in the public sector give considerable impetus to the search for a reliable measurement of, normally hidden, corruption. So far, aggregate indices based primarily on international expert assessments are the best known and most widely used measurement tools, but validity concerns persist. Critics charge that global corruption indices do not necessarily reflect local views. Although aware of the problem, academic literature has only recently paid attention to the existence, causes, and consequences of a perception gap between international experts and the local citizens concerning corruption in a country (Roca 2010).

This study's objective is to compare international experts' and domestic citizens' perceptions of corruption in East and Southeast Asia and develop a typology of perception differences for future research. Using Asian Barometer Survey data for 13 countries/territories in the region, local citizens' responses to questions about the prevalence of corruption in their national and local government were examined. The study found the correlation between citizens' perceptions and experts' assessments in these selected Asian countries/territories to be only moderately strong. The result is consistent with previous studies using the Latinobarometro or Afrobarometer to test the congruity between expert ratings and mass perceptions of government effectiveness in Latin American and African countries (Kurtz and Schrank 2007). The observed perceptual disparity between the two perspectives did not always have the same direction: in some countries the international experts reported higher levels of corruption, while in others local citizens rated corruption higher. Given these results, a different question naturally emerged: why don't global experts and local citizens agree (more often) in their corruption perceptions?

ABS data limitations do not allow a more in-depth investigation of the factors causing the incongruity between global and local perceptions of corruption; thus, there are more questions than answers. It is fair to say that just as global expert assessments have their particular predispositions and idiosyncrasies, local perceptions have their own dynamics as well. A few possible reasons for the divergence were derived from the extant literature: personal ideology, cultural bias, and the echo chamber problem on the international experts' side; respondent reticence (to give truthful answers to sensitive questions), the effect of media or government influence, and greater tolerance for corruption on the domestic citizens' side. Clearly, this list of explanations is neither definitive nor exhaustive. A more immediate challenge would be finding ways to disentangle and later test these various factors. The result would be a better understanding about the perceptions of corruption itself, and a narrowing of the chasm between international expert and domestic citizen corruption assessments.

In conclusion, four implications can be drawn regarding the future of corruption measurement. First, a multi-measure of corruption that incorporates both global (expert-based) and local (citizen-based) perspectives is necessary. A measure that includes the views of different groups and stakeholders would better approximate the actual levels and trends of corruption in a country. Second, future corruption measures need to be ongoing, not one-shot studies. By having time-series data, scholars and officials can be more confident in measuring corruption and in suggesting anti-corruption initiatives. Time-series data would also allow one to test for the presence of time period-related variables. Third, to the extent that local perspectives are valuable in and of themselves, these perspectives cannot simply be added onto existing corruption indices such as CPI for cross-national comparisons without reasonable adjustments, because (a) practices and behaviors that are acceptable in one country may be viewed as corrupt in another (problem of definition), and (b) the quality and validity of local surveys may be difficult to control over a large number of countries and territories (problem of data collection). Finally, if local perspectives of corruption are to be taken into account for global comparison, they should be entered as *relative changes* to enhance cross-national comparability, in order to reduce potential confounding factors.[11] Although no measure of corruption currently features all of the above requirements, the creation of a more inclusive measure of corruption is a goal that should be supported and encouraged by both academic and practitioner communities.

Notes

1. In all fairness, just as corruption perception indices became popular and near-permanent fixtures in cross-national studies of corruption in the late 1990s and early 2000s, researchers began to argue about the need to go beyond perception-based measures and people's impressions. One approach is to examine the actual experience of people exposed to bribery and corruption, as mentioned in the text. However, some scholars contend that even these experience-based measures of corruption may not be accurate enough (see Johnston 2010; Hawken and Munck 2011). They suggest taking steps to develop more sophisticated objective measures of corruption, such as the time required to obtain permits and licenses, the amount of funds leakage in public works projects, and whether prices paid to suppliers and charged to the public for basic services are reasonable (Johnston 2010). Viewed in this manner, corruption measurement research has indeed nearly come full circle.
2. In the most recent update (2011) of World Bank's CC governance indicator, five out of its 30 sources were surveys of individual citizens: Afrobarometer, Latinobarometro, Vanderbilt University's AmericasBarometer, Gallup World Poll, and TI's Global Corruption Barometer.
3. To be specific, the Pearson's correlation coefficient (r) between global expert evaluations in the 2009 CPI and the local people's perception scores in the 2010 GCB was 0.54 ($p < 0.01$).
4. The Pearson's correlation coefficient between the 2009 CPI scores and the percentage of local citizens who report paying bribes was -0.66 ($p < 0.01$). The coefficient has a negative sign because CPI scores are scaled from 10 (very clean) to 0 (highly corrupt).
5. These experts include, "researchers, development workers, decision-makers, high-ranking public officials, politicians, etc." (Razafindrakoto and Roubaud 2010: 1062).
6. The ABS is a collaborative effort encompassing research teams from 13 political systems in East and Southeast Asia. Each administering team was responsible for survey sampling and implementation in its

area. Most individual national surveys used a variation of multi-stage cluster sampling design (sometimes in combination with probability-proportional-to-size sampling) to select the primary geographic sampling units, households, and respondents, except for four areas which used multi-stage random sampling (Japan, Hong Kong, Mongolia, and Singapore), and mainland China, which used multi-stage stratified area sampling methods. In all countries, target respondents represented a cross-section of voting-age adult citizens, and all interviews were conducted face-to-face by trained fieldworkers in the language of the respondent's choice. The ABS uses a standard questionnaire with identical or functionally equivalent questions, which made comparison of results possible across different areas.
7. While there exist several modern remedies for missing data problems (such as multiple imputation techniques), these approaches were ultimately not considered here because a key assumption of those models – that the data was missing completely at random – was probably not met in the China ABS survey.
8. Although there is no consensus in the literature regarding at what point the amount of missing information becomes problematic for inference and estimation, researchers have suggested that a cutoff point between 5 and 20 per cent is acceptable (see Schlomer et al. 2010).
9. The CPI used data from the previous two years to calculate a country's or territory's annual corruption perception score. As such, the CPI is a lagged index, which may not reflect the most recent developments or situations in a country/territory. To correct for this lag, the subsequent two-year average CPI score was compared with the ABS scores.
10. The formula for computing z-scores is $z = \frac{x_i - \mu}{\sigma}$, where μ is the mean and σ is the standard deviation.
11. The formula for computing relative change is: $\frac{this\ year's\ score - last\ year's\ score}{last\ year's\ score}$.

Acknowledgements

Data analyzed in this article were collected by the Asian Barometer Project (2005-2008), which was co-directed by Professors Fu Hu and Yun-han Chu and received major funding support from Taiwan's Ministry of Education, Academia Sinica, and National Taiwan University. The Asian Barometer Project Office (www.asianbarometer.org) is solely responsible for the data distribution. The authors appreciate the assistance by the institutes and individuals aforementioned. They are also grateful to Transparency International (TI) and TI's chapter in Taiwan for providing additional data used in the article. Lastly, they thank the editor and three anonymous reviewers for their constructive comments and suggestions. The views expressed herein are solely the authors' responsibility.

References

Andersson, S. and Heywood, P., 2009, The politics of perception: Use and abuse of Transparency International's approach to measuring corruption. *Political Studies*, **57**(4), pp. 746–767.
Arndt, C. and Oman, C., 2006, *Uses and Abuses of Governance Indicators* (Paris: OECD Development Centre).
Bertrand, M. and Mullainathan, S., 2001, Do people mean what they say? Implications for subjective survey data. *American Economic Review*, **91**(2), pp. 67–72.
Bhargava, V. and Bolongaita, E., 2004, *Challenging Corruption in Asia* (Washington, DC: The World Bank).
Bostrom, A., 1997, Risk perceptions: 'Experts' vs. 'lay people'. *Duke Environmental Law & Policy Forum*, **8**, pp. 101–113.
Brown, A. J., 2006, What are we trying to measure? Reviewing the basics of corruption definition, in: C. Sampford, A. Shacklock, C. Connors and F. Galtung (Eds) *Measuring Corruption* (Burlington, VT: Ashgate Publishers), pp. 57–79.
Caiden, G., 2001, Corruption and governance, in: G. Caiden, O. P. Dwivedi, and J. Jabbra (Eds) *Where Corruption Lives* (Bloomfield, CT: Kumarian Press), pp. 15–37.
Canache, D. and Allison, M., 2005, Perceptions of political corruption in latin american democracies. *Latin American Politics and Society*, **47**(3), pp. 91–111.
Chu, Y.-H., 2007, Taiwan in 2006: A year of political turmoil. *Asian Survey*, **47**(1), pp. 44–51.
Darmofal, D., 2005, Elite cues and citizen disagreement with expert opinion. *Political Research Quarterly*, **58**(3), pp. 381–395.

Diamond, L., 1999, *Developing Democracy* (Baltimore: Johns Hopkins University Press).
Donchev, D. and Ujhelyi, G. 2013, *What Do Corruption Indices Measure?* Working Paper. University of Houston.
Fritzen, S., 2006, Beyond "political will": How institutional context shapes the implementation of anti-corruption policies. *Policy and Society*, **24**(3), pp. 79–96.
Galtung, F., 2006, Measuring the immeasurable: Boundaries and functions of (Macro) corruption indices, in: C. Sampford, A. Shacklock, C. Connors and F. Galtung (Eds) *Measuring Corruption* (Burlington, VT: Ashgate Publishers), pp. 101–130.
Hawken, A. and Munck, G. 2011, *Does the Evaluator Make a Difference? Measurement Validity in Corruption Research*. Working Paper. The Committee on Concepts and Methods, International Political Science Association (IPSA).
Heinrich, F. and Hodess, R., 2011, Measuring Corruption, in: A. Graycar and R. G. Smith (Eds) *Handbook of Global Research and Practice in Corruption* (Cheltenham: Edward Elgar), pp. 18–33.
Hengkietisak, K. 2010, Tolerance of corruption is too ceeply ingrained. *Bangkok Post*, 20 November. Available at http://www.bangkokpost.com/learning/learning-from-news/208707/tolerance-of-corruption.
Jain, A., 2001, Corruption: A review. *Journal of Economic Surveys*, **15**(1), pp. 71–121.
Johnston, M., 1996, The search for definitions: The vitality of politics and the issue of corruption. *International Social Science Journal*, **149**, pp. 321–335.
Johnston, M., 2001, The definitions debate: Old conflicts in new guises, in: A. Jain (Ed.) *The Political Economy of Corruption* (New York: Routledge), pp. 11–31.
Johnston, M., 2002, Measuring the new corruption rankings: Implications for analysis and reform, in: A. Heidenheimer and M. Johnston (Eds) *Political Corruption: Concepts & Contexts* (New Brunswick, NJ: Transaction Publishers), pp. 865–884.
Johnston, M., 2005, *Syndromes of Corruption: Wealth, Power, and Democracy* (Cambridge: Cambridge University Press).
Johnston, M., 2010, Assessing vulnerabilities to corruption: Indicators and benchmarks of government performance. *Public Integrity*, **12**(2), pp. 125–142.
Kaufmann, D. and Kraay, A., 2008, Governance indicators: Where are we, where should we be going?. *The World Bank Research Observer*, **23**(1), pp. 1–30.
Kaufmann, D., Kraay, A. and Mastruzzi, M. 2010, *The Worldwide Governance Indicators: A Summary of Methodology, Data and Analytical Issues*. World Bank Policy Research Working Paper No. 5430.
Kaufmann, D., Kraay, A. and Zoido, P. 1999, *Governance Matters*. World Bank Policy Research Working Paper No. 2196.
Knack, S., 2007, Measuring corruption: A critique of indicators in Eastern Europe and Central Asia. *Journal of Public Policy*, **27**(3), pp. 255–291.
Ko, K. and Samajdar, A., 2010, Evaluation of international corruption indexes: Should we believe them or not. *The Social Science Journal*, **47**(3), pp. 508–540.
Kurer, O., 2005, Corruption: An alternative approach to its definition and measurement. *Political Studies*, **53**, pp. 222–239.
Kurtz, M. and Schrank, A., 2007, Growth and governance: A defense. *The Journal of Politics*, **69**(2), pp. 563–569.
Lambsdorff, J., 2006, Causes and consequences of corruption: What do we know from a cross-section of countries?, in: S. Rose-Ackerman (Ed.) *International Handbook on the Economics of Corruption* (Cheltenham: Edward Elgar), pp. 3–51.
Lambsdorff, J., 2007, *The New Institutional Economics of Corruption and Reform: Theory, Evidence and Policy* (Cambridge: Cambridge University Press).
Lancaster, T. and Montinola, G., 2001, Comparative political corruption: Issues of operationalization and measurement. *Studies in Comparative International Development*, **36**(3), pp. 3–28.
Langbein, L. and Knack, S., 2010, The world wide governance indicators: Six, one, or none?. *Journal of Development Studies*, **46**(2), pp. 350–370.
Luong, H., 2006, Vietnam in 2005: Economic momentum and stronger state-society dialogue. *Asian Survey*, **46**(1), pp. 148–154.
Miller, W., 2006, Perceptions, experience and lies: What measures corruption and what do corruption measures measure?, in: C. Sampford, A. Shacklock, C. Connors and F. Galtung (Eds) *Measuring Corruption* (Burlington, VT: Ashgate Publishers), pp. 163–185.

Mishler, W. and Rose, R. 2008, Seeing Is Not Always Believing: Measuring Corruption Perceptions and Experiences. Paper prepared for the Elections, Public Opinion and Parties 2008 Annual Conference, University of Manchester, UK, September.

Ockey, J., 2007, Thailand in 2006: Retreat to military rule. *Asian Survey*, **47**(1), pp. 133–140.

Philip, M., 2006, Corruption definition and measurement, in: C. Sampford, A. Shacklock, C. Connors and F. Galtung (Eds) *Measuring Corruption* (Burlington, VT: Ashgate Publishers), pp. 45–56.

Pollitt, C., 2010, Simply the best? The international benchmarking of reform and good governance, in: J. Pierre and P. Ingraham (Eds) *Comparative Administrative Change and Reform: Lessons Learned* (Montreal & Kingston: McGill-Queen's University Press), pp. 91–113.

Quah, J., 2006, Curbing Asian corruption: An impossible dream?. *Current History*, **105**, pp. 176–179.

Razafindrakoto, M. and Roubaud, F., 2010, Are international databases on corruption reliable? A comparison of expert opinion surveys and household surveys in sub-Saharan Africa. *World Development*, **38**(8), pp. 1057–1069.

Roca, T. 2010, *Assessing Corruption: Expert Surveys versus Household Surveys, Filling the Gap*. Working Paper, Universite Montesquieu-Bordeaux IV.

Sampford, C.Shacklock, A.Connors, C. and Galtung, F. (Eds), 2006, *Measuring Corruption* (Burlington, VT: Ashgate Publishers).

Schlomer, G., Bauman, S. and Card, N., 2010, Best practices for missing data management in counseling psychology. *Journal of Counseling Psychology*, **57**(1), pp. 1–10.

Sik, E., 2002, The bad, the worse and the worst: Guesstimating the level of corruption, in: S. Kotkin and A. Sajo (Eds) *Political Corruption in Transition: A Skeptic's Handbook* (Budapest: Central European University Press), pp. 91–113.

Sjoberg, L., 1999, Risk perception by the public and by experts: A dilemma in risk management. *Human Ecology Review*, **6**(2), pp. 1–9.

Soreide, T. 2006, *Is It Wrong to Rank? A Critical Assessment of Corruption Indices*. Working Paper, Chr. Michelsen Institute, Norway.

Svensson, J., 2005, Eight questions about corruption. *Journal of Economic Perspectives*, **19**(3), pp. 19–42.

Transparency International (TI), 2010, *Global Corruption Barometer 2010*. Available at http://www.transparency.org. (Accessed 29 August 2013).

Treisman, D., 2007, What have we learned about the causes of corruption from ten years of cross-national empirical research? *Annual Review of Political Science*, **10**, pp. 211–244.

United Nations Development Programme (UNDP), 2008, *A User's Guide to Measuring Corruption* (Oslo: Olso Governance Center).

Yu, C., Chen, C.-M., Juang, W.-J. and Hu, L.-T., 2008, Does democracy breed integrity? Corruption in Taiwan during the democratic transformation period. *Crime, Law and Social Change*, **49**, pp. 167–184.

Introduction – Public Personnel Policies: Impact on Government Performance

GRETA NASI

The presumption underlying this special issue is that creating a body of professional and effective public officials is paramount in public policy and that sharing and comparing scholarship on this topic can make a significant contribution. Personnel policies simply influence all other government activities. The quality of personnel recruited and selected, how well they are compensated and rewarded, the benefits they receive, their professionalism, their training and their degree of trust in their organization and among peers affect the capacity of governments to achieve their policy goals (Perry et al. 2006, Ingraham and Rubaii-Barrett 2007).

The implementation of policies in the public service has always been considered problematic and contentious, mainly because of the gap between decision makers' intent and the capacity of those in charge of carrying it out: in this case the civil servants. These have often been seen as inefficient, ineffective and over-bureaucratized professionals negatively contributing to public sector performance (Pollitt and Bouckaert 2000, Kellough 2006, Bellè 2010).

Yet, while governments seek to introduce new personnel policies, and public sector reform findings suggest that the empowerment of employees is crucial to obtain better policy adoption or implementation results, the impact of human resource management reforms on policy implementation productivity and performance – both at the individual and agency level – is largely debated (Perry et al. 2006, Moyninan and Pandey 2007, Vandenabeele 2009).

The purpose of this special issue is to take different perspectives on the contribution of public personnel policies to government performance, addressing both determinants and implementation issues. Part of the authors involved support the contention that public personnel policies drive better performance in government (Huff, and Randma-Liiv and Järvalt), while others emphasize the role of internal and external factors that contribute to a successful implementation of personnel reforms

(Dussauge Laguna), or focus on the importance of addressing attributes that influence performance such as absenteeism and trust (respectively Cristofoli, Turrini and Valotti; Serritzlew and Svendsen).

This Introduction briefly describes the various modes of addressing the relationship between public personnel policies and government performance in different countries, showing similarities and differences that appear to be relevant for a comparative policy dialogue as well as for lesson drawing purposes. The contributing authors were selected among a number of scholars who responded to the Call for Papers on the topic of Public Personnel Policies and Performance and whose proposals were refereed and shortlisted for the Fifth International Comparative Policy Analysis Forum held at SDA Bocconi School of Management in 2008. In particular, the selected papers discuss public personnel policies providing evidence from different levels of governments that can be useful for cross-national analyses.

Richard Huff's paper "Measuring Performance in US Municipalities: Do Personnel Policies Predict System Level Outcomes?" looks at the relationship between public personnel policies and government performance. Performance is measured through a single measure, namely the ranking used by rating agencies for issuing municipal bonds. He argues that simply transplanting managerial practices, as new personnel policies, from the private sector into the public one does not necessarily lead to *powerful connections* and tangible positive results. The contrary is the case: this might result in *deadly combinations* and un-satisfactory effects, especially if governments are not creative in adopting and implementing complementary and mutually reinforcing practices for their organizations. In his analysis based on over 350 US municipalities he finds that intensive and articulated recruitment procedures, family oriented work practices (for example maternity and paternity leave, relocation expenses, onsite daycare), job flexibility and open communication (including suggestion programs and periodic employee attitude surveys) are significantly correlated with higher performance in the public service.

On the other hand, decentralized human resource management decisions, pay for performance programs and incentives for group participation are not associated with higher bond ratings. Whereas awards and financial incentives are usually considered powerful tools in other sectors, Huff suggests that a number of contextual and cultural issues might mitigate their expected effects and result in failures. To overcome potential deadly combinations, he suggests a variety of complementary actions that governments might want to consider, whilst improving public personnel policy formulation and implementation, and in particular when introducing performance-based pay systems.

Randma-Liiv and Järvalt's article "Public Personnel Policies and Problems in the New Democracies of Central and Eastern Europe" focuses on the role of public personnel policies in contributing to a better performing government. They offer a comprehensive analysis of the evolving nature of public personnel policies of some selected Central and East European countries in relation to different institutional objectives from the 1990s until recent years: institution building after gaining independence from the former Soviet Union, Europeanization before acceding to the European Union, and further adjustment after accession. Their assessment is based on public personnel policies at central government level where, despite differences in context and instruments chosen, common patterns of human resource management are found.

Radma and Järvalt note two periods and respective approaches: at the end of the 1990s, human resource recruitment practices changed substantially in these countries, shifting from patronage (spoil) systems based on political decisions to the adoption of public personnel Acts, based on merit principles. The objective was to support political stabilization and create a culture for civil servants. In fact, contrary to what was happening in Western countries, the objective was to build distinctive characteristics of public personnel rather than just trying to reduce the differences with private sector employees. However, the dilemma between continuity and replacement (of personnel with people coming from the private sector) in countries without a strong tradition of civil servants continued and resulted in different practical choices. The authors further discuss a second period, namely that of Europeanization. They emphasize how poor policy coordination across countries facing similar reform objectives has resulted in uneven development of personnel policies, managed either at central or decentralized levels and with different degrees of politicization. Furthermore, they discuss some instruments of personnel policies that have been implemented, mainly by laws, highlighting how their intent to create favorable conditions for a better government is somehow limited by concurrent contextual conditions. For example, professional development and training programs are not necessarily offered due to budgetary constraints, whereas performance measurement and pay-per-performance systems are poorly applied due to lack of adequate and proper policy implementation competences. To conclude, they suggest a strategic approach to public personnel policies that has to adjust to the evolving needs of government. Moreover, they emphasize the crucial role of individuals as key actors in successfully implementing new managerial practices.

Dussauge Laguna, in his paper "The Challenges of Implementing Merit-Based Personnel Policies in Latin America: Mexico's Civil Service Reform Experience" discusses how design and implementation of policies of public personnel reforms can be affected by multiple concurring internal and external factors which might influence their actual capacity to contribute to a higher performing government. His paper recalls some of the issues highlighted by Randma and Järvalt, such as the degree of politicization and the role of a traditional culture of human resource management affecting public personnel policies.

Nevertheless, while he presents the case of Mexican federal agencies and discusses the two phases of the civil servant reform that started in 2003 and was revised in 2007, his discussion offers a different perspective than that of Central and East European countries. In particular, he focuses on merit-based personnel policies introduced by law as guiding principles for guaranteeing adequate public services provision, promoting economic growth and reducing corruption. In describing the first phase of the reform, the author focuses on a set of concurring causes that affect both the design and the implementation as the values and informal rules of the Mexican administrative tradition, that were driven mainly by patronage and personal loyalties rather than by the safeguard of the public interest.

Dussauge Laguna also focuses on the actual capacity of government to implement the reform agenda. In particular, he questions whether the multi-agency governance structure adopted to implement the civil servant reform contributes to moving towards their common objective. In addition he argues that co-presence of various administrative modernization efforts might be drowning resources and shifting priorities away from the public personnel policy reform. He argues that time and resources are more complex issues than they appear and questions the degree of understanding of the objectives of the merit-based public personnel reform. He highlights how the second wave of reform tries to fix some of these open-ended issues through the governance and degrees of coordination among the agencies involved. However, he points out that the degree of politicization and the traditional culture of patronage appointments are hard to face and describes how instruments of reform, such as decentralization of authority, were introduced with the aim to mitigate the above problematics.

Cristofoli, Turrini and Valotti focus on a determinant of personnel productivity and good public performance: absenteeism. Their paper "Coming Back Soon: Assessing the Determinants of Absenteeism in the Public Sector" investigate a laissez-faire characteristic of personnel behavior in certain bureaucracies and question whether individual characteristics of the workforce might actually be the cause that affects absenteeism behavior. Understanding what causes absenteeism therefore becomes particularly important for public personnel policy formulation, as it might result in actions that can contribute to mitigating its effects on productivity and performance.

The analysis focuses on the local level public service including data from a number of municipalities, provinces and regions of Italy. In particular, the authors look at different determinants of absenteeism: (a) personal characteristics of the workforce such as employee seniority, gender issues and external appointments that senior managers might have (e.g., academic positions); (b) the context agency, such as its size, its location in lower income per capita areas and the degree of civicness of its population; and (c) organizational characteristics such as wages, internal controls and supervision mechanisms, as well as performance-based incentives. The results show that both personal and context characteristics are significantly correlated with absenteeism, whereas organizational characteristics and merit-based instruments are not. What can be learned from these findings for personnel policies? As Huff would say, this calls for powerful connections, among public policies at the local level. Mainly, the lesson drawn is that in formulating personnel policies governments should take into account the socio-economic and demographic characteristics of their territory and population and implement converging policies.

Serritzlew and Svendsen, in their paper "Does Education Produce Tough Lovers? Trust and Bureaucrats", focus on another determinant of performance that should be taken into account when relating to personnel policies in the public service. In particular, they argue that higher performance is achieved if public personnel enforce trust and cooperate, whilst reducing opportunities for corrupt behaviors. In particular, they define two types of trust: social trust, generically defined as trusting other (anonymous) people in general, and institutional trust such as trust in different types of institutions, e.g., the police and governments. Their analysis is based on selected middle-income countries and focuses on the relationship between education and trust. They argue that more trusting individuals are more likely to invest in their higher education, and this leads to higher levels of trust. Furthermore, they assert that more highly educated individuals are more likely to be trusting in less corrupt countries. While the former hypothesis is not confirmed in the study presented, the other two show positive correlations.

The articles included in this Special Issue offer many opportunities for comparative policy analysis focusing on different macro and institutional settings that might influence policy formulation and implementation in and by the public service. Also, the studies focus on micro attributes that are common to the public service and issues of public service policies in many countries. The lessons learnt are that private personnel practices do not necessarily lead to positive effects in governments, since their environment, their organizational context and their culture play an important role affecting public personnel policy formulation and implementation.

While not all concerns raised by this Special Issue articles may be relevant in all contexts, they surely provide insights for practitioners and policy makers interested in designing and adopting personnel policies with the promise of facilitating better government results.

At the scholarly level, the contribution of this Special Issue to scientific work and literature is twofold: the articles discuss different aspects of public personnel policies that are widely relevant in most countries' reform agendas, and provide insights and a grounding for further comparative policy studies. I suggest that the myriad of novel aspects and findings presented in this Special Issue can be further investigated in relation to the role of contextual factors and how they can be mitigated in implementing public policies. Another such study may be about the locus of personnel policies as the determinants of successful policy implementation. Further studies may also examine and define models that assess the actual contribution of public service policies to government performance.

Acknowledgments

I would like to make some acknowledgements in publishing this special issue. First, I would like to thank Iris Geva-May for supporting me in organizing the workshop and for managing this special issue, for the encouragement, her precious advice and her vigorous contributions throughout the process that has led to this JCPA Special Issue. Second, I would like to thank Diana Walker, assistant to the editor, for her valuable work, for her courtesy, her collaboration and patience. Third, I would like to acknowledge the SDA Bocconi School of Management Research Division "Claudio Demattè" for sponsoring and hosting the Fifth ICPA Forum workshop, which eventually led to this special issue. Finally, I would like to express my gratitude to all colleagues, authors, discussants at the workshop and reviewers for making this publication possible.

References

Bellè N., 2010, Così fan tutte? Adoption and rejection of performance-related pay in Italian municipalities: a cross-sector test of isomorphism. *Review of Public Personnel Administration* **30**(2), 166–188.

Kellough, J. E., 2006, Employee Performance Appraisal in the Public Sector: Uses and Limitations, in: N. M. Riccucci (Eds) *Public Personnel Management: Current Concerns, Future Challenges* (New York: Longman), pp. 177–189.

Ingraham, P. W. and Rubaii-Barrett, N., 2010, Human resource management as a core dimension of public administration, Foundations of Public Administration Series, Public Administration Review Website, available from http://www.aspanet.org (accessed November 5, 2010).

Moynihan D. P. and Pandey S. K., 2007, The role of organizations in fostering public service motivation. *Public Administration Review*, **67**(1), 40–53.

Pollitt, C. and Bouckaert, B., 2000, *Public Management Reform: A Comparative Analysis* (Oxford: Oxford University Press).

Perry, J., Mesch, D. and Paarlberg, L., 2006, Motivating employees in a new governance era: the performance paradigm revisited. *Public Administration Review*, **66**(4), 505–514.

Vandenabeele, W., 2009, The mediating effect of job satisfaction and organizational commitment on self-reported performance: more robust evidence of the PSM-performance relationship. *International Review of Administrative Sciences*, **75** (1), 11–34.

Comparative Statistics

Editor: FRED THOMPSON

Government Effectiveness in Comparative Perspective

SOO-YOUNG LEE and ANDREW B. WHITFORD

ABSTRACT *In this paper we offer an approach for conceptualizing and measuring government effectiveness or performance in which the focus is on the whole government's effectiveness. We examine data that portray how countries compare in terms of perceived government effectiveness using the World Bank Governance Indicators dataset, which cover 212 countries from 1996 until 2006. We also offer and interpret a new measure of perceived government effectiveness that accounts for the economic development of each country. We argue that the comparative study of government effectiveness (in terms of both multiple measures and across countries) benefits the study of public administration, public management, and public policy.*

Introduction

In her *Beyond Machiavelli: Policy Analysis Comes of Age*, Beryl Radin (2000: 168) asserts "If there is a single theme that characterizes the public sector in the 1990s, it is the demand for performance". Likewise, for many firms in the private sector attention to enhanced effectiveness has become critical to survival at the same time that global competition has become more intense (Scott 1998). Performance (or effectiveness) of organization has become a central line of research for academics interested in both the public and the private sectors. For scholars and practitioners in public administration, public management, and public policy, though, the search for government performance or effectiveness has intensified with the frequent and widely adopted reforms of the last quarter century (Ingraham and Moynihan 2000). In sum, studying effectiveness or performance helps us better understand the role of accountability in governance.

Research on organizational effectiveness divides into several types: the development of measurement criteria, and studies that predict organizational effectiveness using sets of independent variables (Campbell 1977). Relatively few studies address questions of measuring government effectiveness (for example, Provan and Milward 2001, Boyne 2002, Selden and Sowa 2004, Brewer 2006), but a variety propose models of or explanations for effectiveness (for example, Wolf 1993, 1997, Provan and Milward 1995, O'Toole and Meier 1999, 2003, Rainey and Steinbauer 1999, Brewer and Selden 2000, Lynn *et al.* 2000, Boyne 2003, Ingraham *et al.* 2003, Kim 2004, Moynihan and Pandey 2005). Ironically, while public officials emphasize measures of organizational effectiveness, scholars have yet to develop clear and conclusive ways of defining and assessing effectiveness (Rainey 2003). Few questions have challenged scholars more than what constitutes organizational performance or effectiveness (Selden and Sowa 2004).

Most studies assess one government agency's effectiveness, the effectiveness of several networked agencies, or the effectiveness of a state or federal government within a single country. Very few have assessed the perceived effectiveness of a country's entire government or compared effectiveness across national governments. There is a distinct lack in public administration research of "outcome measures of institutional performance at the jurisdictional level" for organizations (Kirlin 2001: 141) – especially at the level of the national government (Yang and Holzer 2006). Of course, there have been several approaches to measure the effectiveness of a whole government, but those approaches have their own limitations. For example, the Government Performance Project (GPP), one of the most elaborate initiatives in assessing effectiveness of governments, developed a process for rating the management capacity of local and state governments and federal agencies in the United States. However, "in spite of its name, the GPP does not measure performance directly, but rather evaluates the capacity of management systems in government entities" (Rainey 2003: 140). In his classic work on government in Italy, Putnam (1993) identified three dimensions of government performance: policy processes (for example, cabinet stability, budget promptness, and statistical and information services), policy pronouncements (for example, reform legislation and legislative innovation), and policy implementation (for example, industrial policy instruments, agricultural spending capacity, local health unit expenditures, housing and urban development, and bureaucratic responsiveness). But even Putnam's index is limited in that it measures capacity more than performance (Yang and Holzer 2006).

In addition, like others, we emphasize the need for comparison in understanding and assessing government effectiveness. For Pfeffer (1977: 133), "the statement that an organization is effective necessarily implies a comparison with some other organization or set of organizations". Comparison is part of what helps public administration achieve scientific status (Dahl 1947), although most of those studies are limited to select countries usually from the developed world. For example, Brewer (2004) analyzed administrative reform and bureaucratic performance in 25 countries from the Organization for Economic Co-operation and Development (OECD) with performance data from the International Country Risk Group. Also,

Van de Walle (2006) critically reviewed performance data from the World Bank, the European Central Bank's public sector efficiency study, the Global Competitiveness Report, and the World Competitiveness Yearbook; he then ranked 36 OECD and European Union countries using World Bank data.

We assess effectiveness by examining entire governments and comparing across countries. We first focus on what is government effectiveness. We offer a description of how to conceptualize government effectiveness or performance, focusing on the effectiveness of the entire government. Our second research question is how perceived effectiveness of entire governments varies across time and countries. In this paper we claim that comparative study helps move forward the literature on government effectiveness. We center our data analysis in this paper on the World Bank dataset Governance Matters VI: Governance Indicators for 1996–2006 to assess perceived effectiveness of governments across 212 countries (Kaufmann et al. 2007).

Our paper proceeds as follows. In the next section, we address different approaches to understanding and conceptualizing organizational effectiveness, especially in the public sector, and we offer a description on World Bank Governance Indicators. In the third section, we analyze the perceived effectiveness data for a wide variety of countries. Finally, we offer a discussion of the measurement and analysis of effectiveness and how this approach pushes the boundaries of the study of governance.

Concepts of Government Effectiveness

While the concept of organizational effectiveness is central to the literature on organizations and management because of its importance to the investigation of organizational structures, processes, and outputs (Cameron and Whetten 1981), we have long struggled with understanding what constitutes the concept (Steers 1975). For instance, for Barnard (1938: 19) an organizational action is effective when "a specific desired end is attained". Osborne and Gaebler (1992: 351) see effectiveness as a measure of the quality of output, answering the question "how well did it achieve the desired outcome?" One detailed answer is that effectiveness refers to whether the agency does well what it is supposed to do, whether people in the agency work hard and well, whether the actions and procedures of the agency and its members help achieve its mission, and, in the end, whether it actually achieves its mission (Rainey and Steinbauer 1999).

However, most agree that there is little consensus regarding what organizational effectiveness means or how to assess it properly (Cameron and Whetten 1983), for effectiveness has long been one of the most pervasive yet least delineated organizational constructs (Goodman and Pennings 1977), leading to a field in "conceptual disarray" (Connolly et al. 1980: 211). Scholars pursue the topic in part because it is the ultimate dependent variable; the construct lies at the center of all models of organizations, and individuals always see the need to judge the effectiveness of organizations (Pfeffer 1977, Cameron and Whetten 1983, Au 1996). In the public sector, virtually all of public management and organizations is concerned with performance and effectiveness, at least implicitly, because effectiveness in pursuing their goals influences the quality of our lives and even our ability to survive (Rainey 2003). As mentioned above, however, there is little consensus as to what organizational effectiveness means and what constitutes a valid set of measurement criteria. Thus, through a literature review on a number of articles and books, we identified three issues (issues of levels of analysis, perceptual measurement, and measurement criteria) that we believe form the foundations of our understanding of organizational effectiveness. We center our discussion of what organizational effectiveness means and how it should be measured on these three key issues.

Levels (Units) of Analysis

"Levels of analysis" refers to the question of the appropriate unit of analysis for measuring the construct of effectiveness. This issue is one source of the inability of researchers to agree on how to define and operationalize this construct (Campbell 1977, Cameron and Whetten 1981). Researchers use units of analysis that work for the purpose of their individual research agendas. Sometimes the unit of analysis is a large organization with personnel located in many places, sometimes it is all the people under one roof, and sometimes the unit of analysis is an organizational subunit corresponding to the immediate work group (Campbell 1977); "performance analysis is done at three levels – the individual employee or small group, the program, and the organizational level" (Boschken 1994: 309). While scholars select units of analysis according to individual tastes, not all make the distinction of unit of analysis clear (Boschken 1994).[1]

It may be as some claim that the debate over levels of analysis is bewildering and futile (Cameron and Whetten 1981), but we believe that clarifying the unit of analysis helps us identify the match between measurement criteria and the unit, and that this matching contributes to our understanding of the concept of effectiveness. Table 1 shows how we categorize the units of analysis examined in previous organizational effectiveness studies based on our review of the scholars' arguments and a search of the literature. We identify two dimensions: the locus of analysis, and the focus of analysis. By locus of analysis we mean the place where the assessment of effectiveness happens; by focus of analysis we mean the subject of effectiveness measurement. We see the assessment of effectiveness in the case of the public sector as taking place at the levels of the individual employee, the subunit of an organization, a single organization, multiple or networked organizations, and the entire government. As the subject of the assessment enterprise, scholars usually choose the performance of either a specific program or the organization as a whole.

Below we review a few relevant studies across these nine combinations of the dimensions, which comprise "units of analysis", but we offer one example here. The Program Assessment Rating Tool (PART) was developed and implemented in the US federal government starting in 2002 to assess and improve program performance of its agencies and programs. This project represents an attempt to assess the effectiveness of a program at the level of the entire federal government. As we describe below, the unit of analysis for the data we analyze in this paper is the effectiveness of the entire government of a country measured through the use of elite perceptions.

Table 1. Units of analysis in effectiveness research

	Locus of analysis				
	Individual employee	Subunit	Single organization	Multiple (networked) organizations	Entire government
Focus of analysis					
Organization	Individual's effectiveness in organization	Organizational effectiveness of subunit in organization	Organizational effectiveness of single organization	Organizational effectiveness of multiple or networked organizations	Organizational effectiveness of entire government
Program		Program performance of subunit in organization	Program performance of single organization	Program performance of multiple/networked organization	Program performance of entire government

Perception or Objective Measure?

One popular way of classifying performance measures has been the distinction between measures that are "objective" and those that are "subjective". We see the difference as one of source material. Objective measures are usually constructed from records that are considered impartial and independent, or from archives of performance; one example source is school exam results. In contrast, subjective measures are constructed from survey responses about performance that are gathered from the members of an organization (such as managers or employees) or from external stakeholders or raters (such as consumers or citizens) (Parks 1984, Andrews et al. 2006b).

One criticism is that subjective measures are biased since they assess effectiveness by using an informant's recall (Golden 1992); a second is that they have the potential for monomethod bias (although recent advances suggest that this perceived bias in self-report surveys is little more than an "urban legend") (Spector 2006). Objective measures are seen as reflecting the real world accurately and minimizing the discretion of the study designer (Meier and Brudney 2002).[2] But objective measures have their own problems. They are often unavailable. They often cannot approximate the complex dimensions of organizational performance; for example, in the public sector no single dimension of performance is paramount because multiple constituencies (for example, consumers, taxpayers, employees, politicians, and so forth) may hold varying interpretations of effectiveness; in contrast, in the private sector strong financial results may serve as a focal point for measurement (Andrews *et al.* 2006a). Objective measures often suffer from instrumentation effects (if the instrument for measuring performance interacts with the organizational processes and changes the meaning of performance), cheating (if cases are selected that produce favorable figures), or reporting false data (Boyne *et al.* 2006).

We center our investigation here on the use of a perception measure drawn from the World Bank's Governance Matters project, an attempt to collect and analyze data that monitor governance and the impact of governments in developing countries. The World Bank's Government Effectiveness Index is a subjective measure of the entire government's effectiveness (the assessment of the perceived effectiveness of the entire government) which draws on data sources that reflect the perceptions of a very diverse group of respondents through surveys. This index was constructed from a broad array of surveys that elicited responses from individual elites, analysts, firms, or agencies with first-hand knowledge of the governance situation in the country. The index was constructed from multiple items, multiple respondents, and multiple survey houses and was carried out in multiple countries so that perceived effectiveness scores are available for up to 212 countries in each of eight time periods (dating from 1996 to 2006).

We rely on subjective measures of government effectiveness in this study for three reasons. First, organizational performance is a concept that is socially constructed by multiple stakeholders (especially in the public sector) (Brewer 2006). Perception measures are more appropriate for capturing the complex and multiple dimensions of an entire government's performance. Second, measures of perceived organizational performance are often positively correlated with objective measures of organizational performance (Pearce *et al.* 1987, Dollinger and Golden 1992, Powell 1992, Delaney and Huselid 1996, McCracken *et al.* 2001); inference from perception data provides a lens into hidden processes of actual (or objective) effectiveness. Last, "except when either subjective or objective measures are distorted by low reliability or deliberate error, neither is an inherently superior estimate of organizational performance in the public sector" (Andrews *et al.* 2006b: 45). In this sense, perception data for measuring effectiveness at this level or units of analysis are probably at least as good as objective data, were they available.

Measurement Criteria

Last, scholars have sought a best way to define and measure organizational performance, but they have not come to agreement on one model or framework for measuring effectiveness (Daft 2001). We briefly review several approaches to assessing effectiveness. In the rational goal (or purposive-rational) model of organizational performance, the key criterion of performance is whether an organization reaches its goals (Pfeffer 1982). The system resource model defines effectiveness using the overall survival of the organization, "the ability to exploit its environment in the acquisition of scarce and valued resources to sustain its functioning" (Seashore and Yuchtman 1967: 393).[3] Participant-satisfaction models involve asking different participants about their satisfaction with the organization (Rainey 2003); organizational effectiveness is defined according to the ability to satisfy key strategic constituencies in its environment (Boschken 1994). The internal process and human resources model centers on factors such as communication systems, stable procedures, motivation, leadership, interpersonal trust, workforce cohesion, etc. (Likert 1967, Selden and Sowa 2004). Quinn and Rohrbaugh (1983) offer a spatial model of effectiveness that acknowledges competing values surrounding the assessment of performance that combines into four models of effectiveness: the human relations model, the open systems model, the rational goal model, and the internal process model.

These are generic approaches for assessing effectiveness. While they can be applied to both the public and private sectors, none offers natural measurement criteria that fit the public sector well. Table 2 reviews the kinds of measurement criteria for effectiveness used in empirical studies of the public, and includes studies on organizational effectiveness that develop measurement criteria and studies that predict effectiveness using independent variables. Through this literature review, we found that there is no common performance measure standard. As Campbell (1977) notes, a particular way to conceptualize and measure effectiveness is useful only for certain purposes; searching for a best measurement scheme is as futile as searching for one best way (Behn 1996). Collections of performance measures should be selected with the characteristics necessary to help achieve eight managerial purposes: evaluation, control, budgeting, motivation, promotion, celebration, learning, and improvement (Behn 2003). World Bank Government Effectiveness data which measure the quality of public services, the quality of the civil service and the degree of its independence from political pressures, the quality of policy formulation and implementation, and the credibility of the government's commitment to such policies are useful for evaluating and improving the entire government's effectiveness.

Table 2. Measurement criteria

Author(s)	Units of analysis	Measurement criteria of effectiveness (performance)
Putnam (1993)	Italian regional governments	Three performance dimensions – Policy processes: indicators such as cabinet stability, budget promptness, and statistical and information services – Policy pronouncements: indicators such as reform legislation and legislative innovation – Policy implementation: indicators such as the number of day care centers or family clinics, industrial policy instruments, agricultural spending capacity, local health unit expenditures, housing and urban development, and bureaucratic responsiveness
Berman and Wang (2000)	U.S. county government	Performance measurement by survey – workload or output, effectiveness or outcome, and service quality
Brewer and Selden (2000)	Multiple federal agencies	Employees' perception of organizational performance – Internal efficiency, internal effectiveness, internal fairness, external efficiency, external effectiveness, and external fairness
Heinrich and Lynn (2000)	Program	Program performance – Earnings of participants in job training program under Job Training Partnership Act (JTPA)
Provan and Milward (2001)	Network	Evaluation at three levels of analysis: community, network, and organization/participant levels – Community level: cost to community, building social capital, aggregate indicators of client well-being, public perceptions that problem is being solved, and changes in the incidence of the problem – Network level: membership growth, range of services provided, absence of service duplication, relationship strength, creation and maintenance of network administrative organization, integration/coordination of services, cost of network maintenance, and member commitment to network goals – Organization/participant level: agency survival, enhanced legitimacy, resource acquisition, cost of services, service access, client outcomes, minimum conflict for multiprogram agencies across multiple networks

(*continued*)

Table 2. (*Continued*)

Author(s)	Units of analysis	Measurement criteria of effectiveness (performance)
Boyne (2002)	English local governments	Dimensions of performance – Outputs: quantity and quality – Efficiency: cost per unit of output – Service outcomes: formal effectiveness, impact, equity, and cost per unit of service outcome – Responsiveness: consumer satisfaction, citizen satisfaction, staff satisfaction, and cost per unit of responsiveness – Democratic outcomes: probity, participation, accountability, and cost per unit of democratic outcome
Knack (2002)	States' entire governments	Government performance project ratings – Overall performance – Performance in financial management, capital management, human resources, managing for results, and information technology
Boyne (2003)	Literature review of performance of public service organization	Seven types of performance indicators – Quantity of output, quality of outputs, efficiency, equity, outcomes, value for money, and consumer satisfaction
O'Toole and Meier (2003)	Program	Program performance – Pass rate on Texas Assessment of Academic Skills (TAAS)
Selden and Sowa (2004)	Multiple public agencies in NY and VA	Assessed by both objective and perceptual measures – Management capacity, program capacity, management outcomes, and program outcomes
Brewer (2004)	25 Western countries' government	International Country Risk Group (ICRG) assessments – Quality of bureaucracy, corruption in government, and rule of law
Andrews et al. (2005)	Multiple English local governments	Two measures of organizational performance – Best Value Performance Indicator (BVPI): percentage of citizens satisfied with the overall service provided by their authority – Core Service Performance (CSP): quantity of outputs, quality of outputs, efficiency, outcomes, value for money, and consumer satisfaction with individual services

(*continued*)

Table 2. (*Continued*)

Author(s)	Units of analysis	Measurement criteria of effectiveness (performance)
Chun and Rainey (2005)	Multiple federal agencies	Perceived organizational effectiveness – Managerial performance, customer service orientation, productivity, and work quality
Walker and Boyne (2006)	Welsh local governments	Subjective and objective measures of the following dimensions – Effectiveness, output quality, output quantity and equity
Light (2006)	Multiple federal agencies	Federal employees' perceptions of organizational performance – Helping people, spending money wisely, being fair in decisions, and running programs and services

Data Description

In this section, we describe our data and how useful they are for assessing perceptions of government effectiveness. Our data come from the World Bank Governance Matters project. Since 1996, the World Bank has built worldwide governance indicators due to a belief that governance matters – in the sense that there are strong causal relationships between good governance and development outcomes such as higher per capita income, low infant mortality, and higher literacy (Kaufmann *et al.* 1999). The Governance Indicators cover 212 countries (territories) and measure six dimensions of governance (voice and accountability, political stability and absence of violence, government effectiveness, regulatory quality, rule of law, and control of corruption) from 1996 to 2006. The Indicators were updated every two years between 1996 and 2002. Since 2002, they have been updated on an annual basis. We center on one of these dimensions – the effectiveness dimension of governance. The World Bank government effectiveness indicator captures the capacity of the state to implement sound policies by measuring the quality of public services, the quality of the civil service and the degree of its independence from political pressures, the quality of policy formulation and implementation, and the credibility of the government's commitment to such policies.

This indicator measures subjective perceptions regarding government effectiveness in different countries. According to Kaufmann *et al.* (1999), these data come from two types of sources: polls (surveys) of experts, which reflect country ratings produced by commercial risk rating agencies and other organizations, and cross-national surveys of residents carried out by international organizations and other non-governmental organizations. Surveys of experts capture the perceptions of country analysts at major multilateral development agencies (such as the European Bank for Reconstruction and Development, the African Development Bank, the Asian Development Bank, and the World Bank), reflecting these individuals' in-depth experience working on the countries they assess (Kaufmann *et al.* 2007). Surveys of residents are surveys of individuals or domestic firms (such as the World Bank's business environment surveys and the World Economic Forum's Global Competitiveness Report) with first-hand knowledge of the governance situation in the country. Kaufmann *et al.* (1999) observe that subjective measurement of the quality of governance can be useful: it is often difficult to obtain objective data for many issues; perceptions may often be as important as objective differences in institutions across countries; and other work shows that subjective perceptions have significant explanatory power for future economic outcomes (for example, through consumer and investor expectations).

Our version of the data relies on 47 individual items taken from 18 different sources that measure different dimensions of government effectiveness. The effectiveness indicator – which is a latent variable – is itself a combination of these many different individual data sources. The aggregation procedure first rescales the individual indicators from each underlying variable's source in order to make them comparable across data sources (Kaufmann *et al.* 2007). It then constructs a weighted average of each of these rescaled data sources to arrive at an aggregate indicator of government effectiveness. The weights assigned to each data source are in turn based on the estimates of the precision of each source that are produced by the unobserved components model. Essentially, this is an "item response theory" model of survey responses. Each measure on the latent scale of "effectiveness" that underlies these different individual items is associated with an estimate, standard error of the estimate, and number of sources used to construct the estimate. The number of sources used to construct an estimate for any country in a given year varies; accordingly, the estimates of the country's position on the latent variable are also noisy. Table 3 provides a detailed description of each data source and individual questions or concepts drawn from these data sources for the aggregate government effectiveness indicator/latent variable.

The wide variety of descriptions of the individual items, the range of countries covered, and the years for which specific sources are available show exactly how difficult it is to measure effectiveness at this level of analysis. The range of considerations shows that in practical terms, different sources and survey houses conceptualize effectiveness differently. Some measures are only available for the most developed countries; others are widely available for an array of countries (although perhaps at the cost of offering fewer measurements per country). In descriptive terms, the average number of sources for a measurement was 6.7 with a standard deviation of 3.4 (minimum of 1 and maximum of 14). The maximum number of sources for a measurement in a given year has fallen over time from at least 13 in the years from 1996–2003 to 7 in the 2006 version. Using an aggregate measure based on the estimation of a latent variable of perceived effectiveness helps overcome the biases inherent in the selection of specific survey instruments carried out in certain geographic regions, as long as the accompanying uncertainty introduced by variation in the number of sources is accounted for in calculating inferential statistics. For our indicator, positive values of the index measure positive assessments of an individual government's effectiveness by respondents across the multiple indicators and surveys.

A Comparison of Government Effectiveness

This section shows how government effectiveness varies across time, regions, and countries; the global mean value of the main effectiveness score is –0.005 with a standard deviation of 1.015. One consequence of visual inspection is that effectiveness appears to vary with the level of economic development of each country. Accordingly, along with the measure of perceived effectiveness, we also present a score of income-adjusted perceived effectiveness across time, regions, and countries; this measure is constructed as the ratio of perceived effectiveness and a country's Gross Domestic Product (GDP) (accounting for purchasing power parity).[4]

Across Time

Figure 1 shows the distribution of the perceived effectiveness index as calculated for up to 212 countries for eight separate time periods. At the aggregate level, there appears to be remarkable stability in these measurements. The boxplots show that the 2006 data have a tighter distribution, although there are a few high outside values

Table 3. Sources and measurements of perceived government effectiveness indicator

Sources (Country coverage)	Items or concepts measured	96	98	00	02	03	04	05	06
African Development Bank Country Policy and Institutional Assessments (52)	Management of public debt			✓	✓	✓	✓	✓	✓
	Policies to improve efficiency of public sector			✓	✓	✓	✓	✓	✓
	Efficiency of public expenditures (revenue mobilization)			✓	✓	✓	✓		✓
	Budget management			✓	✓	✓	✓		✓
Afrobarometer (18)	What proportion of the country's problems do you think the government can solve?								
	Based on your experiences, how easy or difficult is it to obtain household services (like electricity or telephone)?				✓	✓	✓	✓	✓
	Based on your experiences, how easy or difficult is it to obtain an identity document (like birth certificate, passport)?				✓	✓	✓	✓	✓
	Government handling of health services								
	Government handling of education							✓	✓
Asian Development Bank Country Policy and Institutional Assessments (25)	Competence of civil service			✓	✓	✓	✓	✓	✓
	Budget management			✓	✓	✓	✓	✓	✓
	Efficiency of public expenditures (revenue mobilization)			✓	✓	✓	✓	✓	✓
	Management of public debt			✓	✓	✓	✓	✓	✓
Bertelsmann Transformation Index (120)	Consensus building						✓	✓	✓
	Governance capability						✓	✓	✓
	Effective use of resources						✓	✓	✓

(continued)

Table 3. (*Continued*)

Sources (Country coverage)	Items or concepts measured	Data availability by year							
		96	98	00	02	03	04	05	06
Business Environment & Enterprise Performance Survey (27)	How problematic are telecommunications for the growth of your business				✓	✓	✓	✓	✓
	How problematic is electricity for the growth of your business				✓	✓	✓	✓	✓
	How problematic is transportation for the growth of your business				✓	✓	✓	✓	✓
Business Environment Risk Intelligence (50)	Operation risk index: Bureaucratic delays	✓	✓	✓	✓	✓	✓	✓	✓
Economist Intelligence Unit (154)	Quality of bureaucracy/institutional effectiveness	✓	✓	✓	✓	✓	✓	✓	✓
	Excessive bureaucracy/red tape	✓	✓	✓	✓	✓	✓	✓	✓
Gallup World Poll (130)	Satisfaction with public transportation system	✓							
	Satisfaction with roads and highways	✓							
	Satisfaction with education system	✓							
Global E-Government Index (196)	Global E-governance Index				✓	✓	✓	✓	✓
Global Insight Business Risk and Conditions (202)	*Bureaucracy*: An assessment of the country's bureaucracy. The better the bureaucracy the quicker decisions are made and the more easily foreign investors can go about their business.		✓	✓	✓	✓	✓	✓	
	Policy consistency and forward planning: How confident businesses can be of the continuity of		✓	✓	✓	✓	✓	✓	✓

(*continued*)

Table 3. (*Continued*)

Sources (Country coverage)	Items or concepts measured	Data availability by year							
		96	98	00	02	03	04	05	06
	economic policy stance – whether a change of government will entail major policy disruption, and whether the current government has pursued a coherent strategy. This factor also looks at the extent to which policy-making is far-sighted, or conversely aimed at short-term economic advantage.								
Global Insight Global Risk Service (142)	*Government Instability:* An increase in government personnel turnover rate at senior levels that reduces the GDP growth rate by 2% during any 12-month period.	√	√	√	√	√	√	√	√
	Government Ineffectiveness: A decline in government personnel quality at any level that reduces the GDP growth rate by 1% during any 12-month period.	√	√	√	√	√	√	√	√
	Institutional Failure: A deterioration of government capacity to cope with national problems as a result of institutional rigidity that reduces the GDP growth rate by 1% during any 12-month period.	√	√	√	√	√	√	√	√

(*continued*)

Table 3. (Continued)

Sources (Country coverage)	Items or concepts measured	96	98	00	02	03	04	05	06
IFAD Rural Sector Performance Assessments (100)	Allocation & management of public resources for rural development	✓					✓	✓	✓
Institute for Management Development World Competitiveness Yearbook (53)	Government economic policies do not adapt quickly to changes in the economy			✓	✓	✓	✓	✓	✓
	The public service is not independent from political interference		✓	✓	✓	✓	✓	✓	
	Government decisions are not effectively implemented		✓	✓	✓	✓	✓	✓	✓
	Bureaucracy hinders business activity	✓	✓	✓	✓	✓	✓	✓	✓
	The distribution infrastructure of goods and services is generally inefficient	✓		✓	✓	✓	✓	✓	✓
	Political System is not adapted to today's economic challenges	✓		✓					
	Policy direction is not consistent								
Latinobarometro (18)	Trust in government				✓		✓	✓	✓
Merchant International Group Gray Area Dynamics (156)	Quality of bureaucracy				✓	✓	✓	✓	✓
Political Risk Services International Country Risk Guide (140)	*Bureaucratic quality.* Measures institutional strength and quality of the civil service, assess how much strength and expertise bureaucrats have and how able they are to manage political alternations without drastic interruptions in government services, or policy changes. Good performers have	✓	✓	✓	✓	✓	✓	✓	✓

(*continued*)

Table 3. (*Continued*)

Sources (Country coverage)	Items or concepts measured	96	98	00	02	03	04	05	06
	somewhat autonomous bureaucracies, free from political pressures, and an established mechanism for recruitment and training.								
World Bank Country Policy and Institutional Assessments (136)	Management of external debt	✓	✓	✓	✓	✓	✓	✓	✓
	Management of development programs		✓	✓	✓	✓	✓		
	Quality public administration	✓	✓	✓	✓	✓	✓	✓	✓
	Efficiency of revenue mobilization/public expenditures	✓		✓	✓	✓	✓	✓	✓
	Budget management	✓	✓	✓	✓	✓	✓	✓	✓
World Economic Forum Global Competitiveness Survey (125)	Competence of public sector personnel	✓	✓	✓	✓	✓	✓	✓	✓
	Quality of general infrastructure	✓	✓	✓	✓	✓	✓	✓	✓
	Quality of public schools	✓	✓	✓	✓	✓	✓	✓	✓
	Time spent by senior management dealing with government officials	✓	✓						
	Public Service vulnerability to political pressure		✓	✓			✓	✓	
	Wasteful government expenditure								✓

Figure 1. Perceived effectiveness over time

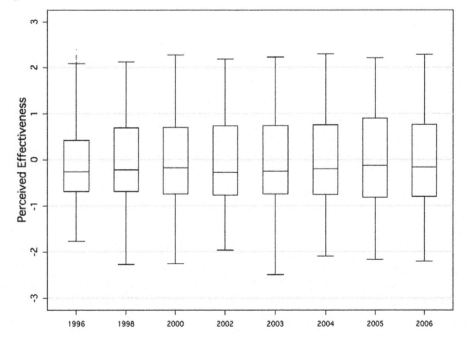

in this time period, too. The medians move slightly upward in 1998 and then downward until reaching a low in 2003; the upward move in 2004 is followed by downward moves in the following two years of measurements. A simple regression of the effectiveness indicator on a year spline shows no significant intercept shifts over time.

Figure 2 shows the distribution of the income-adjusted perceived effectiveness index across time.[5] The boxplots show that both maximum and minimum of perceived effectiveness are decreased across time after income adjustment. However, the interquartile range and median over time appear to be very stable except in the case of 2004; we note, though, that fewer observations are available for 2004 given the lack of complete GDP data.

Across Regions

Figure 3 organizes the data across seven standard geographic regions; for simplicity Canada and the US are lumped together with Western Europe. Differences emerge both in terms of the location of the distributions and their variability. Western Europe/North America appears to have higher measurements of government effectiveness on average, which perhaps calls into question the generalizability of the broad array of studies that have examined a variety of measures of effectiveness in predominately western or industrialized countries. In contrast, South Asia shows greater homogeneity of measurements, although the median is much lower than that

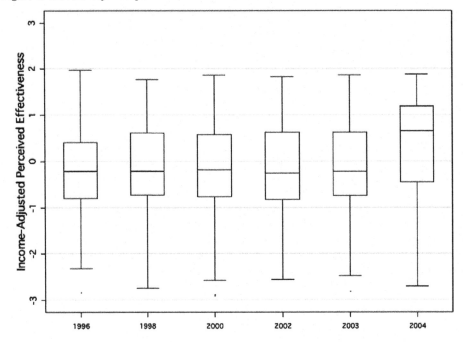

Figure 2. Income-adjusted perceived effectiveness over time

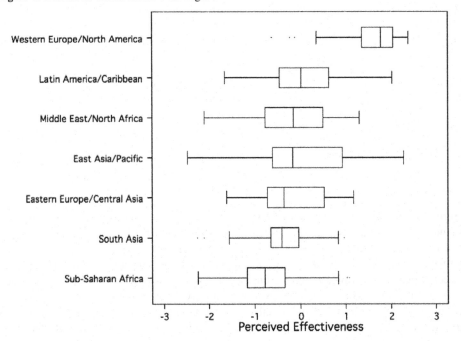

Figure 3. Perceived effectiveness over region

for Western Europe/North America. East Asia and the Pacific exhibit the greatest variability, with the support of the distribution covering virtually the entire range of the variable. However, a simple regression of the indicator on the region indicator variables (with East Asia as the omitted case) shows differences. Western Europe/ North America has significantly higher scores, Latin America/Caribbean scores are no different, and the other regions are all significantly lower.[6]

Figure 4 presents income-adjusted perceived government effectiveness across the regions. Western Europe/North America has the highest median score and Sub-Saharan Africa has the lowest. Western Europe/North America reveals homogeneity of measurement while East Asia/Pacific has the greatest variation. After income adjustment, the median scores for the Middle East/North Africa and East Asia/ Pacific are larger than that for Latin America/the Caribbean.

Across Countries

Figures below show the distribution of the individual scores for countries within each of the seven regions. Western Europe/North America shows unusual variance for what is often considered to be a fairly homogenous set of governments. Denmark records the highest median score in this region; Switzerland records the highest score in the entire dataset. Perhaps not surprisingly, countries like Iceland and the Netherlands follow Switzerland's lead. At the other end of the distribution, Monaco records scores significantly below the global mean of –0.005. In the Latin America/ Caribbean region small islands like the Cayman Islands, the US Virgin Islands, and

Figure 4. Income-adjusted perceived effectiveness over region

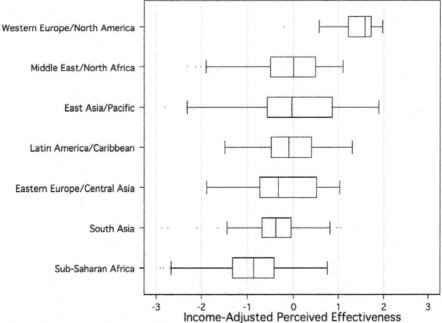

Aruba are counterbalanced by Venezuela, Paraguay, and Haiti. Note the variation in the steepness of the curves in Figures 5 and 6.

Figure 7 shows the income-adjusted perceived effectiveness in the Western Europe/ North America region.[7] Denmark has the highest median score in this region and Switzerland has the highest score in the entire dataset. Yet Greece has the lowest median score and Luxembourg' s ranking fell considerably after income adjustment. The shape of the curve in Figure 7 is steeper than that in Figure 5. Figure 8 shows income-adjusted perceived effectiveness in the Latin America/Caribbean region; countries such as Venezuela, Paraguay, and Haiti still have lower scores of income-adjusted perceived effectiveness.

Figure 9 shows a distinct shift in the distribution when the focus moves to the Middle East/North Africa. Israel, the United Arab Emirates, and Qatar are balanced by (perhaps not surprisingly) Iraq and the West Bank/Gaza, and also Syria. Note that the individual variability in the estimates for this region seems smaller than those for regions like Latin America/Caribbean. In contrast, Figure 10 shows even greater variability in the East Asia/Pacific region, with Singapore, New Zealand, and Australia recording scores that rival Switzerland's. North Korea records some of the lowest scores in the entire dataset. The scores for Myanmar and some of the Pacific Island nations are probably not surprisingly low (the Solomon Islands have the lowest single-year score in the entire dataset).

Figure 11 shows income-adjusted perceived effectiveness in the Middle East/North Africa region. Israel, the United Arab Emirates, and Tunisia are balanced by Iraq

Figure 5. Perceived effectiveness, Western Europe/North America

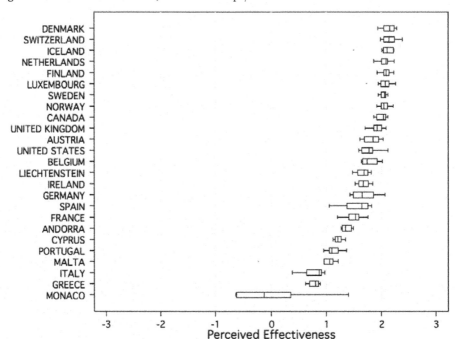

Figure 6. Perceived effectiveness, Latin America/Caribbean

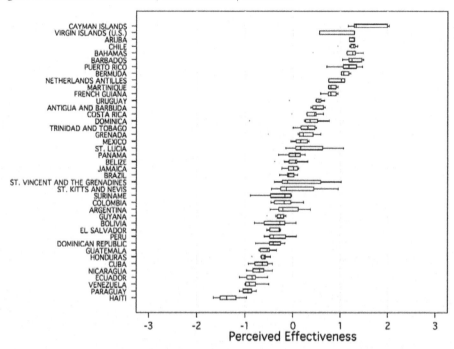

Figure 7. Income-adjusted perceived effectiveness, Western Europe/North America

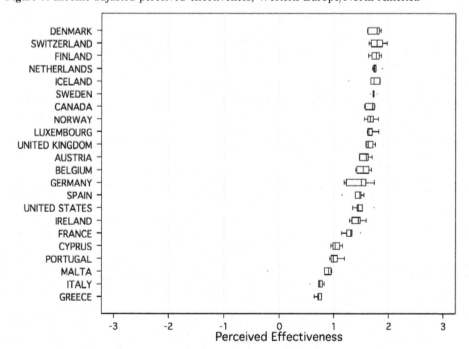

Figure 8. Income-adjusted perceived effectiveness, Latin America/Caribbean

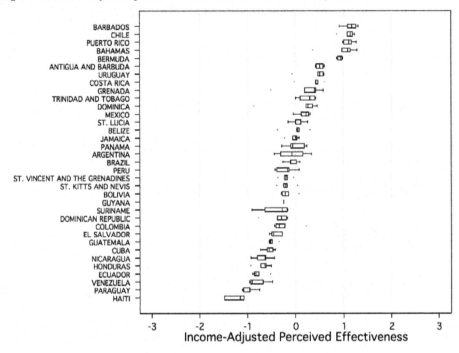

Figure 9. Perceived effectiveness, Middle East/North Africa

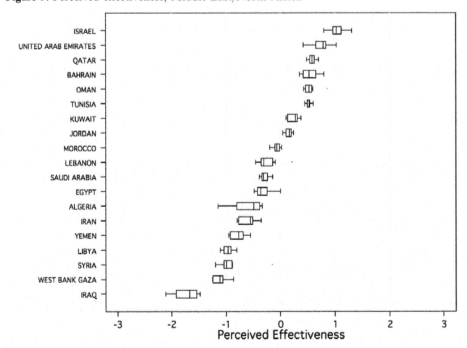

Figure 10. Perceived effectiveness, East Asia/Pacific

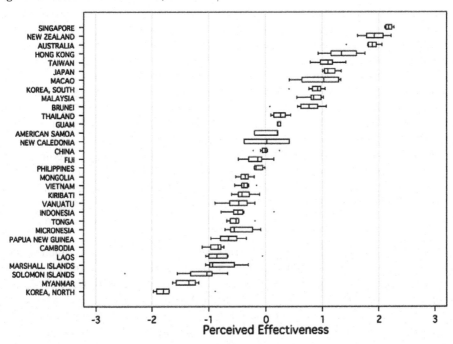

Figure 11. Income-adjusted perceived effectiveness, Middle East/North Africa

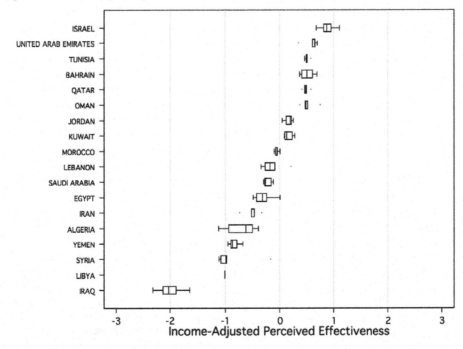

and Libya, and also Syria. Figure 12 shows reduced variability in the East Asia/Pacific region after income adjustment, although Singapore and New Zealand still record scores that rival Switzerland's. The median perceived effectiveness score of North Korea fell after income adjustment and is one of the lowest scores overall.

Figures 13, 14, and 15 continue the theme of within-region differences. Afghanistan in the South Asia region shows the difficulties for countries that are first autocratic and then essentially failed states. Interestingly, in South Asia only the Maldives and Bhutan ever record single-year scores higher than the 75th percentile of the entire dataset. India's scores are all uniformly in the region of the 50th percentile of the entire data distribution. Eastern Europe/Central Asia is a region of contrasts, with Estonia scoring in the upper region of the best-scoring countries in Western Europe/North America; yet a number of former Soviet states score well in the range of the 10th percentile of the entire data. The shape of the curve in the case of Eastern Europe/Central Asia is roughly similar to that in South Asia (an F test cannot reject the null of no differences in their means in the regional regression reported above ($F = 1.97$)).

This is not the case in Sub-Saharan Africa. The shape of the curve is much steeper, indicating greater within-region differences. There is a shift, too, in the levels of perceived effectiveness. The average score for Eastern Europe/Central Asia is significantly higher than that for Sub-Saharan Africa even given the experiences of the former Soviet states like Turkmenistan ($F = 66.95$ in the regional regression). Some of the lowest total scores in the data are recorded in Somalia, again a failed state. Yet Reunion also records scores in the top 20 percent of the entire dataset, and

Figure 12. Income-adjusted perceived effectiveness, East Asia/Pacific

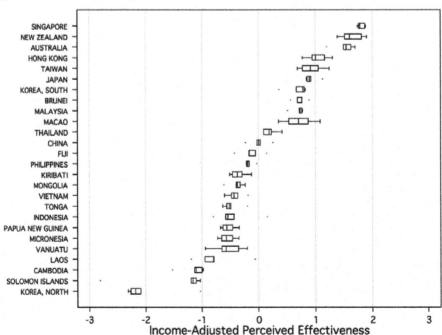

Figure 13. Perceived effectiveness, South Asia

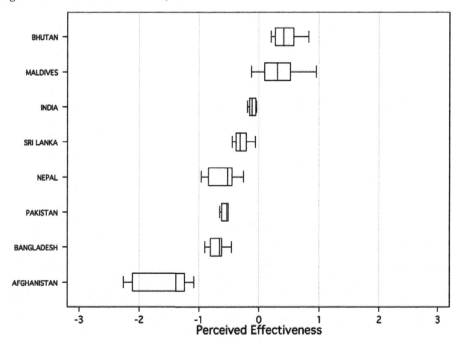

Figure 14. Perceived effectiveness, Eastern Europe/Central Asia

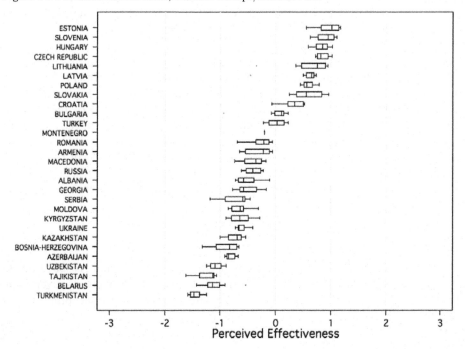

Figure 15. Perceived effectiveness, Sub-Saharan Africa

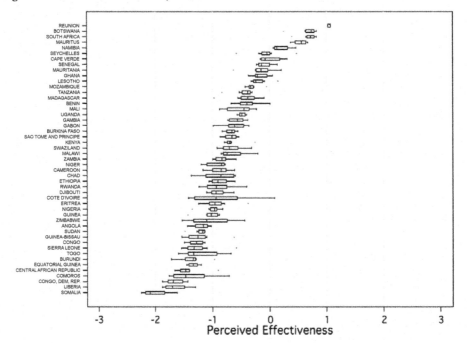

Botswana records scores almost in the top 25 percent, due to governance events that rarely receive coverage in discussions of the difficulty of running effective governments in Africa. Figure 15 shows that Reunion is clearly an unusual case in this region, although Botswana's scores are not so different from those for South Africa.

Figure 16 shows income-adjusted perceived effectiveness in the South Asia region. The score for Afghanistan is considerably lower after income adjustment. Nepal and Bangladesh exhibit less variability than before income adjustment. Figure 17 shows the scores in the Eastern Europe/Central Asia region. The shape of the curve is almost the same. Estonia still has high scores and Tajikistan reports the lowest perceived effectiveness. Last, Figure 18 shows the income-adjusted perceived effectiveness in the Sub-Saharan Africa region. The rankings of Swaziland and Equatorial Guinea fell remarkably after income adjustment. The scores for the Democratic Republic of Congo, Liberia, and Somalia are much lower than perceived effectiveness without income adjustment.

Discussion

The purpose of this paper is to explore the questions: what is government effectiveness, and how do countries compare in terms of perceived government effectiveness? The first research question relates to how we conceptualize and measure government effectiveness in terms of the whole government, not just in terms of an agency or several networked agencies. We discuss three important

Figure 16. Income-adjusted perceived effectiveness, South Asia

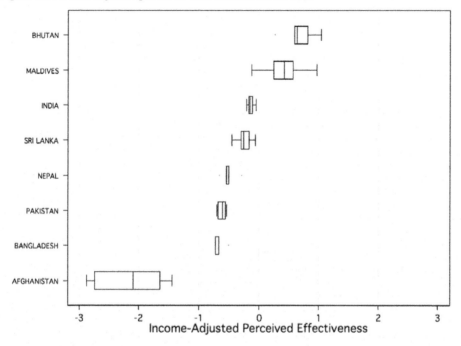

Figure 17. Income-adjusted perceived effectiveness, Eastern Europe/Central Asia

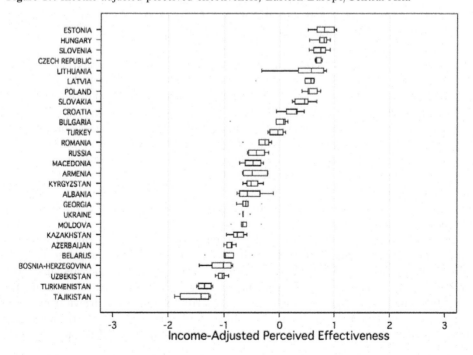

Figure 18. Income-adjusted perceived effectiveness, Sub-Saharan Africa

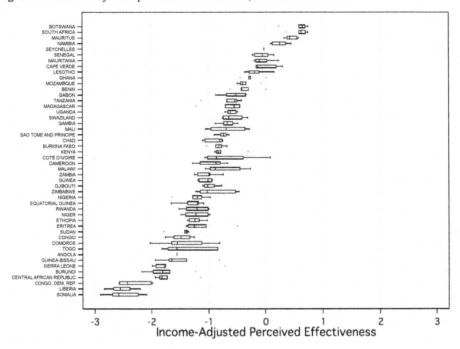

issues – i.e., issues of levels of analysis, perceptual measurement, and measurement criteria – related to the concept of organizational effectiveness and its measurement to get a better grasp on organizational effectiveness, instead of directly providing a specific definition of organizational effectiveness and measurement.

For the second research question, this paper uses data from the World Bank – data that are used by decision makers around the world to form inferences about the performance of other governments – that are drawn from thousands of respondents polled by multiple survey houses about a number of key attributes of government effectiveness. We show that the use of these data can serve an important role in extending our understanding of effectiveness in a comparative perspective through the comparison of government effectiveness across time, regions, and countries with and without income adjustment. Several inferences can follow. Perhaps the most compelling inference is that the comparative study of effectiveness reveals the limitations in what an already limited literature can say about governments, their effectiveness, and the role of the public sector around the globe.

We conclude by describing the central impact that comparison can have in the study of effectiveness and performance. Dahl argued in 1947 that comparison is part of what helps public administration achieve scientific status. Over 50 years later most studies in public administration and public policy are limited to select countries usually from the developed world. The vast majority of studies are drawn from cases located in the top boxplot in Figure 3 – and even in that case many of the countries that contribute to variation in performance in North America and Western Europe are largely unrepresented in the literature. The problem, of course, is the cost of high-risk studies located in countries outside of Western Europe, North America, and/or Northeast Asia. Our claim is that using the comparative method does not require fieldwork – that we should at least take advantage of the full variation available in public domain datasets like those produced by the World Bank. This is made even clearer by the importance of understanding the outcomes these data measure given that they form the basis for rankings countries receive in the Millennium Challenge Account process for allocating foreign aid. Understanding the behavior of countries only within the context of the OECD or other groups provides only a limited glimpse into the full range of effectiveness governments around the world experience.

Notes

1. For example, Wolf (1997: 355) is clear about his selection of the federal agency or bureau as the unit of analysis and what that means for his research.
2. Walker and Boyne (2006: 379) argue that judgments of performance based on archival information or individual perceptions are not objective – that "some subjectivity and political bias are likely to be present in both archival and perceptual data".
3. This definition is seen in the literature on agency survival (see Carpenter and Lewis 2004).
4. These data were obtained from the Penn World Table. See http://pwt.econ.upenn.edu/.
5. Figure 2 does not include 2005 or 2006 due to missing GDP data.
6. Estimates for all of the bivariate regressions reported here are available from the authors.
7. Some countries have missing GDP data.

References

Andrews, Rhys, Boyne, George A., Meier, Kenneth J., O'Toole, Laurence J. and Walker, Richard M., 2005, Representative bureaucracy, organizational strategy, and public service performance: an empirical analysis of English local government. *Journal of Public Administration Research and Theory*, **15**, 489–504.

Andrews, Rhys, Boyne, George A. and Walker, Richard M., 2006a, Strategy content and organizational performance: an empirical analysis. *Public Administration Review*, **66**, 52–63.

Andrews, Rhys, Boyne, George. A. and Walker, Richard M., 2006b. Subjective and objective measures of organizational performance: an empirical exploration, in: George A. Boyne, Kenneth J. Meier, Laurence J. O'Toole and Richard M. Walker (Eds) *Public Service Performance: Perspectives on Measurement and Management* (Cambridge: Cambridge University Press), pp. 14–34.

Au, Chor-fai, 1996, Rethinking organizational effectiveness: theoretical and methodological issues in the study of organizational effectiveness for social welfare organizations. *Administration in Social Work*, **20**, 1–21.

Barnard, Chester I., 1938, *The Functions of the Executive* (Cambridge, MA: Harvard University Press).

Behn, Robert D., 1996, The futile search for the one best way. *Governing*, July, p. 82.

Behn, Robert D., 2003, Why measure performance? Different purposes require different measures. *Public Administration Review*, **63**, 586–606.

Berman, Evan and Wang, Xiaohu, 2000, Performance measurement in U.S. counties: capacity for reform. *Public Administration Review*, **60**, 409–420.

Boschken, Herman L., 1994, Organizational performance and multiple constituencies. *Public Administration Review*, **54**, 308–312.

Boyne, George A., 2002, Concepts and indicators of local authority performance: an evaluation of the statutory frameworks in England and Wales. *Public Money & Management*, **22**, 17–24.

Boyne, George A., 2003, Sources of public service improvement: a critical review and research agenda. *Journal of Public Administration Research and Theory*, **13**, 367–394.

Boyne, George A., Meier, Kenneth J., O'Toole Jr., Laurence J. and Walker, Richard M., 2006, Public management and organizational performance: an agenda for research, in: George A. Boyne, Kenneth J. Meier, Laurence J. O'Toole, and Richard M. Walker (Eds) *Public Service Performance: Perspectives on Measurement and Management* (Cambridge: Cambridge University Press), pp. 295–311.

Brewer, Gene A., 2004, Does administrative reform improve bureaucratic performance? A cross-country empirical analysis. *Public Finance and Management*, **4**, 399–428.

Brewer, Gene A., 2006, All measures of performance are subjective: more evidence on US federal agencies, in: George A. Boyne, Kenneth J. Meier, Laurence J. O'Toole and Richard M. Walker (Eds) *Public Service Performance: Perspectives on Measurement and Management* (Cambridge: Cambridge University Press), pp. 35–54.

Brewer, Gene A. and Selden, Sally Coleman, 2000, Why elephants gallop: assessing and predicting organizational performance in federal agencies. *Journal of Public Administration Research and Theory*, **10**, 685–712.

Carpenter, Daniel C. and Lewis, David E., 2004, Political learning from rare events: poisson inference, fiscal constraints and the lifetime of bureaus. *Political Analysis*, **12**, 201–232.

Cameron, Kim S. and Whetten, David A., 1981, Perceptions of organizational effectiveness over organizational life cycles. *Administrative Science Quarterly*, **26**, 525–544.

Cameron, Kim S. and Whetten, David A., 1983, Organizational effectiveness: one model or several?, in: Kim S. Cameron and David A. Whetten (Eds) *Organizational Effectiveness: A Comparison of Multiple Models* (Academic Press: New York), pp. 1–24.

Campbell, John P., 1977, On the nature of organizational effectiveness, in: Paul S. Goodman and Johannes M. Pennings (Eds) *New Perspectives on Organizational Effectiveness* (San Francisco, CA: Jossey-Bass, Inc.), pp. 13–55.

Chun, Young H. and Rainey, Hal G., 2005, Goal ambiguity and organizational performance in U.S. federal agencies. *Journal of Public Administration Research and Theory*, **15**, 529–557.

Connolly, Terry, Conlon, Edward J. and Deutsch, Stuart Jay, 1980, Organizational effectiveness: a multiple-constituency approach. *Academy of Management Review*, **5**, 211–217.

Daft, Richard L., 2001, *Organization Theory and Design* (Cincinnati, OH: South-Western College).

Dahl, Robert A., 1947, The science of public administration: three problems. *Public Administration Review*, **7**, 1–11.

Delaney, John T. and Huselid, Mark A., 1996, The impact of human resource management practices on perceptions of organizational performance. *Academy of Management Journal*, **39**, 949–969.

Dollinger, Marc J. and Golden, Peggy A., 1992, Interorganizational and collective strategies in small firms: environmental effects and performance. *Journal of Management*, **18**, 695–715.

Golden, Brian R., 1992, Is the past the past – or is it? The use of retrospective accounts as indicators of past strategies. *Academy of Management Journal*, **35**, 848–860.

Goodman, Paul S. and Pennings, Johannes M., 1977, Perspectives and issues: an introduction. In: Paul S. Goodman and Johannes M. Pennings (Eds) *New Perspectives on Organizational Effectiveness* (San Francisco, CA: Jossey-Bass, Inc.), pp. 1–12.

Heinrich, Carolyn J. and Lynn, Laurence E., Jr., 2000, Governance and performance: the influence of program structure and management on Job Training Partnership Act (JTPA) program outcomes, In: C. J. Heinrich and Laurence E. Lynn Jr. (Eds) *Governance and Performance: New Perspectives* (Washington, DC: Georgetown University Press), pp. 68–108.

Ingraham, Patricia W. and Donald P., Moynihan, 2000, Evolving dimensions of performance from the CSRA to the present, in: James P. Pfiffner and Douglas A. Brook (Eds) *The Future of Merit: Twenty Years after the Civil Service Reform Act* (Baltimore, MD: Johns Hopkins University Press), pp. 103–126.

Ingraham, Patricia W., Joyce, Philip G. and Donahue, Amy K., 2003, *Government Performance: Why Management Matters* (Baltimore, MD: Johns Hopkins University Press).

Kaufmann, Daniel, Kraay, Aart and Zoido-Lobatón, Pablo, 1999, Governance matters. World Bank Policy Research Working Paper, No. 2196 (Washington, DC: World Bank).

Kaufmann, Daniel, Kraay, Aart and Mastruzzi, Massimo, 2007, Governance matters VI: aggregate and individual governance indicators 1996–2006. World Bank Policy Research Working Paper, No. 4280 (Washington, DC: World Bank).

Kim, Sangmook, 2004, Individual-level factors and organizational performance in government organizations. *Journal of Public Administration Research and Theory*, **15**, 245–261.

Kirlin, John, 2001, Big questions for a significant public administration. *Public Administration Review*, **61**, 140–143.
Knack, Stephen, 2002, Social capital and the quality of government: evidence from the states, *American Journal of Political Science*, **46**, 772–785.
Light, Paul C., 2006, The tides of reform revisited: patterns in making government work, 1945–2002, *Public Administration Review*, **66**, 6–19.
Likert, Rensis, 1967, *The Human Organization* (New York: McGraw-Hill).
Lynn, Laurence E., Jr., Heinrich, Carolyn J. and Hill, Carolyn J., 2000, Studying governance and public management: challenges and prospects. *Journal of Public Administration Research and Theory*, **10**, 233–261.
McCracken, Melody J., McIlwain, Thomas F. and Fottler, Myron D., 2001, Measuring organizational performance in the hospital industry: an exploratory comparison of objective and subjective methods. *Health Services Management Research*, **14**, 211–219.
Meier, Kenneth J. and Brudney, Jeffrey L., 2002, *Applied Statistics for Public Administration* (Orlando, FL: Harcourt College).
Moynihan, Donald P. and Pandey, Sanjay K., 2005, Testing how management matters in an era of government by performance management. *Journal of Public Administration Research and Theory*, **15**, 421–439.
Osborne, David and Gaebler, Ted, 1992, *Reinventing Government: How the Entrepreneurial Spirit is Transforming the Public Sector* (Reading, MA: Addison-Wesley Pub. Co.).
O'Toole, Laurence J., Jr. and Meier, Kenneth J., 1999, Modeling the impact of public management: implications of structural context. *Journal of Public Administration Research and Theory*, **9**, 505–526.
O'Toole, Laurence J., Jr. and Meier, Kenneth J., 2003, Plus ça change: public management, personnel stability, and organizational performance. *Journal of Public Administration Research and Theory*, **13**, 43–64.
Parks, Roger B., 1984, Linking objective and subjective measures of performance. *Public Administration Review*, **44**, 118–127.
Pfeffer, Jeffrey, 1977, Usefulness of the concept, in: Paul S. Goodman and Johannes M. Pennings (Eds) *New Perspectives on Organizational Effectiveness* (San Francisco, CA: Jossey-Bass, Inc.), pp. 132–145.
Pfeffer, Jeffrey, 1982, *Organizations and Organization Theory* (Boston, Ma: Pittman).
Pearce, John A., II, Robbins, D. Keith and Robinson, Richard B., Jr., 1987, The impact of grand strategy and planning formality on financial performance. *Strategic Management Journal*, **8**, 125–134.
Powell, Thomas C., 1992, Organizational alignment as competitive advantage. *Strategic Management Journal*, **13**, 119–134.
Provan, Keith G. and Milward, H. Brinton, 1995, A preliminary theory of interorganizational network effectiveness: a comparative study of four community mental health systems. *Administrative Science Quarterly*, **40**, 1–33.
Provan, Keith G.and Milward, H. Brinton, 2001, Do networks really work? A framework for evaluating public-sector organizational networks. *Public Administration Review*, **61**, 414–423.
Putnam, Robert, 1993, *Making Democracy Work* (Princeton, NJ: Princeton University Press).
Quinn, Robert E. and Rohrbaugh, John, 1983, A spatial model of effectiveness criteria: towards a competing values approach to organizational analysis. *Management Science*, **29**, 363–377.
Radin, Beryl A., 2000, *Beyond Machiavelli: Policy Analysis Comes of Age* (Washington, DC: Georgetown University Press).
Rainey, Hal G., 2003, *Understanding and Managing Public Organizations* (San Francisco, CA: Jossey-Bass).
Rainey, Hal G. and Steinbauer, Paula, 1999, Galloping elephants: developing elements of a theory of effective government organizations. *Journal of Public Administration Research and Theory*, **9**, 1–32.
Scott, W. Richard, 1998, *Organizations: Rational, Natural, and Open Systems* (Upper Saddle River, NJ: Prentice Hall).
Seashore, Stanley E. and Yuchtman, Ephraim, 1967, Factorial analysis of organizational performance, *Administrative Science Quarterly*, **12**, 377–395.
Selden, Sally Coleman and Sowa, Jessica E., 2004, Testing a multi-dimensional model of organizational performance: prospects and problems, *Journal of Public Administration Research and Theory*, **14**, 395–416.

Spector, Paul E., 2006, Method variance in organizational research: truth or urban legend? *Organizational Research Methods*, **9**, 221–232.

Steers, Richard M., 1975, Problems in the measurement of organizational effectiveness. *Administrative Science Quarterly*, **20**, 546–558.

Van de Walle, Steven, 2006, The state of the world's bureaucracy. *Journal of Comparative Policy Analysis*, **8**, 437–448.

Walker, Richard M. and Boyne, George A., 2006, Public management reform and organizational performance: an empirical assessment of the U.K. labour government's public service improvement strategy. *Journal of Policy Analysis and Management*, **25**, 371–393.

Wolf, Patrick J., 1993, A case survey of bureaucratic effectiveness in U.S. cabinet agencies: preliminary results. *Journal of Public Administration Research and Theory*, **3**, 161–181.

Wolf, Patrick J., 1997, Why must we reinvent the federal government? Putting historical developmental claims to the test. *Journal of Public Administration Research and Theory*, **7**, 353–388.

Yang, Kaifeng and Holzer, Marc, 2006, The performance–trust link: implications for performance measurement. *Public Administration Review*, **66**, 114–126.

Federalism, Political Structure, and Public Policy in the United States and Canada

BERYL A. RADIN AND JOAN PRICE BOASE

ABSTRACT *Two of the three large countries on the North American continent—the United States and Canada—share a number of similarities that often make it difficult for the untrained observer to differentiate between the two nations. On the surface, the two are structured similarly as federal systems that, by definition, exhibit shared power between the national government and provincial or state political entities.*

Although there are other important social and economic characteristics of the two countries that help explain differences in policy processes and outcomes, it is the contention of this article that one gets the clearest sense of what Elazar has called "thinking federal" by utilizing an analytical approach that joins questions related to federalism with some conceptual frameworks of the public policy field. Two frameworks undergird the argument in this article—the Lowi typology of different types of policies and Deil Wright's typology of different models that describe the American intergovernmental system.

In both countries, policies must be sensitive to the greater interdependencies between units of government as well as to linkages between policy areas. The mechanisms or instrumentalities for dealing with policy issues are intrinsically complex. It is also clear that the intergovernmental networks that exist in both the U.S. and Canada are composed of an array of actors. The differing political structures of the systems do impact the types of intergovernmental policies that have emerged in the two countries. The executive dominance so imbedded in Canadian governments has contributed to their ability to adopt and implement certain controversial redistributive policies, such as a national health insurance program. By contrast, the fragmentation of the U.S. system makes redistributive policies more difficult.

Two of the three large countries on the North American continent—the United States and Canada—share a number of similarities that often make it difficult for the untrained observer to differentiate between the two nations. On the surface, the two are structured similarly as federal systems that, by definition, exhibit shared power between the national government and provincial or state political entities. Both these political systems have evolved from earlier British colonial rule, yet they have adopted very different political structures. In the United States, government structures (at both the federal and state levels) were designed as a deliberate rejection of the unchecked power of the British king, and they embraced the Madisonian concept of checks and balances. Canada, on the other hand, chose to emulate (at both federal and provincial levels) the strong British Parliamentary system that had developed by the mid-nineteenth century. The influx of British Empire Loyalists escaping the American revolution in the eighteenth century strengthened the British ties. These fundamentally different political systems are the major explanation for the strikingly distinct forms of policy development evident in these two federal states.

Although there are other important social and economic characteristics of the two countries that help explain differences in policy processes and outcomes (such as relative size, industrial base, ethnic makeup, distribution of wealth, and overall history), it is the contention of this article that one gets the clearest sense of what Elazar has called "thinking federal" by utilizing an analytical approach that joins questions related to federalism with some conceptual frameworks of the public policy field. Two frameworks undergird the argument in this article—the Lowi typology of different types of policies (Lowi, 1964) and Deil Wright's typology of different models that describe the American intergovernmental system (Wright, 1988).

As Dale Krane (1993) has noted, the intertwining of federalism with policymaking enriches both fields. Most importantly, it provides a sense that "American federalism is more than a maze of institutions; it is a matrix of reciprocal power relations" (p. 187). Elazar (1987) has commented:

> In any federal system, it is likely that there will be continued tension between the federal government and the constituent polities over the years and that different "balances" between them will develop at different times. The existence of this tension is an integral part of the federal relationship, and its character does much to determine the future of federalism in each system. The questions of intergovernmental relations which it produces are perennially a matter of public concern because virtually all other political issues arising in a federal system are phrased in terms of their implication for federalism as part of the public discussion surrounding them. In this way, federalism imposes a way of looking at problems that stands apart from the substantive issues raised by the problems themselves (p. 185).

The tensions of which Elazar speaks define Canadian federalism, and the competitive dynamics of policymaking reflect the imbedded nature of the federal fact. Despite this high degree of "thinking federally," however, policymaking in Canada has not been fragmented to the extent that it has in the U.S. In a brief discussion of the consequences of federalism for public policy in Canada, Donald Smiley (1987) said that "to the extent that effective government requires the rationalization of public policy, federalism stands squarely in the way of this goal" (p. 22), yet he concluded that "in general, federalism in its Canadian variant contributes both to the preservation of certain key democratic values *and* to effective public policy" (p. 22). That is, the often distressing nature of federal-provincial competition tends to obscure an underlying unity of purpose, and public policy outcomes are best understood by examining the particular manifestation of relationships in political structure, political culture, and public administration.

The present article seeks to provide a reader with a overview of an approach that draws from both the policy and federalism literatures. It provides a sketch of the policy landscape in the U.S. and Canada, the relationships between levels of government, and the variety of structures and behaviors that characterize the two federal systems. It focuses on the substantive direction of policies that have emerged from the policy adoption process as well as on the behaviors that occur through the policy implementation stage. Lowi's typology— differentiating between (1) redistributive, (2) regulatory, and (3) distributive or developmental policies (see discussion in Wright, 1988, p. 293; see also Lowi, 1972; Peterson, 1981; Beer, 1973)—provides a way to capture the differences between the two countries. This approach also emphasizes what has been called *intergovernmental relations*—the activities and relationships between governmental units or the ways and means of operationalizing a system of government.

The composite picture that emerges from this approach is one that emphasizes the differences between the two federal systems. The U.S. appears to be full of contradictions, is usually pragmatic rather than ideological in its spirit and substance, is open to a range of political and economic trade-offs, and is constantly changing. The Canadian picture that emerges is one of a decentralized, competitive, yet functional federal system. Canada's propensity to engage in extensive negotiation, compromise, and collaboration is perhaps in large part due to the need for high-level political involvement in the pursuit of nationwide redistributive policymaking.

The United States: fragmented powers as the point of departure

Political institutions in the U.S., wherever they are found and whatever they are called, are constructed to minimize or, if possible, avoid the exertion of concentrated power. Power and authority are separated and shared across all aspects of the political landscape. This occurs horizontally through the delineation of separate institutions charged with executive, legislative, and judicial functions, as well as vertically through the assumption of shared or separate powers between the national, state, and sometimes local levels of government. The principle of fragmentation is carried on within institutions (e.g., bicameral legislatures and separation of authorizing and appropriations functions within the legislative branch) as well as across most levels of government (e.g., shared powers between a state governor and a state legislature or between a city mayor and a city council). Divided government is a reality today in Washington, and in many states, with the executive branch represented by one political party and the legislative branch (in at least one of the bicameral bodies) represented by another party. Unlike many other countries, the American system did not begin with the reality of a strong national government. Rather, the American state developed largely from a bottom-up distribution of power.

As a result, unlike a parliamentary system, there is no institutional actor with authority to look at the government as a whole. Except in emergency situations such as wartime, the American system would not create a national planning commission such as that in many countries or even a body charged with allocating funds within program areas to the separate states. The political process, with its vagaries, determines the allocation pattern. This results in striking disparities between the 50 states.

Disparities between states and cities are considered through the process of designing specific policies or programs, rather than a comprehensive approach to relationships between or among levels of government. A dialectic pattern has emerged in which debate about federalism issues within the U.S. occurs at two often contradictory levels: a general, macro, and sometimes symbolic approach (which is usually opposed to any increase in national governmental powers) and a specific policy approach (which focuses on specific problems and specific solutions that may or may not directly involve an increased role for the national government). The assumption about the role of government has been historically defined through partisan political conflict, with one party (the Democrats) representing more activist government and the other (the Republicans) advocates of less government.

The cumulative effect of individual, incremental actions may suggest that policies are moving in a consistent direction although, in reality, they have not been crafted through a planned, rational approach. For example, social policy programs for the poor and minorities were developed in the 1960s that, combined with programs of the Roosevelt New Deal, created a fabric of social programs similar to that found in some of the European welfare states (Edelman and Radin, 1991). Acknowledgment of the significant role of the national government in providing services reflected a "crazy quilt" design rather than an orderly pattern, and the optimism of the 1960s reinforced a belief that a coordinated system would emerge from these bits and pieces. Individual actions are taken for a variety of reasons that cut across the Lowi framework: crisis conditions; unresponsive lower levels of government; problems that are considered to be of national concern; provision of equity or equality of opportunity for individuals, states, and localities; assisting or provoking activity in other parts of the society; or simply because of pressure from interest groups.

With these structural "givens," it is not surprising that fragmentation of authority within the American system has reinforced the tendency of the culture to associate liberty with limited government and to venerate (indeed, sometimes romanticize) the concept of "local control," even when in practice it does not occur.

Canada: executive dominance institutionally imbedded

The exercise of governmental power in Canada is quite unlike the singularly pluralistic and fragmented polity that has evolved in the United States, for there is no deliberate diffusion of governmental authority through the doctrine of the separation of power. The British Parliamentary system in Canada is characterized by an excessive adherence to party discipline, and this has reinforced the potential for a dominant executive that is inherent in the fusion of executive and legislative power; thus, the government of Canada is the party that holds a majority of seats in the House of Commons. The point of departure for an understanding of the Canadian system is an appreciation of the almost unchecked power, in practice, of a united cabinet that commands a majority in the legislature.[1] This power is only slightly ameliorated by the bicameral nature of the federal Parliament, and it is strengthened at the provincial level by unicameral systems. Unlike the American system, the Canadian system was predicated upon a strong faith in government, a top-down approach to the development of policy, and an historical acceptance of government intervention.

This is not to say that the combination of a strong executive and acceptance of government intervention has permitted the federal government to dominate policymaking, although it has often tried. The opposite is actually true. While there have been periods of central domination (during war, depression, and early forays into Keynesian economics post-World War II), policy development is very much a federal-provincial dialogue. However, social and economic expectations are frequently tied to federal government activity (with the possible exception of French-speaking Quebeckers); jobs and the future of social programs are central to the election platforms of federally based parties.

The Constitution Act of 1982 (Part III, s. 36) brought both subtle and clear changes to the federal relationship. For example, the reliance on unanimity in the amending formula for changes in several areas reinforces the developing sense of provincial autonomy. The Act also requires that the federal government preside over equalization payments to the seven "have-not" provinces to enable them to provide social services comparable to those of the three "have" provinces.[2] These are direct government transfers according to an agreed-upon formula. The federal government has also established crown corporations and focused agencies to address regional-provincial disparities and to encourage economic development. These agencies, such as the Atlantic Canada Opportunities Agency, are charged with specific mandates, and their programs can be jointly funded by the federal and provincial governments. The federal government, however, cannot issue mandates to the provincial governments in the areas of provincial jurisdiction; it must negotiate, compromise, and exploit its superior spending power to convince the provincial governments to pass legislation.

The development of policy instruments has therefore been driven by both federal-provincial cooperation as well as by federal-provincial conflict. This development is characterized by strong governments pursuing their own priorities, and it should not be surprising, then, that the highly centralized nature of political power at both levels of government has led to policy development and intergovernmental activity quite dissimilar from what occurs in most other federal countries.

The United States: relationships between and among actors

Although most students of federalism in the U.S. will agree that fragmented powers are a point of departure for understanding the American system, they have differing opinions about the conceptual model that may be used to "map" the relationships between the national (usually called federal), state, and local levels of government. Deil Wright (1988, p. 40) has advanced three models to describe these relationships. The *inclusive authority* model assumes that the national government plays the superior role and will control dealings with other levels of government. The *coordinate authority* model emphasizes the autonomy of states; local governments are viewed as a total creature of the state, and the national government's dealings with the state assumes that both parties are separate and distinct. The *overlapping authority* model, by contrast, conveys several messages: (1) that many areas of policy require national, state, and local involvement; (2) that the areas of autonomy and discretion for any single jurisdiction are limited; and (3) that levels of governments require bargaining and negotiation to obtain adequate power and influence to carry out programs.[3] These models only begin to describe the complex relationships between levels of government in the U.S. when viewed over time (Wright, 1988, p. 67). It is clear that the relationships between levels of government in the U.S. are constantly changing and redefined.

Similarly, this analysis indicates the span of instrumentalities that have been used to develop relationships between levels of government. These instrumentalities reflect social expectations that produce diverse and often conflicting goals. Policies that emerge as a result of bargaining between parties with different interests are more likely to contain multiple expectations. In addition, these multiple expectations are continued (and sometimes actually increased) when the policy moves from the design or adoption phase to implementation in diverse settings. In effect, the structure of federalism reinforces the political and functional complexity of the system.

The instrumentalities that are used to convey these expectations may be formal and direct or informal and indirect, depending on the trade-offs that are devised. This variation makes it clear that the search for the "appropriate" relationship between centralized and decentralized units of government is, in effect, an eternal quest. Solutions are temporal, at best, and are often devised with limited knowledge of their consequences and effects.

A scrutiny of relationships *among* rather than *between* levels of government is also important to an understanding of American federalism. The differences among states and localities in the U.S. are not based on language[4] or religious differences. However, there are striking differences in the political cultures of jurisdictions within the U.S., which are related to population characteristics, geographical and regional patterns, type of governmental structures, and, of course, past experience. While some argue that Americans—wherever they live—are more alike than dissimilar, the system that has been created provides latitude for the differences between jurisdictions (e.g., it gives to all levels of government the ability to tax). The level of analysis that focuses on relationships between levels of government sometimes glosses over the incredible variation that is found in the U.S. when one compares states, regions, or localities. This variation becomes more obvious when the society has committed itself to a national policy (e.g., civil rights) that must be implemented in very different political cultures.[5]

But perhaps the least well understood and most invisible differences among jurisdictions relate to political structures and authority. The relationships between the executive and legislative branches are not consistent across the U.S. States vary strikingly in the degree to which governors have formal authority vis-à-vis the state legislature. Some states have extremely weak governors who do not have the ability to establish their own cabinets, to veto legislation, or, in one case, even to submit a budget. Other states have strong governors. States also vary in terms of the extent of the aggregate role of government within the society. Some states have weak governors and legislative bodies that are limited in the number of days that they may meet in a year. This variety also exists at the local level in terms of the relationship between a mayor, a county executive, and the local legislative body.

This variety of structural relationships has both positive and negative aspects to it. On one hand, the variety provides the setting for "natural experiments" in which one or two states are able to incubate or experiment with new ways of doing the government's business. It is in this sense that states are described as *laboratories of democracy*. These experiments might be used as the demonstration sites for national policies or serve as examples for other states to adopt as they see fit. The problems of individual states are different and, as well, states vary in their willingness to try solutions.[6] These settings also provide a training ground for elected and appointed officials.[7] At the same time, this variety also leads to a sense of chaos and difficulty in talking about *"the* states" or *"the* localities."

Canada: federal provincial interdependence

When the fathers of Canadian Confederation decided in 1867 on an uneasy reconciliation of a British Parliamentary system with a federal system,[8] defined in a constitution that contained many unitary features,[9] they could not have imagined the state of federal-provincial relations in the late twentieth century. Judicial interpretation soon forced into disuse the centralizing constitutional features, and the confidence thus instilled in provincial governments was reinforced by their almost unfettered executive power. Serious jurisdictional disputes have long been a feature of Canadian intergovernmental relations and have defined the formulation of many public policies.

Models that have been developed to describe approaches to Canadian federalism are similar to those Deil Wright (1988) has used to describe federal-state-local relationships in the U.S. While these models may appear to be contradictory or even mutually exclusive, they have nonetheless co-existed in Canada, in constant flux. Wright's models of inclusive, coordinate, and overlapping authority have been called in Canada *centralist, coordinate,* and *executive* or *functional federalism.* To these has been added the *compact* theory, which in its late twentieth-century variant stresses the equality of the provinces, thus undermining federal authority and implicitly rejecting the historical dualist concept of Canadian federalism (the perception of two founding nations—French and English).[10] There is no parallel in the U.S. to the dualist concept that has been so pervasive in Canada and that has added such complexity to federal-provincial relations and the determination of public policy.

In the eyes of many provincial governments, the use of the federal spending power to develop national policy within provincial jurisdiction amounts to coercion. Like many U.S. state officials, provincial governments argue that their priorities are frequently distorted by the constraints of federal moves. Their jurisdictional strength and their resistance to federal encroachment has resulted in what Richard Simeon (1980) has called *political independence/policy dependence?*[11] This has been manifest in the development of an elaborate system of federal-provincial interaction: the federal-provincial conference.

Federal-provincial conferences in Canada have been raised to a fine art, and the media duly note the drama, conflict, compromise, and coercion that occur. This extraconstitutional manifestation of executive federalism has led to attempts to constitutionalize a requirement for a yearly conference (now referred to as *first ministers conferences*) in the most recent failed efforts at constitutional reform. At least two or three conferences at the highest level already take place each year. Although there is no formal decision-making mechanism, Alan Cairns (1977) has suggested that these conferences have developed into a unique Canadian-style variation of the American separation of powers. It is a compelling argument. Although there is no legal veto power, it is nevertheless clear that the extensive federal-provincial negotiation that occurs during the development of public policy circumscribes, in a de facto sense, the exercise of executive power that is so prevalent in a British Parliamentary system. Thus far, such negotiation has served to restrain federal power to a greater extent than provincial power, since the federal government feels constrained to consult provincial governments even when developing policy in an exclusive federal jurisdiction.[12] This is one important example of the increasing prominence of provincial governments in the Canadian federal system, which have successfully "asserted their right to be consulted by Ottawa in respect to a range of matters like trade and tariffs and interprovincial transportation and communication" (Smiley, 1987, p. 85). The latter are all matters within the exclusive federal legislative power.

The evolution in provincial assertiveness—and federal deference—became clear during economic development talks during the decade of the 1970s.[13] It became more evident in the various GATT discussions (and more recently in the World Trade Organization) and in the extensive federal-provincial consultations engaged in by the Mulroney government during its 1980s negotiations with the U.S. in the Free Trade Agreement and the subsequent negotiations with the U.S. and Mexico leading to NAFTA. Broad consultation also occurs in areas of concurrent jurisdiction (pensions, immigration, and agriculture) and in unemployment insurance, which is an exclusive federal jurisdiction. Further, in the concurrent area of pensions, changes to legislation must be approved by two thirds of provincial governments representing two thirds of the Canadian population (Smiley, 1987, p. 86).[14]

There is no parallel in the U.S. system to the extensive Canadian reliance on executive federalism. In fact, Douglas Verney (1986) has said that in the United States, the separation of powers combined with the Supreme Court, the Senate, and the state legislatures has "effectively prevented the transformation of the American system into anything like executive federalism" (pp. 353–354). Although the legitimacy of executive federalism in Canada as an approach to constitutional politics has recently been challenged,[15] it remains institutionalized in the development of public policy. That is, according to Donald Smiley (1980), because in the latter twentieth century, all governments have taken on a greater role in the economy, the federal government has pursued national standards in fields of exclusive provincial jurisdiction, there has been escalating competition among governments for tax dollars, activity has increased in subjects covered by concurrent legislation, provincial resentment of federal encroachment has grown, and there has been increased interprovincial interaction (Smiley, 1980, pp. 92–94).

All these aspects of federal provincial relations came together in the mid to late 1990s, when the federal government, without prior consultation, announced in its 1995 budget a new formula for the financing of social programs that would see the federal contribution drop to zero by the year 2008. The reaction of provincial governments was immediate, vociferous, bitter, and acrimonious. The shock drove them together, and with one voice they argued that federal standards in social policy fields would therefore no longer be tolerable. The federal government backed down and reinstated its (somewhat reduced) funding, and most of the provinces were appeased. Subsequently, in a clear example of executive federalism, the premiers and the prime minister met over several months to develop a carefully guarded agreement that was announced in February 1999 as Canada's new social union. It included a firm commitment by the Chretien government to maintain its share of stable and predictable funding for health care, welfare, and postsecondary education. Several provincial representatives, however, continued to pursue an agreement that would see provincial governments as equal partners with the federal government in the development of standards in social policy. The federal government has resisted this.

Not all observers have found the competitive federalism of the latter part of the twentieth century to be destructive, and there are some compelling arguments in favor of the creative dynamics sometimes evident in this competition. The British Parliamentary system is fundamentally an adversarial system, and there are some who argue that there are advantages in a certain amount of tension—and even conflict—in intergovernmental relations. For example, in a 1984 lecture at York University, former premier of Alberta, Peter Lougheed, found this tension to be healthy, as did several members of the, important Macdonald Royal Commission in the 1980s. The Commission suggested that "economic development in federations is likely to exceed that in centralized states as a result of the beneficial effects of competition in the public sector" (Smiley, 1987, p. 94). One member, in a supplementary statement, considered conflict to be more democratic than the cooperative federalism of the 1960s (see Smiley, 1987, p. 96), but other members argued that any reforms to the system must "increase incentives for intergovernmental collaboration and develop counterweights to the strong political incentives for provincial leaders to see policies primarily in terms of territorial impacts" (Fletcher and Wallace, 1985).

As another manifestation of executive federalism and competitive federalism,[16] interprovincial interaction has become increasingly more institutionalized. In addition to the many ministerial level meetings, there is a formal conference of the premiers in August of each year. The federal government sends only a few observers to this conference.

The conference is chaired by the premiers on a rotating basis, and its purpose is not unlike that of the first such meeting in 1887—to develop common policy positions with which to confront the federal government. Although these meetings do not receive the same media emphasis as the first ministers meetings, they are nevertheless thoroughly covered by the news media. This is especially true when there are controversial issues to be discussed. The communiques that emerge from these meetings are broad, often vague approaches to policy development. They attempt to mask real disagreements among the provincial governments, although the provincial governments were apparently united in their rejection of the thrust of the 1995 budget, discussed above.

The premiers do occasionally rise above their partisan political differences and parochial provincial rivalries at these meetings and issue a statement that has a genuinely national dimension. For the most part, however, little important substantive policy results from the annual premiers' conference, although the more informal and frequent meetings at the ministerial and administrative level do affect policy outcomes.

There is another level of ministerial meetings that affects public policy: the regional meetings, particularly in Atlantic Canada. Representatives of the governments of the Atlantic provinces meet to discuss educational, health, transportation, and economic issues that affect their constituents, and substantive policy is frequently the outcome. In 1996, for example, the four premiers met to discuss Ottawa's proposal to harmonize its unpopular Goods and Services Tax with the provincial sales taxes (as had already occurred in Quebec). Prince Edward Island chose not to participate, but the premiers of Newfoundland, Nova Scotia, and New Brunswick held a joint press conference to announce their agreement to harmonize. This policy target was achieved by Ottawa in a familiar use of its spending power, for each province was to be compensated for lost revenue, but no further harmonization of this unpopular tax was achieved. The four western provinces also have an annual western conference, but their cooperation is less institutionalized, perhaps reflecting the pronounced ideological and political culture differences among these provinces.

Canadian political parties and political culture

As in the United States, there are geographical, demographic, economic, and resource-dependency differences among the Canadian provinces. While to outside observers the most striking difference is that of language between Quebec and the other provinces, equally notable differences exist in the areas of party formation and political culture that have profound implications for policy development and implementation. This becomes more apparent when the federal government defines national programs in areas of provincial jurisdiction and uses its spending power to ensure compliance.

Unlike the U.S., Canada has not, since the 1920s, been a stable two-party system of government, and the links between the federal and provincial wings of the parties are loose; they are more confederal than integrated (see Smiley, 1987, chapter 5, for a discussion of this phenomenon). Many third parties, mostly from the western provinces, have formed to challenge the perceived policy inequities pursued by the two dominant parties in parliament. Most of these parties withered and died, but the social democratic New Democratic Party (NDP), with its roots in the 1930s Saskatchewan Cooperative Commonwealth Federation (CCF), survived to hold the balance of power for several years in Ottawa and to form the government or opposition in four of the provinces. In the 1990s, the Reform Party, an Alberta and British Columbia-based neo-liberal party, made impressive inroads into the House of Commons, and in the 1997 election, it became the official opposition, although it had only one member east of Manitoba.

During many of the years that the NDP held the balance of power in Ottawa, growth of the Canadian welfare state occurred in response not only to the efforts of the NDP but also to an awareness of increasing public support for social programs. In the decade of the 1960s, for example, federal-provincial agreements led to expansion of pension and income support programs, and in 1966 Ottawa passed the Medical Care Act.

The implementation of this last Act underlined the disparate political cultures among the provinces and the opportunities for experimentation that can be one of the strengths of a federal system. Several provinces had already experimented with various aspects of hospital and medical insurance, and in Saskatchewan (under a social democratic government) a publicly administered medical care act had been in place since 1962. Saskatchewan was therefore an early supporter of the federal move, as were British Columbia and Newfoundland.

By contrast, Alberta—Saskatchewan's entrepreneurial neighbor—has long been governed by determinedly conservative governments, and it "loudly proclaimed its opposition to a universal government plan on the grounds that it involved compulsion" (Taylor, 1986, p. 338). Ontario, with its extensive private insurance business and strong medical lobby, was defiantly opposed, as was the Quebec government and its medical associations. The power of the federal purse prevailed, and all the provinces joined the plan by 1971. This plan (and the hospital one before it in 1957), although considered offensive coercion by some of the provinces, was in fact a prime example of effective federal-provincial compromise. Although the provincial governments were required to pass legislation that conformed with Ottawa's five enunciated medical insurance standards in order to qualify for funding, they were left with considerable flexibility to determine details. Consequently, there are many asymmetries among the provincial plans, in accordance with provincial priorities.

Influential actors in the U.S. federal system

The multiple centers of authority that are found in the U.S. system mean that the range of characters involved in some aspect of policymaking is both numerous and varied. Devising a "map" of the system requires attention to actors with both formal and informal powers. One can also shift the focus of the unit of analysis from internal decisionmaking within a level of government to the interrelationships between and among jurisdictions. The actors within the "map" include governmental units as well as specialized policy actors.

Governmental units

At the national level, one might identify the cast of actors by following the formal structure of the three branches of government: the legislative, the judicial, and the executive. Members of Congress deal with issues involving relationships between levels of government in two ways: in the context of the specific needs of their own states or through policy or programmatic issues that arise in their committee assignments. The judiciary branch has had a strong impact on the federal system but, because of the way that it makes decisions, has done so on a case-by-case basis.

The role of the executive branch is, perhaps, the most dense. As we have learned over the past several decades, the executive branch of the U.S. government does not move with a single voice or set of actions. Within the White House there are organizational units that exist across changes in presidents, while there are other units that totally change with the change in the presidency. Although the vast apparatus of the bureaucracy appears as a part of the organizational chart of the executive branch, in reality the system of shared powers means that career public servants have dual masters: the two houses and multiple organizations within the legislature, and the president and the various functions of the White House (such as the Office of Management and Budget).

Relationships between the executive branch and other levels of government come in several forms. The White House itself is usually attentive to governors, mayors, and other elected officials, particularly those of the same political party as the president. While political parties in the U.S. do not have the level of discipline associated with a parliamentary system, there is still a special relationship and patterns of influence between national and state and local officials from the same political party. In addition, each of the executive branch agencies and departments usually has a staff member given specialized responsibility for dealing with intergovernmental matters.

In addition to the national level institutions, governmental units from both state and local levels have an impact on national policy.[17] *Individual states* speak through the governor, members of the legislature, and other directly elected or appointed state level officials. In addition, congressional members of both the House and the Senate from the state will represent the state interest. Much of what has been described regarding Canadian provincial resistance is expressed in the U.S. through the Congress, particularly through the Senate. The interests *of individual localities* can be articulated through a mayor, a county commission, a city council, a township board, or the member of the House from the locality.[18]

While individual units of government may deal independently with other units of government, their involvement with the national government frequently occurs through collective action. Each of the state and local actors within the federal system has an organization that represents its interests in Washington (see Haider, 1974). These groups— known as the PIGs (the public interest groups)— provide information to their members about national developments of interest to the group, take positions on relevant policy issues, and sometimes offer technical assistance to their constituencies. While these groups expanded and prospered in the 1960s and 1970s, it is sometimes forgotten that they were organized during the early decades of this century (Anton, 1984, p. 28). At times these groups work in coalition; often, however, they oppose one another in national debate.

The major organizations at the national level include the National Governors' Association, the National League of Cities, the International City Management Association, the Council of State Governments, the National Association of County Officials, the U.S. Conference of Mayors, and the National Conference of State Legislatures. Many of the groups are also active at the regional or state level (e.g., the California League of Cities or the Western Governors' Association).

While these "general-purpose" government organizations are an important part of the intergovernmental landscape, their influence is limited in several ways. Each of these organizations attempts to represent an array of officials who, in turn, represent jurisdictions with quite different populations as well as economic and social realities. To avoid divisiveness within the organization, policy agreement across this span may require the "lowest common denominator" approach, a position that stays at a rhetorical rather than a substantive level, or a strategy that removes the debate on an issue from elected officials and, instead, places it in the hands of technical specialists.

Specialized policy actors in the U.S.

Although the general-purpose government organizations just described can be defined as *interest groups,* the more common characterization of interest groups in the U.S. refers to organizations that represent participants in the policy process that are usually without formal government positions. From deToqueville on, observers of the American political culture have pointed to the country's predilection to form organizations of a voluntary or a quasi-voluntary nature. The fragmented nature of the policy decision process has reinforced this tendency and created actors up and down the decision-making process who represent various perspectives on the issue at hand. The concept of the *iron triangle* has been used to describe the relationships that develop around specific policy areas involving executive bureaus, congressional committees, and interest group clienteles. Recent analysts of interest-group behavior have characterized the relationships as more fluid than the concept of the iron triangle suggests. Relationships are thought to be more fluid and are described as a "web" of largely autonomous participants with variable degrees of mutual commitment or dependence on each other (see Heclo, 1979).

Each policy issue has a group of specialized policy actors that represent economic interests, constituency groups, professional groups, administrators, and others with some interest in the specific field.[19] Depending on one's perspective, the array of specialized policy actors can be viewed as a help or a hindrance to the development of effective policy. Some have viewed interest groups as public mouthpieces for private interests (see Lowi, 1979). Others have emphasized the role that interest groups play as the thread that holds a fragmented system together (see Radin and Hawley, 1988).

Canadian specialized policy actors

As in the United States, Canada has a plurality of groups and organizations whose purpose is to influence government decision makers in the interests of their members. Their structure and activities reveal much about the political system within which they operate, since the character of these groups will "in any particular system... be the product of interaction between the internal resources of the groups themselves and the political system in which they are found" (Pross, 1986, p. 109). They are highly adaptive and thus are able to adjust their activities to the power structures of the state itself.

In both Canada and the U.S., many groups have been forced to federalize their internal organization to reflect the federal nature of government structure. Their chosen methods of interaction, however, have been adapted to their particular political systems. In the United States, for example, the fragmented nature of the political system and the separation of power provides interest-group representatives with multiple points of access and influence. In Canada, these points of access are more limited, due to the executive dominance of the system. It has been argued that interest groups are essentially shut out of the process once an issue reaches the intergovernmental stage, since the closed and secretive nature of executive federalism in Canada tends to severely restrict access to government decision makers (Simeon, 1972).[20]

The policy communities that develop around each policy issue include vested interests such as professional or industry associations, *government departments* and public servants (at both levels), interested individuals, community organizations, and any other concerned parties who might be affected by the development of policy. The activities of these numerous actors reflect the power relationships within the policy community. Their activities also reveal the expectations of the various interests, based on their historical experience and their perception of the relative influence of different actors. As Robert Presthus (1973) has commented, the focus of group activity is an indication of where decision-making power resides.

In the Canadian case, where the administrative arm has had much responsibility for policy initiation and development delegated to it by the executive (Pross, 1986, p. 110), it has become the principal focus for interest-group activity. Unlike in the U.S., the legislative branch is much less frequently targeted, although some groups attempting to legitimize their activities may work to achieve multiparty support in the legislature (see Boase, 1982). Many groups are also constrained to appeal to the public for support for their policy preferences. The sophisticated groups in Canada, like interest groups in other polities, have learned to identify the locus of influence and power and to cope with the complexities of modern government. They often must become more bureaucratic (in the sense of technological, legal, and public relations skills) rather than political in order to reflect the bureaucratic environment with which they interact (Pross, 1986, p. 110).

The processes of decision making in the United States

Elazar (1987, pp. 195–196) reminds us that American federalism plays the function of a mediating institution within a diverse society with multiple and conflicting interests. Given this point, it is not surprising that students of the intergovernmental system have recently emphasized the importance of bargaining, compromise, and networking as essential processes of decision making rather than traditional hierarchical command-and-control approaches that rely on formal structures as venues for decision making. This path also highlights a movement away from a sorting out of intergovernmental roles to an interdependent approach—the overlapping authority model, in Wright's (1988) terms. It focuses on the development of interorganizational networks that include both governmental and nongovernmental actors and proceeds along a path that includes the acceptance of the independent and separate character of the various members, avoidance of superior-subordinate relationships, interlacing of political and career actors, inclusin of appropriate specialists (when needed) to focus on technical issues, and agreement to abide by tasks and goals (see Agranoff, 1986). This process is intrinsically political and may be viewed as a substitute for strong national political parties that in other societies may be able to play the role of mediator of multiple interests.[21]

The U.S. policy process: policy design and policy implementation

The intergovernmental actors that have been described play a role in the multiple stages of the policy process. They assist in getting an issue onto the policy agenda. They are often involved in designing and formulating methods of carrying out the policy or program. They are themselves the appropriate actors, with authority to adopt policies or, alternatively, to attempt to influence those with the authority. They are often called upon to play a major role in the implementation or delivery of the policy or program, and they may be involved in evaluating the effort. For the purposes of this article, the policy design and the policy implementation roles are highlighted.

Policy design

There are several predictable questions that are asked during the policy design stage that impact intergovernmental relationships. These deal with the appropriate role of government in an issue, the level of government dealing with a particular aspect of the issue, the mechanisms and resources that would carry out responsibility, and the rules to allocate resources.[22]

It is not always intuitively obvious how various actors in the policy process view the intergovernmental system. Recently, all the governors of the U.S. states unanimously called for changes in the welfare and Medicaid systems. Despite political, ideological, geographic, and demographic differences between chief state elected officials and their states, a unified voice was heard during a meeting of the National Governors' Association advocating increased state flexibility in these two programs. The pronouncements were general enough to avoid scrutiny of the impact of policies that could create problems in some of those state settings. In this case, it appeared that at least some of the governors failed to act in the interest of their states.

In many instances, interest groups that represent economic interests will argue against any increased role for government—particularly the national government—in those areas where it seeks to regulate their behavior and potential profit capacity. However, in some instances, economic interests would rather deal with one national governmental unit than 50 states. The pharmaceutical industry, for example, has argued for regulation by the national Food and Drug Administration rather than by 50 individual states. The national focus not only gives the industry more consistency and reliability as the point of policy departure but also allows the industry to expend fewer resources for policy influence by establishing a single venue for action.

Policy implementation

It is not surprising, given the political, economic, and social culture of the U.S., that most of the major domestic programs and policies in the U.S. provide an important implementation role for states, localities, or even nongovernmental sectors. This reality has its roots in the nation's skepticism about governmental action, its commitment to pluralism, and the diversity of settings within the U.S. The tradition of American pragmatism has pushed for a constant redefinition of what is appropriate for the national government to do—but it has frequently expanded the national role by providing new implementation responsibilities for the actual delivery of services to other levels of government.[23]

At least three elements involving implementation are worthy of emphasis: (1) the diversity of predictable state responses to an initiative; (2) expectations about national commitment to some kind of action; and (3) the role to be played by the national bureaucracy responsible for implementing the program. Implementation analysis—an aspect of policy analysis that began in the mid-1970s—has focused on these (and other) issues and has emphasized the conflict between the perspective of those charged with national administration of a program (the macro level) and those charged with the actual service or program delivery (the micro level).

Given diversity, what does it mean to have a national program or policy? If variability can be anticipated across the U.S. in the implementation process, it is difficult to determine the appropriate expectations for a national program or policy. There are several approaches to this dilemma. Some students of the implementation process suggest that national policy should be viewed as a set of general principles, guidelines, or values that guide others who carry out the program. Others, by contrast, believe that the principles of accountability in a governmental system demand that the national government find ways to hold others accountable for implementation of programs or policies. The current movement for the development of performance indicators suggests that fiscal stringencies demand that information be made available about the implementation of a policy or program to justify its continuation. In some instances, those at the state or local level with implementation responsibility resist the imposition of such performance standards, arguing that these measures impose an inflexible and rigid definition on very different settings. At the same time, the model for federal government activity actually was drawn from state and local experience.

Public concern about the growth of bureaucracies is closely related to this accountability drive. At the present time, there seems to be an inverse relationship between the amount of money allocated to a program area and the number of federal bureaucrats assigned responsibility for administering the program. The federal staff depend on the information provided to the national government by those who are implementing the programs; the federal officials have very limited ability to verily this data. This pattern seemed to be the case in many domestic policy areas in the late 1990s. As federal officials deal with their state or local counterparts, their posture in a bargaining situation is often less powerful than one might expect, and, at times, the federal staff revert to a strategy of bluffing to hide their dependence on their intergovernmental partners.

U.S. federal bureaucrats are different from their Canadian counterparts in at least five respects. First, because there is not a strong central bureaucracy, policy proposals rarely emanate from the federal bureaucracy. Second, because political appointees within the American system permeate into several levels of the bureaucracy, turnover at the policy level has more impact on bureaucratic behaviors. Third, American federal bureaucrats—with several exceptions[24]—rarely deliver services themselves but instead provide regulations and resources to others who actually provide the services to citizens. Fourth, rather than being viewed as an elite institution within the nation, the American public service is often described a *representative* bureaucracy that is drawn from many elements within the society. Although top officials do have higher educational attainments than those of the whole population, their training is often in specialized fields, and they have moved to generalist administrative roles from specialized jobs. And fifth, few federal officials have first-hand experience at the state (or local) level, despite some attempts to encourage exchange between bureaucrats at the three levels of government.

The Canadian bureaucratic structure

The nature of the bureaucracy that supports the Canadian executive further strengthens the centralization of political power at both the federal and provincial levels. Unlike the American system, where the bureaucracy has a tier of senior political and temporary appointments, the Canadian public service is overwhelmingly a career public service. With the exception of small Ministerial staffs, which are political and transient appointments, the highest public service positions are held by long-time public servants who have frequently served under more than one political party. In the British tradition, they are expected to be neutral (in the partisan political sense) and to efficiently serve whatever political party controls state power.[25]

This expectation flows from the Canadian constitutional and political tradition of adhering to the British Parliamentary convention of responsible government. It brings a profound difference to the meaning of public service in Canada compared to the United States, and it is manifested in both the collective and the individual sense. Collectively, the central convention requires that the government resign if it cannot win a Parliamentary vote of confidence on important legislation (usually supply).[26]

In its individual sense, responsibility (legal and political) for all acts within departmental jurisdiction is assigned to the department Minister. In theory, the Minister is expected to resign in the event of grave departmental error, thus ensuring the neutrality and anonymity of the public servant in the administration of the department's business and the proffering of policy options and policy advice.[27] In short, the public service in Canada is a trusted source of policy proposals, and the public service "administers established policy, implements policies devised by politicians (and retouched by bureaucrats) and even *develops* both minor and major policies" (Sutherland, 1993, p. 86).

At both the federal and provincial levels, much of the public service is dominated by highly centralized agencies that service the cabinet committees and important ministries, such as finance. If knowledge is power, then much power resides with the high-level public servants in Canada. The permanent nature of their employment means that they have developed strong ties with societal actors active in their field of public policy. They also develop a close working relationship with their policy counterparts at the other level of government. This last is evident in the extensive administrative intergovernmental negotiations that occur; these are an important source of policy initiative and advice.

As is clear from the discussion of executive federalism and intergovernmental relations, officials at both levels of government in Canada perform indispensable roles in the federal-provincial policy process. AH provincial governments have groups of employees—or specific offices—that conduct intergovernmental negotiations on their behalf. The role of these public servants is to explore policy possibilities, to be sensitive to the implications for their own jurisdiction, and to produce background and discussion papers for their ministers. They also can be called upon to smooth relations between the two levels when policy decisions provoke tension. As Sutherland (1993) says, "It is not surprising then that there are civil-servant 'fixers' in both federal and provincial governments, officials whose specialty is federal-provincial diplomacy and intergovernmental machinery" (p. 110). The level of competition and sense of offence is often so high that the "interpersonal skills" and the "capacity to think strategically and tactically" (p. 110) of these public servants are necessary to preserve some degree of intergovernmental civility.

Conclusion

There are several themes that one can discern in the way that federalism and public policy are joined in the U.S. and in Canada. In both countries, policies must be sensitive to the greater interdependencies between units of government as well as to linkages between policy areas. Few policy issues stand alone either in terms of problem causation or in the way that they are tackled. The mechanisms or instrumentalities for dealing with policy issues are intrinsically complex.

It is also clear that the intergovernmental networks that exist in both the U.S. and Canada are composed of an array of actors. While the formal government jurisdictional actors are important, participants in the policy process include others as well, including private sector actors. The differing political structures of the systems do impact the types of intergovernmental policies that have emerged in the two countries.

The executive dominance so imbedded in Canadian governments has contributed to their ability to adopt and implement certain controversial redistributive policies (see Wright, 1988, p. 293; Lowi, 1972; Peterson, 1981; Beer, 1973) such as a national health insurance program. Since "issues that involve redistribution cut closer than any others along class lines and activate interests in what are roughly class terms" (Lowi, 1964, p. 707), high-level intergovernmental decision making was required to realize the implementation of a redistributive program such as Medicare. By contrast, the fragmentation of the U.S. system makes redistributive policies more difficult. While at various times the U.S. has adopted policies that provide income and service support for citizens in poverty or provide special education funds for Native American or limited-English-speaking children, there are countervailing pressures articulated within the system that make these policies rare. In other cases, the U.S. has constructed policies that focus on a particular element of the society (such as the elderly) but have done so by creating universal eligibility criteria. Canada has found it easier to adopt redistributive programs that address territorial discrepancies within the country (e.g., disparities between regions) or particular groups within a geographic area.

Regulatory policies—policies that impose limitations or control the behavior of certain individuals or groups for the benefit of the broader society— have emerged from the U.S. system and have imposed limitations on individuals, private groups, or other governments. These limitations are often referred to as *mandates,* whereby grantees are provided funds conditioned by their agreement to accept certain requirements or standards. In the intergovernmental area, national standards can be imposed on other levels of government through direct orders, crosscutting requirements (such as nondiscrimination, environmental protection), crossover sanctions (linking requirements in one to the benefits in another), and partial preemption (when national standards are created but administration is delegated to states with equivalent policies) (Wright, 1988, p. 368).

In Canada, regulatory policies and agencies abound, for the most part carefully preserving the federal-provincial distinction. National standards in areas outside federal jurisdiction cannot be imposed on other levels of government, but must be adopted by bodies or governments within each jurisdiction. Even regulations that are agreed to in international treaties cannot be imposed if the issue falls within provincial jurisdiction. Many important areas of regulation such as trucking, labor relations, and telephone communication in most provinces are controlled by provincial governments, and although the federal government cannot transfer its legislative power in an area to a provincial government, it can and does delegate regulatory power to provincial agencies (for example, regulation of the interprovincial and export sale of some agricultural products).

The U.S. has tended to emphasize distributive or developmental policies— policies for which the benefits or results are concentrated or clearly focused. These include policies that provide subsidies to encourage private activities; convey tangible governmental benefits to individuals, groups, or firms; appear to produce only winners, not losers; are typically based on decisions guided by short-run consequences; involve a high degree of cooperation and mutually rewarding logrolling; are marked by low visibility; and are fairly stable overtime (Wright, 1988, p. 339).

Programs in this area included economic development efforts as well as general funds for local governments. Distributive policies in Canada have targets and purposes similar to those in the U.S., although these policies do not include the transfer of funds to local governments. They also tend in some instances to have clear, high-profile, politically determined winners and losers, such as when the Mulroney government chose in 1986 to give an areospace contract to a Montreal firm over a Winnipeg firm that had submitted a lower bid.

Federalism in Canada has had a profound effect on public policy development. While it has shown, in its adoption of national health insurance, that the polity is capable of embracing the innovative and pioneering efforts of an individual province, in other instances, "federalism is clearly a conservative force in welfare politics" (Banting, 1987, p. 174). Given the strength of the provincial governments (reinforced by their executive power) that "follows inevitably from Quebec's continuing concern to occupy fully its sphere of jurisdiction" (McRoberts, 1993, p. 174), it is difficult to imagine how the Canadian political system could have developed differently. Policymaking in Canada will continue to be excessively dominated by federal provincial negotiations.

Although the U.S. system does not operate on the basis of executive power in either the states or the national government, it does exhibit some similar elements to Canada. Many innovative efforts within the American system have been drawn from pioneering efforts within an individual state or even a few states. However, there is likely to be less political momentum that emerges from one (or even two or three) of 50 states than is found in Canada. Relationships between the national government and the states are, thus, diverse and highly variable across different policy areas, reflecting separate political realities in a particular policy field. Federalism in the U.S. frames political debate, but it is less accurate to describe it as a set of negotiations than as a variegated system of power plays.

Acknowledgments

This article resulted from an exchange between the authors at a Festschrift for Douglas Verney at York University in Toronto. Joan Boase was the respondent to a paper presented by Beryl Radin, and both of the individuals were struck by the parallels and differences between the two countries.

Notes

1. Legally, of course, the Governor General and the Lieutenant Governors safeguard the system from the exercise of almost dictatorial power. In practice, these positions are largely ceremonial.
2. The three provinces that do not receive equalization payments are Alberta, British Columbia, and Ontario.
3. This model has been used to describe intergovernmental relationships in other countries as well. See the Introduction in Hanf and Scharpf (1978) and Agranoff (1990).
4. Some analysts believe that the increase in the number of Spanish speaking individuals in the U.S. may create a language problem in the future. At the present time, however, there appears to be a swing away from encouragement of bilingual efforts to a push to require English to be used as the only language of the U.S.
5. These diverse elements are a part of the explanation for different responses to a recent inter-governmental coordination experiment involving rural development. See Radin (1992).
6. Several examples illustrate this variety. North Dakota is the only state with a state-owned bank; no other state has sought to emulate it. Over the years, California has been a leader in the environmental field, serving to push the national government in certain directions. By contrast, for more than a decade, Arizona was the only state that chose not to participate in the federal-state Medicaid program. Over the years, the national government has invested both funds and technical assistance to increase the capacity of state and local governments to deal with issues.
7. The current Clinton administration, for example, has a number of individuals within it who had experience in state and local government before coming to Washington.
8. D.V. Verney (1986) has argued that there is a fundamental contradiction between these two systems of government.
9. These included sections that permitted federal government reservation and disallowance of provincial legislation, as well as the federal responsibility to appoint the provincial lieutenant governors.
10. In the 1990s to the chagrin of the French Quebeckers, this concept was expanded to include three nations: French, English and Native.
11. A variation on this dynamic is also found in the U.S.; however, it is a combination of political and policy independence and fiscal dependence.
12. Provincial governments suffer no such challenge to their authority within their borders, since their municipalities have only delegated power.
13. Smiley (1987) says that Gordon Robertson, secretary to the federal cabinet for federal provincial relations, found the Western Economic Opportunities Conference of 1972 to be the "watershed" in this evolution. He deplored this result in Smiley (1979).
14. The federal Finance Minister, Paul Martin, held lengthy meetings with his provincial counterparts before announcing planned changes to the Canada/Quebec Pension Plan in February 1997.
15. This is a result of what was perceived to be unacceptable elite domination ("eleven men in a room") of the constitutional process following the Meech Lake and Charlottetown Accords.
16. The competitive aspects of interprovincial relations can have some nasty results. For example, Premier Frank McKenna of New Brunswick was accused by his fellow premiers of deliberately luring business and jobs from their jurisdiction to his. He made no apology.
17. Deil Wright (1988, p. 17) has noted that there are over 80,000 governmental units in the U.S. with power to tax, spend, and carry out public functions.
18. Even though local governments in the U.S. are legally creatures of the state, they vary in terms of their historical and political independence.
19. Specialized policy actors play a role in state as well as national policy development.

20. There is some debate about this point, however (see Pross, 1986, p. 165). There are important examples of instances when important legislation was changed even after tabling in the House— for example, the Canadian Health Act, 1984 (see Boase, 1994).
21. Increasingly, however, participants in some variant of this process are recognizing the need for the creation of specific venues for bargaining and networks, as was recognized by John Bryson in Bryson and Crosby (1992).
22. Questions that are similar to these have been posed in the Canadian policy design stage as well, especially in the recent move toward decentralization.
23. This is not unique to the U.S. One can discern a similar pattern in India as the national government has devised new programs and policies that are actually delivered by state governments.
24. The domestic policy exceptions are the Social Security Administration, some aspects of the Public Health Service, and the Internal Revenue Service.
25. While the U.S. career service is also based on principles of responsiveness and neutrality, the system is quite different from that in Canada.
26. The most recent example of this was the defeat of the minority Convervative government under Prime Minister Joe Clark in 1979, which resigned when its budget was defeated in the House. This never occurs when there is a majority government, although theoretically, it could.
27. This aspect of ministerial responsibility has fallen into disuse in recent years and some public servants have suffered the consequences. See Sutherland (1993) for glaring examples.

References

Agranoff, Robert J. (1986). *Intergovernmental Management: Human Services Problem-Solving in Six Metropolitan Areas*. Albany: State University of New York Press.

Agranoff, Robert. (1990). "Frameworks for Comparative Analysis of Intergovernmental Relations." Occasional Paper #26, School of Public and Environmental Affairs, Indiana University, August.

Anton, Thomas J. (1984). "Intergovernmental Change in the United States: An Assessment of the Literature." In Trudi C. Miller (ed.), *Public Sector Performance: A Conceptual Turning Point*. Baltimore: Johns Hopkins University Press.

Atkinson, Michael M. (1993). *Governing Canada: Institutions and Public Policy*. Toronto: Harcourt Brace Jovanovich Canada.

Banting, Keith. (1987). *The Welfare State and Canadian Federalism*, 2nd ed. Montreal/Kingston: McGill-Queen's University Press.

Beer, Samuel H. (1973). "The Modernization of American Federalism." Publius 3(Fall), 49–96.

Boase, Joan. (1982). "Regulation and the Paramedical Professions: An Interest Group Study." *Canadian Public Administration* 25(3), 339–361.

Boase, Joan Price. (1994). *Shining Sands; Government-Group Relationships in the Health Care Sector*. Montreal/Kingston: McGill-Queen's University Press.

Bryson, John M., and Barbara C. Crosby. (1992). *Leadership for the Common Good*. San Francisco: Jossey-Bass Publishers.

Cairns, Alan. (1977). "The Governments and Societies of Canadian Federalism." *Canadian Journal of Political Science* 10, 695–725.

Edelman, Peter B., and Beryl A. Radin. (1991). *Serving Children and Families Effectively; How the Past Can Help Chart the Future*. Washington, D.C.: Education and Human Services Consortium.

Elazar, Daniel J. (1987). *Exploring Federalism*. Tuscaloosa: The University of Alabama Press.

Haider, Donald H. (1974). *When Governments Come to Washington*. New York: The Free Press.

Hanf, Kenneth, and Fritz W. Scharpf. (1978). *Interorganizational Policy Making: Limits to Coordination and Central Control*. London and Beverly Hills: Sage.

Heclo, Hugh. (1979). "Issue Networks and the Executive Establishment." In Anthony King (ed.), *The New American Political System*. Washington, D.C.: American Enterprise Institute for Public Policy Research.

Krane, Dale. (1993). "American Federalism, State Governments, and Public Policy: Weaving Together Loose Theoretical Threads." *PS: Political Science & Politics*, June, pp. 186–190.

Lowi, Theodore. (1964). "American Business, Public Policy, Case Studies and Political Theory." *World Politics* 16, 677–715.

Lowi, Theodore J. (1972). "Four Systems of Policy, Politics and Choice." *Public Administration Review* 32(July/August), 298–310.
Lowi, Theodore J. (1979). *The End of Liberalism,* 2nd ed. New York: Norton.
McRoberts, Kenneth. (1993). "Federal Structures and the Policy Process." In Michael M. Atkinson (ed.), *Governing Canada: Institutions and Public Policy.* Toronto: Harcourt Brace Jovanovich Canada.
Peterson, Paul E. (1981). *City Limits.* Chicago: University of Chicago Press.
Presthus, Robert. (1973). *Elite Accommodation in Canadian Politics.* Toronto: MacMillan.
Pross, A. Paul. (1986). Group *Politics and Public Policy.* Toronto: Oxford University Press.
Radin, Beryl A. (1992). "Rural Development Councils: An Intergovernmental Coordination Experiment." *Publius: The Journal of Federalism* 22(3), 111–128.
Radin, Beryl A., and Willis D. Hawley. (1988). *The Politics of Federal Reorganization: Creating the U.S. Department of Education.* New York: Pergamon Press.
Simeon, Richard. (1972). *Federal-Provincial Diplomacy.* Toronto: University of Toronto Press.
Simeon, Richard (ed.). (1979). *Confrontation and Collaboration—Intergovernmental Relations in Canada Today.* Toronto: IPAC.
Simeon, Richard. (1980). "Intergovernmental Relations and the Challenges of Canadian Federalism." *Canadian Public Administration* 23(2).
Simeon, Richard (ed.). (1985). *Division of Powers and Public Policy.* Toronto: University of Toronto Press.
Smiley, D.V. (1979). "The Role of Interministerial Conferences in the Decision-Making Process." In Richard Simeon (ed.), *Confrontation and Collaboration—Intergovernmental Relations in Canada* Today. Toronto: IPAC, pp. 78–88.
Smiley, D.V. (1980). *Canada in Question,* 3rd ed. Toronto: McGraw-Hill Ryerson.
Smiley, D.V. (1987). *The Federal Condition in Canada.* Toronto: McGraw-Hill Ryerson.
Sutherland, Sharon L. (1993). "The Public Service and Policy Development." In Michael M. Atkinson (ed.), *Governing Canada: Institutions and Public Policy.* Toronto: Harcourt Brace Jovanovich Canada, pp. 81–114.
Taylor, Malcolm. (1986). *Health Insurance and Canadian Public Policy: The Seven Decisions that Created the Canadian Health Insurance Program.* Montreal/Kingston: McGill-Queen's University Press.
Verney, D.V. (1986). *Three Civilizations, Two Cultures.* Durham: Duke University Press.
Wright, Deil. (1988). *Understanding Intergovernmental Relations,* 3rd ed. Pacific Grove, CA: Brooks/Cole.

Towards Harmonization or Standardization in Governmental Accounting? The International Public Sector Accounting Standards Board Experience

ILUMINADA FUERTES

ABSTRACT *The main difference between harmonization and standardization processes lies in the degree of strictness of the accounting standards. Harmonization involves a reduction in accounting variations, while standardization entails moving towards the eradication of any variation. This distinction provides the basis for the present study. The purpose of this study is twofold: to analyse the degree of strictness of the IPSASs and to identify the sources of accounting diversity so that the potential of comparability of that international accounting framework can be evaluated. The methodology used enables areas of harmony or disharmony to be identified for IPSASB harmonization purposes. The results show that, given its high degree of regulatory strictness, the IPSASs model is a standardizing model. Potential sources of diversity are identified in areas such as capital assets as well as new research directions in the public sector formal harmonization.*

Introduction

In response to the growing internationalization of governmental accounting and in an attempt to overcome the obstacle of accounting diversity, since the 1990s the International Federation of Accountants (IFAC) has undertaken a major standardization programme aimed at issuing a single set of international public sector accounting standards and promoting their introduction at all levels of government (national, regional and local). The task of drafting the set of international public accounting standards falls to the International Public Sector Accounting Standards Board (IPSASB), set up in 1987.

To date, a total of 25 International Public Sector Accounting Standards (IPSASs) have been issued (a list of which is shown in Table 1). One of the characteristics of

Table 1. List of International Public Sector Accounting Standards

International Public Sector Accounting Standards (IPSAS)		IAS* of reference
IPSAS-1	Presentation of Financial Statements	IAS-1
IPSAS-2	Cash Flow Statements	IAS-7
IPSAS-3	Net Surplus or Deficit for the Period, Fundamental Errors and Changes in Accounting Policies	IAS-8
IPSAS-4	The Effects of Changes in Foreign Exchange Rates	IAS-21
IPSAS-5	Borrowing Costs	IAS-23
IPSAS-6	Consolidated Financial Statements and Accounting for Controlled Entities	IAS-27
IPSAS-7	Accounting for Investments in Associates	IAS-28
IPSAS-8	Financial Reporting of Interests in Joint Ventures	IAS-31
IPSAS-9	Revenue from Exchange Transactions	IAS-18
IPSAS-10	Financial Reporting in Hyperinflationary Economies	IAS-29
IPSAS-11	Construction Contracts	IAS-11
IPSAS-12	Inventories	IAS-2
IPSAS-13	Leases	IAS-17
IPSAS-14	Events After the Reporting Date	IAS-10
IPSAS-15	Financial Instruments: Disclosure and Presentation	IAS-32
IPSAS-16	Investment Property	IAS-40
IPSAS-17	Property, Plant and Equipment	IAS-16
IPSAS-18	Segment Reporting	IAS-14
IPSAS-19	Provisions, Contingent Liabilities and Contingent Assets	IAS-37
IPSAS-20	Related Party Disclosures	IAS-24
IPSAS-21	Impairment of Non Cash-Generating Assets	IAS-36
IPSAS-22	Disclosure of Financial Information about the General Government Sector	–
IPSAS-23	Revenue from Non-exchange Transactions (Taxes and Transfers)	IAS-20/41
IPSAS-24	Presentation of Budget Information in Financial Statements	–
IPSAS Cash Basis	Financial Reporting Under The Cash Basis of Accounting	–

*International Accounting Standards.

these standards is their status as *recommendations*, thus requiring the IFAC to seek the support of public authorities for their application in different countries, mainly in those of the zone of influence of continental Europe, because of its "codified Roman law" legal system.[1] Most of these standards are designed to be applied under the *accrual basis of accounting* to governments and other public sector entities (other than government business enterprises). Given the wide use of cash basis, the IFAC has also developed a cash basis standard as well as a guide on the transition to accrual basis. Two further noteworthy characteristics of the IFAC accounting model is its *similarity to the IASs* and its marked *bias towards the Anglo-Saxon philosophy*. The first feature is due to the fact that the harmonization of accounting information between the governments and private companies is one of the basic aims of the IPSASB, following the experiences of countries such as Australia and New Zealand (Wallace 2004). With regard to the influence of the Anglo-Saxon model in the public sector standard project, this is explained not only by the importance that this culture has always had in the private and public accounting sphere, but also by the international harmonization experience noted in the private sector where this model has been used as a reference to develop international business accounting standards. Correspondence between the two sets of standards is also reported in Table 1.

The regulatory effort made by the IPSASB started in the mid-1990s, although the first results were not observed in practice until the start of the present century when the most representative international organizations – the European Union, the Organization for Economic Co-operation and Development (OECD) and the North Atlantic Treaty Organization (NATO) – decided to include the IPSASs to elaborate their accounting statements. Because the experience of the IPSASB is relatively recent, we cannot yet speak of an "evolution" in the standardization process as we can with the International Accounting Standards Board (IASB). The harmonization process undertaken by the IASB has been going on for a substantially longer time, and since its creation a series of stages can be identified. These stages mark the efforts made to improve the set of accounting regulations for private companies, taking them towards an increased degree of comparability (Garrido *et al.* 2002). To this end, the accounting alternatives have gradually been reduced, matters of application have been clarified and consistency in wording and style improved (Wallace 2004).

In an attempt to avoid errors experienced by the IASB in the past, the IFAC public sector standard project is built on the most recent and least flexible stage of the IASB model.[2] Based on such, and coherent with the reference framework, it is logical to expect a certain *regulatory strictness* and a *poor margin for option* in the IPSASB's international public standards model.

This "intuitive" regulatory strictness of the accounting framework which the IPSASs represent leads us to consider the hypothesis that the process driven by the IFAC to improve the comparability of the government's economic and financial reports, actually comes closer to a standardization process than to a harmonization process, in accordance with the definitions set out in the next section.

As already stated, the objective of this work is to empirically confirm the hypothesis set out by analyzing the degree of strictness or flexibility within the international public accounting standards. On the other hand, this work also attempts to evaluate the comparability potential of this model, adopted by the IFAC as an instrument to reduce diversity among accounting practices in the public sector.

Presently, even though many authors and works address the matter of comparability of financial reporting from a wide range of perspectives, very few empirical works have analyzed the public sector with its accounting practices and regulations. Among these we highlight those by Jones and Pendlebury (1982), Monsen (1994), Montesinos *et al.* (1998), Pina and Torres (1999), Christiaens (2000), Torres and Pina (2003), Benito and Brusca (2004) or Benito *et al.* (2005), which study comparability using methods like cluster analyses or different indices to group and quantify the similarities among the various accounting systems.[3] Most of these indices (the H, C and I indices) originate from the seminal contributions of Van der Tas (1988). These indices were meant to measure the degree of de facto or material harmonization, rather than de jure or formal harmonization. Nonetheless, they have been mainly used to measure formal harmonization in governmental accounting. This study, however, proposes an alternative methodology to analyze comparability from a perspective based on the strictness/flexibility of accounting requirements which is more appropriate to the reasoning and objectives considered.

From this approach, this work starts by justifying the relationship established between the comparability of information and the strictness of regulations. This aspect is covered in the second section. The rest of the study is arranged as follows: section three introduces us to the most relevant aspects of the public sector's international accounting regulation process, which is the setting of this work. Then we go on to analyze the strictness/flexibility of the regulatory framework which upholds this process and which will allow us to evaluate its potential comparability. Thus, sections four and five are the first analysis of the model's strictness broken down into the subsystems it is comprised of, these being disclosure and measurement. This analysis process is achieved by identifying the different accounting items as well as their associated treatments. It aims to detect the subsystem which contributes more strictness or flexibility to the model. The analysis of strictness by items and subsystems is completed in section six with the analysis per category or standard. The method used here has been a comparison of the real model with the totally strict theoretical model by means of a tool based on the Euclidean distance, an instrument already used in international accounting by Garrido *et al.* (2002) to measure the formal harmonization achieved by the IASB throughout its harmonization trajectory. According to Garrido *et al.* (2002: 19), other than being simple and easy to interpret, this methodology allows the similarities or differences in the two models under various categories to be measured in order to identify the standards which present more strictness (less distance) and greater flexibility (more distance) when detecting future diversity in international public accounting practices. Finally, the main conclusions summarize the results and their implications.

Regulatory Strictness and Comparability

Tay and Parker (1990: 73–74) have pointed out that it is precisely the degree of strictness associated with the accounting regulations which is the aspect that marks the difference between the concepts of harmony and harmonization versus standardization and uniformity.[4] Following Van Hulle (1989), harmonization seeks to guarantee that accounting regulations are comparable and equivalent, but it does not involve establishing uniform standards in all countries, a process that is more closely linked to the concept of standardization. It may be said that harmonization is a movement away from total diversity of practice, while standardization involves progressing towards global uniformity.

Therefore, the main difference between a harmonization process and a standardization process lies in the degree of strictness of the accounting regulations that uphold them.[5] While the regulatory framework upon which a harmonization process is developed is characterized by greater flexibility, the regulating framework which upholds the standardization process is fundamentally strict or rigid.

As García points out, both process types have a different impact on the comparability of financial reporting. A harmonization-addressed process helps make the task of comparing information easier, but it does not create comparability, unlike a standardization process. In other words, the skill or potential of comparability differs depending on the process. Even though harmonization is not a strong enough condition to achieve comparability, it is necessary (García 1995: 40).

Comparability can be considered as an increase in the degree of consensus concerning the choice between the alternatives of accounting requirements for an item in financial reports, so that it depends on two aspects: 1) the number of alternative accounting requirements and 2) the extent to which each requirement is applied (Van der Tas 1988: 159). According to the number of alternative accounting requirements, a standard may be "strict", a concept associated with uniformity – or "less strict", associated with harmony (Tay and Parker 1990: 73). Depending on the extent – that is to say, the way accounting requirements are expressed – a standard may contain a precise definition (with mandatory provisions that prescribe or forbid one or more accounting requirements) or a discretionary one (with non-mandatory provisions, such as benchmark or permitted requirements).

Consistently, as the accounting requirements associated with a single accounting item have been reduced, and are of a fundamentally required or forbidden nature, the international public sector regulations could be considered "strict". Therefore we could associate the IFAC regulatory framework not only with a marked standardization profile, but also with a high implicit comparability potential (if not with a total uniform capacity). If, on the contrary, the number of accounting alternatives were high, and the treatments suggested and permitted predominate over the rest, the capacity of the model to accomplish the comparability of economic-financial information in the public sector would be inferior.

The Role of the International Public Sector Accounting Standards Board

The IFAC was set up in 1977 and replaced the previous ICCAP (International Co-ordination Committee for the Accountancy Profession). It works with 155 members and associates in 118 countries to protect public interest by encouraging high quality practices among accountants worldwide. The IFAC develops international standards on ethics, auditing and assurance, education, and public sector accounting standards. It also issues guidelines to support professional accountants in business, small and medium practices, and developing nations. To this end, this organization has different boards and committees (http://www.ifac.org/About).

As previously pointed out, the task of drafting the set of international public accounting standards falls to the International Public Sector Accounting Standards Board, set up to coordinate at an international level the needs of all those involved in the accounting, auditing and communication of public sector accounting information. Over recent years, the IPSASB has developed a series of strategies: a) *standardization strategy*, through the establishment of a set of accounting and auditing standards that are generally accepted by the public sector; b) *promotion strategy*, to make the IPSASB the main international accounting standard setter for the public sector; c) *harmonization strategy*, designed to harmonize accounting information across jurisdictions and, as far as possible, between the public and private sectors.

The importance of the standardization project undertaken by the IFAC basically lies in three aspects: a) in the meaning it accomplished as a starting point of the international public accounting standardization process; b) in the leading role that the IFAC plays to drive the aforementioned process; and c) in the benefits that the IFAC itself offers to improve governmental accounting information and its international comparability. The advantages of having financial reports that compare at an international level would benefit users such as *supranational organizations* which make decisions about those aspects exceeding national barriers, potential *international investors* interested in the public sector, policy makers and participants involved in *common markets* (like that of the EU), since freely flowing information is an important part of the infrastructure of such markets. Furthermore, the standardization project serves as a *common reference* framework for those countries which are starting to modernize their public accounting systems.

Despite its importance, implementing a regulatory body on an international scale, like that of the IPSASs, is actually a slow process due to certain factors, among which we find: 1) a lack of the legal range of regulations, primarily when they have to be applied to contexts in which the legal framework has a considerable influence, that is continental Europe; 2) a heterogeneous starting point to accounting reforms in the public sector which range from a cash basis (Russia and Germany) and hybrid systems of accounting and budgeting combinations on a modified accruals basis (Spain, France), to resource accounting and budgeting (Great Britain, Sweden or New Zealand); 3) a low involvement in lobbying for the comparability of the pressure groups interested in comparing public accounting information from different countries (such as international investors and audit companies) compared with the IASB experience; 4) the fact that politicians and public administrators in many countries still base their decision-making on budgetary information; 5) the cost involved in renouncing the accounting system itself given the influence that each country's specific social, political and economic environment has on accounting systems (Lüder 1992, Fuertes and Vela 2000).

In view of the advantages, and despite the aforementioned difficulties, more and more public organizations recognize the advantages of a standardization project like the present one, and several international organizations, as well as many countries, have done so. Some examples of international institutions are the World Bank, the Asian Bank of Development, the International Monetary Fund or the United Nations Development Programme, which have all offered financial support to such a project. Beyond what is the merely economic support, the OECD has already adopted the IPSASs, the European Union has done so since 2005, and, in a parallel fashion, NATO has applied them to elaborate its financial statements since January 2006. With regard to countries, there is an increasing number of governments that have adopted, or are in the process of adopting, this international accounting framework to face some unsolved but increasingly demanded questions, such as the growing national and international emphasis on improved governmental financial reporting and government accountability. In many cases, these accounting strategies are integrated into broader public management reforms. Thus, along with pioneering countries which adopt full accruals (Australia, New Zealand, the United Kingdom or the United States of America), the number of countries worldwide that are currently implementing IPSASs, or are in process of doing so, is quite significant (see http://www.ifac.org).

Data and Methodology

The present empirical analysis is developed on a sample that includes all the *accounting items* regulated in the IPSASs (published before December 2006) and its associated *accounting requirements* classified according to its nature (or degree of extent). A total of 216 accounting items were identified and classified into categories according to 22 IPSASs (IPSAS-1 to 21 and cash basis). Each standard is one *category* of accounting items.

For the analysis to be exhaustive, the disclosure and measurement items are considered separately. Another reason to separate the two types of items is that Australian, New Zealander and other Anglo-Saxon accounting policy makers have seen more criticism in measurement areas than in disclosure (Rahman *et al*. 1996: 328). The disclosure items refer to requirements about information to be disclosed in the economic and financial reports; in other words, *what* is recognized, *where* and *how*; and the second group, measurement items, refers to the measurements devoted to quantifying the accounting items, in other words, by *how much* they are recognized. Thus, for instance, in the "Foreign currency operations" category (C4), the item "*Valuation of foreign currency operations*" would be a measurement item, whereas the concept "*Recognition of exchange rate differences*" would be a disclosure item, as would the concept "*Information to be provided*" on these differences (Table 2).

After a thorough analysis of the IPSASs, every item is assigned to four feasible requirements. Following Rahman *et al.* (1996: 328) the typology used for identifying the nature of the requirements is as follows: 1) *required*: compulsory for all units covered by the IPSAS; 2) *recommended or benchmark treatment*: suggested by the standard; 3) *allowed*: not required but not prohibited; 4) *forbidden*: not permitted by the IPSASs.

A total of 261 different accounting requirements associated with the 216 accounting items were classified according to this typology. As there are cases in which alternative requirements are established for the same item, the number of items is slightly lower. For example, the measurement item "Global valuation of

Table 2. Example of accounting item classification

Category (C4):	The Effects of Changes in Foreign Exchange Rates	
Disclosure item (D4-1)	Measurement item (M4-1)	Disclosure item (D4-2)
Recognition of exchange differences	*Valuation of foreign currency transactions*	*Information to be provided*
Where?	How much?	How?
In the balance or income statement	At the exchange rate at the date of the transaction Monetary items should be adjusted at closing rate...	Differences included in the net surplus or deficit for the period, differences classified as net assets or equity, explanatory reasons, etc. should be presented

Source: IPSAS no. 4, paragraphs 20, 24–28 and 61–65.

final stock" has assigned two possible accounting requirements: the First Input First Output and the Weighed Average Price methods. Of the 261 treatments that regulate international public sector accounting standards, 201 refer to disclosure items and 60 to measurement items (see Table 3).

Having identified and classified the items and requirements contained in the IPSASs, a descriptive analysis was undertaken to identify the profile of the IFAC accounting model (standardizing or harmonizing) according to its regulatory strictness or flexibility. First, the global model comprising all the accounting items and treatments was analysed. A similar analysis was then undertaken on the disclosure subsystem and, finally, the measurement subsystem was addressed. Thus, a triple analysis was undertaken to identify the subsystem with the greatest levels of strictness or flexibility.

Analysis and Results

Global Model: Disclosure and Measurement Items

As can be appreciated from Figure 1, the largest proportion of international public sector accounting standards content is represented by information disclosure requirements (77.31%), while a notably lower proportion (22.69%) represents aspects related to measurement.

These results show that the IPSASs body proposed by the IFAC to improve the comparability of governmental economic and financial reporting at an international level *is predominantly a disclosure model* because most of the accounting items refer to aspects associated with the type of information to be reported in the financial statements (*where* an item is recognised, *what* aspects are to be disclosed and *how*). This fact reveals the IPSASB efforts to enhance comparability and consistency by clarifying matters of application and style at a very detailed level, following the IASB experience. Then, last but not least, it implies putting into practice the consensus in the public sector around the benefits of accrual versus cash basis and the relevance of the economic and financial information in order to demonstrate accountability in the public sector, to assess the governments' performance in terms of economy and efficiency, as well as to assess the economic impact of the governments financial activities in relation to the overall economy. Following the Anglo-Saxon accounting tradition, the IPSASs involve an attempt to converge towards a greater disclosure by overcoming the restrictions that budgetary information imply, traditionally considered as high priority (given the relevance of the budget on the governmental accounting systems).

On the other hand, recognition and measurement areas are more conflictive for governmental accounting policy makers because cultural factors such as conservatism (Nobes and Parker 1995: 47), and the specific governmental characteristics of certain elements such as assets (IPSASB 1995), both influence the recognition criteria to either include or exclude the value of the assets in financial reports as well as opting for a specific value. Clear examples are the current diversity of accounting practices related to the recognition, valuation and disclosure of capital assets that are not completely clarified in the IPSASs (Pallot 1997, Stanton and Stanton 1997, Rowles and Hutton 1998, Scheid and Lande 2000, Christiaens 2004) as well as the

Table 3. Alternative accounting requirements assigned to total, disclosure and measurement accounting items

Items Total	Alternatives				Items Disclosure	Alternatives				Items Measurement	Alternatives			
	1	2	3	4		1	2	3	4		1	2	3	4
C1 (17 items)	14	9	2	1	D1 (17 items)	14	9	2	1	—				
C2 (12 items)	10	1	2	0	D2 (12 items)	10	1	2	0	—				
C3 (5 items)	3	2	2	0	D3 (5 items)	3	2	2	0	—				
C4 (3 items)	2	1	1	0	D4 (2 items)	1	1	1	0	M4 (1 item)	1	0	0	0
C5 (6 items)	0	2	5	0	D5 (5 items)	0	2	4	0	M5 (1 item)	0	0	1	0
C6 (5 items)	4	2	0	0	D6 (3 items)	3	2	0	0	M6 (2 items)	1	2	0	0
C7 (3 items)	2	2	0	0	D7 (1 item)	1	0	0	0	M7 (2 items)	1	2	0	0
C8 (10 items)	9	1	2	0	D8 (9 items)	8	0	1	0	M8 (1 item)	1	1	1	0
C9 (5 items)	5	0	0	0	D9 (4 items)	4	0	0	0	M9 (1 item)	1	0	0	0
C10 (3 items)	3	0	0	0	D10 (1 item)	1	0	0	0	M10 (2 items)	2	0	0	0
C11 (5 items)	5	0	0	0	D11 (3 items)	3	0	0	0	M11 (2 items)	2	0	0	0
C12 (5 items)	4	2	0	0	D12 (2 items)	2	0	0	0	M12 (3 items)	2	2	0	0
C13 (25 items)	22	6	1	2	D13 (21 items)	18	6	1	2	M13 (4 items)	4	0	0	0
C14 (3 items)	1	4	0	2	D14 (3 items)	1	4	0	2	—				
C15 (10 items)	10	0	0	0	D15 (10 items)	10	0	0	0	—				
C16 (11 items)	8	4	0	0	D16 (8 items)	6	2	0	0	M16 (3 items)	2	2	0	0
C17 (13 items)	10	4	2	0	D17 (9 items)	8	0	1	0	M17 (4 items)	2	4	1	0
C18 (13 items)	11	5	1	0	D18 (7 items)	5	5	1	0	M18 (6 items)	6	0	0	0
C19 (21 items)	19	0	2	3	D19 (13 items)	12	0	0	2	M19 (8 items)	7	0	0	1
C20 (3 items)	3	0	0	0	D20 (3 items)	3	0	0	0	—				
C21 (20 items)	19	19	19	19	D21 (13 items)	13	0	0	0	M21 (7 items)	6	3	0	0
C0 (18 items)	18	0	2	1	D0 (16 items)	16	0	2	1	M0 (2 items)	2	0	0	0
216	182	48	22	9		142	32	19	8		40	16	3	1
	261					201					60			
	167										49			

lack of specific standards of a more measuring nature, such as those relating to the valuation of financial assets (the present IPSASs only regulate aspects related to the information to be reported on these assets).

When the analysis focuses on the accounting items and their associated accounting requirements, the results also indicate a high level of regulatory strictness in the IFAC accounting model (see Figure 2). Then 84.26 per cent of all the accounting items identified have an associated accounting solution, the application of which is *required*, and 4.17 per cent are expressly *forbidden*. The margin for option is therefore relatively low and does not exceed 33 per cent (22.22% are items with recommended or benchmark requirements, and 10.19% are allowed requirements).

Figure 2 also provides the distribution of accounting items between the disclosure and measurement subsystems. The results show that 65.74 per cent of the disclosure

Figure 1. Characteristics of the IPSASs content

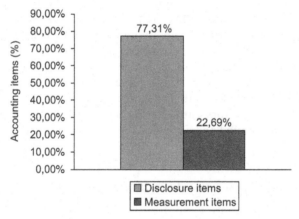

Figure 2. Regulated accounting items

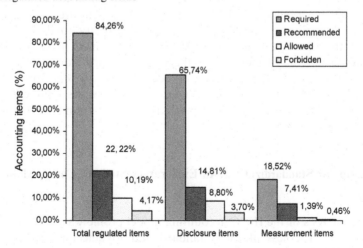

items are associated with "required" treatments, and that the percentage drops to 18.52 per cent when focusing on measurement items. If we examine the "recommended" accounting requirements with a lower requirement for compliance, the percentages fall considerably to 14.81 per cent for aspects related to disclosure, and to 7.41 per cent for those relating to measurement items. Allowed requirements are associated with the aforementioned items by 8.80 per cent and 1.39 per cent, respectively. Forbidden requirements are practically non-existent (3.7% in disclosure items and 0.46% in measurement items). The above results are confirmed when analyses are carried out separately for both disclosure and measurement items.

Disclosure Items and Associated Accounting Requirements

When the sample is restricted to disclosure items, the results are very similar to those detailed above, as seen in Figure 3. Once again, these figures show the high level of regulatory strictness as a major feature of the international governmental accounting model, as 89.82 per cent of disclosure items are associated with mandatory requirements that lead to uniformity (required – 85.03%, forbidden – 4.79%). Hence, the margin for accounting flexibility, represented by benchmark and allowed treatments (19.16% and 11.34%, respectively), is very limited. It reveals the significant step made by the IPSASB to reduce the diversity of disclosure practices and to move towards a greater convergence in governmental accounting. By following Tay and Parker (1990), this convergence comes very close to the state of uniformity given the mandatory nature of the accounting methods (74.61%), which indicates a clustering around these methods and the reduced number of methods available.

Measurement Items and Associated Accounting Requirements

Following the same analysis done for the global system and the disclosure subsystem, Figure 4 offers a detailed view of the different accounting requirements associated with the measurement items. The results obtained indicate that the behaviour pattern shown by the global model, measured in terms of strictness or flexibility, remains practically the same when the disclosure and measurement practices are examined separately. Once again, flexibility totals 38.77 per cent (benchmark and allowed requirements related to measurement items are 32.65% and 6.12% respectively), thus demonstrating the high standardization of the model which mandatorily regulates 81.63 per cent (required) and 2.04 per cent (forbidden) of the items considered. The percentage of mandatory requirements represents 68.34 per cent of the total measurement requirements, a lower proportion than that reached by disclosure practices (74.61%).

Harmonization or Standardization? An Exploratory Study of Comparability

Methodology

Finally, the analysis of the IFAC accounting model profile was taken a step further to quantify the strictness of each standard and to detect potential sources of

Figure 3. Disclosure items

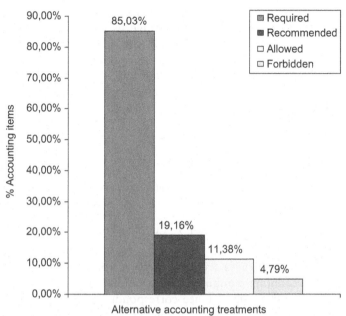

Figure 4. Measurement items

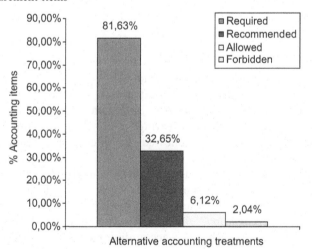

accounting diversity. This was carried out by measuring the distance between the IFAC model (labelled Model A) and an "absolute standardization" theoretical model with forced (required or forbidden) provisions and no possible alternative accounting methods. Because this model, termed Model B, lacks any alternative accounting methods, it is an entirely strict or standardizing model that leads to global comparability or uniformity in financial reports (although this does not necessarily mean it is the most appropriate or the best model). The extent to which there are null differences between Models A and B will enable us to identify the standards that increase the strictness of the model, and those with a more flexible profile.

The methodology used to measure the differences between the two models is that proposed by Garrido et al. (2002). These authors, as Rahman et al. (1996) did previously, use the concept of distance between groups of observations as a measure of discrimination:

$$D_A^B = \sum_{k=1}^{H} d_{k,A}^B$$

where $d(X,Y)$ is the Euclidean distance between two points defined as follows:

$$d(X, Y) = \left[\sum_{j=1}^{J} (x_j - y_j)^2 \right]^{1/2}$$

where $X=(x_1,x_2,\ldots,x_J)$ and $Y=(y_1,y_2,\ldots,y_J)$ vectors of the order J. In our case, j are the various accounting requirements, a total of 4 ($J=4$).

The measurement D_A^B is the distance corresponding to each category, obtained from the sum of the individual distances of the items identified in each category. Hence, H represents the number of items that make up each category and k are the various accounting items.

Following these authors, we first defined as vectors each of the disclosure and measurement accounting items with their respective alternative accounting treatments, that is,

$$A_k, B_k \, k=1,2,\ldots,216$$

where k is the number of accounting items.

The accounting items are classified into categories (a total of 22) in such a way that each category coincides with an IPSAS. Each category has two types of item: disclosure and measurement items. Bearing in mind the accounting requirement typology (required, recommended, allowed, forbidden), the resulting vectors are fourth-order vectors.

As shown in Table 3 for example, the category C17 or IPSAS "Property, Plant and Equipment" covers a total of 13 items, 9 of which are disclosure items and 4 are measurement items. One of the measurement items in this category ("*Measurement subsequent to initial recognition*": *paragraphs 38, 39*) takes the following values (0,1,1,0). The standard establishes two accounting requirements for property, plant and equipment: 1) cost (the benchmark treatment) or revaluations to fair value (the allowed alternative treatment). The vector therefore takes value 0 for the first vector component, as no required treatment is established, 1 for the second, 1 for the third and 0 for the fourth, as no prohibited requirement is established (0,1,1,0). The equivalent vector in the theoretical Model B is (1,0,0,1).

Having defined the vectors, the individual Euclidean distances of each one are calculated and the measure D_A^B is applied, which is simply an aggregation, in our case, at the category level (C1, C2,..., C21, C0) which coincides with the standards (IPSAS1, IPSAS2...). The measurement D_A^B was calculated three times for each category:

1. globally (with all the category items);
2. only with the category disclosure items;
3. with the measurement items.

In this way, we can evaluate the regulatory strictness or flexibility of each public accounting standard and, within these standards, of their disclosure and measurement items, bearing in mind that if $D_A^B = 0$ the standard is totally strict, and consequently, rather than harmonizing, it applies total uniformity, so the degree of comparability arising from its application is maximum (total harmonization). The joint evaluation of all the standards enables us to characterize the IFAC accounting model within the parameters of strictness or flexibility that have been mentioned.

Analysis and Results

On comparing each standard separately with Model B (defined as a standardizing model), the results presented in Table 4 are obtained. The first three columns of Table 4 show the distances for each category or standard measured by means of index D. The values obtained indicate the proximity or distance of each IPSAS to or

Table 4. Distance between Model A and Model B

Category	Global	Distance	Disclosure Category	Distance	Measurement Category	Distance
C1	IPSAS 1	14.24	D1	14.24	–	
C2	IPSAS 2	3.41	D2	3.41	–	
C3	IPSAS 3	4	D3	4	–	
C4	IPSAS 4	2	D4	2	M4	0
C5	IPSAS 5	9.07	D5	7.66	M5	1.41
C6	IPSAS 6	2.45	D6	0	M6	2.45
C7	IPSAS 7	2.45	D7	0	M7	2.45
C8	IPSAS 8	3.86	D8	1.41	M8	2.45
C9	IPSAS 9	0	D9	0	M9	0
C10	IPSAS 10	0	D10	0	M10	0
C11	IPSAS 11	0	D11	0	M11	0
C12	IPSAS 12	2.45	D12	0	M12	2.45
C13	IPSAS 13	9.76	D13	9.76	M13	0
C14	IPSAS 14	4.90	D14	4.9	–	
C15	IPSAS 15	0	D15	0	–	
C16	IPSAS 16	5.28	D16	2.83	M16	2.45
C17	IPSAS 17	7.16	D17	1.41	M17	5.74
C18	IPSAS 18	7.4	D18	7.4	M18	0
C19	IPSAS 19	2.83	D19	2.83	M19	0
C20	IPSAS 20	0	D20	0	–	
C21	IPSAS 21	3.16	D21	0	M21	3.16
C0	IPSAS 0	2.83	D0	2.83	M0	0

from the hypothetical model B, which relates to a standardization process and represents uniformity, that is to say, global comparability. Distance 0 indicates the totally strict profile of a standard that establishes only required or forbidden treatments. The application of these standards consequently leads to absolute harmonization or uniformity in the areas it regulates. The greater the number of standards with this profile, the higher the harmonization level achieved by the IPSASs as financial reports will be more globally comparable.

Standards no. 9, no. 10, no. 11, no. 15 and no. 20 present the highest levels of strictness with a distance of 0 from the alternative model B. By contrast, the most flexible standards are IPSAS no. 17, no. 18, no. 5, no. 13 and no. 1. These standards have a higher number of accounting alternatives and provide the model with a source of accounting diversity, thus reducing its harmonizing quality. Specifically, these standards regulate aspects such as capital assets (a traditionally controversial area in public bodies as noted before), borrowing costs, leases or general aspects of financial statement presentation which evidence the need for the IPSASB to continue working towards greater comparability.

When only disclosure items and their associated accounting requirements are considered, the number of standards with a strict profile increases to include standards no. 6, no. 7, no. 12 and no. 21 (Table 4). The requirements for disclosure contained in these standards are mandatory (required or forbidden), unlike the aspects related to measurement. By contrast, standards no. 18, no. 5, no. 13 and no. 1 once again reveal a more flexible profile, with a wider range of alternatives for disclosure information about activity segments, borrowing costs, leases or general aspects of financial statements. The most outstanding difference is seen in IPSAS no.17, which, when only aspects related to the disclosure are analysed, takes on a stricter profile.

Finally, when we apply index D to the sample of measurement items, the regulatory strictness of the IFAC model in aspects of measurement is also shown (Table 4). Eight standards show 0 distances, of which standards no. 4, no. 13, no. 18, no. 19 and no. 21 do so exclusively for measurement practices, and not for disclosure practices. Once again, IPSAS no. 17 relating to Property, Plant and Equipment shows a greater distance from model B and is therefore more flexible. The valuation of capital assets seems to represent a significant source of accounting diversity in current international standards, thereby reducing the comparability effect of the model.

To sum up, the model's flexibility essentially derives from: a) disclosure aspects related to activity segments, borrowing costs, leases and reporting of financial statements; and b) capital assets. Both are identified as important obstacles that can hinder material harmonization. Although some efforts have been made in the last 20 years, governmental capital assets are still the subject of many unresolved questions, and IPSAS 17 is an important internationally driven milestone in relation to capital assets, although it lacks a conceptual framework.

The IPSASB will have to continue working towards greater comparability, extending its standard setting concern by clarifying matters of application to the above-mentioned concepts, achieving consistency in wording and style, updating IPSASs to converge with the equivalent International Financial Reporting and issuing new standards that address the projects on its current agenda (budget information, taxes and transfers, financial information about the general government sector, employee benefits or impairment of cash-generating assets).

Concluding Remarks

This work has analyzed the accounting model profile proposed by the IPSASB-IFAC and its implicit potential to accomplish comparability. The results obtained corroborate the initial hypothesis. Firstly, the international public sector accounting model proposed by the IFAC and its IPSASB has a *high degree of regulatory strictness*. Most of the regulated accounting solutions are mandatory so the model can be considered as a standardization model that lies close to a rigid uniformity. This characteristic is appreciated both when the model is considered as a whole and when it is separated into its disclosure and measurement components. Flexibility, evaluated in this study in terms of benchmark or allowed treatments, is certainly scarce when the set of standards is taken as a whole, although it is proportionally higher in standards regulating the key aspects of public bodies (for example, valuing of capital assets, reporting of information on operating or finance lease operations and general aspects of financial statement reporting).

Other than strictness, the model presents a *highly potential comparability*. The enforced way of increasing the degree of consensus concerning the choice between the alternative methods of accounting in financial reports and the reduced number of alternative accounting methods are key factors which enhance the degree of comparability. This means that the regulatory framework designed by the IPSASB is an instrument that can contribute significantly to the harmonization of international accounting practices.

In line with the majority opinion sustained by academics, politicians and professionals of the private and public sectors, we believe that the advisability of the harmonization processes for the effective worldwide transmission of accounting information is widely demonstrated.

In a governmental context, however, it is convenient to indicate several factors which can delay the final objective of a standard setting project such as the IPSASB's. We refer to the role played by international users of budgetary and financial information (international investors, financial markets, audit companies, etc.) in the governmental accounting reforms, with much less prominence than the role played in the equivalent process within the private sector. Along with this factor, it is necessary to consider the barriers derived from the different national environments. The underlying values in the social, political and administrative culture determine a series of special features in the governmental accounting practices which make de facto or material convergence more complicated at an international level. Furthermore, these characteristics also produce a negative reaction to introducing accounting reforms given the associated implementation costs involved. Evidently, all the aforementioned factors play an important role in the speed with which accounting reforms are adopted, implemented and consolidated. They slow down the process of material convergence, and they undermine neither its advisability nor its long-term feasibility. It is in this context that the regulatory strictness of the accounting model proposed by the IPSASB can be better understood. Doubtless, the role of the IPSASB is as a driving force of *de jure* convergence across the world because the IPSASs are becoming an increasingly generalized common reference framework for most governmental accounting modernization efforts. Although the most representative examples of accounting reforms (UK, Sweden, New Zealand, Australia or Canada) have always shown a common orientation toward accruals accounting, they obeyed separate (isolated) initiatives. For this reason, it is very difficult to think that the evolution itself of the accounting reforms in each country could lessen the heterogeneity in accounting practices.

In summary, this empirical study highlights the major effort undertaken by the IPSASB-IFAC to achieve the global comparability of the public sector economic and financial reporting. Evidence has emerged that, rather than seeking harmony of financial reports – a point on the continuum between total diversity and uniformity – the IPSASB has chosen a more rigid state, closer to uniformity, as a way of guaranteeing a higher degree of comparability of financial reporting in national, regional and local governments. Therefore, it can be stated that the IFAC's regulatory model, characterized as having a rigid profile, is basically orientated towards uniformity. So in harmonization terms its quality is high.

We should stress that implementing the IPSASs presents a considerably lower number of obstacles in countries with traditional Anglo-Saxon accounting systems since the accounting model is clearly influenced by the Anglo-Saxon accounting philosophy linked to this tradition. To ensure this harmonization quality in the practice on an international scale, it is necessary that the IPSASB continues to make efforts in developing an ample strategy to implement the IPSASs. These efforts must be based on seeking support from professional organizations and public authorities and must take into account the aforementioned factors, the non-legal nature of the international public accounting standards and the importance of budgets in the public accounting system.

The study presented herein opens up new research approaches that could advance the study of formal harmonization in the public sector. For example, given the new initiatives of the current IPSASB agenda, at least two stages in the IPSASB harmonization experience could soon be identified. The methodology used will enable the formal harmonization progress achieved from the initial stage to a second state or to a hypothetical state of uniformity to be measured. In addition, comparisons with the progress made by the IASB in the private sector can be made with a similar sample size.[6]

Notes

1. Most studies on the classification within international accounting, irrespective of the classification criterion chosen (accounting practices, areas of influence or factors within the setting), agree on the fact that differences exist between an Anglo-Saxon accounting tradition and a continental European tradition in both business accounting systems (see Mueller 1968, American Accounting Association 1977, Da Costa *et al.* 1978, Nair and Frank 1980, Gray 1988, Gernon and Bindon 1992, Mueller *et al.* 1994, Nobes and Parker 1995) and government accounting systems (see Lüder 1992, Fuertes and Vela 2000, Benito and Brusca 2004). The main differences centre around whether a conceptual framework exists or not, the influence of the accounting profession and the degree at which regulations are codified (these differ according to the legal system in question, that is, whether it is based on the common law or on the Roman codified law). Such differences are particularly relevant in the public sector where the weight of lawfulness is greater because of the importance given to budgets and to the public nature of the organizations which are subjected to a greater control (Brusca and Cóndor 2002)
2. Following the agreement signed between the IOSCO and the IASC in 1995.

3. See the works by Cañibano and Mora (2000) and Taplin (2004) which analyze the more generalized indices and methodologies.
4. According to Tay and Parker (1990: 73), harmonization and standardization are processes while total diversity, harmony and uniformity are discrete states. Harmony is any point in the continuum between the two states of total diversity and uniformity.
5. This statement is based on the wide range of meanings contributed by authors' studies on international accounting for harmonization and standardization terms (Tay and Parker 1990, Choi and Mueller 1992, Nobes and Parker 1995, Cañibano and Mora 2000). Nonetheless and just as García points out, despite the many terminology accuracies existing in this matter, meanings are exchanged in most cases in such a way that the term harmonization is associated with the European Union process and standardization is related to the IASB (García 1995).
6. Garrido et al. (2000) used this approach for measuring the IASB harmonization progress throughout the three stages considered. The results show an advance in terms of comparability since the distances gradually decrease (46.29; 22.47; 15.40). The last distance refers to the stage from the IOSCO-IASB Agreements, to a hypothetical "ideal harmonization", which is similar to our Model B. Both studies have this stage in common, as explained in section 1, although the differences are not comparable since the design of the D-index depends on the number of items considered in the sample. The IASB study is based on only 20 items (D = 15.40) while our IPSASB study is based on 216 items (D = 87.25).

References

American Accounting Association, 1977, Report of the Committee on international accounting operations and education 1975–76. *The Accounting Review*, **52**, 65–132.

Benito, Bernardino and Brusca, Isabel, 2004, International classification of local government accounting systems, *Journal of Comparative Policy Analysis*, **6**(1), 57–80.

Benito, Bernardino, Brusca, Isabel and Montesinos, Vicente, 2005, Local government accounting: an international empirical analysis, in: Anatoli Bourmistrov and Frode Mellemvik (Eds) *International Trends and Experiences in Government Accounting* (Oslo: Cappelen Akademisk Forlag Publishers), pp. 146–156.

Brusca, Isabel and Condor, Vicente, 2002, Towards the harmonization of local accounting systems in the international context, *Financial Accountability and Management*, **18**(2), 129–162.

Cañibano, Leandro and Mora, Araceli, 2000, Evaluating the statistical significance of de facto harmonization: a study of European global players, *The European Accounting Review*, **9**(2), 329–369.

Choi, Frederick D. and Mueller, Gerhard, 1992, *International Accounting*, 2nd Edition (Englewood Cliffs, NJ: Prentice Hall).

Christiaens, Johan, 2000, Municipal accounting reforms in Flanders: an empirical study of the outcomes, in: Enrico Caperchione and Riccardo Mussari (Eds) *Comparative Issues in Local Government Accounting* (London: Kluwer Academic Publishers), pp. 103–123.

Christiaens, Johan, 2004, Capital assets in governmental accounting reforms: comparing Flemish technical issues with international standards *European Accounting Review*, **13**(4), 743–770.

Da Costa, Richard C., Bourgeois Jacques, C. and Lawson, William M., 1978, Classification of international financial accounting practices, *International Journal of Accounting* (Spring), 37–85.

Fuertes, Iluminada and Vela, José M., 2000, La contabilidad de la Administración Local en Europa: heterogeneidad y armonización, *Revista Española de Financiación y Contabilidad*, **105**, 657–686.

García, María A., 1995, *Armonización de la información financiera en Europa* (Madrid: Instituto de Contabilidad y Auditoria de Cuentas).

Garrido, Pascual, León, Angel, and Zorio, Ana, 2002, Measurement of formal harmonization progress: the IASC experience, *The International Journal of Accounting*, **37**, 1–26.

Gernon, Helen and Bindon, Kathleen R., 1992, *Bounded Diversity: Accounting Measurement and Disclosures Practices of the European Community 1992* (Madrid, Spain: Proceedings of the annual meeting of the European Accounting Association).

Gray, S. J., 1988, Towards a theory of cultural influence on the development of accounting systems internationally, *Abacus*, **24**(1), 1–15.

International Public Sector Accounting Standards Board-IPSASB, 1995, *Definition and Recognition of Assets. Study 5* (New York: International Federation of Accountants).

Jones, Rowan and Pendlebury, Maurice, 1982, Uniformity versus flexibility in the published accounts of local authorities: the UK problem and some European solutions, *Accounting and Business Research* (Spring), 129–135.

Lüder, Klaus, 1992, A contingency model of governmental accounting innovations in the political administrative environment, in: James L. Chan and James M. Patton (Eds) *Research in Governmental and Nonprofit Accounting Vol. 7* (Greenwich: Jai Press), pp. 99–127.

Monsen, Norvald, 1994, Regional accounting harmonization – a case for regional accounting standards, in: Ernst Buschor and Kuno Schedler (Eds) *Perspectives on Performance Measurement and Public Sector Accounting* (Bern: Paul Haupt), pp. 291–308.

Montesinos, Vicente, Pina, Vicente, Torres, Lourdes and Vela, José M., 1998, Análisis comparado de los principios y prácticas contables de los sistemas contables públicos de los países de la OCDE: una aproximación empírica, *Revista Española de Financiación y Contabilidad*, **96**, 787–820.

Mueller, Gerhard G., 1968, Accounting principles generally accepted in the United States versus those generally accepted elsewhere. *International Journal of Accounting*, **3**(2), 91–103.

Mueller, Gerhard, Gernon, Helen and Meek, Gary, 1994, *Accounting: An International Perspective* (Chicago: Richard D. Irwin).

Nair, R. D. and Frank, Werner G., 1980, The impact of disclosure in measurement practices on international accounting classifications, *The Accounting Review*, **55**(3), 426–450.

Nobes, Christopher W. and Parker, Robert H., 1995, *Comparative International Accounting*, 4th Edition, (London: Prentice Hall).

Pallot, June, 1997, Infrastructure accounting for local authorities: technical management and political context. *Financial Accounting and Management*, **13**(3), 225–242.

Pina, Vicente and Torres, Lourdes, 1999, *An Empirical Study about the Degree of Coincidence of Central Governmental Financial Reporting in the EU, USA, Canada, N. Zealand and Australia with the IPSAS of the IFAC* (Tilburg, The Netherlands: Proceedings of the 7th Comparative International Governmental Accounting Research-CIGAR Conference).

Rahman, A., Perea, H. and Ganeshanandam, S., 1996, Measurement of formal harmonization in accounting: an exploratory study, *Accounting and Business Research*, **26**(4), 325–339.

Rowles, T. and Hutton, B., 1998, *Accounting for Land under Roads: Towards Resolution of Conceptual and Measurement Issues* (Antwerp, Belgium: Proceedings of the 21st annual meeting of the European Accounting Association).

Scheid, Jean C. and Lande, Evelyne, 2000, Accounting for capital assets: the IPSAS approach and the main issues. Working paper. Workshop Comparative International Governmental Accounting Research, Speyer.

Stanton, P. J. and Stanton, P. A., 1997, Governmental accounting for heritage assets: economic, social implications, *International Journal of Social Economics*, **24**(7), 988–1006.

Taplin, Ross H., 2004, A unified approach to the measurement of international accounting harmony, *Accounting and Business Research*, **34**, 57–73.

Tay, J. S. W. and Parker, Robert H., 1990, Measuring international harmonization and standardization. *Abacus*, **26**(1), 71–88.

Torres, Lourdes and Pina, Vicente, 2003, Local government financial reporting in the USA and Spain. A comparative study. *Revista Española de Financiación y Contabilidad*, **115**, 153–183.

van der Tas, Leo G., 1988, Measuring harmonization of financial reporting practice, *Accounting and Business Research*, **18**(70), 157–169.

Van Hulle, Karel, 1989, The EC experience of harmonization. *Accountancy* (October), 96–97.

Wallace, Wanda, 2004, Inter-country public sector comparisons and harmonization of international accounting, auditing and regulation. *Journal of Government Financial Reporting* (Fall), 10–17.

Trust and Distrust as Distinct Concepts: Why Studying Distrust in Institutions is Important

STEVEN VAN DE WALLE & FRÉDÉRIQUE SIX

ABSTRACT *Scholarship of trust in institutions has tended to see trust and distrust as opposites on one continuum. Theoretical advances have challenged this view and now consider trust and distrust as different constructs, and thus as constructs with different characteristics and partly different determinants. Current empirical research on trust in government has so far done little to incorporate these findings, and has largely continued to rely on traditional survey items assuming a trust–distrust continuum. We rely on the literature in organization studies and political science to argue in favour of measuring citizen trust and distrust as distinct concepts and discuss future research challenges.*

Citizen trust and distrust in government and the public sector are receiving increasing attention. A common motivation for such studies has been the supposed decline in public trust. Notwithstanding limited empirical evidence about low or declining trust (Van de Walle et al. 2008), two things stand out in the public administration and political science literature: one is an active debate about the need for trust; where some argue that citizen trust is good and distrust destructive, while others argue that citizen distrust in government is rational and trust naïve (Parry 1976; Hardin 2002). The other is the assumption that trust and distrust are polar opposites on one continuum. In this article we argue, in line with Lewicki et al. (1998), that trust and distrust should be treated as separate constructs and that both trust and distrust may be present at the same time. This observation from organization studies has not been adopted yet by trust research in public administration and public policy. This has important implications for the way empirical data are collected and interpreted. This debate is not unlike the conceptual arguments about the relationship between trust and control. Most authors in public policy and public administration appear to assume that the presence of controls equals presence of distrust (e.g. Krouwel and Abts 2007; Rosanvallon 2008).

In this article we use insights from trust research in other fields to develop an argument that clarifies distinctions between trust and distrust in government. An important consequence of our argument is that in public administration and public policy research trust and distrust should be measured using different survey items, and more qualitative research is needed to explore possible differences in antecedents and consequences of trust versus distrust. This will allow a more in-depth analysis of the determinants and effects of trust and distrust in institutions. It might for instance be possible that absence of corruption is a factor that reduces distrust in the public sector, but not one that creates active trust. We use recent discussions in organization studies and e-commerce to argue for making a theoretical and empirical distinction between trust and distrust.

In the first section we argue that to overcome the contradictions in the theories about citizen trust in government we need to clarify definitions. We start with a definition of trust that captures most of the different perspectives on citizen trust in government. We then introduce different democratic theories in relation to trust and distrust. In the following section we address how empirically to study citizen trust and distrust, their antecedents and consequences, referring to empirical work done in organization research. We conclude in the final section with implications for government policies and academic research in a comparative perspective.

Conceptual Clarifications

Defining Trust and Distrust

Some authors define trust as an attitude (e.g. Rousseau et al. 1998), others as an action or as a process (e.g. Möllering 2006). Trust has been studied in many disciplines, such as psychology, economics, sociology, political science and organization studies. Möllering (2006) has studied trust in all these disciplines, except political science, and concluded that trust may have three different bases yet none may provide certainty about the trustees' future behaviour. Möllering's key point is that none of the three bases – reasons, routines or reflexivity – can ever provide certainty about the trusted party's future actions. Trust, therefore, inevitably requires a "leap of faith" in which the irreducible uncertainty and vulnerability are suspended. According to Möllering (2006: 111) trust is based on

> reason, routine and reflexivity, suspending irreducible social vulnerability and uncertainty *as if* they were favourably resolved, and maintaining thereby a state of favourable expectation towards the actions and intentions of more or less specific others.

In political science, citizen or public trust in government has in fact also been defined using these different bases of trust. Hardin and his colleagues, in many of the Russell Sage Foundation's publications on trust and distrust, have focused on the cognitive bases, i.e. reason (e.g. Hardin 2002; Ullmann-Margalit 2002; Larson 2004). Other authors have focused on the cultural and moral foundations of trust, i.e. routines (e.g. Fukuyama 1995). Krouwel and Abts (2007) have explicitly brought the reflexive basis of trust and distrust to our attention.

The "as if" in the definition refers to actors who "interact with each other as if ignorance, doubt and dangers that exist alongside knowledge, convictions and assurances are unproblematic and can be set aside, at least for the time being" (Möllering 2006: 115). When the actor cannot make the leap of faith, this is not automatically distrust, but rather low trust. Distrust also has bases in reason, routines and reflexivity that lead to negative expectations towards the actions and intentions of more or less specific others. Distrust, however, does not require a leap of faith or suspension. We discuss this in more detail in the next section.

Citizen Trust or Distrust as More Appropriate?

Democratic and public administration theories contradict each other in what citizens' attitude towards government should be. Some argue that trust is positive and distrust is destructive, while others argue that distrust is rational and trust naïve.

A dominant assumption in the current public administration debate about citizen trust in government is that it is considered important to have high-trusting citizens. Low trust is seen as an indicator that the government must be doing something wrong or that public services do not deliver, and is a reason for worry because low trust is seen to be associated with a decrease in civic behaviour and undesirable voting behaviour (e.g. Nye et al. 1997). High levels of public trust are regarded as evidence that the government performs effectively, efficiently and democratically. Trust is inevitably important in democratic society, because democracies rely on the voluntary compliance of citizens to authorities' rules (Lenard 2008). This makes trust central. Citizens must trust that government officials have the public interest in mind; and citizens must trust each other to abide by the democratically agreed laws. Yet this trust is not blind nor naïve. Citizens must remain vigilant, without this being distrust. This vigilance "is reflected in a set of institutions and active citizenry" (Lenard 2008: 312). The specific role of distrust in political and administrative systems is often ignored in these debates.

The political literature, especially classical liberal theory, suggests that high levels of public trust are risky because they hollow out checks and balances in a democratic polity. Many political systems are therefore explicitly built on distrust (Parry 1976). A certain level of public distrust with government is thus not a problem, because it guarantees control (Kim 2005). Having too much trust in government can be potentially dangerous as it leads to an absence of control. Whether trust is desirable and necessary for a political-administrative system to function actually depends on how this system defines itself. In a classic-liberal approach it would be inappropriate to actually trust a government (Parry 1976). It may therefore be rational not to trust the government (Levi 1998; Hardin 2002). According to Hardin (2002), a decline of levels of citizen trust may not be a problem. "Indeed, it may even be a sign that citizens are becoming increasingly sophisticated about the conditions of trust" (Warren 1999c: 6). In terms of the bases of trust in Möllering's definition, increased knowledge about government erodes the basis of routine generalized trust in government. Routine trust in government, in this perspective, is naïve.

Warren points to the innovative impact of distrust, "democratic progress is most often sparked by distrust of authorities" (Warren 1999b: 310). The innovations this distrust triggers usually involve "new ways of monitoring and controlling those in power, on the assumption that, as a rule, those with power cannot or ought not to be trusted" (Warren 1999b: 310). He recognized though, that there are also "kinds of trust that are good for democracy ... [they] are necessary to [democracy's] stability, viability and vitality" (Warren 1999b: 310).

Krouwel and Abts (2007) continuum of five attitudes of citizens towards government is indicative of how many political scientists approach trust and distrust (confidence/trust–scepticism–distrust–cynicism–alienation). The first attitude on the trust end of the continuum is called confidence. "Confidence, despite its conditionality, frees individuals from the need of constant monitoring and thus can ultimately take the form of a naïve and unquestioned leap of faith" (Krouwel and Abts 2007: 258). This is close to blind or naïve trust, based on routine only and not on reasons or reflexivity (Möllering 2006). Scepticism is described as "an attitude of reserve, where both trust and distrust are temporarily suspended" (Krouwel and Abts 2007: 259). This appears to be a state of both low trust and low distrust. While routine and reason provide insufficient basis for trust, or distrust, reflexivity is very important: sceptics monitor, differentiate and are receptive to observation (Krouwel and Abts 2007). On the other end of the spectrum, both cynicism and alienation are firmly based on routine generalized distrust of government and low reflexivity. Reasons have no effect (Krouwel and Abts 2007). The middle ground is called distrust and is considered a desirable state, as distrusting citizens "will voice discontent, participate in the political debate and mobilize themselves against the government of the day" (Krouwel and Abts 2007: 268). Most theories would agree that citizens who act like this are desirable for a vibrant democracy, but we question whether it is correct to call them distrusting citizens. In Möllering's (2006) terminology, they are reflexive trusters.

Trust and Distrust as Polar Opposites or Separate Constructs?

Early trust scholarship has treated trust and distrust in institutions as two polar opposites on a continuum (Bigley and Pearce 1998). It regards distrust mainly as an absence of trust. More recent research treats them as conceptually different concepts (Bigley and Pearce 1998; Liu and Wang 2010). Theoretical advances have challenged this one-dimensional view from the early 1990s on (Sitkin and Roth 1993; Lewicki and Bunker 1996). Trust and distrust are now increasingly being considered as different constructs. It has also been proposed that trust and distrust have different characteristics and determinants (Lewicki et al. 1998). Many of these insights from organization studies have not yet filtered through to public administration or public policy research. Current empirical research on trust in government has as yet done little to incorporate these findings, and has largely continued to rely on traditional survey items assuming a trust–distrust continuum.

Although Hardin (e.g. 2002, 2004) did not see trust and distrust as separate constructs, he did emphasize that low trust is not the same as active distrust. In his cognitive account of trust: "If I trust you, I have specific grounds for the trust. In parallel, if I distrust you, I have specific grounds for the distrust. I could be in a state of such ignorance about you, however, that I neither trust nor distrust you" (Hardin 2002: 90).

An early distinction between trust and distrust as different concepts can be found in organization studies. Sitkin and Roth suggested in 1993

> that in organizations, trust rests on a foundation of expectations about an employee's ability to complete task assignments reliably (task reliability), whereas distrust is engendered when expectations about the compatibility of an employee's beliefs and values with the organization's cultural values are called into question (generalized value incongruence). (Sitkin and Roth 1993: 367–368)

Thus, rather than merely being an expression of low trust, "distrust is engendered when an individual or group is perceived as not sharing key cultural values" (Sitkin and Roth 1993: 371).

In their 1998 article on institutional trust, organization scholars Lewicki, McAllister and Bies argued that "low distrust is not the same as high trust, and high distrust is not the same as low trust" (Lewicki et al. 1998: 425), thereby giving rise to a new stream of research in organization studies and e-commerce. Because of this difference, they argue, reasons for trusting and distrusting are different as well.

> We argue that trust and distrust are separate but linked dimensions. Moreover, we propose that trust and distrust are not opposite ends of a single continuum. There are elements that contribute to the growth and decline of trust, and there are elements that contribute to the growth and decline of distrust. (Lewicki et al. 1998: 339–340)

In making this distinction, they refer to the German sociologist Niklas Luhmann. In Luhmann's classic work on trust, distrust (*Mißtrauen*) is described not as the opposite of trust, but as a functional equivalent. He explains this by referring to trust's and distrust's main social function: the reduction of social complexity. With trust, this is done through positive expectations. If there is distrust, this reduction cannot take place in the same way (Luhmann 1968: 69). Reduction of uncertainty is then done using negative strategies (e.g. defining the other as the enemy, building up emergency reserves, attacking, etc.). Reductions of complexity/uncertainty are generally more complex when based on negative expectations than on positive expectations – trusting is just a much easier way of living (Luhmann 1968: 70).

The fundamental difference between trust and distrust becomes visible when we treat trust and distrust as fundamental dispositions. A "disposition to trust means the extent to which one displays a consistent tendency to be willing to depend on general others across a broad spectrum of situations and persons" (McKnight and Chervany 2001: 38). Contrary to trust, distrust can thus be seen as "an actor's assured expectation of intended harm from the other" (Lewicki et al. 1998: 446), something which obviously goes beyond a mere absence of trust. A mere absence of trust, or not trusting someone (or an institution) does not mean actively distrusting that person or institution (Ullmann-Margalit 2002). It follows that the opposite of trust is an absence of trust; the opposite of distrust is, likewise, an absence of distrust.

This means that distrust is not the absence of trust, but an attitude in itself. It is an actual expectation that another actor cannot be relied upon, and will engage in harmful behaviour. While trust consists of "confident positive expectations regarding another's conduct", distrust consists of "confident negative expectations regarding another's conduct" (Lewicki et al. 1998:439). These expectations colour all aspects of interaction, and influence even the most basic perceptions of the other, resulting in a very biased view of "reality". Just like trust, the decision to distrust may be an established way of thinking, of life, that gets strengthened in social life, through a self-fulfilling prophecy (Luhmann 1968: 73). The same objective situation can lead to a decision to trust or to distrust, through selective use of proofs and clues, instigated by one's basic disposition (*Einstellung*) to trust or distrust (Luhmann 1968: 74–75). This disposition is not just a personal one, but one that is reinforced by one's environment. Sztompka, in his research on new democracies in Central Europe, also stresses this social context within which decisions to trust or distrust are taken:

When a culture of trust -or culture of distrust- appears, the people are constrained to exhibit trust or distrust in all their dealings, independent of individual convictions, and departures from such a cultural demand meet with a variety of sanctions. (Sztompka 1996)

A culture of distrust is characterized by "a pervasive, generalized climate of suspicion" (Sztompka 1998: 22), leading to alienation and passivism.

Simultaneous Trust and Distrust in Interpersonal Relationships

When trust and distrust are different concepts, this means that trust and distrust can co-exist because they are not opposites. "Trust and distrust are separate constructs that may exist simultaneously." (McKnight and Chervany 2001: 29). McKnight and Chervany illustrate this apparent contradiction by giving the World War II collaboration between Stalin and Roosevelt as an example (McKnight and Chervany 2001), where both parties trust each other, yet distrust each other at the same time. Trust and distrust may coexist in a relationship, both referring to a different aspect or quality of the relationship (Six 2005; Liu and Wang 2010).

Lewicki et al. even go as far as saying that the combination of high trust/high distrust might be more prevalent in relationships than originally expected, where a combination between high trust/low distrust has generally been seen as logical (Lewicki et al. 1998: 477). This combination, however, means people experience a certain level of ambivalence in their relationships (Lewicki et al. 1998:449). The large degree of middle category or "don't know" responses in most surveys on trust in institutions provide further evidence of such ambivalence (Van de Walle 2004: 233–4). Consider for instance this extract from Eliasoph's micro-level study of on political engagement:

When I asked the standard survey question "How much of the time do you think you can trust the government in Washington to do what is right?" many volunteers said something like what Carolyn said, "Most of the time. Well, at least I'd like to think it's most of the time. Of course, I'm not so sure it really *is*. But I hope it is. So, I'd say "most of the time". Yes, put "most of the time". (Eliasoph 1998: 20)

A similar misconception exists around the relationship between trust and control. Many theories appear to assume that trust and control are substitutes – in other words, if you control you do not trust and if you trust you do not control. Control appears to directly imply distrust. More specifically, we argue that those theories that propose that citizen distrust is the rational, appropriate approach to democratic governance appear to assume that trust and control are substitutes and that control is seen as a sign of distrust (e.g. Warren 1999a; Krouwel and Abts 2007; Rosanvallon 2008), So as soon as one puts in place controls, one distrusts. Lenard (2008), on the other hand, appears to assume that trust and control may strengthen each other in creating vigilant democratic governance. Recent organization theory supports the perspective that trust and control may complement each other. Control may positively affect and strengthen trust, provided certain conditions are met (Das and Teng 1998, 2001; Weibel 2007; Weibel et al. 2009). Although he did not study the relationship between trust and control explicitly, Lindenberg (2000) addressed the same issue by arguing that you first need to take away distrust before you can begin to build trust. He introduced the notion of legitimate distrust situations, situations where "any explicit or implicit promise ... is blatantly against the self-interest of the promising party" (Lindenberg 2000: 12). Because the distrust is seen as legitimate, that is "reasonable observers would say that any other reasonable person put into this situation" would judge similarly, remedies can be relationally neutral, meaning that the distrusting individual can "claim the necessity of remedies, pinpoint to a menu of solutions and show good faith at the same time" (Lindenberg 2000: 12). In other words, the introduction of certain controls may be considered legitimate and not a sign of distrust if the temptations are considered too great. This is the case in democratic theory and public administration theory where citizens grant wide powers to government and public officials. Thus, the controls that need to be put into place in democracies allow citizens to no longer actively distrust government. This would suggest that these controls – e.g. measures to combat corruption and theft of public monies, cronyism, conflict of interests – will mainly act to reduce distrust and not, or to a lesser extent, increase trust.

Lenard's (2008) notion of citizen vigilance mentioned above is an illustration of how legitimate distrust situations in democracies may be dealt with. "Vigilance *does not require* an attitude of distrust towards our legislators and the vigilance we display in constraining our legislators *is not inconsistent* with trusting them" (Lenard 2008: 326, italics in original).

Rosanvallon came to solutions similar to Lenard's for the problem that democracies face, but called them "ways in which distrust may be expressed" (Rosanvallon 2008: xi). He calls it organizing distrust. We prefer Lenard's position, because of the effect of a distrusting attitude vis-à-vis a trusting attitude. A distrusting attitude sets in motion different perceptions and expectations and leads to distrusting behaviours, whereas a trusting attitude sets in motion trusting and more constructive behaviours (cf. Zand 1972). This has important implications for government actions, which will be discussed in the conclusion.

So, just as trust and distrust are not two ends of one continuum, trust and control are also not substitutes. Both may be high at the same time. In fact, controls may be needed to take away legitimate distrust and create the space for active trust to be built. When citizens thus retain some trust and avoid active distrust, they are likely to stay engaged with the democratic and political processes, voicing their support or concerns and possibly showing some degree of loyalty (Hirschman 1970). This is generally considered positive for democracy and public administration. If, on the other hand, their active distrust causes them to become disengaged (Braithwaite et al. 2007; Braithwaite 2009) or alienated (Krouwel and Abts 2007), they are likely to exit the regular democratic processes. This is generally considered destructive to democracy and public administration.

Thus, what Krouwel and Abts (2007) call distrusting citizens, we would call trusting and vigilant citizens, with their trust based on reason and reflexivity, not on routine generalized trust. Their constant vigilance keeps them alert that controls are in place to take away legitimate distrust situations, so that active distrust is taken away and active trust may be built.

In sum, we argue that trust and distrust should be conceptualized as two separate constructs and that the presence of controls does not imply the presence of active distrust. Controls may help to take away active distrust and thus enable the building up of active trust.

Empirically Studying Trust and Distrust

In empirical studies of trust and distrust, the above argument leads to three issues: Measuring trust and distrust separately; exploring differences in determinants of trust and distrust; and exploring differences in the consequences of trust and distrust.

One important implication of our, so far conceptual, argument is that researchers should start to measure citizen trust and distrust in government as separate constructs and stop interpreting low scores on trust measures as indications of the presence of active distrust. If we, as we did in the previous sections, assume that (absence of) trust and distrust are different constructs, then they also require a different operationalization and different items (see Dietz and Den Hartog 2006). The effect of the empirical tradition in public trust research is that low trust is treated as high distrust, and high trust as absence of distrust. In other words, trust and distrust as two polar opposites on a continuum. While the theoretical debate on the difference between trust and distrust (and their antecedents) started in the early 1990s in organizational research (Sitkin and Roth 1993; Lewicki and Bunker 1996), it appears not yet to have fully reached empirical public trust research (Markova et al. 2008):

> This might stem from the fact that the past literature has implicitly treated distrust as being at the opposite end of trust on the same conceptual spectrum. Consequently, evidence of high trust was always regarded as being that of low distrust, and outcomes of high trust would be identical to those of low distrust. (Cho 2006: 25)

Empirical Evidence from Organization Research

Some initial empirical steps are being taken to empirically test the theoretical idea that trust and distrust are separate concepts. Most of this research is currently being done in the field of marketing (McKnight et al. 2004; Cho 2006). Cho, using Lewicki et al.'s distinction between trust and distrust, developed two distinct scales for measuring trust and distrust in internet-based customer–vendor relations, and found that factors fostering trust (notably benevolence) are different from those reducing distrust (notably competence) (Cho 2006). This appears to confirm Sitkin and Roth's (1993) findings. The consequence of this finding is that different strategies are needed to stimulate commercial internet transactions. Liu and Wang used a simple 2×4-item scale to distinguish between trust and distrust, and found that trust and distrust have different roles in negotiations during commercial transactions in generating the anger of compassion (Liu and Wang 2010). McKnight et al. (2004) for example, studied differential effects on dispositional trust and distrust on perceptions in e-commerce transactions. They argue that trust and distrust are based on different sets of emotions. More specifically, they speak about trust as being "cool and collected" and distrust as "fiery and frenzied". Or they state that "distrust is based on fear and worry, while trust is based on feelings of calm and security" (McKnight et al. 2004: 37).

Empirical Evidence from Public Administration and Political Science

While political science has devoted considerable attention to concepts such as alienation, cynicism, scepticism etc. as concepts different from trust, these theoretical distinctions only occasionally make it to empirical studies (Cook and Gronke 2008), and such distinctions are still largely absent from public administration research. Approaches to measuring public trust in public administration research have been relatively one-dimensional, often using a single trust item. One major cause for this phenomenon is the relative scarcity of primary data in public administration research, leading to a necessary reliance on secondary datasets developed for policy and not for research purposes (Bouckaert et al. 2005).

Contrary to theoretical and conceptual developments, which now tend to see trust and distrust as different constructs with both high and low values (Saunders and Thornhill 2004), distinctions between trust and distrust have received considerably less attention in empirical research. Where attention has explicitly gone to the concept of distrust in social and political research, this happened indirectly. One stream of such research has focused on conceptually distinguishing between trust and related concepts such as political inefficacy, cynicism, alienation, etc., where the latter are generally treated as dimensions of the wider trust concept, or as trust antonyms, signifying an absence of trust (Hetherington 1998: 792).

The second stream is mainly interested in the behavioural effects of distrust (Levi and Stoker 2000). This includes abstaining from the vote, voting for non-incumbents (Hetherington 1998), lower tax and legal compliance (Braithwaite and Levi 1998), participation in protest movements, or in new types of political participation or system-challenging behaviour (Muller and Jukam 1977; Levi and Stoker 2000), or other types of resistance against government influence (Kim 2005: 628). In most of these approaches, it has been assumed that there is a trust–distrust continuum, where attitudes such as cynicism and alienation, and various types of protest behaviour emerge when trust sinks below a certain level.

There is a relatively long empirical tradition in measuring trust. Researchers have devoted considerable attention to testing items and to comparing alternative survey items. This has resulted in two main traditions in the measurement of trust in institutions. One is very common in European social and political research, and in policy research. This approach relies on a Likert scale ranging from low to high trust or confidence, or vice versa. It exists both as a generic single item construct, and as a list of items measuring trust in a series of institutions. In this approach, low levels of trust are seen as distrust. This approach is also common in international surveys such as the European Social Survey, the World Values Surveys, or Eurobarometer, partly because of the relative ease of administering these items.

The other tradition is pioneered in the American National Election Studies (NES) from the 1950s on. The NES uses a political trust scale based on a number of items. It consists of one dimension, running from high trust to high distrust (also referred to as political cynicism) (Miller 1974). The NES index has been extensively tested for reliability and validity (Craig et al. 1990), and consists of four items. The strong tradition in the measurement of trust has led to scales and items that have been thoroughly tested, and that allow for cross-sectional and longitudinal comparisons. At the same time, they have had a fossilizing effect on trust research, because they inhibited change. The desire to maximize comparability has resulted in a situation where much of the trust research and resulting questionnaire construction is measurement-driven rather than theory-driven, resulting in a strong "imbalance between measurement and theory" (Weatherford 1992: 151). Specific issues with the NES items relate to their focus on short-term evaluations, and a tendency to exaggerate disaffection (Cook and Gronke 2005). Additional issues relate to the problems with purely quantitative measurements of trust and distrust. We know for instance that survey answers on trust in institutions can be very sensitive to issues such as question order and question wording (Van de Walle and Van Ryzin 2011), or the reversal of answering scales (Friedman et al. 1994). Few of the theoretical advances in trust research, as outlined in the previous section, have therefore been introduced to the more empirical social and political research, which has continued to rely on conventional indicators.

Exploring Differences in Determinants of Trust and Distrust

Sitkin and Roth (1993) suggested that trust and distrust are different concepts, and that therefore they are created by different determinants. Remedying distrust and responding to trust violations requires different approaches. More specifically, they emphasized that legalistic and regulatory approaches may be helpful for restoring trust, but not for remedying distrust (Sitkin and Roth 1993). Liu and Wang demonstrated empirically that "it is evident that trust and distrust are associated with distinct antecedents and consequences" (Liu and Wang 2010: 28). If trust and distrust are distinct constructs, then the determinants are likely to be distinct as well. This means we need instruments not just to measure the extent of trust, but also the extent of distrust, and especially what causes trust and distrust.

This is especially important for two reasons. One is that the predisposition to trust or distrust is generally correlated with other orientations (Kramer 1999). The frequent finding of correlations of trust (in government) with feelings of insecurity, or with dissatisfaction with one's own life, is good evidence in this respect. Further, explaining distrust requires more insight into the types of distrust. Trust has been analysed, and different types of trust have been distinguished, with for instance Lewis and Weigert's distinction between cognitive, emotional and behavioural dimensions of trust (Lewis and Weigert 1985), or Lewicki and Bunker's calculus-, knowledge- and identity-based types of trust (Lewicki and Bunker 1996; see Van de Walle 2010 for an application of this distinction to public management). Yet the same has not happened to this extent for distrust (see also McKnight and Chervany 2001: 44, for an exception).

Just as was the case in Lewicki et al.'s (1998) seminal paper, our trigger to start looking into differences between trust and distrust also comes from Herzberg's distinction between satisfiers and dissatisfiers in his work on job attitudes. Rather than treating job motivation as a single construct, Herzberg distinguishes between factors that cause job satisfaction, and those that cause dissatisfaction. The work was based on a review of earlier studies on job attitudes (Herzberg et al. 1957). In their actual studies, they "decided to ask people to tell ... stories about times when they felt exceptionally good or bad about their jobs" (Herzberg et al. 1959: 17). More specifically, they approached workers with the following question:

"Think of a time in the past when you felt especially good or bad about your job. It may have been on this job or any other. Can you think of such a high or low point in your feelings about your job? Please tell me about it." (Herzberg et al. 1959: 20)

These interviews led them to distinguish between satisfiers and dissatisfiers. Satisfiers or motivators are factors that lead to satisfaction. In job attitudes research, such factors include recognition, the work itself, or responsibility. Dissatisfiers or hygiene factors are factors that do not create satisfaction, but merely help to avoid dissatisfaction. Examples of dissatisfiers are company policy, supervision, salary etc. (Herzberg et al. 1959).

This means satisfaction and dissatisfaction are not opposites. Taking away dissatisfiers therefore does not lead to satisfaction, but merely reduces dissatisfaction. Herzberg et al. concluded "that the satisfier factors are much more likely to increase job satisfaction than they would be to decrease job satisfaction but that the factors that relate to job dissatisfaction very infrequently act to increase job satisfaction" (Herzberg et al. 1959: 80).

The distinction made by Herzberg et al. offers the possibility to draw parallels with trust research: what are the drivers that determine the public trust in government, and are these drivers different from those that determine active distrust? In other words, rather than using a trust–distrust continuum, we propose to distinguish between trust/no-trust and distrust/no distrust.

Exploring Differences in Consequences of Trust and Distrust

A second reason why it is important to not just study trust but also distrust, is that levels of trust and distrust are also related to behaviours, and do not just remain attitudes. Evidence from the political trust literature suggests that those with low political trust are more permissive towards tax-breaking behaviour (Mariën and Hooghe 2011), more likely to participate in protest politics (Mariën and Hooghe 2010), and more likely to vote for extreme right parties or cast a blank or invalid vote (Hooghe et al. 2011). Low levels of trust (generally mistakenly called "distrust" in political science) do not necessarily lead to changes in behaviour. When there is no change in behaviour, then there appears to be little reason for government to worry about distrust. When, however, there is active distrust, and citizens alter their behaviour, such distrust has important consequences for government.

The different responses in terms of voice and exit mentioned above are also about different consequences.

Conclusion and Implications

In this article, we reviewed the emerging literature in organization studies and political science that treats trust and distrust as different constructs. Whereas most scholarship of trust in institutions has tended to consider trust and distrust as opposites on a continuum, more recent advances have focused more explicitly on distrust as a concept different from trust. In this article, we clarified the conceptual distinction between trust and distrust, and challenged the dominant approach that tends to view trust as the normatively desirable option. It shows that distrust is not the opposite of trust. Luhmann (1968) showed how trust and distrust provide two functional equivalents for coping with dealing with social complexity, which lead to different expectations and actions. Lewicki et al. (1998) showed how both constructs may be present simultaneously and hypothesized that each may have different antecedents and consequences. Subsequent empirical research in organization and marketing provide support for their model.

This has implications for research on the effects of trust and distrust on citizens' behaviours, and on the determinants of such attitudes. These findings have important implications both for governments that wish to remedy low trust or high distrust, and for researchers who wish to obtain a deeper insight into what causes distrust, and who those are who have a fundamentally distrusting attitude towards government.

Implications for Government Actions

Our argument has important implications for governments. Active distrust is different from mere low trust, and may therefore have different consequences, and may require a different set of policy solutions. The policy options available across countries also depend on the national trust or distrust dispositions; thus this is relevant in comparative policy analysis.

Actively distrusting citizens are a risk factor for governments, because their basic attitude towards government is one of distrust, which impacts on their perceptions and possibly also on their behaviours. Such a disposition to distrust generates suspicion vis-à-vis all government communications and actions. Whereas trusting citizens resolve uncertainty in their interaction with government through trust, distrusting people use suspicion as their basic attitude. Finishing one's relationship with the other is the most certain way to eliminate dependence, and this uncertainty. Whereas trust lowers transaction costs, distrust increases them or even makes transactions impossible. While trust helps governments to implement policies, or to find support for policies, a mere lack of trust does not necessarily hinder the implementation. Distrust, however, may make the implementation of certain policies that infringe upon people's lives quasi-impossible. Research on trust in government has revealed effects of low trust on rule compliance, tax paying, voting behaviour etc. Most research up to now has tended to focus on more moderate expressions of low trust, such as declining tax discipline or voting for protest parties. In a situation of distrust, some of these behaviours may become more extreme, eventually even resulting in a withdrawal from the state. Such a withdrawal can be full or partial, and may consist of behaviours such as abstaining from voting, tax evasion, non-take-up of public services, refusing to be registered in government databases, or a physical withdrawal. It is therefore crucial to know whether citizens merely display a low level of trust, or are actually actively distrusting. Such extreme disaffection has received little attention in research, partly because deep suspicion makes access to research subjects difficult.

Finding "solutions" for distrust is harder than finding "solutions" for low trust. In a case of low trust, the basic disposition towards government is still one of trust. In the case of distrust, this basic trusting disposition is no longer present: all government actions are interpreted from a basic disposition of distrust and suspicion, which influences attitudes and perceptions. Well-intended actions by government are hence either not perceived at all, or perceived as malicious. These dispositions are different across countries and this impacts on the scope of policy alternatives available to governments. Compare for instance the low levels of trust in government in Central European countries, to very high levels in the Nordic area.

Because we are talking about broad dispositions to trust or distrust, identifying specific reasons for such trust or distrust is difficult. A "Disposition to trust means the extent to which one displays a consistent tendency to be willing to depend on general others across a broad spectrum of situations and persons" (McKnight and Chervany 2001: 38). A disposition to distrust, therefore, is a general tendency to be suspicious of any government actions, also when such actions are initiated by government in order to remediate distrust. Distrusting citizens are unlikely to believe in government's good intentions. Traditional fixes for low trust, such as increasing transparency, initiating anti-corruption legislation, or closing the gap between politicians and citizens through involving the latter in decision making are therefore unlikely remedies for reversing active distrust. Such actions are seen as factors further confirming the distrusting citizen's suspicions about government ("if they initiate anti-corruption laws, it must mean they are corrupt", "if politicians want to talk to us, this must mean they want something from us"). Beginning to trust government is considered by these citizens to be a very risky strategy that only increases the uncertainty in their environment.

Because active distrust (just as trust) is part of a disposition, specific actions and information will do little to change it in the short term, because all such specific action will be interpreted within the broader disposition. We for instance often see in research on trust in government a strong relationship between attitudes towards government and more general attitudes such as satisfaction with one's own life, ethnocentric attitudes, feelings of insecurity, or other emotions. Combating distrust therefore requires a strategy that is not limited to factors directly related to government or government–citizen interactions. Actions needed for trust building are different from actions effective in combating distrust.

Implications for Research

Our suggestion to treat trust and distrust as different concepts, based on a theoretical-conceptual review, has a number of implications for future research on trust and especially distrust. Current research has a predilection for large-N quantitative research, and tends to concentrate on general trends in an entire population. A wealth of empirical survey-based data has become available in recent decades, allowing for an analysis of covariates and determinants of levels of trust. Much of the political science research has in addition also concentrated on dimensions in trusting behaviour, through distinguishing between concepts such as cynicism, scepticism, alienation, etc. (Cook and Gronke 2005; Krouwel and Abts 2007). In public administration, such conceptual distinctions are not common, or are even non-existent. A first avenue for improving research would be to develop a much more comprehensive way of measuring trust and distrust in public administration and government questionnaires, beyond the commonly used one-dimensional trust Likert scale. These new scales also need to take cross-national equivalence of concepts into account (see also Miller and Mitamura 2003). One such common conceptual distinction, the distinction between trust and distrust, to give but one example, is for instance entirely irrelevant in some languages, simply because the two concepts are translated into the same word. Recent large-N studies are often comparative across nations. Such comparative research would benefit from distinguishing trust and distrust explicitly to allow for much more fine-grained analyses of antecedents and consequences of trust and distrust.

A second expansion of trust research would be to devote more attention to measurement equivalence issues in international comparative research. This includes treating ambivalence, non-opinions and middle categories in scales seriously if a questionnaire is only using one single trust item (Eliasoph 1998; Martinez et al. 2007). In addition, when measuring trust in international comparative surveys, recent developments in the survey literature concerning the use of anchoring vignettes need to be taken on board, in order to calibrate findings internationally, and to make cross-national comparisons more meaningful (King et al. 2004).

An additional complication is that survey non-response behaviour tends to co-vary with levels of trust, meaning that distrusting sample units are also those who do not participate in surveys (Loosveldt and Carton 2002), making in-depth study of distrust difficult. This calls for a different approach to studying distrust. Earlier, we referred to Herzberg et al.'s research into satisfiers and dissatisfiers. This research was based on in-depth interviews with workers. Such an approach may also be quite useful for research into distrust. Given that distrust as a separate concept is only recently emerging in organization studies, there may be some relevance in organizing a series of in-depth interviews with extremely distrusting respondents – ideally leading to the design of a formal set of items to be included in future large-N studies. Such in-depth interviews allow the researcher not just to look at generic attitudes and their inter-correlations, but also to explore the genesis of general dispositions to trust or to distrust, through reconstructing individual histories of life experiences and interactions with government.

A final implication of our review is that public sectors need to take distrust seriously as a concept mediating the relationship between citizens and government. Most current government surveys tend to consider trust in government as a normatively superior attitude, and a lack of trust is generally interpreted as a call to action for governments. From such observations of low trust (and distrust, where measured) follow a series of "fixes" to remedy low trust. Such an approach has led to an excessive focus on trusting citizens and what makes them trusting, to the detriment of studies focusing on distrusting citizens and what makes them distrustful. It furthermore ignores many of the realities governing political and administrative systems, which are grounded in profound distrust. We need to take away legitimate distrust to enable trust. This may be done by institutionalising controls that limit the opportunities to benefit from positions of power. Such an approach is a very common feature in the design of democratic systems which are built on a series of checks and balances, including periodic elections, independent courts and rule of law, or law enforcement institutions (Sztompka 1998). These points are especially important in an internationally comparative context. First because base-line levels of trust differ substantially across countries. Trust – both in institutions and between people – tends to be very low in some countries, and very high in others. This means that the interpretation of trust and distrust needs to take this context into account. Second, political and administrative systems in some countries are to a larger extent based on an assumption of trust than they are in other countries.

References

Bigley, G. A. and Pearce, J. L., 1998, Straining for shared meaning in organization science: Problems of trust and distrust. *Academy of Management Review*, **23**(3), pp. 405–421.

Bouckaert, G., Van de Walle, S. and Kampen, J. K., 2005, Potential for comparative public opinion research in public administration. *International Review of Administrative Sciences*, **71**(2), pp. 229–240.

Braithwaite, V. A., 2009, *Defiance in Taxation and Governance: Resisting and Dismissing Authority in a Democracy* (Cheltenham: Edward Elgar Publishing).

Braithwaite, V. and Levi, M., 1998, *Trust and Governance* (New York: Russell Sage Foundation).

Braithwaite, J., Makkai, T. and Braithwaite, V. A., 2007, *Regulating Aged Care: Ritualism and the New Pyramid* (Cheltenham: Edward Elgar Publishing).

Cho, J., 2006, The mechanism of trust and distrust formation and their relational outcomes. *Journal of Retailing*, **82**(1), pp. 25–35.

Cook, T. E. and Gronke, P., 2005, The skeptical American: Revisiting the meanings of trust in government and confidence in institutions. *Journal of Politics*, **67**(3), pp. 784–803.

Craig, S. C., Niemi, R. G. and Silver, G. E., 1990, Political efficacy and trust: A report on the NES pilot study items. *Political Behavior*, **12**(3), pp. 289–314.

Das, T. K. and Teng, B. S., 1998, Between trust and control: Developing confidence in partner cooperation in alliances. *The Academy of Management Review*, **23**(3), pp. 491–512.

Das, T. K. and Teng, B. S., 2001, Trust, control, and risk in strategic alliances: An integrated framework. *Organization Studies*, **22**(2), pp. 251.

Dietz, G. and Den Hartog, D. N., 2006, Measuring trust inside organisations. *Personnel Review*, **35**(5), pp. 557–588.

Eliasoph, N., 1998, *Avoiding Politics: How Americans Produce Apathy in Everyday Life* (Cambridge: Cambridge University Press).

Friedman, H. H., Herksovitz, P. J. and Pollack, S., 1994, Biasing Effects of Scale-Checking Styles on Responses to a Likert Scale, in: *Proceedings of the American Statistical Association Annual Conference: Survey Research Methods*, pp. 792.

Fukuyama, F., 1995, *Trust: The Social Virtues and the Creation of Prosperity* (New York: The Free Press).

Hardin, R., 2002, *Trust and Trustworthiness* (New York: Russell Sage Foundation).

Hardin, R., 2004, Distrust: Manifestations and management. *Distrust*, **8**, pp. 3–33.

Herzberg, F., Mausner, B. and Bloch Snyderman, B., 1959, *The Motivation to Work*, 2nd ed. (New York: John Wiley & sons Inc).

Herzberg, F., Mausner, B., Peterson, R. O. and Capwell, D. F., 1957, *Job Attitudes: Review of Research and Opinion* (Pittsburgh: Psychological Service of Pittsburgh).

Hetherington, M. J., 1998, The political relevance of political trust. *American Political Science Review*, **92**(4), pp. 791–808.

Hirschman, A. O., 1970, *Exit, Voice, and Loyalty: Response to Decline in Firms, Organizations and States* (Cambridge, MA: Harvard University Press).

Hooghe, M., Mariën, S. and Pauwels, T., 2011, Where do distrusting voters turn to if there is no viable exit or voice option? The impact of political trust on electoral behaviour in the Belgian Regional Elections of June, 2009. *Government and Opposition*, **46**(2), pp. 245–273.

Kim, S., 2005, The role of trust in the modern administrative state: An integrative model. *Administration and Society*, **37**(5), pp. 611–635.

King, G., Murray, C. J. L., Salomon, J. A. and Tandon, A., 2004, Enhancing the validity and cross-cultural comparability of measurement in survey research. *American Political Science Review*, **98**(February), pp. 191–205.

Kramer, R. M., 1999, Trust and distrust in organizations: Emerging perspectives, enduring questions. *Annual Review of Psychology*, **50**, pp. 569–570.

Krouwel, A. and Abts, K., 2007, Varieties of Euroscepticism and populist mobilization: Transforming attitudes from mild Euroscepticism to Harsh Eurocynicism. *Acta Politica*, **42**(2–3), pp. 252–270.

Larson, D. W., 2004, Distrust: Prudent, if not always wise. In R. Hardin (ed.) *Distrust*, (New York: Russell Sage Foundation) pp. 34–59.

Lenard, P. T., 2008, Trust your compatriots, but count your change: The roles of trust, mistrust and distrust in democracy. *Political Studies*, **56**(2), pp. 312–332.

Levi, M., 1998, A state of trust, in: V. Braithwaite and M. Levi (Eds) *Trust and Governance* (New York: Russell Sage Foundation), pp. 77–101.

Levi, M. and Stoker, L., 2000, Political trust and trustworthiness. *Annual Review of Political Science*, **3**(1), pp. 475–507.

Lewicki, R. J. and Bunker, B. B., 1996, Developing and maintaining trust in work relationships, in: R. M. Kramer and T. R. Tyler (Eds) *Trust in Organizations: Frontiers of Theory and Research* (Thousand Oaks, CA: Sage Publications), pp. 114–139.

Lewicki, R. J., McAllister, D. J. and Bies, R. J., 1998, Trust and distrust: New relationships and realities. *The Academy of Management Review*, **23**(3), pp. 438–458.

Lewis, D. J. and Weigert, A., 1985, Trust as a social reality. *Social Forces*, **63**(4), pp. 967–985.

Lindenberg, S., 2000, It takes both trust and lack of mistrust: The workings of cooperation and relational signaling in contractual relationships. *Journal of Management and Governance*, **4**(1), pp. 11–33.

Liu, M. and Wang, C., 2010, Explaining the influence of anger and compassion on negotiators' interaction goals: An assessment of trust and distrust as two distinct mediators. *Communication Research*, **37**(4), pp. 443–472.

Loosveldt, G. and Carton, A., 2002, Utilitarian individualism and panel nonresponse. *International Journal of Public Opinion Research*, **14**, pp. 428–438.

Luhmann, N., 1968, *Vertrauen: Ein Mechanismus Der Reduktion Sozialer Komplexität* (Stuttgart: Ferdinand Enke Verlag).

Mariën, S. and Hooghe, M., 2010, Political trust, conventional and unconventional political participation. A comparative analysis. *European Consortium for Political Research Joint Sessions*, 22–27 March, Münster, Germany.

Mariën, S. and Hooghe, M., 2011, Does political trust matter? An empirical investigation into the relation between political trust and support for law compliance. *European Journal of Political Research*, **50**(2), pp. 267–291.

Markova, I., Linell, P. and Gillespie, A., 2008, Trust and distrust in society, in: I. Markova & A. Gillespie (Eds) *Trust and Distrust: Sociocultural Perspectives* (Charlotte, NC: Information Age Publishing), pp. 3–27.

Martinez, M. D., Gainous, J. and Craig, S. C., 2007, Measuring Ambivalence about Government in the 2006 ANES Pilot Study. *ANES Pilot Study Report, No.nes011905*.

McKnight, D. H. and Chervany, N., 2001, *Trust and Distrust Definitions: One Bite at a Time, Trust in Cybersocieties* (London: Springer-Verlag), pp. 27–54.

McKnight, D. H., Kacmar, C. J. and Choudhury, V., 2004, Dispositional trust and distrust distinctions in predicting high-and low-risk internet expert advice site perceptions. *E-Service*, **3**(2), pp. 35–58.

Miller, A. H., 1974, Political issues and trust in government: 1964–1970. *American Political Science Review*, **68**(3), pp. 951–972.

Miller, A. H. and Mitamura, T., 2003, Are surveys on trust trustworthy? *Social Psychology Quarterly*, **66**(1), pp. 62–70.

Muller, E. M. and Jukam, T. O., 1977, On the meaning of political support. *American Political Science Review*, **71**, pp. 1561–1577.

Möllering, G., 2006, *Trust: Reason, Routine, Reflexivity* (Amsterdam: Elsevier).

Nye, J. S., Zelikow, P. D. and King, D. C., 1997, *Why People Don't Trust Government* (Cambridge, MA: Harvard University Press).

Parry, G., 1976, Trust, distrust and consensus. *British Journal of Political Science*, **6**(2), pp. 129–143.

Rosanvallon, P., 2008, *Counter-Democracy: Politics in an Age of Distrust* (Cambridge: Cambridge University Press).

Rousseau, D. M., Sitkin, S. B., Burt, R. S. and Camerer, C., 1998, Not so different after all: A cross-discipline view of trust. *Academy of Management Review*, **23**(3), pp. 393–404.

Saunders, M. N. K. and Thornhill, A., 2004, Trust and mistrust in organizations: An exploration using an organizational justice framework. *European Journal of Work and Organizational Psychology*, **13**(4), pp. 493–515.

Sitkin, S. B. and Roth, N. L., 1993, Explaining the limited effectiveness of legalistic remedies for trust/distrust. *Organization Science*, **4**(3), pp. 367–392.

Six, F., 2005, *The Trouble with Trust, the Dynamics of Interpersonal Trust Building* (Cheltenham: Edward Elgar).

Sztompka, P., 1996, Trust and emerging democracy: Lessons from Poland. *International Sociology*, **11**(1), pp. 37–62.

Sztompka, P., 1998, Trust, Distrust and Two Paradoxes of Democracy. *European Journal of Social Theory*, **1**(1), pp. 19–32.

Ullmann-Margalit, E., 2002, Trust, distrust, and in-between, in: R. Hardin (Ed) *Distrust* (New York: Russell Sage Foundation), pp. 60–82.

Van de Walle, S., 2004, *Perceptions of Administrative Performance: The Key to Trust in Government?* (Leuven: Instituut voor de Overheid).

Van de Walle, S., 2010, New Public Management: Restoring the public trust through creating distrust?, in: T. Christensen & P. Laegreid (Eds) *Ashgate Research Companion to New Public Management* (Aldershot: Ashgate), pp. 309–320.

Van de Walle, S., Van Roosbroek, S. and Bouckaert, G., 2008, Trust in the public sector: Is there any evidence for a long-term decline?. *International Review of Administrative Sciences*, **74**(1), pp. 45–62.

Van de Walle, S. and Van Ryzin, G. G., 2011, The order of questions in a survey on citizen satisfaction with public services: Lessons from a split-ballot experiment. *Public Administration*, **89**(4), pp. 1436–1450.

Warren, M. E., 1999a, *Democracy and Trust* (Cambridge: Cambridge University Press).

Warren, M. E., 1999b, Democratic theory and trust, in: M. E. Warren (ed.) *Democracy and Trust* (New York: Russell Sage Foundation), pp. 310–345.

Warren, M. E., 1999c, Introduction, in: M. E. Warren (ed.) *Democracy and Trust* (New York: Russell Sage Foundation), pp. 1–21.

Weatherford, M. S., 1992, Measuring political legitimacy. *American Political Science Review*, **86**(1), pp. 149–166.

Weibel, A., 2007, Formal control and trustworthiness: Shall the twain never meet? *Group and Organization Management*, **32**(4), pp. 500.

Weibel, A., Searle, R., Den Hartog, D., Six, F., Hatzakis, T., Skinner, D. and Gillespie, N., 2009, Control as a Driver of Trust in the Organization?, in: *Academy of Management Meeting*, 7–11 August, Chicago.

Zand, D. E., 1972, Trust and managerial problem solving. *Administrative Science Quarterly*, **17**(2), 229–239.

Sustainable Development and Transnational Communication: Assessing the International Influence on Subnational Policies

SANDER HAPPAERTS and KAROLINE VAN DEN BRANDE

ABSTRACT *Sustainable development needs to be tackled at different levels of governance. An important role is put aside for subnational entities (such as provinces, states or regions), because of their often large implementation responsibilities. Sustainable development is to a large extent decided in multilateral organizations, such as the UN, the OECD or the EU. Yet unlike nation-states, subnational governments are not formally bound by international commitments. This article uses the concept of transnational communication as a perspective to examine the extent to which international policy and decision-making resonates at the subnational level. Building on the tradition of policy convergence studies, theoretical and methodological refinements are made to explore how the concept can be applied to sustainable development and to subnational governments. Subsequently, the results are presented of a comparative analysis investigating how international initiatives have triggered and shaped sustainable development policies in Quebec (Canada), North Rhine-Westphalia (Germany) and Flanders (Belgium). The findings suggest that international events play a key role in triggering sustainable development policies at the subnational level, but that their impact on policy content is not uniform. It is also stated that political will is needed for sustainable development initiatives to gain ground and that the presence of a strong identity determines whether or not subnational governments are receptive to international influences.*

Introduction

From the beginning of the 1970s, the international community increasingly realized that continued economic growth without concern for social and environmental objectives would be unsustainable. It became clear that the world's development trajectory was causing large-scale environmental degradation, irreversible loss of natural resources, social injustice between and within societies, rapid depletion of certain energy sources, and even troubling changes to the Earth's climate. In response, the concept of "sustainable development" was put forward by the Brundtland Report, which defines it as "development that meets the needs of the present without compromising the ability of future generations to meet their own needs" (WCED 1987: 43). Since the publication of the Report, the concept and policies of sustainable development have continually been discussed and designed in the international arena. Global summits in Rio (1992) and Johannesburg (2002) were important milestones in governance for sustainable development. A significant part of policy- and decision-making for sustainable development still takes places in multilateral organizations such as the United Nations (UN), the Organization for Economic Cooperation and Development (OECD) or the European Union (EU). Since the major policy requirements of sustainable development are developed at global summits and by multilateral organizations, sustainable development scholars consider it an "outside-in" policy: a policy of which the main elements are internationally decided and subsequently need to be "brought home" by lower-level governments (O'Toole 2004: 34; Meadowcroft 2008: 108).

At the national level of governance, it is clear that international policy developments have triggered the institutionalization of sustainable development. For instance, over 100 national sustainable development strategies have by now been developed, in accordance with the Rio and Johannesburg commitments (UNDESA 2009). Yet subnational governments have also taken up the challenge to institutionalize sustainable development. We define a *subnational entity* as "a coherent territorial entity situated between local and national levels with a capacity for authoritative decision-making" (Marks et al. 2008: 113). This entails entities such as provinces, states or regions.[1] Although they have only rarely been the object of research – in contrast to local authorities (for example Ng 2007) – subnational governments have an important role to play in the sustainable development agenda. Problems related to sustainable development (e.g. with regard to energy, transport, spatial planning) often become tangible precisely at the subnational level, and in many countries subnational governments are responsible for a large part of the implementation of policies directed towards sustainable development (OECD 2002: 19).

Governance for sustainable development, the research domain to which this article aims to contribute, refers to "processes of socio-political governance oriented towards the attainment of sustainable development" and it encompasses "public debate, political decision-making, policy formation and implementation, and complex interactions among public authorities, private business and civil society" (Meadowcroft 2008: 107). In this article we do not look at the specific policy issues that are important for sustainable development – which are manifold, for example climate change, sustainable consumption and production, and so forth. We rather approach sustainable development as a meta-policy or "a policy designed to guide the development of numerous more specific policies" (O'Toole 2004: 38). We look at the transversal policy initiatives that subnational governments have taken to institutionalize sustainable development (for example sustainable development plans or strategies), and whether or not they have responded to the global call for sustainable development in doing so. Two main research questions are addressed. First, how has the government's sustainable development policy been *triggered* by international developments? Second, how is the content of the policy *shaped* by international policy?[2]

The next section presents the theoretical literature on policy convergence and applies one of its central concepts, transnational communication, to subnational governments and sustainable development. We then present the main international policy developments regarding sustainable development. Subsequently, the methodology and results of a comparative policy analysis are elaborated. We compare the influence of international developments on the policies of three subnational governments: Quebec (Canada), North Rhine-Westphalia (Germany) and Flanders (Belgium). Finally, the concluding section presents the answers to our research questions.

Policy Convergence and Transnational Communication

In order to study the influence of international policy- and decision-making on lower levels of governance, several theoretical traditions could be tapped. Implementation theory, for instance, is used to investigate the domestic implementation of international commitments and the possible difficulties associated with it (for example Hanf 2000). Related to implementation theory are Europeanization studies, which aim to explain the impact of the EU on the domestic policies of its member states (Saurugger and Radaelli 2008). Alternatively, for reasons that are elucidated below, we think that the mechanisms described by the literature on policy convergence offer a useful approach for the theoretical framing of our topic. Policy convergence is a concept that emerged in comparative policy analysis in the 1960s, driven by the hypothesis that societies are becoming more and more similar under the influence of industrialization and technological modernization (Wilensky 1975; Kerr 1983). Contemporary policy convergence studies investigate the factors that determine the processes according to which policies converge across (mostly national) jurisdictions (Knill 2005: 764).[3] Within that literature, international governance processes are given an important explanatory value (Bennett 1988: 420; Holzinger and Knill 2008: 404).

Several mechanisms concerning the influence of the international level of governance are cited, such as regulatory competition, international harmonization and transnational communication. The two former, however, are not expected to be very relevant for the analysis of sustainable development policies of subnational governments. Regulatory competition explains the mutual adjustment of policies across jurisdictions, stimulated by the increased economic integration of markets and the abolition of trade barriers. Since it is only expected for trade-related policies (Holzinger and Knill 2005: 789), it cannot offer a valid explanation for our research questions. International harmonization refers to the situation in which national governments are legally required to adopt certain policies in order to comply with binding international commitments (Holzinger et al. 2008: 556). Yet international negotiations on sustainable development mainly result in soft law (such as political declarations, policy recommendations, guidelines and strategies) rather than hard law[4] (Snyder 1994; Kraemer et al. 2003). Therefore international harmonization processes do not fit the purpose of our research.

We think rather that the different mechanisms studied under the denominator of transnational communication are useful for our analysis. *Transnational communication* refers to a set of mechanisms that presuppose nothing but information exchange and communication (rather than competitive pressure or legal requirements) with other governments or international organizations (Holzinger et al. 2008: 559). It focuses, inter alia, on learning processes and networking, which makes it an interesting perspective in a sustainable development context. Indeed, sustainable development poses particular challenges to policy-makers due to its conceptual vagueness, its complexity and the uncertainty related to policy choices and their outcomes (Bruyninckx 2006: 270–271; Meadowcroft 2008: 113). Learning is crucial for managing uncertainty with regard to sustainable development policy (O'Toole 2004) and it encourages subnational governments to participate in transnational networks (Happaerts et al. 2010b). By focusing on transnational communication and by conducting an in-depth analysis of the role of transnational communication processes in three specific subnational cases, we follow the findings of Holzinger et al. about transnational communication as an area for future and more detailed research in comparative policy analysis:

> the high relevance of transnational communication indicates a further issue that deserves particular attention in future research. In this regard the focus should be on a more detailed analysis of concrete processes through which transnational communication has its convergent effects. (Holzinger et al. 2008: 585)

Three mechanisms of transnational communication can be distinguished. A first mechanism is the *promotion of policy models by international organizations*. In order to accelerate the diffusion of certain policy innovations, international organizations disseminate information on best practices, evaluations of existing models, propositions on broad goals or standards, or benchmarks of their members' performances. They thus function as mediators of policy transfer without legal pressure or enforcement (Kern et al. 2001: 9; Tews et al. 2003: 573; Holzinger and Knill 2008: 405). If governments adopt the promoted policies, it is rather because of legitimacy pressures exerted by international organizations (Holzinger and Knill 2005: 785). In the area of sustainable development, global organizations such as the UN or the OECD, and regional organizations such as the EU, are expected to play a role. Moreover, in the context of promotion of policy models by international organizations, we believe a significant role is put aside for key international meetings, such as the Rio and Johannesburg Summits (see also Kern et al. 2001: 23; Tews et al. 2003: 572). Those meetings attract a large number of governmental delegations and create publicity and political momentum for certain topics. Moreover, at such international events (non-binding) political agreements are often negotiated and policy solutions are promoted by the organizing institutions. We believe that the promotion of policy models by international organizations can be as relevant for subnational governments as it is for national governments, especially if the subnational governments in question show an interest in international policy and aim to be involved in multilateral decision-making.

A second mechanism of transnational communication is *policy copying*, either through lesson-drawing or policy emulation (Holzinger and Knill 2008: 410).

Lesson-drawing denotes a rational learning process through which a government uses policy experiences of other governments to solve domestic problems (Holzinger and Knill 2005: 783). Since governments will most especially turn to lesson-drawing in cases of uncertainty (Tews et al. 2003: 594; Holzinger and Knill 2008: 410), learning processes are highly relevant in the context of sustainable development. While lesson-drawing is mostly studied at the level of national governments, it has already been acknowledged that it is used by subnational governments as well (for example Jörgensen 2007). Policy emulation is a similar process, but instead of being motivated by the value of the policy solution in question, it is driven by a desire for conformity. Through policy emulation governments do not copy a policy because they believe it is a valuable innovation, but because they observe others around them adopting that policy and do not want to be left behind. In some cases the emulation can be used to legitimize decisions the government had already made (Kern et al. 2001: 10; Tews et al. 2003: 575; Holzinger and Knill 2005: 784–785, 2008: 405). When emulation is merely used for reasons such as seeking credibility or conformity with international trends, some authors speak of "symbolic imitation" (Meseguer 2005: 73). It is our belief that policy emulation can be applied by subnational governments as well. Lesson-drawing and policy emulation are very similar processes, differing only with regard to the government's motivation.

Besides the promotion of policy models by international organizations and processes of policy copying, transnational communication includes mechanisms based on communication through *networking* (Bennett 1991: 224; Brans et al. 2003: 124–125; Holzinger et al. 2008: 559). The argument departs from the observation that different governments or governmental officials join together in formal or informal transnational networks (whether or not in combination with non-governmental stakeholders) with regard to specific policy areas or themes. Those networks facilitate information-sharing, deliberation and learning with regard to certain policy problems (Tews et al. 2003: 573; Holzinger et al. 2008: 559). In addition, they engage in joint problem-solving activities (Holzinger and Knill 2005: 784), driven by the belief that joint or similar responses are more effective in dealing with common challenges. Like other actors, subnational governments have created many such transnational networks, including for the issue of sustainable development (Happaerts et al. 2010b).

We believe that these three mechanisms of transnational communication are useful analytical categories to study the influence of international policy-making on the sustainable development policies of subnational governments. Unlike in other theoretical traditions, they do not focus on the required implementation of binding international requirements by national governments, but offer a useful perspective for international policy issues that result in soft law. While the first mechanism focuses more on a top-down impact, and the other two assume a proper initiative by the government, the three mechanisms display important interrelations. International organizations are promoters of policy models, but they can also facilitate deliberation and information-sharing (networking) between the officials of the participating governments. Insofar as those governmental delegations include subnational officials, that mechanism is relevant for subnational governments too. Moreover, policy copying (through lesson-drawing or emulation) is facilitated by the activities of international organizations and by networking. Various international organizations (e.g. the EU) promote learning through benchmarking and through procedures such as the Open Method of Co-ordination (OMC) (Nedergaard 2006). International organizations as well as networks invest in the identification and diffusion of best practices, which stimulates policy copying. Networks, in addition, are often linked to the activities of international organizations. Indeed, many transnational networks are created with the aim of influencing decision-making in international organizations (Happaerts et al. 2010a: 129).

The "Outside" Character of Sustainable Development Policy

The global sustainable development debate was shaped at important global summits, the starting shot of which was given by the Brundtland Report in 1987. That report was the outcome document of the World Commission on Environment and Development (WCED), or "Brundtland Commission". The WCED was established to address the deterioration of the environment and its consequences on human development, and to reconcile the concerns of the global North and the global South by emphasizing the common character of the challenges both are facing. It advanced the view that environmental challenges lie at the heart of economic development, social problems and even international peace and security. Besides formulating a definition of sustainable development (see above), the Brundtland Report's main merit was the launch of the global sustainable development debate, and the awareness it raised among policy-makers, scholars and civil society. In 1992 the world met at the UN Conference on Environment and Development (UNCED) in Rio de Janeiro, Brazil. The focus in Rio shifted from defining the concept to shaping policies through policy principles in order to achieve sustainable development worldwide (Bruyninckx 2006: 268). The most important outcome document of the Rio Summit was Agenda 21, an action programme with concrete recommendations on a wide range of mechanisms to implement the policy principles of sustainable development.[5] For instance, national governments were asked to develop sustainable development strategies (UNCED 1992: §8.7). Those strategies are meant to harmonize the existing plans and strategies of a government and direct them towards the attainment of sustainable development (Steurer and Martinuzzi 2005: 457–458; Meadowcroft 2007: 153–155). Other means of implementation included in Agenda 21 are financial mechanisms, international cooperation and capacity-building, technology transfer, science, education, information for decision-making and international law (UNCED 1992: §33–40). The Rio Summit also generated widespread support for the vision that sustainable development entails three dimensions: economic, social and environmental (UNCED 1992: §8.41). Ten years later, at the World Summit on Sustainable Development (WSSD) in Johannesburg, the lack of implementation of Agenda 21 was the main agenda item. For instance, the Johannesburg Plan of Implementation included a pledge of national governments to implement their sustainable development strategies by 2005 (WSSD 2002: §162b). In the margins of the Johannesburg Summit, subnational governments organized a parallel conference to denounce their lack of representation in the multilateral debate. In the resulting Gauteng Declaration, the signatory governments committed to developing a subnational sustainable development strategy (Gauteng Declaration 2002: §7).

In the periods before and after important global summits, the sustainable development debate is kept alive in different multilateral organizations. Those organizations, where sustainable development issues are discussed on a regular basis, play an important role in agenda-setting and the formulation of global sustainable development goals. In contrast to high-level summits, discussions within those multilateral organizations are to a large extent left to technocrats and the level of political involvement is usually much lower. Three multilateral organizations play an important role for sustainable development: the UN and the OECD at the global level and the EU at the regional level. Within the UN system, the Commission on Sustainable Development (CSD) is responsible for following up the implementation of Agenda 21 and it has to provide policy recommendations and diffuse best practices in order to guide governments in their pursuit of sustainable development (UNDESA 2008a). For instance, the CSD has done authoritative work in promoting sustainable development indicators (UNDESA 2008b). Since 1997, sustainable development is also discussed by the industrialized countries in the OECD. The OECD's Annual Meeting of Sustainable Development Experts (AMSDE), established in 2004,[6] monitors how sustainable development is integrated in the work of the OECD. It also aims to share best practices on sustainable development strategies in the OECD member states (AMSDE 2009). Considering the various recommendations, guidelines and background notes it publishes on sustainable development (for example OECD 2002, 2007; OECD and UNDP 2002), it could be assumed that the OECD, a prime example of an "ideas-mongering institution" (Rose 1993: 69), might play a role in diffusing similar sustainable development policies through transnational communication. Finally, as a regional organization, the EU has made a significant effort to institutionalize sustainable development. In 1997, the Treaty of Amsterdam recognized sustainable development as an objective for the EU. In 2001, in preparation for the Johannesburg Summit, the EU adopted its Sustainable Development Strategy (EUSDS) (Tanasescu 2006: 54). The EUSDS, which aims to promote the long-term objectives of sustainable development, proposes actions in six priority fields.[7] It was renewed in 2006, defining seven key challenges. The sustainable development activities of the EU do not belong to its legislative work, but largely rely on soft law measures, such as Commission communications, Council conclusions, or on benchmarks and procedures similar to the OMC (von Homeyer 2002: 295, 297; Kraemer et al. 2003). Nevertheless, concrete recommendations are given to the member states, for example to take into account the EUSDS for reviews of the national sustainable development strategy (Council of the European Union 2006: §40).

Methodological Considerations and Selection of the Cases

Previous analyses account for a high relevance of transnational communication in processes of policy convergence (Holzinger et al. 2008). Many of those policy convergence studies apply a large-N quantitative research method (for example

Holzinger et al. 2008). Such a method is appropriate for assessing the relevance of the different factors that explain policy convergence. However, there is still limited knowledge about how exactly policy convergence, including through transnational communication, takes place within cases (see also Holzinger and Knill 2008: 403). An in-depth analysis of the different mechanisms of transnational communication requires another methodology. That is why we opt for a comparative case study design. Through a detailed comparison of a small number of cases, a thorough analysis of the processes of transnational communication becomes possible. Such a qualitative analysis goes further than many policy convergence analyses, which do not move beyond the identification of the *presence* of a certain policy (for example, is there a sustainable development strategy or not?), while we want to investigate the *content* of those policies as well. In addition, a qualitative comparison of a small number of cases allows consideration of the contextual features of the policies (Bennett 2004: 34), which is necessary to understand why certain aspects have been influenced by international dynamics. A comparative case study design can thus be used to uncover all factors – both expected and unexpected – which might explain the nature of the influence of international policy (Mahoney 2007: 125–126). Finally, a qualitative method is more appropriate for the type of exploratory research we intend to do here, since the theoretical framework we presented has not yet been applied to subnational governments and sustainable development. The comparative case study analysis we propose is both structured and focused (George and Bennett 2005: 67–70. It is *structured* because the same questions (the three mechanisms of transnational communication) guide the data collection and analysis in all cases, and *focused* because it deals with the same aspects across cases (the policy content, comprising the interpretation of sustainable development, the policy goals and the policy instruments).

For the purpose of this exploratory small-N study, we selected three subnational governments from different OECD countries: Quebec (Canada), North Rhine-Westphalia (Germany) and Flanders (Belgium). Operating in three federal systems, they have legislative power and a relatively large share of competences in various domains, such as environment, economy, transport, energy or education.[8] As a consequence of that broad range of competences, they have a sufficient degree of autonomy to formulate a proper sustainable development policy, which makes them relevant units of analysis. The fact that two cases operate in an EU context, while Quebec does not, allows the importance of the EU in the promotion of policy models to be controlled. The analysis is based on an extensive study of policy documents and on 42 interviews with political officials (i.e. cabinet advisors, ministers, former ministers and members of parliament) and civil servants of the subnational governments of Quebec, North Rhine-Westphalia and Flanders, the national governments of Canada, Germany and Belgium, and of international organizations (UN, OECD and EU), and with non-governmental stakeholders (NGOs and academics).[9] The data was gathered between July 2007 and January 2010. In the next section, the sustainable development policies of the three cases are first introduced. Subsequently, the results of the comparative analysis are presented in an analytically informed way, structured by the three mechanisms of transnational communication. Conclusions are drawn in a final section.

Results of the analysis

The Sustainable Development Policies of Quebec, North Rhine-Westphalia and Flanders

In Quebec, sustainable development has been on the agenda since 1988, when the government financed the French version of the Brundtland Report. However, it was not until 2003 that a comprehensive sustainable development policy was carried out. Its main elements are the Sustainable Development Act (Assemblée Nationale 2006), the creation of the Sustainable Development Commissioner within the office of the Auditor General of Quebec, and the government's Sustainable Development Strategy (Gouvernement du Québec 2007). The Strategy, which is translated into about 140 Sustainable Development Action Plans by all governmental departments and public organisms, defines 29 objectives in nine themes (ranging from sustainable production and consumption to addressing demographic changes).

In North Rhine-Westphalia, a coalition of Socialists and Greens established the state-wide Agenda 21 project, called "Agenda 21 NRW", to institutionalize sustainable development. The process, conducted between 2000 and 2005, was based on an extensive consultation of citizens and stakeholder groups, aimed at making sustainable development concrete through a series of projects. It was supported by an interministerial "green cabinet" and by the Future Council, an advisory body composed of prominent personalities from different societal groups. The Agenda 21 NRW resulted in concrete recommendations for a subsequent sustainable development strategy (MUNLV 2005), but they were never enacted by the coalition of Christian Democrats and Liberals that came into power in 2005.

Flanders and the other Belgian subnational governments are required to conduct a sustainable development policy within the scope of their competences, by an article in the Belgian Constitution adopted in 2007 (Belgische Senaat 2010: §7bis). Flanders had already adopted a sustainable development strategy in 2006, as the first subnational government in Belgium (Vlaamse Regering 2006). Since then, a small unit within the administration of the Flemish Prime Minister – who was given the responsibility for sustainable development in 2004 – oversees the coordination between departments on a series of sustainable development projects (e.g. sustainable housing and living). It also aims at increasing the presence and visibility of Flanders in national, European and global policy forums (van den Brande et al. 2011). The Flemish sustainable development policy was given legal continuity by a Sustainable Development Act in 2008 (Vlaams Parlement 2008).

Promotion of Policy Models by International Organizations

The theoretical framework states that international organizations can play a triggering role with regard to the institutionalization of sustainable development policies at the subnational level. Legitimacy pressures that they exert can be an important factor. Furthermore, international organizations can have an influence on shaping subnational sustainable development policies.

Global summits such as Rio and Johannesburg and key events such as the publication of the Brundtland Report have clearly played a role in triggering the institutionalization of sustainable development in our three cases. With regard to Quebec and North Rhine-Westphalia, the trigger was rather indirect. In Quebec, several structures were established in the late 1980s and in the 1990s as a response to the Rio Summit and the activities of the Brundtland Commission. Those included the establishment of Canada's first Round Table on Environment and Economy, and the creation of the Interministerial Committee on Sustainable Development and of a sustainable development unit within the Environment Ministry. When the Quebec Liberals came to power in 2003 and decided to establish a sustainable development policy, those foundations allowed for a sound institutionalization. In North Rhine-Westphalia, the process of establishing the state-wide Agenda 21 followed a similar track. The plan was initiated by the Green party in 2000 – after several years of debate and bargaining with its Socialist coalition partner – and fuelled by bottom-up initiatives (interviewees). The latter were all stimulated by the Rio Summit, for instance the numerous Local Agenda 21 initiatives (and the establishment of a horizontal agency to support them), or the publication of the authoritative report *Zukunftsfähiges Deutschland* (Sustainable Germany) by the North Rhine-Westphalia-based Wuppertal Institute (Kern et al. 2007; interviewees). In short, both in Quebec and North Rhine-Westphalia international developments laid some important foundations for a sustainable development policy, but did not directly trigger the institutionalization of sustainable development. In Flanders, the triggering role was much more direct. In 2003, Flemish officials launched the initiative of an informal working group on sustainable development. The working group was meant in part to coordinate international sustainable development activities and resulted from the activities at the Johannesburg Summit, where a large Flemish delegation (including the Environment Minister) was present. In addition, the Flemish government had been actively involved in the Belgian Presidency of the EU in the second half of 2001, when the Johannesburg Summit was prepared and the member states were negotiating the first EUSDS. The institutionalization of sustainable development in Flanders was thus directly triggered by international developments, especially by the momentum created by the Johannesburg Summit. Yet an intervening factor was the composition of the ruling coalition between 1999 and 2004. That included the Green party, which attached particular importance to the sustainable development agenda and invested many resources in active participation at Johannesburg (interviewees).

The data of the three cases suggest that the involvement of subnational entities in international governance processes is a key factor explaining which processes can have a triggering role. The earliest influence is visible in Quebec, where the government actively participated in the activities of the Brundtland Commission (for example by financing the first official French translation of the Brundtland Report) and has been present at both the Rio and Johannesburg Summits. North Rhine-Westphalia was influenced mostly by Rio, which was attended by North Rhine-Westphalian representatives. Flanders, in contrast, was not influenced until Johannesburg. That is explained by the fact that the Belgian subnational governments only gained the constitutional opportunity to be involved in multilateral decision-making after the state reform of 1993.[10]

International organizations can exert legitimacy pressures on governments to adopt certain policies. Those legitimacy pressures are manifestly observable in

Quebec and Flanders, which have both issued a sustainable development strategy as one of the cornerstones of their sustainable development policies. Those strategies explicitly invoke the UN commitments on "national" sustainable development strategies as the reason behind their adoption (Gouvernement du Québec 2004: 12; Vlaamse Regering 2006: 14). In the Flemish discourse, in addition, the EU framework and the engagement made in the Gauteng Declaration are frequently emphasized (Leterme 2004: 6; Vlaamse Regering 2006: 16, 31; interviewees). In contrast, those legitimacy pressures by international organizations are not observed in the North Rhine-Westphalian policy. Rather the impression was that the Agenda 21 NRW sprouted from the bottom up (Landtag NRW 1997; interviewees). The difference seems to be explained by the attitude towards the international level and the presence of a territorial identity. North Rhine-Westphalia is a subnational government without a strong identity. Quebec and Flanders, in contrast, have strong territorial identities and frequently express the ambition to manifest those identities at the international level (Paquin 2004). We argue that, as a consequence, they are susceptible to legitimacy pressures exerted by international organizations. Through compliance with international commitments, they thus legitimize their presence in a certain international community.

When it comes to policy content, the influence of summits and international organizations through the dissemination of guidelines, best practices or other kinds of information varies. The definition of sustainable development in all three cases is affected by the Brundtland formulation and the three pillar model promoted in Rio. In Quebec, moreover, the Sustainable Development Act defines 16 principles which need to be taken into account by the Quebec administration. The principles are said to be Quebec's response to the 27 principles enshrined in the Rio Declaration (Gouvernement du Québec 2004: 21).[11] The goals of Quebec's sustainable development policy mostly focus on the domestic context. Yet with regard to certain policy instruments, concrete influence is noticeable in the form of lesson-drawing from international organizations (see below). Also the Flemish case bears clear signs of international influences on policy content, albeit on a more abstract level. The Flemish policy is founded on five of the Rio principles (Vlaamse Regering 2006: 35). Furthermore, the Flemish sustainable development strategy is centred around seven themes, which are a literal translation of the challenges distinguished in the first EUSDS. Flanders is very receptive to policy developments coming from the EU level (see below). The Flemish government has also developed three reports with sustainable development indicators borrowed from Eurostat (Studiedienst van de Vlaamse Regering 2006, 2008, 2009), but those indicators, surprisingly, are not related to the themes or goals of its strategy. Global summits and EU documents thus play a significant role in offering a strategic framework for the Flemish policy, but they do not have a substantive impact on concrete policy content. The international influence on the policy content in North Rhine-Westphalia seems to have been minimal. While the idea of "bringing Rio home" is prevalent, references to Brundtland or Johannesburg are not found. The EUSDS did not seem to have had any impact either. That is partly explained by the timing of the North Rhine-Westphalian Agenda 21, but it could also be due to a general German culture of not according a large role to the EU unless very specific (hard law) policy issues are at stake (Niestroy 2005: 152–153).

Policy Copying

With regard to lesson-drawing, the case of Quebec is the only one that accounts for a real effort towards learning from other experiences. With regard to the design of the set of policy instruments for sustainable development, it is frequently emphasized in the policy discourse that Quebec's approach was distilled from foreign experiences (Gouvernement du Québec 2004: 12; interviewees). The major sources for lesson-drawing were other Canadian provinces, countries (including the Canadian federal government) and international organizations. The most substantive lessons were drawn from the Canadian federal government. For instance, the position of the Sustainable Development Commissioner was copied from it. With regard to lesson-drawing from international organizations, Quebec's sustainable development indicators were influenced by the work of the UN, the OECD and the EU (interviewees). That is a remarkable finding, since it shows that a government does not need to be a member of an international organization (in this case the EU) in order to be influenced by it. This type of influence is not captured by statistical studies on policy convergence, in which the membership of an international organization is usually one of the major variables (for instance Holzinger et al. 2008: 557). Although Quebec learned from policy models promoted by international organizations and drew lessons from foreign experiences, the government always emphasizes that it wants to do better. That fits into the prominent discourse on leadership of the Quebec government. With regard to sustainable development and related issues such as climate change, Quebec is increasingly profiling itself as a leader in North America and as an example to learn from (Gouvernement du Québec 2004: 6, 2006: 1; interviewees).

In the cases of Flanders and North Rhine-Westphalia, interviews and policy documents show no sign of lesson-drawing. Flanders could have copied elements of the Belgian federal sustainable development policy, which was institutionalized in 1997, but it did not, because that policy is generally perceived as a failure in Flanders (interviewees). In North Rhine-Westphalia, it was frequently emphasized that the government took an initiative in the absence of federal leadership on sustainable development (Landtag NRW 1998), that the policy of the red–green government was different from that of certain other German states (dominated by Christian Democrat governments) and that some of its features were "without precedent" (MUNLV 2005: 9).

Instances of policy emulation or "symbolic imitation" were not prominent in the analysis. Yet it is worth repeating how the thematic challenges of the EUSDS were "blindly" appropriated by the Flemish sustainable development strategy. In general, references to global and European commitments are commonplace in Belgian politics, because it is easier to agree on external requirements than to rely on intra-Belgian negotiations (see also Niestroy 2005: 77, 97). Especially the EU has a strong normative power, meaning that what the EU says or does is rarely criticized or even questioned by Belgian politicians – unlike in many other EU member states (Happaerts et al. 2012). Flanders is thus very receptive to EU policy-making.

Networking Activities

Quebec, North Rhine-Westphalia and Flanders are among the subnational governments that are most active in various networking activities. Networking can be done through involvement in decision-making within multilateral organizations. All three cases display efforts to be present in multilateral decision-making. Flanders has the easiest access through intra-state routes, as its presence in Belgian delegations to international meetings is constitutionally guaranteed (Van den Brande et al. 2011: 73). Quebec has the biggest difficulties in gaining access and needs to rely most on routes that bypass the Canadian government if it wants to be present at multilateral meetings (interviewees). Furthermore, all three cases are active participants in transnational networks of subnational governments. Those networks offer subnational governments direct access to multilateral organizations – in contrast to being part of a national delegation. In addition, they have a strong internal dimension focused on information-sharing, policy learning and joint problem-solving (Happaerts et al. 2010b). For instance, the three cases are members of the Network of Regional Governments for Sustainable Development (nrg4SD). Nrg4SD was set up following the event of subnational governments at the Johannesburg Summit which resulted in the Gauteng Declaration (see above).[12] However, in the three cases examined, no tangible result of networking was found with regard to the three governments' sustainable development policies. Interviewees confirm that, although networking activities offer many benefits to subnational governments (e.g. gaining contacts with other governments and access to multilateral decision-making), their impact on domestic policies is actually quite rare.

Comparative Patterns and Conclusions

International developments clearly play a key role in triggering sustainable development policies at the subnational level. In this process, global summits and major events, in other words the three milestones of Brundtland, Rio and Johannesburg, were much more important than the day-to-day activities of international organizations. The analysis presented here suggests that the two necessary conditions for sustainable development to truly gain ground as a consequence of international influence, are the involvement of the subnational governments in international decision-making (see above), and the presence of political will. Indeed, in all of our cases the capacity of a certain political actor was proved essential. In the European cases, that political actor was the Green party. In Quebec, the return to power of the Liberals in 2003 was the key moment. Moreover, the attitude of subnational governments towards international policy-making and their receptiveness for international influences play a decisive role. Especially subnational governments with a strong identity are susceptible to legitimacy pressures produced by international organizations and events. That is why Quebec and Flanders have issued a sustainable development strategy, a typical *national* instrument, and why North Rhine-Westphalia places more emphasis on the idea that the state's Agenda 21, which is rather a *local* instrument, sprouted from bottom-up initiatives.

While international events have largely triggered subnational policies, their influence in shaping the content of those policies is less uniform. We notice the greatest impact in Quebec, where the will to emerge as a leader has pushed the government to learn from international policy models and best practices. In Flanders, international policy-making only has a framing role, i.e. in the definition of the themes and broad goals of the sustainable development strategy. In North Rhine-Westphalia, where international legitimacy pressures were felt less strongly, the impact on policy content seems minimal. In general, the activities of the UN and the OECD seem less important than the work of the EU. In contrast to the promotion of policy models by international organizations, the two other mechanisms of transnational communication (policy copying and networking) appear less relevant. Only in Quebec is a genuine effort observed to draw lessons from other governments. With regard to networks, a high level of involvement in networking activities is observed in all three cases, but influence on policy content has not taken place. It appears that subnational governments do not invest in such networks with the intention of using them for the benefit of their own internal policies. In shaping the content of subnational sustainable development policies, domestic conditions seem more relevant. Even in the cases where international influence is strong, it mostly remains limited to a strategic level and diminishes when goals and policies become concrete. That finding could be explained by the fact that sustainable development is a meta-policy, and that international influence is less evident at the level of specific policy measures.

Transnational communication has appeared to be a useful perspective to approach this topic. Although it remains hard to distinguish between references to international developments and genuine influences, the use of a qualitative method has allowed for the identification of important explanatory factors. Further research into this topic should analyze international factors in conjunction with those other factors. For instance, the relation between international policy influence and party politics deserves more attention. Moreover, in some cases the territorial identity needs to be taken into account. Further research could also focus on the interplay between the subnational and the national level, and on the specific competences allocated to the subnational governments. While international developments clearly play the key triggering role, those national contexts could help to explain specific policy contents.

Although global policy documents on sustainable development largely ignore subnational governments, their message does resonate at the subnational level. Subnational governments feel concerned about global problems such as sustainable development and they respond to the international call for action. The largest resonance has come from the global summits of Rio and Johannesburg. Although their influence can be belated or indirect, their impact is real. This finding hints at the importance of the future Rio +20 Summit in Brazil in 2012, the successor of the Rio and Johannesburg Summits. A new momentum for sustainable development could trigger other initiatives at the subnational level and become a new milestone in the pursuit of sustainable development.

Acknowledgements

This research was funded by the Flemish Policy Research Centre for Sustainable Development (www.steunpuntDO.be). A previous version was presented at the 2010 convention of the International Studies Association, 17–20 February, at New Orleans. The authors would like to thank Michele Betsill, and three anonymous referees of this journal, for their helpful comments.

Notes

1. Although in many countries subnational governments are referred to as "regions", we reserve the term "region(al)" to denote the level of governance above the nation-state, for example the EU, as is common in international relations theory and the literature on global governance.
2. We identify the presence of a sustainable development policy by a high-level executive decision made by the government to institutionalize sustainable development in its policy-making. A *governmental policy* is understood as an intentional course of action or inaction designed by governmental bodies and officials, that consists of a set of interrelated decisions concerning the selection of goals and the means of achieving them, in dealing with a problem or matter of concern (Adolino and Blake 2001: 10; Howlett and Ramesh 2003: 5–8). *Policy content* comprises policy goals and policy instruments, but in this case also the interpretation of sustainable development.
3. Policy convergence studies are closely related to other theoretical traditions, such as policy learning, policy diffusion and policy transfer. Those concepts focus more on processes, while the concept of policy convergence is centred more on outcomes (Knill 2005). However, the mechanisms that those different traditions describe, are to a large extent similar.
4. According to Snyder (cited in Trubek et al. 2005: 1), *soft law* refers to the "rules of conduct which in principle have no legally binding force but which nevertheless may have practical effects". Abbott and Snidal (2000: 421) define *hard law*, in contrast, as "legally binding obligations that are precise (or can be made precise through adjudication or the issuance of detailed regulations) and that delegate authority for interpreting or implementing the law".
5. After the Rio Declaration defined 27 policy principles for sustainable development, many authors have developed lists and prioritizations of principles. Bruyninckx (2006: 268–269) argues that five principles have achieved a large consensus: horizontal and vertical policy integration (between different policy domains, and among different levels of policy-making), equity, intergenerational solidarity (the need for a long-term perspective), the internalization of social and environmental costs, and participatory policy-making.
6. After sustainable development came on the OECD agenda in 1997 (Eppel 1999: 41), the issue has been discussed within various formats with different mandates. The current setting, the AMSDE, was established in 2004.
7. Those are combating poverty and social exclusion; dealing with the economic and social implication of an ageing society; limiting climate change and increase use of clean energy; addressing threats to public health; managing natural resources more responsibly; and improving the transport system and land-use management (European Commission 2002).
8. According to a recently developed index by Hooghe et al. (2008), Quebec, Flanders and North Rhine-Westphalia score 15, 13 and 12 respectively (out of a maximum of 15) on the degree of self-rule. That measures the autonomy subnational governments have with regard to policy-making in their own jurisdictions.
9. The list of interviewees can be obtained from the authors.
10. Part of the reform was the adoption of the "in foro interno, in foro externo" principle, according to which the Belgian subnational governments are permitted to carry out foreign policies for those policy subjects for which they are internally competent. That implies, inter alia, that they can take part in the national delegation to international negotiations (van den Brande et al. 2011: 73).
11. Indeed, ten of the 16 principles bear very close resemblance to the Rio principles, while six others appear to have been added to accommodate domestic priorities, for example subsidiarity or protection of cultural heritage.
12. Flanders was a founding member of nrg4SD and is still one of its most active members (Happaerts et al. 2010a: 136). North Rhine-Westphalia joined the network shortly after its creation, but withdrew as a result of a shift of government in 2005 (Happaerts et al. 2010a: 140). Quebec joined nrg4SD in 2010.

References

Abbott, K. W. and Snidal, D., 2000, Hard and soft law in international governance. *International Organization*, **54**(3), pp. 421–456.
Adolino, J. R. and Blake, C. H., 2001, *Comparing Public Policies: Issues and Choices in Six Industrialized Countries* (Washington, DC: CQ Press).
Annual Meeting of Sustainable Development Experts (AMSDE), 2009, *Horizontal Sustainable Development Programme in the Post-2010 Period* (Paris: OECD).
Assemblée Nationale, 2006, *Loi sur le développement durable (Projet de loi n° 118)* (Québec: Éditeur officiel du Québec).
Belgische, Senaat, 2010, *De Belgische Grondwet* [cited 5 May 2010]. Available at http://www.senate.be/doc/const_nl.html
Bennett, A., 2004, Case study methods: design, use, and comparative advantages, in: D. F. Sprinz and Y. Wolinsky-Nahmias (Eds) *Models, Numbers and Cases. Methods for Studying International Relations* (Ann Arbor: The University of Michigan Press), pp. 19–55.
Bennett, C. J., 1988, Different processes, one result: the convergence of data protection policy in Europe and the United States. *Governance*, **1**(4), pp. 415–441.
Bennett, C. J., 1991, Review article: What Is policy convergence and what causes it? *British Journal of Political Science*, **21**(4), pp. 215–233.
Brans, M., Facon, P. and Hoet, D., 2003, *Beleidsvoorbereiding in een lerende overheid. Stand van zaken in en uitdagingen voor de Belgische federale overheid* (Gent: Academia Press).
Bruyninckx, H., 2006, Sustainable development: the institutionalization of a contested policy concept, in: M. M. Betsill, K. Hochstetler and D. Stevis (Eds) *Palgrave Advances in International Environmental Politics* (Houndmills: Palgrave Macmillan), pp. 265–298.
Council of the European Union, 2006, *Review of the EU Sustainable Development Strategy (EU SDS) – Renewed Strategy* (Brussels: Council of the European Union).
Eppel, J., 1999, Sustainable development and environment: a renewed effort in the OECD. *Environment, Development and Sustainability*, **1**, pp. 41–83.
European Commission, 2002, *A European Union Strategy for Sustainable Development* (Luxembourg: Office for Official Publications of the European Communities).
Gauteng Declaration, 2002, Johannesburg. Available at http://www.nrg4sd.org
George, A. L. and Bennett, A., 2005, *Case Studies and Theory Development in the Social Sciences* (Cambridge, MA and London: MIT Press).
Gouvernement du Québec, 2004, Plan de développement durable du Québec. Document de consultation, Bibliothèque nationale du Québec, Québec.
Gouvernement du Québec, 2006, Plan d'action 2006-2012. Le Québec et les changements climatiques. Un défi pour l'avenir, Ministère du Développement durable, de l'Environnement et des Parcs, Québec.
Gouvernement du Québec, 2007, Un projet de société pour le Québec. Stratégie gouvernementale de développement durable 2008-2013, Bibliothèque et Archives nationales du Québec, Québec.
Hanf, K., 2000, The domestic basis of international environmental agreements, in: A. Underdal and K. Hanf (Eds) *International Environmental Agreements and Domestic Politics. The Case of Acid Rain* (Aldershot: Ashgate), pp. 1–19.
Happaerts, S., van den Brande, K. and Bruyninckx, H., 2010a, Governance for Sustainable Development at the Inter-subnational Level: The Case of the Network of Regional Governments for Sustainable Development (nrg4SD). *Regional & Federal Studies*, **20**(1), 127–149.
Happaerts, S., van den Brande, K. and Bruyninckx, H., 2010b, Subnational governments in transnational networks for sustainable development. *International Environmental Agreements: Politics, Law and Economics*, Online First (DOI 10.1007/s10784-010-9128-4).
Happaerts, S., Schunz, S. and Bruyninckx, H., 2012, Federalism and Intergovernmental Relations. The Multi-level Politics of Climate Change Policy in Belgium. *Journal of Contemporary European Studies*, **20** (forthcoming).
Holzinger, K. and Knill, C., 2005, Causes and conditions of cross-national policy convergence. *Journal of European Public Policy*, **12**(5), pp. 775–796.
Holzinger, K. and Knill, C., 2008, The interaction of competition, co-operation and communication: Theoretical analysis of different sources of environmental policy convergence. *Journal of Comparative Policy Analysis: Research and Practice*, **10**(4), pp. 403–425.

Holzinger, K., Knill, C. and Sommerer, T., 2008, Environmental policy convergence: The impact of international harmonization, transnational communication, and regulatory competition. *International Organization*, **62**, pp. 553–587.

Hooghe, L., Marks, G. and Schakel, A. H., 2008, Special Issue: Regional Authority in 42 Countries, 1950–2006: A Measure and Five Hypotheses. *Regional and Federal Studies*, **18**(2–3).

Howlett, M. and Ramesh, M., 2003, *Studying Public Policy. Policy Cycles and Policy Subsystems* (Don Mills: Oxford University Press).

Jörgensen, K., 2007, Sub-national trans-Atlantic lesson-drawing related to governance for sustainable development, in: M. Jänicke and K. Jacob (Eds) *Environmental Governance in Global Perspective. New Approaches to Ecological and Political Modernisation* (Berlin: Freie Universität Berlin, Department of Political and Social Sciences), pp. 145–164.

Kern, K., Jörgens, H. and Jänicke, M., 2001, The diffusion of environmental policy innovations: A contribution to the globalisation of environmental policy (discussion paper FS II 01-302), Wissenschaftszentrum Berlin für Sozialforschung, Berlin.

Kern, K., Koll, C. and Schophaus, M., 2007, The diffusion of Local Agenda 21 in Germany: Comparing the German federal states. *Environmental Politics*, **16**(4), pp. 604–624.

Kerr, C., 1983, *The Future of Industrial Societies. Convergence or Continuing Diversity?* (Cambridge, MA and London: Harvard University Press).

Knill, C., 2005, Introduction: Cross-national policy convergence: concepts, approaches and explanatory factors. *Journal of European Public Policy*, **12**(5), pp. 764–774.

Kraemer, R. A., Klasing, A. and von Homeyer, I., 2003, The EU Open Method of Co-ordination: Risks and Chances for Environmental Policy. Paper presented at the Conference "Sustainable Development in an Enlarged Union – Linking National Strategies & Strengthening European Coherence", April, Vienna.

Landtag NRW, 1997, CDU: Umweltpakt für NRW. Plenarprotokoll 12/64, 10.09.1997, Landtag Nordrhein-Westfalen, Düsseldorf.

Landtag NRW, 1998, Agenda 21 NRW – Bündnis für Umwelt, Innovation und Beschäftigung. Plenarprotokoll 12/96, 11.09.1998, Landtag Nordrhein-Westfalen, Düsseldorf.

Leterme, Y., 2004, Vlaanderen, het Noorden én het Zuiden duurzaam ontwikkelen. Beleidsnota Duurzame Ontwikkeling 2004–2009, Ministerie van de Vlaamse Gemeenschap, Brussel.

Mahoney, J., 2007, Qualitative methodology and comparative politics. *Comparative Political Studies*, **40**(2), pp. 122–144.

Marks, G., Hooghe, L. and Schakel, A. H., 2008, Measuring regional authority. *Regional and Federal Studies*, **18**(2–3), pp. 111–121.

Meadowcroft, J., 2007, National sustainable development strategies: Features, challenges and reflexivity. *European Environment*, **17**, pp. 152–163.

Meadowcroft, J., 2008, Who is in charge here? Governance for sustainable development in a complex world, in: J. Newig, J.-P. Voß and J. Monstadt (Eds) *Governance for Sustainable Development. Coping with Ambivalence, Uncertainty and Distributed Power* (London and New York: Routledge), pp. 107–122.

Meseguer, C., 2005, Policy learning, policy diffusion, and the making of a new order. *The Annals of the American Academy*, **598**, pp. 67–82.

Ministerium für Umwelt und Naturschutz; Landwirtschaft und Verbraucherschutz des Landes Nordrhein-Westfalen (MUNLV), 2005, Agenda 21 NRW. Gemeinsame Ideen mit Zukunft. Zusammenfassender Bericht des Landesregierung zur Nachhaltigen Entwicklung in NRW, MUNLV, Düsseldorf.

Nedergaard, P., 2006, Which countries learn from which? A comparative analysis of the direction of mutual learning processes within the Open Method of Coordination Committees of the European Union and among the Nordic countries. *Cooperation and Conflict: Journal of the Nordic International Studies Association*, **41**(4), pp. 422–442.

Ng, M. K., 2007, Introduction: Sustainable development and governance in East Asian world cities. *Journal of Comparative Policy Analysis: Research and Practice*, **9**(4), pp. 317–320.

Niestroy, I., 2005, Sustaining sustainability. A benchmark study on national strategies towards sustainable development and the impact of councils in nine EU member states, *EEAC series, Background study no. 2* (Utrecht: Lemma).

O'Toole, L. J., Jr, 2004, Implementation theory and the challenge of sustainable development: The transformative role of learning, in: W. M. Lafferty (Ed.) *Governance for Sustainable Development. The Challenge of Adapting Form to Function* (Cheltenham and Northampton: Edward Elgar), pp. 32–60.

OECD, 2002, *Governance for Sustainable Development. Five OECD Case Studies* (Paris: OECD Publications).
OECD, 2007, *Institutionalising Sustainable Development* (Paris: OECD Publications).
OECD and UNDP, 2002, *Sustainable Development Strategies. A Resource Book*. Ed. B. Dalal-Clayton and S. Bass (London and Sterling, VA: Earthscan Publication Ltd).
Paquin, S., 2004, La paradiplomatie identitaire: le Québec, la Catalogne et la Flandre en relations internationales. *Politique et Sociétés*, **23**(2–3), pp. 203–237.
Rose, R., 1993, *Lesson-drawing in Public Policy. A Guide to Learning Across Time and Space* (Chatham: Chatham House Publishers).
Saurugger, S. and Radaelli, C. M., 2008, The Europeanization of public policies: Introduction. *Journal of Comparative Policy Analysis: Research and Practice*, **10**(3), pp. 213–219.
Snyder, F., 1994, Soft law and institutional practice in the European Community, in: S. Martin (Ed.) *The Construction of Europe: Essays in Honour Emile Noël* (Dordrecht, Boston and London: Kluwer Academic Publishers), pp. 197–225.
Steurer, R. and Martinuzzi, A., 2005, Towards a new pattern of strategy formation in the public sector: first experiences with national strategies for sustainable development in Europe. *Environment and Planning C: Government and Policy*, **23**, pp. 455–472.
Studiedienst van de Vlaamse Regering, 2006, Omgevingsindicatoren duurzame ontwikkeling. Eerste indicatorennota, Studiedienst van de Vlaamse Regering, Brussel.
Studiedienst van de Vlaamse Regering, 2008, Omgevingsindicatoren duurzame ontwikkeling in Vlaanderen 2008. Tweede indicatorennota, Studiedienst van de Vlaamse Regering, Brussel.
Studiedienst van de Vlaamse Regering, 2009, Omgevingsindicatoren duurzame ontwikkeling in Vlaanderen 2009. Derde indicatorennota, Vlaamse overheid, Brussel.
Tanasescu, I., 2006, The political process leading to the development of the EU sustainable development strategy, in: M. Pallemaerts and A. Azmanova (Eds) *The European Union and Sustainable Development* (Brussels: VUBPress), pp. 53–77.
Tews, K., Busch, P.-O. and Jörgens, H., 2003, The diffusion of new environmental policy instruments. *European Journal of Political Research*, **42**, pp. 569–600.
Trubek, D. M., Cottrell, P. and Nance, M., 2005, *"Soft Law", "Hard Law", and European Integration: Toward a Theory of Hybridity*, University of Wisconsin-Madison.
United Nations Conference on Environment and Development (UNCED), 1992, *Agenda 21: Programme of Action for Sustainable Development* (United Nations Department of Public Information).
United Nations Department of Economic and Social Affairs (UNDESA), 2008a, *Commission on Sustainable Development. About CSD*. United Nations [cited 4 January 2008]. Available at http://www.un.org/esa/sustdev/csd/aboutCsd.htm
United Nations Department of Economic and Social Affairs (UNDESA), 2008b, *Indicators of Sustainable Development* [cited 25 September 2008]. Available at http://www.un.org/esa/sustdev/natlinfo/indicators/isd.htm.
United Nations Department of Economic and Social Affairs (UNDESA), 2009, *National Sustainable Development Strategies*. United Nations [cited 14 February 2011]. Available at http://www.un.org/esa/dsd/dsd_aofw_nsds/nsds_index.shtml.
Van den Brande, K., Happaerts, S. and Bruyninckx, H., 2011, Multi-level interactions in a sustainable development context. Different routes for Flanders to decision-making in the UN Commission on Sustainable Development. *Environmental Policy and Governance*, **21**(1), pp. 70–82.
Vlaams Parlement, 2008, Ontwerp van decreet ter bevordering van duurzame ontwikkeling. Tekst aangenomen door de plenaire vergadering, 9 juli 2008, Vlaams Parlement, Brussel.
Vlaamse Regering, 2006, Samen grenzen ver-leggen. Vlaamse strategie duurzame ontwikkeling (fase 1). Ontwerptekst goedgekeurd door de Vlaamse Regering, Vlaamse Regering, Brussel.
Von Homeyer, I., 2002, The impact of enlargement on EU environmental governance. *Intereconomics*, **37**(6), pp. 293–297.
Wilensky, H. L., 1975, *The Welfare State and Equality: Structural and Ideological Roots of Public Expenditures* (Berkeley: University of California Press).
World Commission on Environment and Development (WCED), 1987, *Our Common Future* (New York and Oxford: Oxford University Press).
World Summit on Sustainable Development (WSSD), 2002, *Plan of Implementation of the World Summit on Sustainable Development*, UN Department of Economic and Social Affairs, New York.

Accountable Climate Governance: Dilemmas of Performance Management across Complex Governance Networks

ASIM ZIA and CHRISTOPHER KOLIBA

ABSTRACT *How can accountability be institutionalized across complex governance networks that are dealing with the transboundary pollution problem of mitigating greenhouse gas emissions at multiple spatial, temporal and social scales? To address this question, we propose an accountability framework that enables comparison of the democratic, market and administrative anchorage of actor accountability within and across governance networks. A comparative analysis of performance measures in a sample of climate governance networks is undertaken. This comparative analysis identifies four critical performance management dilemmas in the areas of strategy, uncertain science, integration of multiple scales, and monitoring and verification of performance measures.*

1. Introduction

Innovative forms of public–public, private–private and public–private partnerships that form the basis of inter-organizational networks operating at multiple geographical scales have recently evolved to create a fragmented system of governance of climate change (Bäckstrand 2008; Biermann 2009). These partnerships typically emerge to address "wicked" and complex public policy problems, such as global climate change, fisheries protection (Kooiman 2008) and public infrastructure provision (Vining et al. 2005). A growing number of studies characterize the range of partnerships as "governance networks" (Klijn 1996; Jones et al. 1997; Kickert et al. 1997; Lowndes and Skelcher 1998; Skelcher 2005; Sorensen and Torfing 2005; Torfing 2005; Bogason and Musso 2006; Klijn and Skelcher 2007; Coen and Thatcher 2008; Koliba et al. 2010). A governance network is defined here as relatively stable patterns of coordinated action and resource exchanges involving policy actors crossing different social scales, drawn from the public, private or non-profit sectors and across geographic levels, who interact through a variety of competitive, command and control, cooperative and negotiated arrangements for purposes anchored in one or more facets of the policy stream (Koliba et al. 2010: 60). While inter-disciplinary enthusiasm for the characterization and analysis of governance networks has grown considerably, much more theoretical and empirical work remains to be done to understand how accountability is institutionalized within and across governance networks (Provan and Milward 1995; Bardach and Lesser 1996; Milward 1996; Agranoff and McGuire 2001; Papadopoulos 2003, 2007; Benner et al. 2004; Slaughter 2004; Fredrickson and Fredrickson 2006; May 2007). We assess these accountability and performance management issues in the context of post-Kyoto international climate policy design and address a specific question: How can accountability be institutionalized across governance networks that are dealing with the transboundary pollution problem of mitigating greenhouse gas emissions (GHGs) at multiple spatial, temporal and social scales?

Notwithstanding its significance as a milestone in global environmental policy, the Kyoto Protocol has failed on many accounts in setting up effective and accountable governance mechanisms for reducing GHGs (Cass 2007; Harrison and Sundstrom 2007). Many large emitters of GHGs did not even bother to sign the treaty, as described in terms of the so-called US–China "suicide pact" (Romm 2007). In this paper, we advance the theoretical and empirical research on climate governance through the comparative analysis of accountability in different types of climate change partnerships. Over the last two decades, a variety of network strategies have been devised to address the need to mitigate the factors that are contributing to climate change. In this analysis we argue that the complexity of these governance networks gives rise to a variety of accountability challenges. These challenges are accentuated by the range of public–public, public–private and private–private partnership arrangements that have arisen from these efforts. We argue that each type of partnership arrangement brings with it certain kinds of accountability challenges. However, we also argue that certain accountability challenges confront all forms of international partnership arrangements being devised to mitigate climate change.

In the recent climate change governance literature efforts have been initiated to develop an accountability framework for evaluating the public–public, public–private and private–private climate change governance networks. Bäckstrand (2008) develops a process-based notion of accountability that includes three accountability criteria: (1) transparency; (2) monitoring mechanisms; and (3) representation of stakeholders. While process-based criteria are important components for evaluating accountability of governance networks, it has been suggested in the broader literature on pluralistic concepts of accountability in governance networks that actors (both individuals and organizations) and outcomes should also be considered as important criteria for comparing the institutionalization of accountability in governance networks (Benner et al. 2004). In section 2, we review the relevant literature on the evolution of the concept of accountability for actors, processes and outcomes in complex governance networks and describe important features of an integrative framework that can be used to comparatively analyze accountability mechanisms across governance networks. In particular, we extend Bäckstrand's (2008) process-based model of accountability for climate change governance networks by incorporating the additional criteria of actor to actor accountability predicated on the nature of ties between them, and then relate these accountability ties to more widely adopted outcome-based forms of accountability. We propose a "Governance Network Accountability Framework" to compare democratic, market and administrative anchorages of actor accountability within and across governance networks. In section 3, we undertake a comparative analysis of performance outcome measures in a stratified sample of public–public, public–private and private–private climate governance networks. This comparative analysis identifies four critical international climate policy design dilemmas that confront humanity for institutionalizing accountability in a global climate governance regime. These dilemmas are related to four questions: First, how to develop consistent performance measures when different governance networks propose different measures. Second, how to incorporate scientific uncertainty into performance measures. Third, how to integrate emission entitlements across multiple space-time scales. Fourth, how to monitor and verify performance benchmarks. Finally, in section 4 we discuss the implications of these performance management and accountability dilemmas in the context of "international democracy-deficit", "politics of knowledge" and "intergenerational accountability" to inform the evolving negotiations on designing international climate policy in the post-Kyoto (post-2012) time frame.

2. The Governance Network Accountability Framework

"Accountability is traditionally defined as the obligation to give an account of one's actions to someone else, often balanced by a responsibility of that other to seek an account" (Scott 2006: 175). In essence, accountability structures arise when a certain measure of interdependency exists between those rendering account (hereafter "accountees") and those to whom accounts should be rendered (hereafter "accounters"). In this paper, we discuss governance as a matter of accountability, with feedback taking place as processes of rendering accounts to particular constituencies, relying on certain explicit standards and tacit norms to do so. This feedback effect of communicating performance information from accountees to accounters has also been characterized as an important feature that distinguishes performance *measurement* from performance *management* systems (Kelman 2006). "Performance management is thus seen as a potentially powerful tool to remedy underperformance in government" (Kelman 2006: 394). Applying Kelman's notion of performance management to accountability in governance networks, we assert that network accountability is a system-level construct involving iterative performance feedback loops between accountees and accounters (Koliba et al.

2010, 2011). The performance feedback loops contain the flow of information on performance measures, which include information on inputs, activities and processes, actors, outputs and outcomes across the system.

Behn (2001), Posner (2002) and Page (2004) have all noted the accountability challenges associated with governance networks, recognizing their complexity and the potential competing aims inherent to the organizations operating within them. Mashaw (2006: 118) calls for the comparison of accountability regimes operating within and across network structures in order to "evaluate their differential capacities, and perhaps articulate hybrid regimes that approximate optimal institutional designs". In cases where a governance network is comprised of non-profit and for-profit organizations working with governments (e.g. most public–private partnerships), the accountability regimes historically ascribed to governments are not sufficient. According to Scott (2006: 190), "conventional accountability narratives, emphasizing ex-post and hierarchical forms of accountability, with only very limited reach beyond the state actors, are unable to support the burden of providing a narrative of accountability that can legitimate governance structures involving diffuse actors and methods".

We present a governance network accountability framework that we have used to study accountability across complex governance networks. Our initial application of this framework focused on the accountability failures found within the response and recovery networks following landfall of Hurricane Katrina in 2005 (Koliba et al. 2011). Within this framework, various state and non-state actors who are perceived as accountees and accounters in governance networks engage in adaptive processes over time to select an evolving set of performance measures. In highly functioning performance management systems, performance outcomes are monitored and verified by some mechanism, some information about which is fed back to accountees and accounters for completing the loop of a performance management system (Moynihan 2008).

We argue that the sustainability of accountability ties within complex governance networks is difficult to accomplish. Radin (2006: 235) warns that, "despite the attractive quality of the rhetoric of the performance movement, one should not be surprised that its clarity and siren call mask a much more complex reality". Performance management is a complicated matter within *individual* organizations, let alone inter-organizational networks. Just what amounts to effective performance within a complex governance network is a matter of perception. It has been noted how performance data and standards come about through the social construction of knowledge that is predicated on a culture of performance fostered within individual organizations (Moynihan 2008) and across complex governance networks (Frederickson and Frederickson 2006; Koliba et al. 2010). Gregory Bateson (1988: 32) has noted that, "the processes of perception are inaccessible; only the products are conscious". Performance data, performance measures and, ultimately, performance management is complicated by the question of whose perceptions matter. We assert that, presumably, accounters are in the best or the most legitimate position to determine what it means for any social entity to "perform" and, presumably, perform effectively.

Many have noted how the shift from a monocentric system of *government* to a polycentric system of *governance* raises complex *actor* accountability challenges

Table 1. Accountability frames for actors in complex governance networks

Accountability frame	Accounters (those "to whom" accounts are rendered)	Relational power	Explicit standards	Implicit norms
Democratic	Elected representatives and courts	Vertical over public sector	Laws, statutes, regulations	Representation of collective interests; policy goals
	Citizens and courts	Horizontal accesses to public sector organizations/ elected officials	Maximum feasible participation; sunshine laws; deliberative forums	Deliberation; consensus; majority rule
	Courts	Vertical legal authority over society	Laws; Statutes; contracts	Precedence; reasonableness; due process; substantive rights
Market	Shareholders/ owners	Vertical over management/ labor	Profit	Efficiency
	Consumers	Horizontal with owners	Consumer law	Affordability; quality; satisfaction
Administrative	Principals; supervisors; bosses	Vertical over agents; subordinates; contractees	Performance measures; administrative procedures; organizational charts	Deference to positional authority; unity of command; span of control
	Partners; peers	Horizontal with peers	Written agreements; decision-making procedures; negotiation regimes	Trust; reciprocity; durability of relationships
	Peers	Horizontal within profession	Codes of ethics; licensure; performance standards	Professional norms; expertise; competence

Source: Adapted from Koliba et al. (2010).

(Behn 2001; Posner 2002; Goldsmith and Eggers 2004; Page 2004; Pierre and Peters 2005; Mashaw 2006; Scott 2006; Mathur and Skelcher 2007). Because it can no longer be assumed that the nation-state possesses the same kind of vertical authority as traditionally ascribed to governments, governing the actors in inter-organizational networks gives rise to new accountability challenges that cannot be simply modeled through conventional mono-centric accountability systems. These challenges arise when nation-states are displaced as central actors, market forces are considered and cooperation and collaboration is recognized as an integral administrative activity.

Table 1 provides an overview of the governance network accountability framework, (Koliba et al. 2010, 2011). The framework is predicated on eight different types of accounters *to whom* accountability must be rendered in a complex governance network that includes actors from government, private and civil society organizations. These accounters, be they elected representatives, citizens, courts, shareholders, consumers, supervisors, professionals or collaborators, are placed in the position of judging the performance of the agents that are being held accountable as accountees. These accountees may come from any number of different kinds of actors. Complex performance management problems arise when accounters prioritize conflicting combinations of policy goals, performance measures and other desired procedures and outcomes in a governance network, placing value on and rendering judgment of performance differently (Gruber 1987; Radin 2006). It is also imperative that accounters are capable of or interested in fulfilling their roles, which in the case of climate governance is a serious problem as a large number of potential accounters are either future generations or non-human species that will face the consequences of climate change under business-as-usual scenarios, as predicted in the IPCC (2007) synthesis report.

Because the governance network accountability framework allows for the mingling of democratic, market and administrative factors, we can view accountability in terms of trade-offs between accountability types – be they trade-offs between democracy and market accountabilities, democracy and administrative accountabilities, or intra-administrative accountabilities, such as those found in trade-offs between bureaucratic–collaborative accountabilities (Koliba et al. 2011).

In the context of climate change mitigation, a governance network's capacity to support or hinder the democratic accountability of its actors hinges on its capacity to be described as "democratically anchored". Sorensen and Torfing (2005: 201) assert that, "governance networks are democratically anchored to the extent that they are properly linked to different political constituencies and to a relevant set of democratic norms that are part of the democratic ethos of society". Democratic anchorage is one of the central governance features of a governance network. However, it has been noted that governance networks that exist at the international scale are confronted with "democratic deficit" because there are no widely accepted, enforceable international democratic norms (Haas 2004). As we consider climate change, international governance needs to be addressed in the light of the network structures that are implicated in certain kinds of climate change mitigation initiatives and the roles that vertical, horizontal and diagonal relations play with regard to the leadership structure and flow of power and authority. Governance thus needs to be understood in the context of the accountability frameworks that persist within each node (or network actor) as well as across the ties forged between accountees and accounters across governance networks. Comparative analysis of different governance networks, especially analysis of their implicit and explicit performance measures and accountability ties, could potentially inform the design of complex policy regimes dealing with transnational pollution control, bio-terrorism, energy security, water sharing and other global public policy problems. Institutionalization of accountability through specific policy designs could be informed by such comparative analyses.

The processes of institutionalizing accountability in governance networks merit special consideration as they explicitly deal with the problem of ensuring procedural fairness in complex situations involving a myriad of private and public sector actors. We believe, as also emphasized by Bäckstrand (2008), three criteria of accountability processes need to be explored: (i) transparency and public provision of information by a governance network is critical for ensuring that accounters are able to access the information in a transparent manner; (ii) monitoring mechanisms ensure whether the governance network has institutionalized monitoring of its stated goals and actions taken to meet those goals; and (iii) representation of stakeholders concerns whether partnerships include government, market and civil society actors. These factors are predicated on the extent to which wide-ranging stakeholder groups participate formally in the network, either as lead or as participating partners (Bäckstrand 2008: 82). We argue that the public, private or non-profit sector characteristics of actors will matter.

Democratic accountability is rendered when elected officials, citizens, courts and interest groups are engaged as stakeholders in a transparent manner with monitoring mechanisms that are trusted by all engaged actors. At the international scale, this calls for the reduction of the "democracy deficit" to enable accountability processes in global climate governance networks. Bäckstrand (2008: 98) presents a comparative analysis of process accountability features for a variety of public–public and public–private climate governance networks. From a governance network accountability framework perspective, these three process criteria – transparency, monitoring and stakeholder representation – may be used to describe the process activities that are adopted to maintain effective accountability ties.

Within effective accountability ties, performance measures are used to ascertain the extent to which explicit standards, such as performance inputs, outputs and outcomes are being met. The definition of what constitutes effective performance measures for a governance network is a critical question to be addressed. There have been some studies conducted that look at the efficacy of network structures in achieving ascribed performance outputs and outcomes (see for example Marsh and Rhodes 1992; Heinrich and Lynn 2000; Koontz et al. 2004; Mingus 2004; Frederickson and Frederickson 2006; Kelman 2006, Rodriguez et al. 2007; Vining et al. 2005). The highly contextual nature of the environments that governance networks operate within, coupled with the highly contextual nature of most of the perceptions of the network actors within the network, render the development of consensus around common definitions of viable network performance measures very difficult to achieve.

This becomes an even more complex problem when performance measures across governance networks are compared and assessed for their accountability regimes. In environmental governance arenas, generally, we hypothesize that governance networks dominated by high greenhouse gas emission countries (i.e. US and China) endeavor to choose performance measures that maintain the status quo (i.e. minimal greenhouse gas abatement). On the other hand, if governance networks give voice to those countries that tend to be victims of the environmental crisis (i.e. African countries and Island nations), the victims tend to choose performance measures that engender maximum feasible change from the status quo (i.e. maximal pollution abatement). Within public–public partnerships, the dominant accountability ties are the elected officials who are responsible for designing and implementing international treaties and protocols. These public–public partnerships are, at least in theory, high in the representation of elected official and citizen interests. Different governance networks are configured with various combinations of high greenhouse gas emitters and those most vulnerable to climate change, for which reason, we postulate that intense conflicts over the choice of performance measures are observed. These performance measures are adaptively updated as performance information flows across governance networks increase, and the science governing the environmental problem matures. In the next section, we apply this theoretical accountability framework to a stratified sample of public–public, public–private and private–private climate governance networks and focus the empirical comparison on their choice of specific performance "outcome" measures vis-à-vis accountability ties of the actors in these different governance networks.

3. Comparative Analysis of Accountability Ties and Performance Outcome Measures across Climate Change Governance Networks

The United Nations Framework Convention on Climate Change (UNFCCC) has driven the international process of addressing climate change mitigation and adaptation at the global scale by relying on the voluntary participation of representative country governments. The UNFCCC process represents an example of a "public–public" governance network. Under the UNFCCC process, the Kyoto Protocol[1] was a first significant step in setting up a global governance regime for reducing GHGs.

From a governance network analysis perspective, there are numerous other public–public, public–private and private–private governance networks that are simultaneously trying to address climate change mitigation and adaptation issues. Some other examples of public–public climate change governance networks include the Asia-Pacific Climate Change Partnership (APP),[2] the International Partnership for the Hydrogen Economy (IPHE),[3] the Carbon Sequestration Leadership Forum (CSLF),[4] Cities for Climate Protection (CCP)[5] and the Clinton Climate Initiative (CCI).[6] Similarly, some "private–private" governance networks addressing climate change include the International Climate Change Partnership (ICCP),[7] the World Business Council for Sustainable Development Climate (WBCSD) Partnerships[8], Combat Climate Change (3C)[9] and the Greenhouse Gas Protocol Initiative (a partnership between World Resources Institute and World Business Council for Sustainable Development).[10] Finally, some examples of "public–private" climate change governance networks include the Renewable Energy Policy Network for 21st Century (REN21),[11] the Renewable Energy and Energy Efficiency Partnership (REEP),[12] Joint Implementation projects (JI) under the Kyoto Protocol (∼170 projects),[13] Clean Development Mechanism (CDM) projects under the Kyoto Protocol (∼1620 projects),[14] World Bank Prototype Carbon Fund (PCF)[15] projects and US EPA's Methane to Markets (M2M)[16] projects. In these examples, regulations, grants and contracts give structure to networks structured through inter-organizational projects or programs.

Table 2. Performance measures (activities and expected outcomes) and their deadlines across sampled climate change governance networks

Type of governance network	Sampled climate governance network	Performance measures	
		Activities and expected outcomes	Deadlines
Private–private	ICCP	Address continued growth of greenhouse gas emissions through mechanisms such as emissions trading. Business and industry expertise are important parts of this process. Technological innovation is crucial	Vague
	3C	Businesses cooperate to reduce emissions for a stable climate by putting a price on carbon emissions, setting minimum efficiency standards, encouraging sustainable forestry and agriculture, and pushing low carbon technologies	Vague
Public–public	UNFCCC	Countries coming together to consider what can be done to reduce global warming and to cope with whatever temperature increases are inevitable. The Kyoto Protocol sets binding targets for 37 industrialized countries and the European community for reducing greenhouse gas emissions by an average of five per cent against 1990 levels over a five-year period. Kyoto mechanisms include emissions trading, Clean Development Mechanism (CDM) and Joint Implementation (JI)	Reductions must be met over the five-year period 2008–2012
	APP	Overall goal is to accelerate the development and deployment of clean energy technologies. There are sub-goals regarding energy security, national air pollution reduction, and climate change. The Partnership will focus on expanding investment and trade in cleaner energy technologies, goods and services in key market sectors	Vague

(*continued*)

Table 2. (*Continued*)

Type of governance network	Sampled climate governance network	Performance measures	
		Activities and expected outcomes	Deadlines
Public–private	CDM Yiyang Xiushan Hydropower Project, P.R. China	Reduce CO_2 emissions by 243,043 metric tons per year by using a consolidated methodology for grid-connected electricity generation from renewable sources	Crediting period of 05/10/09–05/09/16 with lifetime of project lasting 33 years from 08/18/05
	Casa Armando Guillermo Prieto - Wastewater treatment facility for a Mezcal distillery	Reduce CO_2 emissions by 15,153 metric tons per year by using thermal energy with or without electricity and methane recovery in wastewater treatment	Crediting period of 05/07/09–05/06/16 with lifetime of project lasting 25 years from 4/23/07
	Heilongjiang Chemical N_2O Abatement Project	Reduce CO_2 emissions by 279,319 metric tons per year by implementing catalytic reduction of N_2O inside the ammonia burner of nitric acid plants	Crediting period of 05/07/09–05/06/16 with lifetime of project lasting 21 years from 07/17/07
	JI Timisoara Combined Heat and Power Rehabilitation for CET Sud location	Upgrade the existing heat production plant CET Timisoara Sud with cogeneration capacity	Project lifetime is 20 years as of September 2005
	Debrecen landfill gas mitigation project	Installation and operation of a new landfill gas collection system. Reduction in CO_2 emissions by 413,866 metric tons over crediting period	Crediting period of 01/01/08–12/31/12, with lifetime of project lasting 10 years from 11/30/07
	Revamping and Modernization of the Alchevsk Steel Mill	Replacement of technology and upgrade of all major components of iron and steel making and finishes processes	Crediting period of 01/01/08–12/31/12, with lifetime of project lasting 40 years from 08/24/05

The governance network accountability framework provides a coherent theoretical tool to compare the design of accountability and performance management systems across public–public, private–private and public–private climate change governance networks. More specifically, we apply this integrative framework to a sub-sample of two governance networks for each of the three governance network types: private–private; public–public and public–private, as shown in Table 2. We coded performance outcome measures from the documents released by these different types of climate governance networks. The third column in Table 2 shows a summary of coded "Performance Outcome and Activity Measures" for the sampled governance networks and their temporal deadlines specified by these governance networks.

We then undertook comparative interpretive analysis (Yanow 1999) of these three governance network types by specific performance outcome and activity measures agreed upon by the sampled governance networks. From this comparative interpretive analysis we derived four performance management dilemmas that currently bedevil the institutionalization of accountability in global climate governance. We call these dilemmas of strategy, uncertain science, integrating multiple scales and verification, each of which is described below along with the findings of comparative interpretive analysis on the performance outcome measures across these governance networks shown in Table 2. We postulate that a meta-level resolution of these dilemmas is critical for institutionalizing accountability in global climate governance; however, there are no global level institutions in place to enable this kind of meta-level resolution across governance networks. The implications of these dilemmas on post-Kyoto international climate policy design are discussed in section 4.

3.1. Dilemma of Strategy

How to develop consistent performance measures when different governance networks propose different measures, such as GHG/year, GHG/BTUs[17] and GHG/capita?

At the international scale, we find that each GHG polluting nation is caught up in proposing a set of performance measures that, by definition, either let that nation free ride or incur minimal abatement costs. Under the UNFCCC negotiated Kyoto Protocol, which represents a public–public type of international governance network dominated by GHG high emission countries, "grandfathering" performance measures were adopted despite calls for GHG/capita-based performance measures by developing countries which are expected to bear the most adverse impacts of climate change (IPCC 2007). The UNFCCC-based public–public governance network was thus co-opted by the strategic goals of rich developed countries into adopting a grandfathered performance measure (reduce GHG/year emissions by a target year below certain baseline year). Interpretive analysis of recent Conference of Parties (COP 15) negotiations in Copenhagen and COP 16 negotiations in Cancun for a post-Kyoto UNFCCC-based international treaty shows that grandfathering-based performance goals are also being considered for a post-Kyoto treaty.

As shown in Table 2, for the public–public climate change governance network of the UNFCCC, a performance outcome measure of reducing GHG/year by ~ 5 per cent below the 1990 level by 2008–12 was set as a binding commitment for Annex I parties that ratified the Protocol. This performance measure is an example of "grandfathering", which has been compared in the literature with some other performance outcome measures, such as GHG/capita that was not adopted by the UNFCCC governance network (Najam and Sagar 1998; Biermann 2005). The choice of performance outcome measures within this public–public governance network is thus fraught with political maneuvering and strategizing by network actors. This is in the interest of rich industrialized countries, which happen to be the major GHG polluters as well, to choose a performance outcome measure that by definition minimizes their GHG emission reduction burdens. Grandfathered targets agreed upon in the Kyoto Protocol, as compared to the GHG/capita type of performance measures, apparently do exactly what serves the interest of rich industrialized countries. The accountability analysis of the UNFCCC governance network thus shows that the choice of performance outcome measure is an artifact of political power and scientific knowledge, which overrides ethical concerns of equity raised by developing countries which have consistently argued that GHG/capita performance measure must be chosen by the UNFCCC (Najam et al. 2003; Cass 2007; Pettenger 2007).

In contrast to the UNFCCC governance network, the APP governance network has remained vague in setting any performance outcome measures, as shown in Table 2. The APP in fact argued that there should be no binding performance measures, which again demonstrates the tragedy of the commons as the APP represents the most sizable GHG polluting countries. Similar vagueness is obvious from the performance measures developed by private–private climate change governance networks – ICCP and 3C – shown in Table 2. Under public–private partnerships of CDM and JI case study projects, there are specific performance outcome measures that have typically very long target dates (as shown in Table 2).

Comparative application of the accountability framework across public–public, private–private and public–private type of climate governance networks reveals variegated patterns of performance outcome measure selection that is contingent upon the type of actor configuration in a particular network. We call it a "dilemma of strategy" in setting up performance standards in complex governance networks. This dilemma is, for example, obvious when we consider the APP governance network. After the Bush administration in the US reneged on the US commitment to sign the Kyoto protocol on the pretext that developing countries were not included in it, the US government, in alliance with other countries that consider the UNFCC process as too burdensome and potentially a costlier enterprise, decided to engineer a governance network of the seven highest GHG polluting countries that they call the APP. These seven countries are responsible for at least 50 per cent of current global GHG emissions. The performance outcome measure that the APP proposes is no binding commitments to reduce GHG emissions. So the APP does not want a performance standard at all. When criticized for this, some APP leaders called for GHG/BTU and BTU/GDP (i.e. intensity-based) performance standards, which are practically business-as-usual scenarios of growing GHG emissions in the atmosphere.

Dilemma of strategy thus demonstrates that different governance networks, based upon the differential goals and accountability frames of accountees and accounters in the governance networks, propose performance standards in tragedy of the commons situations that minimize actor level costs of pollution abatement. When there are multiple governance networks in public, private and public–private domains with variegated performance outcome measures, it becomes very difficult to hold any governance network accountable on a common performance outcome measure because they do not agree with a common performance outcome measure to begin with. A more serious and intractable horn of the dilemma concerns the fact that the accounters for multi-actor configurations in different governance networks are not interested in holding network actors responsible on some unified performance outcome measures due to the inherent nature of their value and goal conflicts or, in the case of future generations, mere absence of actors. Furthermore, the inherent trade-offs that persist in complex governance networks may be viewed in terms of competing perspectives from the elected officials of national governments in public–public governance networks or as trade-offs between democratic accountabilities and market accountabilities in public–private partnerships.

3.2. Dilemma of Uncertain Science: How to Incorporate Scientific Uncertainty in Policy Design

In this unfolding tragedy of the commons, actors across various climate governance networks have strategically deployed scientific uncertainty to their advantage. In the UNFCCC governance network, for example, the controversy of whether to consider existing forests as carbon stocks or not, and by how much, provides an interesting case study of this dilemma (e.g. Hirsch et al. 2011). While there is great scientific uncertainty about the carbon uptake functions of forest systems in evolving climatic conditions, some network actors with large standing forests argued for inclusion of forests as carbon sinks. However, other network actors argued against the inclusion of forests, citing scientific research showing diminishing carbon uptake in higher CO_2 concentrations. Inclusion or exclusion of forests as carbon sinks presents one example of the dilemma of uncertain science, as it might be too late to take policy action for or against deforestation by the time scientific uncertainty is reduced.

Another example of this dilemma concerns the differential weights that are accorded to different GHGs based on their CO_2 equivalency. While the UNFCCC aimed at standardizing these weights, there has been a severe critique of the methods used to standardize the weights (IPCC 2007). Some private–private governance networks have expressed their concern that industrial gasses are accorded much higher weights, while some other governance networks have argued the opposite, i.e. the industrial gases should have been accorded even higher weights due to their higher radiation potential. Additional questions about "latent" GHG emissions and their inclusion in the UNFCCC basket of post-Kyoto gasses remain largely unaddressed as well.

The scientific uncertainty about climatic change impacts and how it translates into different positions, especially trade-offs between mitigation and adaptation, pose another set of problems in setting up accountability mechanisms. For some governance networks, increased investments in adaptation strategies will entail higher benefits for future generations of citizens (accounters in our accountability model). Other networks argue for higher investment in mitigation strategies. The lack of scientific certainty about the nature and extent of climate impacts poses daunting challenges for designing efficient and fair policies at multiple generational time scales.

From the comparative perspective, the dilemma of uncertain science may be viewed in terms of trade-offs between professional accountability and either elected official or market accountabilities across various types of governance networks. A country's failure to take climate change seriously may be fueled by allusions to a scientific uncertainty that is being tied to climate change models. In the midst of this scientific uncertainty, debates over how to value carbon sinks may be exploited by certain stakeholders as a lack of professional consensus in the scientific community.

3.3. Dilemma of Integrating Multiple Scales: How to Integrate Emission Entitlements across Multiple Space–Time Scales

Climate change mitigation actions are being proposed at multiple space–time scales by different governance networks, which imply that the accountability challenges of measuring their respective performances also multiply with multi-scalar mitigation actions. Double, or even triple accounting of the same "mitigation action" is the biggest concern here. Consider the example of a wind turbine installed in a small town in Europe, for which a city in the CCP governance network claims credit, a firm in ICCP claims credit, and a country in UNFCCC claims credit. In fact, in some voluntary air travel GHG emission offset systems, gross instances of double or triple accounting have been reported for the same set of carbon sinks that are used as GHG emission offsets.

Resolving this dilemma at the inter-governance network level will pose a huge challenge as each governance network and its respective actors have the incentives to undertake double or triple accounting. There has been some movement towards unifying these cross-scalar mitigation activities in terms of a consistent scale, but this remains a huge challenge on many fronts. Consider the example of a huge multinational corporation operating in many countries. Should its mitigation actions in countries where it operates be ascribed to host countries or the country of the corporation's headquarters? Given the typical accounter goals of profit maximization in private–private climate governance networks, we postulate that public–public or public–private partnerships might be more effective in reducing multiple accounting of the same emission reduction credits. In purely private–private partnerships, there is essentially no democratic accountability and very little, if any, market accountability driving voluntary compliance of mutually determined performance measures.

Different governance networks operate at different geographic and social scales, as shown in Table 2. The question of multi-scalar accountability may be viewed as trade-offs between accounters and accountees at these different geographic and social scales. The public–private partnerships developed for CDM and JI projects operate in specific geographical conditions and temporal scales that are different from the performance outcome measures agreed upon in public–public and private–private types of governance networks. Integration of performance outcome measures across these multiple space–time scales is, perhaps, impossible, while issues of double or triple accounting pose daunting challenges for comparing "observed" performance outcomes claimed by different governance networks.

3.4. Dilemma of Monitoring and Verification: How to Monitor and Verify Performance Benchmarks

Monitoring and verification of claimed mitigation actions poses another set of challenges. There has been a movement towards third party verification of emission reductions (e.g. growing California Climate Action Registry Contracts). In a third party verification system, accounters hire an independent third party to verify whether accountees have actually reduced the claimed emissions. Despite the proliferation of third party verification systems, there are some monitoring and verification issues that cannot be easily resolved. Consider the example of CDM public–private partnerships established under the flexibility mechanisms of the Kyoto protocol. There is no consensus about how to establish baseline "reforestation" or "afforestation" scenarios in developing countries that are eligible to claim CDM-based emission reduction credits because they are so dependent upon how one calculates baseline scenarios. Some critics argue that CDM has provided perverse incentives to many developing countries to enhance their GHG emission rates so that they could receive more GHG emission reduction credits when lower emission rates (as opposed to exaggerated baseline rates) are verified. Similar challenges exist for the REDD+(Reduced Emissions from Degradation and Deforestation) policy mechanism negotiated in Cancun COP 16.

Verification of some GHGs is relatively easy (e.g. some industrial gasses), while other GHGs pose persistent dilemmas. Point sources of GHG emissions (e.g. industries) can be easily tracked, but non-point sources (e.g. transportation systems) are not easily amenable to verification. Accurate measurement of transportation activities and transportation behaviors poses age-old modeling dilemmas. The variance of estimates tends to be high. There are also strategic problems with respect to some transportation activities, e.g. military-based transportation operations are typically not reported. Accurate quantities of energy consumed by military activities are not verifiable due to strategic security problems with revealing the nature and extent of these activities. Overall, the governance networks need to develop the capacity to become more effective in verification processes, especially third party certifications. However, as recently evidenced during the Copenhagen negotiations of COP 15, GHG polluting countries such as China refused to institutionalize third party verification mechanisms because they considered these independent verification measures as "infringements on their sovereignty".

The dilemma of verification is fueled by some of the same trade-offs found in the dilemma of uncertain science. Gaps in the scientific models may be exploited by detractors of climate change, thereby undermining the authority of professional accountability. Scientific verification is also confounded by a range of administrative burdens that accompany verification processes. Which actors have the administrative authority to collect, analyze and verify data? To what extent should self-reported data be accepted? These challenges suggest that the administrative lines of accountability (both bureaucratic and collaborative) are hard to clarify and put into practice. These questions speak to the authenticity of administrative accountabilities that exist in climate change mitigation governance networks.

4. Accountability Framework and Post-Kyoto Climate Governance Regime

We have demonstrated that climate change mitigation strategies are perceived to be undertaken by a large variety of governance networks that present particular accountability challenges. The inherent complexity of climate change governance is fueled by a range of perverse incentives that lead to global "tragedy of commons" for economically vulnerable actors as well as future generations. Our comparative analysis reveals that less transparent processes, ineffective monitoring mechanisms, inadequate stakeholder representation and lack of consistent performance outcome measures across governance networks gives rise to at least four chronic dilemmas that require meta-level resolutions for institutionalizing inter-governance network level accountability mechanisms. We call these the dilemmas of strategy, uncertain science, multiple scale integration and verification.

If the post-Kyoto climate governance regime that is now being negotiated across a range of governance networks attains the same performance levels as prior efforts, human civilization is very likely to initiate a dangerous spiral of positive feedback loops of GHGs under business-as-usual scenarios. The resulting cascading effects will be difficult to reverse due to atmospheric complexity and non-linear lagged effects (IPCC 2007). More recent climate science, since the fourth assessment IPCC report, presents an even grimmer picture (Raupach et al. 2007; The Copenhagen Diagnosis 2009). It is critical that a post-Kyoto climate governance regime incorporates accountability-driven design features which ensure that anthropogenic GHGs stay well within planetary resilience, prior to the initiation of dangerous positive feedback loops.

If humanity remains trapped in these dilemmas, worst-case climate change scenarios are very likely to materialize. We have argued that this trap need not be inevitable. The climate change governance networks, at both the political and strategic levels, could design governance networks by drawing on the systematic accountability frameworks presented here. Transparent processes need to be promoted to enable cooperative resolutions of these dilemmas. However, this will require meta-level comparative policy analytical thinking and political resolution. The reduction of "democracy deficit" in international/global governance networks could be the first step in this journey. Acknowledgement of inter-generational accountability issues could be another step. The challenges of asymmetric power and knowledge distribution among the actors in governance networks will nevertheless continue to bedevil meta-level political efforts aimed at resolving these dilemmas. More comparative policy analytical research is needed to understand how the feedback loops of institutionalized accountability mechanisms across climate change governance networks affects the emergence of power and knowledge distribution asymmetries at the global scale. Understanding global climate change policy design problems like those discussed here can inform the development of a coherent accountability framework that simultaneously takes into account actors, processes and outcomes.

Acknowledgments

We are grateful to UVM's James Jefford Center of Policy Research for sponsoring part of this research.

Notes

1. The Kyoto protocol is available at http://unfccc.int/kyoto_protocol/items/2830.php
2. http://www.app.gov/
3. http://www.iphe.net/
4. http://www.cslforum.org/

5. http://www.iclei.org/index.php?id=800
6. http://www.clintonfoundation.org/what-we-do/clinton-climate-initiative/
7. http://www.iccp.net/
8. http://www.wbcsd.org
9. www.combatclimatechange.org
10. http://www.ghgprotocol.org/
11. http://www.ren21.net/
12. http://www.reeep.org/
13. http://ji.unfccc.int/index.html
14. http://cdm.unfccc.int/index.html
15. http://wbcarbonfinance.org
16. http://www.epa.gov/methanetomarkets/
17. BTUs stand for British Thermal Units and GHG/BTU is a type of performance outcome measure that measures GHG emission intensity per unit of energy consumed.

References

Agranoff, R. and Mcguire, M., 2001, Big questions in public network management research. *Journal of Public Administration Research and Theory*, **11**, pp. 295–326.

Bäckstrand, K., 2008, Accountability of networked climate governance: The rise of transnational climate partnerships. *Global Environmental Politics*, **8**, pp. 74–102.

Bardach, E. and Lesser, C., 1996, Accountability in human services collaboratives: For what? And for whom? *Journal of Public Administration Research and Theory*, **6**, pp. 197–224.

Bateson, G., 1988, *Mind and Nature* (New York: Bantam).

Behn, R. D., 2001, *Rethinking Democratic Accountability* (Washington, DC: Brookings Institution Press).

Benner, T., Reinicke, W. H. and Witte, J. M., 2004, Multisectoral networks in global governance: Towards a pluralistic system of accountability. *Government and Opposition*, **39**, pp. 191–210.

Biermann, F., 2005, Between the USA and the south: Strategic choices for European climate policy. *Climate Policy*, **5**, pp. 273–290.

Biermann, F., 2009, The fragmentation of global governance architectures: A framework for analysis. *Global Environmental Politics*, **9**, pp. 14–40

Bogason, P. and Musso, J. A., 2006, The democratic prospects of network governance. *The American Review of Public Administration*, **36**, pp. 3–18.

Cass, L. R., 2007, *The Failures of American and European Climate Policy: International Norms, Domestic Politics, and Unachievable Commitments* (New York: State University of New York Press).

Coen, D. and Thatcher, M., 2008, Network governance and multi-level delegation: European networks of regulatory agencies. *Journal of Public Policy*, **28**, pp. 49–71.

Frederickson, G. D. and Frederickson, H. G., 2006, *Measuring the Performance of the Hollow State* (Washington, DC: Georgetown University Press).

Goldsmith, S. and Eggers, W., 2004, *Governing by Network* (Washington, DC: Brookings).

Gruber, J., 1987, *Controlling Bureaucracies: Dilemmas in Democratic Governance* (Berkeley, CA: University of California Press).

Haas, P. M., 2004, Addressing the global governance deficit. *Global Environmental Politics*, **4**, pp. 1–15.

Harrison, K. and Sundstrom, L. M., 2007, The comparative politics of climate change. *Global Environmental Politics*, **7**, pp. 1–18.

Heinrich, C. J. and Lynn Jr., L. E. (Eds), 2000, *Governance and Performance: New Perspectives* (Washington, DC: Georgetown University Press).

Hirsch, P. D., Adams, B., Brosius, J. P., Zia, A., Bariola, N. and Dammert, J. L., 2011, Acknowledging conservation trade-offs and embracing complexity. *Conservation Biology*, **25**, pp. 259–264.

IPCC, 2007, *Climate Change 2007* Synthesis Report. Intergovernmental Panel on Climate Change, Fourth Assessment Report. Available at http://www.ipcc.ch.

Jones, C., Hesterly, W. S. and Borgatti, S. P., 1997, A general theory of network governance: Exchange conditions and social mechanisms. *Academy of Management Review*, **22**, pp. 911–945.

Kelman, S., 2006, Improving service delivery performance in the United Kingdom: Organization theory perspectives on central intervention strategies. *Journal of Comparative Policy Analysis*, **8**, pp. 393–419.

Kickert, W. J. M., Klijn, E.-H. and Koppenjan, J. F. M., 1997, Introduction: A management perspective on policy networks, in: W. J. M. Kickert, E.-H. Klijn and J. F. M. Koppenjan (Eds) *Managing Complex Networks* (London: Sage), pp. 1–11.
Klijn, E.-H., 1996, Analyzing and managing policy processes in complex networks. *Administration and Society*, **28**, pp. 90–119.
Klijn, E.-H. and Skelcher, C., 2007, Democracy and governance networks: Compatible or not? *Public Administration*, **85**, pp. 587–608.
Koliba, C., Meek, J. and Zia, A., 2010, *Governance Networks: Public Administration and Policy in the Midst of Complexity* (Abingdon, UK: Taylor and Francis).
Koliba, C., Mills, R. M. and Zia, A., 2011, Accountability in governance networks: An assessment of public, private, and nonprofit emergency management practices following hurricane Katrina. *Public Administration Review*, **71**, pp. 210–220.
Kooiman, J., 2008, Exploring the concept of governability. *Journal of Comparative Policy Analysis*, **10**, pp. 171–190.
Koontz, T. M., Steelman, T. A., Carmin, J., Korfmacher, K. S., Moseley, C. and Thomas, C. W., 2004, *Collaborative Environmental Management: What Roles for Government?* (Washington, DC: RFF Press).
Lowndes, V. and Skelcher, C., 1998, The dynamics of multi-organizational parternships: An analysis of changing modes of governance. *Public Administration*, **76**, pp. 313–333.
Marsh, D. and Rhodes, R. A. W., 1992, *Policy Networks in British Government* (Oxford: Oxford University Press).
Mashaw, J. L., 2006, Accountability and institutional design: Some thoughts on the grammar of governance, in: M. W. Dowdle (Ed.) *Public Accountability: Designs, Dilemmas and Experiences* (Cambridge: Cambridge University Press), pp. 115–156
Mathur, N. and Skelcher, C., 2007, Evaluating democratic performance: Methodologies for assessing the relationship between network governance and citizens. *Public Administration Review*, **67**, pp. 228–237.
May, P. J., 2007, Regulatory regimes and accountability. *Regulation and Governance*, **1**, pp. 8–26.
Milward, H. B., 1996, Symposium on the hollow state: Capacity, control, and performance in interorganizational settings. *Journal of Public Administration Research and Theory*, **6**, pp. 193–195.
Mingus, M. S., 2004, Validating the comparative network framework in a Canada/United States context. *Journal of Comparative Policy Analysis*, **6**, pp. 15–37.
Moynihan, D. P., 2008, Learning under uncertainty: Networks in crisis management. *Public Administration Review*, **68**, pp. 350–361.
Najam, A. and Sagar, A., 1998, Avoiding a cop-out: Moving towards systematic decision-making under the climate convention. *Climatic Change*, **39**, pp. iii–ix.
Najam, A., Huq, S. and Sokona, Y., 2003, Climate negotiations beyond Kyoto: Developing countries concerns and interests. *Climate Policy*, **3**, pp. 221–231.
Page, S., 2004, Measuring accountability for results in interagency collaboratives. *Public Administration Review*, **64**, pp. 591–606.
Papadopoulos, Y., 2003, Cooperative forms of governance: Problems of democratic accountability in complex environments. *European Journal of Political Research*, **42**, pp. 473–501.
Papadopoulos, Y., 2007, Problems of democratic accountability in network and multilevel governance. *European Law Journal*, **13**, pp. 469–486.
Pettenger, M. E. (Ed.), 2007, *The Social Construction of Climate Change* (Burlington, VT: Ashgate).
Pierre, J. and Peters, G., 2005, *Governing Complex Societies: Trajectories and Scenarios* (New York: Palgrave Macmillan).
Posner, P., 2002, Accountability challenges of third-party government, in: L. Salamon (Ed.) *The Tools of Government: A Guide to the New Governance* (New York: Oxford University Press), pp. 53–71.
Provan, K. G. and Milward, H. B., 1995, A preliminary theory of inter-organizational effectiveness: A comparative study of four community mental health systems. *Administrative Science Quarterly*, **40**, pp. 1–33.
Radin, B., 2006, *Challenging the Performance Movement: Accountability, Complexity and Democratic Values* (Washington, DC: Georgetown University Press).
Raupach, M. R., Marland, G., Gais, P., Le Quere, C., Canadell, J. G., Klepper, G. and Field, C. B., 2007, Global and regional drivers of accelerating CO_2 emissions. *Proceedings of the National Academy of the Sciences (PNAS)*, **104**, pp. 10288–10293.

Rodriguez, C., Langley, A., Beland, F. and Denis, J.-L., 2007, Governance, power, and mandated collaboration in an interorganizational network. *Administration and Society*, **39**, pp. 150–193.

Romm, J., 2007, *Hell and High Water: Global Warming – The Solution and the Politics – and What We Should Do* (New York: Harper Collins).

Scott, C., 2006, Spontaneous accountability, in: M. W. Dowdle (Ed.) *Public Accountability: Designs, Dilemmas and Experiences* (Cambridge: Cambridge University Press), pp. 174–194.

Skelcher, C., 2005, Jurisdictional integrity, polycentrism, and the design of democratic governance. *Governance: An International Journal of Policy, Administration, and Institutions*, **18**, pp. 89–110.

Slaughter, A.-M., 2004, Disaggregated sovereignty: Towards the public accountability of global government networks. *Government and Opposition*, pp. 159–190.

Sorensen, E. and Torfing, J., 2005, Network governance and post-liberal democracy. *Administrative Theory and Praxis*, **27**, pp. 197–237.

The Copenhagen Diagnosis, 2009, *Updating the World on Latest Climate Science* (Sydney, Australia: The University of New South Wales Climate Change Research Centre).

Torfing, Jacob, 2005, Governance network theory: Towards a second generation. *European Political Science*, **4**, pp. 305–315.

Vining, A. R., Boardman, A. E. and Poschmann, F., 2005, Public–private partnerships in the US and Canada: "There are no free lunches". *Journal of Comparative Policy Analysis*, **7**, pp. 199–220.

Yanow, D., 1999, Conducting interpretive policy analysis (Sage, London).

Comparative Statistics

Editor: FRED THOMPSON

Beyond Welfare Effort in the Measuring of Welfare States

JON OLASKOAGA, RICARDO ALAEZ-ALLER & PABLO DIAZ-DE-BASURTO-URAGA

ABSTRACT *Welfare effort (social spending as a percentage of GDP) has conventionally been the preferred measure for comparisons in space and time of the level of development of welfare states. However, frequent mentions are made in the relevant literature of the drawbacks of this measure as an empirical reference (e.g. it can be demonstrated that in certain conditions it provides a distorted picture of the relative levels of development of social protection systems). This study sets out to determine the extent of the shortcomings of the welfare effort measure for quantifying the relative standards of social protection.*

Introduction

For over 30 years it has been claimed that the welfare state is in crisis. We now have more information on events in the last quarter of the twentieth century, which may be sufficient for us to draw up a practically definitive assessment of this topic. However, it is difficult to find evidence in the relevant literature of any basic consensus on recent trends in welfare states. In a similar context of lack of consensus concerning the determinant factors in the development of the welfare state between the end of the Second World War and the recession of the 1970s, O'Connor and Brym (1988) claimed to have found the cause of that lack of consensus in the fact that the various theories sought empirical support for their assertions based on different measures and indicators which therefore provided different pictures and led to different conclusions concerning the relative development of welfare states. This is due at least in part to what has come to be called the "dependent variable problem" (Green-Pedersen 2007; Kühner 2007).

In research into the consequences of the crisis of welfare states there is also a curious link between the type of measures used and the conclusions drawn from analyses. For example, most studies that postulate the resilience of the welfare state use a measure of the weight of social spending in the economy (welfare effort measured in terms of social spending as a percentage of GDP – Gross Domestic Product), while those that highlight the magnitude of cutbacks base their conclusions on the degree to which social needs are covered by social welfare provisions.

Welfare effort is by far the most widely used measure in empirical literature for gauging trends in welfare states. Since the papers by Wilensky (1975), most classical research on the determining factors in the expansion of social protection has used this measure as a dependent variable (Cameron 1978; Stephens 1979; Schmidt 1983; Pampel and Williamson 1988; Schmidt 1997); and many more recent contributions to the field have followed suit (Iversen 2001; Alesina and Glaeser 2004). Similarly, welfare effort has played a leading role in debates on the retrenchment of the welfare state and the consequences of globalisation for public-sector policies in developed countries (Alber 1988; Castles 2001; Glyn 2004; Brady et al. 2005; Jahn 2006). In this context, the present study has been developed to point out the evident shortcomings of using welfare effort alone to describe social spending trends, and as a result to compare the hypotheses concerning trends in the welfare state.

Changes in Magnitude of Social Protection Described Via Welfare Effort, 1980–2004

This heading is intended to assess the validity of changes in the welfare effort as a measure of the scope of the welfare state reforms during the crisis period.

Table 1 gives a general view of the performance of welfare effort between 1980 and 2004. An analysis of these data results in the following conclusions, among others:

– No generalised reduction in welfare effort is observed. Indeed if the countries are considered as a whole, effort increases by 4.3 per cent over the full period, which can be seen as evidence of the health of the welfare state in the developed world.
– Some correction in welfare effort is observed in some countries, e.g. Ireland and the Netherlands.
– The frequency of spending cuts is higher from the 1990s onwards. It can also be observed that where adjustments were not made the rate of growth in effort fell to below that of the 1980s, especially in the social-democratic area, where the figure for this indicator in 2004 is very similar to that of 1990.
– Elsewhere, by contrast – especially in the southern Europe area – there have been major increases in social protection efforts. The increase in social spending in these countries over the 20 years of the study period has been interpreted in the context of a process of

Table 1. Public social spending as a percentage of GDP

Country	1980	1990	2000	2004	1990–2004	1980–2004
Australia	10.6	13.6	17.8	17.7	4.1	7.0
Canada	13.7	18.1	16.5	16.6	−1.5	2.9
United States	13.1	13.4	14.5	16.1	2.7	2.9
Ireland	16.7	14.9	13.6	16.2	1.3	−0.5
New Zealand	17.2	21.8	19.4	18.0	−3.7	0.8
United Kingdom	16.7	17.0	19.2	21.1	4.0	4.4
Liberal[a]	**13.6**	**14.2**	**15.4**	**16.8**	**2.6**	**3.3**
Denmark	24.8	25.1	25.8	27.7	2.5	2.9
Finland	18.0	24.2	24.3	26.0	1.8	7.9
Norway	16.9	22.3	21.3	23.2	0.9	6.4
Sweden	27.1	30.2	28.5	29.9	−0.3	2.8
Social-democratic[a]	**23.0**	**26.4**	**25.4**	**27.1**	**0.7**	**4.0**
Germany	22.7	22.3	26.2	26.7	4.4	3.9
Austria	22.5	23.9	26.4	27.3	3.5	4.9
Belgium	23.5	24.9	25.3	26.6	1.7	3.1
France	20.8	25.1	27.9	29.1	4.0	8.3
The Netherlands	24.8	25.6	19.8	21.1	−4.5	−3.7
Conservative[a]	**22.3**	**23.8**	**26.1**	**27.0**	**3.1**	**4.7**
Spain	15.5	19.9	20.3	21.2	1.2	5.6
Greece	10.2	16.5	19.2	19.9	3.4	9.6
Italy	18.0	19.9	23.3	24.7	4.7	6.7
Portugal	10.2	12.9	19.6	23.1	10.2	12.9
Southern Europe[a]	**16.3**	**19.2**	**21.8**	**22.9**	**3.7**	**6.6**
Japan	10.6	11.4	16.5	18.2	6.8	7.7
Switzerland	13.5	13.4	17.9	20.3	6.9	6.8
OECD (21)	**15.6**	**16.6**	**18.6**	**19.9**	**3.3**	**4.3**
Coefficient of variation[b]	29.4	26.1	20.4	19.4		

Notes: [a]The figures given for each family or regime and for the "OECD (21)" category indicate the level of spending as a whole in the aggregate category in question, measured in US dollars as a percentage of aggregate GDP in the same accounting unit.[a]**Families of countries are widely used in the literature on comparative social policy.** See Jon Olaskoaga (2007) for a detailed discussion on the choice of the families used here and for the location of each country in its group.[b]The coefficient of variation is expressed in percentage terms.
Sources: SOCX – OECD Social Expenditure Database – (1980–2005), OECD – Organisation for Economic Co-operation and Development.

adaptation and homologation to bring them into line with their more highly developed neighbours in Europe.
- The combination of downward adjustments in the countries with the highest spending levels in the initial period and strong upward adjustments in other countries results in a narrower dispersal of welfare effort across countries.
- In short, an analysis of changes between 1980 and 2004 provides a relatively optimistic picture of the future of welfare states. Reductions in welfare effort are observed in only two of the 21 countries considered, and the average level continues to rise. However, there are elements that indicate otherwise: at first glance the data give the impression that a more widespread adjustment took place at the end of the period under study. Between 1990 and 2004 reductions are observed in four countries, including one from the social-democratic world.

The Drawbacks of Welfare Effort as a Measure

Welfare effort is by far the most widely used measure in empirical literature on the relative levels of development of social policies. Its attractiveness probably lies in the readily apparent advantages of aggregation, availability and comparability with other measures that refer to GDP. However, it has major shortcomings which limit its usefulness and make maximum caution advisable in interpreting it. Jensen (2011) gives an exhaustive discussion of these problems. The two main problems are examined below.

First of all, it may be unsuitable as a measure of the level of development of social policy, i.e. changes in the measure may be caused by factors other than increases in social rights, such as the demographics of the population, so an increase in social spending measured in relation to GDP does not necessarily indicate an improvement in social citizenship status (Korpi 1989: 314). Clayton and Pontusson (1998: 70) make a similar complaint concerning welfare effort, stating that "such measures fail to take account of changes in societal welfare needs". Secondly, welfare effort shows changes in social spending and GDP simultaneously, so it is influenced by the performance of the denominator.

These shortcomings have been described frequently in the relevant literature, so it seems logical to wonder how far the relative trends in welfare effort are the result of factors other than the way in which systems deal with and provide for the social needs of citizens. Surprisingly, as far as we are aware, the relevant literature contains no systematic attempts to determine this. An initial proposal along these lines is made below, based on a fairly straightforward relationship between welfare effort and its immediate determinants:

$$\frac{SS}{GDP} = \frac{SS}{DepPop} \times \frac{DepPop}{Pop} \times \frac{Pop}{GDP}$$

where:

- "SS" is social spending;
- "DepPop" is the dependent population calculated as the sum of those aged 65 or more and the unemployed population;
- "Pop" is the total population;
- and "GDP" is gross domestic product.

The identifying elements can be renamed as follows:

$$\text{Welfare effort} = \frac{SS}{GDP}; \text{Welfare standard} = \frac{SS}{DepPop}; \text{Incidence}$$

$$= \frac{DepPop}{Pop}; \frac{1}{Income} = \frac{Pop}{GDP}$$

and can therefore be rewritten as:

$$\text{Effort} \equiv \text{Welfare standard} \times \text{Incidence} \times \frac{1}{\text{Income}} \qquad (1)$$

This expression highlights the fact that the social spending effort in a given country depends not only on the extent to which protection systems cover situations in need but also on other factors. More specifically, welfare effort is:

- directly proportional to the standards of spending (measured in spending per dependant);
- directly proportional to the incidence of situations covered by protection;
- indirectly proportional to income in the country: all else being equal, the lower the income is, the greater the effort is.

The welfare effort for each country is the result of its situation in each of these immediate determinants. A lower level of effort may, a priori, be due to a low incidence or to a high level of income per capita, and not chiefly to any failure to protect persons suffering social contingencies. On the other hand, a relatively high welfare effort could be due to low levels of prosperity or to a higher incidence of social need. In other words, identical welfare effort levels may conceal very different situations.

To determine the extent to which these situations are found in the OECD 21 group, the determinants of the welfare effort in each country can be calculated in relative terms. The reference used in all cases is the value of the determinants calculated for the 21 countries considered as a whole. Deviations in welfare effort can be expressed as the sum of the deviations in each of the determinants plus the crossed products of those deviations. In view of the data obtained, some of the conclusions drawn at first sight from the analysis of welfare effort need to be qualified.

Events in Ireland in 1980–2004 provide a good example of the extent to which the effort indicator is influenced by factors other than protection levels. According to welfare effort, there is a fall of 26 percentage points in the relative position of Ireland in the period 1980–2004. However, the reasons for this drop do not lie in a worsening of the attention given to each situation covered by protection: indeed, Ireland's position improves substantially in this respect, climbing from 27 points below the average figure in 1980 to 30 points above it in 2004 (see Figure 1). The absolute and relative reductions in effort levels in Ireland are explained by the reduction in the incidence of situations covered by protection and the considerable economic growth that the country enjoyed over the period considered. In the Netherlands, however, the situation is very different and the results for welfare effort do correspond with the figures for standards of protection.

The second conclusion obtained from the analysis of welfare effort is that adjustments were concentrated in the social-democratic world, which is one of the bastions of social democracy but is nevertheless the area where effort has grown least: indeed, since 1990 it has almost ceased to grow altogether. These data support the hypothesis that it is precisely those countries where the tax burden of the welfare state is greatest that have concerned themselves most with controlling social spending (Swank 2002; De Grauwe and Polan 2005). However, it is harder to arrive at that conclusion when the immediate determinants of welfare effort are considered. Over the period as a whole the fall in the relative effort level conceals the fact that the standard of protection rises not only in absolute terms in this area but also relative to the trend in the group of countries analysed as a whole. This rise is not reflected in welfare effort due to the considerable reduction in relative incidence

Figure 1. Deviations in effort, standards of protection, incidence and income measures for Ireland

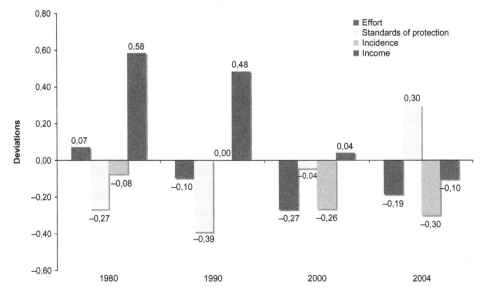

Source: For social spending: OECD, SOCX. For population: OECD, SOCX. For unemployed population: OECD, LFS – Labour Force Statistics. The "Deviation in Income" shows the deviations for the inverse value of income per capita. Positive figures in this one indicate under-average per capita income levels. GDP and public social spending are measured in current PPP – Purchasing Power Parity – units referring to the US dollar.

levels for the contingencies of old age and unemployment, and to a slight correction in relative per capita income levels (Figure 2). This case and that of Ireland provide the clearest examples of just how unfortunate appreciations based exclusively on welfare effort can be.

In southern Europe the situation is similar. If welfare effort levels alone are considered, the conclusion drawn is that the biggest rise in spending in relative terms takes place among this group of countries, with rises in every country in the group. However, more detailed observation reveals that improvements in adjusted standards are actually far more modest, and that the major rise in effort is due largely to the increased incidence of the situations covered by protection (Figure 3). A look at events in each country reveals two very different paths: on the one hand there are relative improvements in the standard of protection in Portugal and Greece, particularly in the former, while on the other hand there are standard decreases in Spain and Italy (following a slight improvement up to 1990 in the former).

Finally, the conclusion on the convergence of protection systems must also be qualified. A comparison between Table 1 and Table 2 shows that the reduction in coefficients of variation is far greater under welfare effort than under the standard of protection measure. Furthermore, Figure 4 shows an increase of the dispersion in the indicator of incidence. This means that is the quality itself of the welfare effort measure which is worsening. Veenhoven (2000: 111) holds that the increase in the ageing population and unemployment occur in approximately the same proportions, at least in first-world countries. By contrast, our analysis here shows that the incidence of these two contingencies is

Figure 2. Deviations in effort, standards of protection, incidence and income measures for the Social-democratic world

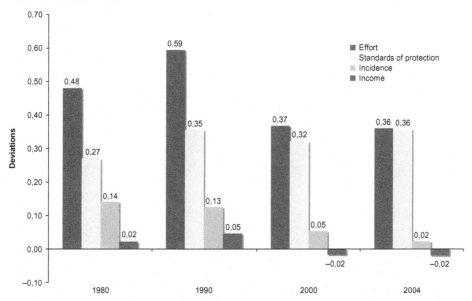

Source: For social spending: OECD, SOCX. For population: OECD, SOCX. For unemployed population: OECD, LFS. The "Deviation in Income" shows the deviations for the inverse value of income per capita. Positive figures in this one indicate under-average per capita income levels. GDP and public social spending are measured in current PPP –Purchasing Power Parity – units referring to the US dollar.

divergent enough over time to influence the conclusions that can be drawn from observing welfare effort.

Alternatives to Welfare Effort

The literature on the welfare state and its recent trends is affected by a peculiar paradox: however far one extends the empirical basis on which it is based, the debate on apparently simple hypotheses is not settled. This is due at least in part to what has come to be called the "dependent variable problem". This problem affects not just measurement itself, as established convincingly by Green-Pedersen (2007), but also the definition of what is to be measured. In other words, all empirical research in this field must answer two questions: what is to be measured and how it is to be measured. The first question is theoretical, so the answer must fit into the theoretical framework and the hypothesis to be checked. The second is operational, and must be determined to ensure that the way in which measurements are taken (e.g. the choice of indicators) fits the purpose of the measurements.

Green-Pedersen (2007) holds that these two questions can only be answered properly if the difference between output and outcome is considered. Output sees social reform in terms of the changes made by political decision-makers in social programmes. Outcome sees the welfare state in terms of the consequences of social programmes for the protection that is actually received by citizens, or of the influence of social programmes on

Figure 3. Deviations in effort, standards of protection, incidence and income measures for Southern Europe

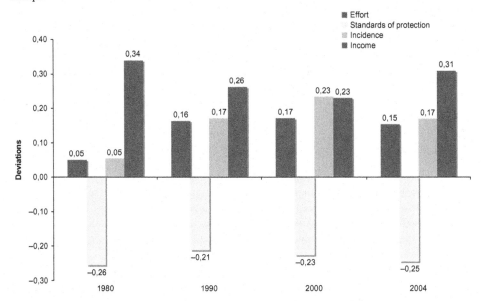

Source: For social spending: OECD, SOCX. For population: OECD, SOCX. For unemployed population: OECD, LFS. The "Deviation in Income" shows the deviations for the inverse value of income per capita. Positive figures in this one indicate under-average per capita income levels. GDP and public social spending are measured in current PPP –Purchasing Power Parity – units referring to the US dollar.

inequality. Developments in these outcomes are influenced by outputs, but other factors such as changes in extent or social need are relevant too.

According to Green-Pedersen (2007: 21), the mechanisms for measuring outputs have developed no further than the direct observation of legal reforms and the construction of indices of reforms, estimation based on budget provisions attached to legislation and the use of simulation methods, which are always complex. Most empirical literature, however, uses outcome indicators. Several such indicators are used, though the most widespread is probably the welfare effort indicator.

Extending the logic used by Green-Pedersen (2007), the question arises of whether there is a single significant dimension in the outcomes of social policy or various facets of welfare states (or social protection systems as their usual empirical referents) can be identified, the measurement of which may legitimately be considered as being of interest in theory.

Table 3 shows what can be considered as the three basic dimensions of social protection systems: effort, intensity (standards of protection) and coverage. Each is influenced by political decisions and by a series of other factors, particularly economic and demographic factors. A good effort indicator will not necessarily be good at measuring the standards of protection or the coverage of protection systems, and vice versa.

Table 3 shows various ways of measuring standards of protection, distinguishing between synthetic methods (which work with all social protection mechanisms, always

Table 2. Standards of protection. Public social spending per dependant[c] in 2000 prices and PPP units referred to the US dollar and average growth rates (Δ%)

Country	1980	1990	2000	2004	Δ% 2004/1990	Δ% 2004/1980
Australia	16,255	20,384	31,725	34,259	3.5	3.0
Canada	22,540	28,527	30,217	30,911	0.5	1.3
United States	19,767	24,282	34,244	37,789	3.0	2.6
Ireland	13,572	13,866	28,449	39,061	7.1	4.3
New Zealand	26,654	26,905	28,202	30,942	0.9	0.6
United Kingdom	16,656	19,736	28,506	34,515	3.8	3.0
Liberal[a]	19,177	23,476	32,658	36,450	3.0	2.6
Denmark	26,109	28,745	43,117	45,540	3.1	2.3
Finland	21,256	35,140	31,374	36,001	0.2	2.1
Norway	23,412	31,395	45,512	52,556	3.5	3.3
Sweden	30,453	38,141	39,401	43,912	0.9	1.5
Social-democratic[a]	26,450	33,982	39,369	43,919	1.7	2.0
Germany	26,015	30,149	31,338	28,070	−0.5	0.3
Austria	26,718	33,813	44,194	45,491	2.0	2.2
Belgium	25,215	30,384	34,820	36,495	1.2	1.5
France	24,468	32,945	37,888	39,952	1.3	2.0
Netherlands	34,246	35,711	38,559	38,430	0.5	0.5
Conservative[a]	26,095	31,897	34,766	33,731	0.4	1.0
Spain	13,853	17,488	19,736	22,978	1.8	2.0
Greece	10,808	15,002	15,971	18,576	1.4	2.2
Italy	20,365	22,947	27,434	29,580	1.7	1.5
Portugal	6,663	10,791	18,197	19,520	4.0	4.4
Southern Europe[a]	16,319	19,552	23,011	25,460	1.8	1.8
Japan	17,761	20,446	21,217	22,133	0.5	0.9
Switzerland	23,940	25,990	31,985	33,836	1.8	1.4
OECD-21[a]	20,409	24,541	29,788	31,769	1.7	1.8
Coefficient of variation[b]	30.7	29.2	25.7	25.4	–	–

Notes: [a]The figures given for each family or regime and for the "All" category indicate the level of spending as a whole in the aggregate category in question, measured in US dollars. [b]The coefficient of variation is expressed in percentage terms. [c]"Dependent population" is understood to mean the population aged 65 and over plus the unemployed population.
Sources: (a) For social spending: OECD, SOCX. (b) For population: OECD, SOCX. (c) For unemployed population: OECD, LFS.

within a conventional definition of their limits) and specific methods (which work only with measures that protect against a given contingency, e.g. unemployment).

The standard of social protection is intuitively understood to be linked to the speed and effectiveness with which protection services deal with the various risk situations incurred by the citizens of a country, and the extent to which they manage to re-establish the quality of life that those citizens enjoyed prior to the appearance of the contingencies in question. Two of the most widely used standards of protection measures are social spending per capita and social spending per dependant (Clayton and Pontusson 1998; Castles 2004; Alsasua et al. 2007). Although they are better suited than welfare effort to measuring the degree of protection provided by institutions, they both have serious drawbacks. Population numbers are not the most appropriate yardstick for measuring the needs covered by protection systems, and nor is the "dependent population", because

Figure 4. Evolution of coefficients of variation in welfare effort and standard of protection

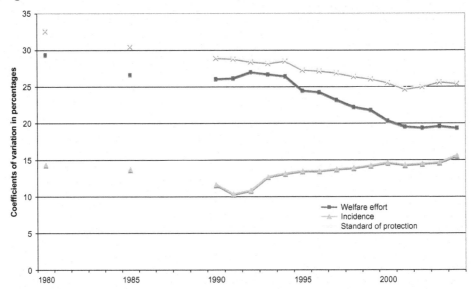

Source: For social spending: OECD, SOCX. For population: OECD, SOCX. For unemployed population: OECD, LFS.

it fails to take into account that some of the contingencies that protection systems were designed to cover are not directly concerned with unemployment or old age. Moreover, this measurement wrongly assumes that the needs of an old person are the same as those of an unemployed person. The problems of synthetic standard of protection measures can be said to stem from the fact that it is not possible to work with a single, homogenous measurement for all the contingencies that social protection institutions were designed to cover.

A second option that has enjoyed considerable support in the relevant literature is to work with replacement rates. These rates measure the extent to which cash benefits restore the purchasing power of individuals and households that have suffered contingencies such as sickness, unemployment or retirement. Unlike the indicators described above, they are based on case-type approach. Replacement rates and other indices based on the same

Table 3. Types of measure for measuring the dimensions of social protection systems

Dimension\\Type of measure	Synthetic measures	Specific measures
Welfare effort	Social spending as a percentage of GDP	X
Standards of protection	Social spending per capita or social spending per dependent Measurements concerned with social spending per capita	Simple indices, e.g. spending on old age per person aged 65 or over Replacement rates for benefits that replace income
Coverage	X	Coverage of certain benefits (health)

Source: Own work.

measurements have been used to describe the extent of the retrenchment of social policies during the period of crisis, to detect the diverse natures of welfare states and to assess the hypothesis of convergence of social protection systems (Montanari 2001; Korpi and Palme 2003; Allan and Scruggs 2004; Scruggs 2006; Starke et al. 2008; Caminada et al. 2010). Replacement rates are a highly precise measurement in this context, because they report on the extent to which an individual and his/her family can maintain their purchasing power when they are unable for any given reason (e.g. sickness, unemployment or old age) to obtain the income provided previously by their participation in the labour market.

Using replacement rates solves some of the problems of the measures described above, but also introduces new ones.

- The main drawback of replacement rates is probably that they can only be applied to benefits that replace income. A large part of the social protection system – including such important areas as disability, housing, social exclusion and healthcare – falls outside the resulting description.
- Moreover, the quality of the results of these measures is affected by the substitutability of some benefits. The problem of substitutability arises when more than one action can be taken to resolve the same type of social need, e.g. retirement pensions and other benefits in kind linked to old age. In the presence of substitutability, considering close aggregates of benefits may reduce the quality of measurements. For example, Scruggs (2006) finds that the replacement rates of standard pensions are higher in the conservative world than in the social-democratic world. This occurs because in the latter much of the attention received by the elderly is provided through benefits in kind linked to residential care or care in the home. When total spending on old age is considered rather than spending on pensions alone, the volume of resources dedicated per elderly person in social-democratic countries exceeds the figure in conservative countries (according to our own calculations, average spending per person aged 65 and over in 2002 was 77 per cent of the average salary of manual workers in conservative countries, and 84 per cent in social-democratic countries).
- Finally, the usefulness of replacement rates is limited by the implicit difficulty of obtaining data for analysis. There are at least two programmes that seek to gather information on replacement rates. The most ambitious is that of the Swedish Institute of Social Research, the Social Citizenship Indicator Program, which compiles data in a series that runs from 1930 to 2000. Also worthy of mention is the *Comparative Welfare Entitlements Dataset* (Scruggs 2007).

It is also possible to resort to the construction of measures that have not been considered so frequently. For instance, simple indexes can be used by working with social expenditure oriented to a specific population group or a specific risk. For example, the social expenditure devoted to the old-age function that a country invests in each person aged 65 or over can also be figured out. This indicator can be improved by relating the result obtained to a salary reference, e.g. the average wage of manual workers. When calculating overall expenditure related to old people, this type of measure solves the problems caused by the substitutability of benefits on a partial basis that affect substitution rates.

However, it is not always easy to find simple indicators of incidence that can be used for this purpose. Health care, housing and social exclusion are cases in point. In this last field, for instance, considerable progress has been made in recent years with the testing of indicators of material deprivation which should, initially, serve to complement the more classical income-based measures. However these good intentions have come to nothing and the new indicators give rise to as many new problems as they solve old ones (see Gilbert 2009 for a full list of these problems). Moreover, indicators of material deprivation are in any event a measurement of poverty that considers living conditions after action by welfare states but not the incidence that protection organisations must deal with.

The foregoing paragraphs may have given readers the impression that empirical work in this field faces a dilemma: if specific indicators are used it is possible to calibrate reasonably well the weight of the objective situations that result from the implementation of protection mechanisms. This helps obtain an appropriate indicator for standards of protection, but the problems of exhaustivity and substitutability arise. When specific indicators are replaced by synthetic indicators, the problems of exhaustivity and substitutability disappear, but the problem of constructing measures suited to objective needs must be faced.

Attempts have been made to overcome this dilemma. For instance, Olaskoaga et al. (2010) develop a method based on the construction of a per capita social spending pattern that permits relative measurements of total spending on protection, taking into account a number of objective conditions that drive spending (levels of activity and unemployment, population aged 65 or over, population aged under 15, etc.). This pattern acts like a table of weights, which gives the appropriate weight for a person depending on height, age, sex, etc., and serves as a benchmark for gauging whether an individual is overweight (or underweight). The practical implementation of this proposal is hindered, however, by the difficulty of finding full, internationally consistent information on the objective factors which are to be isolated.

Conclusions

This article contains a brief outline of the pros and cons of welfare effort and other measures available for comparing the relative state of development of social policies.

No doubt, the welfare effort has been the one most frequently used in literature, but it may be said to have serious drawbacks, the main consequence of which is that the image obtained from it does not match reality. For instance, the welfare effort overvalues the effect of spending cuts in the social-democratic world, where the incidence has been reduced in relative terms, or in those countries such as Ireland where economic growth has been faster. On the other hand, the welfare effort overestimates the convergence of the southern European countries towards the expenditure level of their neighbouring northern countries, since it disregards the fact that in most of the former, the incidence of social problems shows a higher increase than in other countries.

Summing up, in the light of the drawbacks relating to the welfare effort measure, this article recommends the use of a wider range of measures. The most intelligent attitude is not to rule out any alternative, since a diversity of approaches may be considered as a virtue in a problem such as this one, where no single optimum solution can be seen. In this context the proposal made here is similar to that of Jensen (2011), an improvised defender of the welfare effort indicator. Jensen holds that welfare effort has been fairly accused of undervaluing the disparities between countries in matters of entitlement criteria and benefit types in some welfare programmes: old-age pensions, sickness insurance and unemployment protection. However, he argues that those who criticise the indicator are forgetting that it is more sensitive to those disparities in other programmes such as health care and education, and that the same could occur with child care and care for the elderly.

In measuring complex phenomena, a diversity of methods is almost always a virtue. In fact, this article shows that there is room to design measures other than those most frequently used in literature. More specifically, one cannot overlook the possibility that the use of these measures might give rise to different conclusions on the recent development of the welfare state from a political, sociological and economic viewpoint.

Acknowledgement

This paper has been supported by the University of the Basque Country research promotion fund under Number GIC 10/28

References

Alber, J., 1988, Is there a crisis of the welfare state? Cross-national evidence from Europe, North America, and Japan. *European Sociological Review*, **4**(3), pp. 181–207.
Alesina, A. and Glaeser, E. L., 2004, *Fighting Poverty in the US and Europe. a World of Difference* (New York: Oxford University Press).
Allan, J. P. and Scruggs, L., 2004, Political partisanship and welfare state reform in advanced industrial societies. *American Journal of Political Science*, **48**(3), pp. 496–512.
Alsasua, J., Bilbao, J. and Olaskoaga, J., 2007, The EU integration process and the convergence of social protection benefits at national level. *International Journal of Social Welfare*, **16**(4), pp. 297–306.
Brady, D., Beckfield, J. and Seeleib-Kaiser, M., 2005, Economic globalization and the welfare state in affluent democracies, 1975–2001. *American Sociological Review*, **70**, pp. 921–948.
Cameron, D. R., 1978, The expansion of the public economy: A comparative analysis. *American Political Science Review*, **72**(4), pp. 1243–1261.
Caminada, K., Goudswaard, K. and Van Vliet, O., 2010, Patterns of welfare state indicators in the EU: Is there convergence?. *Journal of Common Market Studies*, **48**(3), pp. 529–556.
Castles, F. G., 2001, On the political economy of recent public sector development. *Journal of European of Social Policy*, **11**(3), pp. 195–211.
Castles, F. G., 2004, *The Future of the Welfare State. Crisis Myths and Crisis Realities* (New York: Oxford University Press).
Clayton, R. and Pontusson, J., 1998, Welfare-state retrenchment revisited. Entitlement cuts, public sector restructuring, and inegalitarian trends in advanced capitalist societies. *World Politics*, **51**(4), pp. 67–98.
De Grauwe, P. and Polan, M., 2005, Globalization and social spending. *Pacific Economic Review*, **10**(1), pp. 105–123.
Gilbert, N., 2009, European measures of poverty and 'social exclusion': Material deprivation, consumption, and life satisfaction. *Journal of Policy Analysis and Management*, **28**(4), pp. 738–744.
Glyn, A., 2004, The assessment: How far has globalization gone?. *Oxford Review of Economic Policy*, **20**(1), pp. 1–14.
Green-Pedersen, C., 2007, More than data questions and methodological issues: Theoretical conceptualization and the dependent variable 'problem' in the study of welfare reform, in: J. Clasen and N. A. Siegel (Eds) *Investigating Welfare Change. The Dependent Variable Problem in Comparative Analysis* (Northampton, MA: Edward Elgar), pp. 13–23.
Iversen, T., 2001, The dynamics of welfare state expansion. Trade openness, de-industrialization, and partisan politics, in: P. Pierson (Eds) *The New Politics of Welfare State* (Oxford: Oxford University Press), pp. 45–79.

Jahn, D., 2006, Globalization as 'Galton's Problem': The missing link in the analysis of diffusion patterns in welfare state development. *International Organization*, **60**, pp. 401–431.

Jensen, C., 2011, Less bad than its reputation: Social spending as a proxy for welfare effort in cross-national studies. *Journal of Comparative Policy Analysis: Research and Practice*, **13**(3), pp. 327–340.

Korpi, W., 1989, Power, politics, and state autonomy in the development of social citizenship: Social rights during sickness in eighteen OECD countries since 1930. *American Sociological Review*, **54**(3), pp. 309–328.

Korpi, W. and Palme, J., 2003, New politics and class politics in the context of austerity and globalization: Welfare state regress in 18 OECD countries, 1975–95. *American Political Science Review*, **97**(3), pp. 425–446.

Kühner, S., 2007, Country-level comparisons of welfare state change measures: Another facet of the dependent variable problem within the comparative analysis of the welfare state?. *Journal of European Social Policy*, **17**(1), pp. 5–18.

Montanari, I., 2001, Modernization, globalization and the welfare state: A comparative analysis of old and new convergence of social insurance. *British Journal of Sociology*, **52**(3), pp. 469–494.

Olaskoaga, J. 2007, Un análisis cuantitativo del sector de la protección social en Europa. La dinámica del gasto social desde el punto de vista de la intensidad y la generosidad de las prestaciones. PhD dissertation, University of the Basque Country.

Olaskoaga, J., Aláez, R. and de Basurto, P. D., 2010, Measuring is believing! Improving conventional indicators of welfare state development. *Social Indicators Research*, **96**(1), pp. 113–131.

O'Connor, J. S. and Brym, R. J., 1988, Public welfare expenditure in OECD countries: Towards a reconciliation of inconsistent findings. *The British Journal of Sociology*, **39**(1), pp. 47–68.

Pampel, F. C. and Williamson, J. B., 1988, Welfare spending in advanced industrial democracies. *American Journal of Sociology*, **93**(6), pp. 1424–1456.

Schmidt, M. G., 1983, The Welfare State and economy in periods of economic crisis: A comparative study of twenty-three OECD Nations. *European Journal of Political Research*, **11**, pp. 1–26.

Schmidt, M. G., 1997, Determinants of social expenditure in liberal democracies: The post world war II experience. *Acta Politica*, **32**(2), pp. 153–173.

Scruggs, L., 2006, The generosity of social insurance, 1971–2002. *Oxford Review of Economic Policy*, **22**(3), pp. 349–364.

Scruggs, L., 2007, Welfare State Generosity across space and time, in: J. Clasen and N. A. Siegel (Eds) *Investigating Welfare Change. The Dependent Variable Problem in Comparative Analysis* (Northampton, MA: Edward Elgar), pp. 133–165.

Starke, P., Obinger, H. and Castles, F. G., 2008, Convergence towards where: In what ways, if any, are welfare states becoming more similar? *Journal of European Public Policy*, **15**(7), pp. 975–1000.

Stephens, J. D., 1979, *The Transition From Capitalism to Socialism* (London: Macmillan).

Swank, D., 2002, *Global Capital, Political Institutions and Policy Change in Developed Welfare States* (Cambridge: Cambridge University Press).

Veenhoven, R., 2000, Well-being in the welfare state: Level not higher, distribution not more equitable. *Journal of Comparative Policy Analysis: Research and Practice*, **2**, pp. 91–125.

Wilensky, H. L., 1975, *The Welfare State and Equality* (Berkley, CA: Berkley University Press).

Research Note

Beyond Compliance: The Europeanization of Member States through Negative Integration and Legal Uncertainty

SUSANNE K. SCHMIDT

ABSTRACT *Europeanization – that is the domestic impact of European integration on member states – is rightly attracting increasing attention, given the extent to which European integration determines domestic policies. However, the debate on Europeanization focuses predominantly on the conditions for successful compliance with European secondary law. This note argues that this focus insufficiently captures the implications of member states being part of a multi-level system. It is largely overlooked how negative integration (market making) and legal uncertainty about the implications of European law constrains domestic policy making.*

Introduction

Research on the impact of integration on the member states has become an important part of European Union studies (Héritier 1997, Schmidt 1997, Börzel and Risse 2003, 2007). Because of the depth of European integration and its impact on the policies, politics, and polities of member states, these studies cover a wide territory, and attempts to arrive at a unified approach face difficulties. This note argues that typologies of Europeanization effects (Knill and Lehmkuhl 2002, Bulmer and Radaelli 2005, Knill and Lenschow 2005) and most Europeanization studies fail to take adequate account of the consequences of negative integration. By overly concentrating on the implementation of directives, Europeanization studies neglect the lessons to be learned by distinguishing between positive and negative integration. As Scharpf (1999, 2006) has convincingly shown, this distinction is important for understanding the dynamics of European integration – and therefore it cannot be neglected when explaining the impact of European integration on member states.

Scharpf (1999) argues that positive measures of market shaping – normally brought about by the Commission, Council, and European Parliament acting together in the legislative process – explain only partially the dynamics of European integration. Rather, the negative integration of market making matters immensely, based on far-reaching provisions of market freedoms and competition law contained in the Treaty. Although the distinction into positive and negative integration is well established in European integration studies and part of most taxonomies of Europeanization effects, a bias exists in Europeanization research in favor of implementation studies (Töller 2004: 1–2).

The issue is not only one of closing an empirical blind spot. There is also a theoretical interest. Negative integration normally occurs in a specific way – through judicial and not through legislative policy making. The dynamics of judicial policy making imply that the extent of EU obligations is often far from clear. There is significant *legal uncertainty* as to the exact domestic implications of European law. The term "legal uncertainty" refers here to the lack of predicting law, which is one central element of the term, next to procedural safeguards. Uncertainty is an analytic concept that is broadly discussed in political science, particularly in international relations (Rathbun 2007). This research note focuses on the lack of predictability, without delving further into the theoretical discussion of uncertainty. Other empirical studies conceptualizing uncertainty in the sense of predictability proceed similarly (Alexander 2002: 1149). Suffice it to add that the concept of uncertainty is one of fundamental uncertainty, where not only computation of information is at issue but relevant information is missing (Dequech 2001: 918–919).

Legal uncertainty arising in the course of negative integration has important consequences for Europeanization: member states have to devise domestic policies in the absence of certainty concerning their precise obligations under European law. This situation invites domestic actors to pursue their private interests; it serves as an opportunity structure. Europeanization effects in the case of negative integration depend much on the specifics of domestic interest constellations, which face the constraints and opportunities of European law. As member states are part of the European multi-level polity, the latter's implications refer not only to the requirement of implementing supranational law. Moreover, all domestic policy making has to conform to European legal obligations. Including the dynamics caused by negative integration at the domestic level into Europeanization research, thus takes arguments about a European multi-level system seriously.

This research note begins by briefly reviewing the Europeanization literature, discussing how the differentiation into positive and negative integration has been reflected so far. It then turns to legal uncertainty and the question why it matters for negative integration. Some empirical examples are briefly mentioned. The note develops several hypotheses that provide a starting point for empirically testing the differential Europeanization impact of negative integration.

Europeanization Resulting from Positive and Negative Integration

There are several different definitions of Europeanization. While early definitions included the perspective of European integration (Risse *et al.* 2001: 3), in the meantime a consensus emerged to restrict Europeanization to "the impact that

European policies in particular and European integration in general have on national polities, politics and policies" (Töller 2004: 1, cf. also Kohler-Koch 2000, Eising 2003).

If we take this definition, it is striking that researchers often equate the consequences of membership with the implementation of secondary law (Töller 2004: 2). But the effects of membership are doubtless more diverse. A first indication for this is given by the important distinction between positive and negative integration (Scharpf 1999: 45). If integration takes these two pathways, it cannot be possible that the implications of membership relate only to the implementation of secondary law. Yet the impact of negative integration is not being analyzed much in the Europeanization literature.

The distinction between positive and negative integration is important because, depending on the thrust of policies (whether they are market shaping or market making), there is a different institutional logic.[1] Typically, positive integration follows the legislative process while negative integration relies much more on the decisions and case law of the Commission and the European Court of Justice (ECJ). Positive decisions in the Council, for instance regarding the regulation of markets, face high agreement costs of qualified majority or unanimous voting in the Council, along with varying degrees of involving the European Parliament. Measures of negative integration, in contrast, are supported by the far-reaching provisions of market freedoms and competition law in the Treaty. Often (but not always!), they can be realized by the Commission and the Court and do not require further decisions of the Council or Parliament. Negative integration is not restricted to facilitating cross-border exchange but may severely threaten domestic institutions:

> But, as was true of dental care abroad, retail price maintenance for books, public transport, or publicly owned banks, the only thing that stands between the Scandinavian welfare state and the market is not a vote in the Council of Ministers or in the European Parliament, but merely the initiation of infringement proceedings by the Commission or legal action by potential private competitors before a national court that is then referred to the European Court of Justice for a preliminary opinion. In other words, it may happen any day. Once the issue reaches the ECJ, the outcome is at best uncertain. (Scharpf 2002: 657)

Secondary law doubtless includes market shaping and making. Competition law regulations, such as Council regulation 1/2003, are obvious examples. Actions of the Commission and the ECJ sometimes also realize positive measures. But primary law is much stronger on market making than on market shaping (Scharpf 2006: 854). Were there not this different institutional background, one would not need to speak of a bias of the European Union in favor of negative integration: the liberalization and the regulation of markets would need the same demanding majorities in the Council and Parliament. For the rest of this research note, negative integration should thus be read as judicial and positive integration as legislative decision making, as this is the underlying importance of the distinction.

Knill and Lehmkuhl (1999) were the first to include negative integration in Europeanization studies. Establishing different types of Europeanization mechanisms, they argued that for the implementation of positive measures the question of institutional fit between European requirements and domestic institutions was dominant. For negative measures, in contrast, demands on the domestic systems were less precise so that it would be more relevant how domestic actors were responding to the opportunity structure resulting from negative integration (Knill and Lehmkuhl 1999: 2, 8). This note expands on the idea of negative integration as presenting an opportunity structure. But it rejects the argument of Knill and Lehmkuhl that the implementation of positive measures is more difficult than that of negative measures (see also Bauer et al. 2007: 411). Member states co-operate in the definition of positive measures, and often manage to include several options in directives. Decisions of negative integration, in contrast, involve member states less prominently, given the role of the Commission and the Court. Thus it is more plausible to expect the very opposite (Schmidt 2003).

In a more recent article, Knill and Lenschow (2005) have taken up the distinction again. Analyzing the potential for cross-national policy convergence, they distinguish three different mechanisms – coercion, competition, and communication. Coercion thereby corresponds to positive integration, while competition relates to negative integration, and communication is linked to the Open Method of Coordination. This differentiation seems to be gaining increasing support (cf. Bulmer and Radaelli 2005). Again, while the liberalizing effect of negative integration can be expected to further competition, it is not plausible that this could be the main mechanism – the obligation of market making can be as coercive on member states as are measures of positive integration.

To conclude, the Europeanization literature takes up the distinction between positive and negative integration. But negative integration is misrepresented and implementation studies dominate the field (Börzel 2001, Mbaye 2001, Falkner et al. 2004).

The Domestic Impact of EU Membership: Including Legal Uncertainty

To summarize the argument so far: to include negative integration in Europeanization studies is not only important because the thrust of policies differs, with market making against market shaping. It is important because the policy-making process differs, with judicial policy making playing a much greater role for negative integration. Judicial policy making forms the backdrop of most negative integration, given that the interpretations of the ECJ are decisive.

When member states are concerned by court rulings, this section argues, a distinct dynamic unfolds as legal uncertainty plays a major role in the impact of judicial policy making. Legal uncertainty serves as an opportunity structure for domestic actors so that member states are affected very differently compared to the implementation of secondary law.

If legal uncertainty matters specifically for negative integration, it is first of all necessary to establish the differences between judicial and legislative policy making. While the Treaty – on which negative integration mostly relies – includes only general statements, European secondary law, more relevant for positive integration, is full of compromises in need of interpretation (Everling 2000: 221). Goldstein and Martin (2000: 606) even argue that governments may not be able to enter international obligations without the "veil of ignorance" over the precise future consequences of international regimes, as otherwise domestic lobbying groups mobilize against them. There are thus reasons to believe that legal uncertainty matters in general, for negative and positive integration alike. While directives include some requirements which are clearly set and easy to monitor (for example, a certain extent of parental leave), others are much less precise. One example would be whether the directive on certain aspects of working time (93/104/EC) prohibits member states from demanding compliance with stricter domestic vacation rules on the part of non-national EU posted workers (Giesen 2003: 156) – which they may do, following C-49/98, C-50/98, C-52/98 to C-54/98 and C-68/98 to C-71 (*Finalarte*, 25 October 2001).

Nevertheless, there are good arguments to believe that legal uncertainty is more closely related to judicial than to legislative policy making. First of all, there are fewer guidelines in primary as opposed to secondary law. While directives delve into specific regulatory topics at great length, Treaty articles cover general topics with comparatively few sentences. There is thus greater need of interpretation when these articles are applied to specific national situations. The following quote makes this point for the freedom of goods and its exception.

> The bulk of the task was, however, left to the Court. It was the Court that had to determine the scope of the prohibition decreed by Article 30. It was the Court that had to decide in what circumstances a measure caught by Article 30 was justified on the grounds set out in Article 36.... The expression "creative jurisprudence", which is often used in mock disparagement of courts that give non-obvious answers to questions for which there is no obvious answer, is especially absurd in this context; for whatever the Court did with such scant material, its jurisprudence was bound to be creative. (Keeling 1998: 512)

Secondly, with the exception of those cases where member states recently acceded, they themselves have negotiated the text of secondary law with regard to specific policies. They can therefore be expected to be more familiar with its implications than with the interpretation of primary law, which is shaped by the ECJ. When interpreting the Treaty, the ECJ generally uses the teleological method and is oriented to the goal of further integration (Pescatore 1983). Moreover, the interpretation of the Treaty is not set in stone but subject to considerable development as integration progresses. This is apparent with all landmark judgments such as Cassis de Dijon (120/78), Francovich (C-6/90), or Keck (C-267/91 and C-268/91), to name but a few.

Thirdly and lastly, legal uncertainty follows from the fact that judicial policy making is much more case-specific than legislative policy making. Courts are only asked to make decisions on contentious problems. In order to do so they must interpret rules. If these rules do not determine the issue at hand, judges use a method of interpretation to adapt the existing rules to their current problem. This interpretation leads to judge-made law (or case law). Necessarily, such law is primarily focused on the case at hand. Judicial policy making progresses normally in a very piecemeal and case-specific way – specific questions are resolved but there is insufficient legitimation to provide a more general policy line. As European law is superimposed on different national legal orders of member states, it may be difficult to assess what the results of one preliminary proceeding of the ECJ imply for other member states. Thus, while legal certainty is enhanced for the state concerned by the ruling, it may decrease for all others. National rules may be similar, but are likely to differ in some – possibly decisive – ways. Consequently, the impact of a preliminary proceeding dealing with a specific national question for other member states is often contentious (Hatzopoulos 2002: 728, Joerges 2005: 20). This discussion leads to the following hypotheses:

H1: Domestic implications of European integration differ, depending on whether they are caused by the impact of secondary law or by court rulings.

H2: The more integration is shaped by court rulings rather than directives and regulations, the more its impact is marked by legal uncertainty for the member states. Legal uncertainty implies that relevant actors disagree on the relevance of European legal integration for the domestic context.

A result of this legal uncertainty is that it is often unclear how far a policy question may still be regulated at the national level. The remaining reach of national competencies is contentious, and member states and supranational institutions may well diverge in their judgment of the situation. Moreover, legal uncertainty also implies that EU obligations are likely to be interpreted differently in different member states.

To summarize, there are many reasons to believe that legal uncertainty plays a greater role in the impact of judicial than of legislative policy making: negative integration relies on the provisions of the Treaty, which are much less detailed than secondary law is; member states have better knowledge of secondary law being involved in its formulation; and judges decide specific cases, not being legitimated to draw general policy guidelines. Given that cases stem from a wide variety of backgrounds, the implications of a specific ruling for another member state are difficult to know.

Domestic Policy Making under Legal Uncertainty

This section summarizes several empirical examples of Europeanization effects of negative integration, and develops further hypotheses.

National actors have an incentive to instrumentalize the European legal and political context to realize goals which do not find sufficient support in the national setting alone. The European legal context selectively strengthens particular interests, and serves as an opportunity structure for these, as has also been analyzed by Knill and Lehmkuhl (1999: 2, 8). The following hypothesis would have to be tested systematically in this context:

H3: The higher the legal uncertainty arising from a Treaty rule and its interpretation, the more opportunities it offers for domestic actors to turn to the European courts in order to press for Europeanization.

Thus, the liberalization of previously regulated or monopolized sectors in Germany was much facilitated through the European context (Schmidt 2003, see also Smith 2001). Those actors who are interested in liberalization were strengthened as they could now find support in European law. The national institutional setting, in contrast, had privileged those actors interested in the status quo. In the liberalization of road haulage, actors instrumentalized the legal uncertainty resulting from a pending preliminary proceeding to abolish the tariff system from January 1994 onwards. It became apparent only later that this had not been necessary; European law would have allowed Germany to keep the tariff system (Teutsch 2001: 143f).

Quite well known is also the complaint to the Commission lodged in 1993 on the part of German private banks about the privileges of German public banks. German public banks, belonging to the *Länder*, traditionally enjoyed significant privileges due to their public ownership status. In the end, after more than a decade of negotiations and a court ruling (C-209/00, 12 December 2002), the German public sector banks were restructured and the German private banks claimed a victory they could hardly have gained on the domestic political scene (Smith 2005).

Not only private actors use the opportunity structure offered at the European level. Public actors may also do so. An interesting example is how the German Federal Cartel Office used European competition law to fight against the existing electricity monopolies in Germany in the early 1990s – despite their legality under German law (see Schmidt 1998: 255–256).

These examples show how the emerging multi-level polity allows actors to use rules originally directed at trans-border activities for pursuing political and economic interests that are primarily domestic. The national systems of member states are thereby Europeanized, but these effects have hardly been captured by Europeanization analyses so far.

Legal uncertainty as to the domestic consequences of European law may not only entice action but also escape routes. If member states have to act under uncertainty as to the European legality of their policy instruments and goals, they sometimes simply choose policy instruments which realize the same policy goals in a less contested way. Töller (2004) terms this "evasion". She mentions several cases from German environmental policy, where domestic environmental goals were achieved by self-regulation, as it was unclear whether official German policies would be possible under European legislation. Examples are the prohibition of dangerous materials such as asbestos which could have been interpreted as a distortion of the free movement of goods. In order to evade this legal uncertainty, an agreement was sought with the relevant economic actors about the phasing out of this material.

In ongoing research about the state-aid regime in the Czech Republic and Poland, Michael Blauberger similarly finds instances of evasion. As the approval of state aid is a cumbersome process, new member states have resorted to regional-aid schemes which allow the notification of the entire program rather than having to clear different acts of aid. He also finds that lengthy notification procedures are avoided by redirecting aid so that it falls under block exemption regulations (Blauberger 2008).

Conclusion

This research note has argued that Europeanization research should take the distinction between positive and negative integration more seriously. This distinction matters not so much because the thrust of policies differs but because of the difference in institutional background. Behind the institutionalist bias of the EU in favor of negative integration is the dominance of judicial policy making for the latter, while positive integration relies mostly on legislative policy making. Rulings by the European courts, more so than legislation, imply legal uncertainty for member states.[2]

Domestic actors interested in changing domestic policies find an opportunity structure in legal uncertainty. In the case of negative integration, therefore, Europeanization effects are less determined top-down by the need to implement specific obligations of European secondary law, as is often analyzed in Europeanization studies. Rather, much depends on domestic actors' interests and features of the polity.

The precise impact of negative integration is subject to further research. This note presented several hypotheses as a starting point for such an undertaking. Possibly, there are also differences among member states when reacting to legal uncertainty.

Acknowledgements

For this note I have profited from my participation in the Integrated Project "New Modes of Governance" (see the website http://www.eu-newgov.org). Funding provided by the 6th Framework Program of the European Union (Contract No CIT1-CT-2004-506392) is gratefully acknowledged. Annette Töller, Claudio Radaelli, Wendy van den Nouland, and Michael Blauberger gave helpful comments on previous drafts. I would also like to thank the participants of the workshop in Grenoble in March 2006 for their valuable feedback. Last not least, the note was fundamentally rewritten following excellent comments from anonymous reviewers, for which I am very grateful.

Notes

1. Note that the focus of the argument is on the implications of institutions and not on their genesis.
2. Another issue touched upon in this note is whether legislative policy making in the EU always results in precise obligations, or to which extent legal uncertainty plays a role in the implementation of secondary law. If this is the case, the question of compliance may become a matter of degree and cannot be dealt with in an either/or distinction.

References

Alexander, Gerard, 2002, Institutionalized uncertainty, the rule of law, and the sources of democratic stability. *Comparative Political Studies*, **35,** 1145–1170.
Bauer, Michael W., Knill, Christoph and Pitschel, Diana, 2007, Differential Europeanization in Eastern Europe: the impact of diverse EU regulatory governance patterns. *European Integration*, **29,** 405–423.
Blauberger, Michael, 2006, Making a virtue of necessity. Soft law in European state aid control. Paper presented at the 1st Newgov-Connex Training Course, EUI Florence.

Blauberger, Michael, 2008, From negative to positive integration? European state aid control through soft and hard law. MPIfG Discussion Paper 08/4, available at http://www.mpifg.de/pu/mpifg_dp/dp08-4.pdf (accessed 7 June 2008).
Börzel, Tanja A., 2001, Non-compliance in the European Union: pathology or statistical artefact? *Journal of European Public Policy*, **8**, 803–824.
Börzel, Tanja A. and Risse, Thomas, 2003, Conceptualizing the domestic impact of Europe, in: Keith Featherstone and Claudio Radaelli (Eds) *The Politics of Europeanisation* (Oxford: Oxford University Press), pp. 57–82.
Börzel, Tanja A. and Risse, Thomas, 2007, Europeanization: the domestic impact of European Union politics, in: Knud Erik Jørgensen, Mark A. Pollack and Ben Rosamond (Eds) *Handbook of European Union Politics* (London: Sage Publications), pp. 483–503.
Bulmer, Simon and Radaelli, Claudio M., 2005, The Europeanization of national policy, in: Simon Bulmer and Christian Lequesne (Eds) *The Member States of the European Union* (Oxford: Oxford University Press), pp. 338–359.
Dequech David, 2001, Bounded Rationality, Institutions, and Uncertainty. *Journal of Economic Issues*, **35**, 911–929.
Eising, Rainer, 2003, Europäisierung und Integration. Konzepte in der EU-Forschung, in: Markus Jachtenfuchs and Beate Kohler-Koch (Eds) *Europäische Integration* (Opladen: Leske und Budrich), pp. 387–416.
Everling, Ulrich, 2000, Richterliche Rechtsfortbildung in der EG. *Juristenzeitung*, **55**, 217–227.
Falkner, Gerda, Hartlapp, Miriam, Leiber, Simone and Treib, Oliver, 2004, Non-compliance with EU directives in the member states: opposition through the backdoor? *West European Politics*, **27**, 452–473.
Giesen, Richard, 2003, Posting: social protection of workers vs. fundamental freedoms? *Common Market Law Review*, **40**, 143–158.
Goldstein, Judith and Martin, Lisa L., 2000, Legalization, trade liberalization, and domestic politics: a cautionary note. *International Organization*, **54**, 603–632.
Hatzopoulos, Vassilis, 2002, Killing national health and insurance systems but healing patients? The European market for health care services after the judgments of the ECJ in Vanbraekel and Peerbooms. *Common Market Law Review*, **39**, 683–729.
Héritier, Adrienne, 1997, Market-making policy in Europe: its impact on member state policies. The case of road haulage in Britain, the Netherlands, Germany and Italy. *Journal of European Public Policy*, **4**, 539–555.
Joerges, Christian, 2005, Rethinking European law's supremacy: a plea for a supranational conflict of laws. *EUI Working Paper Law* 2005/12.
Keeling, David, 1998, In praise of judicial activism, in: Seminario Giuridico della Università di Bologna (Ed) *Scritti in onore di Giuseppe Federico Mancini* (Milano: Dott. A. Giuffrè Editore), pp. 505–536.
Knill, Christoph and Lenschow, Andrea, 2005, Compliance, competition and communication: different approaches of European governance and their impact on national institutions. *Journal of Common Market Studies*, **43**, 583–606.
Knill, Christoph and Lehmkuhl, Dirk, 1999, How Europe matters. Different mechanisms of Europeanization. *European Integration Online Papers* (EIoP), **3**, available at http://eiop.or.at/eiop/texte/1999-007a.htm (accessed 7 June 2008).
Knill, Christoph and Lehmkuhl, Dirk, 2002, The national impact of European Union regulatory policy: three Europeanization mechanisms. *European Journal of Political Research*, **41**, 255–280.
Kohler-Koch, Beate, 2000, Europäisierung: Plädoyer für eine Horizonterweiterung, in: Michèle Knodt and Beate Kohler-Koch (Eds) *Deutschland zwischen Europäisierung und Selbstbehauptung* (Frankfurt/Main: Campus), pp. 11–31.
Mbaye, Heather A. D., 2001, Why national states comply with supranational law. *European Union Politics*, **2**, 259–281.
Pescatore, Pierre, 1983, La carence du législateur communautaire et le devoir du juge, in: Gerhard Lüke, Georg Ress and Michael R. Will (Eds) *Rechtsvergleichung – Gedächtnisschrift für Léontin-Jean Constantinesco* (Köln, Berlin, Bonn, München: Heymanns), pp. 559–580.
Rathbun, Brian C., 2007, Uncertain about uncertainty: understanding the multiple meanings of a crucial concept in international relations theory. *International Studies Quarterly*, **51**, 533–557.
Risse, Thomas, Green Cowles, Maria and Caporaso, James A., 2001, Europeanization and domestic change: introduction, in: Maria Green Cowles, James A. Caporaso and Thomas Risse (Eds) *Transforming Europe* (London: Cornell University Press), pp. 1–20.

Scharpf, Fritz W., 1999, *Governing in Europe: Effective and Democratic?* (Oxford: Oxford University Press).
Scharpf, Fritz W., 2002, The European social model: coping with the challenges of diversity. *Journal of Common Market Studies*, **40**, 645–670.
Scharpf, Fritz W., 2006, The joint-decision trap revisited. *Journal of Common Market Studies*, **44**, 845–864.
Schmidt, Susanne K., 1998, *Liberalisierung in Europa. Die Rolle der Europäischen Kommission* (Frankfurt: Campus).
Schmidt, Susanne K., 2003, Die nationale Bedingtheit der Folgen der europäischen Integration. *Zeitschrift für Internationale Beziehungen*, **10**, 43–68.
Schmidt, Vivien A., 1997, European integration and institutional change: the transformation of national patterns of policy-making, in: Gerhard Göhler (Ed) *Institutionenwandel* (Opladen: Westdeutscher Verlag), pp. 143–180.
Smith, Mitchell P., 2001, Europe and the German model: growing tension or symbiosis? *German Politics*, **10**, 119–140.
Smith, Mitchell P., 2005, *States of Liberalization: Redefining the Public Sector in Integrated Europe* (Albany, NY: State University of New York Press).
Teutsch, Michael, 2001, Regulatory reforms in the German transport sector: how to overcome multiple veto points, in: Adrienne Héritier, Dieter Kerwer, Christoph Knill, Dirk Lehmkuhl, Michael Teutsch and Anne-Cécile Douillet, *Differential Europe* (Lanham: Rowman & Littlefield Publishers), pp. 133–172.
Töller, Annette Elisabeth, 2004, The Europeanization of public politics – understanding idiosyncratic mechanisms and contingent results. *European Integration Online Papers* (EiOP), **8**, available at http://eiop.or.at/eiop/texte/2004-009a.htm (accessed 7 June 2008).

Governance in the European Union: A Policy Analysis of the Attempts to Raise Legitimacy through Civil Society Participation

EVA G. HEIDBREDER

ABSTRACT *The article focuses on two flagship initiatives – the open method of co-ordination and online consultations – in which the European Union aimed to improve democratic legitimacy through collaborative governance. Offering an analytical framework to scrutinize the large body of existing theoretical and empirical research, the article concludes that not only were the high expectations on the effects of applied governance disappointed, the results also hint at larger, more general implications for the governance concept that, in contrast to the high expectations, appears to be indeed strongly dependent on government-like conditions to operate successfully.*

Introduction: Approaches to Legitimizing Governance

Revisiting conceptual and empirical notions of governance, the present article focuses on attempts of the European Union to improve the democratic quality of its rule through collaborative forms of decision-making. The aim is to contrast theoretical research on how EU governance ought to work with empirical findings about two key initiatives that promote collaborative governance. Rather than presenting a genuine empirical analysis of a certain policy tool, the goal of the article is to link the findings offered by, on the one hand, theoretical research and, on the other hand, empirical studies conducted roughly since the turn of the millennium (for a complete literature review see below). The methodological approach of this article is to develop an analytical framework that will serve to distil from the large body of literature more specific insights about governance in the EU and beyond.

The subject of analysis this article tackles is the EU because, short of a government proper, it is actively applying and promoting other forms of governance. The bias of having to steer with other tools than traditional government has motivated countless studies on EU governance – which have mutually influenced political practice that has tried to apply governance approaches in a more ideal-typical way than usually observable. The rather close epistemic community that pushed governance concerns on both the academic and political EU agenda in the early 2000s (Kohler-Koch 2010a: 103) makes the initiatives ever more interesting from a conceptual angle. The selection of the two flagship initiatives allows us, first, to illustrate the theoretical expectations linked to alternative governance approaches by practitioners. Second, contrasting the various research findings regarding the actual success or failure of these initiatives allows us to draw some more general conclusions about certain functioning logics of governance – and hence contribute to the purpose of the special issue, which is the conceptualization of governance more generally, in improving the conceptual distinctiveness of governance, which is often used as a catch-all term for ruling without delineating it clearly.

The selected cases both aim at improving the democratic quality of EU policymaking through participatory governance. More than 10 years ago, the European Commission launched its *White Paper on European Governance* (Commission of the European Communities 2001), a veritable blueprint to enact the alleged prospects of "new" governance. Just a year before, the European Council had formally inaugurated the open method of co-ordination (OMC), an attempt to jointly tackle sensitive social policies without conferring policymaking powers from the state to the EU level. Whilst the cases share the normative assumption that stakeholder involvement enhances the democratic value to policymaking, they differ with respect to the initiating actors and their more encompassing motives. While the Commission wanted to raise its legitimacy as political agent, the member state governments aimed primarily at co-ordinating policies at the EU level without conferring substantive powers to the EU. Moreover, both initiatives have been central to the EU agenda and have entailed the creation of policy tools which have by now become widely applied, even though not necessarily due to their overwhelming success in achieving the underpinning goals. The cases illustrate two different theoretical mechanisms being applied in actual policymaking. Although the comparison of only two cases does not allow for broad generalizations, bringing together the findings about crucial advances can enhance our understanding about systematic inconsistencies between conceptual and applied governance.

The remainder of the article proceeds as follows. The next section will set the theoretical scene and closes with the introduction of an analytical framework, which is subsequently used to scrutinize the applied and academic use of governance in the EU. The article closes by summarizing the results of the collective research on the mechanisms and outcomes of governance the EU has produced and returns to the questions the editors raise, namely, which legitimizing effect governance does indeed have, and what consequences this has for the conceptual development of governance.

Setting the Scene, Basic Definitions and Analytical Frame: Governance in the EU

To capture the notion of governance in academia and policymaking and to measure the expectations on governance against its eventual occurrence, I will first briefly review central definitions of governance with special attention to the EU context. Against this background, the high-flying expectations scholars and practitioners attributed to the use of collaborative governance will be illustrated along the selected initiatives, and a framework to explore the findings offered by EU scholarship will be introduced.

Definitions of Governance and Governance in the EU: Governing without Government

The term *governance* has been excessively applied in social sciences and political practice. As an analytical perspective, governance accounts systematically for non-hierarchical co-operation that differs from the traditionally attributed internal and external roles of the state. Across the sub-disciplines of public administration and public policy, international relations, and comparative research, governance "refers to something broader than government, and it is about steering and the rules of the game" (Kjær 2004: 7). Inside the state, the perspective serves to account for co-operative steering, or network governance, involving public and private actors (Rhodes 1997). Between states, increased internationalization has given a boost to the governance perspective in international relations as "governance without government" (Rosenau and Czempiel 1992). From the multiple scholarly references to governance, we can discern a wide and a narrow definition of the term. In its narrow definition, governance is limited to co-ordination modes distinct from coercive hierarchical steering exercised by public authorities. The wide definition of governance encompasses, in contrast, all forms of intentional collective co-ordination and every mode of political steering involving public and private actors. The broadest shared meaning of governance in all these variants is "how to steer, but also how to improve accountability" (Kjær 2004: 11). To grasp the core of the governance concept in actual policymaking, I will apply the narrow definition of the concept in order to scrutinize to what extent the envisaged legitimizing gains pass the empirical test by juxtaposing the expected and actual legitimizing potential of "new" governance.

Turning to empirical analytical research, the European Union has been one of the preferred objects of governance research; indeed much conceptual development resulted from EU scholarship. The so-called governance turn in EU studies (Kohler-Koch and Rittberger 2006) was connected to a shift in the research agenda away from questions of polity formation and causes of regional integration, to queries of how a multilevel and non-hierarchical system involving multiple public and private actors produces public policies. In the multilevel setting of the EU that has established the direct effect of supranational law and joint supranational decision-making bodies but no genuine governmental centre of power, the distinctions between the subjects and objects of political steering are blurred and the procedural feature of *governance* in contrast to a state-centered static notion of authoritative *government* moves to the center of attention. Although there is wide scholarly agreement that governance is the most suitable concept to capture EU policymaking, the terminology and definitions are still multiple. A wide range of concepts and notions circulate that include most prominently notions of governance as network, multilevel, informal, new modes, innovative, co-ordinated or experimental. The reason for the strong affinity of EU scholars for governance concepts lies in the specificities of the EU polity that lacks a single center of authority, ultimate coercive enforcement tools, and hence the means for traditional hierarchical steering associated with "government". Building on the insights of international relations and public policy research on co-ordinating public policies beyond the state, the "European Union, then, is conceptualized as a multi-level system of 'governance', where private and public actors of the supranational, national, and subnational level interact within highly complex networks to produce policy outcomes" (Börzel 2011: 53).

In addition to the notable reception in academia, practitioners in the EU have increasingly applied governance approaches in day-to-day policymaking. Governance beyond hierarchical steering was first evoked in order to prevent the conferral of coercive powers to the EU level during the 1990s. Ever since, it has been expanded and increasingly soft steering modes are applied instead of harmonizing state policies in binding EU regulation. Especially since the early 2000s, different collective actors in the EU have – for varying reasons – devised concrete governance instruments. Two initiatives that promote collaborative policymaking stick out, sponsored by different collaborative notions: the Council as the representative body of the member states, and the Commission as the independent secretariat with an exclusive right to initiate EU legislation. First, the European Council (body of the heads of member states and governments) introduced the so-called open-method of co-ordination to implement the goals of a 10-year development plan, the Lisbon Strategy (European Council 2000: para. 37). Building on earlier mechanisms of the European Employment Strategy, the focal points of the OMC were social policies in which member states showed great reluctance regarding binding EU regulation, yet stuck to intergovernmental co-ordination mechanisms that rest on policy learning and voluntary exchange and the adoption of best practices among peers. The inclusion of non-state actors was an integral part of the OMC. The second initiative referred to the governance concept as a term that "corresponds to the so-called post-modern form of economic and political organisations". Issuing the White Paper on European Governance (Commission of the European Communities 2001), the European Commission established its conception of governance: "the term 'European governance' refers to rules, processes and behaviour that affect the way in which powers are exercised at European level, particularly as regards openness, participation, accountability, effectiveness and coherence".[1] The White Paper served as a document of general policy orientation for the Commission that subsequently established various collaborative governance tools, whose most elaborated form, the Commission's online consultations, will be reviewed here. As will be illustrated below, the Commission's consultation regime had existed for a long time but underwent decisive changes in connection to the governance agenda. The decisive innovation of introducing online consultations was that participation was essentially opened up to every citizen. The fact that instead of exclusive Brussels-based representative groups, all kinds of actors are offered access to policy documents and are invited to provide input resulted in high expectations that online consultations would increase participation and reduce the distance between EU policymakers and citizens.

Expectations on Governance in Academia and Practice: Enhancing the Democratic Quality

To evaluate the output of these collaborative governance approaches, it is necessary to put the theoretical presumptions that underpin both the Council's and the Commission's initiatives into perspective. As Büchs elaborates, the most ambitious normative expectations put on the OMC are derived from the framework of directly deliberative polyarchy (Cohen and Sabel 1997). The most pronounced proponents of "directly-deliberative polyarchy emphasize the OMC's potential to provide a blueprint for a new model of EU democracy and are therefore optimistic that the OMC could contribute to an enhanced quality of democracy within the EU. Directly-deliberative polyarchy is perceived as an alternative to representative and constitutional democracy" (Büchs 2008: 773–774). This is linked to a cognitive dimension "to which many scholars ascribe cognitive and discursive shifts in member states" (Stiller and van Gerven 2012: 119). All in all, the first generation of OMC scholarship "was relatively optimistic regarding both its legitimacy and potential to increase the European Union's democratic quality" (Büchs 2008: 776). The consultation with civil society and stakeholders, which was initially an integral part of the OMC, also stands at the center of the Commission's approach to raise its accountability and legitimacy vis-à-vis EU citizens. The driving theoretical logic is that stakeholder involvement in policy formulation improves both the quality of policy solutions and their acceptance, which in turn fosters the success of policy implementation of the collaborate results. In other words:

> First, the new modes of governance were envisaged as a means for improving problem-solving capacity at the European Union level ... Secondly, the new modes of governance are designed with the aim of addressing complex and long-standing policy problems with a new, more collaborative approach. This is based on the double understanding that such a collaborative approach would solve some of the complex problems across the EU and bring the EU closer to its citizens. (Borras and Ejrnæs 2011: 108)

Keeping in mind that the EU falls short of the basic competence of a state to attribute itself hierarchical steering instruments and coercive tools, both the OMC and the consultation regime were in practice not only an addition to existing democratic procedures: they had to serve as alternatives to other means, or a second-best option.

Following these academic assessments, policymakers also entertained high expectations regarding the legitimizing potential of (new) governance. The introduction of the OMC was driven by an "initial optimism that the OMC would broaden participation, improve transparency and cross-sectoral learning and increase the potential for experimental governance involving a broad range of stakeholders (Sabel and Zeitlin 2007) has turned into concern about the democratic legitimacy of European policy coordination and its impact on national policy-making" (Michalski 2012: 298). To this end, the European Council explicitly stressed the wide, collaborative definition of the OMC as decentralized approach in "which the Union, the Member States, the regional and local levels, as well as the social partners and civil society, will be actively involved, using variable forms of partnership" (European Council 2000). Similarly, the Governance White Paper formulated a straightforward normative understanding of collaborative governance promoted by the Commission. The Commission has since expanded long-standing tools to interact with civil society – especially organized groups – and developed new collaborative instruments. Building on the White Paper and a discussion paper focusing explicitly on NGOs (Prodi and Kinnock 2000), Quittkat (2013a: 79) exemplifies in her examination of two Directorate Generals of the Commission "that the spectrum of instruments has diversified within the past few years and that policy forums and policy networks have been added to conferences and online consultations". Since of these four instruments online consultation is the most accessible for non-public actors and is by far the most extensively used tool, it serves as a representative case here. Devising three generations of the Commission's consultation regime, Quittkat and Finke identify changed normative claims about civil society participation. Starting with the early days of European economic integration, the Commission relied on intense, informal and usually ad hoc dialogue with economic experts. During the mid-1980s, it moved on to a "partnership" notion of the EU–civil society relationship, leading to the vitalization of the EU's Social Dialogue with the social partners, and its extension under the guise of "civil dialogue" to non-governmental actors in various areas, backed also by the establishment of a "social platform". The third generation, on which our main focus lies, builds on the White Paper's move to concepts of "participatory democracy" and more embracing demands on partnership with civil society. The introduction of an online consultation instrument in the aftermath of the White Paper marks a substantive change in public access to the EU policymaking processes and a break from earlier strategies toward a declared collaborative approach (Quittkat and Finke 2008).

In sum, there are two distinct expectations about democracy-enhancing effects. The underlying mechanism the OMC depends on is mutual learning in a process of open and voluntary exchange, theorized as deliberative processes. Policymakers relied on this expectation when inaugurating the OMC procedure as a process of voluntary exchange. Online consultations improved stakeholder inclusion, which is expected to support system effectiveness because "it can help to overcome problems of implementation by considering motives and by fostering the willingness of policy addressees to comply as well as through the mobilization of the knowledge of those affected" (Gbikpi and Grote 2002: 23). The legitimacy-enhancing expectation linked to this approach rests on the assumption that by intensifying the exchange between the Commission and CSOs, the latter would serve as a transmission belt between the EU and citizens and thus enhance the overall legitimacy of the policymaking process.

A Framework to Capture Governance Concepts and Use: Actors, Actions and Achievements

How then can the results on the actual use of governance be put into an analytical perspective in order to draw more far-reaching conclusions about the conceptual reach and implications of the term? To capture motivations behind the recourse to governance, the actual application of governance instruments and the impact of the two, I propose to structure the debate along three basic dimensions: actors, actions and achievements. To account for the networked nature of governance (Rhodes 1997: 109), we need to review who the participating actors are, how they are formally and informally linked, and what objectives they pursue by involving themselves in collaborative governance. Additionally, in order to capture governance, we need to examine tangible actions and which center of authority is dominant. Finally, closing the circle and returning to the question of the practical and theoretical value added, it is indispensable to scrutinize the achievements in terms of performance of policy outputs – measured against high-flying normative and theoretical expectations.

Yet these three dimensions provide only a descriptive framework. In order to evaluate to what extent expectations about governance have been met – that is, the improved "democratic quality" of EU policy-making – the three dimensions do not suffice. To link the large range of normative claims and causal mechanisms, the distinction of input, output and throughput legitimating processes will serve to evaluate the findings of the following analysis. Scharpf's much-cited distinction argues that the EU featured traditionally strongly in legitimizing itself through policy outputs while the input side – that is, the democratic involvement of citizens in decision-making – remained weak, and even underdeveloped to justify the expansion of redistributive policies on the EU level (Scharpf 2003). Adding the notion of "throughput", Schmidt opens the black box of decision-making itself and ascribes these processes a distinct role for legitimate policy-making (Schmidt 2010). Accordingly, independent of input and output, policy-making that rests on corrupt, illegal or otherwise harmful processes is not legitimate. Notably, the author does not claim that throughput can replace either input or output mechanisms, but that it can nonetheless discredit both. Even though Scharpf's – and Schmidt's extended – distinction has been criticized, in particular with respect to the notion of output legitimacy (Fuchs 2011: 30), it is considered of use here because it mirrors the same benchmarks that operate by and large in the background of the expectations discussed above. Therefore, for the purpose of this paper, input, output and throughput, as theorized by EU scholars and absorbed by EU policy-makers, are used as yardsticks to estimate the intended and actual effect of the two initiatives under examination. Accordingly, we can formulate more concrete expectations. If collaborative governance is to indeed enhance the democratic quality of EU policy-making:

- input legitimacy should be enhanced through more accountability and/or a more deliberative decision-making process;
- output legitimacy should be enhanced through some tangible policy change ;
- and throughput legitimacy should be enhanced through higher inclusiveness of the policy process.

The next section will summarize relevant findings in the EU scholarship within this framework. On this basis, we can then estimate the repercussions on the input, output and throughput dimensions in the final section of the article.

Collaborative Governance in EU Policy-Making: Actors, Actions and Achievements

How does collaborative governance play out in a multilevel polity and which effects does it produce? In order to answer these questions, we will review three basic dimensions: actors, actions and achievements introduced in the last section. The two initiatives will be discussed in turn in each paragraph.

Actors: The Union's Top-down Bias

The instruments of collaborative governance in the EU were introduced mainly as an activation strategy designed by EU public actors. The underlying aim was to motivate and include civil society actors to improve the input and output legitimacy of policy-making. Collaborative governance in these instances is accordingly marked by a top-down bias with little – if any – bottom-up involvement for participatory rights, not least due to the absence of an integrated cross-European civil society. I will review the main actors in ordinary EU decision-making, whose involvement in participatory procedures we should expect in the EU system. The focus is on the motivations and observable involvement in each of the two initiatives.

The most prominent proponent of collaborative governance is the European Commission. The motivation for opting for collaborative governance is, above all, the absence of other means to raise its legitimacy and accountability and establish direct links between the Brussels-based administration and EU citizens. Since the Commission has no legal powers to change its formal institutional status, the collaborative elements in the process of policy formulation in particular were introduced as tool to boost its legitimacy by offering throughput participation to citizens. As co-ordinator and interlocutor the Commission is relevant in both initiatives. In the OMC, the Commission formally has mainly a monitoring role since decision-making power rests exclusively with national governments. Since the Commission co-ordinates the definition of shared standards and benchmarks, as well as the monitoring of national reform programs, it has been shown that it actually has considerable informal influence in various OMCs. For instance, in education and technology "the role of the Commission should not be overlooked, as the Commission is often the initiator, driver, and main agenda setter in the OMC process" (Warleigh-Lack and Drachenberg 2010: 220). The Commission's relevance in the OMC is centrally based on the capacity to make extensive use of a co-ordinating role. In contrast, it sits formally in the driving seat in the consultation procedures. In addition, it can arguably exert informal influence on civil society organizations (CSOs) in the framework of the consultation regime by offering substantive funding to enable non-profit CSOs to participate. The extension of consultation procedures was not foreseen in the Treaties or imposed by member states. Instead it follows the self-defined logic spelled out in the Commission's Governance White Paper. The declared aim of the Commission is to involve citizens during the policy formulation phase – however, without giving up its exclusive power to initiate legislation. The way the Commission is involved in both initiatives, the Commission seems to "want more" than its formal powers allow it to do; governance is applied as means to act and develop strategies to reach beyond its formally ascribed role. With a view to institutional competition among EU organizations "the Commission is eager for close cooperation with societal groups to gain expert knowledge, to test stakeholder readiness to comply, and to strengthen its position when it is in conflict with the European Parliament or the member states" (Kohler-Koch 2013a: 11). Rather than fostering deliberation or mutual exchange, the Commission's motivation is goal-oriented to benefit from expertise and enhance stakeholder support and thereby to lend itself more direct support and legitimacy.

The European Council's role is, due to its institutional setup, decisively different. It is the highest representative body of the member states without a formal legislative role in day-to-day policy-making. This means that it is not involved in consultations about specific policy initiatives. Composed of the heads of state and government, it serves as the main agenda setter that formulates the broad policy goals of the EU. The Council's motivation to opt for collaborative governance in the framework of the Lisbon Strategy as a long-term strategy was above all to prevent more binding legislation in the social policy arena. Pressured to co-ordinate on the EU level in areas of social policy, the state representatives had a strong incentive to find an alternative to the conferral of official competences to the EU. The OMC offered a new, non-binding instrument as alternative to binding EU law. In everyday policy-making, national line ministers interact in the Council of the EU to implement the OMC on the member states' behalf. The Council of Ministers therefore shapes the different stages of the OMC. In terms of co-ordination logic, the Council fell back on governance because it "wanted to do less" than harmonization in the EU framework – but more than no co-ordination in sensitive social, fiscal and welfare policies. The institutional challenge for the Councils is not so much on the EU level but inside the member state polities whose traditional steering has to accommodate more participatory mechanisms in the OMC framework. The motivation of the member state governments is hence in part negatively defined. While the pressure to co-ordinate certain policies is recognized, the objective is to do so in a deliberative process and through lesson drawing and peer pressure.

Notably, the European Parliament (EP), which has developed into the EU's central legislator together with the Council of the EU, is by and large marginalized in the Union's collaborative governance. Listing the EP as an actor in this section therefore serves the purpose of delineating the new governance modes from traditional democratic representation, although the EP is usually neglected in this debate. Especially the OMC has long been a thorn in the Parliament's side because the EP remained completely excluded. As the EU's Glossary, explaining basic mechanisms of EU policy-making, points out: "The European Parliament and the Court of Justice play virtually no part in the OMC process".[2] For obvious reasons, the EP, like the Council, remains outside the consultation regime, which the Commission developed as a purely internal practice. However, the EP has advanced to the main target for interest groups to lobby for certain policy outputs (Marshall 2010), where it has come to play de facto an important informal – albeit often questionable – role for special interest representatives. As body of directly elected citizens' representatives the EP "reacted rather defensively to the topic of 'better involvement.' It commented skeptically on the revaluation of civil society through consultations and participation. Understandably, it emphasized the significance of representative democracy and warned to take great care when introducing elements of participatory democracy into the political system" (Kohler-Koch 2013b: 26).

Taking a look at non-state/non-EU actors, these "collaborators" in EU governance show a set of specific features, even though their role obviously varies in the two initiatives under scrutiny. Reviewing the OMC in education and training, Warleigh-Lack and Dracheberg (2010: 220) conclude that although "the involvement of non-state actors besides government representatives is officially promoted, the practical participation of social partners, regional governments, and civil society at large depends very much on the national traditions and political structures in the member states". This finding of territorial and resource-dependent participation biases is also reflected in other areas of the OMC and in the participation patterns of the consultation procedures (Altides 2011). Considering incentives, apart from the flourishing lobbying communities in Brussels, it is relevant that it was not civil society that pushed bottom-up for either the introduction of the OMC or the extension of informal consultations. Turing to the question of who participates in the consultation procedure, the expectation was that online consultations would offer wider access for citizens. However, as will be discussed in a moment, this has not materialized so far. There is a clear bias in favor of organized, professional groups rather than grassroots-level initiatives or individuals reflected in a "double distortion, namely in terms of region and specific interests" (Quittkat 2013b: 109). In order to increase the involvement of non-state actors with few of their own resources, the Commission offers regular funding to civil society organizations, raising the question of CSO independence from public funders. Crucial for the motivation of participating civil society actors is that both initiatives attempt to activate non-state actor participation by imposing a top-down approach. Neither the OMC nor online consultations were introduced in response to bottom-up pressure from citizens; on the contrary, both initiatives aim to activate and include organized civil society.

Actions: Activation and Informal Consultation of Organized Civil Society

Following the academic expectations that dominated at the beginning of the 2000s, and which were actively taken up by practitioners, inclusion of non-state actors is a necessary condition of system effectiveness and is eventually expected to improve the quality of the Union's legitimacy. Let us briefly review how the OMC and direct citizens' consultations have taken shape in the EU. The first use of the OMC goes back to 1997 when it was introduced by the Luxemburg Summit that created the OMC mechanism as an instrument to implement the European Employment Strategy (EES) through soft, non-binding law. The most important expansion of the OMC was the Lisbon Council, which installed it as the prime tool to achieve the ambitious social and welfare goals of the Lisbon Agenda (European Council 2000). According to the Lisbon European Council, the OMC was to contribute to grand social and welfare goals and ultimately the modernization of the European Social Model to achieve more social cohesion (Teló 2002). The Treaty of Lisbon (2009) finally gave the OMC a consolidated constitutional status. From the EES the OMC has been expanded to various areas of economic, monetary and social policies in which the member states seek to co-ordinate without conferring hard powers to the EU. In the area of Economic and Monetary Union, the Growth and Stability Pact, established to guarantee fiscal compliance of member states in the monetary union (Eurozone), follows the voluntary OMC design. Other areas include social inclusion, immigration, education, research and technology, the internet, health care and pensions. The general working practice across the different OMCs proceeds in stages. First, the Council of Ministers fixes shared guidelines and a timetable for action; second, benchmarks and measurable indicators to compare national performance are defined; third, the EU guidelines are transposed into specific national reform programs in the member states; fourth and finally, states compare their results in periodic monitoring and peer review exercises in order to promote mutual learning. In the decentralized approach to developing national responses and reforms, civil society and stakeholders are expected to play a key participating role and to "ensure the input legitimacy of OMCs, openness was made one of the defining elements of OMCs, resulting in a promise to involve stakeholders and national parliaments" (de Ruiter 2012: 3). While the general procedure of the OMC has not changed, the role of civil society has de facto been downgraded substantially after the first midterm review (Kok 2004), due to its limited achievements that will be elaborated below. In terms of actions taken, the OMC was designed to enhance both its own success in triggering learning and its legitimacy through non-public actor involvement at the state level. The participatory element was soon rolled back whilst national parliaments and media have not taken on an independent leading role, leaving state governments as the sole dominant actors.

The European Commission's consultation regime is the most significant and visible follow-up tool of the Governance White Paper. The White Paper itself did not spell out concrete measures but stressed the need to enhance the legitimacy of EU policy-making through more inclusive participation. Notably, the emphasis of the White Paper was on "throughput". The document did not call for more representative democratic tools and to improve the input legitimacy by further empowering the EP; nor did it limit itself to the notion that good output alone was sufficient to legitimate EU policies. Based on better throughput as a principle of "good governance", the Commission elaborated a system of voluntary inclusion of civil society. The basic assumption was that more collaborative governance would improve input and output, in other words: "Participation is supposed to enhance both the efficiency and the legitimacy of European governance" (Magnette 2001). This goal was practically enacted in the consultation policy that had developed from the 1990s (Kohler-Koch and Finke 2007). A major innovation was the introduction of online consultation tools, which substantially widen the accessibility and possibility for decentralized groups to participate. Since 2002, the Commission has applied an online tool, developing step-by-step the modes by which individuals and CSOs can feed in their views on policy proposals. To this end, the website "Your Voice in Europe" serves as an access point where proposals, contributions and results of hearings, academic studies or other information are collected and made publicly available. In the Commission's words: "Your Voice in Europe is the European Commission's 'single access point' to a wide variety of consultations, discussions and other tools which enable you to play an active role in the European policy-making process".[3] Even though the website still falls far short of offering a real single point of access (Quittkat 2013b), compared to most national policy-making, the provision of information and attempt at broad collaboration is indeed ambitious and extensive. In terms of action, the online consultation infrastructure provides a potential platform for civil society actors to feed into policy-making processes, even if in the end all decision-making power rests with the Commission. We will now turn to the question of to what degree the tool fulfills its promise in practice – and why neither the expectations put into the OMC nor the consultation regime can really succeed in improving the democratic quality of the EU.

Achievements: The Failure of Governance as Alternative Approach

Turning to the balance sheet of achievements two questions are to be raised: have the OMC and the consultation regime increased collaborative governance, and has this increased the democratic quality of the EU's policymaking on the input, output or throughput dimension? Despite the OMC clauses on stakeholder involvement in the national implementation of EU law, the actual inclusion of civil society focused predominantly on supranational policy formulation (Trubek and Trubek 2005). It is illustrated by a

> large number of academic studies that national governments have tended to centralize the consultation processes as flexibility (in particular, temporal) and secrecy (purportedly to improve the conditions for a genuine peer review among national officials) have come to dominate the process. Centralization and bureaucratization, rather than transparency and inclusiveness, are the rule in many national contexts as national executives have become "the 'gate-keepers' of local participation" (Dawson 2009, 10) and "the functioning of the OMC depends on closure". (Michalski 2012: 411)

In sum, empirical studies have been rather sobering with respect to the legitimacy enhancing impact of this new governance mode either in improving the (deliberative) input or (efficiency enhancing) output of EU policies, not least because a broad activation of civil society in the OMC has largely failed. In consequence, as from the first midterm review offered by the Kok report, the participatory element of the OMC has systematically been cut back. For the follow-up policy agenda to the initial Lisbon Strategy, Agenda

2020, Armstrong claims that the OMC as an instrument to promote social policy has been largely pushed into irrelevance at the expense of a co-operative co-ordination between the Commission and national governments. He therefore concludes that "[i]t is not yet clear how much or how little of the social OMC will be absorbed into the economic and employment policy coordination framework that now forms part of the European Semester. Whether or not the social OMC will itself continue as a discrete process is even more uncertain" (Armstrong 2012: 298).

More than disillusioning tangible policy output, the OMC appears to have failed with respect to the expectations in the promotion of deliberative decision making in a more subtle way, which puts the mechanism as theoretical expectation into question. Benz (2007: 505) argues accordingly that in practice of the OMC "the dominating 'deliberative' mode does not improve accountability, the 'competitive' mode seems to be more promising". According to Benz, the value added of the OMC can be exploited best when it triggers market mechanisms between states that involve regular peer reviews. Other scholars give more credit to possibly more long-term learning effects (Zeitlin 2005). These competing views also reflect different theoretical assumptions, outlined above. Therefore, "[m]uch of the work undertaken on the OMC to date reflects a divide between optimists and pessimists concerning its effectiveness and legitimacy ... However, the lack of convincing empirical proof of policy learning and problems of definition leaves critics to stress that claims about learning remain tentative" (Stiller and van Gerven 2012: 119). Yet even if, as the proponents of incremental learning and the experimental potential of the new governance tools argue, it is still too early to observe more incremental learning effects, the collaborative elements are predominantly limited to central governments' administrative actors. Also, the "soft governance school's criticism of the OMC's democratic legitimacy, therefore, refers to the lack of systematic and qualitative involvement of sub-national actors and national parliaments in the coordination processes and their unsatisfactory embeddedness in the framework of multilevel governance, which undermine the OMC's legitimacy on grounds of both deliberative and participatory democracy" (Michalski 2012: 399). Büchs (2008: 777) concludes most pessimistically "that current arrangements for stakeholder participation within the OMC are detrimental to the OMC's transparency and accountability. In general, Member State citizens are not well informed regarding OMC processes or the roles played by different institutions and actors at the EU and national levels within the OMC. The majority of EU citizens are furthermore unaware that the OMC and Lisbon strategy even exist". This finding is put into perspective by a sophisticated comparative analysis of national parliamentary and media control of states' OMC involvement which reaches less negative conclusions regarding the availability and use of OMC information inside national parliaments. "However, the finding that OMC-related parliamentary activity in the Netherlands and the UK takes place in parliamentary committee meetings and not in plenary debates limits the visibility of the OMC-related shaming by MPs and, hence, its contribution to increasing the democratic accountability of OMCs" – let alone the basically complete absence of media coverage (de Ruiter 2012: 17). Despite evidence for some national debate around OMC measures, parliamentary involvement is strong only if the EU's involvement is not limited to the OMC – that is, if it is in parallel involved in regulation. This finding supports the evidence that a "shadow of hierarchy" is necessary to activate the voluntary mechanisms of new governance modes (Börzel 2010). In sum, the research findings confirm that the OMC has not activated broad arrays of non-state actors but privileges clearly national governmental actors. In reaction, the Agenda 2020 relies to a much lesser degree on the OMC than the original Lisbon Strategy did. Nor can much evidence be found that the OMC succeeded in deliberating better outcomes. The OMC appears to have brought forth concrete results only when fostering competition between states under the shadow of hierarchy – that is, when the EU can act as a functional equivalent to coercive and hierarchical government.

The evaluation of the Commission's White Paper's principles in the consultation regime is concerned with the direct activation of civil society by the Commission. The most critical point is the top-down approach and the limits of the Commission-driven participation of civil society. In this vein, Magnette (2003: 14, in electronic version) acknowledges that collaborative governance forms can promote accountability through openness, transparency, consultation, communication and other tools but stresses at the same time that "this conception of governance does not in itself encourage citizens to become active, because the policy-making process remains complex – and is even made more complex by governance practices". More critically expressed, in its very design "the White Paper undermines the normative claims made for a civil society premised upon the voluntary nature of its associative forms and its distinctive open, communicative and deliberative rationality" (Armstrong 2002: 102). More concretely regarding online consultations, the fact that the consultation regime is purely informal implies that stakeholders have no options to hold the Commission formally accountable. It remains exclusively up to the latter whether to include or dismiss consultation inputs. The actual impact of consultations therefore remains controlled by public actors, which partially discredits the legitimating input side. The emphasis is fully on throughput – that is, the voluntary hearing of civil society even if the Commission has no formal obligation to do so. Another, more critical reading of the activation strategy is that to improve its performance, the Commission "takes advantage of the private actor resources to increase its action capacity. At the same time, however, the Commission seeks to preserve its autonomy and has no interest in extending the involvement of private actors beyond informal and formal consultations. Against this background, it seems likely that the executive dominance in the EU will prevail" (Börzel 2011: 54).

Regarding the improvement of policy outputs through consultation, Persson and Lindgren (2010: 449) find evidence for positive effects on output legitimacy through raising the input legitimacy of the EU. However, citizens who aim to participate are faced with structural challenges inherent to the EU multilevel policy-making. On the one hand, there is a great need for professionalization to be able to exert influence, which renders direct communication between the EU-level civil society organization and the grassroots level extremely difficult (Kohler-Koch and Buth 2013). On the other hand, the top-down approach clashes with the self-understanding of non-governmental organizations and the collaborative approach.

> What links Brussels' non-profit associations from the perspective of its members down to the single citizen is the shared concern to be fighting for a "good purpose". This is an understanding of representation that is not compatible with a model of delegation. The European NGOs are not delegated to implement the interests of their organizational members but see themselves as executers of a mission and communicate with their member organizations and basis to fulfill this mission together. (Kohler-Koch 2011: 266; own translation)

Kohler-Koch and Buth (2013) therefore conclude that, in the end, due to the structural features of the EU policy-making system and the top-down design of collaborative governance CSOs cannot meet the expectation to serve as a transmission belt between EU policy-making and grassroots activists. Based on an analysis of online consultations between 2001 and 2011, Rasmussen and Carroll come to a less rigid conclusion. Examining that there is indeed more participation in politically salient areas, the authors state that what "we can say with confidence is that organised interests should have at least the potential to act as an additional transmission belt between the public and the decision makers" (Rasmussen and Carroll 2014a: 265). The reproduction of a bias towards an overrepresentation of well-resourced CSOs, mainly business interests, is however also confirmed by this data. Although it has not given a dramatic boost to the perceived legitimacy of the Commission, the potential of the tool may still be further exploited (Hüller 2010). So far, the pre-existing territorial and resource-dependent bias that privileges certain CSOs over other, less organized, less professionalized and more locally anchored civil society seem to persist also in the online consultation system. The findings by Rasmussen and Carroll (2014) which show biases to persist over time are in line with a large-n study by Quittkat (2011) which indicates that although the involvement of interested parties and formal opportunities to give an input have increased, the online consultations fail evidently when it comes to inclusiveness and transparency. The positive effect of reducing the resource dependency for participation that was expected from the introduction of online consultations is thus not confirmed, but there is no clear agreement whether the reasons for it are enshrined in the governance structure of the EU and hence institutional givens, or if it is rather a matter of stronger activation. To date, electronic access has not changed the pattern of who participates and it has to an even lesser degree led to a wider civil society basis for participatory governance across Europe.

Therefore, although the online tool has raised participation numbers, three decisive caveats remain. First, once input has been collected it stays exclusively up to the Commission whether and how to use the information. Civil society cannot issue any binding input. Second, and more importantly, the exclusive role of the Commission implies that the process remains nontransparent. In the end, it remains unclear what is taken on board or ignored by the Commission, which undermines the communicative participatory purpose. Third, despite the larger number of people that can theoretically be reached with the shift to online consultations, the pattern of who is represented (especially an overrepresentation of business interests) is clearly reproduced. Therefore, "the use of this new tool in practice does not achieve the aims of a stronger involvement of (organized) European civil society and the resulting strengthening of European democracy" (Quittkat 2013b: 110). In consequence, keeping up its formal legislative rights, the Commission plays the traditional gatekeeper role of the state. Finally, the top-down approach to render civil society the Commission's collaborator not only undermines CSOs' independent capacity to hold the Commission accountable, it also conflicts with the raison d'être of organized non-state actors who can accordingly hardly serve as a direct link between the EU and civil society.

Conclusions: Governance and Legitimacy without Government?

The concluding section takes up two of the central questions the editors of this special issue raise. First, to which extent does governance succeed as a normative framework that assumes specific legitimizing effects? Second, what does the empirical analysis teach us about the conceptual distinction between government and governance? To start with, how does EU collaborative governance perform if measured against academic and real-life expectations? Overall the image of collaborative governance, promoted by the OMC and the Commission's consultation regime, is predominantly grim. The empirical balance sheet on civil society involvement in the application of new modes of governance provides, at best, a mixed record. Measured by the high political and theoretical expectations, actual achievements have been rather disappointing and "the promise of 'involving civil society' has not bridged the gap between Europe and the people, but rather sponsored a Brussels-based CSO elite working in the interest of deeper integration" (Kohler-Koch 2010b: 335).

Table 1 summarizes the findings gathered in the conceptual and empirical literature on governance in the two flagship EU initiatives. As far as actors are concerned, despite the variance in emphasis that focuses more on deliberation and learning (OMC) or policy efficiency through stakeholder inclusion (consultation regime), on the input side the initiatives remained essentially closed. By formal design, authority to take binding decisions remained in the hands of governments and the Commission. Even though actions tackling the input side do include national parliaments in the OMC, the actual achievements show that this right is not being used unless at least some hard regulatory action is being taken in parallel. The consultation regime does not foresee an inclusion of the EP, yet it also has not managed to establish CSOs that participate as a transmission belt to citizens. In consequence, the central expected impact, that citizens would move closer to EU decision making, was not achieved. Measuring tangible policy change on the output dimension is methodologically difficult and may be challenged. Overall, the evaluations of the OMC are critical. Given the actor constellations on the input and throughput dimensions, success or failure depends in the end on individual government action. Decisive for the OMC achievements in terms of output is that research has found little evidence for mutual learning among member states. Whilst some scholars hold onto the theoretical potential for learning and experimental governance, others provide theoretical reasons about the underlying co-ordination mechanisms of the OMC and argue that behavioral change can only be expected in competitive settings or under the shadow of hierarchy but not as pure voluntary adaptation. Turning to online consultations, we actually lack studies that test how much civil society input changes the position of the Commission. Existing research is, however, critical due to the design of the consultation regime that attributes a strong gatekeeping role to the Commission.

Throughput, finally, is the central dimension in which collaborative governance comes to bear – given that on the other dimensions non-public actors remain secondary. While the initial design of the OMC foresaw civil society inclusion on the national level, online consultations did so on the EU level. Putting aside the question whether this throughput participation can and ought to replace input participation, how does it perform by its own standards? The achievements on this dimension are arguably the most disappointing vis-à-vis the high expectations attached to the initiatives. In the OMC framework, civil society participation was soon scrapped from the process, while national parliaments are not exploiting their potential powers. This leaves the initiative fully under the control and influence of national governments – without the crucial external control of non-state actors. The consultation regime, although indeed offering a potentially more inclusive infrastructure by going online, has similarly failed to meet expectations. It is striking that

Table 1. Findings on implementation and delivery of collaborative governance

	Input accountability/deliberation		Output tangible policy change		Throughput inclusiveness of process	
	OMC	CR	OMC	CR	OMC	CR
Actors	Member state governments	Commission	Member states	Commission, alone	CSOs in MS	CSOs on EU level
Actions	Limited inclusion of national parliaments	No formal inclusion of EP or other bodies	Dependent on member state	Indirect impact on "better regulation"	Inclusion in national planning	Input to policy formulation COM
Achievements	National public scrutiny not enhanced, no public debate on performance of MS	CSO as transmission belt not fulfilled COM remains gatekeeper	Little evidence for policy learning	No tangible change in implementation (gatekeeper role Commission, inputs cannot be traced)	Soon eliminated from OMC → co-operative co-ordination between COM/MS instead	Same participation patterns as before

different studies highlight the potential of the instrument but confirm that so far the biases in representation are not changed but reproduced in the online consultations. Most relevantly, the transmission belt between the EU level and citizens has not been established by throughput mechanisms and "the rhetoric of CSOs and the explicit request of EU institutions convey an image of representation that is in contrast with reality ... and direct communication down to the grassroots level is – except for extraordinary events – marginal" (Kohler-Koch 2010a: 112). Both conceptually and in practice, "throughput" cannot provide an alternative to input and output. On the one hand, governance only produces results if backed by governmental mechanisms and a shadow of hierarchy. On the other hand, the strong top-down activating logic behind collaborative governance in the EU creates a dilemma in that the legitimizing logic of civil society as distinct from the state is turned on its head if CSOs serve as integral part of the decision-making machinery.

Finally, what does the analysis of collaborative governance tell us about the conceptual distinction between governance and government? Even though both the member states and the Commission designed collaborative governance in the EU as shared, networked decision-making whose instruments are voluntary and informal in order to promote a normative agenda, in practice "government" is inherent in governance practices that are marked by strong gatekeeping and public power preserving mechanisms. This observation raises further research questions about legitimate representation and strategic reference to interest representation, which inevitably change if state and non-state boundaries are systematically blurred (Pérez-Solórzano Borragán and Smismans 2012). In turn, the sobering empirical outcomes have by no means led to a retreat from governance and a return to hierarchical steering. In consequence, research needs to scrutinize further the hybrid political, social and individual actors' roles in multilevel governance that ultimately is based on representative democracy (Kröger and Friedrich 2011). The experience of collaborative governance in the EU has not led to a return to government, on the contrary, "governance" has become an integral and persistent element of government.

Notes

1. Both citations are taken from the online achieves see: http://ec.europa.eu/governance/index_en.htm (accessed January 27, 2013).
2. See: http://europa.eu/legislation_summaries/glossary/open_method_coordination_en.htm (accessed April 2, 2014).
3. See the Commission website: http://ec.europa.eu/yourvoice/index_en.htm (accessed January 6, 2013).

References

Altides, C., 2011, Der Beitrag der organisierten Zivilgesellschaft zur Veröffentlichung europäischer Politik, in: B. Kohler-Koch and C. Quittkat (Eds) *Die Entzauberung der Zivilgesellschaft bei der Demokratisierung von EU-Governance* (Frankfurt: Campus), pp. 211–240.

Armstrong, K. A., 2012, EU social policy and the governance architecture of Europe 2020. *Transfer: European Review of Labour and Research*, **18**(3), pp. 285–300.

Armstrong, K. A., 2002, Rediscovering civil society: The European Union and the White Paper on Governance. *European Law Journal*, **8**(1), pp. 102–132. doi:10.1111/1468-0386.00144

Benz, A., 2007, Accountable multilevel governance by the open method of coordination? *European Law Journal*, **13**(4), pp. 505–522. doi:10.1111/j.1468-0386.2007.00381.x

Borras, S. and Ejrnæs, A., 2011, The legitimacy of new modes of Governance in the EU: Studying national stakeholders' support. *European Union Politics*, **12**(1), pp. 107–126. doi:10.1177/1465116510380282

Börzel, T. A., 2010, European governance: Negotiation and competition in the shadow of hierarchy. *JCMS: Journal of Common Market Studies*, **48**(2), pp. 191–219. doi:10.1111/j.1468-5965.2009.02049.x

Börzel, T. A., 2011, Networks: Reified Metaphor or governance panacea? *Public Administration*, **89**(1), pp. 49–63. doi:10.1111/j.1467-9299.2011.01916.x

Büchs, M., 2008, How legitimate is the open method of co-ordination? *JCMS: Journal of Common Market Studies*, **46**(4), pp. 765–786. doi:10.1111/j.1468-5965.2008.00804.x

Cohen, J. and Sabel, C., 1997, Directly-deliberative polyarchy. *European Law Journal*, **3**(4), pp. 313–342. doi:10.1111/1468-0386.00034

Commission of the European Communities (2001) 'European Governance'. A White Paper Vol. Brussels, 25.7.2001: COM(2001) 428 final.

de Ruiter, R., 2012, Full disclosure? The open method of coordination, parliamentary debates and media coverage. *European Union Politics*, **October**(online first), pp. 1–20.

European Council, 2000, Presidency conclusions'. Lisbon European Council: 23 and 24 March.

Fuchs, D., 2011, Cultural diversity, european identity and legitimacy of the EU: A theoretical framework, in: D. Fuchs and H.-D. Klingemann (Eds) *Cultural Diversity, European Identity and the Legitimacy of the EU* (Cheltenham: Edward Elgar), pp. 27–60.

Gbikpi, B. and Grote, J., 2002, From democratic government to participatory governance, in: J. Grote and B. Gbikpi (Eds) *Participatory Governance: Political and Societal Implications* (Opladen: Leske + Budrich), pp. 17–34.

Hüller, T., 2010, *Demokratie und Sozialregulierung in Europa: Die Online-Konsultationen der EU-Kommission* (Frankfurt: Campus).

Kjær, A. M., 2004, *Governance* (Cambridge: Polity Press).

Kohler-Koch, B., 2010a, Civil society and EU democracy: 'astroturf' representation? *Journal of European Public Policy*, **17**(1), pp. 100–116. doi:10.1080/13501760903464986

Kohler-Koch, B., 2010b, Civil society and the European Union, in: H. K. Anheier and S. Toepler (Eds) *International Encyclopedia of Civil Society* (New York: Springer), pp. 332–338.

Kohler-Koch, B., 2011, Zivilgesellschaftlich Partizipation: Zugewinn an Demokratie oder Pluralisierung der europäischen Lobby?, in: B. Kohler-Koch and C. Quittkat (Eds) *Die Entzauberung der Zivilgesellschaft bei der Demokratisierung von EU-Governance* (Frankfurt: Campus), pp. 241–270.

Kohler-Koch, B., 2013a, Civil society and democracy in the EU: High expectations under empirical scrutiny, in: B. Kohler-Koch and C. Quittkat (Eds) *De-Mystification of Participatory Democracy* (Oxford: Oxford University Press), pp. 1–17.

Kohler-Koch, B., 2013b, Governing with the civil society, in: B. Kohler-Koch and C. Quittkat (Eds) *De-Mystification of Participatory Democracy* (Oxford: Oxford University Press), pp. 18–40.

Kohler-Koch, B. and Buth, V., 2013, The balancing act of European civil society: Between professionalism and grass roots, in: B. Kohler-Koch and C. Quittkat (Eds) *De-Mystification of Participatory Democracy* (Oxford: Oxford University Press), pp. 114–148.

Kohler-Koch, B. and Finke, B., 2007, The institutional shaping of EU-society relations: A contribution to democracy via participation? *Journal of Civil Society*, **3**(3), pp. 205–221. doi:10.1080/17448680701775630

Kohler-Koch, B. and Rittberger, B., 2006, Review article: The 'governance turn' in EU studies. *JCMS: Journal of Common Market Studies*, **44**(Annual Review), pp. 27–49. doi:10.1111/j.1468-5965.2006.00642.x

Kok, W. (High Level Group chaired by) (2004) *Report - Facing the Challenge: The Lisbon Strategy for Growth and Employment* Luxembourg: Office for Official Publications of the European Communities, November

Kröger, S. and Friedrich, D. (Eds), 2011, *The Challenge of Democratic Representation in the European Union* (Houndsmill: Palgrave Macmillan).

Lindgren, K. -O. and Persson, T., 2010, Input and output legitimacy: Synergy or trade-off? Empirical evidence from an EU survey. *Journal of European Public Policy*, **17**(4), pp. 449–467. doi:10.1080/13501761003673591

Magnette, P.. (2001) *European Governance and Civic Participation: Can the European Union be Politicised?* Jean Monnet Working Papers. Available at http://centers.law.nyu.edu/jeanmonnet/papers/01/010901.html (accessed 31 November 2011).

Magnette, P., 2003, European governance and civic participation: Beyond elitist citizenship? *Political Studies*, **51**(1), pp. 144–160. doi:10.1111/1467-9248.00417

Marshall, D., 2010, Who to lobby and when: Institutional determinants of interest group strategies in European Parliament Committees. *European Union Politics*, **10**(4), pp. 553–575.

Michalski, A., 2012, Social welfare and levels of democratic government in the EU. *Journal of European Integration*, **34**(4), pp. 397–418. doi:10.1080/07036337.2011.638066

Pérez-Solórzano Borragán, N. and Smismans, S., 2012, Representativeness: A tool to structure interest intermediation in the European Union? *JCMS: Journal of Common Market Studies*, **50**(3), pp. 403–421. doi:10.1111/j.1468-5965.2011.02236.x

Prodi, R. and Kinnock, N.. (2000) *The Commission and Non-governmental Organisations*. Commission Discussion Paper Vol. COM 2000/11: 18 January (Brussels: European Commission).

Quittkat, C., 2011, The European Commission's Online Consultations: A Success Story? *Journal of Common Market Studies*, **49**(3), pp. 653–674.

Quittkat, C., 2013a, Consultation in daily practice, in: B. Kohler-Koch and C. Quittkat (Eds) *De-Mystification of Participatory Democracy* (Oxford: Oxford University Press), pp. 61–84.

Quittkat, C., 2013b, New instruments serving democracy: Do online consultations benefit civil society?, in: B. Kohler-Koch and C. Quittkat (Eds) *De-Mystification of Participatory Democracy* (Oxford: Oxford University Press), pp. 85–113.

Quittkat, C. and Finke, B., 2008, The EU Commission Consultation Regime, in: B. Kohler-Koch, D. De Bièvre and W. Maloney (Eds) *Opening EU-Governance to Civil Society: Gains and Challenges* (Mannheim: CONNEX).

Rasmussen, A. and Carroll, B. J., 2014a, Representatives of the public? Public opinion and interest group activity. *European Journal of Political Research*, **53**(2), pp. 250–268.

Rasmussen, A. and Carroll, B. J., 2014b, Determinants of upper-class dominance in the heavenly chorus: Lessons from European Union online consultations. *British Journal of Political Science*, **44**(2), pp. 445–459. doi:10.1017/S0007123412000750

Rhodes, R. A. W., 1997, *Understanding Governance: Policy Networks, Governance, Reflexivity, and Accountability* (Buckingham: Open University Press).

Rosenau, J. and Czempiel, E.-O. (Eds), 1992, *Governance Without Government* (Cambridge: Cambridge University Press).

Sabel, C. F. and Zeitlin, J., (2007) *Learning from Difference: The New Architecture of Experimentalist Governance in the European Union*. European Governance Papers (EUROGOV): No. C–07–02.

Scharpf, F. W.. (2003) *Problem-Solving Effectiveness and Democratic Accountability in the EU*.

Schmidt, V. A.. (2010) *Democracy and Legitimacy in the European Union Revisited: Input, Output and Throughput*. KFG Working Paper Vol. 21: November. http://www.polsoz.fuberlin.de/en/v/transformeurope/publications/working_paper/WP_21_November_Schmidt1.pdf?1367706585

Stiller, S. and van Gerven, M., 2012, The european employment strategy and national core executives: Impacts on activation reforms in the Netherlands and Germany. *Journal of European Social Policy*, **22**(2), pp. 118–132. doi:10.1177/0958928711433652

Teló, M., 2002, The new knowledge economy in Europe, Elgar, London, September 2001, in: M. J. Rodriguez (Ed) *The New Knowledge Economy in Europe: A Strategy for International Competitiveness and Social Cohesion* (London: Edward Elgar), pp. 242–268.

Trubek, D. M. and Trubek, L. G., 2005, Hard and soft law in the construction of social Europe: The role of the open method of co-ordination. *European Law Journal*, **11**(3), pp. 343–364. doi:10.1111/j.1468-0386.2005.00263.x

Warleigh-Lack, A. and Drachenberg, R., 2010, Policy making in the European Union, in: M. Cini and N. Perez-Solorzano Borragan (Eds) *European Union Politics* (Oxford: Oxford University Press), pp. 209–224.

Zeitlin, J., 2005, Social Europe and experimental governance: Towards a new constitutional compromise?, in: G. de Búrca (Ed) *EU Law and the Welfare State: In Search of Solidarity* (Oxford: Oxford University Press), pp. 213–241.

Policy Transfer and Accession: A Comparison of Three International Governmental Organisations

PETER CARROLL

ABSTRACT *This article compares the extent of policy transfer related to the accession processes of three international governmental organisations (IGOs), the European Union (EU), the Organisation for Economic Cooperation and Development (OECD) and the World Trade Organisation (WTO). It is argued that this is necessary as there is a tendency for studies of IGOs as agents of transfer to focus primarily upon the transfer that occurs after a state has acceded to membership, neglecting the extent of transfer that can take place during the accession process. The key findings are: one, policy transfer occurs during the accession process in all three organisations and, to varying extents, in all three stages of the accession process; two, the extent of transfer varies by accession stage and over time for all three organisations; three, the greatest extent of transfer occurs in the pre-accession and formal accession stages; four, the greater the degree of isomorphism between an applicant's policies and institutions and those of the IGO, the less the extent of policy transfer in the accession process.*

The aim of this article is to compare, on a preliminary basis, the extent of policy transfer related to the accession processes of three international governmental organisations (IGOs), the European Union (EU), the Organisation for Economic Co-operation and Development (OECD) and the World Trade Organization (WTO). It is argued that this is necessary as there is a tendency for studies of IGOs in relation to policy transfer to focus primarily upon the transfer that occurs after a state has acceded to membership, neglecting the extent of transfer that can take place during the accession process.

The three IGOs were selected on the basis that they had differing goals and histories with varying memberships, whose accession processes might exhibit varying types and volumes of transfer over time. In particular, the EU and the OECD were selected as their work covers a very wide range of policy areas in which transfer might occur. In contrast, the WTO was selected because of its primary focus on one area of policy, trade, although this expanded substantially following the Uruguay Round to include agricultural subsidies, trade-related investment, intellectual property, trade in services, customs valuation and phyto-sanitary policies. This, it was felt, might result in a somewhat different pattern and volume of transfer to the EU and OECD. In summary, the three IGOs were selected as it was felt they would reveal differences as regards policy transfer in relation to accession that would enrich the study and its findings, perhaps leading to further research work on the topic, as well as increasing our understanding of the extent and role of policy transfer.

The article is divided into four major sections and a conclusion. The first provides the working definitions and briefly outlines the framework used for the analysis. The framework is based on that used for an examination of accession and policy transfer in relation to the OECD (Carroll and Kellow 2011, pp. 147–166). The second, third and fourth sections examine transfer in the various stages of the accession process and are divided into two parts. The first part of each provides a description and assessment of accession-related transfer in the three IGOs. The second part summarises the major findings regarding the relevant accession stage and transfer, findings that are somewhat tentative, but which could provide a basis for the development of theoretical propositions and future empirical work. The conclusion draws together the major findings. The paper is based primarily upon the secondary literature related to accessions, supplemented by interviews with staff of the organisations. The interviews were granted on the condition of anonymity for those interviewed.

Definitions, Concepts and a Framework

The definition of policy transfer provided by Dolowitz and Marsh is the most commonly employed and it is the one used in this article. It is the process by which actors imitate or emulate policies developed in one setting to develop programmes and policies within another resulting in a policy innovation (Dolowitz and Marsh 1996, p. 357). In 2000 Dolowitz and Marsh further developed their conceptual framework, noting the importance of global economic forces, combined with the growth of rapid communications of all types, and the growing role of international organisations in advocating and sometimes enforcing similar policies across countries (Dolowitz and March 2000, pp. 6–7). Again, in 2006 Dolowitz elaborated on the role of national actors in globalisation processes, using a policy transfer framework, emphasising the opportunities for policy learning and more effective governance that can arise. He also noted that there was still little empirical evidence concerning the role of public and private actors in globalisation (Dolowitz 2006, p. 267). In a later article Dolowitz extended his analysis of the links between policy learning and transfer, arguing that the learning involved in transfer varied from softer to harder learning, the former leading to little more than mimicking or copying, while the latter leads to deeper, more fundamental understandings, with the type of learning being determined by a wide range of factors (Dolowitz 2009). The collection of articles edited by Evans in 2009 aimed at providing a detailed response to the critics of policy transfer, suggesting a variety of new directions for studying processes of policy transfer. In particular, and in conclusion, Evans argued that the concept of policy transfer provides a valuable context for integrating research concerns across the domains of domestic, comparative and international politics (Evans 2009, p. 397).

While all of these studies rightly drew attention to the importance of global forces and international organisations in regard to policy transfer, none focused on the processes of accession to international organisations and their role in the international dynamics of policy transfer and learning. This study represents an early attempt to explore that role, illustrating how transfer takes place in the negotiated accession process, where candidates voluntarily undertake a complex process of learning that subjects them to a variety of domestic and international pressures.

The term accession has a relatively narrow definition in law referring to the situation where a state which has not signed a treaty already in existence, though it has been signed by other states, formally accepts the provisions of the treaty. In this article we adopt a broader definition, understanding accession as the *process* of discussion, bargaining and negotiation that occurs leading up to, and including, the formal acceptance of the provisions of a treaty or its equivalent and the post-accession bargaining, implementation and enforcement of agreements entered into during the accession process. In most cases the formal process of accession and the associated decision rules are broadly outlined in the relevant treaty or convention. In practice, as with most IGOs, the OECD, WTO and EU have each developed and revised over time a more detailed accession process, including decision rules and the criteria that need to be satisfied.

As defined, it is assumed that the process of accession to IGOs involves varying extents of policy transfer. This is because many of the agreements reached by states during that process may require the introduction at the national and, for federal states, the sub-national level of a range of new or modified policies and related institutions by the applicant state if it is to gain membership. The agreements are often referred to as the legal instruments or the acquis of the IGO in question. In many cases the accession agreements provide the applicant state with some discretion as to the form and content of the policy to be transferred, provided it achieves the intent of the agreement. Hence, it is not surprising that accession processes are in essence bargaining processes, often complex and somewhat "messy", involving intensive periods of discussion in relation to difficult areas of the proposed agreements, spread over varying time periods. Moreover, several IGOs prescribe different sets of criteria and related processes for accession for different types of state, as noted below (for descriptions of the accession processes of the three IGOs see EU 2012a; OECD 2012a; WTO 2012a).

Accession to IGOs takes place in political, economic and social contexts that vary over time and that, in turn, may have a variety of impacts, both formal and informal, on accession processes and policy transfer. Hence, while the merits of applicants in relation to the formal criteria of accession are of importance in determining successful accession, the process is fundamentally political in nature, characterised by intensive bargaining. Thus, factors unrelated to the specified accession criteria may come into play, sometimes speeding up or delaying the process, sometimes enabling an applicant state that clearly does not satisfy one or more of the specified criteria to gain entry, or vice versa. As a result, in turn, the extent, type and duration of transfer required of an applicant state might vary, depending on the particular context in which the accession process takes place, including any significant changes in that context during the process.

In order to simplify the above complexity, for analytical purposes the article uses a simple framework that assumes that each accession consists of three basic stages, in each of which policy transfer might occur. The stages are: pre-accession, accession and post-accession, as outlined below. Each accession stage may be associated with a varying degree of policy transfer, determined by a range of factors, some common between the stages, some different (A fuller description can be found in Carroll and Kellow 2011, pp. 147–166.)

The Pre-accession Stage and Policy Transfer

The first, pre-accession, stage refers to a period varying in duration that commences when a country's government makes a decision to proceed to accession, but *before* any formal application is made to the IGO in question. It should be noted that this is a different definition to that applied by the European Commission, where pre-accession activities and transfer are those that occur before the final decision to accede, but *after* the formal application for membership is submitted. It is a stage that involves a period of varying duration with often heated domestic discussion and bargaining about the desirability of accession, its costs and benefits. The secretariats of the IGOs in question and their key members often play a role in the domestic politics regarding potential accession, but usually in a relatively discreet fashion. It is not assumed that the motivation for membership derives only from governments, though this might be the case (Tsogtbaatar 2005). It might, for example, spring from demands by businesses in the export sector aimed at increasing their access to overseas markets.

The focus for much of the domestic discussion that takes place is on the extent of policy change likely to be required in the applicant state by the IGOs' members, and which groups seem likely to benefit, or not, from the policy changes identified. It is in this period of policy change that varying degrees of transfer may occur, based on the changes likely to be required by the IGO and agreed to by the applicant state. It should be stressed that it is not assumed that all policy change which takes place in the accession process is based on the need to undertake required policy transfer. Nor is it assumed that the transfer that does take place is one of simple emulation.

The greater the policy and related institutional changes, the greater and more difficult will be the discussions and negotiations that result, especially where the changes involve ruling elites and major interest groups. In addition, the discussions are made more difficult the greater the degree of uncertainty as to what conditions for access will be specified by the IGO and its members and, hence, the degree of transfer and policy change necessary.

It is sometimes difficult in practice to clearly distinguish pre-accession transfer to a specific IGO from transfer aimed at securing accession to a different IGO, or, indeed, cases of transfer that are not associated with the motive of IGO membership. This is especially the case for policy areas in which different IGOs have similar, possibly overlapping interests and agreements, as is the case for the WTO, EU and OECD, all of which have agreements, often very similar, in relation to the freeing up of trade and the opening of markets.

Comparisons of Formal Accession Transfer

A first, preliminary, examination of pre-accession transfer related to the General Agreement on Tariffs and Trade (GATT)/WTO, EU and OECD indicates a trend common to both the EU and the OECD, which is a substantial increase over time in the extent of policy transfer in the pre-accession stage. There are some signs that this might also be the case for the GATT/WTO.

There have been successive "waves" of accession to the EU, with each wave characterised by varying extents of pre-accession transfer, in large part because of the very different political and economic circumstances of the states in the successive waves of accession. The first set of applications for entry to what was then the EEC, in 1961, was from states with functioning democracies and largely market-based economic systems, the UK, Denmark, Norway and Ireland, broadly similar in those respects to the existing members of the EEC. Their applications failed, as did the applications of 1967, for reasons that had little or nothing to do with the accession criteria. There is little evidence of any pre-accession transfer in relation to the 1961 applications, with Ireland, for example, having little in the way of even a formal policy as regards the EEC in the late 1950s, deciding to apply for membership in 1961 only because the UK had indicated that it would shortly do so (Murphy 2003; Girvin 2008).

However, the failure of these first applications did lead to varying degrees of limited pre-accession transfer over the next 12 years, policy change aimed at more closely aligning policies with those likely to be required by the EEC. This is, perhaps, most obvious in relation to the 1965 Anglo-Irish Free Trade Agreement, which was seen by the Irish government as an important first step towards reducing the various tariff barriers and other protectionist measures in place around its economy, measures that it would have had to undertake had its first application been successful (Lemass 1966).

Accession to the EEC in the 1982 to 1986 period involved three countries, Greece, Spain and Portugal, that had only just emerged from military rule, so they faced significant requirements regarding their progress to stable, functioning democracies, as well as changes to economic policies, with substantial pre-accession transfer. However, it is difficult to determine the transfer which came about because of the decision to apply for membership of the EEC, or that which was determined by a more general concern to promote economic development, democratic government and political stability (Powell 2011).

The next wave of EU accession, in 2004, saw ten new members, eight of them recently members of the Soviet Bloc (Cyprus, Malta, the Czech Republic, Estonia, Hungary, Latvia, Lithuania, Poland, Slovakia and Slovenia), with radically different political and economic structures and related policies. The latter eight were keen to gain EU membership and had commenced major constitutional, institutional and economic changes as soon as the Soviet ties had been broken. In this sense they undertook very rapid and extensive pre-accession change, some of it guided by a general desire to achieve stable, democratic, free market systems, as well as by a desire for EU membership. Levitz and Pop-Eleches, in a study aimed primarily at assessing whether or not the implementation and enforcement of EU requirements had declined after accession, found that there were a number of pre-accession changes aimed at democratisation, at least in part, and that were focused on helping to gain EU accession (Levitz and Pop-Eleches 2010, p. 468).

The first wave of accessions to the OECD after its establishment in 1961 involved Japan (1964), Finland (1969), Australia (1971) and New Zealand (1973). Their experiences reveal little by way of pre-accession transfer compared to later accessions. In Australia, for example, the bulk of pre-accession activity focused on domestic discussions as to the reasons why Australia should seek OECD membership and the benefits that an OECD affiliation would bring, rather than the identification of areas needing change, largely because existing Australia legislation and policy was substantially consistent with the OECD's acquis (Carroll and Kellow 2011, p. 152). In contrast, the break-up of the Soviet Bloc in the early 1990s, as with the EU, brought about a significant increase in pre-accession transfer on the part of the Central and Eastern European countries (CEEC) applying for accession. In comparison with Australia and New Zealand, the accession task for the CEEC was far more challenging, involving the development, implementation and enforcement of entirely new policy in areas such as competition, or making wide-ranging changes to existing policy that had been created, for the most part, when they were centrally planned, socialist economies, if they were to gain accession. In many cases they also needed to develop the institutional capacity to effectively administer these policy changes.

The mixture of motives that can drive decisions to apply for accession is well illustrated in the case of the accession of the Republic of Korea to the OECD. The application for membership was portrayed by the Korean government as a fundamental element in its broader, strategic goal of deeper global integration, and engagement as a fully competitive participant in international finance and commerce (Harris 2002, p. 140). It represented Korea's aspiration for the status of "developed" country, seen as an important political achievement, as well as enabling the Korean government to introduce a series of financial and economic reforms that would otherwise have been difficult. In 1995 the Korean Foreign Minister stated that internationalisation was

> an inevitable process which every nation must undergo to ensure sustained stability and prosperity ... by ... trying to induce foreign investment, liberalizing its financial market and preparing to join the Organization for Economic Cooperation and Development. (Hyun-Chin and Jin-Ho 2006, p. 10)

In preparation for potential OECD accession the Korean government, with advice and assistance from the IMF and World Bank, developed a blueprint and schedule for financial liberalisation and market opening (Harris 2002; Hyun-Chin and Jin-Ho 2006) which also included Korea's position in relation to the OECD's Codes of Liberalisation. The Codes contain many of the key agreements entered into by OECD members in a wide variety of economic sectors and related transactions. They were and are regarded as at the core of the OECD's purpose and activities (OECD 2002).

As with Australia, there is little evidence of pre-accession change and transfer for Japan in relation to its accession to the OECD, it largely taking the form of reductions to regulatory barriers to trade. Several of these changes, however, were also prompted by other factors, including multilateral peer group pressure for policy changes resulting from its earlier membership of the IMF, World Bank and the GATT, as well as traditional diplomatic pressures maintained by its allies, notably the USA (Forsberg 1998).

There is evidence of some pre-accession policy transfer in the later case of Mexico's accession to the OECD (1994), although it was required as much by its accession to the North American Free Trade Agreement (NAFTA) as to the OECD, with many of the NAFTA requirements being similar to those required for the OECD (Poret 1989). The Salinas government (1988–94) commenced a series of major reforms of the Mexican economy in the 1980s, with two major intentions: export-led economic growth via a series of macro- and microeconomic reforms and unilateral trade liberalisation; and the political aim of "locking-in" the reforms by gaining Mexican membership of NAFTA in particular, but also of the OECD. Membership of both institutions entailed legal and quasi-legal obligations and commitments that would make it difficult, if not impossible, for future Mexican governments to undo the economic reforms that had been implemented (Moreno-Brid 2007). While the NAFTA membership requirements were stricter than those of the OECD, they applied to a narrower range of policy areas.

There have been no detailed studies that relate to pre-accession transfer in relation to GATT/WTO of which the author is aware and the limited evidence that exists suggests that up to the establishment of the WTO in 1995, relatively little pre-accession transfer took place, for at least two reasons. First, until the establishment of the WTO those states that were or had been colonies or territories of existing GATT members were able to accede to GATT without going through the normal, more detailed and lengthier process of accession as specified in Article XXXIII (Copelovitch and Ohls 2012). While many did not take up this advantage for several decades, there was a virtual stampede for membership using Article XXVI: 5(c) in the early 1990s, when it became clear that the same "fast-track" access would be terminated in the WTO agreement. In these cases there is little evidence as to any significant, pre-accession transfer focused on gaining GATT membership, which is not surprising as, for the most part, it was simply not necessary.

Second, the GATT/WTO, unlike the OECD and the EU, has no formal provision in its accession process that requires applicants to have democratic political systems. Thus, the extent of transfer required is less, confined largely to trade-related matters. Even during the Cold War, the GATT had only limited difficulties in agreeing to the accession of non-democratic and authoritarian states to its membership. This was evident, for example, in the applications of Poland and Yugoslavia in the late 1950s, neither of which seems to have undertaken any pre-accession transfer, economic or governmental, although both were granted observer status, a first step to full membership (McKenzie 2008). Hence, there was no great incentive for potential applicants to make major changes to their political systems before commencing the formal accession process, so no policy transfer.

Davis and Wilf in their study of the determinants of accession to the GATT/WTO do not find any conclusive evidence that policy changes aimed at the liberalisation of trade occurred prior to applications for membership, suggesting that pre-accession policy transfer was very limited or absent (Davis and Wilf 2011). This may have been because most acceding countries have already established most-favoured-nation treatment on the basis of bilateral agreements with their major trading partners before applying for GATT/WTO membership – agreements whose contents are typically consistent with WTO agreements, so that, for the most part, they may not need to alter existing trade policies to any great extent in order to gain admission (Gibbs 2001).

Findings

In general there seems to have been an increase in the extent of pre-accession transfer, earliest in the case of the EU, followed later by the OECD and GATT/WTO. In the case of the EU and the OECD, this was associated also with the general desire to create democratic, market-based economies by the CEEC. Hence, it is difficult to distinguish that transfer which resulted from this more general desire and that associated with membership of the IGOs, or both. What is clear is the use of the accession decision by CEEC to help "lock in" desired economic and political reforms, justifying the reforms by reference to their need if accession was to be successful, especially in the case of the EU and the OECD (see, for example, Vernon 1992; Mattli and Plumper 2002).

Both the OECD and the EU cases also provide examples of policy transfer in relation to the building of institutions necessary to sustain working democracies, stimulated by the fact that both IGOs required such changes for accession. This has not been the case to the same extent for the more narrowly focused GATT/WTO, where it has been common for non-democratic states to gain membership, notably China, and the accession criteria are primarily trade-related. This is not to argue that political factors have not played a part in accession decisions. McKenzie, for example, provides a convincing analysis of the impact of political factors in GATT accession decisions during the Cold War (McKenzie 2008).

The Formal Accession Stage and Policy Transfer

The second, formal, accession stage commences with the IGO's acceptance of the formal application for accession, concluding with the deposit of the legal instrument of accession. While all of our IGOs have a formal accession process they also indicate that those processes might be varied, depending upon the country in question, and, in addition, the OECD and WTO do not require that candidates participate in all of their activities upon accession.

Comparisons of Formal Accession Transfer

The formal accession stage process for all three IGOs varies in a number of regards, with differing impacts upon the extent of transfer that is agreed and implemented. The OECD and WTO, for example, do not require that new members participate in all of their activities upon accession. In effect they can opt out of some agreements and related activities, in contrast to the EU. Hence, if, for example, a candidate does not wish to participate in the OECD's Development Assistance Committee or the International Energy Authority, this can be negotiated during the formal accession stage and there is unlikely to be any following, related policy transfer. The same is the case as regards the WTO's plurilateral agreements, for example those relating to trade in civil aircraft or that on government procurement. Hence, the extent of policy transfer that will take place on accession will also vary.

As well as a total opting out from some activities, candidates can also derogate or make reservations (in the sense of not applying or excluding a part of an agreement) in relation to a varying number of items, thus not engaging in transfer as regards the item in question. The OECD seems the most generous in this regard, permitting both temporary and, in effect, permanent reservations and derogations regarding a number of its agreements, although many of these are approved in relation to the OECD's recommendations, which are not legally binding, rather than to its decisions. Decisions are binding upon all members other than those that abstained at the time of their adoption (see OECD 2012b for a list of reservations for Estonia). Nevertheless, at times the OECD members do permit derogations or permanent exceptions from its Decisions (see, for example, OECD 2012c, Annex 4). Where it is agreed that a decision or recommendation will be implemented, but over a number of years after accession, the accession Agreement indicates the time period and the need for regular progress reports to the relevant OECD committee, so that any related policy transfer occurs over the agreed period (see OECD 2012b).

The EU is less generous than the OECD, for the most part accepting only derogations that are temporary in nature. The one EU exception seems to have been the permanent derogation agreed to for Malta in relation to the purchase of second homes on that small island state. More typical, for example, was the derogation permitted for Spain in relation the European Patent Convention. While it signed the Convention in 1986, it was agreed that there would be derogation for a transitional period until 1992. A limited number of similar derogations of a temporary nature have been granted to more recent candidates. Hence, the actual degree of policy transfer that occurs as a result of the accession process will vary over time, depending on the extent of derogations or reservations that are operational at any point in time.

It is noticeable that policy transfer *during* the formal accession stage initially was less frequent in relation to all three IGOs, with substantial post-accession transfer being common. Instead, the formal accession stage consisted of a period of bargaining during which agreement was reached as to what changes would be required. Much of the agreed transfer then took place *after* the deposit of the legal instrument of accession. However, the increasingly detailed formal accession processes and criteria adopted by all three IGOs now require that the bulk of the agreed policy transfer take place during the formal accession stage. This change in emphasis happened for the most part in the 1990s, especially as regards the EU, which was faced with the task of managing rapidly increasing numbers of applications from the CEEC.

In summary, what was put in place by the EU in the 1990s was an increasingly elaborate, multi-stage process of proposals, assistance, bargaining, agreement, implementation, monitoring and assessment before accession was finally agreed (see EU 2012a). Based on regular progress reports from the European Commission, each candidate country was, and is, required to have progressively implemented and enforced policy changes across all of the specified areas during the formal accession stage. The progress reports provide, in effect, a formal list of all of the items transferred to the country in question and, most importantly, those that have not been transferred, despite agreements to that end. The OECD also adopted, in 2007, a more detailed enlargement strategy and related accession process, based loosely on that developed by the EU (OECD 2007a). Similarly, the WTO's accession process became both more complex and demanding in the later 1990s and 2000s, especially for less developed countries (LDCs) (Catteneo and Braga 2009, pp. 12–15). In turn, and in response to increasing pressure from its LDC members, the WTO has provided greater technical assistance to acceding members.

The increasingly complex nature of the accession processes for all three of our IGOs, combined with the increasing extent of the acquis over time, has tended to extend the formal accession stage for at least two reasons: one, the increased time it takes for potential members and the secretariats of the IGOs to discuss, bargain and conclude agreements in relation to the acquis; two, the increased awareness of existing members that it is in the formal accession stage that greatest pressure can be placed upon potential members to agree to, implement and enforce the acquis, with the process of gaining post-accession agreement more difficult, as the incentive of membership no longer exists.

It is possible that the extended duration of accession processes, combined with the growing practice of providing assistance to less wealthy potential members during and after the accession process, has increased the rate of policy transfer by all three IGOs, though the author is not aware of any hard evidence supporting this conjecture.

An additional factor that seems likely to have increased transfer and compliance is the phenomenon of parallel accession processes, especially where adherence to similar agreements is required. Mexican accession to the OECD, for example, took place in the same period as its accession to another treaty, NAFTA. Similarly, the accession of Poland, Hungary and the Czech and Slovak Republics to the EU overlapped with their respective accession negotiations with the OECD and, most recently, the OECD has required the

Russian Federation's membership of the WTO as a precondition for accession (OECD 2007b, p. 5). The OECD's Environmental Policy Committee, similarly, has been keen to ensure that accession states are parties to significant multilateral environmental agreements, especially those that draw a distinction between OECD members and non-OECD members (such as the Basel agreements, the Framework Convention on Climate Change and Kyoto). In other words, where a potential member of two or more IGOs is subject to similar pressures by the secretariats and members of those IGOs to sign up to a particular agreement then there is a greater likelihood that they will agree.

Findings

Unlike the pre-accession stage, formal accession involves, as the phrase suggests, formal, as well as informal discussion and bargaining between government representatives, the IGO's secretariat and, to varying extents, the members of the IGO in question. In the case of GATT/WTO, bilateral discussions with individual members of the Working Party established to consider the application are a central part of the accession process, unlike the OECD or the EU, where it seems far less frequent.

It is clear that it is a process of bargaining in which the IGOs can and do exercise a degree of discretion as to their requirements in the way of policy change that is required for accession. At times the extent of discretion might extend to dropping a condition that otherwise might be required, especially if so desired by one or more powerful IGO members. In regard to accession to the EU, for example, the Badinter Commission was given the responsibility of determining which former republics of Yugoslavia deserved recognition for accession based, in part, on their treatment of minorities. The Commission recommended against recognition of Croatia's and Bosnia's efforts, but found that Slovenia and Macedonia were suitable candidates. However, the European Commission chose to recognise Croatia, but not Macedonia, largely because of the influence of Germany and Greece (Saideman and Ayres 2007).

In summary, the major characteristics of transfer in the formal accession stage tentatively identified are:

- One, varying degrees of "opting out" of IGO-related activities and associated agreements, resulting in variations in the extent of transfer that takes place, with the EU being most restrictive in this regard.
- Two, an increasing degree of transfer being required in the formal accession stage, especially in relation to the EU.
- Three, increasingly detailed accession processes and criteria for all three IGOs.
- Four, the increasing provision of technical assistance during all stages of the accession process, most notably by the EU, to a lesser extent by the WTO and least of all by the OECD.
- Five, a trend to parallel accession processes, largely restricted to CEEC, that might have resulted in greater rates of agreed policy transfer.

The Post-Accession Stage and Policy Transfer

The third, post-accession, stage occurs after membership has been achieved. It is focused on the transfer that derives from the formal agreements reached during the formal accession stage, either subject to a specific timetable, or, rarely, on an open-ended basis. It does not include transfer that occurs once the country in question is a member of the IGO and that is not included in, or directly derived from, the accession process and agreement. Such latter transfer might be described as operating transfer. Post-accession and operating transfer might, of course, take place in this same period of time and some of the implications of this are examined in the conclusion.

Comparisons of Post-Accession Transfer

While all three of the IGOs developed systems for monitoring relevant policy transfer and compliance by their members, there was little study of post-accession transfer and the related phenomenon of post-accession compliance of new member states in IGOs until the creation of the WTO and the fifth enlargement of the EU (see, for example, Sasse 2008, and the various articles in Schimmelfennig and Trauner 2009, part of the increasingly large "Europeanisation" literature). The accession of China to the WTO stimulated a further acceleration in studies of post-accession compliance as regards the WTO, focused primarily upon China, but also, to a more limited extent, upon more recent accession by developing countries.

As with the pre-accession and formal accession stages, the extent of post-accession transfer has varied considerably and a number of characteristics are apparent. The first trend, for the OECD and the WTO, from the 1990s, has been an increase in the extent of post-accession transfer as new, acceding members have been required to meet the greater number of obligations contained in their accession agreements, compared to the lesser number in earlier agreements (Cattaneo and Braga 2009, pp. 16–26; Carroll and Kellow 2011). In regard to the WTO, the extent of post-accession transfer agreed varies substantially between states and over time, though it has increased, in line with the increase in the additional agreements reached by GATT and WTO members. The accession agreement (Protocol) for China, for example, consisted of 11 pages, nine annexes and 143 paragraphs incorporated by reference to the relevant sections of the Working Party's report. In contrast, the main text of several other countries has extended to no more than two pages (Cattaneo and Braga 2009, p. 12).

In regard to the OECD, Poland, Hungary and the Czech Republic at times failed to meet obligation deadlines in the later 1990s, especially in relation to the opening up of their economies to foreign investors, financial institutions and banks. The Czech Republic, for example, was strongly criticised by the OECD for its failure to meet several obligations (Trajlinková 2001).

While there has been a substantial increase in transfer associated with accession to the EU in the 2000s, as noted above, the bulk of that transfer has taken place during the EU's formal accession stage, as a condition for accession, although a limited amount of post-accession transfer has always been agreed to and has taken place (Tallberg 2002; Sedelmeier 2008). Further, Sedelmeier's work indicates that non-compliance is relatively low, with the countries most recently acceding complying to a slightly greater extent than those that acceded earlier, indicating, in turn, that the extent of agreed policy transfer is relatively high. This is not to suggest that all acceding members have fully complied, with a number of studies demonstrating where transfer and compliance have been incomplete (see, for example, Pridham 2007; Schimmelfennig and Trauner 2009).

However, recent studies suggest that post-accession transfer in the EU may be growing somewhat, in particular in areas where agreements for policy change reached in the formal accession period have not been concluded, as was the case for Bulgaria and Romania (see Gateva 2010). Initially, the two countries were part of the fifth enlargement process but, unlike the other states that acceded in 2004, the European Commission decided that further progress as regards policy change was needed in relation to the judiciary, the control of corruption and organised crime, and two agreements to that end were put in place. The first, a "super safeguard" gave the EU the power to delay their accession by one year – a power that was not used, although the two countries did not join the EU until 2007. The second, which has been used, was the Cooperation and Verification Mechanism (CVM). This specified a set of criteria or benchmarks against which there would be annual reports as to progress (EU 2012b). While the CVM was backed with very limited power to sanction recalcitrant states, in 2011 several key EU (notably Germany) states blocked the entry of both Bulgaria and Romania into the Schengen free travel zone pending further progress in their meeting the criteria laid down for the CVM, a more effective sanction (Vachudova and Spendzharova 2012).

The use of new mechanisms for the monitoring and control of post-accession transfer and compliance is also apparent in the WTO, with the introduction of the Transitional Review Mechanism (TRM) in relation to China. The sheer extent of the policy changes needed for China to achieve compliance with the obligations it entered into on gaining WTO membership, combined with varying degrees of suspicion by WTO members as to whether Chinese governments would have the commitment and capacity to comply, led to WTO members establishing an annual monitoring mechanism, the TRM. This oversaw and reported on China's implementation of its obligations. The USA, in particular, made an annual review of China's compliance a condition of its agreement to China's accession, as required by Congress. It was agreed that there would be eight annual reviews, followed by a final review in the tenth year after China's accession.

While, to date, the TRM has been unique to China, it has emphasised the growing importance WTO members attach to post-accession transfer and compliance (in addition to formal and pre-accession transfer), an importance further highlighted by the increasing, post-accession assistance that has been made available to new members (including China), so as help them achieve effective implementation and enforcement of the policy changes agreed at accession. The WTO and its predecessor, the GATT, have had mandates for the provision of technical assistance and training for developing countries for many years, assistance that has grown over time. Similarly, the EU has made available continuing, post-accession assistance to new members going back to the accessions of Greece, Spain and Portugal. In the case of the fifth enlargement of the EU, for example, a "Transition Facility" was made available to the new members. It provided financial assistance aimed at improving the new members' administrative capacity to implement and enforce EU legislation, to a total of €380 million, from 2004 to 2006 (European Commission 2012).

Findings

The limited evidence available, as noted above, indicates that post-accession transfer is not always a simple matter of implementing the agreements reached in the second, accession transfer stage, though this is often the case. Rather, post-accession transfer falls into at least two possible phases. The first phase is characterised by the transfer, implementation and enforcement by the new member of several of the items specified in the accession agreement. The second phase, varying in extent and duration, which might run in parallel with the first phase, consists of a period of continued, post-accession *bargaining* over at least some of the items that were contained in the agreement, later followed by a further, limited degree of transfer.

There are at least three situations in which this second, bargaining phase of the post-accession process seems to arise. The first is where the IGO and its members have agreed to the applicant state joining the IGO even where there is no final agreement over all policy changes regarded as necessary, as was the case for Bulgaria and Romania in the EU. The result is that the agreement notes the requirement for further discussion. Such an agreement enables, at least in principle, the applicant state and the IGO to reach an acceptable level of agreement as to the terms of entry while leaving the door open for further bargaining and negotiation after accession (see Jonsson and Talberg 1998). The second is where there are unanticipated differences of interpretation over one or more aspects of the accession agreement on the part of the acceding member and the IGO, so that what is transferred to the national or sub-national level is regarded as unacceptable by the IGO, necessitating a period of discussion and bargaining before they can be resolved. The third is that of simple non-compliance by the new member, either because of a lack of will to engage in the necessary transfer, especially in its domestically difficult implementation and enforcement stages, or because of a lack of political and administrative capacity, or both.

This second phase of post-accession bargaining and its outcomes, especially as regards the final extent of transfer, also has important implications for operating transfer, as noted above. The first is that the new member might attempt to link its final agreement to undertake the extent of policy transfer required by the accession agreement to its support for a separate, unrelated, proposed agreement being discussed by IGO members, by threatening to vote against the proposed agreement. The impact of such a threat will vary, depending on the IGO's specific voting rules. If unanimity is required for adoption of new agreements or the modification of existing ones, then the threat is a serious one, even though it is likely to have an adverse impact upon the threatening state's future reputation. The author has not been able to identify, to date, any such cases for our three IGOs.

The second implication is that, depending on what is finally agreed in the post-accession stage and the extent to which the new member and other members of the IGO view the final agreement as appropriate and fair, then their future propensity to comply with agreements by undertaking policy transfer might change. If, for example, other members regard the outcome as unfair or unreasonable, or both, they might reduce their general degree of compliance with future agreements, especially where they also feel that the secretariat or other unit of the IGO in question has been ineffective in dealing with the issue. In essence, post-accession bargaining may tend to result in a new or modified understanding of what constitutes an acceptable level of compliance and of non-compliance by members and, in turn, the level of transfer that they will undertake. The third implication is that the experience of monitoring, identifying and bargaining over non-compliance as regards the new member might suggest ways of improving the accession process that, if implemented, might lead to greater compliance and the required transfer.

It is also argued that it is as regards monitoring and judging cases of non-compliance that one of the great values of membership of an IGO can be seen, at least from the point of view of complying members. This is the fact that IGO membership means that individual states do not have to undertake, alone, the diplomatically difficult task of identifying cases of non-compliance, bargaining on a one-to-one basis with the non-compliant state and bearing all of the costs of any sanctions that might be involved. Instead, at least formally, it is the staff of the IGO that has to undertake these tasks, assisted to varying extents by interested member states.

Conclusion

The findings of this study are tentative, largely based on the secondary literature, as well as publications by the IGOs. However, they do suggest that accession to IGOs is closely associated with a varying degree of policy transfer and worthy of further, more systematic study. They also indicate what seems to be an increase, again varying, in the extent of transfer associated with accession over time and that the extent of transfer varies by accession stage.

Unsurprisingly, the extent or "breadth" of transfer indicated is largest for the EU and the OECD, primarily because their mandates cover a far wider range of policy areas and related issues than does that of the WTO, with its focus on trade. However, the extent of transfer in relation to the WTO is characterised by its "depth", in the sense that new members sign up to a greater number of agreements within the one policy area, trade.

As regards the stages of the accession process, in general there seems to have been an increase in the extent of pre-accession transfer over time, increasing firstly in the case of the EU, followed later by the OECD and GATT/WTO. A similar increase is apparent in the extent of transfer in the formal accession stage, especially in the case of the EU. The extent of transfer in the post-accession stage seems to have declined, notably for the EU, and is generally far more limited than is the case for the pre-accession and formal accession stages. IGOs have been increasingly keen to ensure that the bulk of required transfer occurs in the pre-accession and formal accession stages, mindful of the greater difficulty of ensuring compliance in the post-accession stage, once a state becomes a member of the IGO in question.

The findings of the study also suggest several major factors are at play in determining the extent and rate of transfer, although their impact has varied by IGO and over time. The first factor is the mandate of the IGOs. The EU and the WTO (including its predecessor, the GATT) have changed their mandates since their establishment, extending them to cover a greater range of policy areas and associated agreements. While the OECD's formal mandate has not changed, its built in flexibility, combined with its members' increasing requirements, has seen its agreements and recommendations extended to cover an increasing range of policy areas. Hence, for the most part, those entering any one of our IGOs in the 1990s or 2000s were required to "sign up" to a greater number of required items than was the case for those entering in the 1960s or 1970s and, correspondingly, the extent of policy transfer also grew.

The second factor is the degree of policy and institutional isomorphism exhibited by the candidates, and the greater the degree of isomorphism, the less the degree of transfer and vice versa. This has been perhaps most apparent in the case of the accession of the CEEC states to the EU, for example Bulgaria and Romania, and of China to the WTO. All lacked the degree of isomorphism with the acquis of either the EU or WTO exhibited by most other members at the time of their earlier accession, necessitating considerable policy and institutional change before accession was approved.

The third factor is the extent of derogation permitted by the members of the IGO. As indicated, there is a considerable difference in the extent of derogation that is permitted by the three IGOs and, as a result, in the extent of policy transfer that takes place during the accession process. The OECD has been the most generous in this regard, followed by the WTO, with the EU being far less generous. Both the EU and the WTO have become less generous over time – the EU, for example, for the most part accepting only derogations that are temporary in nature.

The combined impact of a government's commitment to, and capacity for, policy change is a fourth factor in determining policy transfer. In general, the greater the commitment and capacity, the more likely that policy transfer will occur. The importance of the capacity for change has been recognised by all three IGOs, with one result being an increase in the extent of technical assistance provided by IGOs and their members to candidates, especially in the pre-accession and formal accession stages. The EU and the WTO have also provided increasing post-accession assistance for states with more limited governance and economic capacities.

A fifth factor in explaining policy transfer is the extent to which IGOs have put in place authoritative, efficient mechanisms for monitoring, reporting and enforcing compliance with the accession agreements, that is, whether or not new members have undertaken the agreed extent and type of policy transfer. All three IGOs have such mechanisms in place, with the EU having recently introduced its Cooperation and Verification Mechanism and the WTO its Transitional Review Mechanism. The OECD continues to rely primarily upon its system of committee-based peer reviews, based upon regular monitoring of members' policies by the Secretariat.

A sixth factor in determining the extent and rate of policy transfer undertaken in the accession process is the bargaining position of at least the key members of the IGO in question. As noted, accession is in essence a bargaining process shaped by the interests of the members and those of the candidates, within the context of the established acquis of the IGO. Where the members have a common, substantial interest in the candidate's accession, then they may be less likely to require either the extent or rate of policy transfer that might otherwise have been the case. Conversely, where the interests of members vary significantly, then the candidate might have to agree to a greater extent and rate of policy transfer in order to satisfy those interests.

Finally, as noted, accession to IGOs takes place in political, economic and social contexts that vary over time and that, in turn, may have a variety of impacts on the extent and rate of policy transfer. The most striking example in this study was the break-up of the Soviet Bloc and the rapidly following applications for membership of the EU, the OECD and the WTO by many of the CEEC states. Their desire for membership was matched by an equally strong desire on the part of existing members of these IGOs to ensure the political and economic stability of those who applied, ideally in the shape of market-based, democratic states. The result was a rapid increase in policy and institutional transfer.

This study offers a number of tentative findings as to the association of policy transfer with accession to IGOs. Those findings need further and more rigorous testing. Also, they suggest a number of areas that warrant further research. Are the trends illustrated, for example, typical of all intergovernmental organisations, including the UN's specialised agencies, or only of those with a limited membership? What is the experience of accession-related policy transfer in other regional organisations with a "lesser" degree of integration than the EU? How does policy transfer during the accession process compare with that which takes place after accession? Are the characteristics of what might be called "unilateral" or "bilateral" policy transfer between states similar to those of transfer in the context of an IGO?

References

Carroll, P. and Kellow, A., 2011, *The OECD a Study of Organisational Adaptation* (Cheltenham: Edward Elgar).

Cattaneo, O. and Braga, C., 2009, Everything You Always Wanted to Know about WTO Accession (But Were Afraid to Ask), Policy Research Working Article 5116, World Bank.

Copelovitch, M. and Ohls, D., 2012, Trade, institutions, and the timing of GATT/WTO accession in post-colonial states. *Review of International Organisations*, 7, pp. 81–107.

Davis, C. and Wilf, M., 2011, Joining the Club: Accession to the GATT/WTO. Paper presented at the American Political Science Association Conference, Seattle, 2011.

Dolowitz, D., 2006, Bring back the states: Correcting for the omissions of globalization. *International Journal of Public Administration*, 29(4), pp. 263–280.

Dolowitz, D., 2009, Learning by observation: Surveying the international arena. *Policy and Politics*, 37(3), pp. 317–334.

Dolowitz, D. and March, I., 1996, Who learns what from whom: A review of the policy transfer literature. *Political Studies*, 44, pp. 343–357.

Dolowitz, D. and March, I., 2000, Learning from abroad: The role of policy transfer in contemporary policy-making. *Governance*, 13(1), pp. 5–23.

EU, 2012a, How Does it Work? Available at http://ec.europa.eu/enlargement/how-does-it-work/index_en.htm (accessed 20 March 2012).

EU, 2012b, Progress Report on the Cooperation and Verification Mechanism – Procedural Aspects. Available at http://europa.eu/rapid/pressReleasesAction.do?reference=MEMO/07/260&format=HTML&aged=0&language=EN (accessed 20 March 2012).

European Commission, 2012, Financial Assistance - Transition Facility. Available at http://ec.europa.eu/enlargement/how-does-it-work/financial-assistance/transition_facility_en.htm (accessed 20 March 2012).

Evans, M., 2009, New directions in the study of policy transfer. *Policy Studies*, 30(3), pp. 237–241.

Forsberg, A., 1998, The politics of GATT expansion: Japanese accession and the domestic political context in Japan and the United States, 1948–1955. *Business and Economic History*, 27, pp. 185–195.

Gateva, E., 2010, Post-accession Conditionality – Support Instrument for Continuous Pressure? KFG Working Article Series, No 18, October, Free University of Berlin.

Gibbs, M., 2001, UNCTAD's role in the WTO accession process, in: *WTO Accessions and Development Policies* (Geneva: United Nations Publication), 161–171.

Girvin, B., 2008, The treaty of Rome and Ireland's developmental dilemma, in: M. Gehler (Ed) *Von Gemeinsamen Markt Zur Europäischen Unionbildung. 50 Jahre Römische Verträge* (Wien: Böhlau Verlag), pp. 573–595.

Harris, S., 2002, South Korea and the Asian Crisis: The impact of the democratic deficit and OECD accession, in: G. Underhill and X. Zhang (Eds) *International Financial Governance Under Stress* (Cambridge: Cambridge University Press).

Hyun-Chin, L. and Jin-Ho, 2006, Between neo-liberalism and democracy: The transformation of the developmental state in South Korea. *Development and Society*, 35(1), pp. 1–28.

Jonsson, C. and Talberg, J., 1998, Compliance and post-agreement bargaining. *European Journal of International Relations*, 4(4), pp. 371–408.

Lemass, S., 1966, A speech delivered in Dáil Éireann. *Dáil debates*, 219, 4 January 1966 cols, pp. 1139–1161.

Levitz, P. and Pop-Eleches, G., 2010, Why no backsliding? The European Union's impact on democracy and governance before and after accession. *Comparative Political Studies*, 43(4), pp. 457–485.

Mattli, W. and Plumper, T., 2002, The demand-side politics of EU enlargement: Democracy and the application for EU membership. *Journal of European Public Policy*, 9(4), pp. 550–574.

McKenzie, F., 2008, GATT and the cold war: Accession debates, institutional development, and the western alliance, 1947–1959. *Journal of Cold War Studies*, **10**(3), pp. 78–109.

Moreno-Brid, J., 2007, Economic Development and Industrial Development in Mexico post-NAFTA, Economic Commission for Latin America and the Caribbean, Mexico. Available at http://www.eclac.org/celade/noticias/paginas/3/28353/JCMoreno.pdf (accessed 20 March 2012).

Murphy, G., 2003, *Economic Realignment and the Politics of EEC Entry: Ireland, 1948–1972* (Bethesda: Academia Press).

OECD, 2002, *Forty Years Experience with the OECD Code of Liberalisation of Capital Movements* (Paris: OECD).

OECD, 2007a, *A General Procedure for Future Accessions, C(2007)31/Final* (Paris: OECD).

OECD, 2007b, *Roadmap for the Accession of the Russian Federation to the OECD Convention* (Paris: OECD).

OECD, 2012a, OECD Enlargement. Available at http://www.oecd.org/document/42/0,3746,en_2649_201185_38598698_1_1_1_1,00.html (accessed 20 March 2012).

OECD, 2012b, *Agreement on the Terms of Accession of the Republic of Estonia to the Convention on the Organisation for Economic Co-operation and Development* (Paris: OECD).

OECD, 2012c, *Agreement on the Terms of Accession of the State of Israel to the Convention on the Organisation for Economic Co-operation and Development* (Paris: OECD).

Poret, P., 1989, Mexico and the OECD codes of liberalisation. *OECD Observer*, No. 189, August/September.

Powell, C., 2011, The long road to Europe: Spain and the European community, 1957–1986, in: J. Roy and M. Lorca-Susino (Eds) *Spain in the European Union the First Twenty Five Years* (Miami: European Union Center), pp. 21–44.

Pridham, G., 2007, Romania and EU membership in comparative perspective: A post-accession compliance problem? – The case of political conditionality. *Perspectives on European Politics and Society*, **8**(2), pp. 168–188.

Saideman, S. and Ayres, R., 2007, Pie crust promises and the sources of foreign policy: The limited impact of accession and the priority of domestic constituencies. *Foreign Policy Analysis*, **3**, pp. 195–196.

Sasse, P., 2008, The politics of EU conditionality: The norm of minority protection during and beyond EU accession. *Journal of European Public Policy*, **15**(6), pp. 842–860.

Schimmelfennig, F. and Trauner, F. (Eds), 2009, Post-accession Compliance in the EU's New Member States, European Integration Online Paper, Special Issue 2, 13/23. Available at http://eiop.or.at/eiop/texte/EIoP_2009_SpecIssue_2.pdf (accessed 17 May 2012).

Sedelmeier, U., 2008, After conditionality: Post-accession compliance with EU law in East Central Europe. *Journal of European Public Policy*, **15**(6), pp. 806–825.

Tallberg, J., 2002, Paths to compliance: Enforcement, management, and the European Union. *International Organization*, **56**(3), pp. 609–643.

Trajlinková, K., 2001, A Review of Slovakia's Accession to the OECD Liberalization Process: Comparisons between Slovakia, Czech Republic, Poland and Hungary, Narodna Banka Slovenska, BIATEC, No 9. Available at http://www.nbs.sk/_img/Documents/BIATEC/trajan.pdf (accessed 24 October 2011).

Tsogtbaatar, D., 2005, Mongolia's WTO accession: Expectations and realities of WTO membership, Case Study 29 in: *Managing the Challenges of WTO Participation*, World Trade Organisation. Available at http://www.wto.org/english/res_e/booksp_e/casestudies_e/case29_e.htm (accessed on 21 December 2011).

Vachudova, M. and Spendzharova, A., 2012, The EU's Cooperation and Verification Mechanism: Fighting Corruption in Bulgaria and Romania after EU Accession, Swedish Institute for European Policy Studies, European Policy Analysis, pp. 1–16.

Vernon, J., 1992, Mexico's accession to the GATT: A catalyst at odds with the outcome? *St Mary's Law Journal*, **24**, pp. 717–735.

WTO, 2012a, Accessions. Available at http://www.wto.org/english/thewto_e/acc_e/acc_e.htm (accessed 20 March 2012).

Agency Fever? Analysis of an International Policy Fashion

CHRISTOPHER POLLIT, KAREN BATHGATE, JANICE CAULFIELD,
AMANDA SMULLEN, AND COLIN TALBOT

ABSTRACT *In the last 15 years, the governments of many OECD countries have transferred a wide range of functions to new, agency-type organizations. Allowing for the fact that, for comparative purposes, it is difficult precisely to define agencies, and further acknowledging that in many countries agencies are far from being new, it nevertheless remains the case that there seems to have been a strong fashion for this particular organizational solution.*

This article investigates the apparent international convergence towards "agencification." It seeks to identify the reasons for, and depth of, the trend. It asks to what extent practice has followed rhetoric. The emerging picture is a complex one. On the one hand, there seems to be a widespread belief, derived from a variety of theoretical traditions, that agencification can unleash performance improvements. On the other hand, systematic evidence for some of the hypothetical benefits is very patchy. Furthermore, the diversity of actual practice in different countries has been so great that there must sometimes be considerable doubt as to whether the basic requirements for successful performance management are being met.

Agency fever: the apparent global convergence on the agency form

Let us for the moment define a government agency as an organization that stands at arm's length from its parent ministry or ministries and carries out public functions, but that is not (primarily) a commercial enterprise. (A more sophisticated definitional discussion follows shortly.) During the last 15 years, this category of public body has become a popular vehicle for executing a wide range of functions in a large number of countries. As the OECD put it as early as 1995, "A number of countries have seen merit in the agency model" (OECD, 1995, p. 32).

In some countries, specific programs have been announced to create agencies that function across the government (Canada, the Netherlands, Jamaica, Japan, New Zealand, Tanzania, the U.K., and the U.S.A.)—even if some of these programs have faded before many agencies were actually up and working. In other countries, substantial numbers of agencies have been created without there necessarily having been a single, umbrella program to shape the exercise (Australia, Denmark, Latvia). In other countries still—such as Finland, Sweden, and the U.S.A.—central government agencies had existed as an important and recognized category of public body for a long time. Yet here too there was considerable change. Agencies were reformed, slimmed down, in some cases merged, and generally subjected to modernization processes intended to make them more performance oriented, more economical, more customer friendly, or some virtuous mixture of these elements. In short, there appears to have been a major international shift of public functions (and employees) into the arm's-length format, combined with an updating of that format itself. If "agency fever" sounds a tad too dramatic, then at the very least we have been witnessing an outbreak of internationally infectious "agency flu."

In the case of the U.K., for example, the Next Steps program has received widespread publicity and has led to more than 81% of civil servants becoming employees of agencies within a period of just one decade (Cabinet Office, 1999; Gains, 1999; O'Toole and Jordan, 1995; Wilson, 1999). Since 1991, the Netherlands has created 22 agencies. These now employ 28% of Dutch civil servants. Canada has its Special Operating Agencies (SOAs: see Aucoin, 1996). New Zealand has dozens of Crown Entities (Boston et al., 1996, chapter 4). President Clinton's administration, evidently not content with its considerable existing portfolio of executive agencies (e.g., the National Aeronautics and Space Administration), proposed to set up a series of Performance Based Organizations (PBOs), although only one of these had got off the drawing board by the time of the 2000 Presidential election. The EU Commission, under pressure to reform, has produced proposals that include elements of externalization to agency-like bodies. The Tanzanian Public Service Reform Program included proposals for more than 30 agencies (although by mid-2000 only 7 had been launched). The Jamaican 1996 Public Service Modernization Program envisaged the creation of 11 to 13 executive agencies. Even Japan—hitherto not a country noted for its enthusiasm for New Public Management (NPM)-type reforms—has announced its intention to create, from April 2000, more than 80 Independent Administrative Corporations (IACs) that will take over approximately 67,000 staff (James, 1999; Yamamoto, 2000). International bodies such as SIGMA/OECD, the IMF, and the World Bank have offered their seal of approval for agency creation in such widely diverse areas as Africa, the Caribbean, and central and eastern Europe (see, e.g., Polidano, 2000; SIGMA, 1999). During 2000/2001, both the OECD (PUMA) and the World Bank acknowledged the pervasiveness of the agency form by launching studies of agency practice intended to draw lessons for the international community. In sum, as SIGMA/PUMA recently put it,

> Since the 1980s there has been an explosion of interest in the agency model in many countries, driven largely by the pressures to restrain spending and make service to citizens more responsive (SIGMA, 2001, p. 8).

In the face of what is apparently such a strong trend, the time seems ripe for some analysis of the phenomenon. How far is policy convergence real and substantial or superficial and rhetorical? What are the main claims and purposes of agencification (an inelegant but increasingly used neologism)? In this article, we will seek to clarify and begin to answer these questions. At the same time, we would wish to acknowledge energetically that the jury is still out on many important aspects or, to put it more positively, that there is still ample room for fresh empirical research on the agency phenomenon.

Defining agency

A *number of* scholars—and more than one *international* organization—have tried to produce short but watertight definitions of agencies. In our judgment, none of these attempts has been entirely successful, at least not in producing a portable, general-purpose definition that will comfortably fit every case. SIGMA/PUMA—an international organization not normally given to harsh words—sums up the status quo as follows:

> As even a cursory review of international experience reveals, the term public agency, when used by a national government, really carries whatever meaning that government wishes to give to it (SIGMA, 2001, p. 14).

There are good reasons why definition is difficult. Not least of these is the variation in public law between countries. The available legal boxes into which different kinds of public bodies may be placed vary widely (as do the processes by which that positioning is brought about). Many foreign observers have regarded the very flexible U.K. system, where agencies can be created without any new statutes being required, with a mixture of envy and distaste. Compare this situation with that of France where, since 1958, about 200 separate legal categories for *établissements public* have been set up in order to pigeonhole the more than 1000 central government bodies that fall into this broad category (SIGMA, 2001, pp. 43–73). Indeed, as has often been noted, the very boundaries and character of administrative law diverge significantly between countries—France and the U.K. being one favorite contrast.

Another problem is language itself. There are subtle shades of difference (we are told by native speakers) between the terms used in, say, Finnish, Japanese, and English for their national variants, but all are bundled together in PUMA or World Bank documents as *agencies* or *les agences*. Important connotations may be lost in translation, and new ones may unintentionally slip in.

A third problem is that the formal and quickly ascertainable features of an organization are, of course, only one part of the story. Two entities with broadly similar legal statuses and formal powers may in fact operate in startlingly different ways because they are embedded in different kinds of political systems (for example, an agency working within the consensual political system of the Netherlands may behave rather differently from an apparently similar agency 200 kilometers away in the intensely adversarial U.K. political system). This important set of behavioral issues can only be very briefly referred to in the present article.

All this having been said, we nevertheless acknowledge the need to offer at least a working definition of what we are writing about. We begin from the idea that one may envisage a two-dimensional spectrum of types of organization running from the center of government out across the public-private borderline (which is increasingly a rather large patchwork *zone* rather than a *line*). Along one dimension, one moves from organizations with no commercial purposes (e.g., central government think tanks) to those that are largely or wholly suffused with commercial purposes—e.g., state enterprises, such as a state railway, and privately owned, profit-seeking companies such as a supermarket chain. These organizations compose what could be termed the *state-market dimension*. Along the other dimension, one moves from wholly state-owned and public law-dominated institutions, such as a ministry, through arm's-length but still public bodies (such as a meterological office, or a driving license agency) to public-private partnership organizations and finally to voluntary organizations existing not in the state sphere but as part of civil society (such as a trade union, or a hiking club, or a local church). These organizations make up the *state-civil society dimension*.

Different definitions of agencies fence off more or less extensive strips along these two dimensions. For example, one thoughtful article includes agencies as a type of *quango* and defines quangos as covering virtually the whole of the state-market dimension except ministries at one end and profit-oriented commercial companies at the other (Greve, Flinders, and van Thiel, 1999). The working definition we are using is broad, but not quite as extensive as this. We define agencies as those bodies that have all or most of the following characteristics:

- They are at arm's length from the main hierarchical spines of ministries, i.e., there is a degree of structural disaggregation
- They carry out public tasks (service provision, regulation, adjudication, certification) at a national level
- Their core staff are public servants (not necessarily civil servants—definitions here again vary enormously between countries)
- They are financed, in principle at least, by the state budget. In practice, some agencies recover a good deal of their financial needs from charges (e.g., charging for a driving or television license). *However, even* in these cases, the state retains the residual financial liability
- They are subject to at least some administrative law procedures (i.e., they are not wholly or predominantly private law bodies)

Thus we see agencies as lying center left on both the state-market dimension and the state-civil society dimension. At the left-hand pole of both dimensions lie ministries themselves. At the right-hand end of the state-market dimension, we exclude state enterprises (because they are predominantly commercial in orientation) and for-profit private sector companies. At the right-hand end of the state-civil society dimension, we exclude *voluntary* associations, even if they are sometimes given public tasks to perform and public money to do it with (sijch as health care, social care, or housing provision). Agencies are part of the state apparatus; voluntary associations, such as the Royal Society for the Protection of Animals in the U.K. or a Montessori school in the Netherlands, are not.

This working definition does not get us out of all difficulties, and readers will already have noticed a certain amount of fudging (e.g., "all or most of the following characteristics"). Nevertheless, it does fence off a sizeable population of public sector organizations and usefully excludes many others, even if a few hard cases remain. Our definition includes, inter alia, traditional American agencies such as NASA and new types such as former vice president Gore's proposed PBOs; British Next Steps agencies and also Non-Departmental Public Bodies (NDPBs); Canadian SOAs; Dutch *agentschappen* and most *zelfstandig bestuur organisaties* (ZBOs); Finnish *virastot*; Japanese lACs; most of New Zealand's Crown Entities; and Swedish *myndigheter*.

Agencification as part of a larger trend

The multiple blooming of the agency form should be seen in context. It is part of a wider trend towards decentralization and autonomization within many public sectors (Kettl, 2000; Hood and Schuppert, 1988; OECD, 1995; Polidano, 2000; Pollitt and Bouckaert, 2000; van Thiel, 2000). Agencies are one species in the genus *public service providers*. However, the setting up of agencies is perhaps of special interest, since agencies generally represent the organizational form closest to the traditional core bureaucracy—the general-purpose ministry or department of state. Other decentralized forms are further out from the core—state enterprises (many countries), previously state-provided services that have been contracted out to private sector providers (many countries), public-private partnership organizations (PPPs: many countries), and so on. In this sense, agencies could be seen as the *marginal case*—as the form of organization considered suitable for activities that can be shifted out from core government departments, but not very far. Perhaps because of this, the numerical significance of agencies is sometimes overlooked. Public management scholars tend to spend more time looking at the theoretically more exciting examples of privatization and contracting out than the perhaps less pure form of the state agency (e.g., Kettl, 2000; Lane, 2000).

Why agencies?

In recent years, there has been a notable convergence of purposes and theories (problems and solutions) that are favorable to agency creation. The purposes have been those of politicians and senior public servants. The theories have come from academics in various disciplines, and also from management consultants. These theories suggest that agencies could assist governments in achieving certain salient and widely held objectives.

Broadly, governments of the period since the global economic upheavals of the 1970s have faced three large problems. The first is financial: the ability to tax seems to have diminished just as the cost of continuing to run welfare states has climbed. We need not go into the widely rehearsed reasons for this here (but see Pollitt and Bouckaert, 2000, Chapter 2 and Appendix). The important point for the present article is that these circumstances have created tremendous pressures to restrain the rate of growth of public expenditure—to economize. However, governments cannot simply slash services, because the biggest spending programs also tend to be the most popular—pensions, health care, and education. The second problem has been an apparent decline in citizen trust in governmental institutions (see, e.g., Norris, 1999; Nye et al., 1997). The third has been rising citizen expectations with respect to the standards of public services. There are many possible reasons for this shift, including generally rising affluence and the "equalling up" of expectations derived from the experience of private sector services and imported into public sector contexts (Pollitt and Bouckaert, 1995). Quality is different from trust. One may trust a government while deploring the low standards of certain services. Or one may recognize that a particular service is good while simultaneously mistrusting the integrity or honesty of a government.

Governments are therefore seeking ways to economize, to restore trust, and to improve the quality of services. While the second and third of these tasks are analytically separable, there is some connection between them, because governments occasionally claim that quality improvement will help restore trust. There are reasons to doubt whether this link is at all straightforward (see Norris, 1999; Pollitt and Bouckaert, 2000, pp. 142–148), but this particular issue is not our main focus here.

The first (financial), second (trust), and third (quality) problems together lead directly to the proposition, articulated most loudly in the U.S.A. but echoed in many other countries, that government must "do more *with less.*" This is where agencies come in. It is believed that agencies can help governments work better, yet more economically. How will they accomplish this trick? The precise answer depends on which theorist one turns to, but overall there is an impressive theoretical convergence towards the hypothesis that more autonomous, more specialized public bodies will improve service quality, efficiency, and perhaps other aspects too. Thus, to summarize, the following hypotheses been variously suggested:

- The specialization of functions (e.g., by taking an agency out of a general, multipurpose ministry or department) will allow for more professional organizations, that are better managed and offer higher quality services (management and organization theories). Osborne and Gaebler, in (famously) recommending that government separate "steering" tasks from "rowing" tasks, opined, "Rowing requires people who focus intently on one mission and perform it well" (Osborne and Gaebler, 1992, p. 35)
- Separating out agencies with defined functions will also improve rank-and-file motivation. Staff will see themselves as belonging to a more identifiable, specialized organization with its own personality and purpose, rather than as just being part of a large amorphous civil service (management theories: property rights variety of rational choice theory—assuming that agency status increases the property rights of staff)
- The "distancing" of agencies from political intervention will further encourage a more professional approach to management ("letting managers manage" among management theories)
- Separation will also lead to more flexible, tailor-made systems of recruitment, training, and promotion. The "iron cage" of civil service central regulations will be relaxed. Thus more appropriate staff will produce a higher quality service (management theories)
- Separation will also permit greater transparency, since an agency can more easily be subject to a contract-like regime, specifying its performance criteria and budgetary limits (principal agent variety of rational choice theory)
- Greater transparency and a contract-like form of relationship will put principals in a better position to apply pressure for efficiency gains (principal agent variety of rational choice theories; "making managers manage" among management theories)
- Separation into distinct, single-purpose organizations will make it easier for key stakeholders to identify, participate in, and be consulted about the work of the organization, i.e., being "close to the consumer" should become easier (communitarian theories, pluralist political theories)

Taken together, the above hypotheses make agencies sound like a Very Good Idea Indeed. However, considerable caution is advisable before accepting these theories at face value. The reasons are various:

1. The validity and applicability of the underlying theories themselves have frequently been called into question. Many management theories have been attacked for either

their pronounced normative biases or their weak evidential base (anecdotalism; absence of validity or reliability checks or both—for example, see Pollitt, 2000, on Osborne and Gaebler, 1992). Rational choice theory, despite its sometime elegance and rigor, has also been subject to extensive criticism. These attacks have been directed both at the underlying epistemological assumptions of the theory (utility maximization, low trust, the ruling-out of altruism) and at its manifest failure to account for certain well-known cases (Gains, 1999, pp. 37–40, provides a useful summary). More generally, a number of public administration scholars have suggested that a good deal of what passes for administrative theorizing is prone to fashionable swings and is fairly unscientific (Hood and Jackson, 1991; Hood, 1998; Pollitt and Bouckaert, 2000, pp. 183–191). Finally, there may be a large cultural bias in the Anglophone management literature. James (1999) argues that the models of corporate management that influenced the architects of the Next Steps report were Anglo-American and that (for example) German and Japanese models of well-functioning corporations diverge significantly from these transatlantic stereotypes.

2. Empirically, there seems to be remarkably little systematic scientific evidence on the results of creating agencies. More than a decade ago, Hood and Schuppert (1989, pp. 23–24) found that "nowhere, it seems, have the doctrinal claims made for the advantages of [autonomized organizations] been put carefully to the proof..." More recently, a research project into Dutch quangos found that "The motives of politicians for their choice of quangos... are not substantiated. An immediate and overall improvement in the efficiency and effectiveness of policy implementation is not found" (van Thiel, 2000, p. 184; see also Bogt, 1999; for New Zealand, see Boston et al., 1996, p. 86; for the U.K., see Gains, 1999, p. 43, and, more generally, Pollitt, 1995, 2000). One should not exaggerate the situation: there are certainly case studies and performance indicator data showing how specific agencies have improved specific aspects of performance year after year (e.g., Chancellor of the duchy of Lancaster, 1997). However, it is usually difficult if not impossible to connect such improvements to agency status per se (just as it would be problematic to connect the manifest *failures* of certain agencies, such as the U.K. Child Support Agency, to agency status alone). And general evidence of agencification as the cause of greater efficiency, higher quality, etc. is conspicuous by its absence.

3. Several pieces of empirical research have suggested that, in practice, the choice of organizational form by ministers and civil servants tends to be fairly ad hoc and that the theoretical propositions mentioned above feature more from lectures and textbooks than from the reality of politico-administrative decision making (e.g., Gains, 1999; van Thiel, 2000, pp. 7–12). Alternatively, other authors demonstrate that, while theoretical ideas have played a role, their application has been haphazard and constantly diluted by practical and political considerations. Evidently, this outcome was true even of the New Zealand reforms, which are commonly held up as examples of unusual theoretical purity (Boston et al., 1996, pp. 82–85).

4. A convergence of theories and purposes still leaves us a long way short of a convergence of actual practices and behaviors. It means that many governments appear to be talking about roughly the same kinds of thing but may not necessarily have made any crucial decisions about these issues. Even where such decisions have been taken, they may not have resulted in specific and identifiable changes in administrative behavior (widely cited publications on modernization—e.g., OECD, 1995, 1997—describe

much of the reasoning behind agencification and refer to various reform decisions and programs, but they tend to be rather short on information about behavioral change). And, finally, changes in behavior do not automatically result in performance improvements. The chain from talk to results is therefore long and complex. These distinctions between *talk* (which we will here treat as including hard copy and electronic texts), *decisions, behavior,* and *results* are based on Brunsson's work, as modified by one of us (Brunsson, 1989; Pollitt, 2001).

Summary: an ideal-type agency

It is easy to picture the ideal New Public Management-style agency. It would be professionally managed, flexible, customer responsive, specialized, efficient, and intensely performance oriented. Its operations would be transparent, and, using the latest IT and accounting techniques, it would render to its democratic watchdogs a "balanced scorecard" of its achievements and weaknesses. It would learn swiftly from its rare mistakes and would always be listening to its stakeholders. Perhaps the two key dimensions in all this are *structural disaggregation* and *performance contracting*. These are explicit, or strongly implicit, in most of the theoretical arguments for agencies set out in the previous section. Structural disaggregation gives the opportunity for flexibility, specialization, staff identification, and a specific customer focus. A performance contract framework ensures that the agency remains accountably focused on politically approved objectives and does not go off the rails. To the extent that either of these elements are missing, one might expect the benefits predicted by management and rational choice theorists also to be absent.

With this ideal type in mind, we can now turn back to the practicalities of real agencies in specific countries in order to form a first estimate of how deep and how uniform recent reforms have been.

Unpacking agencification

The diversity of statuses and powers

In the U.K., most Next Steps agencies continue to be responsible to individual ministers, and the official line is that the constitutional doctrine of ministerial responsibility remains unaffected by the decanting of four out of every five civil servants into this relatively new type of organization (O'Toole and Jordan, 1995; Wilson, 1999). Agencies, although at arm's length, are still constitutionally part of their parent ministries.

The main task of Next Steps agencies is supposed to be the execution of operational tasks—*rowing,* in Osborne and Gaebler-speak. They carry on their businesses within framework agreements with their parent departments (these are contractlike but *not,* legally, contracts). They work within specified budgets and targets that can be seen in their annual reports and/or in the government's annual review of agencies (e.g., Chancellor of the Duchy of Lancaster, 1997). Generally speaking, agencies have delegated authority to recruit and manage their own staff (although these staff are still civil servants) and have their own budgets. They answer questions from MPs about operational issues directly, although the extent to which these replies are actively screened by the parent department varies a good deal (Hogwood et al., 2000).

Yet even within the Next Steps agencies as a set, significant variations occur. Many of the Ministry of Defense's 40-odd agencies formally report to senior officials, not to the minister. Some agencies are definitely involved in *steering* as well as *rowing*. The Director of the Prison Service, for example, had it written into his contract that he provided policy advice to the minister (Gains, 1999, p. 34). The Director of the Benefits Agency has always had a similarly substantial policy role. The larger agencies are self-sufficient in terms of the traditional management functions of finance and human resource management, but others still rely extensively on their parent ministries. Although agencies have formally received a great deal of delegated authority over personnel issues, even this authority is still constrained by (often hidden) central controls and "guidance" that operates differently for different agencies (Talbot, 1997). This variety seems to be closely related to the huge differences between the sizes of different agencies (see next section). Finally, a few agencies are frequently in the headlines, while others attract virtually no interest from MPs or the mass media (Hogwood et al., 2000).

In Sweden, matters are very different:

> It is an important tenet in the Swedish constitutional tradition that agencies are not subject to the command of individual ministers but only to the decisions of the cabinet as whole. Civil servants in the agencies take some pride in the relative autonomy of their institutions and are well aware of their right to resist informal suggestions from the ministries (Tarchys, 1988, p. 73).

The position of individual ministers within the Swedish system is in fundamental contrast to that of the U.K. system. In general, relative to individual ministries, Swedish agencies have much greater freedom than their U.K. counterparts, and they are not constrained by any equivalent of the British constitutional doctrine of individual ministerial responsibility. Indeed, a recent OECD survey identified the weakness of ministries with regard to setting performance targets and other guidelines for agencies as a continuing source of concern (OECD, 1998). Rather like some of the larger U.S. federal agencies, Swedish agencies have built up their own sets of political connections, which they sometimes use to protect themselves from attempts by "their" ministry to intervene.

Compared with the sturdy autonomy of Sweden's agencies, the first-generation SOAs created in Canada in the early 1990s were somewhat feeble creatures (Aucoin, 1996). They had even less protection from continuous ministerial interference—and less flexibility to depart from general civil service rules— than their U.K. counterparts. The SOA heads were the direct subordinates of the Deputy Ministers (Permanent Secretaries/top civil servants) of their parent departments. Delegation of authority to these "special" organizations was "half-hearted" (Aucoin, 1996, p. 10). A study of a slightly more recent creation— the Canadian Food Inspection Agency—described it as "not really at arm's length" but as having some financial and personnel "elbow room" (Prince, 2000, p. 217).

Latvia regained its independence from the Soviet Union in 1991. Within 10 years, 2.5 million Latvian citizens were enjoying the services of more than 170 central government agencies (the exact number is uncertain, because there is no single, authoritative, central register). The talk was all of escaping from the dead hand of bureaucracy and of adopting more entrepreneurial approaches. The resulting agencies took a bewildering variety of legal forms— nonprofit organizations, nonprofit joint stock companies, nonprofit state enterprises, nonprofit limited companies, and so on. Parent ministries tend to be poorly equipped to guide and monitor, and performance frameworks were the exception rather than the rule. Procedural relations between ministries and agencies took a variety of forms, some of them quite vestigial. A number of undesirable financial practices have arisen, and in some cases years go by without a particular agency filing proper accounts. The ministry of finance and the state exchequer have not yet acquired the political clout to discipline strongly either the agencies or their parent ministries. Credible evidence concerning efficiency and quality is, with a few honorable exceptions, nonexistent. International funding and development bodies have become unhappy about this semichaos, and in 2000, a new law on agencies was introduced to the *Saiema* (parliament) to try, retrospectively, to regularize the situation. An uncharitable commentator might observe that, less than 10 years ago, some of these international bodies were among those supporting Latvian agencification.

One could go on with such contrasts, drawing in other countries, but the basic point has been made. Across countries, and even sometimes within individual countries, agencies vary so much in terms of their powers and statuses that it hard to think of many generalizations that could possibly fit every member of the species. In particular, both structural disaggregation and the degree of performance measurement may be low, medium, or high. The settings for these two theoretically crucial variables seem to depend on a multitude of constitutional and contextual factors. If this is convergence, then the zone converged upon is a large and varied terrain.

The diversity of size and functions

According to classical organization theory, size is an important predictor of many features of organizations and their behavior. For example, Donaldson (1985) argues that cumulative research into a wide range of organizations indicates that size tends to have an important influence on the degree of functional specialization, of centralization, and of formalization, and on the number of levels in the organizational hierarchy. Other research suggests that size affects the speed and nature of the diffusion of decentralizing reforms (Pollitt, Birchall, and Putman, 1998, pp. 174–175).

The type of activity (function) in which an organisation is involved is another significant variable. Again, research has pointed to the tendency for the type of function to influence both the culture of organizations and the specific methods of organizing (e.g., James, 1994; Stewart, 1992). Since agencies display a huge range of sizes and functions, both among different countries and within individual countries, it would be surprising if their organizational structures and cultures were not also widely divergent.

A few brief national examples will illustrate the scale of some of these differences. In the U.K., at the beginning of 1997, the Benefits Agency employed 74,925 staff and had a running costs budget of over £2600M. (Interestingly, in most European countries, the payment of social security benefits is not regarded as a function suitable for the executive agency form.) At the same time, the Wilton Park Conference Center, another agency, had a staff of 32 and a running costs budget of £1.6M. In the Netherlands, the prison service (DJI) was an agency with a staff of over 16,000 and an expenditure of over 2400M NLG, while the Central Archive Service (CAS) employed just over 100 people and spent 12M NLG.

Comparisons of countries with substantial agency populations show that many functions are allocated to different types of bodies in different countries. This finding can be construed as a blow to any strong version of functional convergence theory. After all, if a function proves suitable for the agency form in one place, the expectation would presumably be that other reform-minded countries would soon follow suit, in order to reap the same advantages.

Let us take just four, tolerably similar European countries—Finland, the Netherlands, Sweden, and the U.K. All have agencies. Do the functions given to these agencies match? The short answer is "only occasionally." Meteorology is a promising start—all four countries have national meteorological offices that have agency status (though the *spread of services* varies somewhat, and, in some cases, certain services have been privatized). The prison service is also an agency in three of the four (and a department that is due to become an agency in the fourth). But differences soon set in. For forestry, the Finns have a state corporation (although it used to be an agency), The Dutch have a ZBO ("self-standing organisation"—a quango), the Swedes have an agency, and the British have a Non-Departmental Public Body. For social security, the Brits are the only ones to have had almost all benefits packaged in a single agency (though at the time of writing, this situation is set to change). In Finland, the task is split between a department of the Ministry of Labor, local authorities, and a National Pensions Agency (KELA) that (unusually) is responsible directly to the Parliament. In Sweden also, various bodies are involved. In the Netherlands, the Sociale Verzekeringsbank (SVB), which administers pensions, is a ZBO, but other organizations are involved in social security as well—for example, local authorities pay out unemployment benefits. Currently planned organizational changes *will, if anything,* bring the SVB *closer* to the parent ministry. For immigration, the Dutch have an agency (probably their most controversial one), but the Finns, Swedes, and Brits all have different types of organizations, usually departments within ministries.

If one extends the analysis to Japan, further differences appear. Many of the *executive* functions that had been considered strong candidates for agency status in the U.K. (such as social security or patents) were ruled out as possible IACs in Japan—despite the fact that the Japanese initiative was to some extent modelled on the U.K. Next Steps program—because it was argued that activities entailing the exercise of coercive power over citizens must remain directly accountable to parliament. As a result, a substantial proportion of IAC candidates were concerned with research, educational, and cultural functions. One might hypothesize that this outcome will lead to performance measurement problems. In the ideal agency, the outputs are discrete and measurable. Unit costs can be confidently monitored. The nature of quality can be agreed upon and assessed. James Q. Wilson (1989) is only one of many scholars who have drawn attention to the importance of having observable, measurable outputs as the foundation for an arm's-length regime of performance management. In the Japanese case, however, it appears that the functions picked for agency status are mainly those where measurement and attribution problems will be considerable.

Contexts and motives—a tale of three countries

An earlier section set out the most prominent theoretical arguments in favor of the agency form. A summary of the recent histories of agency development in Finland, the U.K., and the Netherlands may help throw light on the actual contexts, as opposed to the theoretical justifications, for agencification.

In Finland, during the mid-1990s, central agencies were *reduced* in function and number on the grounds that they were bureaucratic and undemocratic (since they could make rules for the citizen but were not directly supervised by elected politicians). They were seen as part of the old-fashioned, heavy, legalistic way of governing, to be culled and reshaped. Agencies performing commercial functions were turned into state enterprises and then, in some cases, privatized (e.g., the postal service, the railways). Other agency functions were actually reabsorbed into central ministries (e.g., some elements of the National Board for Agriculture). This process could be termed structural reaggregation. The remaining central agencies—fewer and smaller—were to have been given research, development, and evaluation tasks, not the kinds of administrative and regulatory work with which agencies were previously most associated (e.g., STAKES, a development center for health and social affairs—more generally, see Ministry of Finance, 1997, pp. 62, 75, and 76). Also, from the end of the 1980s, agencies were increasingly drawn into a system of *results-oriented budgeting* in which their parent departments were supposed to set them challenging, measurable performance targets. In practice, not all ministries were particularly energetic or skillful at this task (Summa, 1995), but the improvement effort patiently persisted from year to year, and the system gradually tightened. In general, one might say that the performance-contracting dimension was given greater emphasis than the structural disaggregation emphasis.

In the U.K., in contrast, agencies were seen as the new answer to a variety of problems that had emerged from earlier rounds of reform. The *Next Steps* report of 1988 recommended the creation of agencies as a way of freeing civil servants engaged in operational tasks to manage in a more flexible and professional way. Many agencies were carved out of central departments, as part of what became a bipartisan program pursuing efficiency and higher quality public services (Gains, 1999; OToole and Jordan, 1995). By the end of 1996, a total of 131 agencies were in existence (and a few had already disappeared through privatization). Elaborate performance measurement and reporting mechanisms were put in place (Chancellor of the Duchy of Lancaster, 1997). In many ways, these were very impressive—and almost certainly represented an increase in transparency relative to the status quo ante. However, this achievement was somewhat qualified by the discoveries both that individual indicators were frequently changed and that some of the agencies' formal objectives lacked corresponding operational measures altogether (Talbot, 1996). In any event, each year each agency publishes a report in which it sets out to what extent it has achieved the targets it has been set and what new targets are being put in place for the year to come. From the mid-1990s, increasing emphasis was placed on interagency performance comparisons, especially those that were made through the use of a benchmarking model derived from private sector practice (Samuels, 1997). Finally, it was widely seen as an advantage that agencies represented partial depoliticization (i.e., almost the opposite of the sentiment in Finland), though there was also, initially at least, some Parliamentary and academic concern about public accountability (Hogwood et al., 2000). In sum, the Next Steps Program stressed *both* structural disaggregation *and* performance contracting, though in legal/constitutional terms disaggregation was modest.

In the Netherlands, the program of agencification was, at least nominally, influenced by the U.K. program. Agencies became a new *category* in the government accounts, and they were granted certain freedoms not available to the ministries themselves (e.g., the ability to introduce accruals-type accounting). However, as in Finland, agencies also represented a partial *retreat* from a more radical form of autonomization—the 1980s fashion for ZBOs. The agency Program developed in the context of a growing political concern for the primacy of politics (i.e., not letting too many public functions get beyond the reach and close scrutiny of elected politicians). In the domestic Dutch political debate, the concept of privatization was used in a more promiscuous fashion than in the U.K., and some commentators even referred to agency creation as *internal privatization,* thus giving the whole process a more controversial tinge.

Furthermore, the new Dutch agencies usually lacked the sophisticated performance measurement regimes that came to characterize the Next Steps. Certainly the need to be able to define and cost products was discussed, but the public domain Dutch documentation shows nothing like the detail available in the U.K. *Next Steps Review.* Systematic sets of performance indicators are only now being developed, five years or more after most of the agencies were set up. In sharp contrast to the plethora of performance indicators that festoon the U.K. Next Steps agencies, a 1998 report on agency performance from the Dutch Ministry of Finance contained only brief references to quantified performance data (Ministerie van Financien, 1998). Current efforts to develop indicator sets seem to be closely tied to more general budgetary reforms, rather than being an exercise in their own right as took place in the U.K. By the end of the 1990s, there seemed to be a lack of enthusiasm in Den Haag for any radical extension of the modest set of agencies that had by then been accumulated. A small number of additional activities were earmarked for greater autonomy, but, interestingly enough, the title *agency* was actually being avoided in cases where it was felt it might give the wrong impression. One might say that the Dutch story is almost the mirror image of that in Finland. The Dutch emphasized the virtue of structural disaggregation but were relatively slow to develop performance contracting.

In short, in three northern European countries, agency reforms were fairly divergent in origins, aims, and the degree of emphasis on managing for performance. In Finland, agencies were seen as part of the old system, to be replaced or slimmed down. In the U.K., they were seen as the spearhead of the new. In the Netherlands, they were seen as a politically more acceptable alternative to more radical forms of autonomization and as an opportunity to escape from the tight budgetary and accounting procedures that applied to the ministries themselves. The performance management regimes varied, from intense and elaborate in the U.K. through a slow, general reorientation towards results in Finland to an initially weak measurement regime for some of the Dutch agencies, later reinforced by more general budgetary reforms. Finally, the relations between agencies and the political process were constructed differently in the different countries. In Finland, the surviving agencies were made more firmly the creatures of their ministries: their tasks were reduced and they were drawn into the framework of "results budgeting." In the U.K., agencies were run by chief executives who also often became accounting officers and were therefore likely to be called before Parliamentary Select Committees. This system of personal accountability to the legislature for finance was unique to the U.K. and is not found in either the Netherlands or Finland. In the Netherlands, the relationship of agencies to the legislature is usually indirect—they are represented by their minister, and communication with him/her is usually through the Director General of the Ministry. The fear of loss of political control—of internal privatization—was pronounced.

Conclusions: variations on a theme

Despite all the differences noted above, one thing that certainly did converge was the hype itself—i.e., the general belief that something (not too well specified) called an *agency* (or equivalent) was a modern thing to have and would symbolize a government's progressive attitude towards the state apparatus. An agency represented modernization that stopped short of privatization. It sounded modern and managerial, but not overtly ideological. Thus agencification infected the conference circuit and the international organizations like an epidemic. One might almost say that agencies became a kind of administrative fashion accessory.

Beyond this trend, there has been—in many but not all countries—a sometimes implicit, sometimes explicit belief that the agency form would lend itself to greater efficiency and quality (through specialization/professionalization of management) and that it might restrain the worst excesses of political interference. For some politicians, agencies may also have held out the possibility of avoiding blame when things went wrong—because operational matters were to be made the responsibility of the agency and the politicians would only be responsible for policy (see, e.g., Pierre, 1995, p. 3, for Sweden; Gains, 1999, for the cases of the Prison Service and the Child Support Agency in the U.K.).

To express this idea more positively, there was a good deal of convergent thinking about the advantages of making a greater separation between strategic/policymaking functions and operational/executive functions. To this extent, it might be said that there was some (but not anything like total) international convergence in general thinking. *However, that convergence did not take decision makers very far when it came to the practicalities of setting up new organizations.* Hence the diversity appeared as soon as the question arose of equipping agencies with statutes, staff, functions, and management systems.

At this point we can reintroduce the distinctions between talk, decisions, actions, and results (Pollitt, 2001). Clearly, there has been an enormous amount of government talk about agencies worldwide. Most of it has been convergent, in the sense of advancing some subset of the propositions listed in the section on purposes and theories (above). In addition, there have been quite widespread worries about fragmentation, accountability, and loss of political control (all interesting and important, but not the main focus of this article). Overall, a dominant view does seem to have developed. This view can be summed up in Osborne and Gaebler's simple and appealing nostrum:

> In today's world, things simply work better if those working in public organizations ... have the authority to make many of their own decisions (Osborne and Gaebler, 1992, p. 251)

Yet even this conclusion does not quite fit the popular geometric image of *convergence* as a set of lines coming together at a point. The focus is too large and woolly to be thought of as a point. It is more like a zone or a section of rough terrain.

Nevertheless, the converging talk has led to some important decisions. The Canadian, Dutch, Japanese, U.K., and U.S. governments are among those which decided to launch specific programs of agency creation. The New Zealanders spawned their Crown Entities. At a very general level, therefore, decisional convergence is obvious.

Beyond this point, however, great caution is advisable. Once one begins to probe the details of the decisions, the influence of national diversity immediately becomes apparent.

Crucial relationships with ministers, ministries, and legislatures are far from uniform. The degree of structural disaggregation varies widely from one country to another, and even, sometimes, within a single country. Reporting requirements and contractual frameworks are also hugely diverse.

Divergence is even more obvious when the focus is shifted from decisions and pronouncements to actions and activities. Those who have imbibed the Osborne and Gaebler version may expect agencies to be small, specialized organizations, working in participatory ways and with professional commitment to deliver high-quality services to a defined group of customers. Even a brief inspection of official documentation shows something much less neat. Some agencies are huge—and quite bureaucratic. Some provide services to identifiable customers, but others are engaged in regulatory or ordering tasks, or in evaluation or research. Some appear to be purely operational, but others have a quite explicit role in policy advice. Some are fairly transparent; some remain opaque. Some attract intense political interest; many others are effectively ignored by members of legislatures. Most fundamentally, perhaps, hard evidence of the superior efficiency of the agency form in practice is very patchy.

Convergence, therefore, is real but often superficial. In the domain of speeches and labels and announcements of programs of organizational reform, agencies are in fashion. In the domain of action, however, convergence is weak and diversity strong. As for results, there is little that can be said. The jury is out (and may well never be in a position to give a confident verdict). When we look at the actual development of agencies in specific countries, what we see is better explained by path-dependency theories and by historically informed institutionalism (Pierson, 2000; Premfors, 1998) than by principal and agent theory or the supposed global imperatives of Osborne and Gaebler's model of entrepreneurial government.

These conclusions are, however, subject to at least one important proviso, namely, that our knowledge of what goes on *inside* agencies is as yet fairly limited. The literature that exists is predominantly based on views from the outside—reports and other accounts by ministers, parliaments, external auditors, academics, and so on. If we wish to understand more of the action, we need more extensive research into the internal management systems and cultures of agencies. Conceivably, this research could reveal another layer of convergence, at what might be called the microlevel. Our expectation, however, would be that such research—in which we are ourselves engaged—is more likely to furnish further confirmation of significant national and local differences.

Acknowledgments

The authors compose the EUROPAIR research team. EUROPAIR is a four-country comparative analysis of the management of agencies.

References

Aucoin, P. (1996). "Designing Public Agencies for Good Public Management: The Urgent Need for Reform." *Choices* (IRPP) 2(4), 5–20.

Bogt, H. ter. (1999). "Financial and Economic Management in Autonomized Dutch Public Organizations." *Financial Accountability and Management* 15(3/4), 329–348.

Boston, J., J. Martin, J. Pallot, and P. Walsh. (1996). *Public Management: the New Zealand Model,* Auckland: Oxford University Press.

Brunsson, N. (1989). The *Organisation of Hypocrisy: Talk, Decisions and Actions in Organisations*. Chichester: Wiley.

Cabinet Office. (1999). *Next Steps Report 1998*, Cm4273. London: The Stationary Office.

Chancellor of the Duchy of Lancaster. (1997). *Next Steps: Agencies In Government: Review 1996*, Cm3579. London: The Stationary Office.

Christensen, J. (1999). "Bureaucratic Autonomy as a Political Asset." Paper presented at the European Consortium for Political Research Joint Workshops, Mannheim, March 26–31.

Donaldson, L (1985). *In Defence of Organisation Theory: A Reply to the Critics*. Cambridge: Cambridge University Press.

Gains, F. (1999). *Understanding Department-Next Steps Agency Relationships*. Ph.D thesis, Department of Politics, University of Sheffield.

Greve, C, M. Flinders, and S. van Thiel. (1999). "Quangos: What's in a Name? Defining Quangos from a Comparative Perspective." *Governance* 12(1), 129–146.

Hogwood, B., D. Judge, and M. McVlcar. (2000). "Agencies and Accountability." In R. Rhodes (ed.), *Transforming British Government, Vol. 1: Changing Institutions*. Basingstoke: Macmillan.

Hood, C. (1998). *The Art of the State: Culture, Rhetoric and Public Management*. Oxford: Oxford University Press.

Hood, C. and G. Schuppert (eds.). (1988). *Delivering Public Services in Western Europe*. London: Sage.

Hood, C. and M. Jackson. (1991). *Administrative Argument*. Aldershot: Dartmouth.

James, O. (1994). "The Agency Revolution in Whitehall: A Bureau-Shaping Analysis." Paper presented at the U.K. Political Studies Association Conference, York, April.

James, O. (1999). *"Varieties of New Public Management: 'Business-Like' Government Agencies— Like What Model of Business?"* Paper presented at the American Political Science Association Annual Conference, Atlanta, Georgia, 2–5 September.

Kettl, D. (2000). *The Global Public Management Revolution: A Report on the Transformation of Governance*. Washington, D.C.: Brookings Institution.

Lane, J. (2000). *New Public Management*. London: Routledge.

Ministerie van Financien. (1998). *VerdermetresultaaUhetagentschapsmodel 1991–1997*. Den Haag: Dutch Ministry of Finance.

Ministry of Finance. (1997). *Public Management Reforms: Five Country Studies*. Helsinki: Ministry of Finance.

Norris, P. (ed.). (1999). *Critical Citizens: Global Support for Democratic Governance*. Oxford: Oxford University Press.

Nye, J., P. Zelikow, and D. King. (1997). *Why People Don't Trust Government*. Cambridge, MA: Harvard University Press.

OECD. (1995). *Governance in Transition: Public Management Reforms in OECD Countries*. Paris: PUMA/OECD.

OECD. (1997). *In Search of Results: Performance Management Practices*. Paris: PUMA/OECD.

OECD. (1998). *Budgeting in Sweden*. Paris: PUMA/OECD.

Osborne, D. and T. Gaebler. (1992). *Reinventing Government: How the Entrepreneurial Spirit is Transforming the Public Sector*. Reading, MA: Addison Wesley.

O'Toole, B. and G. Jordan. (1995). *Next Steps: Improving Management in Government*. Aldershot: Dartmouth.

Pierre, J. (ed.). (1995). *Bureaucracy in the Modem State: An Introduction to Comparative Public Administration*. Aldershot: Edward Elgar.

Pierson, P. (2000). "Increasing Returns, Path Dependence and the Study of Politics." *American Political Science Review* 94(2), 251–267.

Polidano, C. (2000). "Administrative Reform in Core Civil Services: Application and Applicability of the New Public Management" In W. McCourt and M. Minogue (eds.), *The Internationalisation of Public Management Reinventing the Third World State*. Cheltenham: Edward Elgar.

Pollitt, C. and G. Bouckaert (eds.). (1995). *Quality Improvement in European Public Services: Concepts, Cases and Commentary*. London: Sage.

Pollitt, C, J. Birchall, and K. Putman. (1998). *Decentralising Public Service Management*. Basingstoke: Macmillan.

Pollitt, C. and G. Bouckaert. (2000). *Public Management Reform: A Comparative Analysis*. Oxford: Oxford University Press.

Pollitt, C. (2000). "Is the Emperor in his Underwear? An Analysis of the Impacts of Public Management Reform." *Public Management: An International Journal of Theory and Research* 2(2), 181–199.

Pollitt, C. (Forthcoming). "Convergence: The Useful Myth?" *Public Administration*.

Premfors, R. (1998). "Reshaping the Democratic State: Swedish Experiences in a Comparative Perspective." *Public Administration* 76(1), 141–159.

Prince, M. (2000). "Banishing Bureaucracy or Hatching a Hybrid? The Canadian Food Inspection Agency and the Politics of Reinventing Government." *Governance* 13(2), 215–232.

Samuels, M. (1997). *Benchmarking Next Steps Agencies—An Evaluation of the Agency Benchmarking Pilot Exercise*. London: Cabinet Office/Office of Public Service.

SIGMA. (1999). *Public Management Profiles of Central and Eastern European Countries: Latvia*. Paris: PHARE/OECD.

SIGMA. (2001). *Financial Management and Control of Public Agencies*. SIGMA Paper No. 32. Paris: CCNM/SIGMA/PUMA (2001)4, April (available at www.oecd.org/puma/sigmaweb).

Stewart, J. (1992). *Managing Difference: An Analysis of Service Characteristics*. Birmingham: Institute of Local Government Studies.

Summa, H. (1995). "Old and New Techniques For Productivity Promotion: From Cheese-Slicing to a Quest for Quality." In A. Halachmi and G. Bouckaert (eds.), *Public Productivity Through Quality and Strategic Management*. Amsterdam: IOS Press, pp. 155–165.

Talbot, C. (1996). *Ministers and Agencies: Control, Performance and Accountability*. London: CIPFA.

Talbot, C. (1997). "UK Civil Service Personnel Reform: Devolution, Decentralization and Delusion." *Public Policy and Administration* 12(4), 14–34.

Tarchys, D. (1988). "PGOs in Sweden." In C. Hood and G. Schuppert (eds.), *Delivering Public Services in Western Europe*. London: Sage, pp. 63–74.

van Thiel, S. (2000). *Quangocratization: Trends, Causes and Consequences*. Ph.D thesis, University of Utrecht, Interuniversity Centre for Social Science Theory and Methodology.

Wilson, J.Q. (1989). *Bureaucracy: What Government Agencies Do and Why They Do It*. New York: Basic Books.

Wilson, R. (1999). "77ie Civil Service in the New Millenium." Speech, May (Sir Richard Wilson is Head of the Home Civil Service).

Yamamoto, H. (2000). "*Comparative Study of Agencification in Britain, the United States and Japan.*" Unpublished paper, Center for National University Finance, Tokyo.

Networks for Regulation: Privacy Commissioners in a Changing World

CHARLES D. RAAB

ABSTRACT *This article discusses the attempt to develop global data protection regulatory activity through the network of privacy commissioners and their agencies at the highest international levels. It describes the trajectory of forming a common outlook, identity, and infrastructure for regulatory enforcement amongst data protection authorities (DPAs) in recent years, and considers the value of analytic approaches to carry research forward.*

Introduction and Aims

Since 1970, regimes for protecting personal data have proliferated in and across states, reflecting an increased salience of privacy as a threatened value and human right. The difficulty of protecting the information of individuals and social groups or categories, and thus their privacy and other important human qualities, has been exacerbated by a number of factors. These include the growth of the Internet and global commercial transactions; states' interest in creating large and detailed databases for law enforcement, counter-terrorist, and public service purposes; and the formation of an "information economy" and "information society", or even a "surveillance society".

Stimulated partly by the work of civil society groups of privacy advocates (Bennett 2008), information privacy protection has emerged as a public issue. It is addressed by laws and policies that are overseen or enforced by designated officials and their offices: the privacy commissioners or supervisory data protection authorities (DPAs) of most countries and lower-level jurisdictions. These DPAs have been created by statute and fulfil crucial regulatory functions despite the often unclear, ambiguous and impotent legal provisions that they enforce and interpret. Laws have been found indispensable but wanting, and other policy instruments have evolved, operating singly or in combinations alongside the law (Bennett and Raab 2006: chs. 4–7). Although DPAs are typically underpowered, their functions go beyond legal enforcement to embrace a variety of promotional and policy-influencing activities, and they engage in relationships with those using non-official or extra-legal instruments for the protection of information privacy and the limitation of surveillance.

As with water and money, personal information flows across jurisdictional boundaries. Dangers and risks are imported and exported without, as yet, the consistent ability of regulators – singly or in concert – to counter them effectively. There has been a great deal of regulatory activity by DPAs over several decades, manifested on paper, in meetings, by legal enforcement and advice, and through other means. These bodies have often expressed alarm in ways that sometimes resemble those of advocacy groups themselves, yet talking the talk is not walking the walk. Possibly, the perceived threats to privacy, civil liberties and human rights are now so unprecedented and grave that only running the run would suffice, but DPAs have only recently learnt to talk and to walk. Possibly, however, efforts to talk, walk and run collectively have been inhibited by factors beyond their control: massive personal data collection and analysis in the interests of combating terrorism, global commerce, law enforcement, and the provision of public services. Despite criticism of weak responses to particular privacy intrusions, few would say that DPAs are universally pusillanimous, or that frequently there are not severe constraints on acting speedily and forcefully together or separately. Although many commissioners might see themselves as advocates, they cannot easily imitate these activists lest they risk being ignored – or perhaps not being renewed in office – by hostile governments or parliaments, or written off by powerful groups which they must often cajole, rather than hector, into more privacy-protective practices.

At the 29th International Conference of the world's data protection and privacy commissioners, held in Montreal in September 2007, privacy and civil liberties groups issued a Declaration calling for more vigorous DPA action. In addition to steps that they urged DPAs to take domestically, they exhorted commissioners, who are "uniquely positioned to defend our societies' core values and rights of privacy", to "increase their own collective efforts" and to make a "concerted, cross-national effort to preserve fundamental human rights". The signatories believed that "stronger, more aggressive action ... is required to tackle this problem – that specific reports, warnings and enforcement actions, while often valuable, are not sufficient to address the enormity of the problem we face".[1]

DPAs have increasingly, but perhaps hesitantly, realized that they cannot each stand alone to fight national or sub-national battles while the threats to privacy become more global. They have recognized the need for mutual support as well as for more institutionalized forms of international collaboration, building upon, but also helping to foster, a variety of emerging networks of relationships that have developed over many years (Raab 2010). We will see later that much of the DPAs' recent activity at the international level has been concerned with establishing the groundwork and infrastructure for co-operation and mutual assistance. Many new departures have aimed at establishing a better basis for the main regulatory work itself, giving evidence of a move towards global regulation that deserves closer description and analysis. Of particular interest in the subsequent discussion is the frequent interpenetration of international, national, and sub-national organizations or levels of activity, often bringing resources and expertise that are available at one level to bear upon decisions at another one. This is indicative of both fluidity and entrepreneurship as DPAs and some of their main actors develop initiatives aimed at institution-building or substantive regulatory change. However, there has been little possibility, so far, of acting together as a global or regional "rapid reaction force", or of exerting definitive preventative influence in policy-making circles.[2]

Some authors have speculated on the future of privacy protection in a globalizing world, and assessed the economic and political factors constraining or promoting either a regulatory "race to the bottom" or a "race to the top". Evidence could be found for both scenarios (Bennett and Raab 2006: ch. 10), and recent DPA developments refresh this question. The activities of groups of privacy activists, the increasing salience of surveillance in the face of terrorist and other threats (Lyon 2003), the contrast between – and the mutual involvement of – private and public sector information processes, are among the factors that must be considered in order to obtain a clearer view of the vagaries of regulation, for they have powerfully influenced the speed and slope of the conflicting trajectories of privacy threats and protections.

Little such analysis can be done within the confines of this largely descriptive article, which attempts to break ground by focusing on the development of networks of relationships amongst DPAs in a complex and overlapping policy space. Based on earlier investigations of the regulatory governance of privacy (Bennett and Raab 2006, Raab and De Hert 2008, Raab and Koops 2009), including developments at the sub-global level (Raab 2010), this article begins to explore DPAs' wider international relations and to map and comprehend the evolving patterns of their activity in transition from network to possible corporate group. The attention given to the activities of privacy commissioners and their changing milieu is meagre in the existing literature, and there is very little account of their relationships, roles, or activity beyond the confines of single countries.[3] Such behaviour has not been investigated in depth before, but it provides much raw material for further analysis, comparison, and theorizing beyond the case-study account that can be given here. While this article emphasizes networks in the "case" of privacy protection in which states and their governments as such – represented through their executives or international officials – may also act through other networks, space limitations prevent discussion of DPAs' complex and crucial relations with these and other actors or "stakeholders". However, the developments highlighted in this article are of some comparative value in the practical world of regulation in the field of information policy and in disparate policy fields as well, where steps are taken towards greater comprehensiveness in the forms of control.

In the broad field of information and communication policy studies within which privacy regulation is situated, there have not been many attempts to analyse and compare the development of regulatory regimes. Murray (2007) has looked at the institutions, processes and networks for the regulation of the Internet, including protocols and standards, domain names, content, and "netiquette" in cyberspace communities, but efforts towards online privacy regulation – however tenuous it may be, in a world inhabited by Google, Facebook and other social networking – is left out of that account. For eventual comparative purposes, it is therefore important to document and understand these processes for institutionalizing countervailing forces against privacy erosion in which official regulators launch collective initiatives beyond their individual jurisdictions.

This field seems to exemplify a growing transgovernmentalism: "horizontal rather than vertical ... decentralized and informal rather than organized and rigid" (Slaughter and Zaring 2006: 178), although those two axes are inadequate to represent alternative positioning of the interactions that have emerged. In turn, research among networks of privacy commissioners and into their (proto-) institutional arrangements may help to fill a gap in our understanding of trends towards global – but therefore multilevel – governance arrangements. This is because the activities and perceptions of these officials (and others) about regulatory possibilities and practicalities, about positions to take (or to eschew) on public issues, and about their influence on public policy, commercial practice, and public attitudes and awareness all have a bearing on the nature of regulatory "races" and their outcome. Beyond its relevance for comparative information and communication policy studies, understanding change in this one field is also a way of learning from, and contributing to, a growing body of descriptive and theoretical work on global regulation and governance that has devoted scant attention to this particular subject matter (e.g. Held and McGrew 2002, Koenig-Archibugi and Zürn 2005).

To the extent that the politics of privacy protection is becoming the international relations of privacy protection, a range of conceptual tools may be useful for investigating them. While this exploration can be seen in terms of the wider literatures on the globalization of regulation, on institutional theory, on the importance of networks in international relations (e.g. Keohane and Nye 1974, Slaughter 2000, Slaughter and Zaring 2006, Farrell and Newman 2010), and on multilevel governance (MLG) (e.g. Hooghe and Marks 2003, Bache and Flinders 2004, Fairbrass and Jordan 2004), it does not seek to construct or test theories that may be derived from these. This is largely because insufficient evidence is as yet available for this, although this may be a fruitful step in further research.

However, a few remarks on the applicability of some conceptual approaches are useful at this point, and should be borne in mind in terms of the case study. MLG may be a promising avenue: it has been used in studying relations within the EU, but it has wider application both within states and in policy domains. Rather than "Type I" governance – general-purpose jurisdictions with non-intersecting memberships, a limited number of jurisdictional levels, and a system-wide, durable architecture – "Type II" governance fits the present case better: task-specific jurisdictions, intersecting memberships, many jurisdictional levels, and flexible design (Hooghe and Marks 2003). But little may be gained by attempting to fit the evidence to a typology. A conceptual framework for making sense of the "levels" of privacy and surveillance regulation should probably be custom-made (Fairbrass and Jordan 2004: 241), and lower-level concepts in general currency can be used instead (Scharpf 2001).

MLG – although not uniquely – at least sensitizes us to the need to concentrate on *relationships* of institutions, roles, tasks and jurisdictions, and turns us away from concentrating only on any one of these. The concept of "level", however, should not be reified: to focus on groups, networks, bodies, and so on is not necessarily to talk about discrete jurisdictional or geographical levels, although these are important as targets or sources of regulatory activity. Although the meaning of "level" is far from clear, it is, in any case, too tidy a concept to embrace activity that is scattered in time and space. Considering jurisdictions, MLG usefully moves the exclusive focus away from single states, and embraces non-public sector participants. Privacy regulation as "governance" involves a mixture of participants of varied provenance. These include DPAs, governments, firms of many kinds, activist groups and standardization bodies (Bennett and Raab 2006: ch. 8). Although non-state participants, including privacy advocates, are not investigated here, the transnational role of privacy officers and their networks should be recognized.[4]

Some observations can also be made about the application of a historical-institutionalist frame, or indeed other versions of new institutionalism, to the present case. The account of privacy regulation given here and elsewhere (Raab 2010) suggests that the institutionalization of potentially important international networks or organizations is taking place, albeit at variable speeds. Their rules, procedures, criteria of membership, and pursuit of common aims are becoming somewhat clearer and more systematized. Several of the networks have crystallized into groupings with some longevity, corporate identity, and likely permanence. In addition, initiatives are being taken by prominent leaders as agents whose actions aim to propel participant DPAs towards infrastructural development for the emergent organizations, and towards the articulation and promotion of substantive regulatory policies for the exercise of regulatory power over the flows of personal information that have brought DPAs' role into being.

Identifying these characteristics of institutionalism[5] in the present case is, of course, to oversimplify and rationalize a welter of activity that is always more complex than can be expressed in these terms; it is in the very nature of theory to abstract from reality in this way. No premature position is taken in this article as between competing or overlapping versions of new institutional theory, although further research into motives, behaviour, sequence, and contexts may allow more refined insights into the applicability of those or other theoretical perspectives to the case of international privacy protection. So far, Newman (2008) has gone the furthest in an exploration of historical institutionalism, centring on the European Union and its data protection Directive 95/46/EC as the main engine for regulatory globalization. Emphasizing expertise, domestically delegated authority, and networks as explanatory factors, he highlights the importance of timing – in this case, stages – and of leadership and activity in enabling European DPAs to promulgate regulations internationally. Newman's identification of horizontal and vertical networks as amplifiers of DPAs' power is germane, although opinions may differ about the extent of different DPAs' leveraging power at the directive-formation stage, and other policy players' resistance to DPAs' advocacy of strong data protection may have been underestimated. While the aim of Newman's institutional analysis and of the present article is not to estimate how much more information privacy the world actually experiences owing to the Directive or to the creation of networks and multilevel organizations, nevertheless the question of "success" needs to be addressed in more dimensions than that which only considers political, legal, or institutional achievements (Bennett and Raab 2006: ch. 9).

Leaving these particular matters aside, the application of this approach holds promise. However, it requires descriptive accounts of the networking itself, the issues around which it crystallizes, and its actors' perspectives and behaviour: elements that the present article tries to illuminate without framing them specifically in terms of historical institutionalism. In addition, the three factors Newman identifies must be separately theorized and investigated. In giving an account of behaviour, the approach should guard against "rational actor" assumptions or *ex post facto* reconstructions, which are tempting if one already knows the outcome in a particular case. Greater recognition must be given not only to the uneven "distribution of power within regulatory networks", as Newman (2008: 151) acknowledges, but also to the sheer difficulty and the pressure of circumstance in creating and institutionalizing the alliances, networks and groups described in this article. As will be seen, narratives are available for chronicling the policy entrepreneurship of certain actors in these networks and the like. But both the policy action and the capacity-building infrastructural development – which are probably best understood as reflexive – should be seen, institutional-historically, in the light of men (and women) making history, but not as they please, and under circumstances existing already, given and transmitted from the past. What, then, is that past?

A Brief Historical Overview

In 1970 the German *Land* of Hesse established the first regime for the protection of personal data, including a regulatory agency headed by a privacy commissioner (Bennett 1992). Since then, the number of such organizations and officials has multiplied, in individual countries and in smaller jurisdictions (Bennett and Raab 2006: ch. 5). Descriptive and explanatory accounts of this history can be found elsewhere (Flaherty 1989, Bennett 1992, 1997, Mayer-Schönberger 1997, Bygrave 2002, Bennett and Raab 2006). Commencing as the "project" of an international informal group of prominent public officials and academics in the 1970s, the initiative continued with a further concretization of rules established by institutions like the Council of Europe and the Organisation for Economic Co-operation and Development (OECD) in 1980/81. They established focal privacy principles as landmarks with, respectively, Convention 108 and Guidelines, and the OECD and the Council of Europe continue their practical work as major players in the global game. An important point is that the growth in numbers and in geographical extension has exerted great influence on the dynamics and possibilities of internationalizing and co-ordinating regulation. Where there were only eight national DPAs in the 1970s (all in Western Europe), the number more than doubled in the 1980s to include other areas of the world, and reached nearly 40 into the 2000s, leaving aside DPAs in the many smaller jurisdictions. It is tempting to apply a "punctuated-equilibrium" theoretical framework (True et al. 1999) to this expansion, but this cannot be explored here in depth; difficult questions about the identification of stability and the factors affecting change caution against a superficial interpretation of the evidence. Yet the spread of regimes has certainly been punctuated by spates of activity, waves and phases; that the USA does not have such an overall agency is a highly significant factor in assessing the prospects for global regulation.

Two events might explain the most recent of these punctuating waves in Europe. Most notable has been the effect or anticipation of the 1995 EU Data Protection Directive, requiring member states to establish supervisory authorities, and also influencing some non-EU countries to follow suit. The passage of the Directive was a major transnational landmark in giving further impetus to the interaction of national and sub-national European DPAs. The Article 29 Working Party, established under the Directive to debate and concert opinions and to advise the European Commission (EC), brings national DPAs together to adopt positions and opinions on prominent issues on policy agendas in Europe and between the EU and elsewhere. The EC is in overall charge of policy and legislative development for data protection, and the European Parliament has, on paper, a strengthened role. A key influential force is the European Data Protection Supervisor (EDPS), who acts and advises independently but also in the midst of the Working Party and other bodies. Within the EU, institutionalization has been manifest in the annual meetings of all DPAs in a Spring Conference. At the EU level and beyond, there are other comings together of commissioners for various purposes relating to policing and criminal justice: for example, in the supervisory work with regard to data protection in Europol, Eurojust, Eurodac and Interpol.

Lack of space prevents a fuller discussion of the prominent international activity carried out at the EU level as a whole or of the functions performed by joint action.[6] We must also leave on one side the effect upon privacy-protection institutions of the development of international co-operation within important fields such as police and judicial co-operation. In those, there have been crucial EU constitutional or structural issues concerning the jurisdictional legitimacy of data protection laws and regulatory powers across the "pillars" of the EU. The second "punctuation" has been the accession of 12 new member states to the EU within a short space of time (2004–2007), entailing anticipatory data protection legislation and the formation of DPAs. This expansion has further ramified the patterns of interaction, and co-operation and interchange amongst the new accession states themselves is developing in concrete forms. Possible further EU accessions, as well as developments in Latin America, Africa and the Middle East, suggest a punctuated future as well.

While DPAs' responsibilities and performance vary, there have been increasing efforts to augment national approaches by creating networks and organizations of DPAs across jurisdictional lines and at different levels. This article can only discuss in any depth the most extensive range of DPA activity, that which exists at the global level and is represented by an annual, long-established conference of DPAs. However, a highly intricate range of sub-global groupings of varying structural coherence is described elsewhere (Raab 2010). There is a particular concentration in Europe but there are also important and growing linkages elsewhere and intercontinentally, sometimes reflecting path-dependent geographical, linguistic, historical and other affinities. These associations exist at levels constituted by various criteria that help to define and place outer limits upon their membership. With different degrees of organization and intensity of activity, and with shifting memberships, they bring together a host of networks DPAs or other agencies and individuals with a shared privacy and data protection interest.

These include the EU as a whole, Central and Eastern Europe amongst new EU member states, the Ibero-American and Francophonic zones, a UK-centric sphere, the Asia-Pacific region, within the federal or decentralized states of Australia, Canada, Germany, Spain and Switzerland, and sometimes across these lines of demarcation. More specialized networks and *ad hoc* concentrations exist in the field of telecommunications privacy and in other domains in which new technological, policy or commercial developments generate privacy issues. Many of these smaller organizations and arenas of activity are perhaps obscure, but they are by no means negligible as intersecting networks or corporate groupings in the global game, often lending a dynamic impetus to further co-operation. There have also been tutelary "twinning" arrangements between established EU jurisdictions and new or candidate members, or other states, including Bosnia-Herzegovina, Bulgaria, Croatia, Israel, Lithuania, Malta and others, where there has been a felt need for learning and development of regulatory capacity. All told, there is a richness of multilevel and multidimensional connections among official data protectors, with many combinatorial possibilities for action, but by the same token, many points for blocking action that would fall foul of one or another national or jurisdictional interest.

Developing a Global Framework for Regulation

Leaving the level of sub-global developments, we can now turn to consider more inclusive ranges of activity and institutionalization. Although the United Nations has lent its moral force to the cause of privacy protection, it has played little part in practical activity. However, in addition to the OECD, the World Trade Organization has played a part in shaping privacy protection in the context of international trade policy. It can only be noted in passing that the movement for the creation of privacy standards has been manifest at international as well as at European and national levels in standardization organizations, and has risen high on the agenda of the world's commissioners, although the term "standard" is often used loosely there.

At the global level and below, a rich array of connections of a variety of frequencies and densities has developed in and around issues, laws and practices of privacy protection. DPAs often now see important business interests as well as privacy advocates' groups as their allies in the movement towards global regulation. In earlier years, many such actors were frequently regarded in a far less favourable light, and there remain fundamental differences of outlook and interest amongst regulators, the regulated and vocal critics. These patterns will be described in greater detail, bearing in mind the question of how far this phenomenon constitutes, or promotes, the institutionalization of a multilevel governance infrastructure, perhaps *en route* to a global regime. Commissioners have called for increasing co-operation, and their conferences at several levels have produced many final communiqués, opinions and resolutions. However, there have sometimes been apparent difficulties in concerting views on issues that affect the national working of all. What the difficulties of institutional structure, context, role or personal interaction have been, and the perceived prospects for overcoming them, are subjects for future investigation.

The most comprehensive group is that of the world's privacy and data protection commissioners, who have met in a movable annual International Conference since 1979: itself indicative of some degree of institutionalization over a long period of time. This is now a major international event and focus of discussion, networking and high-level consideration of current issues, and has now expanded to include companies, privacy NGOs and countries as yet unqualified to join the global DPA "club". One of the longest-standing international groupings, the International Working Group on Data Protection in Telecommunications – known as the "Berlin

Group" – began in 1983 in the framework of the International Conference, with the Berlin DPA – which instigated the initiative – as its secretariat. It comprises legal and technical telecommunications experts drawn from DPAs and others from national administrations and international as well as industry organizations, and meets twice yearly in Berlin or elsewhere. It has produced many working papers and non-binding resolutions ("common positions") on issues related to privacy in telecommunications and on the Internet, leading to other resolutions passed by the annual international conference.[7] In terms of this article's interest in levels of activity, it is noteworthy that this international group has as its main hub the DPA of a sub-national jurisdiction, a pattern also visible in other contexts.

The activities of the international conference group are necessary but insufficient for achieving global regulatory capacity and effectiveness. In the years since 2000, and most prominently culminating in the 2009 Madrid Resolution on international standards,[8] a number of DPAs and their commissioners have evidently been seized of the necessity to move their vehicle into higher gear, equipping it with the ability to speak and act as an institution with the rules, procedures, boundaries and infrastructure of corporate existence. The group's procedural rules have been slow to develop, as it was not until the conferences in 2000 and 2001 that guidelines on procedures for passing resolutions had been codified and amended.[9] Reflected in these measures, the pace of movement towards more comprehensive and assertive universal regulation has quickened in more recent years. In closing the 27th International Conference in Montreux in 2005, the commissioners issued the "Montreux Declaration" to "express their will to strengthen the international recognition of the universal character" of data protection principles, and to "collaborate ... with the governments and international and supra-national organisations for the development of a universal convention" for personal data protection.[10] For support, they appealed to the United Nations, all governments, the Council of Europe, international NGOs (including consumer and business groups), and to the then forthcoming 2005 World Summit on the Information Society. DPAs agreed to intensify their information exchange and co-ordination of supervisory standards, the development of common standards, and other collaborative measures. One of these concerned a common permanent website, which will be discussed later. Further, they resolved regularly to assess progress, starting with the 28th Conference in 2006, to be held in London in November 2006.

That Conference's "Closing Communiqué" emphasized the need for commissioners to reassess their role, resources and strategies for combating the growing dangers of the "surveillance society". It urged them to develop better communication strategies, to re-assess and adapt their practices, to gain greater technological understanding and avoid an excessively "legal" approach, to institutionalize their collective activities, to help develop global protective instruments, and to develop strategic partnerships with NGOs and other stakeholders.[11] Some of these items were elaborated in a further seven-page statement, the "London Initiative".[12] Illustrative of the important part played by leading protagonists, it had originated in a speech by Alex Türk, President of the *Commission Nationale de l'Informatique et des Libertés* (CNIL, the French Data Protection Authority), after which Peter Hustinx, the EDPS, had asked the CNIL to develop the initiative – supported by the UK Information Commissioner – for the London meeting. The three DPAs contributed to the statement that inter alia saw data protection challenged by the discrepancy between the globalization of data transfers and the limited scope of the rule of law, anti-terrorism laws and technological change. It lamented some DPAs' low reputation, which affected compliance as well as the salience of data protection and its associated rights and freedoms.

The London Initiative therefore proposed action including shared work on technological developments and better institutional recognition of DPAs' action at the international level. Because "[g]lobal challenges need global solutions", the Initiative declared that the annual conferences themselves must spearhead action by functioning better, by being more visible and efficient, and by forming an action plan and communication programme. In terms of further institutional development, the "thinking about the creation of a permanent secretariat" was especially significant. Moreover:

> The Conference must become an unavoidable interlocutor in all international initiatives which have an incidence on data protection. It must allow room for discussion and allow concrete suggestions to emerge, in order to better follow up on international initiatives, to harmonize practices and adopt common positions.[13]

The Montreux call for an international convention for data protection was renewed. The international level also sought to influence behaviour in lower-level arenas: DPAs were urged to promote this call, especially in their linguistic or regional zones, and to seek global solutions in specific sectors such as Internet governance, financial transactions and air transport.

It is important to note a parallel departure towards institutionalization and collective activity taking place in sites at the sub-global level, among regional groupings. For example, and perhaps under Spanish tutelage and assisted by Spain's provision of a permanent secretariat and website facilities, in the mid-2000s the Ibero-American network of DPAs was rapidly gaining an organizational structure, a Directive on regulatory harmonization within the group, as well as the formulation of common positions. By 2008, its Colombia conference deliberated on the "Globalisation of Privacy: Towards Common Standards"; along with the earlier gains, this was arguably a staging post for the Madrid Resolution on the same subject in 2009. Although slightly later, somewhat similar institutional developments were taking place in the Francophonic association of DPAs (Raab 2010: 297–298).

A further stage in the development of at least the "talk" of international regulation was the Resolution on International Co-operation, promulgated at the 29th conference in Montreal in 2007.[14] It mentioned that practical information had meanwhile been shared in London Initiative workshops in Paris and Brussels, and acknowledged that much co-operative activity was underway in sub-global arenas. Among these were the Council of Europe, the OECD, Asia-Pacific Economic Cooperation (APEC), the Asia Pacific Privacy Authorities (APPA), the Ibero-American Data Protection Network, the new Association of Francophone Data Protection Authorities, and the EU's Article 29 Working Party (Raab 2010). The resolution urged stronger co-operation, supported the continuation of London Initiative work, and welcomed the OECD's 2007 Recommendation on Cross-Border Co-operation in the Enforcement of Laws Protecting Privacy.[15]

The OECD Recommendation illustrates the synergy of DPAs and other international bodies whose work is also essential. It was prepared by a working party led by Jennifer Stoddart, the Canadian privacy commissioner and host of the Montreal conference, and sought to leverage a more global and comprehensive regulatory reach than that afforded by narrower groupings. Overlooking national differences, it emphasized common interests in protecting privacy and ensuring the free flow of information. Its practical recommendations adhered to the largely infrastructural and capacity-building path: thus OECD countries should:

a) Improve their domestic frameworks for privacy law enforcement to better enable their authorities to co-operate with foreign authorities.
b) Develop effective international mechanisms to facilitate cross-border privacy law enforcement co-operation.
c) Provide mutual assistance to one another in the enforcement of laws protecting privacy, including through notification, complaint referral, investigative assistance and information sharing, subject to appropriate safeguards.
d) Engage relevant stakeholders in discussion and activities aimed at furthering co-operation in the enforcement of laws protecting privacy.[16]

The focus was mainly on regulating the private sector, but public sector regulatory co-operation was considered desirable; for example, mutual assistance in privacy law enforcement through bilateral and multilateral agreements. In addition,

> Member countries should foster the establishment of an informal network of Privacy Enforcement Authorities and other appropriate stakeholders to discuss the practical aspects of privacy law enforcement co-operation, share best practices in addressing cross-border challenges, work to develop shared enforcement priorities, and support joint enforcement initiatives and awareness raising campaigns.[17]

Arguably, the most important infrastructural matters considered at Montreal in 2007 were those dealt with in the Resolution on Conference Organisational Arrangements,[18] based on the report of a working group led by Marie Shroff, the New Zealand Commissioner, and four subgroups;[19] perhaps a telling point is that the term "conference" not only referred to a meeting but also served as a collective noun, akin to "group", for the world's DPAs. Steps had been taken to regularize arrangements, for example on the accreditation of DPAs and other bodies[20] and on procedures for passing resolutions. This Resolution pressed for co-operative activity, leadership and machinery to provide continuity between the dates of the annual conferences.[21] Making a serious attempt to shape quasi-constitutional and formal structures, the Resolution seemed to suggest a network taking stock of its corporate identity, its membership boundaries, and its potentially authoritative voice as a group. It is also instructive that it had taken nearly 30 years to come to this degree of institutionalization, which seems to indicate change undertaken in response to the new pressure of privacy and surveillance issues faced globally in the twenty-first century as well as to the simultaneous promulgation of the critical Montreal Declaration by civil society groups, mentioned earlier.

Financial and organizational burdens borne by the annual conference host, and the necessity of corporate sponsorship, are among the practical difficulties of promoting a more strongly organized conference and platform for decisive activity. Indeed, the 2006 conference, scheduled for Buenos Aires, had to be cancelled and hastily re-scheduled for London late in the year. The working group's Resolution dealt with annual hosting, smoother transition and continuity; the formation of a permanent website; language translation; the status of international organizational observers[22] and rules on their speaking; and, conversely, the representation of the DPAs' group at conferences of, for example, OECD, APEC, and the International Organization for Standardization (ISO).[23] Some of these departures aimed at facilitating closer relations with other bodies, possibly including NGOs, travelling roughly in the same direction. But only as recently as the seventh annual meeting of the Credentials Committee in 2008 at the (30th) Strasbourg International Conference was the question aired of finding a permanent and accessible home for the committee's "several kilos" of archives – application forms, documentation, correspondence, decisions and the like – which required to be shipped from one DPA to the next when the chairmanship changed hands. The committee said that "a permanent organization in terms of both location/accessibility and of a person in charge of its management is urgently needed",[24] and recommended that this matter be studied in consultation with the conference's website matters working group (discussed below), aiming at a solution by 2009.

New transnational co-ordinated initiatives were acclaimed in Montreal's Resolution on International Co-operation: the APPA Privacy Awareness Week[25] and the Council of Europe's Data Protection Day.[26] Building on the London Initiative and declaring these events successful, the 2008 Strasbourg Conference escalated the celebration to the global level through a resolution asking for an Australian-chaired working party to explore the establishment of an international day or week, and to report to the 2009 31st International Conference in Madrid.[27] Noting that APPA in 2008 had seen profile-raising value and cost-effectiveness in global co-ordination of these events and had agreed to promote the idea at Strasbourg, this resolution suggested that "a key theme each year would be a demonstration of the community of data protection authorities speaking with one voice".[28] Following the spirit of London and Montreux, possibilities for external bridge-building with like-minded privacy groups were anticipated, even in the composition of the working party.

Contrasting evaluations of such celebratory events are possible. On the one hand, their adoption and promotion absorb the time, energy and material resources of Commissioners and their international networks and organizations: meetings, preparing declarations and resolutions, and staging the annual "day" or "week" are not cost-free. Some could argue that these events are merely beside the point and symbolic, offering circuses instead of bread. Awareness-raising, some might say, is not the main event of regulation, even if it is industry and governments whose awareness needs raising, not just the general public. Moreover, mounting these occasions is only a quick – and facile – win. On the other hand, it could be argued that awareness-raising and promotional activities are an inherent part of the DPA role, even inscribed in laws governing their functions. Catching miscreants and influencing the policies of states and firms, in this line of thought, is not the only important bottom line in regulating privacy or in evaluating achievement, and nurturing a supportive public constituency for their work is politically astute for regulators who often feel isolated in their mission. Less persuasively, awareness activities may, in the long run, reduce the need for enforcement if database controllers, information technology designers, and the public better understand "information society" risks and dangers. It could also be held that quick wins benefit fledgling organizations and networks as they move towards more effective and "serious" dimensions of international regulatory co-operation.

Websites are among the promotional devices used by individual European DPAs and sub-global groupings in public communication as well as in their networks.[29] The desire to develop a global one was declared at Montreux, where it was seen as, in particular, an infrastructural tool for information and resources management. The website issue is evidently of more significance to DPAs than might be supposed for a technical move towards better information and communication in support of regulatory activities. As a public repository for documents, it can help to establish an elementary common memory and history for the global group and for outside enquirers, and its links can help to consolidate connections to the wider privacy policy community. Its private space can be used for protected communications regarding enforcement operations. In 2008, the Strasbourg Conference received a Resolution, proposed by David Loukidelis, the British Columbia Commissioner, that built on the work of the Website Working Group (WWG) under the mandate it had received at Montreal.[30] This resolution mentioned "enforcement co-operation" as another practical aim of direct benefit to DPAs, and collaboration with OECD was then being explored towards a shared-cost hosted website. The chairing of an international working group comprising five national DPAs by a Canadian provincial commissioner further illustrates how international action has been led by DPAs at different jurisdictional levels. The existence of the WWG indicates, again, that the world's commissioners sought a more corporate presence and identity, albeit on a functionally specific and ad hoc matter of common interest.

However, the achievement of a corporate will on a wider front remains a main aim. In this connection, the 2008 Strasbourg Conference's adoption of an ambitious resolution on international standards seems highly significant in promoting national accession to the Council of Europe Convention 108 as a platform for co-operation.[31] The resolution was supported by a long list of co-proposing DPAs, traversing a wide multilevel range. Apart from the two proposers, 20 others were drawn from three continents, including three Spanish sub-national jurisdictions, one of the German *Länder*, and the small jurisdictions of Guernsey and Andorra, in addition to the supra-national EDPS. It called for a new working group to present international privacy and data protection standards for decision in 2009 at the Madrid annual conference. This proposal would aim at the global acceptance of a set of principles and rights ensuring a high level of protection, as well as defining sectors of application, considering self-regulation and defining the criteria guaranteeing effective implementation.

The 2009 Madrid Resolution was much heralded and many speakers and chairs in the conference sessions gave exhortations about the glaring need for global privacy standards. The Resolution was adopted on November 5, and printed copies of a large document were distributed. The main parts consisted of basic, general principles and rights derived from the familiar ones of the OECD, the Council of

Europe and the Directive, and enshrined in innumerable pieces of national legislation. But there were additional sections on proactive measures that were suggested for better compliance with laws, on DPA monitoring, on international co-operation and co-ordination, and on data controllers' liability, and several principles were elaborated in greater detail. The somewhat confusing title, "Joint Proposal for a Draft of International Standards on the Protection of Privacy with regard to the processing of Personal Data", implied that the Resolution itself did not establish these "standards" – if indeed they were that – but that a further draft would be put in hand. However, the preamble by the Spanish Commissioner, Artemi Rallo Lombarte, indicated that the document would now be promoted by DPAs without mentioning any further drafting process.

Nevertheless, the value of the Resolution was arguably more in the fact of its promulgation at the global level as a consensual document and rallying cry, supported very widely by DPAs and "civil society",[32] than in its formal recitation of conventional principles. Reaching this level of consensus on an enhanced set of principles, as a precursor to a more effective regulatory future, was a significant achievement. This may be especially so insofar as in the USA – which has no comprehensive Federal data protection legislation, but whose stance on privacy regulation is all-important to any global achievement – the conception of principles has narrowed, in many instances, to those of giving notice to individuals, seeking consent and pledging technical security for personal data. The USA's Center for Democracy and Technology's simultaneous briefing pointed this out in pressing the Federal Trade Commission to move beyond its espousal of this narrow conception and to embrace the fuller set of principles to underpin its enforcement activities.[33]

Discussion

Where, then, are the world's DPAs on a hypothetical journey towards global regulation? A great deal of actual regulatory activity is conducted with legal and other instruments at and among various jurisdictional levels: sub-national, national and international. Most privacy regulation has occurred nationally and sub-nationally, but with the growing importance of global flows and processing of personal information, and the increased international movement of people and goods, regulation at one or even two levels looks much less effective than hitherto, if indeed it ever was effective. Important questions can be asked about the adequacy of single-level instruments, such as national laws or national codes of practice. Although these questions are not addressed in this article, the welter of international regulatory activity implicitly indicates that strategies as well as instruments must be created at other levels as well. DPAs have thus emphasized the development of infrastructures for collaboration and have generated a tapestry of interlocking relationships for mutual sharing and regulatory action, but the efficacy of DPAs concerting as watchdogs beyond jurisdictional boundaries is not yet proven and their reputation remains somewhat fragile. The main issue is whether there is, as yet, much regulatory effect, beyond the tooling-up of the machinery, at whatever level.

Newman's account of the EU policy outcome of the issue of data retention, in which a compromise was reached that was unwelcome in terms of strong privacy protection, points up DPAs' limitations in winning major battles (Newman 2008:

125–132). More generally, measurement of the effectiveness of privacy regimes, including DPAs, is notoriously difficult. Whilst the aim of Newman's institutional analysis and of the present article is not to estimate how much more information privacy the world actually experiences owing to the Directive or the creation of networks and multilevel organizations, nevertheless the question of "success" needs to be addressed in more dimensions than that which only considers political, legal or institutional achievements (Bennett and Raab 2006: ch. 9).

What we have seen does not testify to a Whiggish or "steady progress" path of development: many factors and complexities have affected national activity, as well as delays and lags (Bennett 1997, Bennett and Raab 2006: ch. 5), and the Madrid Resolution may turn out to have been a plateau rather than a springboard for further institutional development or for more rigorous regulation. What happens in the USA, China, India and other major data-processing countries lacking robust information privacy protection will be crucial. As international data protection moves into a future marked by increasing surveillance-related threats to privacy, there is as yet no permanent organizational infrastructure, such as a secretariat, to manage common practical relationships, to represent DPAs to the world and to aid communication: the Madrid Conference agreed a resolution to develop options aimed at creating a secretariat, but remitted the question to a working group to report back. However, DPAs decided on a common website with OECD hosting, and its governance structure and financial formula were outlined.[34]

The relatively slow pace of development – albeit accelerating somewhat – exemplifies and signifies the restriction of the formation of global regulation: a trajectory that lags behind the globalization of the threats. Such institution-building, including "bureaucratization", would be a significant although controversial milestone; its depth and effectiveness are not yet certain, for we may expect the continuation of inhibiting factors even among the post-Madrid participants in the new consensus. The question of "who pays for what" among DPAs of different-sized countries does not appear settled, but resource considerations are not the only ones perceptible in the continuing relative informality of arrangements. National or regional power differentials and differences of approach to privacy questions and their relation to other political objectives sought by countries or regions may be too much to bridge or suppress in favour of an overarching global framework. The slow tempo of change is likely to reflect, particularly among some DPAs and especially their governments, a certain felt restraint, or indeed proscription, regarding further institutionalization and the possible transfer of power or policy initiative that this may entail, as well as the collective decision-making costs of such institutionalization.

In sum, many spheres of activity, networks of varying density and closure, and cross-cutting or partly isomorphic coalitions bring the "usual suspects" together with others in a shifting array of contexts and for many purposes at various levels of geographical and functional scale. For greater public visibility, policy influence over national and international governments, and regulatory effectiveness, steps have been taken to institutionalize this commingling more formally and to support it with infrastructure. We can discern a sometimes piecemeal and entrepreneurial emergence of new initiatives potentially yielding a weightier and more institutional presence and better coherence of regulatory strategies, both in individual jurisdictions and in a more co-ordinated international environment. Growing institutionalization and interaction reflect internal dynamics within the regulatory community and is a response to external pressures that have not been analysed here. The descriptions of this transformation given here are only indicative, for there are other mutual involvements of DPAs along dimensions including, or beyond, the ones discussed earlier. Moreover, these connections may vary in their openness or closure to other participants, their general or specific focus on functions or purposes, their longevity, their formality and their extent; a closer analysis would employ these variables. Further activity may be more, or less, structured than those described; the more informal and fleeting they are, the more elusive and difficult to investigate.

Does the spate of procedural, organizational and public relations initiatives constitute merely the actions of an aspiring global regulatory force getting all dressed up with rules and procedures, establishing an identity and a "mission", but with nowhere to go? Or are they the necessary groundwork preparations for more effective global regulation? As mentioned, regional or sub-global bodies and networks have also proliferated, and the same questions pertain to them, although some collective identities seem clearer at this level. More research and the passage of time are needed before they, and other research questions, can be answered. Using available materials as well as interview techniques, it should be fruitful to compare the various networks – particularly the sub-global groupings – in search of explanations for their different or similar trajectories of development, for example; or for their choice of different targets for collaborative regulation. Beyond that, comparative analysis of the "case" of information privacy protection with other areas of information policy – for example, developments within each of the many facets of Internet regulation – could similarly be constructed if there were sufficient "thick descriptions" as well as analytical questions in play. But the social science of information policy is not yet so well developed for these to be straightforward comparative research aims to fulfil in the very near future; that, however, should be a stimulus, not a deterrent.

Acknowledgements

This article is a companion piece to Raab (2010). It has not been possible to update the information it contains beyond the end of 2009. I would like to thank the Hanse-Wissenschaftskolleg (Institute for Advanced Study) in Delmenhorst, Germany for the excellent facilities available to me during my Fellowship in May and June 2009; the Carnegie Trust for the Universities of Scotland for financial assistance; and current and former members of Data Protection Authorities, including Alexander Dix, Peter Harris, Hansjürgen Garstka, David Loukidelis, Peter Schaar, Marie Shroff, David Smith, Blair Stewart, Nigel Waters and Thilo Weichert, for discussions and other assistance.

Notes

1. http://www.privacyconference2007.gc.ca/Terra_Incognita_resolutions_ngo_E.html (accessed May 28, 2009).
2. The Article 29 Working Party, established by the 1995 European Union Data Protection Directive 95/46/EC, is a partial exception. Space does not permit extensive discussion of its role, but see Newman (this issue).

3. But see Flaherty (1989), Bennett (1992), Stewart (1997), Bennett and Raab (2006), Newman (2008), and Newman (this issue).
4. See the activity under the auspices of Privacy Laws & Business, at: http://www.privacylaws.com/templates/Events.aspx?id=364 (accessed May 25, 2009). The International Association of Privacy Professionals (IAPP) "is the world's largest association of privacy professionals, representing more than 6,000 members from businesses, governments and academic institutions across 47 countries"; see https://www.privacyassociation.org/index.php (accessed May 25, 2009). They offer a credentialing scheme and host international conferences.
5. See Stone Sweet et al. (2001), and Steinmo (2008), summarizing institutionalist approaches.
6. For some of this, see Newman (2008), Raab (2010) and Newman (this issue).
7. See http://www.edps.europa.eu/EDPSWEB/edps/site/mySite/pid/99 (accessed May 12, 2009); http://www.privacycommission.be/en/international/berlin-telecom (accessed June 7, 2009); http://www.datenschutz-berlin.de/content/europa-international/international-working-group-on-data-protection-in-telecommunications-iwgdpt (accessed June 7, 2009). The latter website links to a large document in German and English, "International Documents on Data Protection in Telecommunications and Media 1983–2006", providing texts of all Common Positions (later called Working Papers) and other outputs from the first 40 meetings, through 2006.
8. http://www.gov.im/lib/docs/odps//madridresolutionnov09.pdf (accessed November 4, 2010).
9. http://www.privacyconference2007.gc.ca/PRIVACY-191481-v1-RESOLUTION_GUIDELINES.pdf (accessed May 28, 2009).
10. http://www.privacyconference2005.org/fileadmin/PDF/montreux_declaration_e.pdf (accessed May 12, 2009).
11. http://www.privacy.org.nz/28th-international-conference-of-data-protection-and-privacy-commissioners/ (accessed May 11, 2009).
12. "Communicating Data Protection and Making it More Effective", available at: http://www.edps.europa.eu/EDPSWEB/webdav/shared/Documents/Cooperation/Conference_int/06-11-03_London_initiative_EN.pdf (accessed May 11, 2009).
13. Ibid., 5.
14. http://www.privacyconference2007.gc.ca/Resolution%20on%20Global%20cooperation%20-English.pdf (accessed May 28, 2009).
15. http://www.oecd.org/dataoecd/43/28/38770483.pdf (accessed May 12, 2009).
16. Ibid., 7.
17. Ibid., 11.
18. http://www.privacyconference2007.gc.ca/Working%20Group%20Resolution_english.pdf (accessed May 28, 2009).
19. http://www.privacyconference2007.gc.ca/country_reports/NEW%20ZELAND%20-%20ENGLISH.pdf (accessed May 28, 2009).
20. A relatively new three-person Credentials Committee was initially chaired for five years by the New Zealand DPA, working with a subgroup to decide on accrediting new DPAs to annual meetings. However, a consolidated list of accredited DPAs is not available at the time of writing. See the document of the 2001 Paris Conference, amended at the 2002 Cardiff Conference, at http://www.privacyconference2007.gc.ca/PRIVACY-190100-v1-Accreditation_principles_and_committee_rules_ENG.pdf (accessed May 28, 2009). Item A7 of this document states that members of the Committee bear their own costs.
21. http://www.privacyconference2007.gc.ca/Working%20Group%20Resolution_english.pdf (accessed May 28, 2009), Section F.
22. See the resolution adopted at the 2005 Montreux Conference, at http://www.privacyconference2008.org/pdf/resolution_concerning_en.pdf (accessed May 29, 2009).
23. A resolution on this, proposing the establishment of a steering group, was passed at the 30th Annual Conference in Strasbourg in 2008. See http://www.privacyconference2008.org/adopted_resolutions/STRASBOURG2008/resolution_steering_group_en.pdf (accessed June 6, 2009).
24. https://www.agpd.es/portalweb/privacyconference2009/documentacion/common/report_credentials_committee_en.pdf (accessed May 28, 2009).
25. The New Zealand Privacy Commissioner's website, http://www.privacy.org.nz/privacy-awareness-week/ (accessed May 12, 2009), explained with respect to the week of May 3–9, 2009, that "Privacy Awareness Week is run in partnership with ... APPA". The week would "see a variety of programs

and initiatives hosted by public and private sector organisations from across the Asia-Pacific region to promote awareness of privacy rights and responsibilities". The first such Week was held in 2007.
26. The third annual Data Protection Day was held on January 28, 2009. The Council of Europe urged that "events should be organised all over Europe to raise awareness on data protection and inform citizens of their rights and of good practices, thereby enabling them to exercise these rights more effectively", see http://www.coe.int/t/e/legal_affairs/legal_co%2Doperation/data_protection/Default_DP_Day_en.asp#TopOfPage (accessed May 12, 2009).
27. http://www.edps.europa.eu:80/EDPSWEB/webdav/site/mySite/shared/Documents/Cooperation/Conference_int/08-10-17_Strasbourg_DPDay_EN.pdf (accessed May 12, 2009). At Madrid, DPAs appeared to be unable to agree on a common date for a global event, and no final decision was taken.
28. Ibid., 1.
29. European Commission (2009), a recent European Commission research report, describes the existing state of promotional and communication activities among EU member states. The author was a sub-contractor to KANTOR for this project.
30. http://www.lda.brandenburg.de/sixcms/media.php/3509/resolution_website_working_group_en.pdf (accessed May 12, 2009).
31. http://www.privacyconference2008.org/adopted_resolutions/STRASBOURG2008/resolution_international_standards_en.pdf (accessed May 12, 2009).
32. See "Global Privacy Standards for a Global World – The Madrid Privacy Declaration, 3 November 2009", http://thepublicvoice.org/madrid-declaration/ (accessed November 10, 2009).
33. See Center for Democracy and Technology, "Policy Post 15.17, November 10, 2009", at: http://www.cdt.org/publications/policyposts/2009/17 (accessed November 16, 2009).
34. See "Resolution Proposed by the Website Working Group", at: http://www.privacyconference2010.org/upload/2009%20-%20Resolution%20proposed%20by%20the%20Website%20Working%20Group.pdf (accessed November 4, 2010).

References

Bache, I. and Flinders, M. (Eds), 2004, *Multi-level Governance* (Oxford: Oxford University Press).
Bennett, C., 1992, *Regulating Privacy: Data Protection and Public Policy in Europe and the United States* (Ithaca, NY: Cornell University Press).
Bennett, C., 1997, Understanding Ripple Effects: The Cross–National Adoption of Policy Instruments for Bureaucratic Accountability. *Governance*, **10**(3), 213–233.
Bennett, C., 2008, *The Privacy Advocates: Resisting the Spread of Surveillance* (Cambridge, MA: MIT Press).
Bennett, C. and Raab, C., 2006, *The Governance of Privacy: Policy Instruments in Global Perspective* (Cambridge, MA: MIT Press).
Bygrave, L., 2002, *Data Protection Law: Approaching its Rationale, Logic and Limits* (The Hague: Kluwer Law International).
European Commission, 2009, Directorate-General Justice, Freedom and Security. Evaluation of the means used by national data protection supervisory authorities in the promotion of personal data protection ã Final report, Framework contract for evaluation and evaluation related services, JLS/2007/C4/040: 30-CE-0185875/00-79 (Request for services No. 18), Submitted by KANTOR Management Consultants SA, 2009, available from: http://ec.europa.eu/justice_home/fsj/privacy/docs/studies/final_report_kantor_management_consultants.pdf (accessed May 12, 2009).
Fairbrass, J. and Jordan, A., 2004, Multi-level governance and environmental policy, in: I. Bache and M. Flinders (Eds) *Multi-level Governance* (Oxford: Oxford University Press), pp. 147–167.
Farrell, H. and Newman, A., 2010, Making global markets: historical institutionalism in international political economy. *Review of International Political Economy*, **17**(4), 609–638.
Flaherty, D., 1989, *Protecting Privacy in Surveillance Societies: The Federal Republic of Germany, Sweden, France, Canada, and the United States* (Chapel Hill, NC: University of North Carolina Press).
Held, D. and McGrew, A. (Eds), 2002, *Governing Globalization: Power, Authority and Global Governance* (Cambridge: Polity Press).

Hooghe, L. and Marks, G., 2003, Unraveling the central state, but how? Types of multi-level governance. *American Political Science Review*, **97**(2), 233–243.

Keohane, R. and Nye, J., 1974, Transgovernmental Relations and International Orgganizations. *World Politics*, **27**(1), 39–62.

Koenig-Archibugi, M. and Zürn, M. (Eds), 2005, *New Modes of Governance in the Global System: Exploring Publicness, Delegation and Inclusiveness* (London: Palgrave).

Lyon, D., 2003, *Surveillance after September 11* (Cambridge: Polity Press).

Mayer-Schönberger, V., 1997, Generational development of data protection in Europe, in: P. Agre and M. Rotenberg (Eds) *Technology and Privacy: The New Landscape* (Cambridge, MA: MIT Press), pp. 219–241.

Murray, A., 2007, *The Regulation of Cyberspace: Control in the Online Environment* (Abingdon: Routledge-Cavendish).

Newman, A., 2008, *Protectors of Privacy: Regulating Personal Data in the Global Economy* (Ithaca, NY: Cornell University Press).

Raab, C., 2010, Information privacy: networks of regulation at the subglobal level. *Global Policy*, **1**(3), 291–302.

Raab, C. and De Hert, P., 2008, Tools for technology regulation: seeking analytical approaches beyond Lessig and Hood, in: R. Brownsword and C. Yeung (Eds) *Regulating Technologies: Legal Futures, Regulatory Frames and Technological Fixes* (Oxford: Hart Publishing).

Raab, C. and Koops, B.-J., 2009, Privacy actors, performances, and the future of privacy protection, in: S. Gutwirth, Y. Poullet, P. De Hert, C. de Terwangne and S. Nouwt (Eds) *Re-inventing Data Protection?* (Dordrecht: Springer).

Scharpf, F., 2001, Notes toward a theory of multilevel governing in Europe. *Scandinavian Political Studies*, **24**(1), 1–26.

Slaughter, A.-M., 2000, Governing the global economy through government networks, in: M. Byers (Ed) *The Role of Law in International Politics: Essays in International Relations and International Law* (Oxford: Oxford University Press), pp. 177–205.

Slaughter, A.-M. and Zaring, D., 2006, Networking goes international: an update. *Annual Review of Law and Social Science*, **2**, 211–229.

Steinmo, S., 2008, Historical institutionalism, in: D. Della Porta and M. Keating (Eds) *Approaches and Methodologies in the Social Sciences: A Pluralist Perspective* (Cambridge: Cambridge University Press), pp. 118–138.

Stewart, B., 1997, Privacy commissioner gatherings. *Privacy Law and Policy Reporter*, **29**, available from: http://www.austlii.edu.au/au/journals/PLPR/1997/29.html (accessed July 9, 2009).

Stone Sweet, A., Fligstein, N. and Sandholtz, W., 2001, The institutionalization of European space, in: A. Stone Sweet, W. Sandholtz and N. Fligstein (Eds) *The Institutionalization of Europe* (Oxford: Oxford University Press), pp. 1–28.

True, J., Jones, B. and Baumgartner, F., 1999, Punctuated-equilibrium theory: explaining stability and change in American policymaking, in: P. Sabatier (Ed) *Theories of the Policy Process* (Boulder, CO: Westview Press).

Four Styles of Regulation and their Implications for Comparative Policy Analysis

CHRISTIAN ADAM, STEFFEN HURKA, & CHRISTOPH KNILL

ABSTRACT *Comparative research crucially depends on the availability of meaningful descriptive concepts capturing the essence of empirical phenomena. In policy analysis, the portfolio of classical concepts describing policy contents and procedures remains unmatched by a similar pool of concepts available for describing patterns of regulatory outputs. Starting from the premise that policy-makers not only create behavioral rules, but also define sanctions for rule violations, this article distinguishes four ideal-typical styles of regulation: authority, lenient authority, punitive permissiveness, and permissiveness. It uses handgun regulation to illustrate the merits of this distinction and discusses the theoretical implications of the approach.*

1. Introduction

One of the major challenges for modern states is to answer the question of how to resolve the tension between citizens' individual freedoms and public intervention in order to reach political goals. How far should individual liberties be limited for the sake of the public good? How far should society be protected from governmental intervention? Yet surprisingly few attempts have been made to discuss more systematically how the actual balance of individual freedom, public intervention and potential changes in this balance can be assessed. The central research question addressed in this paper is hence how to describe and measure the way in which this balance has shifted in different countries.

It is well-recognized that the normative foundations of how to balance individual rights and collective intervention vary across countries. This variation becomes apparent in different state traditions that can be understood as deeply institutionalized norms specifying the relationship between state and society. These norms typically emerged during historical "watersheds" of state formation, implying that – depending on the underlying historical conditions and interest constellations – state traditions vary considerably across countries. The UK, for instance, has been classified as "stateless society", with the role of the government being restricted to mediating societal conflicts rather than directly intervening in society "from above". This latter approach, by contrast, has been identified as crucial feature of the French *etatist* tradition (Dyson 1980; Badie and Birnbaum 1983; Knill 2001).

However, state traditions are highly abstract concepts hardly sufficient to capture the variety and complexity of governmental decision-making over time and across a range of different policy sectors. To get a better, empirically grounded understanding of how different countries balance individual rights and collective intervention, it is necessary to focus on distinctive policy areas in which this basic conflict appears most clearly and even constitutes a defining characteristic, namely regulatory policies. Regulatory policies refer to policies that specify conditions and constraints for individual and collective behavior. In contrast with distributive or redistributive policies that extract and allocate resources between different societal actors, the basic objective of regulatory policies is to influence human conduct (Lowi 1972, 2011). Regulation can hence be conceived as a policy type in which the balance between governmental intervention and the preservation of individual liberties is, by definition, most clearly pronounced. The common feature of regulatory policies is that they define rules for human behavior and sanctioning regimes to enforce compliance with these rules. These arrangements, regardless of their concrete design and content, entail more or less far-reaching restrictions for individual behavior. In other words, a clear understanding of national patterns of regulation tells us a lot about underlying conceptions of state–society relationships and their change over time.

The identification of stable country- or sector-specific policy patterns has been at the heart of the public policy literature, which analyzed the prevalence of different policy styles from the early 1980s onwards. These policy styles capture "standard operating procedures" of governments in making and implementing public policies (Richardson et al. 1982, p. 2). Put differently, policy styles relate to durable and systematic approaches to policy problems (Freeman 1985, p. 474, Feick and Jann 1988). In this regard, central emphasis was placed on procedural characteristics. The focus was on the question of whether politics in countries have some persistent characteristics that predispose them to formulate and implement public policies in certain distinct ways, irrespective of the issue concerned or the policy sector they belong to.

The study of national policy styles started with influential contributions authored and co-authored by Jeremy Richardson, who contrasted national policy styles by distinguishing active and reactive government approaches to problem-solving as well as by distinguishing a consensual from an impositional style of policy-making (Richardson et al. 1982). Along similar lines, van Waarden (1995) proposed that national policy styles can be characterized by distinguishing between high and low formalization of the relationship between public and private actors as well as between strong and weak participation of societal actors in policy-making. While the term policy style has been used as the most general and widespread term to identify such process patterns, some authors (in particular Vogel 1986; Vogel and Kagan 2004) refer to similar phenomena as styles of regulation. Since these approaches simply refer to "regulation" as one specific policy type, the findings of this strand of literature allow us to better describe and understand stable policy-making patterns. While styles of regulation hence concentrate on a specific policy type, the concept of administrative styles developed by Knill (1998, 2001) explicitly focuses on traditional behavioral patterns of a specific player in the political administrative system, namely the public administration (see also Zysman 1994; Howlett 2002, 2003).

Notwithstanding this long research tradition, it is striking that the specification of policy styles has always been based on the politics dimension: i.e. typical features characterizing the process of policy-making. By contrast, issues of policy content and policy design have been neglected. However, it is especially this latter category of *regulatory outputs* in which the boundaries between individual rights and collective intervention are most clearly visible.

It is the objective of this paper to address this research deficit. In so doing, we develop an innovative concept that enables us to identify and describe central characteristics of regulatory policy outputs. Rather than focusing on the politics dimension, our concept allows for precisely assessing the boundaries between the protection of individual freedoms and collective intervention, as it becomes apparent in the output dimension. More precisely, we focus on two dimensions of regulatory outputs. On the one hand, we consider the extent to which individual freedoms are conditioned and constrained by regulatory rules. On the other hand, we analyze the extent to which deviations from these rules are actually sanctioned. Based on the combination of these two dimensions, we identify four ideal-typical styles of regulatory policy output. We argue that this concept offers an innovative tool for mapping and assessing regulatory change over time and to compare regulatory outputs across countries and sectors.

In the following, we first present four ideal-typical styles of regulatory policy output. Secondly, we propose a way to measure output in terms of these styles. Thirdly, we highlight the advantages of this approach for describing regulatory output in the context of handgun regulation. Finally, the paper discusses several implications of this approach for the explanation of regulatory change.

2. Four Styles of Regulatory Output

One of the central goals of democratic systems is to protect the individual freedoms of their citizens. At the same time, democratic systems regularly seem to feel the need to influence individual behavior to protect the freedoms, order, and welfare of society as a whole. The tension between individual freedoms and the collective good is particularly evident in the context of regulatory policies, which – according to Lowi's classic typology (Lowi 1972, p. 300) – are policies that define behavioral constraints.

Yet, behavioral constraints can take different forms. They are closely related to the underlying governance principles through which governments seek to motivate such changes (Hood 1986; Hood and Margetts 2007; Holzinger and Knill 2008; Bauer and Knill 2014). Governments might restrict their intervention to merely offering information to policy addressees in order to stimulate behavioral change (e.g. campaigns against drug consumption). They might also offer positive or negative financial incentives to encourage such changes, such as taxes, fees or subsidies. If, for example, policy-makers want to keep citizens from driving overly pollutant cars, they have at least two options. Either policy-makers encourage citizens not to drive such cars, for example cars without a catalytic converter, by informing them about the damaging environmental effects. Alternatively, they may choose to adopt tax reductions for drivers of cars with catalytic converters. Both of these governance principles try to affect individual behavior only in an indirect way. They rely on cognitive or financial means to encourage behavioral change. They do not prescribe behavioral change. The latter element – direct prescription – of behavioral change constitutes the most far-reaching intervention into individual liberties, as it relies on direct legal specification of constraints for individual behavior. In the example introduced above, the most severe form of such a direct constraint would be to prohibit cars without catalytic converters. Less severe measures in this context could be locational (e.g. prohibition in inner cities) or temporal (e.g. on Sundays). It is exactly this pattern – what Hood (1986) refers to as authority – that builds the starting point for our analysis. We argue that it is especially via these direct ways of governmental prescription through which the balance between individual rights and collective intervention can be assessed.

Yet, just as normative encouragements are typically flanked with financial incentives such as taxes or subsidies, behavioral boundaries are usually not only reinforced by attempts to persuade citizens of the importance of the boundary. Instead, legal boundaries are complemented by sanctions. Although some might consider both sanctions and incentives to be costs of certain behavior, sanctions and incentives differ in an important way. In the case of incentives flanking behavioral encouragements, citizens pay a financial price for engaging in certain behavior. For example, they pay taxes for smoking or for drinking alcohol. If they pay this financial price, they are free to smoke and drink. Sanctions, in contrast, are not mere costs whose payment legalizes an otherwise prohibited behavior. If, for instance, driving a car without a catalytic converter was sanctioned with a fine, paying this fine will not legalize the activity, to stick to the example from above. The prohibition of certain activities is thus the most drastic form in which policy-makers can interfere with individual behavior. By taking some behavioral options off the table, they effectively define the borders of individual freedom. These borders can be complemented with no, low, or rather severe sanctions. Depending on those degrees of severity, crossing behavioral boundaries can be inconsequential or highly consequential.

Therefore, just as the concept of coercion is at the heart of Lowi's definition of regulatory policy (Lowi 1972, p. 300), it informs our classification of regulatory output: policy-makers do not only decide how strongly regulations interfere with individual liberties by setting legal boundaries, they also delineate how accepting societies are of noncompliant behavior by defining sanctions for rule violations. This distinction between the interference with individual liberties through the formulation of behavioral boundaries and the consequentiality of noncompliance forms the basis of our concept of regulatory policy output. Accordingly, we identify four ideal-typical styles of regulation (see Table 1).

If narrow boundaries (i.e. boundaries which greatly restrict individual freedom) are combined with severe sanctions, the corresponding style of regulation is authority. The opposite situation occurs if policy-makers grant citizens wide boundaries and even the disrespect of these boundaries is not subject to meaningful sanctions. In such a scenario,

Table 1. Four styles of regulation

		Consequentiality of noncompliant behavior	
		Low	High
Behavioral boundaries	Narrow	*Lenient authority*	*Authority*
	Wide	*Permissiveness*	*Punitive permissiveness*

we speak of a permissive style of regulation. This dichotomy of ideal types, however, does not provide us with sufficient vocabulary to describe all empirically relevant types of regulatory output. In fact, two additional categories reflect styles of regulation that appear somewhat less consistent in the way they combine rules with sanctions. One such additional style of regulation is what we call "lenient authority". Here, strict and far-reaching prohibitions are combined with low or even nonexistent sanctions. For example, this style of lenient authority is clearly evident in the context of Portugal's drug policy reform in 2000 (Chatwin 2011; Hughes and Stevens 2012; Adam and Raschzok 2014). Here, the existing authoritarian style of drug regulation was perceived to be utterly ineffective. Yet even the leftist government coalition did not want to lift the behavioral constraints from citizens by rendering the possession of drugs legal. Since the perceived need for reform coincided with a lack of political will to ease behavioral constraints, reform efforts were directed towards the consequentiality of rule violations – i.e. the sanctions imposed for the possession of illegal drugs. In fact, Portuguese policy-makers decided to drop all custodial sanctions for such an offense. Portuguese drug policy thus moved from authority to lenient authority. This category of lenient authority represents a style of regulation that remains prohibitive in terms of individual freedoms but is inconsequential where those prohibitive rules are violated.

This pattern strongly contrasts with a style we refer to as punitive permissiveness. In this scenario, policy-makers only impose minor constraints on individual freedoms by granting individuals wide behavioral boundaries. Yet they also decide to make any misuse of these far-reaching freedoms highly consequential. They do so by adopting severe sanctions in cases where the few constraints are not complied with. Another example from the context of drug policy helps to illustrate the empirical relevance of this style. Specifically, Spain's drug regime throughout the 1980s was based on a regulatory style of punitive permissiveness. While individuals were allowed to possess cannabis and even heroin for personal use (wide behavioral boundaries), they faced severe sanctions of mandatory prison sentences if they carried more than could plausibly be considered to be intended for personal use (high consequentiality of rule violations). Punitive permissiveness thus refers to regulatory output that is permissive in the sense that it only introduces minor constraints on individual freedoms, but punitive in the sense that severe sanctions are imposed on anyone overstepping the defined boundaries.

Both drug policies – the Spanish throughout the 1980s and Portuguese after 2000 – could be described as "liberal" policies. However, this description would either cover up the existing differences evident in both policy regimes or require additional definitions of what the term "liberal" implies. Our conceptualization of regulatory styles captures the difference between both regimes directly. While the Portuguese style of lenient authority combines narrow behavioral boundaries with low sanctions for rule violations, the

Spanish style of punitive permissiveness foresees relatively wide behavioral boundaries while punishing rule violations severely. Both systems are liberal, yet in very different ways. This difference finds expression in our concept of regulatory styles.

3. Measuring Styles of Regulation

This section proposes a way to measure regulatory output in terms of our two-dimensional concept. We start by presenting our approach to measuring the width of behavioral boundaries. These boundaries can be measured with varying degrees of complexity. In its simplest form, a measure of this concept could take a binary form and capture whether a certain behavior is prohibited (1) or not (0). Yet in most policy sectors, this crude distinction will fail to capture the essence of the legal provisions in place and will leave us blind to empirical variation between countries. Accordingly, we propose a hierarchical measure that differentiates between three aspects of a policy's behavioral boundaries. This measure relies on the assumption that not all aspects of existing regulation reflect the same severity of governmental intervention. Scholars have to decide which aspects and how many aspects to include as well as how to order them according to the severity of intervention. In our illustration, we propose to differentiate between the general regulatory paradigm, additional personal requirements, and additional procedural boundaries.

On the first level, we capture the general approach, or paradigm, towards the object of regulation by distinguishing between prohibition, narrow permission, and wide permission. These categories capture whether policy-makers generally prohibit certain behavior or restrict it to specific circumstances. In the latter case, our measurement also incorporates how narrowly these circumstances are defined. Of course, especially the categories of wide and narrow permission can hardly be defined without a clearer understanding of a certain policy field under investigation. Nevertheless, it is possible to define general criteria to differentiate between both categories. In this regard, the decisive feature is whether the underlying approach is one that generally seeks to minimize certain activities or not. Does certain behavior, although not prohibited in general, constitute the exception (narrow permission) or the rule (wide permission)?

While this differentiation might already be sufficient for some purposes, the first level of measurement can be complemented with a second level that takes account of additional, more specific characteristics of the regulatory output. Specifically, we propose to include boundaries concerning characteristics of the policy addressees. After policy-makers have defined their general approach towards a given behavior, they can define hurdles that individuals must overcome in order to engage in that behavior legally. Even if a state allows a certain conduct in principle, there are still many secondary adjustments it can impose in terms of personal eligibility. For instance, while most states permit the consumption of tobacco, they usually define age thresholds in order to prevent minors from smoking.

In case further refinement of measurement of the scope of behavioral constraint is required, the existing measure can be complemented by a third level. Here, we propose to capture whether regulatory output contains procedural constraints. Again, such measures can take various forms capturing different procedural aspects of the regulated behavior. Returning to the tobacco example from above, such procedural hurdles have recently materialized in the form of locational restrictions. Thus, even if smoking is

Table 2. Generic example of measuring behavioral boundaries

Level 1 General approach towards the object of regulation	Level 2 Personal constraints	Level 3 Procedural requirements	Category
Prohibition	n/a	n/a	3.00
Narrow permission	High	High	2.84
		Low	2.67
	Medium	High	2.50
		Low	2.33
	Low	High	2.17
		Low	2.00
Wide permission	High	High	1.84
		Low	1.67
	Medium	High	1.50
		Low	1.33
	Low	High	1.17
		Low	1.00

allowed in principle and cigarettes can be obtained by every individual in compliance with the personal requirements, states can still limit individual freedoms to smoke by defining smoke-free areas in, for example, bars, gas stations, or hospitals.

Table 2 summarizes our measurement concept with the help of a generic example. In principle, the concept is guided by the assumption that the general approach to the regulation of the policy object is more fundamental than personal requirements defined for addressees of the regulation or mere procedural constraints. This assumption finds its expression in the values we assign to different alterations of the regulatory status quo. In other words, if a state changes its general approach on a given regulatory issue, this is reflected in greater shifts of the corresponding index value than a change on the subordinate levels. If, for example, a state moves from an approach of narrow permission with low personal and procedural hurdles towards prohibition, the corresponding value changes from 2.00 to 3.00. If, however, the state retains its narrowly permissive approach, but increases personal hurdles to medium, the value only changes from 2.00 to 2.33. If the state decides to tighten procedural rules in addition, the value changes from 2.33 to 2.50. Thus, fundamental shifts on level 1 are mirrored more strongly in the index value than changes on secondary or tertiary levels.

Next to this hierarchical conception of state interference with individual liberties, we measure the severity of sanctions imposed for such rule violations to capture the extent to which governments are willing to tolerate individual misconduct. Generally, prohibitive regulatory arrangements define a series of punishable offenses related to behavioral boundaries on all levels of measurement: Offenses can include violations of both personal and procedural requirements. To reduce complexity and sharpen the analytical focus, we propose to focus on the sanctions for the most typical offense within a given area of regulation. Of course, what counts as a punishable offense is not necessarily constant across the different policy configurations. An activity that is legal in a situation of wide permission may become illegal if permission is narrowed down and vice versa. In such situations, we consider it the most practicable solution to capture the most typical offense in the respective general approach.

For the technical implementation of the measurement, we propose an ordinal scale consisting of 16 categories (see Table 3). The most severe punishment for individual misconduct is the death penalty. We also include the possibility of a life sentence in this most extreme category. The ordering of the remaining categories is based on a range of assumptions. First, we generally conceive of a deprivation of liberty as a more severe sanction than of the imposition of a monetary fine, regardless of the length of the jail sentence or the amount of the fine. This assumption does not only make intuitive sense, there is also broad consensus in the criminological literature and scholars of penal policies that it is reasonable. As Lappi-Seppälä (2008, p. 321) notes: "Imprisonment has uncontested prominence as the principal and most severe sanction in European and industrialized Western countries (with the unfortunate exception of the United States)". Thus, we regard even a short prison sentence to be a more severe sanction than a high monetary fine. Secondly, we conceive of a monetary fine as being more severe than a purely administrative sanction, like the withdrawal of a license or the closure of an establishment. Thirdly, (penal) laws mention both the possibility of imposing a jail sentence *and* a fine or they prescribe jail sentences, which can be substituted for a fine. We generally consider the former more severe than the latter, regardless of the precise calibrations of the sentences. Fourthly, sanctioning provisions sometimes include "and/or" provisions as far as fines and imprisonment are concerned, leaving the ultimate decision of substitutability to the judge. We argue that it makes sense to assume that such types of penalties fall in between the mandatory and substitutable categories. Finally, there is a distinction made between long, medium, and short jail sentences in order to keep some of the information of the calibration of jail sentences but at the same time do justice to the need to reduce complexity. Thus, we conceive of a short mandatory jail sentence as a more severe punishment than a long jail sentence, which can be substituted for a monetary fine. The main challenge associated with this categorization rests with the definition of thresholds between short, medium and long jail sentences. Where the lines should be drawn between the respective categories is ultimately an empirical question, which cannot be answered without deeper knowledge of the regulatory area under study. In any case, the decision should be based on both theoretical considerations and empirical evidence. Accordingly, the sanctioning dimension runs from "no sanction" to "death penalty/life imprisonment", differentiating between more finely grained penal categories in between.

If we combine both measures introduced above – the one for behavioral boundaries and the one for the consequentiality of noncompliance – we can place countries in a two-dimensional regulatory space within which the four ideal types are located at the corners. The following sections will illustrate why we think it is worthwhile to engage in this exercise. To do so, we illustrate that our approach helps us to improve the description of regulatory policy output by capturing differences we would have overlooked otherwise.

4. Improving Our Description of Regulatory Output: An Illustration

To make our two-dimensional measurement approach more accessible and to illustrate its advantages over one-dimensional approaches, this section focuses on the empirical example of handgun regulation in 12 European countries. The data used for this illustration

Table 3. Generic example of measuring the consequentiality of noncompliance

Basic punishment	Substitutability	Calibration	Additional fine	Category
Death/life	n/a	n/a	n/a	15
Prison	Mandatory	Long	Yes	14
			No	13
		Medium	Yes	12
			No	11
		Short	Yes	10
			No	9
	Substitutable (and/or)	Long	n/a	8
		Medium	n/a	7
		Short	n/a	6
	Substitutable (or)	Long	n/a	5
		Medium	n/a	4
		Short	n/a	3
Fine	n/a	n/a	n/a	2
Administrative	n/a	n/a	n/a	1
No sanction	n/a	n/a	n/a	0

were collected in the context of the Comparative Analysis of Morality Policy Change (MORAPOL) project (Knill 2013).

We start this exercise with our measurement of behavioral boundaries for individuals interested in the possession of a handgun.[1] On the first level of these boundaries, we capture the general approach towards the object of handgun regulation: is the possession of this object completely prohibited (prohibition), is the right of possession granted to privileged citizens able to prove that they have a genuine need for it (narrow permission), or can handguns be possessed by anyone as long as authorities cannot prove that the person cannot be trusted (wide permission)?

This rather crude measure can be fine-tuned by adding another aspect of handgun regulation that reflects an additional and less severe intervention in individual freedoms than the general paradigms formulated on the first level. On this second level, we focus on constraints concerning the addressee of the regulation. Given that handguns are not prohibited as such, the question is whether there are any personal requirements a person should meet to be allowed to own a handgun. To demonstrate the flexibility of the measurement approach, we create a composite measure on this level. In the context of handgun regulation, second-level constraints can be interpreted as licensing requirements, i.e. the personal requirements a potential customer must fulfill in order to qualify for a gun purchase. Such personal constraints are not only relevant in systems of narrow permission but also in systems of wide permission. We thus construct a ten-point additive index capturing the height of the qualification hurdles a prospective handgun owner must overcome before being able to acquire a weapon.[2] The respective items generally refer to the applicant's *maturity* (age threshold), *health* (mental and physical), *character* (criminal record, addiction to drugs), and *technical capability* (the need to provide a safety training or similar technical tests). Two additional items measure whether the applicant must prove regular employment and/or income and whether third party character references or the consent of cohabitants must be produced.

Table 4. Indicators used on the three levels of state intervention in handgun regulation

Level 1 General regulatory approach	Level 2 Personal requirements	Level 3 Procedural requirements
Prohibition	n/a	n/a
Privilege Permission	Age threshold	Safe storage
	Mental health	
	Physical health	
	Criminal history	
	Drug addiction	
	Practical or theoretical exam	
	Proof of employment/income	
	Third party reference(s)	

If scholars feel that the measure of behavior boundaries should be even more fine-grained to capture relevant differences and changes, they can include the relevant aspect of regulation on an additional third level in the hierarchy. In our example, we do so by including additional procedural constraints of individual liberties relevant in the context of handgun regulation. Even when the general policy paradigm allows for the possession of a handgun, and after individuals have cleared all of the relevant personal requirements, possession of handguns is still tied to further procedural requirements in the form of safe storage provisions. We distinguish between no, basic, and advanced storage requirements. For the purpose of this illustration, we do not engage in a more detailed discussion of the indicators here. Table 4 summarizes the measure.

Taken together, this yields an ordinal scale of behavioral constraints of 67 ordinal categories. As outlined above, changes in the behavioral boundaries on the first level lead to a larger shift than changes on the second level. A change on the second level is in turn more consequential for the index value than a change on the third level.

To assess the consequentiality of noncompliance in the context of handgun regulation, we focus on the most relevant criminal offense: the possession of a handgun while lacking the authority to do so. Depending on the general approach towards the regulatory object, this can simply be any possession of a handgun (prohibition), or the possession of a handgun without the respective authorization (narrow permission and wide permission). Furthermore, we consider any prison sentence below one year as short, any sentence between one and three years as medium, and any sentence above three years as long. While any classification in this regard is somewhat arbitrary, we choose these categories so as to make the most out of our two-dimensional measurement. This means that we choose values that ensure the ability to observe a certain degree of empirical variation.

One advantage of our conceptualization relying on both of these dimensions can be shown with the help of Figure 1. This figure combines two plots. In the left plot, we solely rely on the measure of behavioral constraints in assessing the regulation of handguns. The plot suggests that there are only minor differences regarding handgun regulation in our sample of countries. Greece (GR) is somewhat of an exception with slightly weaker constraints. Yet all countries in the sample foster a general regulatory approach of narrow permission. There are several differences in terms of personal and procedural constraints within this approach. However, Germany (DE) and Portugal (PT) as well as France (FR) and Norway (NO) seem to maintain identical handgun

Figure 1. Illustration of cross-national variation

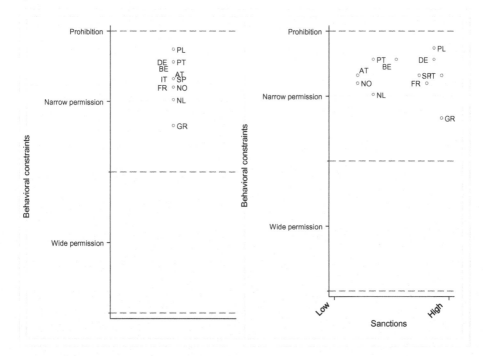

Source: Data is taken from the MORAPOL project.

policies. While this picture might be good enough for some purposes, the right-hand plot in Figure 1 indicates how our approach can improve our assessment of regulatory output. Specifically, the right-hand plot shows that particularly countries previously perceived to maintain identical handgun regulations in fact uphold quite different regulations when the consequentiality of noncompliance is taken into account. While Portugal and Germany constrain the legal possession of handguns in a fairly similar way, they differ greatly in the degree of sanctions applying in case of illegal possession of handguns. German policy-makers have equipped judges with the ability to choose from a much more severe set of sanctions than Portuguese policy-makers have. The same holds true for French policy-makers when compared to Norwegian policy-makers. These differences were covered up in the one-dimensional assessment of handgun regulation. Uncovering such additional variation might not be necessary for all purposes, but it can be helpful in some circumstances. If we choose our analytical research question based on the left-hand-side description, we might be tempted to ask why Austria and Italy were equally restrictive in terms of handgun regulation despite their different gun cultures. If we choose the analytical research question based on the right-hand-side description, we would not find their handgun regulations to be strikingly similar and would choose another theoretical puzzle.

Figure 2 highlights the advantages of our approach for the assessment of regulatory change. Again, the left-hand plot in Figure 2 represents a one-dimensional assessment of change in handgun regulation as captured by behavioral constraints. Based on this one-

Figure 2. Illustration of temporal variation

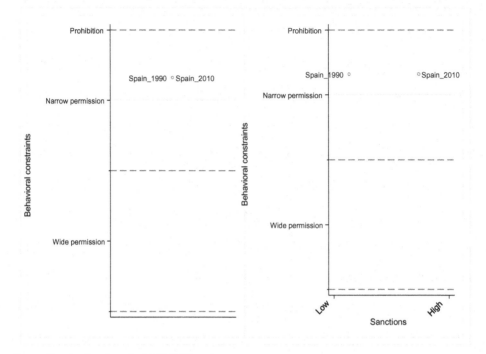

Source: Data is taken from the MORAPOL project.

dimensional assessment, handgun regulation in Spain did not change between 1990 and 2000. This assessment changes completely when looking at the plot located at the right-hand side in Figure 2. This two-dimensional plot shows that persistence in Spain only concerned the behavioral constraints on handgun possession. Yet the consequentiality of illegal handgun possession was greatly enhanced. Our explanations of change in handgun regulation will greatly depend on whether we try to explain the left-hand or the right-hand plot in Figure 2. Is the analytical challenge to explain persistence (left-hand plot) or to explain regulatory change (right-hand plot)?

A similar point can be made with the help of Figure 3. In this case, the one-dimensional plot on the left-hand side in Figure 3 indicates that the Netherlands changed its handgun regulations between 1980 and 1990. Specifically, the Dutch seem to have introduced more restrictive handgun regulations as they have increased the constraints on handgun possession. In case our goal was to explain change in handgun regulation, we would look for explanations able to account for the introduction of stricter rules in the Netherlands. However, if we relied on the picture drawn by the right-hand plot in Figure 3 the analytical challenge would be different. Specifically, the right-hand plot in Figure 3 shows that while the Netherlands has enhanced constraints on legal handgun possession, it has relaxed the sanctions applying in case of illegal handgun possession. In our terms, the Netherlands moved towards a style of lenient authority regarding handgun regulation. While the explanation of this shift does not necessarily have to depend on whether we rely on the one-dimensional or the two-dimensional description, it certainly can. This is

Figure 3. Illustration of cross-national and temporal variation

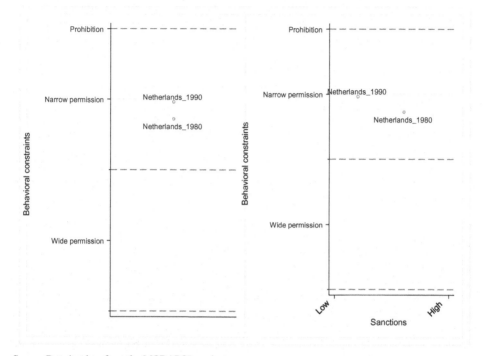

Source: Data is taken from the MORAPOL project.

because the simpler one-dimensional description might hide relevant actor constellations and bargaining dynamics underlying the observed regulatory change.

In sum, the comparisons above highlight how our conceptualization of different styles of regulatory output helps to uncover empirical variation that would be lost otherwise. This improvement is accomplished without adding excessive complexity. At the same time, we should emphasize that we conceive of this scheme as an analytical tool for uncovering the direction of regulatory changes rather than exactly measuring regulatory outputs in absolute terms. In other words, we should be careful when trying to classify individual countries into our fourfold conception of regulatory styles without an external point of reference. The handgun example above shows that it is often futile to attribute regulatory output to one of our four ideal-typical categories. This will only be fruitful for extreme cases with extreme values on both dimensions of our measures. Instead, the ideal types are always helpful in determining shifts in the direction of regulatory outputs. Thus, our concept is particularly useful for studies interested in sophisticated descriptions of patterns of regulatory change and convergence.

5. Implications for Explaining Regulatory Change

A two-dimensional conception of regulatory output can thus improve our *description* of regulatory change. At the same time, however, such a conception does also have certain implications for our attempts to *explain* the phenomenon. The main challenge in this regard presents itself in the following way. We need to clarify the conditions under which regulatory styles shift along the diagonal axes. Which factors facilitate coordinated reform efforts leading to simultaneous adjustments of both behavioral constraints and sanctions for noncompliance? Which factors lead to one-dimensional shifts (vertical or horizontal)? Secondly, we have to answer when and why regulatory change reflects a compromise between the two dimensions. On the one hand, such a compromise can be reflected by regulatory shifts towards a style of lenient authority. Here, narrow behavioral boundaries are combined with low consequentiality of noncompliance. On the other hand, such compromises are reflected by shifts towards a style of punitive permissiveness – where a reduction of behavioral constraints is combined with an increasing consequentiality of rule violations. When and why do policy-makers turn to such compromises? We argue that two conditions can stand in the way of two-dimensional regulatory changes: goal ambiguities and procedural differences.

Goal Ambiguities Can Impede Two-Dimensional Shifts

Whether regulatory shifts occur simultaneously on both dimensions depends on whether the goals of reform proponents align on both dimensions. Quite intuitively, if the actor coalition pushing for reform wants to change behavioral constraints and the consequentiality of violations of these constraints, regulatory output is more likely to shift along both dimensions (if the coalition is successful in adopting a reform) than when the proponents of reform only want to change one dimension. The ambiguity of policy goals is one factor that might impede this willingness of actor coalitions to push for such diagonal change of regulation.

Take, for example, the German regulation of female circumcision practiced by some cultures for ritual reasons. In the spring of 2013, opposition parties tried to push for a reform of the current regulation of female circumcision. While this practice was already illegal in Germany, it was not illegal to conduct such a circumcision abroad (while on vacation) and then return to Germany. This could be changed by including this practice in §5 of the German penal code, summarizing offenses punishable in Germany that were committed abroad. The Social Democrats and the Greens, as the two main opposition parties, jointly pushed for this increase in behavioral constraints. While they were united on this dimension, they were divided on the question about the "right" consequences for noncompliance with the behavioral constraints. The Green party demanded that the sanctions applying to such violations be increased to a minimum of three years' imprisonment (http://dip21.bundestag.de/dip21/btd/17/047/1704759.pdf). The Social Democrats objected that while a strict punishment was indeed the right way to go, setting a prison sentence of a minimum of three years would automatically lead to the deportation of the offender and their family. In case of such offenses, girls would thus not only suffer from circumcision but also from deportation. The actual goal of protecting young girls would therefore be undermined by such a severe sentence. In consequence, the Social Democrats pushed for lower minimal sanctions of one year instead of three years (http://dip21.bundestag.de/dip21/btd/17/123/1712374.pdf), joining the proposals of the governing coalition consisting of the Christian Democrats and the Liberal party (http://dip21.bundestag.de/dip21/btd/17/137/1713707.pdf). The example shows how goal ambiguities can lead to actor heterogeneity. Due to such goal ambiguities, actors forming a coalition for change on the question of how to constrain behavior can be separated on the question of how to sanction the disrespect of these constraints. This will affect the probability of two-dimensional change.

Yet even if proponents of reform want to change both dimensions of regulation, this willingness does not necessarily translate into two-dimensional shifts. One additional factor that can impede such two-dimensional shifts is procedural differences.

Procedural Differences Can Impede Two-Dimensional Shifts

Actor coalitions pushing for two-dimensional regulatory change are not always able to change both dimensions simultaneously. Procedural differences can impede this ability to adopt diagonal changes. Specifically, the institutional environment within which policy-makers have to act when they want to adjust behavioral boundaries might not be the same institutional environment as when they try to adjust the consequentiality of noncompliance. Legislative procedures and the relevance of certain veto players might be different for each dimension. These factors are likely to affect the direction of regulatory change.

Let us first consider a situation without procedural differences, i.e. a situation in which the procedural requirements to change rules on behavioral constraints are identical to the procedural requirements to change sanctions. An example for such a situation is the German weapons law (Waffengesetz), which is one law consisting of a first part delineating boundaries for individual behavior (in particular the licensing process) and a second part specifying penal sanctions for rule violations. Changing either element of this law (constraints or sanctions) imposes identical procedural requirements. Specifically, such changes require a simple majority in the first chamber (Bundestag) and the second chamber (Bundesrat). This implies that the regulation of weapons takes place under a common legislative framework and the specification of sanctions is neither "outsourced" to the penal code nor delegated to other (sub-national) levels of government. Any group of actors *willing* to change both dimensions of the weapons law and actually *able to change one dimension* should thus also be *able to change the other dimension*. If regulatory change occurs, this change is more likely to reflect a diagonal shift than when procedural differences existed between the two dimensions rendering it much more difficult to change one of them.

To see how the existence of procedural differences can complicate diagonal regulatory shifts, a look at German sports betting regulation can be informative. In this context, the competences to define behavioral boundaries and the consequentiality of noncompliance are spread across different levels of government. Specifically, the question of what kinds of sports betting are legal and illegal falls within the competence of the regional governments (Länder). They decide whether citizens are kept from placing sports bets by prohibiting the activity completely, whether citizens can legally engage in sports betting through a (regional) monopolist, or whether they can legally access sports bets offered by private operators located in Germany and abroad.[3] Currently, the Länder define these behavioral boundaries through an Interstate Treaty (Glücksspielstaatsvertrag) which they negotiate among each other. While this treaty defines behavioral constraints, it does not define the sanctions imposed on participants in illegal sports betting. These sanctions are defined at the federal level. Specifically, paragraph 285 of the German penal code defines that the participation in illegal gambling is sanctioned with six months of imprisonment. This prison sentence can be substituted with a fine. The institutional environment within which behavioral constraints in Germany in the context of sports betting are defined thus differs greatly from the institutional environment within which the consequentiality of noncompliance is defined. The group of actors which is able to adopt a reform of behavioral constraints is thus not automatically able to also change the sanctioning dimension. These procedural differences make the coordinated diagonal shift of sports betting regulation unlikely or at least more difficult than in other policy sectors. From this perspective, it is thus not surprising that the latest reforms of sports betting regulation in Germany have shifted regulatory output in a vertical direction and not in a diagonal direction.[4]

6. Conclusion

Balancing the protection of individual liberties and collective intervention for the sake of the public good constitutes a fundamental challenge for modern states. The ability of any theory to explain shifts in this balancing process crucially depends on what we perceive these shifts to be. The need for thorough conceptual tools is what motivated this paper.

Essentially, the paper is structured into two main parts. In the first part, we presented our conceptual approach. In the second, theoretical, part, we discussed under what conditions two-dimensional regulatory shifts become more or less likely.

Conceptually, we presented a measurement scheme capturing the degree to which governments interfere with individual liberties across different fields of regulation. Specifically, we proposed a two-dimensional concept taking account of (a) the degree of behavioral restrictions by rules and (b) the level of sanctions in case of rule deviations. This distinction reveals four styles of regulatory outputs: authority, lenient authority, punitive permissiveness, and permissiveness. We have demonstrated that this scheme offers a highly differentiated assessment of regulatory change and, in particular, sheds light on dimensions that might otherwise be overlooked, hence avoiding potentially misleading conclusions with regard to the cross-national similarity of regulatory approaches.

We consider our contribution a first step towards improving our understanding of regulatory change and, in particular, as a tool for identifying and comparing changes in regulatory styles. Thus, we are well aware of the fact that our concept focuses on a specific dimension of public regulation, namely the balance between individual rights and collective goals. While this dimension is certainly crucial, our approach at the same time is not sensible to other dimensions that might be of equal relevance, such as, for instance, issues of social equality.

Moreover, we should emphasize that we restricted our analysis to regulatory outputs, hence excluding the dimensions of policy outcomes and policy impacts. A systematic integration of the implementation stage into our analysis constitutes an important aspect that should be addressed in future research. In this context, especially the link between different regulatory styles and implementation effectiveness might be a promising research avenue.

Notes

1. See Knill et al. (2015) for the application of the measurement concept to a broad range of sectors including the regulation of prostitution, euthanasia, abortion, gambling, homosexuality, drugs, and pornography
2. This relates to possession licenses, not to carriage licenses.
3. This option is usually more attractive than bets offered by state monopolists because private operators are able to offer much better odds.
4. Specifically, behavioral constraints have been relaxed since the former monopoly was abolished and citizens were granted legal access to 20 licensed private operators of sports bets while the sanctions for participation in illegal sports betting (i.e. participation in bets offered by operators other than the 20 licensed operators) were kept at the same level.

References

Adam, C. and Raschzok, A., 2014, Explaining trends in addictive behaviour policy – the role of policy coherence. *International Journal of Drug Policy*, **25**(3), pp. 494–591. doi:10.1016/j.drugpo.2014.02.013

Badie, B. and Birnbaum, P., 1983, *The Sociology of the State* (Chicago: University of Chicago Press).

Bauer, M. W. and Knill, C., 2014, A conceptual framework for the comparative analysis of policy change: Measurement, explanation and strategies of policy dismantling. *Journal of Comparative Policy Analysis: Research and Practice*, **16**(1), pp. 28–44. doi:10.1080/13876988.2014.885186

Chatwin, C., 2011, *Drug Policy Harmonization and the European Union* (Basingstoke: Palgrave Macmillan).

Dyson, K. H. F., 1980, *The State Tradition in Western Europe: A Study of an Idea and Institution* (Oxford: Oxford University Press).

Feick, J. and Jann, W., 1988, „Nations matter" — Vom Eklektizismus zur Integration in der vergleichenden Policy-Forschung? in: M. G. Schmidt (Ed) *Staatstätigkeit* (Wiesbaden: VS Verlag für Sozialwissenschaften), pp. 196–220.

Freeman, G. P., 1985, National styles and policy sectors: Explaining structured variation. *Journal of Public Policy*, **5**(4), pp. 467–496. doi:10.1017/S0143814X00003287

Holzinger, K. and Knill, C., 2008, The interaction of competition, co-operation and communication: Theoretical analysis of different sources of environmental policy convergence. *Journal of Comparative Policy Analysis: Research and Practice*, **10**(4), pp. 403–425. doi:10.1080/13876980802468857

Hood, C., 1986, *The Tools of Government* (Chatham: Chatham House).

Hood, C. and Margetts, H. Z., 2007, *The Tools of Government in the Digital Age* (Basingstoke: Palgrave Macmillan).

Howlett, M., 2002, Understanding national administrative styles and their impact upon administrative reform: A neo-institutional model and analysis. *Policy and Society*, **21**(1), pp. 1–24. doi:10.1016/S1449-4035(02)70001-5

Howlett, M., 2003, Administrative styles and the iimits of administrative reform: A neo-institutional analysis of administrative culture. *Canadian Public Administration/Administration Publique Du Canada*, **46**(4), pp. 471–494. doi:10.1111/capa.2003.46.issue-4

Hughes, C. E. and Stevens, A., 2012, A resounding success or a disastrous failure: Re-examining the interpretation of evidence on the Portuguese decriminalisation of illicit drugs. *Drug and Alcohol Review*, **31**(1), pp. 101–113. doi:10.1111/dar.2012.31.issue-1

Knill, C., 1998, European policies: The impact of national administrative traditions. *Journal of Public Policy*, **18**(1), pp. 1–28. doi:10.1017/S0143814X98000014

Knill, C., 2001, *The Europeanisation of National Administrations: Patterns of Institutional Change and Persistence* (Cambridge: Cambridge University Press).

Knill, C., 2013, The study of morality policy: Analytical implications from a public policy perspective. *Journal of European Public Policy*, **20**(3), pp. 309–317. doi:10.1080/13501763.2013.761494

Knill, C., Adam, C. and Hurka, S., 2015, *On the Road to Permissiveness? Change and Convergence of Moral Regulation in Europe* (Oxford: Oxford University Press).

Lappi-Seppälä, T., 2008, Trust, welfare, and political culture: Explaining differences in national penal policies. *Crime and Justice*, **37**(1), pp. 313–387. doi:10.1086/525028

Lowi, T. J., 2011, Foreword: New dimensions in policy and politics, in: R. Tatalovich and B. W. Daynes (Eds) *Moral Controversies in American Politics* (4th ed.), (Armonk: M.E. Sharpe), pp. xi–xxiii.

Lowi, T. J., 1972, Four systems of policy, politics, and choice. *Public Administration Review*, **32**(4), pp. 298–310. doi:10.2307/974990

Richardson, J., Gustafsson, G. and Grant, J., 1982, The concept of policy style, in: J. Richardson (Ed) *Policy Styles in Western Europe* (Winchester: George Allen & Unwin), pp. 1–16.

Van Waarden, F., 1995, Persistence of national policy styles, in: B. Unger and F. Van Waarden (Eds) *Convergence or Diversity? Internationalization and Economic Policy Response* (Aldershot: Avebury), pp. 333–372.

Vogel, D., 1986, *National Styles of Regulation: Environmental Policy in Great Britain and the United States* (Ithaca: Cornell University Press).

Vogel, D. and Kagan, R. A. (Eds), 2004, *Dynamics of Regulatory Change: How Globalization Affects National Regulatory Policies* (Berkeley: University of California Press).

Zysman, J., 1994, How institutions create historically rooted trajectories of growth. *Industrial and Corporate Change*, **3**(1), pp. 243–283. doi:10.1093/icc/3.1.243

Global Governance Indices as Policy Instruments: Actionability, Transparency and Comparative Policy Analysis

TERO ERKKILÄ

ABSTRACT *Global country rankings have faced criticism for their normative character and methodology. Because of this, there have been attempts at creating so-called actionable governance indicators that provide more detailed and reform-oriented measurements of governance. This article analyzes the policy process behind the rise of actionable governance indicators and related changes in the production and use of indicators. It argues that the evolution of measurements can be understood as a process of field structuration, where various actors are entering the field of global governance assessments with rival indicator sets. But as the new actors tend to reproduce ideas and practices that already exist in the field, there are rather limited methodological improvements in the indices. However, the new actionable indicators are likely to become more influential policy instruments than rankings. This can be seen as an unintended outcome of the critique of ranking that has sparked the development of actionability. Measurements of transparency are used for analyzing the changes in the field of global governance indicators.*

Introduction

Economic globalization has intensified countries' competition for investment and wealth (Garrett 1998; Drezner 2004). Many view public institutions as a core element of economic competitiveness (Fukuyama 2004; North 2005), and countries are ranked globally with regard to their state of "governance". Such measurements are tightly linked to the notion of good governance, most notably promoted by the World Bank (Erkkilä and Piironen 2014). Since their emergence in the 1990s, governance indices have become a central policy instrument of transnational governance. While more traditional means for "transnational governance" build on direct interaction between actors (Mahon and McBride 2009), the rankings function largely indirectly through public naming and shaming. Even though there is no apparent mechanism of influence, the governance indices are said to have a strong steering effect on the countries that are being ranked, as policy actors adhere to the perceived norm (Löwenheim 2008; Erkkilä and Piironen 2009; Buduru and Pal 2010; Merry 2011; Davis et al. 2012).

Recently, there has been a shift in the way governance is assessed globally, as more nuanced and detailed numerical assessments, often referred to as second-generation or actionable indicators, are challenging rankings (Knack et al. 2003; Trapnell 2011). According to Knack et al. (2003), second-generation indicators are characterized by four criteria: (1) transparency, meaning that they should be replicable, well-documented and that the data sources are not politically controversial; (2) availability, meaning that the data has broad country coverage and continuity over time; (3) quality and accuracy, meaning consistency across countries and validity of measurements; and (4) specificity, meaning that indicators measure specific institutions or output and that exogenous factors do not unduly affect the measurements. Index-producers have also called these new types of indicators "actionable" governance indicators because they – unlike rankings – allow close monitoring and development of specific aspect of governance, providing guidance on reforms (World Bank 2009; Trapnell 2011). Actionable indicators are also often referred to as "mappings", as they allow different representation of data, instead of just single aggregate number. To summarize, the key characteristics of actionable indicators are their detailed non-aggregated measurements and explicit aim of causality – in other words, an established link between the use of indicators and the subsequent actions.

We can understand this shift in the production of governance indicators as field structuration, where new actors are joining the field of global governance assessments with competing sets of indicators (Kauppi and Erkkilä 2011). In trying to secure a position in the field, the actors engage in the production of competing classifications of reality. Such classification struggles also entail political conflict. But for the political conflict to become manifest, it first has to be discovered.

Palonen identifies "politicization" as a process where the political character of some phenomena or process is detected (Palonen 2003). This opens a new horizon for action as the previous status quo is challenged, making the issue a subject of renegotiations. Numbers are seemingly neutral and their political character often remains tacit (Porter 1996; Desrosierères 1998). Their politicization is therefore important in the evolution of governance measurements, as it opens an opportunity for change, allowing new actors and ideas to enter the field. As this article will show, the shift towards actionable governance indicators was sparked by the politicization of country rankings.

One characteristic of structuration is the unintentional reproduction of practices already existing in the field (Giddens 1984). This can have unintended consequences for governance reform, as actors claiming to change existing practices come (often unconsciously) to replicate them (Baert 1991). New actors wishing to join the activity of governance measurements need to legitimate their knowledge products according to the criteria set by the epistemic community existing in the field (Haas 1992). As a result, the new indicators are likely to conform to the existing normative and causal beliefs and criteria of validity.

The indicators are also policy instruments, functioning as means for collecting information but also as effective tools of government in trying to influence the outside world (Hood and Margetts 2007, p. 3). Hence, changes in their outlook have implications for their mechanisms of influence. With regard to ranking, we could understand the mechanism of influence as Foucauldian governmentality, where actors adhere to a perceived norm constructed by the rankings (Löwenheim 2008; Erkkilä and Piironen 2009). Such "government at a distance" (Miller and Rose 1990), where the actors external to the governed body are creating norms and setting goals that come to steer activities, is particularly evident in the actionable governance indicators that explicitly aim to become effective tools of policymaking by creating goals of governance that can be observed from a distance. This resembles the social and institutional practices of accounting and auditing (Hopwood and Miller 1994; Power 1999), which we now see in the new domain of global indicators.

In the following, I explore the shift from rankings to actionable governance indicators with regard to (1) the underlying policy process, (2) the evolution of the field of (good) governance indicators, and (3) their changing character as policy instruments. My aim is to answer the following two questions: (i) how has the field of global governance measurements evolved as the result of the shift towards actionable governance indicators; and (ii) how does this shift influence governance indicators as policy instruments?

I will focus on measurements of transparency, which is widely acknowledged to be a key component of good governance (Drechsler 2004; Zanotti 2005). Nevertheless, few governance indices or country rankings have actually measured transparency in the past, an indication of its poor measurability. Because of the shift from rankings to actionable governance indicators, transparency has also become a measurable attribute of good governance assessments. There is no universal definition of government transparency, but it is generally understood as access to government documents, involving also public information on statistics, budget and government performance, as well as an uncensored internet. Broadly, transparency concerns democratic control, freedom of speech and press, and economic performance (Stiglitz 1998; Best 2005; Fung et al. 2008). This broad understanding of transparency is reflected in the indicators selected for analysis.[1] This article uses a qualitative content analysis of public documentation of global governance indices, supplemented with process tracing based on additional interview material and selected news items.[2] The process tracing used triangulation, meaning that the observations had to be confirmed by other data sources or at least be consistent with the general narrative.

I will begin by looking at the policy process behind global ranking and related political controversies. I then examine the recent turn away from aggregate rankings towards the so-called actionable governance indicators that provide more detailed and customized data on governance. I conclude that actionability is leading the field towards more advanced measurements of good governance. But as the new actors entering the production of governance indicators are also replicating ideas and practices already existing in the field, changes in measurements remain limited. Actionable indicators are likely to become more influential policy instruments: they can be directly used to steer and monitor the policies of countries concerned, unlike rankings whose effects on national policies tend to be indirect. We can see this as an unintended consequence of the partially politically motivated critique of ranking that sparked the change towards actionable indicators, as it further embeds numerical assessment in transnational governance.

Policy Process: Governance Indicators and Critique of Ranking

Junctures in activities due to political conflicts are important in the development of the field of global governance assessments. As I show, the critique of country rankings, which is in part politically motivated, has been an important turning point in the structuration of the field.

Global governance indicators differ from the previous social-scientific attempts at comparing countries (Erkkilä and Piironen 2009). Whereas large country comparisons were previously done mostly by academics, the practice today is largely in the hands of international governmental organizations (the World Bank, United Nations Development Programme [UNDP], Organisation for Economic Co-operation and Development [OECD]), non-governmental organizations (NGOs, such as Transparency International, Freedom House), private businesses (such as Standard & Poor's) and linked associations (including the World Economic Forum [WEF] and Bertelsmann Foundation). Some are engaged in administrative or economic development, others are purely profit-making.

Also, the subject of measurement has shifted. Whereas previous academic assessments centered on the notion of democracy, the current country comparisons focus on good governance (Erkkilä and Piironen 2009, pp. 130–132). Many assessments root the notion of "good governance" in market liberalist and efficiency-seeking perceptions of institutions (Erkkilä and Piironen 2014) put forward by international organizations of economic development (Seppänen 2003; Drechsler 2004; Zanotti 2005).

We can connect the rise of the governance indices with the global concern over good governance and corruption (Ivanov 2009). In the World Bank, the issue of corruption was put firmly on the agenda in the mid-1990s, with the Director General referring in a public speech to the "cancer of corruption". The previously unspeakable word "corruption" was now out in the open, paving the way for attempts at assessing good governance globally. Another issue placing governance firmly on the agenda of the World Bank was the collapse of communism in Europe, leading to problems in building state capacity amid corruption and state capture in the former communist countries (for terminology, see Bagashka 2014).[3]

Coinciding with the general pressures for economic globalization, the concern over good governance led to the development of governance indicators. The first of its kind, and a model for many, was the World Bank Institute's *Worldwide Governance Indicators* (WGI). While the World Bank has used its *Country Policy and Institutional Assessment* (CPIA) tool since the mid-1970s for assessing eligibility for funding, the WGI were developed as a tool for general assessment on governance globally. This initially targeted specific problems of global governance, such as corruption. In the interviews conducted for this study, the developers of the WGI stated that as several existing measurements of corruption and accountability were not always coherent in their results, they devised the WGI to neutralize this variance by creating an aggregate number of available measurements. But the unanticipated effect of this technical solution was that it gave the figures high media visibility.

Aggregation allows ranking of nations based on their relative position on the various measurements, and the league table format has drawn a fair amount of media attention on certain global measurements. At the same time, the rankings have come in for criticism. Most notably, rankings have been controversial in countries that fare poorly in them, indicating the politicization of governance indicators. The WGI rankings have caused opposition within the World Bank and there have been mounting political pressures from countries receiving funding to abolish the rankings. In 2007, nine executive directors of the World Bank representing countries such as China, Russia, Mexico and Argentina expressed concerns about the WGI. Their criticism was not so much about the accuracy of the measurements but whether the World Bank should be producing such indices in the first place. One of the concerns was China's low ranking in the voice and accountability component of the WGI (Guha and McGregor 2007; see also Harding 2013). In the interviews I conducted for this study, the respondents stated that there had been a political controversy regarding the WGI rankings at the World Bank, which was also linked to the rise of actionable indicators within the organization. This can be interpreted as the politicization of governance indicators and rankings.

According to Palonen (2003), politicization means discovering the political potential of some existing phenomena or processes that were previously not acknowledged. Numbers are seemingly neutral and often perceived as social facts (Desrosierères 1998). Hence, the political character of the figures often tends to go unnoticed. Their politicization creates a new realizable horizon of chances and opportunities for action (Palonen 2003, p. 181–182). We can identify elements of politicization in the field of global governance indicators where the critique of ranking has led to attempts not only to readjust the methodology but also to redefine the goal of measurement.

The most visible critique of the rankings has been methodological, sparking a lively debate with and among the developers (Thomas 2010; Kaufmann et al. 2010, 2011). The criticism of the existing rankings – WGI in particular – has led to attempts to develop indicators that are more appropriate and methodologically advanced (McFerson 2009; Andrews et al. 2010; Gramatikov et al. 2011; Joshi 2011). Aggregation, the aim to produce single ranking numbers, has drawn much attention to the first generation of governance indicators (Langbein and Knack 2010). While the conceptualization of good governance, which is inclined towards market liberalism, has not been a broadly politicized topic, aggregation as a methodological choice has become a subject of political controversy. The WGI have been criticized for the use of aggregate figures by the OECD, which has been creating its own non-aggregated dataset. The development team of the WGI has also over time downplayed its optimism about aggregation (Erkkilä and Piironen 2014), and ultimately denounced ranking as a technique for comparing individual countries (Kaufmann et al. 2008, p. 5).

Another methodological debate addresses the validity of the measurements and the measurability of abstract issues (van de Walle 2006; Andrews 2008; Neumann and Graeff 2010; Barendrecht 2011; Ginsburg 2011). Moreover, the global indices might not always be apt for observing grassroots developments, and therefore even undemocratic events or crises might remain under their radar (Hinthorne 2011; Morgan 2011).

Also, the use of the good governance indicators has attracted interest, most notably concerning development funding (Hammergren 2011; Saisana and Saltelli 2011; Knoll and Zloczysti 2012). Here, observers have seen indicators such as the WGI to be relevant to development aid (Stubbs 2009). While the World Bank has not used the WGI in its allocation of funding, others have used the index for such purposes. The most prominent user of the governance indices in development funding has been the US government through its Millennium Challenge Corporation (MCC), established in 2004.

Concerning the politicization of rankings, we should note that the producers of rankings are not equally politically accountable for their activities. Transparency International as a transnational NGO has not been affected much by the critique of ranking, whereas the critique has caused international public organizations such as the World Bank and OECD to steer away from ranking, which is seen as politically controversial. As an NGO, Transparency International has little incentive to give up its rankings. On the contrary, its *Corruption Perception Index* (CPI) attracts wide media attention, which has also given the organization its prominent global position.

Nevertheless, criticism of rankings has led to a shift in the global field of governance assessment. The politicization of governance indicators and the related methodological debate has also enabled new actors to enter the field through their criticism of the old indicators. I will now turn to the qualitative shift towards "second-generation" or "actionable" (good) governance indicators through the case of transparency metrics.

Good Governance Indicators' Shift from Ranking to Actionability: The Case of Transparency

This section explores how the field of global governance measurements has evolved as a result of the shift towards actionable governance indicators. Transparency is now measured in global comparisons and this reflects the changes in the policy process of governance indicators and the related political controversies. We can see that the methodological development of transparency metrics can be understood in the context of field structuration in global measurements of good governance. The developments in the field not only demonstrate collaboration between the knowledge producers but also competition that becomes apparent only sporadically. On the one hand, the index producers are best described as an epistemic community that shares a policy enterprise with common normative and causal perceptions as well as data sources (Haas 1992; Erkkilä and Piironen 2009). On the other hand, different producers of governance indices compete with each other for visibility and users, and therefore create differing reality maps (Kauppi and Erkkilä 2011).

The development towards more "actionable" governance indicators has drawn attention to particular aspects of governance, instead of the ranking of countries. As the name indicates, the organizations behind actionable indicators are actively attempting to influence and improve the measured aspects of governance (Trapnell 2011). Whereas the early rankings did not necessarily measure transparency, the new second-generation rankings increasingly include various concrete assessments of it. The shift can be observed from Tables 1–4, showing development on the global measurements of good governance with regard to assessments of transparency. There are also new actors on the scene.

Good Governance Rankings and Transparency

The first rankings of good governance largely built on the ideas of the so-called "Washington Consensus", a notion that comprised the key causal beliefs of economic development of past decades, including the idea of avoiding information asymmetries in the market through transparency (Stiglitz 2002). The concept of "transparency" is referred to in Transparency International's fight against corruption and in the WEF's attempts at enhancing economic competitiveness (Lopez-Claros et al. 2006, p. 6). Still, only a few of the early governance indices specifically measure transparency. One reason for this has been that transparency is very difficult to operationalize and measure (cf. Hazell and Worthy 2010). Another reason for the absence of measurements on transparency has been the predominance of aggregate figures in the early governance indicators, leading to assessments that are highly abstract.

Table 1. Good governance indices measuring transparency

	Freedom in the World	Freedom of the Press	Corruption Perception Index (CPI)	Worldwide Governance Indicators (WGI)	Global Competitiveness Index (GCI)
Type of assessment	Ranking (single accumulated score)	Ranking (accumulated score)	Ranking (single accumulated number)	Six aggregate indicators	Ranking (single accumulated number)
Institution Year	Freedom House First year covered 1972 (launched in 1973) (annual)	Freedom House 1980 (annual)	Transparency International 1995 (annual)	World Bank Institute 1996–2002 (biennial), since 2002 annually	World Economic Forum Beta published in 2004–2005 report, official annual index since WEF 2005–2006 report
What is assessed?	Liberal Democracy	Freedom of media	Perceptions of corruption (bribery)	Governance performance	Economic performance
Criteria	Civil liberties and political rights as experienced by individuals	23 methodology questions and 109 indicators divided into three broad categories: the legal environment, the political environment, and the economic environment	Overall extent of corruption (frequency and/or size of bribes) in the public and political sectors	Voice and accountability, political stability, government effectiveness, regulatory quality, rule of law, control of corruption	Institutions, infrastructure, macroeconomy, health and primary education, higher education and training, market efficiency, technological readiness, business sophistication, innovation
Assessment of transparency	Assessment of government openness and transparency	Assessment of legal, political and economic environment for media	Precondition	Precondition	Precondition

Table 2. Good governance indices measuring transparency

	Fringe Special	Press Freedom Index	UN e-Government survey; the e-Government Readiness/Development Index (EGRI/EGDI)	UN e-Government survey; the e-Participation Index	Global Integrity Report; Global Integrity Index
Type of assessment	Mapping of freedom of information (FOI) legislation around the globe	Ranking	Ranking	Ranking complementing EGRI/EGDI	Yearly country-by-country ranking (since 2010 only a mapping)
Institution	Roger Vleugel and network of Dutch and foreign freelance journalists ("stringers")	Reporters without Borders	United Nations	United Nations	Global Integrity
Year	2001	2002 (annually)	Annually 2003–2005, since 2008 biannually	Annually 2003–2005, since 2008 biannually	As an index 2006–2009 (annually)
What is assessed?	The introduction, adoption, and approval of freedom of information laws in national, sub-, inter-, super- and supranational settings	The state of press and media freedom in countries	The government's efforts and application of transparency-enhancing ICT	Level of government provision of information to citizens (e-information) Interaction with stakeholders (e-consultation) and level of engagement in decision-making processes (e-decision-making)	Anticorruption mechanisms and government accountability at the national level

(*continued*)

Table 2. (*Continued*)

	Fringe Special	Press Freedom Index	UN e-Government survey; the e-Government Readiness/ Development Index (EGRI/EGDI)	UN e-Government survey; the e-Participation Index	Global Integrity Report; Global Integrity Index
Criteria	Stage and level of adopting FOI law according to three stages: (1) FOI laws in power (2) Government close to adopting FOI act (3) No sign of FOI act	Questionnaire with 44 indicative criteria regarding the state of press freedom	Composite index, based on three other composite indicators: 1/3 Online service index 1/3 Telecommunication infrastructure index 1/3 Human capital index	Level of government provision of information to citizens, interaction with stakeholders, level of engagement in decision-making processes	Quantitative data from country teams based on 300 actionable indicators regarding existence, effectiveness, and citizen access to key governance and anticorruption mechanisms
Assessment of transparency	Assessment of the adoption of FOI acts	Assessment of media, journalist and "netizen" freedom	Assessed under the "Online service index" as availability and accessibility of government information, policies, laws, regulation and databases	Assessment of online transparency aimed at involving and enhancing deliberative and participatory democracy	Assessment of access to government, access to monitor government and access to advocate for better governance

Table 3. Good governance indices measuring transparency

	Global Integrity Report; Integrity Scorecard	Open Budget Index	Open Net Initiative	Actionable Governance Indicators – Public Accountability Measures	Government at a Glance (GG)
Type of assessment	Mapping (successor of the index)	Mapping	Mapping	Mapping	Mapping
Institution	Global Integrity	International Budget Partnership	Open Net Initiative	World Bank	Organisation for Economic Co-operation and Development (OECD)
Year	Since 2010 (annually)	2006 (biannually)	Since 2007 (annually)	2008 (biannually)	2009 (first published)
What is assessed?	Existence, effectiveness and accountability of anticorruption mechanisms and citizen access to these	Public availability of budget information	Government-run internet filtration and censorship	Government transparency and accountability	Government performance
Criteria	(1) the existence of laws, anticorruption mechanisms and institutions that promote public accountability (2) the effectiveness of these (3) citizen access to mechanisms	Public access to budget information, opportunities for public participation in the budget process, and the ability to hold the executive accountable	Internet access to provocative or objectionable global website (constant for each country) and to provocative or objectionable local website (different for each country)	Income and asset disclosure, conflict of interest, freedom of information, immunity protections, ethics training	Political and institutional frameworks of government, government revenues and expenditures, employment, and compensation, government policies and practices on integrity, e-government and open government, human resources management, budgeting, procurement, and regulatory management

(*continued*)

Table 3. (Continued)

	Global Integrity Report; Integrity Scorecard	Open Budget Index	Open Net Initiative	Actionable Governance Indicators – Public Accountability Measures	Government at a Glance (GG)
Assessment of transparency	Assessment of transparency as an electoral issue, public administration and professionalism issue and budgetary oversight issue	Availability and comprehensiveness of budget documents	Measure of government censorship, government filtration and access to information	Assessment of legal framework, coverage of information, procedures of accessing information, exemptions to disclosure, FOI law's enforcement mechanism, deadlines for release of information, sanctions for non-compliance	Assessment of transparency as a legal principle and practice, in public procurement, and as clarity of regulations

Table 4. Good governance indices measuring transparency

	Global Right to Information (RTI) Rating	**Implementation Assessment Tool (IAT)**
Type of assessment	Rating	Rating
Institution	Center for Law and Democracy	Carter Center
Year	2011 (published first time)	2011 (piloted)
What is assessed?	RTI, access to information and strength of the legal framework for guaranteeing the RTI	Government compliance with adapted RTI laws and extent to which persons who request information can receive it
Criteria	61 indicators measuring seven overall categories: right of access, scope, requesting procedures, exceptions and refusals, appeals, sanctions and protections, promotional measures	Over 70 indicators related to government activities (leadership, rules, systems, and resources) and functions (responding to requests, automatic publication, and records management)
Assessment of transparency	Assessment of legal framework for guaranteeing the RTI	Assessment of the extent and quality of implementation of access to information legislation

In Tables 1–4, selected governance indices are classified for their type of assessment, producing institution, focus of assessment, assessment criteria and, in particular, their assessment of transparency or openness. The first ranking to assess transparency has been the *Freedom in the World* ranking by the Freedom House. Published as early as 1973, the ranking assesses liberal democracy, concentrating mainly on civil liberties and political rights. This has involved assessment of government openness and transparency. Then came another Freedom House ranking produced in 1980 – *Freedom of the Press* – that assesses transparency as an element of media environment, with regard to legal, political and economic conditions. These two rankings were for a long time only global rankings to address the issue of transparency, even measuring it.

Subsequently, two prominent rankings of good governance emerged in the mid-1990s, the *Corruption Perception Index* (CPI) by Transparency International and the WGI by the World Bank.[4] These two rankings are related to the general rise of good governance as a global concern in development economics coinciding with the paradigm shift in economics that stressed the role of information in the functioning of markets (Stiglitz 1998, 2002). However, neither of these rankings actually measures transparency. Instead, they refer to transparency as an explanation for the results of the rankings. The CPI and WGI are tightly linked to the WEF's *Global Competitiveness Index* (GCI) that was first published with the Forum's 2005–2006 report. These three rankings largely sum up the current standing of good governance: low corruption and transparency are keys to economic competitiveness. The links between the figures are not only ideological, as the GCI, CPI and WGI also share data sources in composing their indicators and validate their work against one another (Erkkilä and Piironen 2009), pointing to their interlinking on practical level.

Several other rankings that assessed transparency also emerged in the early 2000s. In 2002, the NGO Reporters without Borders launched its *Press Freedom Index*, which ranks countries on press freedom. Transparency is embedded in the rankings assessment of freedom in information media, journalism and internet use. Looking at transparency from the perspective of electronic government, the United Nations e-Government survey produced two rankings in the early 2000s, *e-Government Readiness Index* and *e-Participation Index* that measure the accessibility of government data and legislative information as well as the participatory aspects of online transparency. The *e-Government Readiness Index* measures the allocation of government information online and its use in digital service provision. The top ten ranked countries are largely the same as in the GCI and CPI. As part of the global drive for anticorruption (Ivanov 2009), Global Integrity launched its *Global Integrity Index* in 2006, assessing governments' anticorruption and accountability mechanisms. Here transparency is understood as citizens' access to government and its monitoring.

However, because of the mounting criticism of the use of rankings, there is a growing demand for non-aggregate figures, which have also influenced the way transparency is measured.

Towards Actionable Governance Indicators

While there have been some rankings to measure transparency, including initiatives by organizations such as Freedom House and Reporters without Borders, they have been complemented and challenged by non-aggregate, actionable governance indicators. This development has also caused shifts in the activities of established index producers. A concrete example of this was Global Integrity's 2010 discontinuation of the *Global Integrity Index*, a widely cited ranking. Instead, Global Integrity now publishes its annual *Global Integrity Report* with an Integrity Scorecard, which maps selected aspects of government integrity. The organization itself referred to two reasons for the shift from ranking to mapping (Global Integrity 2011). First, the number of countries ranked by Global Integrity had diminished over time, thereby losing the assessment's global element. Second, the rankings were seen as too blunt in their assessment of governance and as bringing no visible effects. This reflects the shift in the field of governance indices, away from the use of single aggregated figures towards more actionable and reform-oriented measurements.

Already in 2001, Roger Vleugel launched his *Fringe Special* initiative that compares freedom of information laws around the globe. While there have been similar initiatives (for example Freedominfo.org), the *Fringe Special* is perhaps the most up-to-date assessment of freedom of information acts, collected by a network of Dutch and foreign journalists. Fringe does not produce a ranking and the *Fringe Special* could be seen as an early form of "mapping" that has come to complement the good governance rankings. Because of the shift towards actionability, the Fringe listing has gained new users recently though it was launched a decade ago.

The transparency of finances has been a topical issue in good governance debates, and the International Budget Partnership has been collecting an *Open Budget Index* since 2006. This basically explores the public access to budget information (Seifert et al. 2013). Since 2007, the Open Net Initiative has produced a mapping of government censorship and filtration of the internet. We can also see the initiative as a representative of the second-generation governance indices that are critical about ranking countries, and instead make non-aggregate measurements of more specific qualities of governance.

Even large organizations of government reform such as the OECD have jumped on the bandwagon by producing second-generation indicators on government performance. The OECD's *Governance at a Glance* (GG, launched in 2009) is more sophisticated than the rankings of governance performance or competitiveness (GCI, WGI, CPI), as it aims for a multidimensional assessment. As a newcomer to the production of governance indices, the OECD has argued strongly for the need of this new knowledge product on the basis that as a non-aggregate figure it marks a methodological improvement to the existing rankings, most notably to the WGI (OECD 2006, pp. 7, 60, 2007, p. 3). Nevertheless, as with WGI, it measures governance in terms of its economic qualities (Erkkilä and Piironen 2014) and the assessments of transparency are centered on the notion of budget transparency, understood as the collection, allocation and use of performance information.

The interviews conducted for this study provided an interesting perspective on the relations of the OECD and the World Bank. Even if the OECD appears somewhat critical towards the work of the World Bank on the level of documentation, some of the people developing the GG at the OECD were actually World Bank staff on leave from the Bank. Experts of the World Bank have also held advisory board positions with Transparency International. Also, a member of the World Bank staff reviewed the transparency component of the OECD's GG. This is a good example of how the actors who join the field are – despite their outspoken criticism of established indicators – actually reproducing many of the existing practices and entering the epistemic community.

Also, the World Bank has developed a systematic response to the methodologically and politically motivated criticism of the WGI. The World Bank's governance and anticorruption strategy of 2007 endorses the use of "disaggregated and actionable indicators" (World Bank 2007, p. ix). Related to this, the World Bank has developed a set of indicators, named *Actionable Governance Indicators* (AGI), alongside its WGI. This new set of indicators is reform-oriented and more nuanced, striving for close observations on selected issues of governance (Trapnell 2011).

As members of an epistemic community, the key actors also share data. This has been the case with the first rankings, such as the WGI, GCI and CPI, but the "second-generation" or "actionable" governance indicators also build on the same logic. Most notably, the World Bank's AGI are fundamentally a collection of data produced by others. They aim to provide single access points to different indices that measure governance on a global scale. The AGI also contain their own *Public Accountability Measures* component that assesses the legal framework of freedom of information, coverage of information and procedures of accessing information. This aims at assessing not only legislation and reported procedures but also their implementation and institutional practices.

According to its developers, the AGI were launched not to compete with but to complement the WGI, though the AGI entered the scene as criticism towards the WGI was gaining ground, both within the Bank and outside. On a general level, the AGI utilize the growing supply of governance indices that is mostly of global nature. There are at present many small NGOs producing detailed measurements of certain aspects of governance that are becoming legitimate sources of information for large international organizations such as the World Bank.

The two last items in the classification of the transparency indices (Table 4), the *Global RTI Rating* by the Center for Law and Democracy and the Carter Center's *Implementation Assessment Tool* (IAT), are representative of this new development. Launched in 2011, they measure the right to information from a legal perspective (*Global RTI Rating*) and government compliance (IAT). These two indicators are clearly part of the new second-generation governance indices that have opened the way for smaller actors in the field. A noteworthy aspect of the new actors' outlook is their North American origin (Global Integrity, Open Net Initiative, Center for Law and Democracy, Carter Center). Concerning the normative and causal beliefs, they all seem to follow the key ideas of good governance and the Washington Consensus, where transparency is seen as a tool for both democracy and efficiency. At present, there seems to be a grassroots-level development in the Washington, DC area, where many NGOs now work on transparency issues.

The new index producers characteristically collect data through collective effort, often utilizing country experts to make the assessments that are then centrally processed. For instance, Fringe relies on country experts and Global Integrity has even publicized its Indaba fieldwork platform for general use, allowing local transparency researchers to collect and exchange unified content. So far, the tool has been used by the Carter Center. While one criticism of rankings was that their methodology was unclear, the second-generation governance indices are considered transparent in terms of methodological choices (Knack et al. 2003).

Table 5 summarizes developments in the field. The actionable governance indicators have resulted in significant improvements in terms of methodology, providing detailed information on institutions and processes of the countries analyzed, whereas the previous rankings were limited to aggregate figures. The actionable indicators only provide disaggregated data, which has shifted the focus towards individual institutional aspects, such as the state of transparency.

While the politicization of the ranking technique may have provided the second-generation index producers an opportunity to enter the field, non-aggregate figures are not likely to create news headlines and the information they provide is aimed more at expert audiences. Therefore, the actionable indicators are not competing for media visibility, which makes it easier to collaborate on data production.

At first glance, the field of governance indices might appear as a competition among different data producers, but it is perhaps best understood as an epistemic community that shares many normative and causal beliefs on good governance as well as related policy objectives. While the rankings were informed by the so-called Washington Consensus and

Table 5. Rankings and actionable governance indicators as policy instruments

	Rankings on (good) governance	Actionable governance indicators
Presentation of results	Single aggregate figure	Disaggregated data
Specificity of results	General information on systemic level	Detailed information on institutions and processes
Producers	International organization in development economics but also NGOs	Mostly NGOs but also international organizations
Data production	Collaboration and competition between major players	Intensified collaboration between data producers
Use of rankings	General level assessments, comparisons	Monitoring
Mechanism of influence	Naming and shaming, adherence to norm	Expert knowledge, peer pressure, funding

had institutional ties to the major organizations of economic development, the second-generation indicators are in many ways part of the same movement, now only produced by smaller NGOs. At least in the case of transparency metrics, there are hardly any challenges to the ideological premises of the rankings and the actionable indicators are in many ways reproducing the market-oriented core beliefs of good governance (cf. Drechsler 2004; Zanotti 2005). In this respect, the critique of ranking may have politicized the aggregate indicators in terms of data presentation, but the attributes of "good governance" as the subject of measurement have remained largely unchallenged.

It is typical of structuration (Giddens 1984) that the new actors involved in measuring governance reproduce, often unintentionally, existing practices by legitimating their knowledge products according to the criteria set by those actors already present (Haas 1992). Consequently, the new indicators conform to pre-existing normative and causal beliefs and criteria of validity. This may be an unintended consequence of the struggle to create alternative figures, as actors claiming to change existing practices of governance measurements end up reproducing them (Baert 1991).

But while the qualitative changes in the rankings are limited, there are significant changes in the uses and mechanisms of influence of governance indicators.

Indicators as Policy Instruments: Uses and Mechanisms of Influence

Although we can see the shift from rankings to actionable governance indicators as a response to the political controversies around the normative coercion related to the early rankings, the second-generation indicators might in fact prove to be more influential policy instruments. As the global governance assessments made by external expert organizations are moving towards more fine-grained analysis, there is in addition an attempt at active improvement, also indicated by the term "actionability". But how does the shift towards actionability influence governance indicators as policy instruments?

One criticism of global rankings is their instrumental character in global governance, because the indicators establish normative hierarchies (Löwenheim 2008; Erkkilä and Piironen 2009; Buduru and Pal 2010; Merry 2011; Davis et al. 2012). Here, scholars have referred to Foucauldian ideas of governmentality in explaining the rankings mechanisms of influence – the rankings construct a norm that the actors on the national level feel obliged to obey (Miller and Nikolas 1990).

Paradoxically, while the index producers have no norm-giving authority over nation states, there seems to be an ideational hierarchy between index producers and the subjects of their measurements, with the former defining the norms of governance. Moreover, measurements tend to carry an idealization of what is being measured (Husserl 1970, pp. 34–35), making them appear as sought-after qualities. While the figures neatly fit the present understanding of global economic competition, measuring different elements of it, they also set policy goals for countries, to either maintain or improve their position. In this sense, the shift away from the aggregated figures could mean the dissolving of ideational hierarchies between index producers and their subjects of measurement. On the other hand, the actionable governance indicators make the assessments even more instrumental, as countries' institutions and policies can now be monitored almost in real time (see Table 5). Here Global Integrity's description of its motivations for discontinuing its ranking in 2010 and instead producing an actionable indicator is revealing:

[T]he decision to cease publishing the Index was a conscious attempt to reinforce a key belief that we have come to embrace after many years of carrying out this kind of fieldwork: indices rarely change things. Publishing an index is terrific for the publishing organization in that it drives media coverage, headlines, and controversy. They are very effective public relations tools. But a single number for a country stacked up against other countries has not proven, in our experience, to be an effective policy-making or advocacy tool. Country rankings are too blunt and generalized to be "actionable" and inform real rebate and policy choices. (Global Integrity 2011)

The same argumentation is also visible in the World Bank's *AGIs* that aim at change:

AGIs reflect actionability, i.e., they establish the link between actions and indicator values. In short, AGIs provide greater clarity regarding the actions that governments can take to achieve better results on assessments of certain areas of governance. (World Bank 2014)

The OECD also cites the need for detailed data for improving governance performance and that its GG dataset allows governments to "benchmark their performance against other countries" (OECD 2011). Despite their disaggregated form, the new actionable datasets provide detailed information that allows country comparisons on specific topics. This expert knowledge creates peer pressure to comply with policy prescriptions (see Table 5). However, there are indications that these new measurements are becoming even more influential as policy instruments, serving as criteria for the allocation of funding.

There are initiatives for using the actionable indicators in the allocation of financial aid. A good example of this is the work of the US government Millennium Challenge Corporation, mentioned above. This is one of the few donors in development funding that bases its decision-making on third-party data such as the WGI, but also increasingly actionable governance indicators.

In the revision of MCC's financing criteria for 2012, the "voice and accountability" component based on WGI data was replaced by a component of "transparency" using data from Fringe and Open Net Initiative. In the interviews conducted for this study, the respondents pointed to the availability of data as a motivation for this change. This shifted the focus towards measuring transparency and using it as a criterion for policy recommendations and development.

The same trend can be observed within the World Bank, as the AGI initiative also includes assessments of freedom of information legislation in different countries through the *Public Accountability Measures* component (produced by the World Bank) as well as several external data sources. Consequently, the AGI function as an observation tool that provides detailed information on transparency from various perspectives. The aims of the AGI are also directly reform-oriented (Trapnell 2011) and the respondents interviewed at the Bank even described it as a potential tool to complement the country visits to the countries receiving funding.

While the first-generation country rankings incurred much criticism from experts and national policy actors, this has been less so with the second-generation indices, even though the indices are likely to be more influential as policy instruments. Bearing in mind that the shift towards actionable indicators was sparked by criticism of rankings, the ensuing reforms have had the paradoxical effect of further strengthening the role of governance indicators in transnational governance.

Conclusions

Global good governance indices are seemingly apolitical, and yet they increasingly steer the debates at domestic level and provide ideas for reform. The rankings have been criticized for imposing policy prescriptions on countries. This politicization of rankings has caused a shift towards non-aggregated indicators that are not presentable in rank order. The measured attributes of "good governance" have gone unchallenged. So-called actionable governance indicators have provided more advanced measurements of governance, and there is now more diversity in the measurements of good governance, as the analysis of transparency metrics shows. But the underlying normative and causal beliefs and desired policy outcomes are mostly unchanged.

The shift towards actionability has also brought in new players to the global field of governance assessment. While the rankings have been produced by international public organizations and larger NGOs, the actionable indicators are mostly produced by smaller NGOs with a very specialized focus. But although there is discernible competition between the old and new actors, there are also indications of ever-tightening collaboration between the knowledge producers through sharing of data. Typical for the process of structuration, the new actors joining the field come to reproduce many of the existing practices. Rather than providing a critical alternative to the existing figures, they have come to join the epistemic community of index producers.

As policy instruments, governance indicators have contributed to the global diffusion of policies that promote good governance. The shift away from rank orders and aggregate figures could be understood as a move away from the hierarchical relations of the index producers and the subjects of measurements. But in reality, actionable governance indicators are potentially more influential policy instruments. They can be directly used in monitoring development on the national level, also having more direct impact on funding of certain countries. At the same time, the production of indicators is shifting towards small NGOs that do not have a stake in the allocation of development funds.

Because the second-generation governance indicators focus on particular aspects of governance, such as transparency, they make it a subject of almost real-time observation. In this respect, actionable governance indicators are more appropriate observation tools than the league tables. The ever-closer observation of specific aspects of governance enables policy intervention, making the actionable indicators part of a process where institutional practices of nation states are constantly evaluated and actively steered by international organizations. While the rankings may have had indirect effects on national policies, through naming and shaming, the actionable indicators are likely to become more influential through their direct use as policy instruments. This can be seen as an unintended consequence of the critique of ranking that initiated the development towards actionable governance indicators.

Acknowledgments

I would like to thank the anonymous reviewers for their helpful comments on earlier drafts. Max Eklund helped with the collection of data. Caroline Werner and Mark Waller helped with editing and proofing the manuscript.

Funding

I would like to thank the Academy of Finland for research funding [grant number 268181].

Notes

1. The indicators analyzed for this study were selected using two criteria. First, the indicators had to have global country coverage. Second, the indicators had to concern (good) governance and transparency.
2. In January 2012, I interviewed six experts in Washington, DC, representing the World Bank, World Bank Institute and Millennium Challenge Corporation.
3. Bagashka has defined state capture as formulation of new laws and regulations for private interest, whereas corruption is understood as implementation of existing rules for personal gain (Bagashka 2014).
4. The WGI do not provide a single ranking but instead only results for six aggregate indicators.

References

Andrews, M., 2008, The good governance agenda: Beyond indicators without theory. *Oxford Development Studies*, **36**(4), pp. 379–407. doi:10.1080/13600810802455120

Andrews, M., Hay, R., and Myers, J., 2010, Can governance indicators make sense? Towards a new approach to sector-specific measures of governance. *Oxford Development Studies*, **38**(4), pp. 391–410. doi:10.1080/13600818.2010.524696

Baert, P., 1991, Unintended consequences: A typology and examples. *International Sociology*, **6**(2), pp. 201–210. doi:10.1177/026858091006002006

Bagashka, T., 2014, Unpacking corruption: The effect of veto players on state capture and bureaucratic corruption. *Political Research Quarterly*, **67**(1), pp. 165–180. doi:10.1177/1065912913492584

Barendrecht, M., 2011, Rule of law, measuring and accountability: Problems to be solved bottom up. *Hague Journal on the Rule of Law*, **3**(2), pp. 281–304. doi:10.1017/S1876404511200071

Best, J., 2005, *The Limits Of Transparency: Ambiguity and the History of International Finance* (Ithaca: Cornell University Press).

Buduru, B. and Pal, L. A., 2010, The globalized state: Measuring and monitoring governance. *European Journal of Cultural Studies*, **13**(4), pp. 511–530. doi:10.1177/1367549410377144

Davis, K. E., Kingsbury, B., and Merry, S. E., 2012, Indicators as a technology of global governance. *Law & Society Review*, **46**(1), pp. 71–104. doi:10.1111/j.1540-5893.2012.00473.x

Desrosierères, A., 1998, *The Politics of Large Numbers: A History of Statistical Reasoning* (Cambridge, MA: Harvard University Press).

Drechsler, W., 2004, Governance, good governance, and government: The case for Estonian administrative capacity. *Trames*, **8**(4), pp. 388–396.

Drezner, D. W., 2004, The global governance of the internet: Bringing the state back. *Political Science Quarterly*, **119**(3), pp. 477–498. doi:10.2307/20202392

Erkkilä, T. and Piironen, O., 2009, Politics and numbers: The iron cage of governance indices, in: R. W. III Cox (Ed) *Ethics Integrity in and Public Administration: Concepts and Cases* (Armonk: M.E. Sharpe), pp. 125–145.

Erkkilä, T. and Piironen, O., 2014, (De)politicizing good governance: The world bank institute, the OECD and the politics of governance indicators. *Innovation: The European Journal of Social Science Research*. doi:10.1080/13511610.2013.850020

Fukuyama, F., 2004, *State-Building: Governance and World Order in the 21st Century*, (Ithaca: Cornell University Press).

Fung, A., Mary, G., and David, W., 2008, *Full Disclosure: The Perils and Promise of Transparency*, (Cambridge: Cambridge University Press).

Garrett, G., 1998, Global markets and national politics: Collision course or virtuous circle? *International Organization*, **52**(4), pp. 787–824. doi:10.1162/002081898550752

Giddens, A., 1984, *The Constitution of Society: Outline of the Theory of Structuration*, (Cambridge: Polity Press).

Ginsburg, T., 2011, Pitfalls of Measuring the Rule of Law. *Hague Journal on the Rule of Law*, **3**(2), pp. 269–280. doi:10.1017/S187640451120006X

Global Integrity, 2011, *The* Global Integrity *Report: 2011 Methodology White Paper*. Available at http://www.globalintegrity.org/report/methodology/white-paper.

Gramatikov, M., Barendrecht, M., and Verdonschot, J. H., 2011, Measuring the costs and quality of paths to justice: Contours of a methodology. *Hague Journal on the Rule of Law*, **3**(2), pp. 349–379. doi:10.1017/S1876404511200101

Guha, K. and McGregor, R., 2007, World Bank Directors Test Zoellick. *Financial Times*, 12 July. Available at http://www.ft.com/intl/cms/s/0/fe1d7ece-30d8-11dc-9a81-0000779fd2ac.html#axzz2883nwxuM.

Haas, P. M., 1992, Introduction: Epistemic communities and international policy coordination. *International Organization*, **46**(1), pp. 1–35. doi:10.1017/S0020818300001442

Hammergren, L., 2011, Indices, indicators and statistics: A view from the project side as to their utility and pitfalls. *Hague Journal on the Rule of Law*, **3**(2), pp. 305–316. doi:10.1017/S1876404511200083

Harding, R., 2013, China Seeks to Water down Key World Bank Report. *Financial Times*, May 6. Available at http://www.ft.com/intl/cms/s/0/a1ca36d2-b654-11e2-b1e5-00144feabdc0.html#axzz2SmcKhrYs.

Hazell, R. and Worthy, B., 2010, Assessing the performance of freedom of information. *Government Information Quarterly*, **27**(4), pp. 352–359. doi:10.1016/j.giq.2010.03.005

Hinthorne, L. L., 2011, Democratic crisis or crisis of confidence? What local perceptual lenses tell us about Madagascar's 2009 political crisis. *Democratization*, **18**(2), pp. 535–561. doi:10.1080/13510347.2011.553371

Hood, C. and Margetts, H., 2007, *The Tools of Government in the Digital Age* (Basingstoke: Palgrave Macmillan).

Hopwood, A. G. and Miller, P., 1994, *Accounting As Social and Institutional Practice* (Cambridge: Cambridge University Press).

Husserl, E., 1970, *The Crisis of European Sciences and Transcendental Phenomenology: An Introduction to Phenomenological Philosophy* (Evanston: Northwestern University Press).

Ivanov, K., 2009, Fighting corruption globally and locally, in: R. W. III Cox (Ed) *Ethics and Integrity in Public Administration: Concepts and Cases* (Armonk: M.E. Sharpe), pp. 146–154.

Joshi, D., 2011, Good governance, state capacity, and the millennium development goals. *Perspectives on Global Development & Technology*, **10**(2), pp. 339–360. doi:10.1163/156914911X582468

Kaufmann, D., Kraay, A., and Mastruzzi, M., 2008, Governance matters VII: Aggregate and individual governance indicators, 1996–2007. *World Bank Policy Research Working Paper No.4654* (Washington, DC: World Bank).

Kaufmann, D., Kraay, A., and Mastruzzi, M., 2010, Response to 'What do the worldwide governance indicators measure?' *European Journal of Development Research*, **22**(1), pp. 55–58. doi:10.1057/ejdr.2009.49

Kaufmann, D., Kraay, A., and Mastruzzi, M., 2011, The worldwide governance indicators: methodology and analytical issues. *Hague Journal on the Rule of Law*, **3**(2), pp. 220–246. doi:10.1017/S1876404511200046

Kauppi, N. and Erkkilä, T., 2011, The struggle over global higher education: Actors, institutions, and practices. *International Political Sociology*, **5**(3), pp. 314–326. doi:10.1111/j.1749-5687.2011.00136.x

Knack, S., Kugler, M., and Manning, N., 2003, Second-generation governance indicators. *International Review of Administrative Sciences*, **69**(3), pp. 345–364. doi:10.1177/0020852303693004

Knoll, M. and Zloczysti, P., 2012, The good governance indicators of the millennium challenge account: How many dimensions are really being measured? *World Development*, **40**(5), pp. 900–915. doi:10.1016/j.worlddev.2011.11.010

Langbein, L. and Knack, S., 2010, The worldwide governance indicators: Six, one, or none? *Journal of Development Studies*, **46**(2), pp. 350–370. doi:10.1080/00220380902952399

Lopez-Claros, A., Porter, M. E., Sala-i-Martin, X., and Schwab, K. (Eds), 2006, *The Global Competitiveness Report 2006-2007* (Houndmills: Palgrave Macmillan).

Löwenheim, O., 2008, Examining the State: A foucauldian perspective on international 'governance indicators'. *Third World Quarterly*, **29**(2), pp. 255–274. doi:10.1080/01436590701806814

Mahon, R. and McBride, S., 2009, Standardizing and disseminating knowledge: The role of the OECD in global governance. *European Political Science Review*, **1**(1), pp. 83–101. doi:10.1017/S1755773909000058

McFerson, H. M., 2009, Measuring African governance: By attributes or by results? *Journal of Developing Societies*, **25**(2), pp. 253–274. doi:10.1177/0169796X0902500206

Merry, S. E., 2011, Measuring the world: Indicators, human rights, and global governance. *Current Anthropology*, **52**(S3), pp. S83–S95. doi:10.1086/657241

Miller, P. and Nikolas, R., 1990, Political rationalities and technologies of government, in: S. Hänninen and K. Palonen (Eds) *Texts, Contexts, Concepts. Studies on Politics and Power in Language* (Helsinki: The Finnish Political Science Association).

Morgan, G., 2011, Traction on the ground: From better data to better policy. *Hague Journal on the Rule of Law*, **3**(2), pp. 380–396. doi:10.1017/S1876404511200113

Neumann, R. and Graeff, P., 2010, A multitrait-multimethod approach to pinpoint the validity of aggregated governance indicators. *Quality & Quantity*, **44**(5), pp. 849–864. doi:10.1007/s11135-009-9238-7

North, D. C., 2005, *Understanding the Process of Economic Change* (Princeton: Princeton University Press).

OECD, 2006, *How and Why Should Government Activity Be Measured in 'Government at a Glance'? OECD GOV Technical Paper 1, GOV/PGC(2006)10/ANN1* (Paris: OECD).
OECD, 2007, Towards better measurement of government. *OECD Working Papers on Public Governance 2007/1* (Paris: OECD).
OECD, 2011, Government at a glance 2011. Available at http://www.oecd.org/gov/governmentataglance2011.htm (accessed 24 May 2014).
Palonen, K., 2003, Four times of politics: Policy, polity, politicking, and politicization. *Alternatives*, **28**(2), pp. 171–186.
Porter, T. M., 1996, *Trust in Numbers*, (Princeton: Princeton University Press).
Power, M., 1999, *The Audit Society: Rituals of Verification*, (Oxford: Oxford University Press).
Saisana, M. and Saltelli, A., 2011, Rankings and ratings: Instructions for use. *Hague Journal on the Rule of Law*, **3**(2), pp. 247–268. doi:10.1017/S1876404511200058
Seifert, J., Carlitz, R., and Mondo, E., 2013, The Open Budget Index (OBI) as a comparative statistical tool. *Journal of Comparative Policy Analysis: Research and Practice*, **15**(1), pp. 87–101. doi:10.1080/13876988.2012.748586
Seppänen, S., 2003, *Good Governance in International Law*, (Helsinki: The Erik Castrén Institute).
Stiglitz, J. E., 2002, Information and the change in the paradigm in economics. *American Economic Review*, **92**(3), pp. 460–501. doi:10.1257/00028280260136363
Stiglitz, J., 1998, Distinguished lecture on economics in government: The private uses of public interests: Incentives and institutions. *The Journal of Economic Perspectives*, **12**(2), pp. 3–22. doi:10.1257/jep.12.2.3
Stubbs, R., 2009, The millennium challenge account: Influencing governance in developing countries through performance-based foreign aid. *Vanderbilt Journal of Transnational Law*, **42**(2), pp. 621–682.
Thomas, M. A., 2010, What do the worldwide governance indicators measure? *European Journal of Development Research*, **22**(1), pp. 31–54. doi:10.1057/ejdr.2009.32
Trapnell, S. E., 2011, Actionable governance indicators: Turning measurement into reform. *Hague Journal on the Rule of Law*, **3**(2), pp. 317–348. doi:10.1017/S1876404511200095
van de Walle, S., 2006, The state of the world's bureaucracies. *Journal of Comparative Policy Analysis: Research and Practice*, **8**(4), pp. 437–448. doi:10.1080/13876980600971409
World Bank, 2007, *Implementation Plan for Strengthening World Bank Group Engagement on Governance and Anticorruption*, 28 September. Available at http://siteresources.worldbank.org/PUBLICSECTORANDGOVERNANCE/Resources/GACIP.pdf (accessed 24 May 2014).
World Bank, 2009, Actionable Governance Indicators | Data. Available at http://data.worldbank.org/data-catalog/actionable-governance-indicators (accessed 24 May 2014).
World Bank, 2014, An explanation of AGIs. Available at https://www.agidata.org/Site/Explained.aspx (accessed 24 May 2014).
Zanotti, L., 2005, Governmentalizing the post-cold war international regime: The UN Debate on democratization and good governance. *Alternatives: Global, Local, Political*, **30**(4), pp. 461–487. doi:10.1177/030437540503000404

Informing Institutional Design: Strategies for Comparative Cumulation

AIDAN R. VINING AND DAVID L. WEIMER

ABSTRACT *Institutional features that vary across countries affect the operation of policy instruments. Researchers often leave these features unstated. The absence of a clear description of relevant institutional features not only interferes with effective borrowing of (first-order) policy instruments across national contexts, but also hinders the cumulation of research that could inform institutional design (second-order policy instruments). The authors propose a framework based on five characteristics of property rights (completeness of allocation, cost of alienation, security from trespass, credibility of persistence, and autonomy) to be assessed at three levels (individual, interorganizational, and intraorganizational) for facilitating accumulation of comparative information.*

Introduction

Political, economic, and social institutions facilitate and constrain the adoption and implementation of public policies. Researchers specializing in the study of public policy in a specific country can reasonably treat these features of the environment as constants generally understood by scholars, policy makers, and other audiences already familiar with that country. Because these constants are commonly known to other specialists, they are usually left unstated. Yet these institutional features vary across countries, so that researchers wishing to learn comparatively about such questions as the feasibility and efficacy of policy instruments face the difficult task of determining relevant institutional features and deciphering their impacts. More generally, scholars interested in understanding institutions face high costs in systematically classifying institutional differences across countries. Researchers can increase the contributions of their work to more appropriate policy "borrowing" and to the more productive study of the effects of institutions on public policy by being explicit about important institutional features that shape the use of the policy instruments that they study. In this essay, we propose a framework to help increase the chances that such reporting will be useful and cumulative.

We define institutions to be the persistent and anticipated sets of rules that affect the behavior of individuals. One tends to think of these rules as formal— constitutional provisions constraining government actions, monetary rules governing the value and use of paper money, laws establishing rights and duties of spouses. But they can also be informal—norms about how people should behave as public officials, employees and employers, and family members. The puzzle of why people submit to such rules, even when doing so appears not to be in their immediate self-interest, has become the project of the rational choice theory of institutions (Schotter, 1991; Milgrom, North, and Weingast, 1990; Kreps, 1990; Miller, 1992; Calvert, 1995). The puzzle of how institutions change, given their general persistence, is being addressed both theoretically and empirically (North, 1990; McChesney, 1990; Knight, 1992; Alston, Eggertsson, and North, 1996; Weimer, 1997). Unraveling these puzzles will ultimately open the door for a more systematic approach to designing institutions to accomplish policy goals.

Cross-country investigations of the consequences of alternative institutions for policy outcomes and the processes by which institutions change, or could be induced to change, offer an interesting basis for empirical research on the relationships between institutions and policy (Olson, 1996). Unfortunately, several factors hamper the comparative study of institutions and institutional change (Riker and Weimer, 1995). Put simply, researchers typically only have detailed familiarity with the institutions of a single country. Unless they share a common conceptual framework, the contributions of their individual efforts are unlikely to cumulate effectively into general knowledge.

Contributors to the *Journal of Comparative Policy Analysis* will be providing a wealth of information about the application of particular policy instruments in a variety of institutional settings. If this information provides adequate descriptions of institutional settings, then perhaps ten or fifteen years from now researchers will have the possibility of making systematic comparisons of the effects of institutional arrangements on the functioning of a number of types of policy instruments. Further, clear accounts of institutional settings may facilitate the empirical study of institutional change by providing a baseline for researchers who revisit particular policy contexts. In order to realize these possibilities, however, contributors must have some guidance on what information is adequate. We hope to open discussion on this question.

We proceed as follows. First, we distinguish between policy design (first-order policy instruments that directly affect behavior) and institutional design (second-order policy instruments that indirectly affect behavior by altering the processes that shape first-order policy instruments) in order to show how institutional design can be thought of in relation to policy instruments. Second, we propose a framework based on the distribution of property rights as a minimal description of institutional features. Within this framework, we consider the salient features of property rights systems operating at the individual, interorganizational, and intraorganizational levels. Third, we briefly illustrate how this framework can help increase the comparability of cross-national studies by sketching its application to organ harvesting and transplant policies in several countries.

First-order and second-order policy instruments

A number of intellectual streams in the policy sciences have drawn attention to policy instruments—the generic ways that governments can do things. Some students of implementation have argued that studying instruments qua instruments, rather than the more complex programs that they comprise, provides a more uniform unit of analysis that better facilitates the accumulation of knowledge about what types of government interventions work best in which particular circumstances (Bardach, 1980; Elmore, 1987; Salamon, 1981). Those interested in policy design from a policy analysis perspective see policy instruments as valuable starting points for crafting policy alternatives (Alexander, 1979,1982; May, 1981; Schneider and Ingram, 1988; Weimer, 1993), and have proposed lists, classifications, and menus of various sorts to organize policy instruments (Balch, 1980; Hood, 1986; Kirschen et al., 1964; MacRae, 1980; Salamon and Lund, 1989; Savas, 1987; Schneider and Ingram, 1990; Stone, 1988; Weimer and Vining, 1989). Other researchers seek to understand the interconnections between policy instruments and policy processes (Doern and Phidd, 1983; Ingraham, 1987; Kingdon, 1984; Linder and Peters, 1984, 1987, 1988, 1989; Lowi, 1972; May, 1991; Sabatier and Jenkins-Smith, 1993; Schneider and Ingram, 1997; Woodside, 1986).

These streams of literature emphasize "first-order" policy instruments—the rules, incentives, and other devices that are aimed directly at prohibiting, requiring, permitting, encouraging, or discouraging various behaviors with the manifest intention of promoting social values. An emphasis on first-order policy instruments directs attention to the final design itself. Further, it tends to place government in a very central role as the selector and implementer of a particular design. Yet, a great variety of processes, involving both public and private actors, can lead to first-order policy instruments. Recognition of these alternatives shifts the design problem from an emphasis on selecting a particular combination of first-order policy instruments as a final design to "second-order" policy instruments that could be used to initiate, facilitate, induce, or impede processes yielding desired incentives and rules. We use the term second-order to convey that these instruments affect the final design indirectly through their impacts on choices about design components rather than directly as the design components themselves.

Second-order policy instruments are the mechanisms of institutional design. Although political scientists and legal theorists have traditionally been interested in issues of institutional design, their emphasis has typically been on the achievement of procedural values rather than substantive outcomes (Gormley, 1987). In parallel with a renewed interest in the theory of institutions in the social sciences has come a growing interest in designing institutions to achieve substantive as well as procedural policy goals (Brandl, 1988; Bromley, 1989; North, 1990; Weimer, 1995; Olson, 1996). Specific applications include self-regulation (Bardach and Kagan, 1982), standard setting (Cheit, 1990), catalytic and hortatory versus coercive controls over bureaus (Gormley, 1989), the design of administrative and legislative procedures (McCubbins, Noll and Wein-gast, 1989), automatic program adjustments through indexing (Weaver, 1988), and inducing third-party monitoring through the creation of appropriable value (Weimer, 1992; Vining and Weimer, 1997), and the governance of policy networks (de Bruijn and ten Heuvelhof, 1995).

Borrowing first-order policy instruments across countries requires sensitivity to differences in institutional features if false steps are to be avoided. Borrowing second-order policy instruments requires an even deeper understanding of the institutional features that are different and their relationship to features that have remained constant. Indeed, this is exactly the challenge that those engaged in designing new institutional frameworks for the former Soviet Union and Eastern Europe face (Weimer, 1997). But how can researchers who wish to facilitate borrowing identify the most salient features from among the great detail they confront in actual institutions?

In the section that follows, we offer a particular framework based on characteristics of property rights. Although it is certainly not the only possible framework, we think it has two important merits. First, it draws on a large body of research that sees the features of property rights as fundamentally important in shaping economic behavior. By marginally adding to these features, and by applying them at both the individual and organizational levels, we arrive at a framework that encompasses political and social, as well as economic, interaction. Second, the framework is simple and therefore relatively easily applied by anyone with sufficient knowledge to write about policy instruments in a particular national context.

An expanded property rights framework

Many economic historians see the evolution of property rights mediated through institutions as a key institutional factor in shaping economic growth and social welfare (Schlatter, 1951; North and Thomas, 1973; Jones, 1981; Olson, 1996; Rosenberg and Birdzell, 1986; North, 1990). Property rights generally refer to relationships among people with respect to the use of things; as James Buchanan (1975, p. 9) puts it "[e]scape from the world of perpetual Hobbesian conflict requires an explicit definition of the rights of persons to do things." We define a property right for the purposes of this essay as follows: A property right is a relationship among people or organized groups of people with respect to the use of some thing. Note that the relationships can be de jure or de facto. Things most notably include tangible or intangible assets, and use encompasses a variety of activities from physical control to claims on the residual income produced by productive assets. What we commonly think of as ownership is typically a bundle of rights that tie together a variety of uses. Classifications of property rights have generally been in terms of the nominal owners of things: state property (owned by the government and overseen by bureaus), private property (owned by individual persons), common property (owned collectively by a defined group of persons), and open access property (owned by anyone who can gain physical access). While helpful for some purposes, such classifications do not do justice to the features of the complex relationships governing the use of things that shape that use. So, for example, economic theory makes clear predictions about the relative efficiency in the use of ideal private property as opposed to pure open access property (Weimer and Vining, 1992, pp. 53–57). But actual property rights rarely fit the ideal—nominally private property may be insecure because of weak legal systems; nominally open access property may be effectively private because a single actor can use force to exclude potential entrants.

A more functional description of property rights isolates those features most relevant for understanding behavior. Among these features are clarity of allocation, cost of alienation, security from trespass, and credibility of persistence (Riker and Weimer, 1993). As we wish to provide a broad framework for describing institutions, we augment Riker and Weimer's characterization with the degree of autonomy enjoyed by individuals and organizations in the exercise of property rights as one of the salient features. By autonomy we mean the extent to which an individual or organization retains discretion over the right in the face of competing duties and claims. Most rights have relatively low autonomy in the sense that they are on an equal footing with possibly competing rights. Nonetheless, individual rights to physical, and often spiritual, self-preservation typically enjoy high levels of autonomy in most societies in the sense that they override the exercise of more mundane claims that would impinge upon them.

Although the analysis here focuses on property rights we do not mean to imply that property rights are the only relevant, or possible, dimension of cross-country institutional comparison. Culture, natural resource endowments, income distribution, education, and many other factors may influence institutional development and efficiency. The literature, for example, on the relationship between democracy and economic growth is implicitly concerned with exactly such questions (Levine and Renelt, 1992; Helliwell, 1994; De Haan and Sierman, 1995; Alesina et al., 1996). Yet property rights as we broadly define them provide the building blocks that shape incentives in more complex institutional arrangements (Federand Noronha, 1987; Federand Feeney, 1991; Frant, 1996; Olson, 1996). Further, property rights are an excellent beginning point for comparative institutional analysis because of their empirical importance (see below), especially when they are interpreted broadly.

These five property right characteristics can be applied at three levels. The first, and broadest, level concerns the rules relevant to the behavior of an individual within the economic, political, and social spheres. It specifies the allocation of rights and duties among individuals. For example, in the case of a government income maintenance program, it would include specifications of eligibility and responsibility. The second level concerns the rules that govern the relationships among organizations. Because so much of what we do is within organizational contexts, these rules are as central as those governing the interaction of individuals. These rules include those that regulate contracting among organizations as well as the regulation of privately owned organizations by government agencies. Thus, they can be thought of as encompassing both horizontal and vertical relationships between organizations. In the case of income maintenance, it specifies the rights and obligations of the myriad public and private organizations that provide services to clients. The third level describes relationships within organizations. Again with respect to income maintenance, it specifies the duties and responsibilities of members of the organization delivering services to clients.

Note that we follow legal and economic theorists in intending property rights to be construed very broadly to include any claim by one party for which some other party has a corresponding duty to respect (Hohfeld, 1919; Buchanan, 1975). However, these claims and corresponding duties need not be formally specified in law. They may also take force informally through social conventions that coordinate behavior among people, as, for example, walking to the right on busy sidewalks, and norms through which individuals constrain their own behavior as, for example, engaging in reciprocity (Young, 1996).

Although we intend the framework to be the basis for systematic description of institutional features, we recognize that it has normative connotations. Especially with respect to the individual and interorganizational levels, the characteristics have a strongly implied normative direction. For example, more secure and credible rights are generally socially preferable to less secure and less credible rights on efficiency grounds. At least among economists, theory and evidence are generally interpreted as indicating that weak property rights (on any of the relevant dimensions) tend to engender wasteful uses of resources in either defending or appropriating them (Feder, Ouchon, and Chalamwong, 1988; Baumol, 1990; Feder and Feeney, 1991; Leblang, 1994; Torstenssen, 1994; Knack and Keefer, 1995; Brunetti, 1997). Additionally, political economists generally recognize that weak property rights open the door for wasteful competition for de facto ownership ("rentseeking," see Buchanan, Tollison, and Tullock, 1980). Nonetheless, these normative assessments are not the primary focus of our framework, which identifies the salient characteristics for understanding the consequences of institutional arrangements regardless of how one values those consequences.

In the discussion that follows, we consider each of the five characteristics for each of the three levels. With reference to Table 1, we consider each row in turn.

Completeness of allocation. The first step in describing institutional features involves identifying the rights to relevant goods. Every society allocates goods through some combination of de jure and de facto property rights. Although de jure rights tend to be clear, because they are explicitly stated, they are rarely exhaustive—statutory or common law cannot anticipate all possibilities of interaction between potential rights holders and potential duty bearers. The remaining goods become allocated through de facto rights based on historical use, ease of access, or other informal mechanisms. In relatively stable

Table 1. Property rights framework for specifying institutional arrangements.

	Private property rights	*Interorganizational property rights*	*Intraorganizational property rights*
Completeness of allocation	How specific are the bundles of rights individuals have over the use of things?	How clear are the rights of organizations vis-a-vis other organizations including the regulatory organs of government?	How clearly defined are rights and obligations within organizations?
Cost of alienation	How easily can individuals transfer rights to other individuals?	How easily can organizations transfer rights?	How easily can rights be transferred among organizational members?
Security from trespass	How costly is it for individuals to enforce legally held rights?	How costly is it for organizations to enforce their legally held rights?	How costly is it for individuals to protect their contractual rights with in organizations?
Credibility of persistence	How confident are individuals that currently held rights will not be involuntarily taken away?	How confident are organizational leaders that currently held rights will not be involuntarily taken away?	How confident are organizational members that currently held rights within the organization will not be taken away?
Autonomy	To what extent do individuals maintain rights over their own persons?	To what extent do organizations maintain rights to their own existence?	To what extent do individuals surrender personal rights as organizational members?

circumstances, de facto rights may become widely recognized and accepted, providing a clear allocation. Either changes in relative prices or the introduction of new technology that create the demand for new rights (Demsetz, 1967), or the influx of new populations that do not share norms supporting existing de facto rights, however, may make allocation, especially that done through de facto rights, incomplete. There was, for example, much less interest in the ownership of body organs prior to the development of medical transplant technology, including immunosuppressive drugs.

At the individual level, the completeness of allocation refers to the comprehensiveness of rights that specify the *recognized duties and claims of persons* with respect to other persons, organizations, and the state. The allocations are likely to be very clear or comprehensive for such simple goods as food, clothing, and shelter; they are likely to much less clear or comprehensive with respect to more complex goods such as parenthood and citizenship. The first step in describing the institutional arrangements in a particular policy area is to identify the relevant goods and determine how the rights to these goods are allocated. In general, unclear and incomplete rights are socially undesirable because they prevent people from anticipating the behaviors of others and engaging in long-run maximizing behavior.

At the inter-organizational level, the completeness of allocation refers to the comprehensiveness of the rights that specify the recognized duties and claims of organizations with respect to other organizations. It focuses on the interaction among corporate bodies, including legally defined corporations, informal organizations, and government agencies. Among the important aspects of this interaction are claims and duties with respect to information, jurisdiction, and resources. For example, what information must organizations provide to government agencies? Which organizations have political jurisdiction such as regulatory power? Which organizations, if any, have economic jurisdiction through franchises or legal monopolies? What obligations does government have to fund organizations or organizational functions? What restrictions, such as rules governing the distribution of financial residuals and assets, are placed on organizations? Mapping out the interorganizational relationships in a particular policy area involves first identifying which organizations are relevant and then specifying their respective claims and duties. As with the individual-level assessment, greater completeness and clarity generally contribute to greater social efficiency as organizations operate in environments that allow them to plan more rationally.

At the intraorganizational level, the completeness of allocation refers to the comprehensiveness of the rights that specify the recognized duties and claims of persons with respect to the organizations to which they belong. In many organizations, a wide range of duties and claims are specified only vaguely in terms of hierarchical relationships. Indeed, one rationale for the existence of firms, as opposed to production through spot-contracts among all the relevant factory owners, is that in many situations hierarchies offer lower transaction costs (Coase, 1937). Employees are likely to have some duties and claims formally specified by labor laws and contracts with their organizations. Many duties and claims, however, are likely to be left formally unspecified, for example, whether and under what circumstances children can visit the workplace of their parents. Similarly, it is unlikely to be formally specified as to whether one employee has a right to tell another employee a sexually suggestive joke. However, effective organizations generally have "corporate cultures" consisting of norms and conventions that create relatively clear expectations among organizational members about these formally unspecified claims and duties (Kreps, 1990; Miller, 1992).

Assessing intraorganizational allocations of goods involves identifying both the formal and informal rights that apply. In the case of government agencies delivering services to clients, for example, the duties and claims set out in civil service laws and manuals of procedures typically provide most of the formal framework, while norms, both specific to the organization and generally held by members of professions, provide the informal framework. In contrast to the individual and intraorganizational levels where greater completeness in terms of allocations through formal rights is often socially desirable, the very nature of organizations means that at the intraorganizational level greater comprehensiveness of formal rights is not necessarily socially desirable because they may generate excessive self-interested behavior and create rigidities that prevent organizations from flexibly responding to changing circumstances (Miller, 1992).

Cost of alienation. The value of specific property rights usually differ across individuals and organizations. An important characteristic of property rights is the ease with which they can be transferred from one party to another to permit gains from trade. The rights to a great many things in most societies can be transferred at low cost through exchanges in organized markets or the execution of standardized contracts. Where rights are complex, or bundled together in complicated ways, the need to negotiate specialized contracts may greatly increase the costs of alienation. So too do legal restrictions that drive transactions to black markets.

In terms of describing institutional arrangements, the relevant questions generally concern the extent to which government facilitates, restricts, or blocks specific transactions. With respect to individual-level rights, for example, most countries prohibit one from selling one's right to vote or selling oneself into slavery. At the interorganizational level, several types of organizations, such as nonprofits, are restricted in how they can use their financial resources. Government agencies usually cannot legally transfer their regulatory authorities to other governmental or private organizations. At the intraorganizational level, employees usually cannot sell their jobs to others, but labor laws typically make it easy for them to leave jobs voluntarily.

Security from trespass. Property rights are only effective if duty bearers respect them. Governments play an important formal legal role in determining how secure rights are from trespass through their administration of criminal, tort, contract, and real and intellectual property law as well their laws on "takings" (Knetsch, 1983; Epstein, 1985; Blume and Rubinfield, 1984; Schwindt and Globerman, 1996). They also play an important role via their toleration of endemic inefficiency, corruption, and cronyism, which may substantially undermine security in spite of high degrees of formal legal protection. Social norms also play an important role by helping to establish limits to behavior that is generally considered as legitimate. To the extent that legal systems and norms fail to protect property rights fully, claims holders can engage in self-protection, accept less than fully effective claims, or abandon the claims altogether. In combination, legal systems, social norms, and self-protection determine to what extent nominally recognized rights can be effectively exercised at each of the levels we consider. In general, greater security from trespass promotes greater social efficiency.

Credibility of persistence. Property rights play a fundamentally important role in allowing individuals and organizations to make efficient use of resources over time. Fear of losing currently held rights to assets sometime in the future discourages investment and conservation to preserve them. One of the central concerns of modern political economy that has immediate consequences for public policy is how governments strong enough to create secure property rights can credibly commit to preserving these rights in the future (North and Thomas, 1973; Rodrik and Zeckhauser, 1988; Diermeier et al., 1997). A meaningful description of institutional features in any policy area requires an assessment of the credibility of the relevant rights.

As almost any change in public policy alters some property rights, especially as viewed in the broader perspective we present here, government often faces a tradeoff between improving the allocation of property rights and the credibility of the property rights system overall. Constitutional protections, to the extent that they themselves are credible, may reassure individuals and organizations that rights will be preserved, or at least not taken without compensation. Political systems that encourage leaders to seek widespread support may also reassure rights holders who can expect such consensus building mechanisms as compensation and the use of "grandfathering" to be part of the policy making process. At the intraorganizational level, corporate cultures can help assure organizational members that norms will persist beyond the tenure of any particular organizational leader (Kreps, 1990). In spite of these mechanisms, the tension between credibility of persistence and efficiency-enhancing changes to property rights regimes raises many conceptual and predictive problems that present a rich research agenda.

Autonomy. In conceiving of property rights broadly, one confronts the limits of the interpretation of individuals as the objects of claims and duties. Certain classes of individuals, such as children and the mentally impaired, are often not granted the same degree of freedom of action as the general population. Other restrictions on claims and duties, such as those prohibiting slavery, apply generally to populations. Most societies view people as autonomous beings whose immediate interests of survival and dignity take precedence over many other claims and duties. Utilitarianism, which is fundamental to the economic perspective on property rights, treats individuals' utility as the cornerstone of both normative and positive analysis. There are, of course, many critics of this perspective. In particular, a variety of objections are raised against the actual or perceived "commodification" of everything that results from such a perspective (Kelman, 1981; Brown, 1992; Anderson, 1993; Radin, 1996).

Yet, even a "strong" view of people as autonomous beings inevitably involves restrictions on their autonomy in some spheres of activity (Buchanan, 1975). Completing a description of institutional arrangements requires an accounting of the degree of autonomy exercised by individuals and organizations. Restrictions related to the use of one's body, including discretion over the circumstances of the termination of its life, obviously arise at the individual-level. At the interorganizational level, autonomy refers to such questions as the rights of organizations to form, select their own leaders and internal property rights, and disband. At the intraorganizational level, one finds circumstances in which much autonomy is transferred from the individual to the organization, most obviously in prisons and the military, but also to some extent in more common contexts such as patients in hospitals and students in schools where choice, including that concerning exit, are somewhat restricted.

Illustrative application of comparison at the individual level

We illustrate cross-national variations in property rights with reference to human organ harvesting and transplant policies. We select this policy arena because property rights differ in important ways across countries. To some extent cross-country variability reflects the difficulty of making firm positive predictions about any particular policy regime. Perhaps more fundamentally, it reflects disagreements about important values such as commodification and autonomy. Almost everyone agrees that public policy must deal in some way with a "shortage" of appropriate organs for transplant (Waller, Haisch, and Skelly, 1992). Yet some observers analyze the shortage treating some aspects of property rights as exogenous, while others insist that it is the property rights regimes themselves that primarily create the shortage. Rather than try to resolve this debate, we seek to show the usefulness of the property rights framework for describing differences in the way countries govern the use of organs.

We briefly compare the property right regimes in Sweden, the United States, India, and China. For these illustrative purposes we focus on comparisons at the individual level and ignore both the interorganizational and intraorganizational levels of analysis, even though both of these levels raise many interesting property rights—and, therefore policy—issues. In the next section we briefly sketch the inter- and intraorganizational levels for the United States.

The individual-level analysis is summarized in Table 2, with the same row labels as in Table 1 and columns for Sweden, the United States, India, and the People's Republic of China. Sweden and the United States are economically developed countries with strong systems of general property rights; India and the People's Republic of China are developing economies with weaker systems of general property rights. De facto individual property rights with respect to human organs are much closerto de jure rights in Sweden and the United States than in India and the People's Republic of China.

For a considerable period of time beginning with the Act on the Use of Tissue and Other Biological Material in 1958, Sweden was typical of countries with "presumed consent" laws. In such countries, the state assumes ownership of organs in the absence of an express wish by the deceased or the next-of-kin that organs not be removed. There was no requirement that next-of-kin be informed about organ removal. In 1975 amendments were adopted that required notification where possible. Additionally, the amendments required that the physician responsible for the potential donor had to be a different individual than the physician of the potential recipient. The Transplant Act of 1987, however, replaced the principle of presumed consent with the principle of nonconsent. Unless there is written authorization by the deceased, explicit permission from the next-of-kin is required for organ harvesting. Neither the donor nor the next-of-kin can designate the potential recipient or, indeed, the institution that will be their agent. Sale of organs is proscribed, and the focus is upon the "unselfish act of giving" (Machado, 1996). Thus, alienation is limited to nonspecific gifts.

In 1995, to the surprise of most observers, the Swedish government proposed a return to presumed consent (Machado, 1996). Atthetime'of writing, legislation had been introduced but not yet adopted.

The property rights system relevant to organs can be summarized as follows: First, with respect to individual donors, the allocation of rights is complete and clear. Second, alienation is limited to nonspecific gifts. Third, largely reflecting the high level of economic legality and strong medical norms in Sweden generally, the rights to organs are highly secure from trespass. Fourth, changes, and proposed changes, in the nature of consent reduce somewhat the credibility of the persistence of rights. Though unlikely to be

Table 2. Organ harvesting for four countries as described by individual-level property rights.

	Sweden	United States	India	People's Republic of China
Completeness of allocation	Clear	Clear	Clear after 1995	Nominally clear for prisoners, unclear for general donors
Cost of alienation	Limited to nonspecific gifts	Generally limited to nonspecific gifts	Sales now banned and non-specific giving restricted, but directed gifts facilitate black market	Generally limited to nonspecific gifts
Security from trespass	Highly secure	Right to keep organ highly secure; right to alienate as gift generally not secure	Poor contract enforcement lowers security from trespass	Alteration of prisoners' wills provides little security from trespass
Credibility of persistence	Somewhat reduced credibility due to law changes	Very credible	Reduced credibility due to uncertainty about future enforcement	International criticism reduces credibility somewhat
Autonomy	Written consent by individual or next-of-kin required	Written consent by individual and, in practice, next-of-kin required	Consent and medical committee review	Prisoners subjected to involuntary medical preparation; coerced consent by prisoners or next-of-kin

very important in this particular context, one could imagine that expectation of a possible switch back to presumed consent might discourage some people from making the effort to give consent under the current system. Fifth, the current system provides a fairly high degree of autonomy in that the state cannot claim ownership without the prior consent of the donor or next-of-kin.

The situation in the United States is somewhat more complex than that in Sweden. Individuals have the right to donate their organs (nonspecifically through an organ donation card or specifically to a relative), but they are proscribed by the National Organ Transplantation Act and state laws from selling their organs. Yet, in practice, hospitals generally will not remove organs from a deceased without the permission of the next-of-kin even if the deceased has expressed a desire to donate (DeJong et al., 1995). If one subscribes to the theory that an individuals' right to dispose of property extends beyond their life, then this practice can be viewed as trespass against donors' rights to alienate organs as nonspecific gifts. Pellegrino (1991), for example, argues that it is the deceased's wishes that should be followed rather than the next-of-kin. Finally, it is important to note that individual potential donees have no property rights to any specific organ until they actually receive it as a transplant (Schwindt and Vining, 1986).

The individual-level property rights for organs in the United States can be summarized as follows: First, allocation is complete and clear. Second, alienation is restricted to gifts. Third, individuals' rights to keep organs is highly secure from trespass, but the deference of hospitals to the wishes of next-of-kin involve trespass against the right of alienation. Fourth, the credibility of the allocated rights is high. Fourth, the requirement of prior written consent provides a high level of autonomy.

Until 1995 India had no transplant law. Many commercial transactions for kidneys were made because organ sellers can function with one kidney, and because the payment could easily represent the equivalent of more than a year's income. At the same time, organ sellers often either had little idea of the seriousness of the operation or had limited means to enforce promised payments. With the passage of the Transplantation of Human Organs Act, the commercial sale of organs was banned. Under the new law people are allowed to make donations only to immediate relatives unless a case is judged by a medical committee to be one of dire need and the donor is willing to act on "humanitarian grounds only" (Stackhouse, 1997). As a result of the law, legal transplants have dropped in number from the thousands to the hundreds. However, it seems that most operations are now performed illegally in small rural hospitals (Stackhouse, 1997). Payments are obviously difficult to enforce because the sale of organs is illegal and because many transactions involve fraudulent documents that claim that the parties are related and that the donation is motivated by humanitarian concerns.

The individual property rights involving organs can be summarized as follows: First, allocation is now nominally complete and clear. Second, the cost of alienation has risen with the prohibition of sale, though given the general legal framework and individual incentives, a black market continues to operate. Third, the right to retain organs is secure, but illegal transactions are vulnerable to trespass. Fourth, the de facto rights are not fully credible as higher levels of enforcement could make costs of participating in the black market higher; nevertheless, the impact is probably not great as most transfers are spot transactions with live donors rather than gifts or sales that become effective after death. Finally, there is a high level of autonomy in terms of the nominal protection of organs, but the high value of organs relative to earnings for many people create the potential for coercive loss of organs.

As is the case in many Asian countries, customs and traditions work against organ donation in China (Woo, 1992). So too does the absence of a definition of brain death that would facilitate the use of organs from patients who die under medical treatment. Anonymous donation by the general public is quite rare, as is donation to relatives. Indeed, despite the symbolic gesture by Deng Xiaoping in bequeathing his corneas, there is little general governmental effort to encourage nonspecific organ donations. Instead, the main source of kidneys and other organs is "donations" by executed prisoners. The next largest source is fetal-embryo organs.

Nearly all the transplant organs that are available in China (somewhere between 2,000 to 3,000 annually) come from executed prisoners; they are allocated to "loyal servants of the revolution and for cash-paying foreigners" (Economist, 1994, p. 40). Nominally, except in the case of unclaimed bodies, prisoners, or their next-of-kin, must give written consent for the post-execution use of their organs. In practice, however, it appears that the organs of executed prisoners are often harvested without their free consent ("Organ Procurement and Judicial Execution in China," 1994). Prisoners awaiting execution are held in extremely coercive circumstances. Although they are allowed to make wills, prison officials are allowed to alter them as they see fit. Not only do prisoners often donate without their consent or even knowledge, they are often subjected to medical preparation for extraction prior to their execution. As bodies are cremated, it is often difficult for the families of those executed to determine if organs have been removed. The families themselves are often coerced into consenting to donation by being presented with various bills for prisoners' board, cremation, and even the bullet used for execution if they do not consent. These circumstances are in stark contrast to those in several Western countries, including the United States, where prisoners are forbidden from donating organs because of the belief that they cannot give free consent in the coercive circumstances of the prison environment.

The individual-level of prisoners as organ donors in China can be described as follows: First, the nominal allocation of rights to the organs of executed prisoners is complete. Second, alienation is generally limited to nonspecific donations. Third, there is little security from trespass, as prison officials can change wills or otherwise coerce donations. Fourth, the possible response of the Chinese government to international criticism somewhat undercuts credibility. Finally, in practice, prisoners have little autonomy over the disposition of their organs.

This brief tour of the characteristics of individual-level property rights related to organ donation provides fundamental description of the institutional environment relevant to public policy in each of the four countries. Effectively conveying an understanding of the design and function of first-order policy instruments, such as public information campaigns, subsidies, and mechanisms to make donation more convenient, to those not already familiar with the countries requires a specification of these characteristics. More obviously, so too does the presentation of second-order policy instruments, which involve changes in one or more of these institutional characteristics.

Application at the inter- and intraorganizational level framework to the United States

As an illustration of the inter- and intraorganizational property rights framework, we very briefly consider the property rights environment for organ harvesting and allocation in the United States. We first examine interorganizational issues.

In the United States the organizational system for harvesting and distributing human organs is governed by the Department of Health and Human Services (DHHS) and the United Network for Organ Sharing (UNOS), a nonprofit membership organization that holds DHHS contracts to administer the national Organ Procurement and Transplantation Network and the Scientific Registry on Organ Transplantation. It can be summarized as follows: "...monopoly of procurement activities by organ procurement organizations in discrete catchment areas...[allocation of organs is regulated by a national, computerized system of organ sharing...[and]...[p]rovision of transplantation services is restricted by DHHS and UNOS regulation to centers that meet certain criteria" (Blumstein and Sloan,

1989, p. 1). The regional transplant organizations have de jure property rights to organs that are collected within their jurisdiction, but UNOS has considerable power over the allocation of organs because of its gate keeping regulatory authority (Blumstein, 1989, p. 18).

Individual regional procurement agencies wish, for a variety of economic and political reasons, to allocate their organs to local transplant hospitals and recipients (Evans, 1993; Barnett and Kasserman, 1995). This has led to concerns by the General Accounting Office about whether there is optimal matching between donors and donees (Wagner, 1993). In response, UNOS has increasingly used its regulatory authority to specify detailed matching criteria and to attempt to "persuade" transplant centers to abide by them. For example, in June, 1997 the board of directors approved a policy whereby transplant centers that do not comply with national guidelines would be removed from participation in UNOS decision making. As the UNOS press release put it: "Both patients and member organizations are looking to us to strengthen the voluntary guidelines by stepping up the costs of failing to comply with national policies" (UNOS, 1997). Thus, although UNOS has no formal property rights to organs it is acquiring some de facto property rights. The situation has been further complicated by statements from an assistant secretary of DHHS that it is his department that will determine transplant policy (in specific reference to liver transplantation policy) (UNOS, 1996). Allocation criteria remain unclear to the media, the public, donors, and potential donees judging by the outcry surrounding recent transplants to Governor Robert Casey of Pennsylvania and Mickey Mantle (Colburn, 1993); as a result there is "public skepticism about the integrity and fairness of the nation's distribution system" (DeJong, 1995, p. 463).

In summary, while formally completeness of allocation is high, in practice it is considerably lower. As in many other contexts in which allocation is not complete, the costs of alienation are inevitably raised. These alienation difficulties probably partly explain the strong reluctance of regional centers to let organs out of their region (Wagner, 1993); they cannot, for example, write contracts with other regions mandating future reciprocity. As one would expect in the United States, there is a high degree of security from trespass. Given the problems described above, the persistence of organizational property rights is not fully credible; however, it is not likely that this has imposed any major costs on the system. Finally, it is important to point out that it is impossible to separate the individual level and the organizational level completely in analyzing organ property rights. Barnett and Kasserman (1995, p. 510) argue that many of the organizational problems are generated by the fundamental restriction on individual autonomy: "because donors are prohibited from receiving payment for the organs they supply, the various other parties involved in the transplant procedure (e.g., the hospitals) may be able to appropriate a portion of the inflated value (or rents)...or it is dissipated in rent-seeking activities."

Finally, we turn to the intraorganizational level. The most important property rights issue revolves around the fact that doctors have no property rights in organs (even as agents for potential donees), but must bear significant costs to acquire them: "[p]hysicians have little motivation to become involved in organ donation because it is a time-consuming and emotionally intensive process to recover organs, while the beneficiaries are transplant teams and patients at other hospitals" (Modarress, 1992, p. 554; see also DeJong et al., 1995). Consequently, hospitals fail to harvest many donations. The design of policies to increase organ supply in the United States would require attention to the intraorganizational property rights that shape the harvesting behavior of physicians.

Conclusion

As institutional arrangements affect the feasibility and effectiveness of policy instruments, researchers seeking to contribute to our general knowledge about policy design must frame their work within an institutional context. Researchers within a national-level community can reasonably assume that their audiences share common knowledge that implicitly provides an adequate institutional framing. Researchers wishing to communicate effectively with those who do not share such common knowledge, however, must provide explicit institutional framing if they wish their insights to travel well internationally. By using the same framework, researchers increase the likelihood that their individual studies will cumulate into a larger body of empirical work relevant to answering general questions about what sorts of policies work best in particular institutional settings. We have set out what we believe to be a relatively simple but nonetheless useful framework for describing institutional arrangements in terms of property rights, broadly defined, at the individual, interorganizational, and intraorganizational levels.

The characteristics of property rights underlying the framework—completeness of allocation, cost of alienation, security from trespass, credibility of persistence, and autonomy—fundamentally affect the choice, operation, and impacts of policy instruments. They also suggest avenues for institutional changes that either directly address policy problems or do so indirectly by affecting the policies that are selected. For example, shifting the interorganizational allocation of property rights in a policy domain can shift the influence of various stakeholders over the selection of policies. Variation across countries in institutional arrangements offers the possibility of discovering insights into how institutional redesign (second-order policy instruments) affects the selection of first-order policy instruments. Here again, effective comparison requires that individual researchers report important institutional features within a common framework.

We have offered what we believe to be an effective and economical framework for facilitating the accumulation of cross-national insight for informing first-and second-order policy design. Whether or not contributors to *Journal of Comparative Policy Analysis* adopt this particular framework, we hope that they will make efforts to convey what they believe to be salient institutional features in their substantive areas of study to the international community of policy researchers interested in policy and institutional design.

References

Alchian, A.A. and H. Demsetz. (1973). "The Property Rights Paradigm." *Journal of Economic History* 33(1), 16–27.

Alesina, A., S. Oezler, N. Roubini, and P. Swagel. (1996). "Political Instability and Economic Growth." *Journal of Economic Growth* 1(2), 189–211.

Alexander, E.R. (1982). "Design in the Decision-Making Process." *Policy Sciences* 14(3), 279–292.

Alexander, E.R. (1979). "The Design of Alternatives in Organizational Contexts: A Pilot Study." *Administrative Science Quarterly* 24(3), 382–404.

Alston, L.J., T. Eggertsson, and D.C. North (Eds.). (1996). *Empirical Studies in Institutional Change*. New York: Cambridge University Press.

Anderson, E. (1993). *Value in Ethics and Economics*. Cambridge, MA: Harvard University Press.

Balch, G.I. (1980). 'The Stick, the Carrot, and Other Strategies: A Theoretical Analysis of Governmental Intervention." *Law and Policy Quarterly* 2(1), 35–60.

Bardach, E. (1980). "Implementation Studies and the Study of Implements." Mimeo. Paper presented at the Annual Meeting of the American Political Science Association, Washington, DC, (August).

Bardach, E. and R.A. Kagan. (1982). Going *by the Book: The Problem of Regulatory Unreasonableness.* Philadelphia: Temple University Press.
Barnett, A.H. and D.L Kaserman. (1995). "The 'Rush to Transplant' and Organ Shortages." *Economic Inquiry* 33(3), 506–515.
Baumol, W.J. (1990). "Entrepreneurship: Productive, Unproductive, and Destructive." *Journal of Political Economy* 89(5/1), 893–921.
Blume, L. and D. Rubinfeld. (1984). "Compensation for Takings: An Economic Analysis." *California Law Review* 72 (July), 569–628,
Blumstein, J A. (1989). "Government's Role in Organ Transplantation Policy." In J.A. Blumstein and F.A. Sloan (eds.), *Organ Transplantation Policy.* Durham, NC: Duke University Press, pp. 5–39.
Blumstein, J.A. and F.A. Sloan. (1989). "Introduction." In J.A. Blumstein and F.A. Sloan (eds.), *Organ Transplantation Policy.* Durham, NC: Duke University Press, pp. 1–4.
Brandl, J. (1988). "On Politics and Policy Analysis as the Design and Assessment of Institutions." *Journal of Policy Analysis and Management* 7(3), 419–424.
Bromley, D.W. (1989). *Economic Interests and Institutions: The Conceptual Foundations of Public Policy.* New York: Basil Blackwell.
Brown, P.G. (1992). "The Failure of Market Failures." *Journal of Socio-Economics* 21(1), 1–24.
Brunetti, A. (1997). "Political Variables in Cross-Country Growth Analyses." *Journal of Economic Surveys* 11 (2), 163–190.
Buchanan, J.M. (1975). *The Limits of Liberty.* Chicago: University of Chicago Press.
Buchanan, J.M., R.D. Tollison, and G. Tullock (Eds.). (1980). *Toward a Theory of the Rent Seeking Society.* College Station: Texas A&M Press.
Cheit, R.E. (1990). *Setting Safety Standards: Regulation in the Public and Private Sectors.* Berkeley: University of California Press.
Coase, R. (1937). "The Nature of the Firm." *Economica* 4 (November), 386–405.
Colburn, D. (1993). "Gov. Casey's Quick Double Transplant: How did He Jump to the Top of the Waiting List?" *Washington Post, Health* June, pp. 8–9.
de Bruijn, J.A. and E.F. ten Heuvelhof. (1995). "Policy Networks and Governance." In D.L. Weimer (ed.), *Institutional Design.* Boston: Kluwer Academic Publishers, pp. 161–179.
De Haan, J. and C. Siermann. (1995). "A Sensitivity Analysis of the Impact of Democracy on Economic Growth." *Empirical Economics* 20(2), 197–215.
DeJong, W., J. Drachman, S.L. Gortmaker, C. Beasley, and M.J. Evanisko. (1995). "Options for Increasing Organ Donation: The Potential Role of Financial Incentives, Standardized Hospital Procedures, and Public Education to Promote Family Discussion." The *Milbank Quarterly* 73(3), 463–481.
Demsetz, H. (1967). "Toward a Theory of Property Rights." *American Economic Review* 57(2), 347–359.
Diermeier, D., J.M. Ericson, T. Frye, and S. Lewis. (1997). "Credible Commitment and Property Rights: The Role of Strategic Interaction Between Political and Economic Actors." In D.L. Weimer (ed.), *Political Economy of Property Rights: Institutional Change and Credibility in the Reform of Centrally Planned Economies.* New York: Cambridge University Press, pp. 20–42.
Doern, G.B. and R.W. Phidd. (1983). *Canadian Public Policy: Ideas, Structure, Process.* New York: Methuen.
Economist (1994). "Of Car and Body Parts." September, p. 40.
Elmore, R.F. (1987). "Instruments and Strategy in Public Policy." *Policy Studies Review* 7(1), 174–186.
Epstein, R. (1985). *Taking, Private Property and the Power of Eminent Domain.* Cambridge, MA: Harvard University Press.
Evans, R.W. (1993). "Organ Procurement Expenditures and the Role of Financial Incentives." *Journal of the American Medical Association* 269 (June), 3113–3118.
Feder, G. and F. David. (1991). "Land Tenure and Property Rights: Theory and Implications for Development Policy." *The World Bank Economic Review* 5(1), 135–153.
Feder, G. and R. Norohna. (1987). "Land Right Systems and Agricultural Development in Sub-Saharan Africa." *World Bank Research Observer* 2 (July), 143–169.
Feder, G., T. Onchon, and Y. Chalamwong. (1988). "Land Policies and Farm Performance in Thailand's Forest Reserve Areas." *Economic Development and Cultural Change* 36(3), 483–502.
Frant, H. (1996). "High-Powered and Low-Powered Incentives in the Public Sector." *Journal of Public Administration Research and Theory* 6(3), 365–381.
Gormley, W.T., Jr. (1989). *Taming the Bureaucracy: Muscles, Prayers, and Other Strategies.* Princeton, NJ: Princeton University Press.

Gormley, W.T., Jr. (1987). "Institutional Policy Analysis: A Critical Review." *Journal of Policy Analysis and Management* 6(2), 153–169.

Helliwell, J. (1994). "Empirical Linkages Between Democracy and Economic Growth." *British Journal of Political Science* 24(2), 225–248.

Hohfeld, W.N. (1919). *Fundamental Legal Conceptions*. New Haven, CT: Yale University Press.

Hood, C.C. (1986). *The Tools of Government*. Chatham, NJ: Chatham House.

Ingraham, P.W. (1987). 'Toward More Systematic Consideration of Policy Design." *Policy Studies Journal* 15(4), 611–628.

Jones, E.L. (1981). *The European Miracle: Environments, Economics, and Geopolitics*. New York: Cambridge University Press.

Kelman, S. (1981). "Cost-Benefit Analysis: An Ethical Critique." *Regulation* (January/February), 33–40.

Knetsch, J. (1983). *Property Rights and Compensation*. Toronto, Ontario: Butterworth and Company.

Kingdon, J.W. (1984). *Agendas, Alternatives, and Public Policies*. Boston: Little, Brown.

Kirschen, E.S., J. Bernard, H. Besters, F. Blackaby, O. Eckstein, J. Faaland, F. Hartog, L. Morissens, and E. Tosco. (1964). *Economic Policy in Our Time: General Theory*, vol. 1. Chicago: Rand McNally and Company.

Knack, S. and P. Philip Keefer. (1995). "Institutions and Economic Performance: Cross-Country Tests Using Alternative Institutional Measures." *Economics and Politics* 7(3), 207–227.

Knight, J. (1992). *Institutions and Social Conflict*. New York: Cambridge University Press.

Kreps, D.M. (1990). "Corporate Culture and Economic Theory." In J.E. Alt and K.A. Shepsle (eds.), *Perspectives on Positive Political Economy*. New York: Cambridge University Press, pp. 90–143.

Leblang, D.A. (1994). "Property Rights, Democracy and Economic Growth." Mimeo. Thomas Jefferson Program in Public Policy Working Paper Number 27, The College of William and Mary.

Levine, R., and D. Renelt. (1992). "A Sensitivity Analysis of Cross-Country Growth Regressions." *American Economic Review* 82(4), 942–963.

Linder, S.H. and B.G. Peters. (1984). "From Social Theory to Policy Design." *Journal of Public Policy* 4(3), 237–259.

Linder, S.H. and B.G. Peters. (1987). "A Design Perspective on Policy Implementation: The Fallacies of Misplaced Prescription." *Policy Studies Review* 6(3), 459–475.

Linder, S.H. and B.G. Peters. (1988). "The Analysis of Design or the Design of Analysis?" *Policy Studies Review* 7(4), 738–750.

Linder, S.H. and P.G. Peters. (1989). "Instruments of Government: Perceptions and Contexts." *Journal of Public Policy* 9(1), 35–58.

Lowi, T.J. (1972). "Four Systems of Policy, Politics, and Choice." *Public Administration Review* 32(4), 298–310.

Machado, N. (1996). "The Swedish Transplant Acts: Sociological Considerations on Bodies and Giving." *Social Science and Medicine* 42(2), 159–168.

MacRae, D., Jr. (1980). "Policy Analysis Methods and Governmental Functions." In S. Nagel (ed.), *Improving Policy Analysis*. Beverly Hills, CA: Sage Publications, pp. 129–151.

May, P.J. (1981). "Hints for Crafting Alternative Policies." *Policy Analysis* 7(2), 227–224.

May, P.J. (1991). "Reconsidering Policy Design: Policies with Publics." *Journal of Public Policy* 11(2), 187–206.

McChesney, F.S. (1990). "Government as Definer of Property Rights: Indian Lands, Ethnic Externalities, and Bureaucratic Budgets." *Journal of Legal Studies* 19(2), 297–335.

McCubbins, M.D., R.G. Noll, and B.R. Weingast. (1989). "Structure and Process, Politics and Policy: Administrative Arrangements and the Political Control of Agencies." *Virginia Law Review* 75(2), 431–482.

Milgrom, P.R., D.C. North, and B.R. Weingast. (1990). "The Role of Institutions in the Revival of Trade: The Law Merchant, Private Judges, and the Champagne Fairs." *Economics and Politics* 2(1), 1–23.

Miller, G.J. (1992). *Managerial Dilemmas: The Political Economy of Hierarchy*. New York: Cambridge University Press.

North, D.C. (1990). *Institutions, Institutional Change and Economic Performance*. New York: Cambridge University Press.

North, D.C. and P.R. Thomas. (1973). *The Rise of the Western World: A New Economic History*. New York: Cambridge University Press.

Olson, M., Jr. (1996). "Big Bills Left on the Sidewalk: Why Some Nations are Rich, and Others Poor." *Journal of Economic Perspectives* 10(2), 2–24.

Organ Procurement and Judicial Execution in China. (1994). *Human Rights Watch/Asia Report: China* 6(9), 1–42.

Pellegrino, E.D. (1991). "Families' Self-interest and the Cadaver's Organ: What Price Consent?" *Journal of the American Medical Association* 265 (March), 1305–1306.

Radin, M.J. (1996). *Contested Commodities*. Cambridge, MA: Harvard University Press.

Riker, W.H. and D.L Weimer. (1993). "The Economic and Political Liberalization of Socialism: The Fundamental Problem of Property Rights." *Social Philosophy and Policy* 10(2), 79–102.

Riker, W.H. and D.L Weimer. (1995). "The Political Economy of Transformation: Liberalization and Property Rights." In J.S. Banks and E.A. Hanushek (eds.), *Modem Political Economy: Old Topics, New Directions*. New York: Cambridge University Press, pp. 80–107.

Rodrik, D. and R. Zeckhauser. (1988). "The Dilemma of Government Responsiveness." *Journal of Public Policy Analysis and Management* 7(4), 175–188.

Rosenberg, N. and L.E. Birdzell, Jr. (1986). *How the West Grew Rich*. New York: Basic Books.

Sabatier, P.A. and H.C. Jenkins-Smith. (1993). Policy *Change and Learning: An Advocacy Coalition Approach*. San Francisco: Westview Press.

Salamon, L.M. (1981). "Rethinking Public Management: Third-Party Government and the Forms of Changing Government." *Public Policy* 29(3), 255–275.

Salamon, L.M. and M.S. Lund. (1989). "The Tools Approach: Basic Analytics." In L.M. Salamon (ed.), *Beyond Privatization: The Tools of Government in Action*. Washington, DC: The Urban Institute Press, pp. 23–49.

Savas, E.S. (1987). *Privatization: The Key to Better Government*. Chatham, NJ: Chatham House Publishers.

Schlatter, R. (1951). *Private Property: The History of an Idea*. New Brunswick, NJ: Rutgers University Press.

Schneider, A.L and H. Ingram. (1990). "Behavioral Assumptions of Policy Tools." *Journal of Politics* 52(2), 510–529.

Schneider, A.L. and H. Ingram. (1988). "Systematically Pinching Ideas: A Comparative Approach to Policy Design." *Journal of Public Policy* 8(1), 61–80.

Schneider, A.L. and H. Ingram. (1997). *Policy Design for Democracy*. Lawrence: University Press of Kansas.

Schotter, A. (1981). *The Economic Theory of Social Institutions*. New York: Cambridge University Press.

Schwindt, R. and S. Globerman. (1996). "Takings of Private Rights to Public Natural Resources: A Policy Analysis." *Canadian Public Policy* 22(3), 205–224.

Schwindt, R. and A.R. Vining. (1986). "Proposal for a Future Delivery Market for Transplant Organs." *Journal of Health Politics, Policy and Law* 11 (Fall), 483–500.

Stackhouse, J. (1997). "Organ Racket Alive and Well in India." *Toronto Globe and Mail*. (August).

Stone, D.A. (1988). *Policy Paradox and Political Reason*. Glenview, IL: Scott, Foresman and Company.

Torstensson, J. (1994). "Property Rights and Economic Growth: An Empirical Study." *Kyklos* 47(2), 231–247.

UNOS. (1996). Statement by Dr. James M. Burdick, transplant surgeon, John Hopkins Medical Center, President, UNOS Board of Directors, News Release, Richmond, VA (December).

UNOS. (1997). "Organ Transplant Network Strengthens Policy Enforcement." Press Release, Position Statements, Richmond, VA (June).

Vining, A.R. and D.L. Weimer. (1997). "Saintly Supervision: Monitoring Casino Gambling in British Columbia." *Journal of Policy Analysis and Management* 16(4), 615–620.

Wagner, L. (1993). "GAO Report Hits Organ Allocation." *Modern Healthcare* (May), p. 20.

Waller, J.A., C.E. Haisch, and J.M. Skully. (1992). "Potential Availability of Transplantable Organs According to Factors Associated with Type of Injury Event." *Accident Analysis and Prevention* 24(2), 193–200.

Weaver, R.K. (1988). *Automatic Government: The Politics of Indexing*. Washington, DC: The Brookings Institution.

Weimer, D.L (1992). "Claiming Races, Broiler Contracts, Heresthetics, and Habits: Ten Concepts for Policy Design." *Policy Sciences* 25(2), 135–139.

Weimer, D.L (1993). "The Current State of Design Craft: Borrowing, Tinkering, and Problem Solving." *Public Administration Review* 53(2), 110–120.

Weimer, D.L. (Ed.). (1995). *Institutional Design*. Boston: Kluwer Academic Publishers.

Weimer, D.L. (Ed.). (1997). *Political Economy of Property Rights: Institutional Change and Credibility in the Reform of Centrally Planned Economies*. New York, NY: Cambridge University Press.

Weimer, D.L. and A.R. Vining. (1989). *Policy Analysis: Concepts and Practice*. Englewood Cliffs, NJ: Prentice Hall.

Woo, K.T. (1992). "Social and Cultural Aspects of Organ Donation in Asia." *Annals of the Academy of Medicine (Singapore)* 21(3), 421–427.

Woodside, K. (1986). "Policy Instruments and the Study of Public Policy." *Canadian Journal of Political Science* 19(4), 775–793.

Young, H.P. (1996). "The Economics of Convention." *Journal of Economic Perspectives* 10(2), 105–122.

Index

Note: **Bold** page numbers refer to tables; *italic* page numbers refer to figures and page numbers followed by "n" denote endnotes.

ABS *see* Asian Barometer Survey
absenteeism 189
absolute standardization 257
Abts, K. 266, 267, 271
accession 364; complex nature 370; EEC 366; formal accession stage 369–371; NAFTA 367; super safeguard 373
accounting regulations, strictness 249–250
Achen, C. H. 96
actionable governance 434
Actionable Governance Indicators (AGI) 446
Adachi, Y. 3
Adam, C. 415–431
Adger, W. N. 155
administrative styles 417
agencies: characteristics 382; convergence 392, 393; definition 381; empirical research 385; global economic problems 383; hypotheses 384; ideal-type 386; microlevel 393; operational/executive functions 392; political interference 392; political systems 381; public body 379–380; public management 383; strategic/policymaking functions 392; unpacking *see* unpacking agencification
Agenda 21 NRW 290, 292
aggregation procedure 202–203
The Alberta Special Waste Management System (ASWMS) 54, 60
Allison, M. 172
Alzira model 42
analysis and results, IPSAS: characteristics of 255; disclosure items and associated accounting requirements **254**, 256; global model, disclosure and measurement items 253, 255, 256; measurement items and associated accounting requirements 256; regulated accounting items 255
Andrews, R. **200**
Anglo-Saxon model 247, 253, 262
Annual Meeting of Sustainable Development Experts (AMSDE) 288

Arato, A. 159
ASEAN 38
Asian Barometer Survey (ABS) 170, 174–177, 181, 182n6
Asia-Pacific Climate Change Partnership (APP) 307
Asia-Pacific Economic Cooperation (APEC) 405
Asia Pacific Privacy Authorities (APPA) 405
Athias, L. 83n13
Atlantic Canada Opportunities Agency 229
Australia–New Zealand Closer Economic Relations Trade Agreement (ANZCERTA) 144
Australia's Cabinet Implementation Unit 125

Bäckstrand, K. 301, 302, 306
Baehler, K. J. 5
Bagashka, T. 451n3
Bajari, P. 69
Baker, K. 110
Bakvis, H. 122
Baldwin, R. 144
Bardach, E. 116–119
Barnard, C. I. 194
Barnett, A. H., 467
Bathgate, K. 379–393
Baumgartner, F. R. 163
Bavinck, M. 159, 163, 165n1
Beattie, P. 117, 125
behavioral constraints 417, 419, 424, 428–430, 431n4
Benito, B. 248
Bennett, C. 412n3
Bennett, J. 83n7
Benz, A. 83n7
Berman, E. **199**
Bhagwati, J. N. 143, 144
Bies, R. J. 269
Biglaiser, G. 92, 101
Biltran, E. 83n11
biotechnology policy decision-making 7–8
Blair, T. 117, 125

Blauberger, M. 339
Boardman, A. 62n1, 70
Boase, A. 7
Borins, S. 56
Boushey, G. 7
BOVAR Inc. 54, 60, 62n10
Boyne, G. A. **200**, **201**, 221n2
Breen, M. 86–103
Breton, A. 131, 133, 134, 135
Brewer, G. A. 193, **199**, **200**
Brundtland Commission 287
Brundtland Report 283, 287, 290, 291
Brusca, I. 248
Brussels-based representative groups 346
Bruyninckx, H. 296n5
Brym, R. J. 320
Buanes, A. 162
Buchanan, J. 136
budgetary savings 46
Build–Operate–Transfer (BOTs) projects 46
Buth, V. 356

Cabinet Implementation Unit (CUI) 125
Caiden, G. 170
Cairns, A. 231
California Private Transportation Company (CPTC) 52–53
Campbell, J. P. 198
Canache, D. 172
Canada: bureaucratic structure 240–241; economic characteristics 226; executive dominance institutionally imbedded 228–229; federal provincial interdependence 230–233, 243n2; federal systems 226; political parties/political culture 233–234; regulatory policies 242; specialized policy actors 236–237
Canadian Food Inspection Agency 387
Cañibano, L. 263n5
Capano, G. 4, 7, 33
capital mobility 94, 103n14
Carbon Sequestration Leadership Forum (CSLF) 307
Carroll, B. J. 356
Carroll, P. 372
Carter, D. B. 95
Casella, A. 136
Caulfield, J. 379–393
CC *see* control of corruption
Central and Eastern European countries (CEEC) 366
Central Archive Service (CAS) 388
Chinn, M. D. 94
Cho, J. 272
Chuenpagdee, R. 156, 159, 165n1
Chun, Y. H. **201**
Cities for Climate Protection (CCP) 307
citizens' perceptions: ABS 175–177; acceptance of corruption 177; anti-corruption legislation 177; economic growth 177; item nonresponse 176; local/municipal government 177, **178**; national government **175**, 176, 177; typology of *180*, 181; z-scores 177, **179**, 180
citizen surveys 174
citizen trust and distrust: culture of 269–270; definition 266–267; dispositions 269, 276–277; empirical evidence, organization research 272; empirical evidence, public administration/political science 272–274; exploring differences in consequences 275; exploring differences in determinants 274–275; implications for government actions 276–277; implications for research 277–278; internet-based customer–vendor relations 272; interpersonal relationships 270–271; 2×4-item scale 272; polar opposites/separate constructs 268–270
citizen trust *vs*. distrust 267–268
civil society organizations (CSOs) 350
Clayton, R. 322
Clean Development Mechanism (CDM) 307
Clifton, J. 103
coercion 231, 234, 336, 418
co-governance 13, 157, 158
Cohen, J. L. 159
collaborative governance 27, 344, 346, 349, 355, **358**; EU, top-down bias (actors) 349–351
Comín, F. 103
Commission on Sustainable Development (CSD) 288
common markets 133, 251
comparability potential 248, 250
comparative implementation research: large-n/small-n comparison 111; macro- *vs*. lower level institutional factors 112–113; MDSD 112; MSSD 112; policy formation 113; variants 110–111; *vs*. longitudinal research design 112
comparative policy analysis (CPA) 3, 13, 164, 165; and governance mantra: capacity 19–20; dynamics 19; MLG 18–19; national systems 20; performance 21; policy instruments 19; strategy 20; streams of research 21; structure 18–19; and institutions 6; macro and institutional settings 190; micro attributes 190; political science 4; scholarship 3; theory and methodology 5–6
conceptual disagreement 107
The Confederation Bridge 56–57
contracting costs 49–50
control of corruption (CC) 171, 172
Cooperation and Verification Mechanism (CVM) 373
Cooperative Commonwealth Federation (CCF) 234
coordinate authority model 229
corporate governance 14
corruption: Asian economies 168–169; citizens' perceptions of (*see* citizens' perceptions);

CPI 169, **169**, 171, 172; measurement (*see* corruption measurement); TI 169, 171, 172
corruption measurement: developing indicators/indices 170–171; experts/citizens 172–174; implications 182
Corruption Perception Index (CPI) 169, **169**, 171, 172, 181, 438, 444
Country Policy and Institutional Assessment (CPIA) 436
crazy quilt design 228
Cristofoli, D. 189
cross-country investigations, 455
cross-national policy analysis 4
Crozier, M. 149

Dahrendorf, R. 135, 136
Danis, M. A. 92, 101
data protection authorities (DPAs): civil liberties and human rights 397; information and communication policy 398; infrastructural development 400, 401; institution-building 410; international collaboration 397; jurisdictional levels 409; Madrid Resolution 410; privacy intrusions 397; rapid reaction force 398; regulation framework (*see* global framework for regulation); regulatory functions 396; regulatory governance 398; social networking 398; structural coherence 402; sub-global groupings 411
Davis, C. 368
De Bettignies, J. -E. 82n5, 83n7
Deil Wright's typology 226
deLeon, P. 3
Delors, J. 139
Department of Health and Human Services (DHHS), 466
dependent variable problem 320, 325
De Vries, M. S. 162
Díaz Fuentes, D. 103
distributive policies 416
distrust 275, 276
Dolowitz, D. 363
Donaldson, L. 388
Donchev, D. 173
Doyle, D. 86–103
Dulles Greenway P3 51–52

ecology of central capabilities: co-ordinating Secretariats 122; downstream co-ordination 123; downstream implementation 124; facilitation advice 123; monitoring and evaluating performance 123; other standing Cabinet Secretariats 122; policy adhocracies in departments 122; scrutiny and challenge 122–123; traditional Cabinet Secretariats 121–122; upstream implementation 123–124
economic globalization 433
economic governance 14

economic integration 145
e-Government Readiness Index 445
Elazar, D. J. 226, 237
EU adopted its Sustainable Development Strategy (EUSDS) 288
European Commission (EC) 402
European Court of Justice (ECJ) 335
European Data Protection Supervisor (EDPS) 402
European Employment Strategy (EES) 352
Europeanization 7, 333; legal uncertainty 334; positive/negative integration 334–335; private actors 339; rans-border activities 339; research note 334; secondary law 335, 338
European Parliament (EP) 351
Evans, M. 363
evidence-based policymaking 6
experience-based measures 170, 182n1
ex post harmonization: economic development 133; entrepreneurial competition 134; European integration 133; instability 132; inter-jurisdictional competition 131; inter-state competition 133; mutual recognition 132; nationalism 131; neoclassical theory 134; OMC 132; supranational level 131

federal-state Medicaid program 243n6
federal systems: Canada 226; definition 225; United States 226
Fifth International Comparative Policy Analysis Forum 187
financial incentives 418
Fink, S. 90, 100
Finke, B. 347
first-order autocorrelation 96
first-order policy instruments (policy design), 455–457
Flaherty, D. 412n3
Flemish childcare voucher system 110
Flemish delegation 291
Foreign currency operations 252
formal accession stage 369–371; Development Assistance Committee 369; findings 371; International Energy Authority 369; Russian Federation's membership 371
Foucault, M. 32
Freedom in the World 444
Freedom of the Press 444
Freeman, G. 8, 20
Fringe Special 445
Froestad, J. 111
functional convergence theory 389
functional *vs.* territorial integration: European integration 135; formal theory 136; monetary policies 137; optimal strategy 137; organizational/managerial problem 138; principles 135; public (or collective) goods 136

Gaebler, T. 194, 384, 392, 393
Garrido, P. 249, 258, 263n6
Gaussian first-order autoregressive process 96
GCB *see* Global Corruption Barometer
GDP *see* gross domestic product
Geddes, A. 40–41
Generalized Least Squares (GLS) 101
German Federal Cartel Office 339
Geva-May, I. 4, 13, 165
Giest, S. 34
Global Competitiveness Index (GCI) 444
Global Competitiveness Report 194
Global Corruption Barometer (GCB) 172
global financial crisis (GFC) 40
global framework for regulation: awareness-raising 407; bilateral and multilateral agreements 406; CNIL 404; collective activity 405; co-operative activity 406; DPA monitoring 409; enforcement co-operation 408; financial and organizational burdens 407; global acceptance 408; information society 408; institutionalization 403, 405; London Initiative 405; multilevel governance infrastructure 403; OECD 406; privacy protection 403; public communication 408; quasi-constitutional and formal structures 406; transnational co-ordinated initiatives 407
global governance indicators 436
Global Integrity Index 445
Global Integrity Report 445
global valuation of final stock 252–253
GLS *see* Generalized Least Squares
Goggin, M. L. 108, 113
Goldberg, V. 83n15
good governance 13–14
governability: concept of 150; definition 150; entities 150; factors 149, 150; integrated framework *151*; public authorities 148; semipolitical movement 149; SG (*see* system-to-be-governed (SG)); societal sector 149
governance 4, 13, 27; arrangements 17; from government to (*see* government to governance); and institutions 6; as minimal State 14; modes 32; non-hierarchical modes 32; problem 35; quality of 19; self-governing 35; as self-organizing system 14; as socio-cybernetic system 14; socio-economic and political processes 13; special issue 32–34; types 13; without government 15, 28
Governance at a Glance (GG) 446
Governance for sustainable development 283
governance interactions (GI) 149–150; governing entities 160–161; impact/effect of GS and SG 163–164; influence of GS and SG 162–163; modalities 161–162
governance in the EU: activation and informal consultation of organized civil society (actions) 352–353; actors/actions/achievements, concept and use 348–349; approaches 343–344; collaborative governance 357, **358**, 359 (*see* collaborative governance, EU); collaborative notions 346; competitive mode 354; consultations 355; definitions 344–346; deliberative mode 354; democratic quality 346–348; empirical analytical research 345; EP 351; failure of governance as alternative approach (achievements) 353–356; flagship initiatives 344; good governance 352; institutional setup 350; legitimizing effects 356–357; non-public actors 347; OMC process 351; participation 356; White Paper 347, 350
governance mantra 14; battle of meaning 14–16; capacity 17; CPA (*see* comparative policy analysis (CPA)), and governance mantra; dynamics 16; policy instruments 17; strategy 17; structure 16
Governance Network Accountability Framework 302–307
governance networks 301; accountability criteria 301–302; accountability frames **304**; accountability processes, criteria 306; climate policy design dilemmas 302; dilemma of strategy 310–312; integrating multiple scales 313; monitoring and verification 313–314; performance measures **308–309**; post-Kyoto climate governance regime 314–315; scientific uncertainty in policy design 312–313
governance system (GS) 148–150; attributes 156–158; structural level 155; sub-systems 159–160
governmentality 32
government effectiveness: across countries 211–212, *212–220*, 216, 218; across regions 209, *210*, 211, *211*; across time 203, 209, *209*, *210*; conceptual disarray 194; data analysis 194; data description 202–203; independent variables 193; levels of analysis 195, **196**; measurement criteria 193, 198, **199–201**; perception/objective measurement 197–198; policy implementation 193; policy processes 193; policy pronouncements 193; public and private sectors 192; sources and measurements **204–208**
government ideology 100
Government Performance Project (GPP) 193
government to governance: actors and interactions 29; central government, crisis 29; decision-making process 30; dichotomy 29; modes 28–29; policy-making process 29–30; political-institutional centres 31; self-governance model 29; symbolic resources 2; transition process 30
government transparency 435
GPP *see* Government Performance Project
green cabinet 290

greenhouse gas emissions (GHGs) 301
Green-Pedersen, C. 6, 325, 326
Greve, C. 39, 82n2
gross domestic product (GDP) 203
Guasch, J. L. 69
Guy, P. B. 3–4

Hall, T. 62n7
Hardin, G. 157
Hardin, R. 266, 267, 268
hard law 296n4
harmonization: definition 130; ex ante 131; ex post 131–134; functional vs. territorial integration 135–138; inter-governmental performance comparisons 135; nations 141–143; normative arguments 138–141; political authority 130; and regional integration 143–146; vs. standardization process 249; Tiebout hypothesis 134; types 130–131
Hart, O. 83n7
Hartz, L. 133
Hawken, A. 172, 173
Heckman, J. J. 95
Heckman selection model 95
Heidbreder, E. 33
Heinrich, C. J. **199**
Helgøy, I. 110
Herzberg, F. 274, 275, 278
hierarchical governance 15, 17, 29, 34, 157, 158
high degree of regulatory strictness 261
highly potential comparability 261
Highway 407 project: design features 55; financial risk 55; Ontario Transport Capital Corporation 55; operational risk 55; RFP 54–55; transfer financing risks 56
Hill, M. 127n1
Hodge, G. 82n2
Hodge, G. A. 39
Holling, C. S. 154
Homme, A. 110
Hood, C. 385, 418
Hooghe, L. 296n8
horizontal governance 13, 31–32
Howard, J. 117, 125
Howlett, M. 4, 119
Hudec, R. E. 143
Huff, R. 187
human relations model 198
human resource management 186–188
Huntington, S. P. 149
Hupe, P. 106–113, 127n1
Hurka, S. 415–431

Ibero-American Data Protection Network 405
ICVS see International Crime Victimization Survey
ideal harmonization 263n6

ideas-mongering institution 288
Implementation Assessment Tool (IAT) 446–447
inclusive authority model 229
Independent Administrative Corporations (IACs) 380
information economy 396
information privacy protection 396
information society 396
institutionalism 400
institutional isomorphism 375
institutional theory 400
institutional features: autonomy, 462; completeness of allocation, 459–461; cost of alienation, 461; credibility of persistence, 461–462; definition, 454–455; inter/intraorganizational level, 459, 466–467; property rights framework, 457–459; security from trespass, 461
institutions 5; arrangements 16; features of 6
interactive governance 151
interconnectedness 120
Intermodal Surface Transportation Efficiency Act 51
internal privatization 391
internal process model 198
International Accounting Standards Board (IASB) 248, 249, 253, 262
International Climate Change Partnership (ICCP) 307, **308**, 313
International Comparative Policy Analysis (ICPA) 124, 126, 190
International Crime Victimization Survey (ICVS) 172
International Federation of Accountants (IFAC) 246; advantages 251; analysis and results **259**, 259–260; disclosure items *257*; harmonization/standardization 256–260; measurement items *257*, 259; methodology, comparability 256–259
international governmental organisations (IGOs) 362
International harmonization 284
international investors 251
International Organization for Standardization (ISO) 407
International Partnership for the Hydrogen Economy (IPHE) 307
international policy developments 283
International Public Sector Accounting Standards (IPSASs) 246, **247**; accounting item classification **252**; analysis and results (*see* analysis and results, IPSAS); data and methodology 252–253; factors 251; high degree of regulatory strictness 261; highly potential comparability 261; requirements 252; role 250–251; strategies 250

International Working Group on Data Protection in Telecommunications 403
inter-regional policy analysis 6–7
Investment Plan for Europe 38
Iossa, E. 83n7, 83n13
item response theory 203
Ito, H. 94

James, O. 385
Jensen, C. 322, 330
Johnson, D. 152
Johnson, H. 145
Joint Implementation projects (JI) 307
Jones, R. 248
Journal of Comparative Policy Analysis (JCPA) 3–5, 455; aim and scope 5; comparative inter-regional policy analysis studies 6–7; CPA 6; policy sectors 7–8; theoretical and methodological approaches 5–6
judge-made law 337
Juillet, L. 122
Juncker, J. -C. 38

Kaserman, D. L., 467
Kaufmann, D. 173, 202
Kellow, A. 372
Kelman, S. 125, 126, 302
Knack, S. 173, **200**
Knill, C. 335, 336, 338, 415–431, 431n1
Knack, S. 434
Knudsen, M. 56
Ko, K. 172
Kohler-Koch, B. 356
Kooiman, J. 148–165, 165n1
Kraay, A. 173
Krane, D. 226
Krouwel, A. 266, 267, 271

Laffont, J. -J. 84n25
Laguna, D. 188
Lanza-Kaduce, L. 58
La Porta, R. 95
Lappi-Seppälä, T. 422
"leading PPP jurisdictions" 39
leap of faith 266
Least-Present-Value-of-Revenue (LPVR) 81
Lee, S. -Y. 192–221
Leebron, D. 130
Leech, B. L. 163
legal heritage 95
legal uncertainty 334; domestic policy making 338–339; hypotheses 338
Lehmkuhl, D. 335, 336, 338
Lenard, P. T. 270, 271
Lenient authority 419
Lenschow, A. 336
less developed countries (LDCs) 370

lesson-drawing 286
level of democracy (POLITY) 101
levels/units of analysis 195, **196**
Lewicki, R. J. 265, 269, 270, 272, 274, 275
Lewis, D. J. 274
Li, B. 61
liberal policies 419
Light, P. C. **201**
Lin, M. -W. 168–183
Lindenberg, S. 270
Lindgren, K. -O. 355
Lindquist, E. A. 116–127
Lisbon Strategy 346
Liu, M. 272, 274
López-de-Silanes, F. 95
Lowi typology 226, 227
Loxley, S. 63n15
LPVR *see* Least-Present-Value-of-Revenue
Luedtke, A. 7
Luhmann, N. 149, 275
Lynn, L. E., Jr. 3, 13, **199**

McAllister, D. J. 269
McDonald, D. 58
Macdonald Royal Commission 232
McGoodwin, J. R. 157
McKnight, D. H. 272
McRae, D. 3
Madisonian concept 225
Madrid Resolution 408
Mahon, R. 165n1
Majone, G. 130–146
March, I. 363
March, J. G. 32
Martimort, D. 83n7, 83n13, 84n25
Mayntz, R. 149, 150
MDSD *see* most-different-systems design
measurement criteria 193, 198, **199–201**
Meier, K. J. **200**
merit-based personnel policies 188, 189
meta-governance 13; in contemporary policy-making 31–32; defining 31
meteorology 389
Mexican federal agencies 188
Millennium Challenge Corporation (MCC) 437
Milward, H. B. **199**
Mintz, J. 62n11
Mitrany, D. 135, 136
mixed enterprises 46, 49
Möllering, G. 266, 267, 268
Monnet, J. 135
Monsen, N. 248
Montesinos, V. 248
Montreux Declaration 404
Mora, A. 263n5
most-different-systems design (MDSD) 112
most-similar-systems design (MSSD) 112

multilateral development agencies 202
multilateral development banks 173
multi-level governance (MLG) 399; and European Public Policy 18; and modes of governance 18; tobacco control policy 19
Munck, G. 172, 173
Murray, A. 398
Mylvaganam, C. 56

Nash bargaining model 71
Nasi, G. 186–190
National Election Studies (NES) 273
National Network for Wind Power project 34
national policymaking 143
national policy styles 416; characterization 416
negative integration 334
networked agencies 193, 218
network governance 14, 34
New Democratic Party (NDP) 234
new governance 30, 34–35
Newman, A. 400, 401, 412n3, 412n6
new public management (NPM) 16, 35, 380
normative arguments: econometric analyses 140; environmental quality 140; jurisdictions 139; multinational firms 140; national autonomy 140; social dumping 138, 140; social protection 139
North American Free Trade Agreement (NAFTA) 144, 145, 232, 367, 370
North Atlantic Treaty Organization (NATO) 248, 251

Obama administration 38
O'Connor, J. S. 320
OECD *see* Organization for Economic Co-operation and Development
Olaskoaga, J. 330
old government 30
OLS *see* ordinary least squares
Olsen, J. P. 32
Open Budget Index 445
open method of coordination (OMC) 132, 287, 344
open systems model 198
opportunism 42, 49, 60
ordinary least squares (OLS) 96
organizational context 190
Organization for Economic Co-operation and Development (OECD) 19, 38, 82n2, 131, 193, 194, 221, 248, 283, 362, 401, 406
organization theory 126
Osborne, D. 194, 384, 392, 393
O'Toole, L. J. Jr. 108, **200**
overlapping authority model 229

Pal, L. A. 4–5
Palonen, K. 437
panel-corrected standard errors (PCSE) 96, 101

Parker, K. 58
PART *see* Program Assessment Rating Tool
participant-satisfaction models 198
PCSE *see* panel-corrected standard errors
Pendlebury, M. 248
perception-based measures 170, 171, 182n1
perception/objective measurement 197–198
performance based organizations (PBOs) 380
performance-based pay systems 187
performance contracting 386, 390
performance management 302
Persson, T. 355
Pfeffer, J. 193
PFI *see* private finance initiative
Pierre, J. 14–15
Pina, V. 248
policy convergence 284–287, 296n3
policy design *vs.* institutional design, 455
policy domains 8; cross-fertilization 4
policy implementation: adhocracies 118; analytical-theoretical framework 107; assessments 108; clusters of variables 108; comparative and longitudinal studies 109; comparative research (*see* Comparative implementation research); cross-national comparison 109; delivery units 117; ecology (*see* ecology of central capabilities); emergence of 117; first generation 107; game-fixing 116; hypotheses 120–121; innovations 119–120; jurisdictions 117; knowledge utilization 119; managerial strategies 119; phases 118; qualitative 107; research 108; research generations 107; second generation 107; third generation 107–108; top-down and bottom-up approaches 118; top-down and bottom-up perspectives 107
policy instruments 19
policy-making 33–34, 417, 418; command and control approach 29; complexity 18; coordinating 30, 35; credibility 4; decentralization 18; EU 33; evidence-based 6; meta-governance and 31–32; policy-makers 29; self-governing 35
policy sectors 7–8
policy styles 416–417; regulatory outputs (*see* regulatory policy output); specification 417
policy transfer: definition 363; pre-accession 365; rate of 375–377
political-administrative system 113
political independence/policy dependence 231
political integration 145
political science 106
political stabilization 188
political union 141
politicization 434
politico-administrative decision making 385
Pollit, C. 379–393

polls (surveys) of experts 202
polluter pays principle 131
Pontusson, J. 322
Porter, M. 141, 142
Portuguese drug policy 419
Poschmann, F. 62n1, 63n12
positive vs. negative integration 335
post accession stage 371–375; bargaining phase 374; Chinese government 373; findings 374–375
post-Kyoto climate governance regime 314–315
Pozen, D. 57
PPPs vs. taditional public procurement: efficiency–flexibility trade-off 77; private interests 75; renegotiation 77; VFM 76
pre-accession stage 365; Australia 367; developed country 367; findings 368–369; formal accession transfer 365–368; Korean government 367; Mexican economy 367; waves of accession 365–366
Pressman, J. L. 106, 107, 113, 116–118
Presthus, R. 237
Prime Minister's Delivery Unit (PMDU) 124–125
privacy commissioners *see* data protection authorities (DPAs)
privacy protection 398, 399, 402, 403
private finance initiatives (PFIs) 47, 82n1, 82n6
privatization 69; checks 100; debt 100; domestic interest groups 92; electoral incentives 91; factors 89; fiscal distress 91; GDP per capita 100; IMF 99, 102; institutional limitations 92; international diffusion and emulation 90; international financial institutions 92; national economy 86; opposition 91; policy adoption 91; quantitative studies 87; regional emulation 95; revenue from 87–89, *88*, 95; robustness 101; 1988–1999 sample 96, **97**; 2000–2008 sample 96, **98**; trade liberalization 90; two-stage process 87, 99; variables 90, 93–95
probit model 87, 95, 99
Program Assessment Rating Tool (PART) 195
project reviews (P3): ASWMS 54; The Confederation Bridge 56–57; Dulles Greenway 51–52; Highway 407 54–56; SR 91; Orange County 52–53; Tampa Bay Seawater Desalination Plant 53–54
property rights framework: allocation, 465; characteristics of, 468; classifications, 457; cross-national variations, 462–463; definitions, 457; emotionally intensive process, 467; individual level, 462–466, **464;** institutional arrangements, **459;** levels, 458; transplant organs, 465–466
Prototype Carbon Fund (PCF) 307
Provan, K. G. **199**
Public Accountability Measures 446, 449
public bureaucracies 120

public good 415
public personnel policies: and government performance 187; implementation of 186; individual and agency level 186; internal and external factors 186; managerial practices 187
public policy problems 301
public–private partnerships (PPPs or P3s) 38, 45, 383; arrangement 40; collection 43; competitive bidding 68; contracting out 46; critical analysis approach 39, 40, 42; critical feature 46; critics of 69; delivery options 39–40; economic stimulus plan 41; economic theory 39; examples 46; firm's optimal effort 72; flexibility 69; GFC 40; government rationales for 47–49; greater transparency 41; infrastructure 38, 46; initial payment 73–74; language 39; legal environments 43; motivations 40; outcomes 46–47; over-indexation, payments 43; positive model 46; positive theory perspective 49–50; project reviews (*see* project reviews (P3)); public policy scholars 39; public procurement 46; public services 67–68; rationales (*see* rationales for P3s), government; relationships 62n3; renegotiation 72–73; risks 41–42; setup 70–71; social infrastructure 68; Spain 42; stakeholders 43; strategic misrepresentation 42; timing 71–72; toll revenue 79–80; trade-off 68; transportation, risk 40; TSS 78–79; US and Canadian cases: asset specificity 59; complexity/uncertainty 58–59; contestability 60; contract management skills 60; cost-effective 61–62; transaction cost theory 59; US prison 57–58; VFM 74–75; VfM 39, 41
public procurement 68, 69
public sector organizations 382
public service providers 383
Pullin, R. 154, 160, 165n1
punctuated-equilibrium theoretical framework 401
Putnam, R. 193, **199**

quadratic disutility function 70
Quah, J. 169
Queensland's Implementation Unit 125
Quinn, R. E. 198
Quittkat, C. 347

Raab, C. D. 396–413, 412n3, 412n6
Radin, B. 3, 7, 192
Ragin, C. C. 4
Rahman, A. 252, 258
Rainey, H. G. **201**
Ramesh, M. 119
Rasmussen, A. 356
rational choice theory 385
rationales for P3s, government 41, 46; capital costs 47; cost-reduction profit incentives 49; faddism 47; health care provider 48; large

multinational firms 48; off-budget 47; political cost 48; private sector firms 48; public balance sheet 48; public sector 49; revenue streams 47; risk charge 48; superior incentives 48–49; technical efficiency cost 49; X-efficiency 47
rational goal model 198
Razafindrakoto, M. 172
redistributive policies 416
Reduced Emissions from Degradation and Deforestation (REDD) 314
Reeves, E. 41
regional integration: economic and legal analyses 143; formal institutional development 144; MERCOSUR 145; multilateralism 144; national policies 144; public policymakers 146; supranational institutionalization 145, 146
regulatory change: description 427; two-dimensional shifts 427–430
Regulatory competition 284
regulatory policies 416; feature 416; standard operating procedures 416
regulatory policy output: advantages 425; behavioral constraints 417; characteristics 417; classification 418; coercion 418; Comparative Analysis of Morality Policy Change (MORAPOL) project 422–423, 425–427; cross-national and temporal variations 425–427; democratic systems 417; financial incentives 418; handgun regulation 422–427; liberal policies 419; Lowi's definition 418; measurement 420–423; policy-makers 419; regulatory change 427–430; styles 418–419
renegotiation process 69
Renewable Energy and Energy Efficiency Partnership (REEP) 307
Renewable Energy Policy Network for 21st Century (REN21) 307
request for proposals (RFP) 54–55
results-oriented budgeting 390, 391
Revesz, R. L. 139, 140
Rhodes, R. A. W 28
Richards, D. 125, 126
risk regulation approach 131
Robinson, J. 153
Rodrik, D. 143
Rohrbaugh, J. 198
Rosanvallon, P. 271
Ross, J. 39–40
Ross, T. W. 67–84, 82n5, 83n7
Roth, N. L. 272, 274
Roubaud, F. 172

Salagrama, V. 165n1
Samajdar, A. 172
Sappington, D. 84n25
SAPs *see* structural adjustment programs
Sætren, H. 106–113

Saussier, S. 83n13
Scharpf, F. W. 333, 334
Schneider, V. 90, 100
Schuppert, G. 385
second-generation/actionable indicators: actionable governance indicators 438; AGIs 449; cancer of corruption 436; criteria 434, 451n1; critique of ranking 435–438; good governance 436; governance indicators 445–448; mappings 434; market-oriented core beliefs 448; methodological debate 437; NGOs 450; policy instruments **447**; policy process 435–438; shift from rankings 435; transparency 438, 444–445; uses and mechanisms of influence 448–449
second-order policy instruments (institutional design), 455–457
Selden, S. C. **199, 200**
Senge, P. 120
Serritzlew, S. 189
Sheingate, A. D. 7, 8
Shleifer, A. 95
Shui-bian, C. 176
Siedentorpf, H. 109
Signorino, C. S. 95
Sinawatra, T. 177
Sitkin, S. B. 272, 274
Smiley, D. V. 226, 232, 243n13
Smith, M. 125, 126
Smullen, A. 379–393
Snyder, F. 296n4
social dumping 138, 140
social insurance motive 143
social networking 398
social protections 133, 139, 143, 320, 326, 329
social security 388, 389
social units 4
societal systems 151
society-centric governance 15, 29
soft law 132, 284, 288, 296n4
Sorensen, E. 305
Sowa, J. E. **200**
Spaak, P. -H. 135, 146
special issue 28, 32; federal political systems 33; geopolitical contexts 33; hierarchical modes 34; liberalization and privatization 34; Open Method of Coordination 33
special operating agencies (SOAs) 380, 382, 387
special purpose vehicle (SPV) 74, 83n12
SPV *see* special purpose vehicle
stand-alone operating firms 61
state-centric governance 15, 29
state-civil society dimension 382
stateless society 416
state-market dimension 381
State Route (SR) 91; Orange County 52–53
state–society relationships 416
state traditions 416

Steinmo, S. 412n5
Stewart, B. 412n3
Stoker, G. 110
Stone Sweet, A. 412n5
Strait Crossing Development Inc. (SCDI) 56–57
Strait Crossing Finance Inc (SCFI) 56–57
structural adjustment programs (SAPs) 90
structural conditionality 90–91
structural disaggregation 386, 390
supranational organizations 251
surveillance society 396, 404
surveys of residents 202
sustainable development 283; comparative patterns 294–295; global policy documents 295; governmental policy 296n2; international organizations 290–293; networking activities 294; policies of Quebec, North Rhine-Westphalia and Flanders 290; policy copying 293; principles 296n5; subnational entity 283
Sutherland, S. L. 244n27
Svendsen, G. T. 189
symbolic imitation 286, 293
system-to-be-governed (SG) 148–150; GI (*see* governance interactions (GI)); GS *see* (governance system (GS)); properties 153–154; resilience 154–155; societal primary processes 152–153; vulnerability 155

Tadelis, S. 69
Talbot, C. 379–393
Tampa Bay Seawater Desalination Plant: components 53; construction 53; contract arrangement 54; desalination process 53; gallons 54; utility and contractor 53; water utility 53
telecommunications 83n11, 402, 404
Tenbücken, M. 90, 100
theory and methodology 5–6
thinking federal 226
third generation research paradigm 113
Thomas, C. 58
TI *see* Transparency International
Tiebout, C. M. 134
time-series cross-sectional (TSCS) 96, 99
Tinker, J. 153
Torfing, J. 305
Torres, L. 248
total social surplus (TSS) 72, 78–79, 81
traditional public policy 27
transaction cost theory 50, 59, 62
transgovernmentalism 399
Transitional Review Mechanism (TRM) 373
Transnational Communication 284–287; mechanisms 286; methodological considerations/selection of the cases 288–289; networking 286

transnational governance 13, 433
Transparency International (TI) 169, 171, 172, 437–438
trust: institutional 189; social 189
TSCS *see* time-series cross-sectional
TSS *see* total social surplus
Turrini, A. 189
two-dimensional shifts: goal ambiguities 428–429; procedural differences 429–430

Ujhelyi, G. 173
UNCAC *see* United Nations Convention against Corruption
UN Conference on Environment and Development (UNCED) 287
unitary decision process 90
unitary national system 126
United Nations Convention against Corruption (UNCAC) 170
United Nations Development Programme (UNDP) 436
United Nations Framework Convention on Climate Change (UNFCCC) 307, 310–313
United Network for Organ Sharing (UNOS), 466, 467
United States: developmental policies 242; economic characteristics 226; federal systems 226; fragmented powers, point of departure 227–228; governmental units 235; influential actors 234–236; laboratories of democracy 230; language 243n4; policy design 238; policy implementation 238–240; processes of decision making 237–238; regulatory policies 241; relationships between and among actors 229–230; specialized policy actors 236
units of analysis 109
unpacking agencification: contexts and motives 389–391; size and functions 388–389; statuses and powers 386–388
USA's Center for Democracy and Technology 409
US General Accounting Office (USGAO) 62n2, 63n17
US prison P3s 57–58

Valotti, G. 189
value for money (VFM) 39, 72, 74–75, 81
Van der Tas, L. G. 248
Van de Walle, S. 194
Van Kersbergen, K. 14
Van Nispen, F. 3
Van Waarden, F. 14, 416
Veenhoven, R. 324
Verney, D. V. 243n8
VFM *see* value for money
Vining, A. 62n1, 62n6, 70, 83n15

Walker, R. M. **201**, 221n2
Wang, C. 272, 274
Wang, X. **199**
Washington Consensus 438
Watanuki, J. 149
Weatherill, S. 143
Website Working Group (WWG) 408
Weigert, A. 274
Weimer, D. 3, 62n6
Weingast, B. R. 133
welfare effort 320; alternatives 325–330; dependent population 327–328; deviations, Ireland *324*; drawbacks 322–325; identifying elements 322; replacement rates 329; social-democratic world 323, *325*; social protection (1980–2004) 320–322, **321**; social protection systems **328**; standards of protection **327**, *328*; uses 330–331; *vs.* determinants 322
Westminster systems 118
WGI *see* Worldwide Governance Indicators
White Paper on European Governance 344
Wildavsky, A. 106, 107, 113
Wildavsky, A. B. 116–118
Wilensky, H. L. 320
Wilf, M. 368
Williamson, O. E. 159
Wilson, C. D. 155
Wilson, J. Q. 389
Winter, S. 108, 109
Wolf, A. 5
Wolf, P. J. 221n1
Wootton, G. 163
World Bank Governance Matters project 202
World Bank's Development Indicators 94, 95
World Bank's Government Effectiveness Index 197
World Bank's Privatization Database 93, 103n2
World Business Council for Sustainable Development Climate (WBCSD) 307
World Commission on Environment and Development (WCED) 287
World Competitiveness Yearbook 194
World Economic Forum (WEF) 436
World Summit on Sustainable Development (WSSD) 287
World Trade Organization (WTO) 19, 131, 362, 403
World Values Survey (WVS) 172
Worldwide Governance Indicators (WGI) 171, 172, 436
Wright, D. 7, 229, 231, 237, 243n17
WVS *see* World Values Survey

X-efficiency 47

Yan, A. 39–40
Yan, J. 67–84
Yescombe, E. R. 83n10
Your Voice in Europe 353
Yu, C. 168–183

Ziller, J. 109